WORD
BIBLICAL
COMMENTARY

WORD

BIBLICAL

COMMENTARY

Volume 35c

Luke 18:35–24:53

JOHN NOLLAND

WORD BOOKS, PUBLISHER • DALLAS, TEXAS

Word Biblical Commentary
Luke 18:35–24:53
Copyright © 1993 by Word, Incorporated

Library of Congress Cataloging-in-Publication Data
Main entry under title:

Word biblical commentary.

   Includes bibliographies.
   1. Bible—Commentaries—Collected works.
BS491.2.W67   220.7'7   81–71768
ISBN 0–8499–1072–2 (v. 35C) AACR2

Printed in the United States of America

The author's own translation of the Scripture text appears in italic type under the heading *Translation.*

8 9 9   AGF   9 8 7 6 5 4

To my mother
and in memory of my father

Editor's Note

For the convenience of the reader, page numbers for volumes one, two, and three of this commentary on Luke (35A, 35B, and 35C) are included in the Contents. Page numbers for the volume in hand are printed in boldface type, while those for the other volumes are in lightface.

In addition, all of the front matter from Vol. 35A but the Introduction has been repeated in Vol. 35C so that the reader may have abbreviations, bibliography, and other pertinent information readily at hand.

Contents

xii CONTENTS

Editorial Preface

The launching of the *Word Biblical Commentary* brings to fulfillment an enterprise of several years' planning. The publishers and the members of the editorial board met in 1977 to explore the possibility of a new commentary on the books of the Bible that would incorporate several distinctive features. Prospective readers of these volumes are entitled to know what such features were intended to be; whether the aims of the commentary have been fully achieved time alone will tell.

First, we have tried to cast a wide net to include as contributors a number of scholars from around the world who not only share our aims, but are in the main engaged in the ministry of teaching in university, college, and seminary. They represent a rich diversity of denominational allegiance. The broad stance of our contributors can rightly be called evangelical, and this term is to be understood in its positive, historic sense of a commitment to Scripture as divine revelation, and to the truth and power of the Christian gospel.

Then, the commentaries in our series are all commissioned and written for the purpose of inclusion in the *Word Biblical Commentary*. Unlike several of our distinguished counterparts in the field of commentary writing, there are no translated works, originally written in a non-English language. Also, our commentators were asked to prepare their own rendering of the original biblical text and to use those languages as the basis of their own comments and exegesis. What may be claimed as distinctive with this series is that it is based on the biblical languages, yet it seeks to make the technical and scholarly approach to the theological understanding of Scripture understandable by—and useful to—the fledgling student, the working minister, and colleagues in the guild of professional scholars and teachers as well.

Finally, a word must be said about the format of the series. The layout, in clearly defined sections, has been consciously devised to assist readers at different levels. Those wishing to learn about the textual witnesses on which the translation is offered are invited to consult the section headed *Notes*. If the readers' concern is with the state of modern scholarship on any given portion of Scripture, they should turn to the sections on *Bibliography* and *Form/Structure/Setting*. For a clear exposition of the passage's meaning and its relevance to the ongoing biblical revelation, the *Comment* and concluding *Explanation* are designed expressly to meet that need. There is therefore something for everyone who may pick up and use these volumes.

If these aims come anywhere near realization, the intention of the editors will have been met, and the labor of our team of contributors rewarded.

General Editors: *David A. Hubbard*
Glenn W. Barker†
Old Testament: *John D. W. Watts*
New Testament: *Ralph P. Martin*

Author's Preface

In 1966 W. C. van Unnik wrote an article under the title "Luke-Acts, A Storm Center in Contemporary Scholarship" (In *Studies in Luke-Acts,* ed. L. E. Keck and J. L. Martyn). It is probably fair to say that the intensity of the storm has since considerably abated, but there has continued to be an immense devotion of scholarly labor dedicated to the elucidation of the Lukan writings. And as some issues in dispute have clarified with the emergence of a good degree of scholarly consensus, other issues have come forward to take their place as matters in hot dispute.

A commentary such as the present one is partly a digest of the present state of this ongoing debate. In this guise it seeks to synthesize the insights that are scattered through the specialist literature and to evaluate in connection with the development of a coherent understanding of the whole Lukan enterprise the competing suggestions that have been offered in the literature for the understanding of individual items. It has, however, also been my intention to offer a fresh reading of each passage of the Gospel. In this guise the perusal of the literature has been a kind of apprenticeship or an initiation, entitling me to move on beyond the place where the accumulated discussion has taken us. Here my ambition has been to improve the answers that have been given to the issues thrown up by the particular features of the individual passages and at points to add my own questions to the scholarly agenda.

I have focused my engagement with the scholarly literature on the journal literature and the specialist monographs rather than upon the existing commentaries, largely because of the greater possibility there for exploring the detailed reasoning that stands behind the particular judgments which have been made. That said, I have learned much from the commentators. Schürmann and Fitzmyer have been constant companions. Marshall and Grundmann have also been of special use, as in different ways have the earlier works of Schlatter, Godet, and Loisy. Other commentators have periodically left their mark upon the present work. D. M. Goulder's recent work (*Luke: A New Paradigm* [2 vols., JSNTSup 20; Sheffield: JSOT, 1989]) did not appear before the manuscript left my hands in January 1989. I have tried to keep an eye constantly upon Luke's second volume, and the scholarship devoted to its elucidation, but here I have necessarily been much more selective.

While I have attempted to take something like comprehensive responsibility for all the issues involved in attempting to provide a modern reading of the ancient Lukan text, inevitably my own sense of the relative importance of things, as well as of my own areas of greater strength, will be reflected in the allocation of space (and of effort). The central paradigm for my work has been provided by seeing the Gospel text as an exercise in communication, deliberately undertaken by the Gospel writer with at least some focused sense of the actual or potential needs of his audience. I use "communication" here in a broad sense to encompass all the ways in which the Gospel may be intended to have an impact upon the reader.

To give one example that goes beyond what we might call the theological message of the book, there is a considerable sense of literature about Luke's work. Some of that will be due to Luke's instincts as artist and in that sense will be an expression of his own person as artist; some of that will be due to the fact that Luke stands heir (from the Old Testament, but also from his Christian context) to a narrative method of doing theology, along with which comes an investment in the artistry of story-telling; but for part of the explanation of this literary phenomenon we need to look in a totally nonliterary direction. Luke's ambition was not to make a name for himself in the literary world of the day (his work probably does not come up to the level). His efforts were directed towards being taken with a certain kind of seriousness in this attempt that he has made to commend and elucidate the Christian faith: Luke seeks to write at a level that would commend itself to the cultural level of his readers and implicitly make certain claims about how they as readers should orient themselves to his work. That is, Luke uses literary means to nonliterary ends. With an eye upon each of these roles for literary technique, I have sought to pay particular attention to the literary strategies of Luke at both the micro-level and the macro-level.

While the main paradigm for inquiry has been provided by a concern for the nexus of communication, the commentary also pays considerable attention to issues concerning the ultimate origin of the materials that Luke has used. Luke seems to have a concern to present his material as capable of standing up to "secular" scrutiny. He is the Gospel writer who is most clearly aware of a distance between his own reporting and the events that it is his concern to report (Luke 1:1–4), and he is the one Gospel writer who seems to work with a fairly clear conceptual distinction between the place for religious testimony and the role of "historical" evidence in commending the Christian faith. His own approach, therefore, invites our attention to the questions of origin.

The commentary may be accessed at various levels. Most readers will find the *Explanation* for each passage the best point of entry. Here the major results of the detailed work of the earlier sections are outlined in nontechnical language. Also important for keeping in view the overall thrust of the Lukan text are the brief summaries which begin each major section of the commentary, and which at the next level down constitute the opening paragraphs for both the *Form/Structure/ Setting* and the *Comment* for each passage.

Libraries are finally what make humanistic scholarship possible, and I am deeply grateful for the library resources that have been made available to me at Regent College, Vancouver; the University of British Columbia; Tyndale House Cambridge; the University of Cambridge; and Trinity College Bristol. I am particularly grateful for the inter-library loan services which have given me access to a great many items not held by the particular libraries where I have worked from time to time. I wish to pay a particular tribute to the series of teaching assistants who in the early years of this project gathered library resources for me and to Su Brown, assistant librarian at Trinity College Bristol, who was of such assistance in the final stages of readying the manuscript for the press.

I owe a debt of gratitude to Regent College, for the year of sabbatical leave in which a considerable part of the manuscript was written.

Finally I pay tribute to my wife Lisa and son David who have borne with my having this project on my mind for many a year, and particularly to my wife who "journeyed [with me to] a foreign land" far "away from [her] country and [her] kindred and [her] father's house" in order that I might be able to stay in the kind of employment that would allow me to continue with this work.

October 1989   JOHN NOLLAND
Trinity College, Bristol

Abbreviations

A. General Abbreviations

A	Codex Alexandrinus	id.	*idem,* the same
ad	comment on	i.e.	*id est,* that is
Akkad.	Akkadian	impf.	imperfect
א	Codex Sinaiticus	infra	below
Ap. Lit.	Apocalyptic Literature	in loc.	*in loco,* in the place cited
Apoc.	Apocrypha	Jos.	Josephus
Aq.	Aquila's Greek Translation	lat	Latin
	of the OT	lit.	literally
Arab.	Arabic	loc. cit.	the place cited
Aram.	Aramaic	LXX	Septuagint
B	Codex Vaticanus	M	Mishna
C	Codex Ephraemi Syri	masc.	masculine
c.	*circa,* about	mg.	margin
cent.	century	MS(S)	manuscript(s)
cf.	*confer,* compare	MT	Masoretic text (of the Old
chap(s).	chapter(s)		Testament)
cod., codd.	codex, codices	n.	note
contra	in contrast to	n.d.	no date
CUP	Cambridge University Press	Nestle	Nestle (ed.), *Novum*
D	Codex Bezae		*Testamentum Graece* [26],
DSS	Dead Sea Scrolls		rev. by K. and B. Aland
ed.	edited by, editor(s)	no.	number
e.g.	*exempli gratia,* for example	n.s.	new series
et al.	*et alii,* and others	NT	New Testament
ET	English translation	obs.	obsolete
EV	English Versions of the	o.s.	old series
	Bible	OT	Old Testament
f., ff.	following (verse or verses,	p., pp.	page, pages
	pages, etc.)	*pace*	with due respect to, but
fem.	feminine		differing from
frag.	fragments	//, par(s).	parallel(s)
FS	Festschrift, volume written	par.	paragraph
	in honor of	passim	elsewhere
ft.	foot, feet	pl.	plural
gen.	genitive	Pseudep.	Pseudepigrapha
Gr.	Greek	Q	Quelle ("Sayings" source
hap. leg.	*hapax legomenon,* sole		for the Gospels)
	occurrence	q.v.	*quod vide,* which see
Heb.	Hebrew	rev.	revised, reviser, revision
Hitt.	Hittite	Rom.	Roman
ibid.	*ibidem,* in the same place	RVmg	Revised Version margin

Sam.	Samaritan recension	UBSGT	The United Bible Societies
sc.	*scilicet,* that is to say		Greek Text
Sem.	Semitic	Ugar.	Ugaritic
sing.	singular	UP	University Press
Sumer.	Sumerian	u.s.	*ut supra,* as above
s.v.	*sub verbo,* under the word	v, vv	verse, verses
sy	Syriac	viz.	*videlicet,* namely
Symm.	Symmachus	vg	Vulgate
Tg.	Targum	v.l.	*varia lectio,* alternative
Theod.	Theodotion		reading
TR	Textus Receptus	vol.	volume
tr.	translator, translated by	x	times (2x = two times, etc.)

For abbreviations of Greek MSS used in *Notes,* see Nestle[26].

B. Abbreviations for Translations and Paraphrases

AmT	Smith and Goodspeed, *The Complete Bible, An American Translation*	Moffatt	J. Moffatt, *A New Translation of the Bible* (NT 1913)
		NAB	The New American Bible
AB	Anchor Bible	NEB	The New English Bible
ASV	American Standard Version, American Revised Version (1901)	NIV	The New International Version (1978)
		NJB	New Jerusalem Bible (1985)
AV	Authorized Version = KJV	Phillips	J. B. Phillips, *The New Testament in Modern English*
GNB	Good News Bible = Today's English Version	RSV	Revised Standard Version (NT 1946, OT 1952, Apoc. 1957)
JB	Jerusalem Bible		
JPS	Jewish Publication Society, *The Holy Scriptures*	RV	Revised Version, 1881–85
KJV	King James Version (1611) = AV	Wey	R. F. Weymouth, *The New Testament in Modern Speech*
Knox	R. A. Knox, *The Holy Bible: A Translation from the Latin Vulgate in the Light of the Hebrew and Greek Original*	Wms	C. B. Williams, *The New Testament: A Translation in the Language of the People*

C. Abbreviations of Commonly Used Periodicals, Reference Works, and Serials

AARSR	American Academy of Religion Studies in Religion	ACNT	Augsburg Commentary on the New Testament
		AcOr	*Acta orientalia*
AAS	*Acta apostolicae sedis*	ACW	Ancient Christian Writers
AASOR	Annual of the American Schools of Oriental Research	*ADAJ*	*Annual of the Department of Antiquities of Jordan*
		AER	*American Ecclesiastical Review*
AB	Anchor Bible	*AfJT*	*African Journal of Theology*
ABR	*Australian Biblical Review*	AFLN-WG	Arbeitsgemeinschaft für
AbrN	*Abr-Nahrain*		Forschung des Landes

	Nordrhein-Westfalen, Geistgewissenschaften	*AnnThéol*	*L'Année théologique*
		AnOr	Analecta orientalia
AfO	*Archiv für Orientforschung*	*ANQ*	*Andover Newton Quarterly*
AGJU	Arbeiten zur Geschichte des antiken Judentums und des Urchristentums	*ANRW*	*Aufstieg und Niedergang der römischen Welt*, ed. H. Temporini and W. Haase, Berlin
AGSU	Arbeiten zur Geschichte des Spätjudentums und Urchristentums	ANT	Arbeiten zur Neutestamentlichen Textforschung
AH	F. Resenthal, *An Aramaic Handbook*	ANTJ	Arbeiten zum Neuen Testament und zum Judentum
AHR	*American Historical Review*		
AHW	W. von Soden, *Akkadisches Handwörterbuch*	*Anton*	*Antonianum*
AION	*Annali dell'istituto orientali di Napoli*	AOAT	Alter orient und Altes Testament
AJA	*American Journal of Archaeology*	AOS	American Oriental Series
AJAS	*American Journal of Arabic Studies*	*AP*	J. Marouzeau (ed.), *L'année philologique*
AJBA	*Australian Journal of Biblical Archaeology*	*APOT*	R. H. Charles (ed.), *Apocrypha and Pseudepigrapha of the Old Testament*
AJBI	*Annual of the Japanese Biblical Institute*		
AJP	*American Journal of Philology*	*ArchLing*	*Archivum linguisticum*
AJSL	*American Journal of Semitic Languages and Literature*	*ARG*	*Archiv für Reformationsgeschichte*
AJT	*American Journal of Theology*	ARM	Archives royales de Mari
ALBO	Analecta lovaniensia biblica et orientalia	*ArOr*	*Archiv orientální*
ALGHJ	Arbeiten zur Literatur und Geschichte des hellenistischen Judentums	ARSHLL	Acta Reg. Societatis Humaniorum Litterarum Lundensis
ALUOS	Annual of Leeds University Oriental Society	*ARW*	*Archiv für Religionswissenschaft*
		ASB	*Austin Seminary Bulletin*
AmCl	*Ami du clergé*	*AshTB*	*Ashland Theological Bulletin*
AnBib	Analecta biblica	*AshTJ*	*Ashland Theological Journal*
AnBoll	Analecta Bollandiana	ASNU	Acta seminarii neotestamentici upsaliensis
ANEP	J. B. Pritchard (ed.), *Ancient Near East in Pictures*		
		ASS	*Acta sanctae sedis*
ANESTP	J. B. Pritchard (ed.), *Ancient Near East Supplementary Texts and Pictures*	*AsSeign*	*Assemblées du Seigneur*
		ASSR	*Archives des sciences sociales des religions*
ANET	J. B. Pritchard (ed.), *Ancient Near Eastern Texts*	*ASTI*	*Annual of the Swedish Theological Institute*
ANF	The Ante-Nicene Fathers	ATAbh	Alttestamentliche Abhandlungen
Ang	*Anglicum*	ATANT	Abhandlungen zur Theologie des Alten und Neuen Testaments
AnnPhil	*Annales de Philosophie* (Beirut)	ATD	Das Alte Testament Deutsch

ATDan	Acta Theologica Danica		*Griechisch*
ATJ	*African Theological Journal*	*BeO*	*Bibbia e oriente*
ATR	*Anglican Theological Review*	*BenM*	*Benediktinische Monatschrift*
AuCoeurAfr	*Au Coeur de l'Afrique: Revue*	*BerlinTZ*	*Berliner Theologische Zeitschrift*
	interdiocésaine (Burundi)		(Berlin)
AugR	*Augustinianum*	BET	Beiträge zur biblischen
AUSS	*Andrews University Seminary*		Exegese und Theologie
	Studies	BETL	Bibliotheca ephemeridum
AzNTT	Arbeiten zur neutestament-		theologicarum
	lichen Textforschung		lovaniensium
		BEvT	Beiträge zur evangelischen
BA	*Biblical Archaeologist*		Theologie
BAC	Biblioteca de autores	BFCT	Beiträge zur Förderung
	cristianos		christlicher Theologie
BAGD	W. Bauer, *A Greek-English*	BGBE	Beiträge zur Geschichte der
	Lexicon of the New Testament		biblischen Exegese
	and Other Early Christian	*BHH*	*Biblisch-Historisches*
	Literature, ET, ed. W. F.		*Handwörterbuch*
	Arndt and F. W. Gingrich;	*BHK*	R. Kittel, *Biblia hebraica*
	2d ed. rev. F. W. Gingrich	*BHS*	*Biblia hebraica stuttgartensia*
	and F. W. Danker (Univer-	BHT	Beiträge zur historischen
	sity of Chicago, 1979)		Theologie
BAH	Bibliothèque archéologique	*Bib*	*Biblica*
	et historique	BibB	Biblische Beiträge
BangTF	*Bangalore Theological Forum*	*BibLeb*	*Bibel und Leben*
BAR	*Biblical Archaeology Review*	*BibLit*	*Bibel und Liturgie*
BASOR	*Bulletin of the American Schools*	*BiblScRel*	*Biblioteca di Scienze Religiose*
	of Oriental Research	*BibNot*	*Biblische Notizen*
BASP	*Bulletin of the American Society*	BibOr	Biblica et orientalia
	of Papyrologists	BibS(F)	Biblische Studien (Freiburg,
BBB	Bonner biblische Beiträge		1895–)
BBudé	*Bulletin de l'Association G.*	BibS(N)	Biblische Studien
	Budé (Rome)		(Neukirchen, 1951–)
BCSR	*Bulletin of the Council on the*	*BIES*	*Bulletin of the Israel Explora-*
	Study of Religion		*tion Society (= Yediot)*
BDB	F. Brown, S. R. Driver, and C.	*BIFAO*	*Bulletin de l'institut français*
	A. Briggs, *Hebrew and*		*d'archéologie orientale*
	English Lexicon of the Old	BILL	Bibliothèque des cahiers de
	Testament (Oxford:		l'Institut de Linguistique
	Clarendon, 1907)		de Louvain
BDF	F. Blass, A. Debrunner, and R. W.	*BiTod*	*The Bible Today*
	Funk, *A Greek Grammar of*	*BJRL*	*Bulletin of the John Rylands*
	the New Testament (Univer-		*University Library of*
	sity of Chicago/University		*Manchester*
	of Cambridge, 1961)	BJS	Brown Judaic Studies
BDR	F. Blass, A. Debrunner, and	*BK*	*Bibel und Kirche*
	F. Rehkopf, *Grammatik des*	BKAT	Biblischer Kommentar: Altes
	neutestamentlichen		Testament

BL	Book List	CB	*Cultura biblica*
BLE	*Bulletin de littérature ecclésiastique*	CBFV	Cahiers biblique de Foi et Vie
BLit	*Bibel und Liturgie*	CBG	*Collationes Brugenses et Gandavenses*
BLS	Bible and Literature Series		
BLT	*Brethren of Life and Thought*	CBQ	*Catholic Biblical Quarterly*
BNTC	Black's New Testament Commentaries	CBQMS	CBQ Monograph Series
		CBVE	*Comenius Blätter für Volkserziehung*
BO	*Bibliotheca orientalis*		
BPAA	Bibliotheca Pontificii Athenaei Antoniani	CCath	Corpus Catholicorum
		CCER	*Cahiers du cercle Ernest Renan*
BR	*Biblical Research*	CChr	Corpus Christianorum
BRev	*Bible Review*	CGTC	Cambridge Greek Testament Commentary
BS	Biblische Studien		
BSac	*Bibliotheca Sacra*	CGTSC	Cambridge Greek Testament for Schools and Colleges
BSO(A) S	*Bulletin of the School of Oriental (and African) Studies*		
		CH	*Church History*
BSR	Bibliothèque de sciences religieuses	ChicStud	*Chicago Studies*
		CHR	*Catholic Historical Review*
BT	*The Bible Translator*	ChrTod	*Christianity Today*
BTB	*Biblical Theology Bulletin*	CHSP	*Centre for Hermeneutical Study in Hellenistic and Modern Culture Protocol of the Colloquy*
BTS	*Bible et Terre Saint*		
BU	Biblische Untersuchungen		
BulBR	*Bulletin for Biblical Research*		
BulCPE	*Bulletin du Centre Protestant d'Études* (Geneva)	CIG	*Corpus inscriptionum graecarum*
BulCRIMGU	*Bulletin of the Christian Research Institute Meiji Gakuin University* (Tokyo)	CII	*Corpus inscriptionum iudaicarum*
		CIL	*Corpus inscriptionum latinarum*
BulSSul	*Bulletin de Saint Sulpice* (Paris)		
BVC	*Bible et vie chrétienne*	CIS	*Corpus inscriptionum semiticarum*
BW	*Biblical World*		
BWANT	Beiträge zur Wissenschaft vom Alten und Neuen Testament	CJT	*Canadian Journal of Theology*
		ClerMon	*Clergy Monthly*
		ClerRev	*Clergy Review*
BZ	*Biblische Zeitschrift*	CLit	*Christianity and Literature*
BZAW	Beihefte zur ZAW	ClQ	*The Classical Quarterly*
BZET	Beihefte zur Evangelische Theologie	ClW	*Classical Weekly*
		CM	*Cahiers marials*
BZNW	Beihefte zur ZNW	CnS	*Cristianesimo nella Storia*
BZRGG	Beihefte zur ZRGG	CNT	Commentaire du Nouveau Testament
CAD	*The Assyrian Dictionary of the Oriental Institute of the University of Chicago*	CollMech	*Collectanea Mechliniensia*
		CollTheol	*Collectanea Theologica*
		ComLit	*Communautes et liturgies*
CAH	*Cambridge Ancient History*	Communio	*Communio: International Catholic Review* (Notre Dame)
CAT	Commentaire de l'Ancien Testament		

ConB	Coniectanea biblica	DS	Denzinger-Schönmetzer,
Concil	Concilium		Enchiridion symbolorum
ConcJ	Concordia Journal	DT	Deutsche Theologie
CongQ	The Congregational Quarterly	DTC	Dictionnaire de théologie
ConNT	Coniectanea neotestamentica		catholique
CQ	Church Quarterly	DTT	Dansk teologisk tidsskrift
CQR	Church Quarterly Review	DunRev	Dunwoodie Review
CRAIBL	Comptes rendus de l'Académie		
	des inscriptions et belles-	EBib	Etudes bibliques
	lettres	EBT	Encyclopedia of Biblical
CRev	Classical Review		Theology
CrisTR	Criswell Theological Review	EcR	Ecclesiastical Review
CrQ	Crozier Quarterly	ED	Euntes Docete (Rome)
CSCO	Corpus scriptorum	EE	Estudios Eclesiásticos
	christianorum	EglT	Église et théologie
	orientalium	EHAT	Exegetisches Handbuch zum
CSEL	Corpus scriptorum ecclesias-		Alten Testament
	ticorum latinorum	EKKNT	Evangelisch-katholischer
CTA	A. Herdner, Corpus des		Kommentar zum Neuen
	tablettes en cunéiformes		Testament
	alphabétiques	EKL	Evangelisches Kirchenlexikon
CTJ	Calvin Theological Journal	EL	Ephemerides Liturgicae
CTM	Calwer Theologische	Emman	Emmanuel
	Monographien	EnchBib	Enchiridion biblicum
CTMonth	Concordia Theological Monthly	EncJud	Encyclopedia judaica (1971)
CTQ	Concordia Theological	EphMar	Ephemerides mariologique
	Quarterly		(Madrid)
CurTM	Currents in Theology and	EpR	Epworth Review
	Mission	ER	Ecumenical Review
CuW	Christentum und Wissenschaft	ErJb	Eranos Jahrbuch
CV	Communio viatorum	EstBib	Estudios biblicos
CW	Die christliche Welt	EstTeol	Estudios teologicos (Guatemala)
		ETL	Ephemerides theologicae
DACL	Dictionnaire d'archéologie		lovanienses
	chrétienne et de liturgie	ETR	Etudes théologiques et religieuses
DBSup	Dictionnaire de la Bible,	ETS	Erfurter Theologische
	Supplément		Studien
Diak	Diakonia	EuA	Erbe und Auftrag
DISO	C.-F. Jean and J. Hoftijzer,	EV	Esprit et Vie
	Dictionnaire des inscriptions	EvErz	Das evangelische Erzieher
	sémitiques de l'ouest	EvJ	Evangelical Journal
DJD	Discoveries in the Judean	EvK	Evangelische Kommentar
	Desert	EvQ	Evangelical Quarterly
DL	Doctrine and Life	EvT	Evangelische Theologie
DOTT	D. W. Thomas (ed.),	EW	Exegetisches Wörterbuch zum
	Documents from Old		Neuen Testament (EWNT),
	Testament Times		ed. H. Balz and G.
DR	Downside Review		Schneider, 3 vols.

	(Stuttgart: Kohlhammer, 1980–83)	GTA	Göttinger Theologische Arbeiten
ExAuditu	*Ex Auditu: An International Journal of Theological Interpretation of Scripture*	*GThT*	*Geformelet Theologisch Tijdschrift*
Exp	*Expositor*	*GTJ*	*Grace Theological Journal*
ExpTim	*The Expository Times*	*GuL*	*Geist und Leben*
FB	Forschung zur Bibel	*HALAT*	W. Baumgartner et al., *Hebräisches und aramäisches Lexikon zum Alten Testament*
FBBS	Facet Books, Biblical Series		
FC	Fathers of the Church		
FilolNT	*Filologia Neotestamentaria* (Córdoba, Spain)	HAT	Handbuch zum Alten Testament
FM	*Faith and Mission*	HB	*Homiletica en Biblica*
FoiTemps	*La Foi et le temps* (Tournai)	*HBT*	*Horizons of Biblical Theology*
FriedIsr	*Friede über Israel: Zeitschrift für Kirche und Judentum* (Nürnberg)	HD	*Heiliger Dienst* (Salzburg)
		HDR	Harvard Dissertations in Religion
FRLANT	Forschungen zur Religion und Literatur des Alten und Neuen Testaments	*HerKor*	*Herder Korrespondenz*
		HeyJ	*Heythrop Journal*
		HibJ	*Hibbert Journal*
FTS	Frankfurter Theologische Studien	HKAT	Handkommentar zum Alten Testament
FV	*Foi et Vie*	HKNT	Handkommentar zum Neuen Testament
FZPT	*Freiburg Zeitschrift für Philosophie und Theologie*	*HL*	*Das heilige Land*
GAG	W. von Soden, *Grundriss der akkadischen Grammatik*	HNT	Handbuch zum Neuen Testament
GBZKA	*Grazer Beiträge: Zeitschrift für die klassischen Altertumswissenschaft*	HNTC	Harper's NT Commentaries
		HR	*History of Religions*
		HSM	Harvard Semitic Monographs
GCS	Griechische christliche Schriftsteller	HTKNT	Herders theologischer Kommentar zum Neuen Testament
GJ	*Grace Journal*		
GKB	Gesenius-Kautzsch-Bergsträsser, *Hebräische Grammatik*	*HTR*	*Harvard Theological Review*
		HTS	Harvard Theological Studies
GKC	*Gesenius' Hebrew Grammar,* ed. E. Kautzsch, tr. A. E. Cowley	*HTS*	*Hervormde Teologiese Studies* (Pretoria)
		HUCA	*Hebrew Union College Annual*
GNT	Grundrisse zum Neuen Testament	HUTH	Hermeneutische Untersuchungen zur Theologie
GOTR	*Greek Orthodox Theological Review*		
GR	*Greece and Rome*	*IB*	*Interpreter's Bible*
GRBS	*Greek, Roman, and Byzantine Studies*	*IBD*	*Illustrated Bible Dictionary,* ed. J. D. Douglas and N. Hillyer
Greg	*Gregorianum*	*IBS*	*Irish Biblical Studies*

ICC	International Critical Commentary		*Theological Society*
		JHS	*Journal of Hellenic Studies*
IDB	G. A. Buttrick (ed.), *Interpreter's Dictionary of the Bible*	*JIBS*	*Journal of Indian and Buddhist Studies*
IDBSup	Supplementary volume to *IDB*	*JIPh*	*Journal of Indian Philosophy*
IEJ	*Israel Exploration Journal*	*JJS*	*Journal of Jewish Studies*
IER	*Irish Ecclesiastical Record*	*JLH*	*Jahrbuch für Liturgie und Hymnologie*
IES	*Indian Ecclesiastical Studies*		
IKZ	*Internationale Kirchliche Zeitschrift*	*JLitTheol*	*Journal of Literature and Theology*
IKZCom	*Internationale Katholische Zeitschrift "Communion"* (Rodenkirchen)	*JMES*	*Journal of Middle Eastern Studies*
		JMS	*Journal of Mithraic Studies*
		JNES	*Journal of Near Eastern Studies*
ILS	H. Dessau (ed.), *Inscriptiones Latinae Selectae* (Berlin, 1892)	*JPOS*	*Journal of the Palestine Oriental Society*
		JQ	*Jewish Quarterly* (London)
Int	*Interpretation*	*JQR*	*Jewish Quarterly Review*
ISBE	*International Standard Bible Encyclopedia*, ed. G. W. Bromiley	JQRMS	Jewish Quarterly Review Monograph Series
		JR	*Journal of Religion*
ITQ	*Irish Theological Quarterly*	*JRAS*	*Journal of the Royal Asiatic Society*
ITS	*Indian Theological Studies*		
		JRE	*Journal of Religious Ethics*
JA	*Journal asiatique*	*JRelS*	*Journal of Religious Studies*
JAAR	*Journal of the American Academy of Religion*	*JRH*	*Journal of Religious History*
		JRomH	*Journal of Roman History*
JAC	*Jahrbuch für Antike und Christentum*	*JRS*	*Journal of Roman Studies*
		JRT	*Journal of Religious Thought*
JAMA	*Journal of the American Medical Association*	*JSJ*	*Journal for the Study of Judaism*
		JSNT	*Journal for the Study of the New Testament*
JANESCU	*Journal of the Ancient Near Eastern Society of Columbia University*	JSNTSup	JSNT Supplement Series
JAOS	*Journal of the American Oriental Society*	*JSOT*	*Journal for the Study of the Old Testament*
JAS	*Journal of Asian Studies*	JSOTSup	JSOT Supplement Series
JBC	R. E. Brown et al. (eds.), *The Jerome Biblical Commentary*	*JSS*	*Journal of Semitic Studies*
		JSSR	*Journal for the Scientific Study of Religion*
JBL	*Journal of Biblical Literature*		
JBR	*Journal of Bible and Religion*	*JTC*	*Journal for Theology and the Church*
JBT	*Jahrbuch für biblische Theologie* (Neukirchen)	*JTS*	*Journal of Theological Studies*
JCS	*Journal of Cuneiform Studies*	*JTSA*	*Journal of Theology for South Africa*
JDS	Judean Desert Studies		
JEA	*Journal of Egyptian Archaeology*	*Jud*	*Judaica*
JEH	*Journal of Ecclesiastical History*		
JerPersp	*Jerusalem Perspectives*	KAI	H. Donner and W. Röllig, *Kanaanäische und aramäische Inschriften*
JES	*Journal of Ecumenical Studies*		
JETS	*Journal of the Evangelical*		

KAT	E. Sellin (ed.), *Kommentar zum Alten Testament*	*LumVieSup*	*Supplement to LumVie*
KatBl	*Katechetische Blätter*	*LVit*	*Lumen Vitae*
KB	L. Koehler and W. Baumgartner, *Lexicon in Veteris Testamenti libros*	*LW*	*Lutheran World*
KD	*Kerygma und Dogma*	*ManQ*	*The Manking Quarterly*
KEK	Kritisch-exegetischer Kommentar über das Neue Testament	*MarStud*	*Marian Studies*
		MC	*Modern Churchman*
		McCQ	*McCormick Quarterly*
KeTh	*Kerken en Theologie*	MDOG	Mitteilungen der deutschen Orient-Gesellschaft
KF	*Der Kirchenfreund*	*MelT*	*Melita Theologica*
KlT	Kleine Texte	MeyerK	H. A. W. Meyer, *Kritisch-exegetischer Kommentar über das Neue Testament*
KM	*Katholischen Missionen*		
KRS	*Kirchenblatt für die reformierte Schweiz*	*MGWJ*	*Monatschrift für Geschichte und Wissenschaft des Judentums*
KTR	*King's Theological Review* (London)	*MilltownStud*	*Milltown Studies* (Dublin)
KuBANT	Kommentare und Beiträge zum Alten und Neuen Testament	MM	J. H. Moulton and G. Milligan, *The Vocabulary of the Greek Testament* (London: Hodder, 1930)
		MNTC	Moffatt NT Commentary
LCC	Library of Christian Classics	*MonPast*	*Monatschrift für Pastoraltheologie*
LCL	Loeb Classical Library	*MPAIBL*	*Mémoires présentés a l'Académie des inscriptions et belles-lettres*
LD	Lectio divina		
LebSeel	*Lebendige Seelsorge*	*MPG*	*Patrologia Graeca*, ed. J. P. Migne, 1844 ff.
Leš	*Lešonénu*		
LexTQ	*Lexington Theological Quarterly*	*MScRel*	*Mélanges de science religieuse*
LingBib	*Linguistica Biblica*	MTS	Marburger theologische Studien
LitMönch	*Liturgie et Mönchtum*		
LitTheol	*Literature and Theology* (Oxford)	*MTZ*	*Münchener theologische Zeitschrift*
LLAVT	E. Vogt, *Lexicon linguae aramaicae Veteris Testamenti*	*MUSJ*	*Mélanges de l'université Saint-Joseph*
LM	*Lutherische Monatshefte*	MVAG	Mitteilungen der vorder-asiatisch-ägyptischen Gesellschaft
LouvStud	*Louvain Studies*		
LPGL	G. W. H. Lampe, *Patristic Greek Lexicon*		
LQ	*Lutheran Quarterly*	NABPR	National Association of Baptist Professors of Religion
LR	*Lutherische Rundschau*		
LS	*Louvain Studies*	*NAG*	*Nachrichten von der Akademie der Wissenschaften in Göttingen*
LSJ	Liddell-Scott-Jones, *Greek-English Lexicon*		
LTK	*Lexikon für Theologie und Kirche*	*NB*	*New Blackfriars*
LTP	*Laval théologique et philosophique*	NCB	New Century Bible (new ed.)
LTSB	*Lutheran Theological Seminary Bulletin*	NCCHS	R. C. Fuller et al. (eds.), *New Catholic Commentary on Holy Scripture*
LUÅ	Lunds universitets årsskrift		
LumVie	*Lumière et Vie*		

NCE	M. R. P. McGuire et al. (eds.), *New Catholic Encyclopedia*	*Numen*	*Numen: International Review for the History of Religions*
NClB	New Clarendon Bible	*NZM*	*Neue Zeitschrift für Missionswissenschaft*
NedTTs	*Nederlands theologisch tijdschrift*	*NZSTR*	*Neue Zeitschrift für systematische Theologie und Religionsphilosophie*
Neot	*Neotestamentica*		
NESTR	*Near East School of Theology Review*		
NewDocs	*New Documents Illustrating Early Christianity, A Review of Greek Inscriptions, etc.*, ed. G. H. R. Horsley, North Ryde, NSW, Australia	*OAK*	*Österreichisches Archiv für Kirchenrecht*
		OberrheinPast	*Oberrheinisches Pastoralblatt*
		OBL	*Orientalia et Biblica Lovaniensia*
NFT	New Frontiers in Theology	OBO	Orbis biblicus et orientalis
NGS	New Gospel Studies	ÖBS	Österreichische Biblische Studien
NHS	Nag Hammadi Studies		
NICNT	New International Commentary on the New Testament	*OCD*	*Oxford Classical Dictionary*
		OCP	*Orientalia christiana periodica*
NieuTS	*Nieuwe theologische studiën*	*OGI*	W. Dittenberger (ed.), *Orientis graeci inscriptiones selectae* (Leipzig: Hirzel, 1903–5)
NiewTT	*Niew theologisch tijdschrift*		
NIGTC	New International Greek Testament Commentary		
NJDT	*Neue Jahrbücher für deutsche Theologie*	OIP	Oriental Institute Publications
NKZ	*Neue kirchliche Zeitschrift*	OLP	Orientalia lovaniensia periodica
NorTT	*Norsk Teologisk Tijdsskrift*		
NovT	*Novum Testamentum*	*OLZ*	*Orientalische Literaturzeitung*
NovTSup	Supplement to *NovT*	*OPTAT*	*Occasional Papers in Translation and Textlinguistics* (Dallas)
NovVet	*Nova et vetera*		
NPNF	Nicene and Post-Nicene Fathers	*Or*	*Orientalia* (Rome)
NRF	*Nouvelle revue française*	*OrAnt*	*Oriens antiquus*
NRT	*La nouvelle revue théologique*	*OrChr*	*Oriens christianus*
NSK	*Neues Sächsisches Kirchenblatt*	*OrSyr*	*L'orient syrien*
NTA	*New Testament Abstracts*	ÖTKNT	Ökumenischer Taschenbuch-Kommentar zum NT
NTAbh	Neutestamentliche Abhandlungen		
NTD	Das Neue Testament Deutsch	OTM	Oxford Theological Monographs
NTF	Neutestamentliche Forschungen	OTS	Oudtestamentische Studiën
NTL	New Testament Library	*PAAJR*	*Proceedings of the American Academy of Jewish Research*
NTR	*New Theology Review*	*Parlit*	*Paroisse et liturgie*
NTS	*New Testament Studies*	*PastB*	*Pastoralblätter*
NTSR	The New Testament for Spiritual Reading	PC	Proclamation Commentaries
NTTS	New Testament Tools and Studies	PCB	M. Black and H. H. Rowley (eds.), *Peake's Commentary on the Bible*

PEFQS	Palestine Exploration Fund, Quarterly Statement	RA	Revue d'assyriologie et d'archéologie orientale
PenHom	La Pensée et les hommes	RAC	Reallexikon für Antike und Christentum
PEQ	Palestine Exploration Quarterly	RArch	Revue archéologique
PerTeo	Perspectiva Teologica	RB	Revue biblique
PFay	Fayûm Papyri	RBén	Revue Bénedictine
PG	Patrologia graeca, ed. J. P. Migne	RCB	Revista de cultura biblica
		RDC	Revue de droit canonique
PGM	K. Preisendanz (ed.), Papyri graecae magicae	RE	Realencyklopädie für protestantische Theologie und Kirche
PhEW	Philosophy East and West		
PhRev	Philosophical Review	REA	Revue des Études Augustiniennes
PJ	Palästina-Jahrbuch		
PLL	Papers on Language and Literature	REAnc	Revue des études anciennes (Bordeaux)
PM	Protestantische Monatshefte	RecAcLég	Recueil de l'Académie de Législation (Toulouse)
PNTC	Pelican New Testament Commentaries	RechBib	Recherches bibliques
PO	Patrologia orientalis	REg	Revue d'égyptologie
POxy	Oxyrhynchus Papyri	REG	Revue des études grecques
ProcCTSA	Proceedings of the Catholic Theological Society of America	REJ	Revue des études juives
		RelArts	Religion and the Arts
		RELiège	Revue Ecclésiastique de Liège
ProcGLBS	Proceedings Eastern Great Lakes Bible Society	RelLif	Religion in Life
		RelS	Religious Studies
ProcIBA	Proceedings of the Irish Biblical Association	RelSoc	Religion and Society
		RelSRev	Religious Studies Review
PRS	Perspectives in Religious Studies	RES	Répertoire d'épigraphie sémitique
PRU	Le Palais royal d'Ugarit		
PSTJ	Perkins (School of Theology) Journal	RestQ	Restoration Quarterly
		RevAfTh	Revue Africaine de Théologie (Kinshasa-Limette, Zaire)
PTMS	Pittsburgh Theological Monograph Series		
		RevApol	Revue Apologétique
PTR	Princeton Theological Review	RevArch	Revue archéologique
PVTG	Pseudepigrapha Veteris Testamenti graece	RevDioc Namur	Revue diocésaine de Namur
PW	Pauly-Wissowa, Real-Encyklopädie der klassischen Altertumswissenschaft	RevDTournai	Revue diocésaine de Tournai
		RevExp	Review and Expositor
		RevistB	Revista biblica
PWSup	Supplement to PW	RevQ	Revue de Qumrân
		RevRef	Revue Réformée
QD	Quaestiones Disputatae	RevRel	Review for Religious
QDAP	Quarterly of the Department of Antiquities in Palestine	RevScRel	Revue des sciences religieuses
		RevSém	Revue sémitique
QLP	Questions liturgiques et paroissiales (Louvain)	RevSR	Revue des sciences religieuses (Strasbourg)
QRev	Quarterly Review (Nashville)	RevThom	Revue thomiste

RevUB	*Revue de l'Université de Bruxelles*	SANT	Studien zum Alten und Neuen Testament
RGG	*Religion in Geschichte und Gegenwart*	SAQ	Sammlung ausgewählter kirchen- und dogmengeschichtlicher Quellenschriften
RHD	*Revue de l'histoire de droit*		
RHE	*Revue d'histoire ecclésiastique*		
RHPR	*Revue d'histoire et de philosophie religieuses*	*SAWB*	*Sitzungsberichte der (königlich preussischen) Akademie der Wissenschaften zu Berlin (phil.-hist. Klasse)*
RHR	*Revue de l'histoire des religions*		
RHS	*Revue d'histoire de la spiritualité*	SB	Sources bibliques
RICP	*Revue de l'Institut Catholique de Paris*	SBB	Stuttgarter biblische Monographien
RIDA	*Revue internationale du droit de l'antiquité*	*SBFLA*	*Studii biblici franciscani liber annuus*
RIL	*Religion and Intellectual Life*	*SBJ*	*La sainte bible de Jérusalem*
RivB	*Rivista biblica*	SBLASP	Society of Biblical Literature Abstracts and Seminar Papers
RM	*Rheinisches Museum für Philologie*		
RNT	Regensburger Neues Testament	SBLDS	SBL Dissertation Series
		SBLMasS	SBL Masoretic Studies
RR	*Review of Religion*	SBLMS	SBL Monograph Series
RSB	*Religious Studies Bulletin*	SBLSBS	SBL Sources for Biblical Study
RSLR	*Rivista di Storiae Letteratura Religiosa* (Turin)	SBLSCS	SBL Septuagint and Cognate Studies
RSO	*Rivista degli studi orientali*		
RSPT	*Revue des sciences philosophiques et théologiques*	SBLTT	SBL Texts and Translations
		SBM	Stuttgarter biblische Monographien
RSR	*Recherches de science religieuse*	SBS	Stuttgarter Bibelstudien
RST	Regensburger Studien zur Theologie	SBT	Studies in Biblical Theology
		SC	Sources chrétiennes
RTL	*Revue théologique de Louvain*	*ScEccl*	*Sciences ecclésiastiques*
RTP	*Revue de théologie et de philosophie*	*ScEs*	*Science et esprit*
		SCR	*Studies in Comparative Religion*
RTQR	*Revue de théologie et des questions religieuses* (Montaublon)	*Scr*	*Scripture*
		ScrB	*Scripture Bulletin*
RTR	*Reformed Theological Review*	SD	Studies and Documents
RUO	*Revue de l'université Ottawa*	*SE*	*Studia Evangelica* 1, 2, 3, 4, 5, 6 (= TU 73 [1959], 87 [1964], 88 [1964], 102 [1968], 103 [1968], 112 [1973]
RUV	*La Revue de l'Université Laval*		
SaatHof	*Saat auf Hoffnung*		
SacPag	*Sacra Pagina*		
SAH	*Sitzungberichte der Heidelberger Akademie der Wissenschaften (phil.-hist. Klasse)*	SEÅ	*Svensk exegetisk årsbok*
		Sef	*Sefarad*
		SeinSend	*Sein und Sendung*
Sal	*Salmanticensis*	Sem	*Semitica*

SémiotBib	*Sémiotique et Bible*		*Testament*, 4 vols.
SHAW	Sitzungsberichte		(Munich: Beck'sche,
	heidelbergen Akademie		1926–28)
	der Wissenschaften	*StudBib*	*Studia biblica*
SHT	Studies in Historical	*StudClas*	*Studii clasice* (Bukarest)
	Theology	*StudMiss*	*Studia Missionalia*
SHVL	Skrifter Utgivna Av Kungl.	StudNeot	Studia neotestamentica
	Humanistika Veten-	*StudPat*	*Studia Patristica*
	skapssamfundet i Lund	*STZ*	*Schweizerische theologische*
SIDJC	*Service international de documen-*		*Zeitschrift*
	tation judéo-chrétienne	SUNT	Studien zur Umwelt des
SJLA	Studies in Judaism in Late		Neuen Testaments
	Antiquity	SVTP	Studia in Veteris Testamenti
SJT	*Scottish Journal of Theology*		pseudepigrapha
SLJT	*St Luke's Journal of Theology*	*SWJT*	*Southwestern Journal of*
SMSR	*Studi e materiali di storia delle*		*Theology*
	religioni	SymBU	Symbolae biblicae
SNT	Studien zum Neuen		upsalienses
	Testament		
SNTA	Studiorum Novi Testamenti	*TantY*	*Tantur Yearbook*
	Auxilia	*TAPA*	*Transactions of the American*
SNTSMS	Society for New Testament		*Philological Association*
	Studies Monograph	*TB*	*Theologische Beiträge*
	Series	TBC	Torch Bible Commentaries
SNTU	*Studien zum Neuen Testament*	*TBl*	*Theologische Blätter*
	und seiner Umwelt	TBü	Theologische Bücherei
SO	*Symbolae osloenses*	TC	Theological Collection
SOTSMS	Society for Old Testament		(SPCK)
	Study Monograph Series	*TD*	*Theology Digest*
SPap	*Studia papyrologica*	*TDNT*	G. Kittel and G. Friedrich
SPAW	Sitzungsberichte der		(eds.), *Theological*
	preussischen Akademie		*Dictionary of the New*
	der Wissenschaften		*Testament*, 10 vols., ET
SPB	Studia postbiblica		(Grand Rapids:
SR	*Studies in Religion/Sciences*		Eerdmans, 1964–76)
	Religieuses	*TE*	*Theologica Evangelica*
SSS	Semitic Study Series	TextsS	Texts and Studies
ST	*Studia theologica*	*TF*	*Theologische Forschung*
STÅ	*Svensk teologisk årsskrift*	*TGeg*	*Theologie der Gegenwart*
StBibT	*Studia biblica et theologica*	*TGl*	*Theologie und Glaube*
STDJ	Studies on the Texts of the	*Th*	*Theology*
	Desert of Judah	*ThA*	*Theologische Arbeiten*
StimmZeit	*Stimmen der Zeit* (Munich)	*ThBer*	*Theologische Berichte*
STK	*Svensk teologisk kvartalskrift*	THKNT	Theologischer
StMon	*Studia Monastica*		Handkommentar zum
StMor	*Studia Moralia*		Neuen Testament
Str-B	H. Strack and P. Billerbeck,	*ThViat*	*Theologia Viatorum*
	Kommentar zum Neuen	*TJ*	*Trinity Journal*

TJT	*Toronto Journal of Theology*		Humanities Monograph
TK	*Texte und Kontexte* (Stuttgart)	*UnaSanc*	Una Sancta (Freising)
TLZ	*Theologische Literaturzeitung*	UNT	Untersuchungen zum
TNTC	Tyndale New Testament		Neuen Testament
	Commentaries	*US*	*Una Sancta*
TP	*Theologie und Philosophie*	*USQR*	*Union Seminary Quarterly*
	(ThPh)		*Review*
TPQ	*Theologisch-Praktische*	*USR*	*Union Seminary Review*
	Quartalschrift		(Richmond, VA)
TQ	*Theologische Quartalschrift*	UT	C. H. Gordon, *Ugaritic*
TRev	*Theologische Revue*		*Textbook*
TrinSemRev	*Trinity Seminary Review*	UUÅ	Uppsala universitetsårsskrift
	(Columbus, OH)	*UUC*	*Unitarian Universalist*
TRRHD	*Tijdschrift voor*		*Christian*
	Rechtsgeschiednis: Revue		
	d'histoire de droit	*VC*	*Vigilae christianae*
TRu	*Theologische Rundschau*	*VCaro*	*Verbum caro*
TS	*Theological Studies*	*VChr*	*Vigiliae Christianae*
TSAJ	Texte und Studien zum	*VD*	*Verbum domini*
	Antiken Judentum	*VetC*	*Vetera Christianorum*
TSFB	*Theological Students Fellowship*	*VF*	*Verkündigung und Forschung*
	Bulletin	VKGNT	K. Aland (ed.), *Vollständige*
TSK	*Theologische Studien und*		*Konkordanz zum griech-*
	Kritiken		*ischen Neuen Testament*
TT	*Teologisk Tidsskrift*	*VoxEv*	*Vox Evangelica* (London)
TTKi	*Tidsskrift for Teologi og Kirke*	VS	Verbum salutis
TToday	*Theology Today*	*VSpir*	*Vie spirituelle*
TTS	Trier theologische Studien	*VT*	*Vetus Testamentum*
TTZ	*Trierer theologische Zeitschrift*	VTSup	Vetus Testamentum,
TU	Texte und Untersuchungen		Supplements
TVers	*Theologische Versuche* (Berlin)		
TWAT	G. J. Botterweck and H.	WA	M. Luther, Kritische
	Ringgren (eds.),		Gesamtausgabe
	Theologisches Wörterbuch		(="Weimar" edition)
	zum Alten Testament	WBC	Word Biblical Commentary
TWNT	G. Kittel and G. Friedrich	WC	Westminster Commentary
	(eds.), *Theologisches*	*WD*	*Wort und Dienst*
	Wörterbuch zum Neuen	*WDB*	*Westminster Dictionary of the*
	Testament		*Bible*
TynB	*Tyndale Bulletin*	WF	Wege der Forschung
TZ	*Theologische Zeitschrift*	*WHAB*	*Westminster Historical Atlas of*
			the Bible
UBSGNT	United Bible Societies Greek	WMANT	Wissenschaftliche
	New Testament		Monographien zum
UCL	Universitas Catholica		Alten und Neuen
	Lovaniensis		Testament
UF	*Ugaritische Forschungen*	*WO*	*Die Welt des Orients*
UFHM	University of Florida	*WortWahr*	*Wort und Wahrheit*

WTJ	*Westminster Theological Journal*	ZKG	*Zeitschrift für Kirchengeschichte*
WUNT	Wissenschaftliche	ZKNT	*Zahn's Kommentar zum NT*
	Untersuchungen zum	ZKT	*Zeitschrift für katholische*
	Neuen Testament		*Theologie*
WW	*Word and World*	ZMR	*Zeitschrift für Missionskunde*
WZKM	*Wiener Zeitschrift für die Kunde*		*und Religionswissenschaft*
	des Morgenlandes	ZNW	*Zeitschrift für die*
WZKSO	*Wiener Zeitschrift für die Kunde*		*neutestamentliche*
	Süd- und Ostasiens		*Wissenschaft*
		ZPE	*Zeitschrift für Papyrologie und*
ZA	*Zeitschrift für Assyriologie*		*Epigraphik*
ZAW	*Zeitschrift für die*	ZRGG	*Zeitschrift für Religions- und*
	alttestamentliche		*Geistesgeschichte*
	Wissenschaft	ZSSR	*Zeitschrift der Savigny Stiftung*
ZDMG	*Zeitschrift der deutschen*		*für Rechtsgeschichte,*
	morgenländischen		*romantische Abteilung*
	Gesellschaft	ZST	*Zeitschrift für systematische*
ZDPV	*Zeitschrift des deutschen*		*Theologie*
	Palästina-Vereins	ZTK	*Zeitschrift für Theologie und*
ZdZ	*Die Zeichen der Zeit*		*Kirche*
ZEE	*Zeitschrift für evangelische Ethik*	ZWT	*Zeitschrift für wissenschaftliche*
ZHT	*Zeitschrift für historische*		*Theologie*
	Theologie		

D. Abbreviations for Books of the Bible, the Apocrypha, and the Pseudepigrapha

OLD TESTAMENT

Gen	2 Chr	Dan
Exod	Ezra	Hos
Lev	Neh	Joel
Num	Esth	Amos
Deut	Job	Obad
Josh	Ps(Pss)	Jonah
Judg	Prov	Mic
Ruth	Eccl	Nah
1 Sam	Cant	Hab
2 Sam	Isa	Zeph
1 Kgs	Jer	Hag
2 Kgs	Lam	Zech
1 Chr	Ezek	Mal

NEW TESTAMENT

Matt	1 Tim
Mark	2 Tim
Luke	Titus
John	Philem
Acts	Heb
Rom	Jas
1 Cor	1 Peter
2 Cor	2 Peter
Gal	1 John
Eph	2 John
Phil	3 John
Col	Jude
1 Thess	Rev
2 Thess	

APOCRYPHA

1 Esd	1 Esdras	Wis	Wisdom of Solomon
2 Esd	2 Esdras	Sir	Ecclesiasticus (Wisdom of
Tob	Tobit		Jesus the son of Sirach)
Jdt	Judith	Bar	Baruch
Add Esth	Additions to Esther	Ep Jer	Epistle of Jeremy

S Th Ch	Song of the Three Children	Pr Man	Prayer of Manasseh
	(or Young Men)	1 Macc	1 Maccabees
Sus	Susanna	2 Macc	2 Maccabees
Bel	Bel and the Dragon		

E. Abbreviations of the Names of Pseudepigraphical and Early Patristic Books

Adam and Eve	Life of Adam and Eve	Barn.	Barnabas
Apoc. Abr.	Apocalypse of Abraham	1–2 Clem.	1–2 Clement
	(1st to 2nd cent. A.D.)	Did.	Didache
2–3 Apoc. Bar.	Syriac, Greek Apocalypse	Diogn.	Diognetus
	of Baruch	Herm. Man.	Hermas, Mandates
Apoc. Mos.	Apocalypse of Moses	Sim.	Similitudes
As. Mos.	(See T. Mos.)	Vis.	Visions
1–2–3 Enoch	Ethiopic, Slavonic,	Ign. Eph.	Ignatius, Letter to the
	Hebrew Enoch		Ephesians
Ep. Arist.	Epistle of Aristeas	Magn.	Ignatius, Letter to the
Ep. Diognetus	Epistle to Diognetus		Magnesians
Jub.	Jubilees	Phil.	Ignatius, Letter to the
Mart. Isa.	Martyrdom of Isaiah		Philadelphians
Odes Sol.	Odes of Solomon	Pol.	Ignatius, Letter to
Pss. Sol.	Psalms of Solomon		Polycarp
Sib. Or.	Sibylline Oracles	Rom.	Ignatius, Letter to the
T. 12 Patr.	Testaments of the Twelve		Romans
	Patriarchs	Smyrn.	Ignatius, Letter to the
T. Abr.	Testament of Abraham		Smyrnaeans
T. Judah	Testament of Judah	Trall.	Ignatius, Letter to the
T. Levi	Testament of Levi, etc.		Trallians
Apoc. Pet.	Apocalypse of Peter	Mart. Pol.	Martyrdom of Polycarp
Gos. Eb.	Gospel of the Ebionites	Pol. Phil.	Polycarp to the
Gos. Eg.	Gospel of the Egyptians		Philippians
Gos. Heb.	Gospel of the Hebrews	Adv. Haer.	Irenaeus, Against All
Gos. Naass.	Gospel of the Naassenes		Heresies
Gos. Pet.	Gospel of Peter	De Praesc.	Tertullian, On the
Gos. Thom.	Gospel of Thomas	Haer.	Proscribing of Heretics
Prot. Jas.	Protevangelium of James		

F. Abbreviations of Names of Dead Sea Scrolls and Related Texts

CD	Cairo (Genizah text of the)		Qumran, yielding written
	Damascus (Document)		material; followed by
Hev	Nahal Hever texts		abbreviation of biblical or
Mas	Masada texts		apocryphal book
Mird	Khirbet Mird texts	QL	Qumran literature
Mur	Wadi Murabbaʿat texts	1QapGen	Genesis Apocryphon of
P	Pesher (commentary)		Qumran Cave 1
Q	Qumran	1QH	Hôdāyôt (Thanksgiving
1Q, 2Q			Hymns) from Qumran
3Q, etc.	Numbered caves of		Cave 1

1QIsa^{a,b}	First or second copy of Isaiah from Qumran Cave 1
1QpHab	*Pesher on Habakkuk* from Qumran Cave 1
1QM	*Milḥāmāh* (War Scroll)
1QS	*Serek hayyahad (Rule of the Community, Manual of Discipline)*
1QSa	Appendix A *(Rule of the Congregation)* to 1QS
1QSb	Appendix B *(Blessings)* to 1QS
3Q15	Copper Scroll from Qumran Cave 3
4QFlor	*Florilegium* (or *Eschatological Midrashim*) from Qumran Cave 4

4QMess ar	Aramaic "Messianic" text from Qumran Cave 4
4QPrNab	Prayer of Nabonidus from Qumran Cave 4
4QTestim	*Testimonia* text from Qumran Cave 4
4QTLevi	*Testament of Levi* from Qumran Cave 4
4QPhyl	Phylacteries from Qumran Cave 4
11QMelch	*Melchizedek* text from Qumran Cave 11
11QtgJob	*Targum of Job* from Qumran Cave 11

G. Abbreviaations of Targumic Material

Tg. Onq.	*Targum Onqelos*
Tg. Neb.	*Targum of the Prophets*
Tg. Ket.	*Targum of the Writings*
Frg. Tg.	*Fragmentary Targum*
Sam. Tg.	*Samaritan Targum*
Tg. Isa.	*Targum of Isaiah*
Pal. Tgs.	*Palestinian Targums*
Tg. Neof.	*Targum Neofiti I*

Tg. Ps. -J.	*Targum Pseudo-Jonathan*
Tg. Yer. I	*Targum Yerušalmi I**
Tg. Yer. II	*Targum Yerušalmi II**
Yem. Tg.	*Yemenite Targum*
Tg. Esth I, II	*First or Second Targum of Esther*

*optional title

H. Abbreviations of Other Rabbinic Works

ʾAbot	ʾAbot de Rabbi Nathan
ʾAg. Ber.	*ʾAggadat Berešit*
Bab.	*Babylonian*
Bar.	*Baraita*
Der. Er. Rab.	*Derek Ereṣ Rabba*
Der. Er. Zut.	*Derek Ereṣ Zuṭa*
Gem.	*Gemara*
Kalla	*Kalla*
Mek.	*Mekilta*
Midr.	*Midraš;* cited with usual abbreviation for biblical book; but *Midr. Qoh.* = *Midraš Qohelet*
Pal.	*Palestinian*
Pesiq. R.	*Pesiqta Rabbati*

Pesiq. Rab Kah.	*Pesiqta de Rab Kahana*
Pirqe R. El.	*Pirqe Rabbi Eliezer*
Rab.	Rabbah (following abbreviation for biblical book: *Gen. Rab.* [with periods] = *Genesis Rabbah*)
Sem.	*Semahot*
Sipra	*Sipra*
Sipre	*Sipre*
Sop.	*Soperim*
S. ʿOlam Rab.	*Seder ʿOlam Rabbah*
Talm.	*Talmud*
Yal.	*Yalqut*

I. Abbreviations of Orders and Tractates in Mishnaic and Related Literature

(Italicized m., t., b., or y. used before name to distinguish among tractates in Mishnah, Tosepta, Babylonian Talmud, and Jerusalem Talmud.)

ʾAbot	*ʾAbot*	*Nazir*	*Nazir*
ʿArak.	*ʿArakin*	*Ned.*	*Nedarim*
ʿAbod. Zar.	*ʿAboda Zara*	*Neg.*	*Negaʿim*
B. Bat.	*Baba Batra*	*Nez.*	*Neziqin*
Bek.	*Bekorot*	*Nid.*	*Niddah*
Ber.	*Berakot*	*Ohol.*	*Oholot*
Beṣa	*Beṣa (= Yom Tob)*	*ʿOr.*	*ʿOrla*
Bik.	*Bikkurim*	*Para*	*Para*
B. Meṣ.	*Baba Meṣiʿa*	*Peʾa*	*Peʾa*
B. Qam.	*Baba Qamma*	*Pesah.*	*Pesahim*
Dem.	*Demai*	*Qinnim*	*Qinnim*
ʿEd.	*ʿEduyyot*	*Qidd.*	*Qiddušin*
ʿErub.	*ʿErubin*	*Qod.*	*Qodašin*
Giṭ.	*Giṭṭin*	*Roš. Haš.*	*Roš Haššana*
Ḥag.	*Ḥagiga*	*Sanh.*	*Sanhedrin*
Hal.	*Halla*	*Šabb.*	*Šabbat*
Hor.	*Horayot*	*Šeb.*	*Šebiʿit*
Ḥul.	*Ḥullin*	*Šebu.*	*Šebuʿot*
Kelim	*Kelim*	*Šeqal.*	*Šeqalim*
Ker.	*Keritot*	*Soṭa*	*Soṭa*
Ketub.	*Ketubot*	*Sukk.*	*Sukka*
Kil.	*Kilʾayim*	*Taʿan.*	*Taʿanit*
Maʿaś.	*Maʿaśerot*	*Tamid*	*Tamid*
Mak.	*Makkot*	*Tem.*	*Temura*
Makš.	*Makširin (=Mašqin)*	*Ter.*	*Terumot*
Meg.	*Megilla*	*Ṭohar.*	*Ṭoharot*
Meʿil.	*Meʿila*	*T. Yom*	*Tebul Yom*
Menaḥ.	*Menahot*	*ʿUq.*	*ʿUqsin*
Mid.	*Middot*	*Yad.*	*Yadayim*
Miqw.	*Miqwaʾot*	*Yebam.*	*Yebamot*
Moʿed	*Moʿed*	*Yoma*	*Yoma (= Kippurim)*
Moʿed Qat.	*Moʿed Qatan*	*Zabim*	*Zabim*
Maʿaś. Š.	*Maʿaśer Šeni*	*Zebah.*	*Zebahim*
Našim	*Našim*	*Zer.*	*Zeraʿim*

J. Abbreviations of Nag Hammadi Tractates

Acts Pet. 12	*Acts of Peter and the Twelve*	*1 Apoc. Jas.*	*First Apocalypse of James*
Apost.	*Apostles*	*2 Apoc. Jas.*	*Second Apocalypse of James*
Allogenes	*Allogenes*	*Apoc. Paul*	*Apocalypse of Paul*
Ap. Jas.	*Apocryphon of James*	*Apoc. Pet.*	*Apocalypse of Peter*
Ap. John	*Apocryphon of John*	*Asclepius*	*Asclepius 21–29*
Apoc. Adam	*Apocalypse of Adam*	*Auth. Teach.*	*Authoritative Teaching*

Dial. Sav.	Dialogue of the Savior	*On Euch. B*	On the Eucharist B
Disc. 8–9	Discourse on the Eighth and Ninth	*Orig. World*	On the Origin of the World
		Paraph. Shem	Paraphrase of Shem
Ep. Pet. Phil.	Letter of Peter to Philip	*Pr. Paul*	Prayer of the Apostle Paul
Eugnostos	Eugnostos the Blessed	*Pr. Thanks.*	Prayer of Thanksgiving
Exeg. Soul	Exegesis on the Soul	*Prot. Jas.*	Protevangelium of James
Gos. Eg.	Gospel of the Egyptians	*Sent. Sextus*	Sentences of Sextus
Gos. Phil.	Gospel of Philip	*Soph. Jes. Chr.*	Sophia of Jesus Christ
Gos. Thom.	Gospel of Thomas	*Steles Seth*	Three Steles of Seth
Gos. Truth	Gospel of Truth	*Teach. Silv.*	Teachings of Silvanus
Great Pow.	Concept of our Great Power	*Testim. Truth*	Testimony of Truth
Hyp. Arch.	Hypostasis of the Archons	*Thom. Cont.*	Book of Thomas the Contender
Hypsiph.	Hypsiphrone	*Thund.*	Thunder, Perfect Mind
Interp. Know.	Interpretation of Knowledge	*Treat. Res.*	Treatise on Resurrection
Marsanes	Marsanes	*Treat. Seth*	Second Treatise of the Great Seth
Melch.	Melchizedek		
Norea	Thought of Norea	*Tri. Trac.*	Tripartite Tractate
On Bap. A	On Baptism A	*Trim. Prot.*	Trimorphic Protennoia
On Bap. B	On Baptism B	*Val. Exp.*	A Valentinian Exposition
On Bap. C	On Baptism C	*Zost.*	Zostrianos
On Euch. A	On the Eucharist A		

Note: The textual notes and numbers used to indicate individual manuscripts are those found in the apparatus criticus of *Novum Testamentum Graece,* ed. E. Nestle and K. Aland et al. (Stuttgart: Deutsche Bibelgesellschaft, 1979[26]). This edition of the Greek New Testament is the basis for the *Translation* sections.

Commentary Bibliography

Barclay, W. *The Gospel of Luke.* Daily Study Bible Series. 2nd ed. Philadelphia: Westminster, 1956. **Barrel, E. V.,** and **Barrell, K. G.** *St. Luke's Gospel: An Introductory Study.* London: Murray, 1982. **Bossuyt, P.,** and **Radermakers, J.** *Jésus, parole de la Grâce selon saint Luc 1: Texte. 2 Lecture continue.* Brussels: Institut d'Études Théologique, 1981. **Bovon, F.** *Das Evangelism nach Lukas.* 1, 1–9, 50. EKKNT 3/1. Neukirchen/Einsiedeln: Neukirchener/Benziger, 1989. **Bratcher, R. G.** *A Translator's Guide to the Gospel of Luke.* Helps for Translators. London/New York/Stuttgart: UBS, 1982. **Busse, U., et. al.** *Jesus zwischen Arm und Reich: Lukas-Evangelium.* Bibelauslegung für die Praxis 18. Stuttgart: Katholisches Bibelwerk, 1980. **Caird, G. B.** *The Gospel of St. Luke.* London: Penguin, 1963. **Craddock, F. B.** *Luke.* Louisville: John Knox, 1990. **Creed, J. M.** *The Gospel according to St. Luke.* London: Macmillan, 1942. **Danker, F. W.** *Jesus and the New Age according to St. Luke.* St. Louis: Clayton, 1972. ————. *Luke.* Proclamation Commentaries, 2nd ed. Philadelphia: Fortress, 1987. **D'Arc, J., Sr.** *Évangile selon Luc: Présentation du texte grec, traduction et notes.* Nouvelle collection de textes et documents . . . G. Budé. Paris: Les Belles Lettres/Desclée de Brouwer, 1986. **Dean, R. J.** *Luke.* Layman's Bible Book Commentary 17. Nashville, TN: Broadman, 1983. **Delebecque, É.** *Évangile de Luc: Texte traduit et annoté.* Études anciennes de l'Association G. Budé. Paris: Les Belles Lettres, 1976. **Dieterlé, C., et al.** *Manuel du traducteur pour l'évangile de Luc.* Stuttgart/Paris: Alliance biblique universelle, 1977. **Drury, J.** *Luke.* J. B. Phillips Commentaries, Fontana Books. London: Collins, 1973. **Easton, B. S.** *The Gospel according to St. Luke: A Critical and Exegetical Commentary.* New York: Scribner, 1926. **Ellis, E. E.** *The Gospel of Luke.* 2nd ed. London: Oliphants, 1974. **Ernst, J.** *Das Evangelium nach Lukas, übersetzt und erklärt.* RNT. Regensburg: Pustet, 1977. **Evans, C. A.** *Luke.* Peabody, MA: Hendrickson Publishers, 1990. **Evans, C. F.** *Saint Luke.* London/Philadelphia: SCM/Trinity, 1990. **Fitzmyer, J. A.** *The Gospel according to Luke.* AB 28, 28A. 2 vols. Garden City, NY: Doubleday, 1981–85. **Geldenhuys, N.** *Commentary on the Gospel of Luke: The English Text with Introduction, Exposition, and Notes.* NICNT. Grand Rapids: Eerdmans, 1951. **Gilmour, S. M.** "The Gospel according to St. Luke." *Interpreter's Bible.* Nashville: Abingdon, 1952. 8:1–434. **Godet, F.** *A Commentary on the Gospel of St. Luke.* Tr. E. W. Shelders. 2 vols. Edinburgh: T. & T. Clark, repr. 1976 (1887, 1889). **Gooding, D.** *According to Luke: A New Exposition of the Third Gospel.* Grand Rapids/Leicester, UK: Eerdmans/Inter-Varsity, 1987. **Goulder, M. D.** *Luke: A New Paradigm.* JSNTSup 20. 2 vols. Sheffield: Sheffield Academic, 1989. **Grundmann, W.** *Das Evangelium nach Lukas.* THKNT 3. 2nd ed. East Berlin: Evangelische Verlaganstalt, 1961. **Harrington, W. J.** *The Gospel according to St. Luke: A Commentary.* Westminster, MD/Toronto: Newman, 1967. **Hauck, F.** *Das Evangelium des Lukas.* Leipzig: Deichertsche Verlagsbuch-handlung, 1934. **Hendriksen, W.** *Exposition of the Gospel according to Luke.* New Testament Commentaries. Grand Rapids, MI: Baker, 1978. **Hobbs, H.** *An Exposition of the Gospel of Luke.* Grand Rapids: Baker, 1966. **Johnson, L. T.** *The Gospel of Luke.* Sacra Pagina 3. Collegeville, MN: Liturgical, 1991. **Karris, R. J.** *Invitation to Luke: A Commentary on the Gospel of Luke with Complete Text from the Jerusalem Bible.* New York: Doubleday, 1977. **Kealy, S. P.** *The Gospel of Luke.* Denville, NJ: Dimension Books, 1979. **Kilgallen, J. J.** *A Brief Commentary on the Gospel of Luke.* New York/Mahwah, NJ: Paulist, 1988. **Klostermann, E.** *Das Lukasevangelium.* HNT 5. Tübingen: Mohr (Siebeck), 1975 = 1929. **Kodell, J.** *The Gospel according to Luke.* Collegeville Bible Commentary 3. Collegeville, MN: Liturgical Press, 1983. **Kremer, J.** *Lukasevangelium: Die Neue Echter Bible, Kommentar zum Neuen Testament mit der Einheitsübersetzung 3.* Würzburg: Echter, 1988. **Lachs, S. T.** *A Rabbinic Commentary on the New Testament: The Gospels of Matthew, Mark, and Luke.* Hoboken, NJ: Ktav, 1987. **Lagrange, M.-J.** *Évangile selon Saint Luc.* 2nd ed. Paris: Gabalda, 1921. **Larson, B.** *Luke.*

Communicator's Commentary 3. Waco, TX: Word Books, 1983. **LaVerdiere, E.** *Luke.* Wilmington, DE: Glazier, 1980. **Leaney, A. R. C.** *A Commentary on the Gospel according to St. Luke.* BNTC. London: A. & C. Black, 1958. **Lenski, R. C. H.** *The Interpretation of St. Mark's and St. Luke's Gospel.* Columbus, OH: Lutheran Book Concern, 1934. **Liefeld, W.** "Luke." In *The Expositor's Bible Commentary,* ed. F. Gaebelein et al. 8:797–1059. **Linden, P. van.** *The Gospel of Luke and Acts.* Message of Biblical Spirituality 10. Wilmington, DE: Glazier, 1986. **Loisy, A.** *L'évangile selon Luc.* Paris: E. Nourry, 1924. **Luce, H. K.** *The Gospel according to St. Luke.* CGTSC. Cambridge: University Press, 1949. **Manson, W.** *The Gospel of Luke.* London: Hodder & Stoughton, 1930. **Marshall, I. H.** *The Gospel of Luke: A Commentary on the Greek Text.* NIGTC. Exeter: Paternoster, 1978. **McBride, D.** *The Gospel of Luke: A Reflective Commentary.* Dublin/Northfort, NY: Dominican Publications/Castello, 1982. **Mentz, H.** *Das Lukas-Evangelium neu erzählt.* Göttingen: Vandenhoeck, 1987. **Meynet, R.** *L'évangile selon saint Luc: Analyse rhétorique. I. Planches; II. Commentaire.* Paris: Cerf, 1988. **Miller, D. G.** *The Gospel according to Luke.* Richmond: John Knox, 1959. **Morris, L.** *The Gospel according to St. Luke: An Introduction and Commentary.* TNTC. London: Inter-Varsity, 1974. ————. *The Gospel according to St. Luke: An Introduction and Commentary.* TNTC. 2nd ed. London: Inter-Varsity, 1988. **Müller, P.-G.** *Lukas-Evangelium.* Stuttgarter kleiner Kommentar, Neues Testament 3. Stuttgart: Katholisches Bibelwerk, 1984. **Obach, R. E.,** and **Kirk, A.** *A Commentary on the Gospel of Luke.* New York/Mahwah, NJ: Paulist, 1986. **Osty, E.** *La Sainte Bible traduite en français sous la direction de l'École Biblique de Jérusalem. L'évangile selon Saint Luc. Traduction, introduction et notes.* Paris: Cerf, 1961. **Plummer, A.** *A Critical and Exegetical Commentary on the Gospel according to S. Luke.* ICC. 5th ed. New York: Scribner, 1922. **Ragg, L.** *St. Luke.* WC. London: Methuen, 1922. **Rengstorf, K. H.** *Das Evangelium nach Lukas.* NTD 3. 9th ed. Göttingen: Vandenhoeck & Ruprecht, 1962. **Rice, E.** *Commentary on the Gospel according to Luke.* Philadelphia: Union, 1900. **Rienecker, F.** *Das Evangelium des Lukas.* Wuppertaler Studienbibel. 4th ed. Wuppertal: Brockhaus, 1972. **Sabourin, L.** *L'évangile de Luc: Introduction et commentaire.* Rome: Gregorian University, 1985. **Schlatter, A. von.** *Das Evangelium des Lukas aus seinen Quellen erklärt.* Stuttgart: Calwer, 1931. **Schmid, J.** *Das Evangelium nach Lukas.* RNT 3. 4th ed. Regensburg: Pustet, 1960. **Schmithals, W.** *Das Evangelium nach Lukas.* Zürcher Bibelkommentar NT 3.1. Zürich: Theologischer Verlag, 1980. **Schneider, G.** *Das Evangelium nach Lukas.* 2 vols. Gütersloh: Mohn, 1977. **Schürmann, H.** *Das Lukasevangelium: Erster Teil: Kommentar zu Kap. 1, 1–9, 50.* HTKNT 3/1. Freiburg/Basel/Vienna: Herder, 1969. **Schweizer, E.** *The Good News according to Luke.* Tr. D. E. Green. London: SPCK, 1984. **Stöger, A.** *The Gospel according to St. Luke.* The New Testament for Spiritual Reading 3. Tr. B. Fahy. London: Sheed, 1977. **Stoll, R.** *The Gospel according to St. Luke.* New York: Pustet, 1931. **Summers, R.** *Jesus the Universal Savior: Commentary on Luke.* Waco, TX: Word, 1972. **Talbert, C. H.** *Reading Luke: A Literary and Theological Commentary on the Third Gospel.* New York: Crossroad, 1982. **Thompson, G. H. P.** *The Gospel according to Luke in the Revised Standard Version.* The New Clarendon Bible. New York/Oxford: Oxford University Press, 1972. **Tiede, D. L.** *Luke.* Augsburg Commentary on the New Testament. Minneapolis, MN: Augsburg, 1988. **Tinsley, E. J.** *The Cambridge Bible Commentary in the New English Bible: The Gospel according to Luke.* New York/London: Cambridge University, 1965. **Title, E.** *The Gospel according to Luke.* New York: Harper and Bros., 1951. **Tresmontant, C.** *Évangile de Luc: Traduction et notes.* Paris: O.E.I.L., 1987. **Wellhausen, J.** *Das Evangelium Lucae, übersetzt und erklärt.* Berlin: Georg Reimer, 1904. **Wiefel, W.** *Das Evangelium nach Lukas.* THKNT 3. Berlin: Evangelische, 1988. **Zahn, T. von.** *Das Evangelium des Lukas ausgelegt.* 4th ed. Leipzig: Deichert, 1930.

General Bibliography

Aalen, S. "St. Luke's Gospel and the Last Chapters of I Enoch." *NTS* 1 (1966) 1–13. **Aarde, A. G. van.** "'The most high God does live in houses, but not houses built by men . . .': The relativity of the metaphor 'temple' in Luke-Acts." *Neot* 25 (1991) 51–64. **Abraham, M. V.** "Good News to the Poor in Luke's Gospel." *Biblebhashyam* 14 (1988) 65–77. **Achtemeier, P. J.** "Towards the Isolation of Pre-Markan Miracle Catenae." *JBL* 89 (1970) 265–91. ————. "The Lukan Perspective on the Miracles of Jesus: A Preliminary Sketch." *JBL* 94 (1975) 547–62. ————. "Carlston's Parables: A Review Article." *ANQ* 16 (1976) 227–31. **Ades, J. I.** "Literary Aspects of Luke." *PLL* 15 (1979) 193–99. **Allison, D. C.** "Was There a 'Lukan Community'?" *IBS* 10 (1988) 62–70. **Arai, S.** "Individual- und Gemeindeethik bei Lukas." *AJBI* 9 (1983) 88–127. **Argyle, A. W.** "'Hypocrites' and the Aramaic Theory." *ExpTim* 75 (1963–64) 113–14. ————. "Evidence for the View That St. Luke Used St. Matthew's Gospel." *JBL* 83 (1964) 390–96. ————. "The Greek of Luke and Acts." *NTS* 20 (1974) 441–45. **Asante, E.** "The Theological Jerusalem of Luke-Acts." *ATJ* 15 (1986) 172–82. **Asting, R.** *Die Verkündigung des Wortes im Urchristentum, dargestellt an den Begriffen "Worte Gottes," "Evangelium" und "Zeugnis."* Stuttgart: Kohlhammer, 1939. **Aune, D. E.** "The Significance of the Delay of the Parousia for Early Christianity." In *Current Issues in Biblical and Patristic Interpretation,* ed. G. F. Hawthorne. Grand Rapids: Eerdmans, 1975. 87–109. ————. "The Gospels, Biography or Theology?" *BRev* 6 (1990) 14–21, 37. **Aurelio, T.** *Disclosures in den Gleichnissen Jesu.* RST. Frankfurt am M./Berne/Las Vegas: Lang, 1977. **Baasland, E.** "Zum Beispiel der Beispielerzählungen: Zur Formenlehre der Gleichnisse und zum Methodik der Gleichnisauslegung." *NovT* 28 (1986) 193–219. **Bachmann, M.** *Jerusalem und der Tempel: Die geographisch-theologischen Elemente in der lukanischen Sicht des jüdischen Kulzentrums.* BWANT 6/9. Stuttgart: Kohlhammer, 1980. **Baer, H. von.** *Der heilige Geist in den Lukasschriften.* BWANT 3/3. Stuttgart: Kohlhammer, 1926. **Bailey, J. A.** *The Tradition Common to the Gospels of Luke and John.* NovTSup 7. Leiden: Brill, 1963. **Bailey, K. E.** *Poet and Peasant: A Literary-Cultural Approach to the Parables in Luke.* Grand Rapids: Eerdmans, 1976. ————. *Through Peasant Eyes: More Lukan Parables, Their Culture and Style.* Grand Rapids: Eerdmans, 1980. **Baird, J. A.** "A Pragmatic Approach to Parable Exegesis: Some New Evidence on Mark 4:11, 33–34." *JBL* 76 (1957) 201–7. **Baker, J.** "Luke, the Critical Evangelist." *ExpTim* 68 (1957) 123–25. **Balch, D. L.** "Comments on the Genre and a Political Theme of Luke-Acts: A Preliminary Comparison of Two Hellenistic Historians." In *SBL 1989 Seminar Papers,* ed. D. J. Lull. 343–61. ————. "The Genre of Luke-Acts: Individual Biography, Adventure Novel, or Political History?" *SWJT* 33 (1990) 5–19. **Baltzer, K.** "The Meaning of the Temple in the Lukan Writings." *HTR* 58 (1965) 263–77. **Bammel, E.** "The Baptist in Early Christian Tradition." *NTS* 18 (1971–72) 95–128. ———— and **Moule, C. F. D.,** eds. *Jesus and the Politics of His Day.* Cambridge: University Press, 1984. **Barr, D. L.** "Speaking in Parables: A Survey of Recent Research." *TSFB* 6 (1983) 8–10. ———— and **Wentling, J. L.** "The Conventions of Classical Biography and the Genre of Luke-Acts: A Preliminary Study." In *Luke-Acts: New Perspectives,* ed. C. H. Talbert. 63–88. **Barraclough, R.** "A Reassessment of Luke's Political Perspective." *RTR* 38 (1979) 10–18. **Barrett, C. K.** *The Holy Spirit and the Gospel Tradition.* London: SPCK, 1947. ————. *Luke the Historian in Recent Study.* FBBS 24. 2nd ed. Philadelphia: Fortress, 1970. ————. *The Gospel according to St. John: An Introduction with Commentary and Notes on the Greek Text.* 2nd ed. London: SPCK, 1978. **Bartsch, H.-W.** *Wachet aber zu jeder Zeit!* Hamburg/Bergstedt: Reich, 1963. ————. "Das Thomas-Evangelium und die synoptischen Evangelien." *NTS* 6 (1959–60) 249–61. ————. "Die stehenden Bilder in den Gleichnissen als Beispiel für eine existentiale Interpretation des Bildes." In *Kerygma und Mythos,* vol. 6. 2, ed. H. W. Bartsch.

TF 31. Hamburg/Bergstedt: Reich, 1964. 103–17. ————. "Early Christian Eschatology in the Synoptic Gospels (A Contribution to Form-Critical Research)." *NTS* 11 (1965) 387–97. **Bauer, J. B.** "Evangelium und Geschichtlichkeit: Vom heutigen Stand der Erforschung des Neuen Testaments." In *Evangelienforschung: Ausgewählte Aufsätze deutscher Exegeten*, ed. J. B. Bauer. Graz: Verlag Styria, 1968. 9–32. ————. "Gleichnisse Jesu und Gleichnisse der Rabbinen." *TPQ* 119 (1971) 297–307. **Bauernfeind, O.** *Die Worte der Dämonen im Markusevangelium*. BWANT 3/8. Stuttgart: Kohlhammer, 1927. **Baumbach, G.** *Das Verständnis des Bösen in den synoptischen Evangelien*. East Berlin: Evangelische Verlagsanstalt, 1963. ————. "Gott und die Welt in der Theologie des Lukas." *BLit* 45 (1972) 241–55. **Bayer, H. F.** *Jesus' Predictions of Vindication and Resurrection: The Provenance, Meaning, and Correlation of the Synoptic Predictions*. WUNT 2/20. Tübingen: Mohr (Siebeck), 1986. **Beardslee, W. A.** "Parable Interpretation and the World Disclosed by the Parable." *PRS* 3 (1976) 123–39. ————. "Parable, Proverb, and Koan." *Semeia* 12 (1978) 151–77. **Beare, F. W.** *The Gospel according to Matthew*. Oxford: Blackwell, 1981. **Beasley-Murray, G. R.** *Baptism in the New Testament*. Exeter: Paternoster, 1972=1962. **Beck, B. E.** "The Common Authorship of Luke and Acts." *NTS* 23 (1977) 346–52. **Becker, J.** *Johannes der Täufer und Jesus von Nazareth*. BS 63. Neukirchen-Vluyn: Neukirchener, 1972. **Behm, J. M.** *Die Handauflegung im Urchristentum: Nach Verwendung, Herkunft und Bedeutung in religionsgeschichtlichen Zusammenhang untersucht*. Darmstadt: Wissenschaftliche Buchgesellschaft, 1968. **Beilner, W.** *Christus und die Pharisäer: Exegetische Untersuchung über Grund und Verlauf der Auseinandersetzungen*. Vienna: Herder, 1959. **Benoit, P., et al.** *Aux sources de la tradition chrétienne*. FS M. Goguel. Bibliothèque théologique. Neuchâtel/Paris: Delachaux et Niestlé, 1950. ———— and **Boismard, M.-E.** *Synopse des Quatre Évangiles en français: Tome 2, Commentaire*. Paris: Cerf, 1972. **Berchmans, J.** "Some Aspects of Lukan Christology." *Biblebhashyam* 2 (1976) 5–22. **Berger, K.** *Die Auferstehung des Propheten und die Erhöhung des Menschensohnes: Traditionsgeschichtliche Untersuchungen zur Geschickes Jesu in frühchristlichen Texten*. SUNT 13. Göttingen: Vandenhoeck & Ruprecht, 1976. ————. "Zum traditionsgeschichtlichen Hintergrund christologischer Hoheitstitel." *NTS* 17 (1970–71) 391–425. ————. "Materialen zu Form- und Überlieferungsgeschichte neutestamentlicher Gleichnisse." *NovT* 15 (1973) 1–37. **Bergquist, J. A.** "'Good News to the Poor'—Why Does This Lukan Motif Appear to Run Dry in the Book of Acts?" *BangTF* 18 (1986) 1–16. **Bernadicou, P. J.** "The Lukan Theology of Joy." *ScEs* 25 (1973) 75–98. **Berry, D. L.** "Revisioning Christology: The Logic of Messianic Ascription." *ATR* 70 (1988) 129–40. **Betz, O.** "The Kerygma of Luke." *Int* 22 (1968) 131–46. **Beyer, K.** *Semitische Syntax im Neuen Testament*. Vol. 1. SUNT 1. 2nd ed. Göttingen: Vandenhoeck & Ruprecht, 1968. **Black, M.** *An Aramaic Approach to the Gospels and Acts*. Oxford: Clarendon, 1946. ————. "The Parables as Allegory." *BJRL* 42 (1960) 273–87. **Blackman, E. C.** "New Methods of Parable Interpretation." *CJT* 15 (1969) 3–13. **Blass, F.** *Philology of the Gospels*. London: Macmillan, 1898. **Blomberg, C. L.** "New Horizons in Parable Research." *TJ* 3 (1982) 3–17. ————. "The Law in Luke-Acts." *JSNT* 22 (1984) 53–80. ————. "When Is a Parallel Really a Parallel? A Test Case in the Lukan Parables." *WTJ* 46 (1984) 78–103. **Böcher, O.** *Dämonenfurcht und Dämonenabwehr: Ein Beitrag zur Vorgeschichte der christlichen Taufe*. BWANT 90. Stuttgart: Kohlhammer, 1970. ———— and **Haacker, K.,** eds. *Verborum Veritas*. FS G. Stählin. Wuppertal: Theologischer Verlag R. Brockhaus, 1970. **Bock, D. L.** *Proclamation from Prophecy and Pattern: Lucan Old Testament Christology*. JSNTSup 12. Sheffield: JSOT, 1987. ————. "The Use of the Old Testament in Luke-Acts." In *SBL 1990 Seminar Papers*, ed. D. J. Lull. Atlanta, GA: Scholars, 1990. 494–511. **Bonnard, P.-E.** "Le psaume 72: Ses relectures, ses traces dans l'oeuvre de Luc?" *RSR* 69 (1981) 259–78. **Borg, M. J.** *Conflict, Holiness, and Politics in the Teaching of Jesus*. Studies in the Bible and Early Christianity 5. New York/Toronto: Edwin Mellen, 1984. **Borgen, P.** "From Paul to Luke: Observations towards Clarification of the Theology of Luke-Acts." *CBQ* 31 (1969) 168–82. **Boring, M. E.** *Sayings of the Risen Jesus: Christian Prophecy in the Synoptic Tradition*. Cambridge: University Press, 1982. **Boucher, M.** *The Mysterious Parable: A Literary Study*. CBQMS 6. Washington: Catholic Biblical Association of America, 1977. **Bouttier, M.**

"L'humanité de Jésus selon Saint Luc." *RSR* 69 (1981) 33–44. **Bouwman, G.** *Das dritte Evangelium: Einübung in die formgeschichtliche Methode.* Tr. H. Zulauf. Düsseldorf: Patmos, 1968. **Bovon, F.** *Luc le théologien: Vingt-cinq ans de recherches (1950–1975).* Le Monde de la Bible. Neuchâtel/Paris: Delachaux et Niestlé, 1978. ————. "Le salut dans les écrits de Luc: Essai." *RTP* 23 (1973) 296–307. ————. "L'importance des médiations dans le projet théologique de Luc." *NTS* 21 (1974) 23–39. ————. "Orientations actuelles des études lucaniennes." *RTP* 26 (1976) 161–90. ————. "Effet de réel et flou prophétique dans l'oeuvre de Luc." In *À cause de l'Évangile,* ed. R. Refoulé. 349–60. ————. "La figure de Moïse dans l'oeuvre de Luc." In *La figure de Moïse: Ecriture et relectures.* Geneva: Publications de la Faculté de Théologie de l'Université de Genève, 1978. 47–65. ————. "Le Dieu de Luc." *RSR* 69 (1981) 279–300. ————. "Luc: portrait et projet." *LVit* 30 (1981) 9–18. ————. "Du côté de chez Luc." *RTP* 115 (1983) 175–89. ————. "Israel, die Kirche und die Völker im lukanischen Doppelwerk." *TLZ* 108 (1983) 403–14. **Boys, M. C.** "The Parabolic Ways of Teaching." *BTB* 13 (1983) 82–89. **Braumann, G.** "Das Mittel der Zeit: Erwägungen zur Theologie des Lukasevangeliums." *ZNW* 54 (1963) 117–45. ————, ed. *Das Lukas-Evangelium: Die redaktions- und kompositionsgeschichtliche Forschung.* WF 280. Darmstadt: Wissenschaftliche Buchgesellschaft, 1974. **Braun, H.** *Qumran und das Neue Testament.* Vol. 1. Tübingen: Mohr (Siebeck), 1966. **Brawley, R. L.** *Centering on God: Method and Message in Luke-Acts.* Literary Currents in Biblical Interpretation. Louisville, KY: Westminster/John Knox, 1990. ————. *Luke-Acts and the Jews: Conflict, Apology, and Conciliation.* SBLMS 33. Atlanta: Scholars, 1987. **Breech, E.** "Kingdom of God and the Parables of Jesus." *Semeia* 12 (1978) 15–41. **Breech, J.** *The Silence of Jesus: The Authentic Voice of the Historical Man.* Philadelphia: Fortress, 1983. **Brown, F. B.,** and **Malbon, E. S.** "Parables as a *Via Negativa:* A Critical Review of the Work of John Dominic Crossan." *JR* 64 (1984) 530–38. **Brown, R. E.** *The Gospel according to John.* AB 29, 29A. 2 vols. Garden City, NY: Doubleday, 1966–70. ————. "Parable and Allegory Reconsidered." *NovT* 5 (1962) 36–45. **Brown, S.** *Apostasy and Perseverance in the Theology of Luke.* AnBib 36. Rome: Pontifical Biblical Institute, 1969. ————. "Precis of Eckhard Plümacher, *Lukas als hellenistischer Schriftsteller.*" In *Society of Biblical Literature. Seminar Papers, 1974,* ed. G. MacRae. 2 vols. Cambridge, MA: Society of Biblical Literature, 1974. 103–13. ————. "'Water Baptism' and 'Spirit Baptism' in Luke-Acts." *ATR* 59 (1977) 135–51. **Brox, N.** *Zeuge und Märtyrer: Untersuchungen zur frühchristlichen Zeugnis-Terminologie.* SANT 5. Munich: Kösel-Verlag, 1961. **Bruce, F. F.** *The Acts of the Apostles.* Grand Rapids: Eerdmans, 1951. ————. *The Book of the Acts.* NICNT. Rev. ed. Grand Rapids: Eerdmans, 1988. **Bruners, W.** "Lukas-Literat und Theologe: Neue Literatur zum lukanischen Doppelwerk." *BK* 35 (1980) 110–12, 141–51. **Büchele, A.** *Der Tod Jesu im Lukasevangelium.* Theologische Studien 26. Frankfurt am Main: Joseph Knecht, 1978. **Bultmann, R.** *Theology of the New Testament.* Tr. K. Grobel. 2 vols. London: SCM, 1952–55. ————. *The History of the Synoptic Tradition.* Tr. J. Marsh. 2nd ed. Oxford: Blackwell, 1972. **Bundy, W. E.** *Jesus and the First Three Gospels: An Introduction for the Synoptic Tradition.* Cambridge, MA: Harvard University, 1955. **Burridge, R. A.** *What are the Gospels? A Comparison with Graeco-Roman Biography.* SNTSMS 70. Cambridge: University Press, 1992. **Busse, U.** *Die Wunder des Propheten Jesus: Die Rezeption, Komposition und Interpretation der Wundertradition im Evangelium des Lukas.* FB 24. Stuttgart: Katholisches Bibelwerk, 1977. ————. *Das Nazareth-Manifest: Eine Einführung in das lukanische Jesusbild nach Lk 4: 16–30.* SBS 91. Stuttgart: Katholisches Bibelwerk, 1978. **Bussman, C.,** and **Radl, W.,** eds. *Der Treue Gottes trauen: Beiträge zum Werk des Lukas.* FS G. Schneider. Freiburg/Basel/Vienna: Herder, 1991. **Buzy, D.** *Les Paraboles: Traduites et commentées.* VS 6. Paris: Beauchesne, 1932. **Cadbury, H. J.** *The Style and Literary Method of Luke.* HTS 6. 2 vols. Cambridge, MA: Harvard University, 1919–20. ————. "The Tradition." In *Beginnings,* ed. F. J. Foakes-Jackson and K. Lake. 2:209–64. ————. *The Making of Luke-Acts.* New York: Macmillan, 1927. ————. "Four Features of Lucan Style." In *Studies in Luke-Acts,* ed. L. E. Keck and J. L. Martyn. ————. "Lexical Notes on Luke-Acts: II. Recent Arguments for Medical Language." *JBL* 45 (1926) 190–209. ————.

"Lexical Notes on Luke-Acts: V. Luke and the Horse-Doctors." *JBL* 52 (1933) 55–65. ————. "Soluble Difficulties in the Parables." In *New Testament Sidelights*. FS A. C. Purdy, ed. H. K. McArthur. Hartford: Hartford Seminary Foundation, 1960. 118–23. ————. "Acts and Eschatology." In *The Background of the New Testament and Its Eschatology*, ed. D. Daube and W. D. Davies. Cambridge: University Press, 1964. 300–321. **Cadoux, A. T.** *The Parables of Jesus: Their Art and Use*. London: Clarke, 1930. **Caird, G. B.** "Eschatology and Politics: Some Misconceptions." In *Biblical Studies*. FS W. Barclay, ed. J. R. McKay. Philadelphia: Westminster, 1976. 72–86. ————. *The Language and Imagery of the Bible*. Duckworth Studies in Theology. London: Duckworth, 1980. **Cambe, M.** "La XAPIΣ chez Saint Luc: Remarques sur quelques textes, notamment le κεχαριτωμένη." *RB* 70 (1963) 193–207. ————. "Bulletin de Nouveau Testament: Études lucaniennes." *ETR* 56 (1981) 159–67. **Carlston, C.** *The Parables of the Triple Tradition*. Philadelphia: Fortress, 1975. ————. "Changing Fashions in Interpreting the Parables." *ANQ* 14 (1974) 227–33. ————. "Proverbs, Maxims, and the Historical Jesus." *JBL* 99 (1980) 87–105. ————. "Parable and Allegory Revisited: An Interpretive Review." *CBQ* 43 (1981) 228–42. **Carroll, J. T.** "Luke's Portrayal of the Pharisees." *CBQ* 50 (1988) 604–21. ————. *Response to the End of History: Eschatology and Situation in Luke-Acts*. SBLDS 92. Atlanta, GA: Scholars, 1988. **Cartlidge, D.,** and **Dungan, D.** *Documents for the Study of the Gospels*. Philadelphia: Fortress, 1980. **Casetti, P., et al.,** eds. *Mélange Dominique Barthélemy*. FS. D. Barthélemy. OBO 38. Fribourg/Göttingen: Editions universitaires/Vandenhoeck & Ruprecht, 1981. **Cassidy, R. J.** *Society and Politics in the Acts of the Apostles*. Maryknoll, NY: Orbis, 1987. ———— and **Scharper, P. J.,** eds. *Political Issues in Luke-Acts*. Maryknoll, NY: Orbis, 1983. **Cave, C. H.** "The Parables and the Scriptures." *NTS* 11 (1964–65) 374–87. **Chance, J. B.** *Jerusalem, the Temple and the New Age in Luke-Acts*. Macon, GA: Mercer University, 1988. **Charlesworth, J. H.** *Jesus within Judaism: New Light from Exciting Archaelogical Discoveries*. Anchor Bible Reference Library. New York: Doubleday, 1988. ————, ed. *The Old Testament Pseudepigrapha*. 2 vols. London: Darton, Longman & Todd, 1983–85. **Chevallier, M.-A.** *L'Esprit et le Messie dans le bas-judaïsme et le Nouveau Testament*. Études d'histoire et de philosophie religieuse 49. Paris: Presses Universitaires de France, 1958. ————. "Luc et l'Esprit saint." *RSR* 56 (1982) 1–16. ————. "Apparentements entre Luc et Jean en matière de pneumatologie." In *À cause de l'Évangile*, ed. R. Refoulé. 377–408. **Chilton, B. D.** *God in Strength: Jesus' Announcement of the Kingdom*. SNTU B, 1. Freistadt: Plöchl, 1979. **Christ, F.** *Jesus Sophia: Die Sophia-Christologie bei den Synoptikern*. ATANT 57. Zürich: Zwingli, 1970. **Clines, D. J. A., et al.,** eds. *The Bible in Three Dimensions: Essays in Celebration of Forty Years of Biblical Studies at Sheffield*. JSOTSup 87. Sheffield: Sheffield Academic, 1990. **Collison, J. G. F.** "Eschatology in the Gospel of Luke." In *New Synoptic Studies*, ed. W. R. Farmer. Macon, GA: Mercer University, 1983. 363–71. **Conzelmann, H.** *The Theology of St. Luke*. Tr. G. Buswell. New York: Harper & Brothers, 1960. ————. *An Outline of the Theology of the New Testament*. NTL. Tr. J. Bowden. London: SCM, 1969. ————. *Die Apostelgeschichte*. Tübingen: Mohr, 1972. **Cook, C.** "The Sense of Audience in Luke: A Literary Examination." *NB* 72 (1991) 19–30. **Cook, D. E.** "A Gospel Portrait of the Pharisees." *RevExp* 84 (1987) 221–33. **Cope, L., et al.** "Narrative Outline of the Composition of Luke according to the Two Gospel Hypothesis." In *SBL 1992 Seminar Papers*, ed. E. H. Lovering, Jr. 98–120. **Cosgrove, C. H.** "The Divine Δεῖ in Luke-Acts: Investigations into the Lukan Understanding of God's Providence." *NovT* 26 (1984) 168–90. **Cranfield, C. E. B.** *The Gospel according to Saint Mark*. CGTC. Cambridge: University Press, 1959. **Crehan, J. H.** "The Purpose of Luke in Acts." *SE* 2 [= TU 87] (1964) 354–68. **Cribbs, F. L.** "A Study of the Contacts that Exist between St. Luke and St. John." In *SBL Seminar Papers 1973*, ed. G. MacRae. Cambridge, MA: Society of Biblical Literature, 1973. 2:1–93. **Crossan, J. D.** *In Parables: The Challenge of the Historical Jesus*. New York: Harper & Row, 1973. ————. *Raid on the Articulate: Comic Eschatology in Borges and Jesus*. New York: Harper & Row, 1976. ————. *Finding Is the First Act: Trove Folktales and Jesus' Treasure Parables*. Philadelphia: Fortress, 1979. ————. *Cliffs of Fall: Paradox and Polyvalence in the Parables of Jesus*. New York: Seabury, 1980. ————. *In Fragments: The Aphorisms of Jesus*.

San Francisco: Harper and Row, 1983. ————. *The Historical Jesus: The Life of a Mediterranean Jewish Peasant.* San Francisco: HarperSanFrancisco, 1991. ————. "Parable as Religious and Poetic Experience." *JR* 53 (1973) 330–58. ————. "The Servant Parables of Jesus." *Semeia* 1 (1974) 17–62. ————. "Parable and Example in the Teaching of Jesus." *Semeia* 1 (1974) 63–104. ————. "Structuralist Analysis and the Parables of Jesus." *Semeia* 1 (1974) 192–221. ————. "Paradox Gives Rise to Metaphor: Paul Ricoeur's Hermeneutics and the Parables of Jesus." *BR* 24–25 (1979–80) 20–37. **Crump, D. M.** "Jesus the Intercessor: Prayer and Christology in Luke-Acts." Ph.D. diss., University of Aberdeen, 1988. **Cullmann, O.** *The Christology of the New Testament.* Tr. S. C. Guthrie and C. A. M. Hall. 2nd ed. London: SCM, 1963. **Culpepper, R. A.** "Paul's Mission to the Gentile World: Acts 13–19." *RevExp* 71 (1974) 487–97. **Dahl, N. A.** "The Purpose of Luke-Acts." In *Jesus in the Memory of the Early Church: Essays.* Minneapolis: Augsburg, 1976. 87–98. **Dalman, G.** *Orte und Wege Jesu.* BFCT 2/1. 3rd ed. Gütersloh: Bertelsmann, 1924. **D'Angelo, M. R.** "Images of Jesus and the Christian Call in the Gospels of Luke and John." *Spirituality Today* 37 (1985) 196–212. **Danker, F. W.** "Imaged through Beneficence." In *Reimaging,* ed. D. D. Sylva. 57–67, 184–86. ————. "Theological Presuppositions of St. Luke." *CurTM* 4 (1977) 98–103. **Darr, J. A.** "Discerning the Lukan Voice: The Narrator as Character in Luke-Acts." In *SBL 1992 Seminar Papers,* ed. E. H. Lovering, Jr. 255–65. **Daube, D.** *The New Testament and Rabbinic Judaism.* London: Athlone, 1956. ————. "Shame Culture in Luke." In *Paul and Paulinism.* FS C. K. Barrett, ed. M. Hooker and S. G. Wilson. London: SPCK, 1982. 355–72. **Dauer, A.** *Beobachtungen zur literarischen Arbeitstechnik des Lukas.* Athenäums Monografien, Theologie. BBB 79. Frankfurt. Hain, 1990. **Davies, W. D.** *The Setting of the Sermon on the Mount.* Cambridge: University Press, 1964. ———— and **Allison, D. C.** *A Critical and Exegetical Commentary on the Gospel according to Saint Matthew: Vol. 1. Introduction and Commentary on Matthew I-VII.* ICC. Edinburgh: Clark, 1988. **Dawsey, J. M.** *The Lukan Voice: Confusion and Irony in the Gospel of Luke.* Macon, GA: Mercer University, 1986. ————. "What's in a Name? Characterization in Luke." *BTB* 16 (1986) 143–47. ————. "The Temple-Theme in Luke." *MelT* 38 (1987) 26–32. ————. "The Unexpected Christ: The Lucan Image." *ExpTim* 98 (1987) 296–300. ————. "The Literary Unity of Luke-Acts: Questions of Style—a Task for Literary Critics." *NTS* 35 (1989) 48–66. **Degenhardt, H.-J.** *Lukas, Evangelist der Armen: Besitz und Besitzverzicht in den lukanischen Schriften. Eine traditions- und redaktionsgeschichtliche Untersuchung.* Stuttgart: Katholisches Bibelwerk, 1965. **Dehandschutter, B.** "The Gospel of Thomas and the Synoptics: The Status Quaestionis." *SE* 7 [= TU 126] (1982) 157–60. **Delebecque, É.** *Etudes grecques sur l'évangile de Luc.* Paris: Société d'édition "Les Belles Lettres," 1976. ————. "L'Hellénisme de la 'relative complexe' dans le Nouveau Testament et principalement chez Luc." *Bib* 62 (1981) 229–38. **Delobel, J.,** ed. *Logia: Les paroles de Jésus—The Sayings of Jesus.* FS J. Coppens. BETL 59. Leuven: Peeters/University Press, 1982. **Delorme, J.,** and **Duplacy, J.,** eds. *La parole de grâce: Études lucaniennes.* FS A. George. Paris: Recherches de Science Religieuse, 1981. **Demel, S.** "Jesu Umgang mit Frauen nach dem Lukasevangelium." *BibNot* 57 (1991) 41–95. **Derrett, J. D. M.** *Law in the New Testament.* London: Darton, Longman, and Todd, 1970. ————. *New Resolutions of Old Conundrums: A Fresh Insight into Luke's Gospel.* Shipton-on-Stour: Drinkwater, 1986. **Descamps, A.,** and **Halleux, A. de,** eds. *Mélange biblique.* FS B. Rigaux. Gembloux: Duculot, 1970. **Diamond, G.** "Reflections upon Recent Developments in the Study of Parables in Luke." *ABR* 29 (1981) 1–9. **Dibelius, M.** *Die urchristliche Überlieferung von Johannes dem Täufer.* FRLANT 15. Göttingen: Vandenhoeck & Ruprecht, 1911. ————. *From Tradition to Gospel.* Tr. B. L. Woolf. London: Ivor Nicholson & Watson, 1934. ————. *Studies in the Acts of the Apostles,* ed. H. Greeven. Tr. M. Ling. London: SCM, 1956. **Dietrich, W.** *Das Petrusbild der lukanischen Schriften.* BWANT 94. Stuttgart: Kohlhammer, 1972. **Dihle, A.** "Die Evangelien und die biographische Tradition der Antike." *ZTK* 80 (1983) 33–49. **Dillon, R. J.** *From Eye-witnesses to Ministers of the Word.* Rome: Biblical Institute Press, 1978. **Dodd, C. H.** *The Parables of the Kingdom.* 3rd ed. New York: Scribner's, 1961. **Dömer, M.** *Das Heil Gottes: Studien zur Theologie des lukanischen Doppelwerkes.* BBB 51. Cologne/Bonn: Peter Hanstein,

1978. **Domeris, W. R.** "The Holy One of God as a Title of Jesus." *Neot* 19 (1985) 9–17. **Donahue, J. R.** *The Gospel in Parable: Metaphor, Narrative, and Theology in the Synoptic Gospels.* Minneapolis, MN: Fortress, 1990. **Downing, F. G.** "Law and Custom: Luke-Acts and Late Hellenism." In *Law and Religion,* ed. B. Lindars. 148–58, 187–91. ———. "Common Ground with Paganism in Luke and Josephus." *NTS* 28 (1982) 546–59. ———. "Freedom from the Law in Luke-Acts." *JSNT* 26 (1986) 49–52. ———. "A bas les aristos: The Relevance of Higher Literature for the Understanding of the Earliest Christian Writing." *NovT* 30 (1988) 212–30. **Drazin, I.** *Targum Onkelos to Deuteronomy: An English Translation of the Text with Analysis and Commentary.* New York: Ktav, 1982. **Drury, J.** *Tradition and Design in Luke's Gospel: A Study in Early Christian Historiography.* London: Darton, Longman & Todd, 1976. ———. *The Parables in the Gospels: History and Allegory.* New York: Crossroad, 1985. ———. "The Sower, the Vineyard, and the Place of Allegory in the Interpretation of Mark's Parables." *JTS,* n.s., 24 (1973) 367–79. **D'Sa, T.** "The Salvation of the Rich in the Gospel of Luke." *Vidyajyoti* 52 (1988) 170–80. **Dschulnigg, P.** "Positionen des Gleichnisverständnisses im 20. Jahrhundert: Kurze Darstellung von fünf wichtigen Positionen der Gleichnistheorie (Jülicher, Jeremias, Weder, Arens, Harnisch)." *TZ* 45 (1989) 335-51. **Dubois, J.-D.** "La figure d'Elie dans la perspective lucanienne." *RHPR* 53 (1973) 155–76. **Dumais, M.** "Ministères, charismes et esprit dans l'oeuvre de Luc." *EglT* 9 (1978) 413–53. ———. "L'évangélisation des pauvres dans l'oeuvre de Luc." *ScÉs* 36 (1984) 297–321. **Dungan, D. L.** "Jesus and Violence." In *Jesus, the Gospels, and the Church.* FS W. R. Farmer, ed. E. P. Sanders. Macon, GA: Mercer, 1987. 135–62. **Dunn, J. D. G.** *Baptism in the Holy Spirit.* London: SCM, 1970. ———. *Jesus and the Spirit: A Study of the Religious and Charismatic Experience of Jesus and the First Christians as Reflected in the New Testament.* London: SCM, 1975. ———. "Pharisees, Sinners and Jesus." In *The Social World of Formative Christianity and Judaism,* ed. J. Neusner et al. 264–89. **Dupont, J.** *Les actes des Apôtres.* Paris: Cerf, 1953. ———. *Les béatitudes.* 3 vols. Louvain: Nauwelaerts, 1958, 1969, 1973. ———. *Le discours de Milet: Testament pastoral de saint Paul (Actes 20, 18–36).* LD 32. Paris: Cerf, 1962. ———. "Die individuelle Eschatologie im Lukasevangelium und in der Apostelgeschichte." In *Orientierung an Jesus.* FS J. Schmid, ed. P. Hoffmann et al. 37–47. ———. *Pourquoi les paraboles? La méthode parabolique de Jésus.* Lire la Bible. Paris: Cerf, 1977. ———. *Études sur les évangiles synoptiques.* BETL 70. 2 vols. Leuven: University Press/Peeters, 1985. ———. "Le salut des Gentiles et la signification théologique du Livre des Actes." *NTS* 6 (1959–60) 132–55. ———. "Le chapître des paraboles." *NRT* 89 (1967) 800–820. ———. "L'après mort dans l'oeuvre de Luc." *RTL* 3 (1972) 3–21. ———. "The Poor and Poverty in the Gospel and Acts." In *Gospel Poverty: Essays in Biblical Theology.* Chicago: Franciscan Herald, 1977. 25–52. ———. "La prière et son efficacité dans l'évangile de Luc." *RSR* 69 (1981) 45–56. **Easton, B. S.** "The Purpose of Acts." In *Early Christianity: "The Purpose of Acts" and Other Papers,* ed. F. C. Grant. London: Seabury, 1955. 33–118. **Ebertz, M. N.** *Das Charisma des Gekreuzigten: Zur Soziologie der Jesusbewegung.* WUNT 1/45. Tübingen: Mohr (Siebeck), 1987. **Edwards, D. R.** "Acts of the Apostles and the Graeco-Roman World: Narrative Communication in Social Contexts." In *SBL 1989 Seminar Papers,* ed. D. J. Lull. 362-77. **Edwards, O. C., Jr.** *Luke's Story of Jesus.* Philadelphia: Fortress, 1981. **Ehrhardt, A.** "The Construction and Purpose of the Acts of the Apostles." *ST* 12 (1958) 45–79. **Ehrhardt, E.** *The Framework of the New Testament Stories.* Manchester: University Press, 1964. **Eichholz, G.** *Einführung in die Gleichnisse.* Neukirchen-Vluyn: Neukirchener, 1963. ———. *Gleichnisse der Evangelien: Form, Überlieferung, Auslegung.* 3rd ed. Neukirchen-Vluyn: Neukirchener, 1979. **Elliott, J. H.** "Temple versus Household in Luke-Acts: A Contrast in Social Institutions." *HTS* 47 (1991) 88–120. ———. "Household and Meals vs. Temple Purity: Replication Patterns in Luke-Acts." *BTB* 21 (1991) 102–8. **Ellis E. E.** "The Making of Narratives in the Synoptic Gospels." In *Jesus and the Oral Gospel Tradition,* ed. H. Wansbrough. 301–24. ———. *Eschatology in Luke.* Philadelphia: Fortress, 1972. ———. "Present and Future Eschatology in Luke." *NTS* 12 (1965–66) 27–41. ———. "'Those of the Circumcision' and the Early Christian Mission." *SE* 4 [= TU 102] (1968) 390–99. **Eltester, W.** "Israel im lukanischen Werk und die Nazarethperikope."

In *Jesus in Nazareth*, ed. W. Eltester. 76–147. ———, ed. *Neutestamentliche Studien*. FS R. Bultmann. BZNW 21. Berlin: Töpelmann, 1954.———, ed. *Jesus in Nazareth*. Berlin: de Gruyter, 1972. **Enslin, M. S.** "Luke, the Literary Physician." In *Studies in New Testament and Early Christian Literature*. FS A. P. Wikgren, ed. D. E. Aune. NovTSup 33. Leiden: Brill, 1972. 135–43. **Ernst, J.** *Herr der Geschichte: Perspektiven der lukanischen Eschatologie*. SBS 88. Stuttgart: Katholisches Bibelwerk, 1978. ———. *Lukas: Ein theologisches Portrait*. Düsseldorf: Patmos, 1985. ———. "Das Evangelium nach Lukas—kein soziales Evangelium." *TGl* 67 (1977) 415–21. **Esler, P. F.** *Community and Gospel in Luke-Acts: The Social and Political Motivations of Lucan Theology*. SNTSMS 57. Cambridge/New York: Cambridge University Press, 1987. **Evans, C. A.** "Is Luke's View of the Jewish Rejection of Jesus Anti-Semitic?" In *Reimaging*, ed. D. D. Sylva. 29–56, 174–83. ———. "Luke's Use of the Elijah/Elisha Narratives and the Ethic of Election." *JBL* 106 (1987) 75–83. **Farmer, W. R.** *The Synoptic Problem: A Critical Analysis*. Macon, GA: Mercer University, 1976. ———. "Luke's Use of Matthew: A Christological Inquiry." *PSTJ* 40 (1987) 39–50. **Feldkämper, L.** *Der betende Jesus als Heilsmittler nach Lukas*. Veröffentlichung des Missionspriesterseminars 29. St. Augustin bei Bonn: Steyler, 1978. **Fiebig, P.** "Jesu Gleichnisse im Lichte der rabbinischen Gleichnisse." *ZNW* 13 (1912) 192–211. **Fiedler, P.** *Jesus und die Sünder*. BET 3. Frankfurt am M./Bern: Lang, 1976. **Fiedler, W.** *Antiker Wetterzauber*. Würzburger Studien zur Altertumswissenschaft 1. Stuttgart: Kohlhammer, 1931. **Finegan, J.** *The Archaeology of the New Testament: The Mediterranean World of the Early Christian Apostles*. Boulder, CO: Westview, 1981. **Fisher, N. F.** *The Parables of Jesus: Glimpses of God's Reign*. New York: Crossroad/Continuum, 1990. **Fitzmyer, J. A.** *Luke the Theologian: Aspects of His Teaching*. New York/Mahwah, NJ: Paulist, 1989. ———. "The Priority of Mark and the 'Q' Source in Luke." In *Jesus and Man's Hope*, ed. D. G. Miller. Perspective Books. 2 vols. Pittsburgh: Pittsburgh Theological Seminary, 1970. 1:131–70. ———. *Essays on the Semitic Background of he New Testament*. Missoula, MT: Scholars, 1974. ———. "Jesus in the Early Church through the Eyes of Luke-Acts." *ScrB* 17 (1987) 26–35. ———. "The Use of the Old Testament in Luke-Acts." In *SBL 1992 Seminar Papers*, ed. E. H. Lovering, Jr. 524–38. ——— et al. *À cause de l'Évangile: Études sur les Synoptiques et les Actes*. FS J. Dupont. LD 123. Paris: Cerf, 1985. **Flanagan, N. M.** "The What and How of Salvation in Luke-Acts." In *Sin, Salvation and the Spirit*, ed. D. Durkin. Collegeville: Liturgical, 1979. 203–13. ———. "The Position of Women in the Writings of St. Luke." *Marianum* 40 (1978) 288–304. **Flender, H.** *St. Luke: Theologian of Redemptive History*. Tr. R. H. and I. Fuller. London: SPCK, 1967. **Foakes-Jackson, F. J.**, and **Lake, K.**, eds. *The Beginnings of Christianity*. Part 1, *The Acts of the Apostles*. 5 vols. London: Macmillan, 1920–33. **Focant, C.** "La chute de Jérusalem et la datation des évangiles." *RTL* 19 (1988) 17-37. **Ford, J. M.** *My Enemy Is My Guest: Jesus and Violence in Luke*. Maryknoll, NY: Orbis, 1984. **France, R. T.** *Jesus and the Old Testament: His Application of Old Testament Passages to Himself and His Mission*. London: Tyndale, 1971. **Francis, F. O.** "Eschatology and History in Luke-Acts." *JAAR* 37 (1969) 49–63. **Frankemölle, H.** "Hat Jesus sich selbst verkündet? Christologische Implikationen in den vormarkinischen Parabeln." *BibLeb* 13 (1972) 184–207. ———. "Kommunikatives Handeln in Gleichnissen Jesu. Historichkritische und pragmatische Exegese. Eine kritische Sichtung." *NTS* 28 (1982) 61–90. **Franklin, E.** *Christ the Lord: A Study in the Purpose and Theology of Luke-Acts*. Philadelphia: Westminster, 1975. **Freire, C. E.** "Jesús profeta, libertador del hombre: Vision lucana de su ministerio terrestre." *EE* 51 (1976) 463–95. **Freyne, S.** *The Twelve: Disciples and Apostles. An Introduction to the Theology of the First Three Gospels*. London: Sheed and Ward, 1968. ———. *Galilee, Jesus and the Gospels: Literary Approaches and Historical Investigations*. Dublin: Gill and Macmillan, 1988. **Fridrichsen, A.** *Le problème du miracle dans le Christianisme primitif*. Strasbourg/Paris: Istra. 1925. ———. "Jesu Kampf gegen die unreinen Geister." In *Der Wunderbegriff im Neuen Testament*, ed. A. Suhl. WF 295. Darmstadt: Wissenschaftliche Buchgesellschaft, 1980. 248–65. **Friedrichsen, T. A.** "The Matthew-Luke Agreements against Mark: A Survey of Recent Studies: 1974–89." In *L'Évangile de Luc* (1989), ed. F. Neirynck. 335–91. **Frye, R. M.** "The Jesus of the Gospels: Approaches through Narrative Structure."

In *From Faith to Faith*. FS D. G. Miller, ed. D. Y. Hadidian. PTMS 31. Pittsburgh: Pickwick, 1979. 75–89. **Fuchs, A.** *Sprachliche Untersuchungen zum Matthäeus und Lukas: Ein Beitrag zur Quellenkritik.* AnBib 49. Rome: Pontifical Institute, 1971. **Fuchs, E.** "Bemerkungen zur Gleichnisauslegung." In *Zur Frage nach dem historischen Jesus: Gesammelte Aufsätze II.* 2nd ed. Tübingen: Mohr, 1960. 136–42. ————. "Die Analogie." In *Die neutestamentliche Gleichnisforschung*, ed. W. Harnisch. 1–19. **Fuller, R. H.** *Interpreting the Miracles.* Philadelphia: Westminster, 1963. **Funk, R. W.** "The Narrative Parables: The Birth of a Language Tradition." In *God's Christ and His People*, ed. J. Jervell and W. A. Meeks. Oslo: Universitetsforlaget, 1977. 42–50. ————. *Parables and Presence: Forms of the New Testament Tradition.* Philadelphia: Fortress, 1982. ————. "Critical Note." *Semeia* 1 (1974) 182–91. ————. "Structure in the Narrative Parables of Jesus." *Semeia* 2 (1974) 51–73. ————. "Parable, Paradox, Power: The Prodigal Samaritan." *JAAR* 48 (1981) 83–97. ————. "From Parable to Gospel: Domesticating the Tradition." *Forum* 1 (1985) 3–24. ————. "Unraveling the Jesus Tradition." *Forum* 5.2 (1989) 31–62. **Fusco, V.** "Tendences récentes dans l'interpretation des paraboles." In *Les paraboles évangéliques: Perspectives nouvelles. XIIe congrès de l'ACEF*, ed. J. Delorme. LD 135. Paris: Cerf, 1989. 19–60 **Gaechter, P.** *Maria im Erdleben: Neutestamentliche Mariestudien.* 3rd ed. Innsbruck: Tyrolia, 1955. **Gager, J. G.** *Kingdom and Community: The Social World of Early Christianity.* Engelwood Cliffs: Prentice-Hall, 1975. ————. *The Origins of Anti-Semitism: Attitudes towards Judaism in Pagan and Christian Antiquity.* New York/Oxford: Oxford University Press, 1985. **Garrett, S. R.** *The Demise of the Devil: Magic and the Demonic in Luke's Writings.* Minneapolis, MN: Fortress, 1989. **Gärtner, B. E.** "The Person of Jesus and the Kingdom of God." *TToday* 27 (1970) 32–43. **Gasque, W. W.** *A History of the Criticism of the Acts of the Apostles.* Grand Rapids: Eerdmans, 1975. **Gaston, L.** *No Stone on Another: Studies in the Significance of the Fall of Jerusalem in the Synoptic Gospels.* NovTSup 22. Leiden: Brill, 1970. **Gault, J. A.** "The Discourse Function of *Kai Egeneto* in Luke and Acts." *OPTAT* 4 (1990) 388-99. **Gaventa, B. R.** "The Eschatology of Luke-Acts Revisited." *Encounter* 43 (1982) 27–42. **Geiger, R.** "Gesprächspartner Jesu im Lukasevangelium." In *Biblische Randbemerkungen.* FS R. Schnackenburg, ed. H. Merklein and J. Lange. Würzburg: Echter, 1974. 150–56. **George, A.** "Miracles dans le monde hellénistique." In *Les miracles de Jésus*, ed. X. Léon-Dufour. 95–108. ————. "Le miracle dans l'oeuvre de Luc." In *Les miracles de Jésus*, ed. X. Léon-Dufour. 249–68. ————. *Études sur l'oeuvre de Luc.* SB. Paris: Gabalda, 1978. ————. "La royauté de Jésus selon l'évangile de Luc." *ScEccl* 14 (1962) 57–69. ————. "Jésus Fils de Dieu dans l'évangile selon Saint Luc." *RB* 72 (1965) 185–209. ————. "Tradition et rédaction chez Luc: La construction du troisième évangile." *ETL* 43 (1967) 100–129. ————. "Israël dans l'oeuvre de Luc." *RB* 75 (1968) 481–525. ————. "L'emploi chez Luc du vocabulaire de salut." *NTS* 23 (1977) 308–20. ————. "L'Esprit-Saint dans l'oeuvre de Luc." *RB* 85 (1978) 500–542. **Gerhardsson, B.** "The Narrative Meshalim in the Synoptic Gospels." *NTS* 34 (1988) 339–63. ————. "If We Do Not Cut the Parables out of Their Frames." *NTS* 37 (1991) 321–35. **Gewalt, D.** "Das 'Petrusbild' der lukanischen Schriften als Problem einer ganzheitlichen Exegese." *LingBib* 34 (1975) 1–22. **Gibbs, J. M.** "Mark 1.1–15, Matthew 1.1–4.16, Luke 1.1–4.30, John 1.1–51: The Gospel Prologues and Their Function." *SE* 6 [= TU 112] (1973) 154–88. **Giblin, C. H.** *The Destruction of Jerusalem according to Luke's Gospel: A Historical-Typological Moral.* AnBib 107. Rome: Biblical Institute, 1985. ————. "Discerning Gospel Genre." *Thought* 47 (1972) 225–52. **Giet, S.** "Un procédé littéraire d'exposition: l'anticipation chronologique." *REA* 2 (1956) 243–53. **Gilbert, A.** "Où fut écrit l'évangile de Luc?" *ScEs* 39 (1987) 211–28. **Giles, K.** "Salvation in Lukan Theology (1)." *RTR* 42 (1983) 10–16. ————. "The Church in the Gospel of Luke." *SJT* 34 (1981) 121–46. ————. "Is Luke an Exponent of 'Early Protestantism'?: Church Order in the Lukan Writings (Part I)." *EvQ* 54 (1982) 193–205. **Gillman, J.** *Possessions and the Life of Faith: A Reading of Luke-Acts.* Zacchaeus Studies: New Testament. Collegeville, MN: Liturgical, 1991. **Gils, F.** *Jésus prophète d'après les évangiles synoptiques.* Orientalia et Biblica Lovaniensia 2. Louvain: Université de Louvain, 1957. **Glen, J. S.** *The Parables of Conflict in Luke.* Philadelphia:

Westminster, 1962. **Glöckner, R.** *Die Verkündigung des Heils beim Evangelisten Lukas.* Walberger Studien der Albertus-Magnus-Akademie. Theologische Reihe 9. Mainz: Grünewald, n.d. (1976). **Glombitza, O.** "Die Titel διδάσκαλος und ἐπιστάτης für Jesus bei Lukas." *ZNW* 49 (1958) 275–78. **Glover, W. W.** "The Kingdom of God' in Luke." *BT* 29 (1978) 231–37. **Gnilka, J.** *Das Matthäusevangelium.* HTKNT. 2 vols. Freiburg/Basel/Vienna: Herder, 1986-88. ————. *Die Verstockung Israels: Isaias 6, 9–10 in der Theologie der Synoptiker.* SANT 3. Munich: Kösel, 1961. **Goudoever, J. van.** "The Place of Israel in Luke's Gospel." *NovT* 8 (1966) 111–23. **Goulder, M. D.** *Midrash and Lection in Matthew.* London: SPCK, 1974. 452–71. ————. *The Evangelists' Calendar.* London: SCM, 1978. ————. "Characteristics of the Parables in the Several Gospels." *JTS,* n.s., 19 (1968) 51–69. ————. "On Putting Q to the Test." *NTS* 24 (1978) 218–34. ————. "Did Luke Know Any of the Pauline Letters?" *PRS* 13 (1986) 97–112. **Gowler, D. B.** *Host, Guest, Enemy and Friend: Portraits of the Pharisees in Luke and Acts.* Emory Studies in Early Christianity 2. New York/Bern: Lang, 1991. ————. "Characterization in Luke: A Socio-Narratological Approach." *BTB* 19 (1989) 54–62. **Grässer, E.** *Das Problem der Parusieverzögerung in den synoptischen Evangelien.* BZNW 22. 2nd ed. Berlin: Töpelmann, 1960. **Grassi, J. A.** *God Makes Me Laugh: A New Approach to Luke.* Wilmington: Glazier, 1986. **Green, J. B.** "'The Message of Salvation' in Luke-Acts." *ExAud* 5 (1989) 21–34. **Grelot, P.** "Miracles de Jésus et la démonologie juive." In *Les miracles de Jésus,* ed. X. Léon-Dufour. 59–72. **Grundmann, W.** *Das Evangelium nach Markus.* THKNT 2. 2nd ed. East Berlin: Evangelische Verlagsanstalt, 1959. ————. "Weisheit im Horizont des Reiches Gottes: Eine Studie zur Verkündigung Jesu nach der Spruchüberlieferung Q." In *Die Kirche des Anfangs.* FS H. Schürmann, ed. R. Schnackenburg, J. Ernst, and J. Wanke. Freiburg/Basel/Vienna: Herder, 1978. 175–200. **Guillet, J.** "Bulletin d'exégèse lucanienne." *RSR* 69 (1981) 425–42. **Gundry, R. H.** *Matthew: A Commentary on His Literary and Theological Art.* Grand Rapids: Eerdmans, 1982. **Güttgemanns, E.** "Narrative Analyse synoptischer Texte." In *Die neutestamentliche Gleichnisforschung,* ed. W. Harnisch. 179–223. **Haaker, K.** "Verwendung und Vermeidung des Apostelbegriffs im lukanischen Werk." *NovT* 30 (1988) 9–38. **Hadidan, D. Y.,** ed. *Signs and Parables.* PTMS 23. Pittsburgh: Pickwick, 1978. **Haenchen, E.** *Der Weg Jesu: Eine Erklärung des Markus-Evangeliums und der kanonischen Parallelen.* Berlin: Töpelmann, 1966. ————. *Die Bibel und wir: Gesammelte Aufsätze.* 2 vols. Tübingen: Mohr (Siebeck), 1968. ————. *The Acts of the Apostles: A Commentary.* Tr. B. Noble and G. Shinn. Oxford: Blackwell, 1971. ————. "Historie und Verkündigung bei Markus und Lukas." In *Das Lukas-Evangelium,* ed. G. Braumann. 287–316. ————. "Petrus-Probleme." *NTS* 7 (1960–61) 187–97. **Hahn, F.** *The Titles of Jesus in Christology: Their History in Early Christianity.* Tr. H. Knight and G. Ogg. London: Lutterworth, 1969. **Hamm, D.** "Sight to the Blind: Vision as Metaphor in Luke." *Bib* 67 (1986) 457–77. **Hammer, R. A.** "Elijah and Jesus: A Quest for Identity." *Judaism* 19 (1970) 207–18. **Hanford, W. R.** "Deutero-Isaiah and Luke-Acts: Straightforward Universalism?" *CQR* 168 (1967) 141–52. **Harnack, A. von.** *Luke the Physician: The Author of the Third Gospel and the Acts of the Apostles.* New Testament Studies 1. Tr. J. R. Wilkinson. New York: Putnam, 1907. ————. *The Acts of the Apostles.* New Testament Studies 3. Tr. J. R. Wilkinson. London/New York: Williams & Norgate/G. P. Putnam's Sons, 1909. ————. "'Ich bin gekommen': Die ausdrücklichen Selbstzeugnisse Jesu über den Zweck seiner Sendung und seines Kommens." *ZTK* 22 (1912) 1–30. **Harnisch, W.** *Die Gleichniserzählungen Jesu: Eine hermeneutische Einführung.* Unitaschenbücher 1343. Göttingen: Vandenhoeck & Ruprecht, 1985. ————. "Die Ironie als Stilsmittel in Gleichnisse Jesu." *EvT* 32 (1972) 421–36. ————. "Die sprachkraft der Analogie: Zur These vom 'argumentativen Character' der Gleichnisse Jesu." *ST* 28 (1974) 1–20. ————. "Die Metaphor als heuristisches Prinzip: Neuerscheinungen zur Hermeneutik der Gleichnisreden Jesu." *VF* 24 (1979) 53–89. ————, ed. *Die neutestamentliche Gleichnisforschung im Horizont von Hermeneutik und Literaturwissenschaft.* WF 575. Darmstadt: Wissenschaftliche Buchgesellschaft, 1982. ————, ed. *Gleichnisse Jesu: Positionen der Auslegung von Adolf Jülicher bis zur Formgeschichte.* WF 366. Darmstadt: Wissenschaftliche Buchgesellschaft, 1982. **Hartman, L.** *Testimonium Linguae:*

Participial Constructions in the Synoptic Gospels: A Linguistic Examination of Luke 21, 13. ConNT 19. Lund: Gleerup, 1963. **Harvey, A. E.** *Jesus and the Constraints of History.* Philadelphia: Westminster, 1982. **Hasler, V.** *Amen.* Zürich/Stuttgart: Gotthelf-Verlag, 1969. **Hastings, A.** *Prophet and Witness in Jerusalem.* Baltimore: Helicon, 1958. **Haubeck, W.,** and **Bachmann, M.,** eds. *Wort in der Zeit: Neutestamentliche Studien.* FS K. H. Rengstorf. Leiden: Brill, 1980. **Hauerwas, S.** "The Politics of Charity." *Int* 31 (1977) 251–62. **Hawkins, J. C.** *Horae Synopticae: Contributions to the Study of the Synoptic Problem.* 2nd ed. Oxford: Clarendon, 1909. **Heard, W.** "Luke's Attitude toward the Rich and the Poor." *TJ* 9 (1988) 47–80. **Heinemann, J.** "The Triennial Lectionary Cycle." *JJS* 19 (1968) 41–48. **Heininger, B.** *Metaphorik, Erzählstruktur und szenisch-dramatische Gestaltung in den Sondergutgleichnissen bei Lukas.* NTAbh n.f. 24. Münster: Aschendorff, 1991. **Hemer, C. J.** *The Book of Acts in the Setting of Hellenistic History,* ed. C. H. Gempf. WUNT 49. Tübingen: Mohr-Siebeck, 1989. **Hengel, M.** *The Charismatic Leader and His Followers.* Tr. J. C. G. Greig. New York: Crossroad, 1981. **Hennecke, E.** *New Testament Apocrypha.* Ed. W. Schneemelcher. Tr. R. McL. Wilson. 2 vols. London: Lutterworth, 1963–65. **Heutger, N.** "Münzen im Lukasevangelium." *BZ* 27 (1983) 97–101. **Hiers, R. H.** *The Kingdom of God in the Synoptic Tradition.* UFHM 33. Gainesville: University of Florida, 1970. ————. "The Problem of the Delay of the Parousia in Luke-Acts." *NTS* 20 (1974) 145–55. **Higgins, A. J. B.** *Jesus and the Son of Man.* London/Philadelphia: Lutterworth/Fortress, 1964. ————. "Non-Gnostic Sayings in the Gospel of Thomas." *NovT* 4 (1960) 292–306. **Hill, E.** "Messianic Fulfilment in St. Luke." *SE* 1 [= TU 73] (1959) 190–98. **Hinnebusch, P.** "Jesus, the New Elijah, in Saint Luke." *BiTod* 31 (1967) 2175–82; 32 (1967) 2237–44. **Hirsch, E.** *Die Auferstehungsgeschichten und der christliche Glaube.* Tübingen: Mohr (Siebeck), 1940. **Hobart, W. K.** *The Medical Language of St. Luke: A Proof from Internal Evidence that "The Gospel according to St. Luke" and "The Acts of the Apostles" Were Written by the Same Person, and that the Writer Was a Medical Man.* Grand Rapids: Baker, 1954 = 1882. **Hoehner, H. W.** *Herod Antipas.* SNTSMS 17. Cambridge: University Press, 1972. **Hoffmann, J. C.** "Story as Mythoparabolic Medium: Reflections on Crossan's Interpretation of the Parables of Jesus." *USQR* 37 (1983) 323–33. **Hoffmann, P.** *Studien zur Theologie der Logienquelle.* Münster: Aschendorff, 1972. ———— et al., eds. *Orientierung an Jesus: Zur Theologie der Synoptiker.* FS J. Schmid. Freiburg/Basel/Vienna: Herder, 1973. **Hollenbach, P. H.** "From Parable to Gospel: A Response Using the Social Sciences." *Forum* 2.3 (1986) 67–75. **Holtz, T.** *Untersuchungen über die alttestamentlichen Zitate bei Lukas.* TU 104. Berlin: Akademie, 1968. **Holtzmann, H. J.** *Die Synoptiker.* HKNT. 3rd ed. Tübingen: Mohr, 1901. **Hooker, M. D.** *The Son of Man in Mark: A Study of the Background of the Term "Son of Man" and Its Use in St. Mark's Gospel.* Montreal: McGill University, 1967. **Horn, F. W.** *Glaube und Handeln in der Theologie des Lukas.* GTA 26. Göttingen: Vandenhoeck & Ruprecht, 1983. **Horsley, R. A.** *Sociology and the Jesus Movement.* New York: Crossroad, 1989. **Houlden, J. L.** "The Purpose of Luke." *JSNT* 21 (1984) 53–65. **House, P.** "Suffering and the Purpose of Acts." *JETS* 33 (1990) 317–30. **Hubbard, B. J.** "Commissioning Stories in Luke-Acts: A Study of Their Antecedents, Form, and Content." *Semeia* 8 (1977) 103–26. ————. "Luke, Josephus, and Rome: A Comparative Approach to the Lukan *Sitz im Leben.*" In *1978 SBL Seminar Papers,* ed. P. J. Achtemeier. Missoula: Scholars, 1978. 1:59–68. **Huffman, N. A.** "Atypical Features in the Parables of Jesus." *JBL* 97 (1978) 207–20. **Hull, J. M.** *Hellenistic Magic and the Synoptic Tradition.* SBT 2/28. London: SCM, 1974. **Hultgren, A. J.** "Interpreting the Gospel of Luke." *Int* 30 (1976) 353–65. **Hunkin, J. W.** "'Pleonastic' ἄρχομαι in the New Testament." *JTS,* o.s., 25 (1924) 390–402. **Hunter, A. M.** *The Parables for Today.* London: SCM, 1983. ————. "Interpreting the Parables." *Int* 14 (1960) 70–84; 167–85; 315–54. **Jackson, D.** "Luke and Paul: A Theology of One Spirit from Two Perspectives." *JETS* 32 (1989) 335–43. **Jellicoe, S.** "St. Luke and the Letter of Aristeas." *JBL* 80 (1961) 149–55. **Jeremias, J.** *Jesus' Promise to the Nations.* SBT 24. Tr. S. H. Hooke. London: SCM, 1958. ————. *Jerusalem in the Time of Jesus.* Philadelphia: Fortress, 1969. ————. *New Testament Theology.* Vol. 1. London: SCM, 1971. ————. *The Parables of Jesus.* Tr. S. H. Hooke et al. 3rd ed. London: SCM, 1972. ————. *Die Sprache des Lukasevangeliums: Redaktion* *und Tradition im Nicht-Markusstoff des dritten Evangeliums.* KEK, Sonderband. Göttingen: Vandenhoeck & Ruprecht, 1980. ————. "Pericopen-Umstellungen bei Lukas?" *NTS* 4 (1958) 115–19. **Jervell, J.** *Imago Dei.* FRLANT 58. Göttingen: Vandenhoeck & Ruprecht, 1960. ————. *Luke and the People of God.* Minneapolis: Augsburg, 1972. ————. *The Unknown Paul: Essays on Luke-Acts and Early Christian History.* Minneapolis: Augsburg, 1984. ————. "Die Mitte der Schrift: Zum lukanischen Verständnis des Alten Testaments." In *Die Mitte des Neuen Testaments,* ed. U. Luz and H. Weder. 79–96. ————. "God's Faithfulness to the Faithless People: Trends in Interpretation of Luke-Acts." *WW* 12 (1992) 29–36. ————. "Retrospect and Prospect in Luke-Acts Interpretation." In *SBL 1991 Seminar Papers,* ed. E. H. Lovering, Jr. 283–404. ————. "The Church of Jews and Godfearers." In *Luke-Acts and the Jewish People,* ed. J. B. Tyson. 11–20, 138–40. **Johnson, L. T.** *The Literary Function of Possessions in Luke-Acts.* SBLDS 39. Missoula, MT: Scholars, 1977. ————. *Luke-Acts: A Story of Prophet and People.* Chicago: Franciscan Herald, 1981. **Johnston, R. M.** "The Study of Rabbinic Parables: Some Preliminary Observations." In *Society of Biblical Literature. 1976 Seminar Paper.* Missoula, MT: Scholars, 1976. 337–57. **Jones, C. P. M.** "The Epistle to the Hebrews and the Lukan Writings." In *Studies in the Gospels.* FS R. H. Lightfoot, ed. D. E. Nineham. Oxford: Blackwell, 1955. 113–43. **Jones, D. L.** "Luke's Unique Interest in Historical Chronology." In *1989 SBL Seminar Papers,* ed. D. J. Lull. 378–87. **Jones, G. V.** *The Art and Truth of the Parables.* London: SPCK, 1964. **Jonge, M. de,** ed. *The Testaments of the Twelve Patriarchs: A Critical Edition of the Greek Text.* Leiden: Brill, 1978. ———— and **Woude, A. S. van der.** "11 Q Melchizedek and the New Testament." *NTS* 12 (1965–66) 301–26. **Jörns, K. P.** "Die Gleichnisverkündigung Jesu: Reden von Gott als Wort Gottes." In *Der Ruf Jesu und die Antwort der Gemeinde.* FS J. Jeremias, ed. E. Lohse. Göttingen: Vandenhoeck & Ruprecht, 1970. 157–77. **Judge, E. A.** "The Social Identity of the First Christians." *JRomH* 11 (1980) 201–17. **Juel, D.** *Luke-Acts: The Promise of History.* Atlanta: John Knox, 1983. **Jülicher, A.** *Die Gleichnisreden Jesu.* 2 vols. 2nd ed. Tübingen: Mohr, 1910. **Jüngel, E.** *Paulus und Jesus: Eine Untersuchung zur Präzisierung der Frage nach dem Ursprung der Christologie.* HUTh 2. 4th ed. Tübingen: Mohr, 1972. 71–215. **Kaestli, J.-D.** *L'Eschatologie dans l'oeuvre de Luc.* Geneva: Labor et Fides, 1969. **Kahlefeld, H.** *Gleichnisse als Lehrstücke im Evangelium.* 2 vols. 2nd ed. Frankfurt: Knecht, 1964–65. **Kähler, M.** *The So-Called Historical Jesus and the Historic Biblical Christ.* Tr. C. E. Braaten. Fortress: Philadelphia, 1964. **Kampling, R.** "Jesus von Nazaret—Lehrer und Exorzist." *BZ* 30 (1986) 237–48. **Karris, R. J.** *Invitation to Luke.* Garden City: Doubleday Image, 1977. ————. *What Are They Saying about Luke and Acts? A Theology of the Faithful God.* New York: Paulist, 1979. ————. *Luke: Artist and Theologian.* New York: Paulist, 1985. ————. "Poor and Rich: The Lukan *Sitz im Leben.*" In *Perspectives on Luke-Acts,* ed. C. H. Talbert. 112–25. ————. "Windows and Mirrors: Literary Criticism and Luke's *Sitz im Leben.*" In *1979 SBL Seminar Papers,* ed. P. J. Achtemeier. Missoula: Scholars, 1979. 1:47–58. ————. "The Lukan *Sitz im Leben:* Methodology and Prospects." In *Society of Biblical Literature. 1976 Seminar Papers.* Missoula, MT: Scholars, 1976. 219–33. ————. "Missionary Communities: A New Paradigm for the Study of Luke-Acts." *CBQ* 41 (1979) 80–97. **Käsemann, E.** *Essays on New Testament Themes.* SBT 41. London: SCM, 1964. **Keathley, N. H.** "The Temple in Luke and Acts: Implications for the Synoptic Problem and Proto-Luke." In *With Steadfast Purpose: Essays on Acts.* FS H. J. Flanders, Jr., ed. N. H. Keathley. Waco, TX: Baylor University, 1990. 77–105. **Keck, L. E.,** and **Martyn, J. L.,** eds. *Studies in Luke-Acts.* FS P. Schubert. Philadelphia: Fortress, 1980 = 1966. **Kee, H. C.** *Christian Origins in Sociological Perspective.* London: SCM, 1980. ————. *Miracle in the Early Christian World: A Study in Sociohistorical Method.* New Haven: Yale University, 1983. **Kellner, W.** *Der Traum vom Menschensohn: Die politisch-theologische Botschaft Jesu.* Munich: Kösel, 1985. **Kelly, J. F.** "The Patristic Biography of Luke." *BiTod* 74 (1974) 113–19. **Kelly, J. G.** "Lucan Christology and the Jewish-Christian Dialogue." *JES* 21 (1984) 688–708. **Kenny, A.** *A Stylometric Study of the New Testament.* Oxford/New York: University Press/Clarendon, 1986. **Kertelge, K.** *Die Wunder Jesu im Markusevangelium: Eine redaktionsgeschichtliche Untersuchung.* SANT 33. Munich: Kösel, 1970. ————. "Die Wunder Jesu in der neueren

Exegese." *TBl* 5 (1976) 71–105. **Kilgallen, J. J.** "The Function of Stephen's Speech (Acts 7,2–53)." *Bib* 70 (1989) 173–93. ———. "Social Development and the Lukan Writings." *StudMiss* 39 (1990) 21–47. **Kilpatrick, G. D.** "The Gentiles and the Strata of Luke." In *Verborum Veritas*, ed. O. Böcher. 83–88. **King, N. Q.** "The 'Universalism of the Third Gospel." *SE* 1 [= TU 73] (1959) 199–205. **Kingsbury, J. D.** *Jesus Christ in Matthew, Mark, and Luke.* Philadelphia: Fortress, 1981. ———. *Conflict in Luke: Jesus, Authorities, Disciples.* Minneapolis, MN: Fortress, 1990. ———. "Ernst Fuchs' Existentialist Interpretation of the Parables." *LQ* 22 (1970) 380–95. ———. "Major Trends in Parable Interpretation." *CTM* 42 (1971) 579–96. ———. "The Parables of Jesus in Current Research." *Dialog* 11 (1972) 101–7. **Kirchschläger, W.** *Jesu exorzistisches Wirken aus der Sicht des Lukas: Ein Beitrag zur lukanischen Redaktion.* OBS 3. Klosterneuburg: Österreichisches Katholisches Bibelwerk, 1981. **Kissinger, W. S.** *The Parables of Jesus: A History of Interpretation and Bibliography.* Metuchen, NJ: Scarecrow and ATLA, 1979. **Kistemaker, S. J.** *The Parables of Jesus.* Grand Rapids: Baker, 1980. **Klauck, H.-J.** *Allegorie und Allegorese in synoptischen Gleichnistexten.* Münster: Aschendorff, 1978. ———. "Neue Beiträge zur Gleichnisforschung." *BibLeb* 13 (1972) 214–30. ———. "Die Armut der Jünger in der Sicht des Lukas." *Claretianum* 26 (1986) 5–47. ———. "Die heilige Stadt: Jerusalem bei Philo und Lukas." *Kairos* 28 (1986) 129–51. **Klein A. F. J.** "Joden en heidenen in Lukas-Handelingen." *KeTh* 13 (1962) 16–24. **Klein, H.** "Zur Frage nach dem Abfassungsort der Lukasschriften." *EvT* 32 (1972) 467–77. **Klinghardt, M.** *Gesetz und Volk Gottes: Das lukanische Verständnis des Gesetzes nach Herkunft, Funktion und seinem Ort in der Geschichte des Urchristentums.* WUNT 2/32. Tübingen: Mohr, 1988. **Klostermann, E.** *Das Markusevangelium.* HNT 3. Tübingen: Mohr, 1926. **Knox, W. L.** *The Sources of the Synoptic Gospels.* Vol. 2, *St. Luke and St. Matthew.* Ed. H. Chadwick. Cambridge: University Press, 1957. **Koch, R.** "Die Wertung des Besitzes im Lukasevangelium." *Bib* 38 (1957) 151–69. **Kodell, J.** "Luke's Use of *laos*, 'People,' Especially in the Jerusalem Narrative (Lk 19,28–24,53)." *CBQ* 31 (1969) 327–43. ———. "The Theology of Luke in Recent Study." *BTB* 1 (1971) 115–44. **Koenig, J.** "Occasions of Grace in Paul, Luke, and First Century Judaism." *ATR* 64 (1982) 562–76. **Koester, H.** *Ancient Christian Gospels: Their History and Development.* Philadelphia, PA: Trinity, 1991. ———. "From the Kerygma-Gospel to Written Gospels." *NTS* 35 (1989) 361–81. **Koet, B. J.** *Five Studies of Scripture in Luke-Acts.* SNTA 14. Leuven: University Press, 1989. **Kopas, J.** "Jesus and Women: Luke's Gospel." *TToday* 43 (1986) 192–202. **Kraybill, D. B.** "Possessions in Luke-Acts: A Sociological Perspective." *PRS* 10 (1983) 215–39. **Kremer, J.,** ed. *Les Actes des Apôtres: Traditions, rédaction, théologie.* BETL 48. Gembloux: Duculot, 1979. **Kühschelm, R.** *Jüngerverfolgung und Geschick Jesu: Eine exegetisch-bibeltheologische Untersuchung der synoptischen Verfolgungsankündigungen Mk 13, 9–13 par und Mt 23, 29–36 par.* OBS 5. Klosterneuburg: Österreichisches Katholisches Bibelwerk, 1983. **Kümmel, W. G.** "Noch einmal: Das Gleichnis von der selbstwachsenden Saat: Bemerkungen zur neuesten Diskussion um die Auslegung der Gleichnisse Jesu." In *Orientierung an Jesus.* FS J. Schmid, ed. P. Hoffmann et al. 220–37. ———. *Promise and Fulfilment: The Eschatalogical Message of Jesus.* SBT 1/23. Tr. D. M. Barton. Naperville/London: Allenson/SCM, 1957. ———. *Introduction to the New Testament.* Tr. H. C. Kee. 2nd ed. London: SCM, 1975. ———. "Futurische und präsentische Eschatologie im ältesten Christentum." *NTS* 5 (1958–59) 113–26. ———. "Current Theological Accusations against Luke." *ANQ* 16 (1975) 131–45. **Kurz, W. S.** "Narrative Approaches to Luke-Acts." *Bib* 68 (1987) 195–220. ———. "Narrative Models for Imitation in Luke-Acts." In *Greeks, Romans and Christians.* FS A. J. Malherbe, ed. D. L. Balch et al. Minneapolis, MN: Fortress, 1990. 171–89. **Lacan, M.-F.** "Conversion et Royaume dans les Évangiles synoptiques." *LumVie* 9 (1960) 25–47. **Ladd, G. E.** "The Life-Setting of the Parables of the Kingdom." *JBR* 31 (1963) 193–99. **Lambrecht, J.** "Les parables dans les synoptiques." *NRT* 102 (1980) 672–91. **Lampe, G. W. H.** "The Holy Spirit in the Writings of St. Luke." In *Studies in the Gospels.* FS R. H. Lightfoot, ed. D. E. Nineham. Oxford: Blackwell, 1955. 159–200. ———. "The Lukan Portrait of Christ." *NTS* 2 (1956) 160–75. **Lane, W. L.** *The Gospel according to Mark.* NICNT. Grand Rapids: Eerdmans, 1974.

——— and **Robertson, M. J., III,** eds. *The Gospels Today: A Guide to Some Recent Developments.* Philadelphia: Skilton House, 1990. **Lategan, B. C.** "Tradition and Interpretation—Two Methodological Remarks." *Neot* 7 (1973) 95–103. **Laufen, R.** *Die Doppelüberlieferungen der Logienquelle und des Markusevangeliums.* BBB 54. Königstein/Bonn: Hanstein, 1980. **LaVerdiere, E.** "The Gospel of Luke." *BiTod* 18 (1980) 226–35. ——— and **Thompson, W. G.** "New Testament Communities in Transition: A Study of Matthew and Luke." *TS* 37 (1976) 567–97. **Légasse, S.** *Jésus et l'enfant: "Enfant," "petits" et "simple" dans la tradition synoptique.* Paris: Gabalda, 1969. **Legrand, L.** "Christ's Miracles as 'Social Work.'" *IES* 1 (1962) 43–64. ———. "The Parables of Jesus Viewed from the Dekkan Plateau." *ITS* 23 (1986) 154–70. **Lemcio, E. E.** *The Past of Jesus in the Gospels.* SNTSMS 68. Cambridge: University Press, 1991. **Léon-Dufour, X.** *Études d'évangile.* Parole de Dieu. Paris: Seuil, 1965. ———, ed. *Les miracles de Jésus selon le Nouveau Testament.* Paris: Seuil, 1977. **Levy, J.** *Neuhebräisches und chaldäisches Wörterbuch über die Talmudim und Midraschim.* 4 vols. Leipzig: Brockhaus, 1876–89. **Lightfoot, R. H.** *Locality and Doctrine in the Gospels.* London: Hodder & Stoughton, 1938. **Lindars, B.** "Elijah, Elisha, and the Gospel Miracles." In *Miracles: Cambridge Studies in Their Philosophy and History,* ed. C. F. D. Moule. London: Mowbray, 1965. 63–79. ———. *Jesus Son of Man: A Fresh Examination of the Son of Man Sayings in the Gospels in the Light of Recent Research.* London: SPCK, 1983. ———, ed. *Law and Religion: Essays on the Place of the Law in Israel and Early Christianity.* Cambridge: J. Clarke and Co., 1988. **Lindeboom, G. A.** "Luke the Evangelist and the Ancient Greek Writers on Medicine." *Janus: Revue internationale de l'histoire des sciences, de la médicine, de la pharmacie et de la technique* 52 (1965) 143–48. **Lindemann, A.** "Erwägungen zum Problem einer 'Theologie der synoptischen Evangelien.'" *ZNW* 77 (1986) 1–33. **Lindeskog, G.** "Johannes der Täufer: Einige Randbemerkungen zum heutigen Stand der Forschung." *ASTI* 12 (1983) 55–83. **Lindsey, R. L.** "A Modified Two-Document Theory of the Synoptic Dependence and Interdependence." *NovT* 6 (1963) 239–63. **Linnemann, E.** *Jesus of the Parables: Introduction and Exposition.* New York: Harper and Row, 1966. ———. *Parables of Jesus.* Tr. J. Sturdy. New York: Harper & Row, 1966. **Linton, O.** "Coordinated Sayings and Parables in the Synoptic Gospels: Analysis versus Theories." *NTS* 26 (1980) 139–63. **Little, J. C.** "Parable Research in the Twentieth Century." *ExpTim* 87 (1975–76) 356–60; 88 (1976–77) 40–44, 71–75. **Lohfink, G.** *Die Sammlung Israels: Eine Untersuchung zur lukanischen Ekklesiologie.* SANT 34. Munich: Kösel, 1975. **Lohmeyer, E.** *Das Evangelium des Markus.* KEK. Göttingen: Vandenhoeck & Ruprecht, 1953. **Lohse, E.** "Missionarisches Handeln Jesu nach dem Evangelium des Lukas." *TZ* 10 (1954) 1–13. ———. "Lukas als Theologe der Heilsgeschichte." *EvT* 14 (1954) 256–75. ——— et al., eds. *Der Ruf Jesu und die Antwort der Gemeinde: Exegetische Untersuchungen.* FS J. Jeremias. Göttingen: Vandenhoeck & Ruprecht, 1970. **Loisy, A.** *Les évangiles synoptiques.* Vol. 1. Cliffonds: Chez l'auteur, 1907. **Loos, H. van der.** *The Miracles of Jesus.* NovTSup 9. Leiden: Brill, 1965. **Lovering, E. H., Jr.,** ed. *Society of Biblical Literature 1991 Seminar Papers.* Atlanta: Scholars, 1991. ———, ed. *Society of Biblical Literature 1992 Seminar Papers.* Atlanta: Scholars, 1992. **Lövestam, E.** *Son and Saviour: A Study of Acts 13, 32–37. With an Appendix: 'Son of God' in the Synoptic Gospels.* ConNT 18. Tr. M. J. Petry. Lund: Gleerup, 1961. **Luck, U.** "Kerygma, Tradition, und Geschichte Jesu bei Lukas." *ZTK* 57 (1960) 51–66. **Lührmann, D.** *Die Redaktion der Logienquelle.* WMANT 33. Neukirchen: Neukirchener, 1969. ———. "The Gospel of Mark and the Sayings Collection Q." *JBL* 108 (1989) 51–71. **Lull, D. J.,** ed. *1989 SBL Seminar Papers.* Atlanta, GA: Scholars, 1989. **Luomanen, P.,** ed. *Luke-Acts Scandinavian Perspectives.* Publications of the Finnish Exegetical Society 54. Helsinki/Göttingen: Finnish Exegetical Society/Vandenhoeck & Ruprecht, 1991. **Luz, U.,** and **Weder, H.,** eds. *Die Mitte des Neuen Testaments: Einheit und Vielfalt neutestamentlicher Theologie.* FS E. Schweizer. Göttingen: Vandenhoeck & Ruprecht, 1983. **Mack, B. L.** *Rhetoric and the New Testament.* Minneapolis: Fortress, 1990. ——— and **Robbins, V. K.** *Patterns of Persuasion in the Gospels.* Sonoma, CA: Polebridge, 1989. **MacRae, G. W.** "The Gospel of Thomas—*Logia Iesou?*" *CBQ* 22 (1960) 56–71. **Maddox, R.** *The Purpose of Luke-Acts.* Edinburgh: Clark, 1982. **Magass, W.**

"Die magistralen Schlusssignale der Gleichnisse Jesu." *LingBib* 36 (1976) 1–20. **Mainville, O.** *L'esprit dans l'oeuvre de Luc.* Héritage et Projet 45. Montreal: Fides, 1991. ————. "Jésus et l'Esprit dans l'oeuvre de Luc: Éclairage à partir d'Ac 2, 33." *ScEs* 42 (1990) 193–208. **Malina, B. J.** *The New Testament World: Insights from Cultural Anthropology.* Atlanta: Knox, 1981. ————. "Interpreting the Bible with Anthropology: The Case of the Rich and the Poor." *Listening* 21 (1986) 148–59. ————. "Wealth and Poverty in the New Testament and Its World." *Int* 41 (1987) 354–67. **Maloney, F. J.** "Reading Eucharistic Texts in Luke." *ProcIBA* 14 (1991) 25–45. **Maly, E. H.** "Women and the Gospel of Luke." *BiTod* 10 (1980) 99–104. **Mánek, J.** "Das Aposteldekret im Kontext der Lukastheologie." *CV* 15 (1972) 151–60. **Mangatt, G.** "The Gospel of Salvation." *Biblebhashyam* 2 (1976) 60–80. **Manson, T. W.** *The Sayings of Jesus.* London: SCM, 1949. ————. *The Teaching of Jesus: Studies in Its Form and Context.* Cambridge: University Press, 1959 = 1935. **Manson, W.** *Jesus the Messiah: The Synoptic Tradition of the Revelation of God in Christ, with Special Reference to Form-Criticism.* London: Hodder & Stoughton, 1943. **Marin, L.** "Pour une théorie du texte parabolique." In *Le récit évangélique,* ed. C. Chabrol and C. Marin. BSR. Paris: Aubrier Montagne/ Delachaux et Niestlé/Cerf/Brouwer, 1974. 165–92. **Marshall, I. H.** *Eschatology and the Parables.* London: Tyndale, 1963. ————. *Luke: Historian and Theologian.* Exeter: Paternoster, 1970. ————. *The Acts of the Apostles.* Leicester: Inter-Varsity Press, 1980. ————. *Luke: Historian and Theologian.* 3rd ed. Exeter Paternoster, 1988. ————. *Luke: Historian and Theologian.* Enl. ed. Grand Rapids: Zondervan, 1989. ————. "The Present State of Lukan Studies." *Themelios* 14 (1988–89) 52–57. ————, ed. *New Testament Interpretation: Essays on Principles and Methods.* Exeter: Paternoster, 1977. **Martin, R. A.** *Syntactical Evidence of Semitic Sources in Greek Documents.* SBLSCS 3. Missoula, MT: Scholars, 1974. ————. *Syntax Criticism of the Synoptic Gospels.* Studies in the Bible and Early Christianity 10. Lewiston, NY/Queenston, Ont.: Mellen, 1987. **Martin, R. P.** "Salvation and Discipleship in Luke's Gospel." *Int* 30 (1976) 366–80. **Marx, W. G.** "Luke, the Physician, Re-examined." *ExpTim* 91 (1980) 168–72. **Marxsen, W.** *Der "Frühkatholizismus" im Neuen Testament.* BibS(N) 21. Neukirchen: Neukirchener, 1958. **März, C.-P.** *Das Wort Gottes bei Lukas: Die lukanische Worttheologie als Frage an die neuere Lukasforschung.* ETS 11. Leipzig: St. Benno, 1974. **Masson, C.** *Vers les sources d'eau vive: Études d'exégèse et de théologie du Nouveau Testament.* Publication de la Faculté de théologie, Université de Lausanne 2. Lausanne: Libraire Payot, 1961. **Matera, F. J.** "Responsibility for the Death of Jesus according to the Acts of the Apostles." *JSNT* 39 (1990) 77–93. **Matthey, J.** "Puissance et pauvreté: Notes sur la mission de l'Eglise à partir de la théologie de Luc." *BulCPE* 30 (1978) 47–54. **Mattill, A. J., Jr.** "The Purpose of Acts: Schneckenburger Reconsidered." In *Apostolic History and the Gospel: Biblical and Historical Essays.* FS F. F. Bruce, ed. W. W. Gasque and R. P. Martin. Exeter/Grand Rapids: Paternoster/Eerdmans, 1970. 108–22. ————. *Luke and the Last Things: A Perspective for the Understanding of Lukan Thought.* Dillsboro, NC: Western North Carolina, 1979. ————. "*Naherwartung, Fernerwartung,* and the Purpose of Luke-Acts: Weymouth Reconsidered." *CBQ* 34 (1972) 276–93. ————. "The Jesus-Paul Parallels and the Purpose of Luke-Acts: H. H. Evans Reconsidered." *NovT* 17 (1975) 15–46. **McArthur, K. H.,** and **Johnston, R. M.** *They Also Taught in Parables: Rabbinic Parables from the First Centuries of the Christian Era.* Grand Rapids: Zondervan, 1990. **McBride, D.** *Emmaus: The Gracious Visit of God according to Luke.* Dublin: Dominican Publications, 1991. **McDowell, E. A.** "The Gospel of Luke." *SWJT* 10 (1967–68) 7–24. **McEachern, V. E.** "Dual Witness and Sabbath Motif in Luke." *CJT* 12 (1966) 267–80. **McLaren, J. S.** *Power and Politics in Palestine: The Jews and the Governing of Their Land 100 B.C.–A.D. 70.* JSNTSup 63. Sheffield: JSOT, 1991. **McLoughlin, S.** "Les accords mineurs Mt-Lc contre Mc et le problème synoptique: Vers la théorie des deux sources." *ETL* 43 (1967) 17–40. **McPolin, J.** "Holy Spirit in Luke and John." *ITQ* 45 (1978) 117–31. **Melbourne, B. L.** *Slow to Understand: The Disciples in Synoptic Perspective.* Lanham, MD/New York/London: UP of America, 1988. **Mellon, C.** "La parabole, manière de parler, manière d'entendre." In *Le récit évangélique,* ed. C. Chabrol and L. Marin. Paris: Aubrier-Montaigne/Delachaux et Niestlé/Cerf/Brouwer, 1974. 147–61. **Menoud, P.-H.** *Jésus-Christ* *et la foi: Recherches néotestamentaires.* Bibliothèque théologique. Neuchâtel/Paris: Delachaux et Niestlé, 1975. ————. *Jesus Christ and the Faith.* PTMS 18. Tr. E. M. Paul. Pittsburg: Pickwick, 1978. ————. "Jésus et ses témoins: Remarques sur l'unité de l'oeuvre de Luc." *EglT* 23 (1960) 7–20. **Menzies, R. P.** *The Development of Early Christian Pneumatology with Special Reference to Luke-Acts.* JSNTSup 54. Sheffield: Sheffield Academic, 1991. **Merk, O.** "Das Reich Gottes in den lukanischen Schriften." In *Jesus und Paulus.* FS W. G. Kümmel, ed. E. E. Ellis and E. Grässer. Göttingen: Vandenhoeck & Ruprecht, 1975. 201–20. **Metzger, B. M.** *A Textual Commentary on the Greek New Testament: A Companion Volume to the United Bible Societies' Greek New Testament. 3rd ed.* United Bible Societies, 1971. **Meyer, A.** *Jesu Muttersprache: Das galiläische Aramäisch in seiner Bedeutung für die Erklärung der Reden Jesu und der Evangelien überhaupt.* Freiburg i. B./Leipzig: Mohr (Siebeck), 1896. **Meyer, B. F.** *The Aims of Jesus.* London: SCM, 1979. ————. *Critical Realism and the New Testament.* Princeton Theological Monograph Series 17. Allison Park, PA: Pickwick Publications, 1989. ————. "How Jesus Charged Language with Meaning: A Study of Rhetoric." *SR* 19 (1990) 273–85. **Meyer, E.** *Ursprung und Anfänge des Christentums.* 3 vols. Darmstadt: Wissenschaftliche Buchgesellschaft, 1962 = 1921–23. **Meynet, R.** *Quelle est donc cette parole? Lecture "rhétorique" de l'évangile de Luc (1–9, 22–24).* LD 99. 2 vols. Paris: Cerf, 1979. ————. *Avey-vous lu saint Luc? Guide pour la rencontre.* Lire la Bible 88. Paris: Cerf, 1990. ————. "Crie de joie, stérile!" *Christus* 33 (1986) 481–89. **Michaelis, W.** *Die Gleichnisse Jesu: Eine Einführung.* 2nd ed. Hamburg: Furche, 1956. ————. "Das unbetonte καὶ αὐτός bei Lukas." *ST* 4 (1950) 86–93. **Michalczyk, J. J.** "The Experience of Prayer in Luke/Acts." *RevRel* 34 (1975) 789–801. **Michiels, R.** "La conception lucanienne de la conversion." *ETL* 41 (1965) 42–78. **Miller, M. H.** "The Character of Miracles in Luke-Acts." Th.D. diss., Graduate Theological Union, Berkeley, 1971. **Miller, R. J.** "Elijah, John and Jesus in the Gospel of Luke." *NTS* 34 (1988) 611-22. **Mills, M. E.** *Human Agents of Cosmic Power in Hellenistic Judaism and the Synoptic Tradition.* JSNTSup 41. Sheffield: JSOT, 1990. **Minear, P. S.** *To Heal and to Reveal: The Prophetic Vocation according to Luke.* Crossroad Books. New York: Seabury, 1976. ————. "Dear Theo." *Int* 27 (1973) 131–50. ————. "Jesus' Audiences, according to Luke." *NovT* 16 (1974) 81–109. **Miyoshi, M.** *Der Anfang des Reiseberichts Lk 9, 51–10, 24: Eine redaktionsgeschichtliche Untersuchung.* AnBib 60. Rome: Biblical Institute, 1974. **Moessner, D. P.** "'The Christ Must Suffer': New Light on the Jesus—Peter, Stephen, Paul Parallels in Luke-Acts." *NovT* 28 (1986) 220–56. ————. "The 'Leaven of the Pharisees' and 'This Generation': Israel's Rejection of Jesus according to Luke." *JSNT* 34 (1988) 21–46 . ————. "Paul in Acts: Preacher of Eschatological Repentance to Israel." *NTS* 34 (1988) 96–104. **Moffatt, J.** *An Introduction to the Literature of the New Testament.* International Theological Library. 3rd ed. Edinburgh: T. & T. Clark, 1918. **Monloubou, L.** *La prière selon Saint Luc: Recherche d'une structure.* LD 89. Paris: Cerf, 1976. **Moore, S. D.** "Luke's Economy of Knowledge." In *1989 SBL Seminar Papers,* ed. D. J. Lull. Atlanta, GA: Scholars, 1989, 38–56. ————. *Literary Criticism and the Gospels: The Theoretical Challenge.* New Haven, CT/London: Yale UP, 1989. ————. "The Gospel of the Look." *Semeia* 54 (1991) 159–96. **Morgenthaler, R.** *Die lukanische Geschichtsschreibung als Zeugnis: Gestalt und Gehalt der Kunst des Lukas.* ATANT 14–15. 2 vols. Zürich: Zwingli, 1949. ————. *Statistik des neutestamentlichen Wortschatzes.* Zürich/Frankfurt am Main: Gotthelf, 1958. **Morris, L.** *The New Testament and the Jewish Lectionaries.* London: Tyndale, 1964. ————. *The Cross in the New Testament.* Grand Rapids: Eerdmans, 1965. ————. "Luke and Early Catholicism." *JTSA* 40 (1982) 4–16. **Morton, A. Q.,** and **MacGregor, H. C.** *The Structure of Luke and Acts.* New York/Evanston, IL: Harper & Row, 1965. **Moscato, M.** "Current Theories regarding the Audience of Luke-Acts." *CurTM* 3 (1976) 355–61. **Most, W.** "Did St. Luke Imitate the Septuagint?" *JSNT* 15 (1982) 30–41. **Moule, C. F. D.** "The Intention of the Evangelists." In *New Testament Essays.* FS T. W. Manson, ed. A. J. B. Higgins. Manchester University, 1959. 165–79. ————. *An Idiom Book of New Testament Greek.* 2nd ed. Cambridge: University Press, 1963. **Moulton, J. H.,** and **Milligan, G.** *The Vocabulary of the Greek Testament, Illustrated from the Papyri and Other Non-literary Sources.* London: Hodder & Stoughton, 1930. **Moxnes, H.** *The Economy of the Kingdom: Social Conflict and Economic Relations in Luke's Gospel.*

Philadelphia: Fortress, 1988. ————. "Meals and the New Community in Luke." *SEÅ* 51–52 (1986–87) 158–67. **Muhlack, G.** *Die Parallelen von Lukas-Evangelium und Apostelgeschichte.* Theologie und Wirklichkeit 8. Bern/Frankfurt/Las Vegas: Lang, 1979. **Mulder, H.** "Theophilus de 'godvrezende.'" In *Arcana revelata.* FS F. W. Grosheide, ed. N. J. Hommes et al. Kampen: Kok, 1951. 77–88. **Müller, P.-G.** "Conzelmann und die Folgen: Zwanzig Jahre redaktionsgeschichtliche Forschung am Lukas-Evangelium." *BK* 28 (1974) 138–42. ————, ed. *Das Zeugnis des Lukas: Impuse für das Lesejahr C.* Stuttgart: Katholisches Bibelwerk, 1985. **Mussner, F.** "Wege zum Selbstbewusstsein Jesu: Ein Versuch." *BZ* 12 (1968) 161–72. **Navone, J.** *Themes of St. Luke.* Rome: Gregorian University, 1971. ————. "Three Aspects of Lucan Theology of History." *BTB* 3 (1973) 115–32. **Neale, D. A.** *"None but the Sinners":* *Religious Categories in the Gospel of Luke.* JSNTSup 58. Sheffield: Sheffield Academic, 1991. **Nebe, G.** *Prophetische Züge im Bilde Jesu bei Lukas.* BWANT 127. Stuttgart/Berlin/Cologne: Kohlhammer, 1989. **Neirynck, F.** "La matière marcienne dans l'évangile de Luc." In *Problèmes.* FS L. Cerfaux, ed. F. Neirynck, 157–201. ————. "Recent Developments in the Study of Q." In *Logia.* FS J. Coppens, ed. J. Delobel. 29–75. ————. *Evangelica. Gospel Studies. Collected Essays.* Ed. F. van Segbroeck. BETL 60. Leuven: University Press, 1982. ————. "The Argument from Order and St. Luke's Transpositions." *ETL* 49 (1973) 784–815. ————, ed. *L'évangile de Luc: Problèmes littéraires et théologiques.* FS L. Cerfaux. BETL 32. Gembloux: Duculot, 1973. ————, ed. *L'évangile de Luc—The Gospel of Luke. Revised and Enlarged Edition of L'Évangile de Luc: Probleme littéraires et théologique.* BETL 32. 2nd ed. Leuven: University Press/Peeters, 1989. ————, ed. *The Minor Agreements of Matthew and Luke against Mark: With a Cumulative List.* In collaboration with T. Hanson and F. van Segbroeck. BETL 37. Leuven: University Press, 1974. **Nelson, P. K.** "Leadership and Discipleship: A Study of Luke 22:24–30." Ph.D. diss., Trinity College, Bristol, 1991. **Nestle, E.** *Philologica Sacra: Bemerkungen über die Urgestalt der Evangelien und Apostelgeschichte.* Berlin: von Reuther und Reichard, 1896. **Neusner, J., et al.,** eds. *The Social World of Formative Christianity and Judaism.* FS H. C. Kee. Philadelphia: Fortress, 1988. **Nevius, R. C.** *"Kyrios* and *Iēsous* in St. Luke." *ATR* 48 (1966) 75–77. **Neyrey, J. H.,** ed. *The Social World of Luke-Acts: Models for Interpretation.* Peabody, MA: Hendrickson, 1991. **Nickelsburg, G. W. E.** "Riches, the Rich, and God's Judgment in I Enoch 92–105 and the Gospel according to Luke." *NTS* 25 (1978–79) 324–44. **Nielsen, H. K.** *Heilung und Verkündigung: Das Verständnis der Heilung und ihres Verhältnisses zur Verkündigung bei Jesus und in der ältesten Kirche.* ATDan 22. Tr. D. Harbsmeier. Leiden/New York: Brill, 1987. **Nodet, E.** "Jésus et Jean-Baptiste selon Josèphe." *RB* 92 (1985) 497–524. **Nolland, J. L.** "Luke's Readers: A Study of Luke 4.22–8; Acts 13.46; 18.6; 28.28 and Luke 21.5–36." Ph.D. diss., Cambridge, 1977. ————. "Luke's Use of χάρις." *NTS* 32 (1986) 614–20. **Norden, E.** *Agnostos Theos: Untersuchungen zur Formgeschichte religiöser Rede.* Stuttgart: Teubner, 1956 = 1923. **Nuttall, G. F.** *The Moment of Recognition: Luke as Story-Teller.* London: Athlone, 1978. **Nützel, J. M.** *Jesus als Offenbarer Gottes nach den lukanischen Schriften.* FB 39. Würzburg: Echter, 1980. **O'Brien, P. T.** "Prayer in Luke-Acts." *TynB* 24 (1973) 111–27. **Oesterley, W. O. E.** *The Gospel Parables in the Light of Their Jewish Background.* New York: Macmillan, 1936. **Ó Fearghail, F.** "Israel in Luke-Acts." *ProcIBA* 11 (1988) 23–43. **Ommeren, N. M. van.** "Was Luke an Accurate Historian?" *BSac* 148 (1991) 57–71. **O'Neill, J. C.** *The Theology of Acts in Its Historical Setting.* 2nd ed. London: SPCK, 1970. ————. "The Six Amen Sayings in Luke." *JTS,* n.s., 10 (1959) 1–9. ————. "The Silence of Jesus." *NTS* 15 (1968–69) 153–67. **Orchard, J. B.** "Some Reflections on the Relationship of Luke to Matthew." In *Jesus, the Gospels, and the Church.* FS W. R. Farmer, ed. E. P. Sanders. Macon, GA: Mercer, 1987. 33–46. **O'Rourke, J. J.** "The Construction with a Verb of Saying as an Indication of Sources in Luke." *NTS* 21 (1975) 421–23. **Osborne, G. R.** "Luke: Theologian of Social Concern." *TJ* 7 (1978) 135–48. **O'Toole, R. F.** *The Unity of Luke's Theology: An Analysis of Luke-Acts.* Wilmington, DE: Glazier, 1984. ————. "Why Did Luke Write Acts (Lk-Acts)?" *BTB* 7 (1977) 66–76. ————. "Parallels between Jesus and His Disciples in Luke-Acts: A Further Study." *BZ* 27 (1983) 195–212. ————. "Luke's Message in Luke 9:1–50." *CBQ* 49 (1987) 74–98. ————. "The Parallels between Jesus and Moses." *BTB* 20 (1990) 22–29.

————. "Poverty and Wealth in Luke-Acts." *ChicStud* 30 (1991) 29–41. **Ott, W.** *Gebet und Heil: Die Bedeutung der Gebetsparänese in der lukanischen Theologie.* ANT 12. Munich: Kösel, 1965. **Parsons, M. C.** "'Allegorizing Allegory': Narrative Analysis and Parable Interpretation." *PRS* 15 (1988) 147–64. **Patte, D.**, ed. *Semiology and Parables: Exploration of the Possibilities Offered by Structuralism for Exegesis.* PTMS 9. Pittsburgh: Pickwick, 1976. **Payne, P. B.** "Metaphor as a Model for Interpretation of the Parables of Jesus with Special Reference to the Parable of the Sower." Ph.D. diss., Cambridge, 1975. **Percy, E.** *Die Botschaft Jesu: Eine traditionskritische und exegetische Untersuchung.* LUÅ 1, 49, 5. Lund: Gleerup, 1953. **Perkins, P.** *Hearing the Parables of Jesus.* New York: Paulist, 1981. **Pernot, H.** *Études sur la langue des évangiles.* Collection de l'Institut Néo-hellénique de l'Université de Paris 6. Paris: Societé d'Édition "Les belles lettres," 1927. **Perrin, N.** *Rediscovering the Teaching of Jesus.* NTL. London: SCM, 1967. ————. *Jesus and the Language of the Kingdom.* Philadelphia: Fortress, 1976. ————. "The Modern Interpretation of the Parables of Jesus and the Problem of Hermeneutics." *Int* 25 (1971) 131–48. ————. "Historical Criticism, Literary Criticism, and Hermeneutics: The Interpretation of the Parables of Jesus and the Gospel of Mark Today." *JR* 52 (1972) 361–75. **Pervo, R. I.** "Must Luke and Acts Belong to the Same Genre?" In *1989 SBL Seminar Papers,* ed. D. J. Lull. 309-16. **Pesch, R.** *Das Markusevangelium.* 2 vols. Freiburg: Herder, 1976–77. ————. *Die Apostelgeschichte.* 2 vols. Neukirchen-Vluyn: Neukirchener, 1986. **Petersen, N. R.** *Literary Criticism for New Testament Critics.* Philadelphia: Fortress, 1978. ————. "On the Notion of Genre in Via's 'Parable and Example Story: A Literary-Structuralist Approach.'" *Semeia* 1 (1974) 134–81. **Petzke, G.** *Das Sondergut des Evangeliums nach Lukas.* Zürcher Werkkommentare zur Bibel. Zurich: Theologischer, 1990. **Pilgrim, W. E.** *Good News to the Poor: Wealth and Poverty in Luke-Acts.* Minneapolis: Augsburg, 1981. ————. "Luke-Acts as a Theology of Creation." *WW* 12 (1992) 51–58. **Piper, R. A.** *Wisdom in the Q-Tradition.* SNTSMS 61. Cambridge: University Press, 1989. **Pittner, B.** *Studien zum lukanischen Sondergut: Sprachliche, theologische und form-kritische Untersuchungen zu Sonderguttexten in Lk 5–19.* ETS 18. Leipzig: St. Beno, 1991. **Plooy, G. P. V. du.** "The Use of the Optative in Luke-Acts: Grammatical Classification and Implications for Translation." *Scriptura* 19 (1986) 25–43. ————. "The Author in Luke-Acts." *Scriptura* 32 (1990) 28-35. **Plümacher, E.** *Lukas als hellenistischer Schriftsteller: Studien zur Apostelgeschichte.* SUNT 9. Göttingen: Vandenhoeck & Ruprecht, 1972. **Plymale, S. F.** "Luke's Theology of Prayer." In *1990 SBL Seminar Papers,* ed. D. J. Lull. Atlanta, GA: Scholars, 1990. 529-51. ————. *The Prayer Texts of Luke-Acts.* American University Studies. 7/118. New York/San Francisco/Bern: Lang, 1991. **Pokorný, P.** "Strategies of Social Formation in the Gospel of Luke." In *Gospel Origins and Christian Beginnings.* FS J. M. Robinson, ed. J. E. Goehring et al. Forum Fascicles. Sonoma, CA: Polebridge, 1990. 106–18. **Portefaix, L.** *Sisters Rejoice: Paul's Letter to the Philippians and Luke-Acts as Seen by First Century Philippian Women.* ConBNT 20. Stockholm: Amlqvist & Wiksell, 1988. **Potterie, I. de la.** "Le titre κύριος appliqué à Jésus dans l'évangile de Luc." In *Mélanges bibliques.* FS B. Rigaux, ed. A. Descamps and A. de Halleux. Gembloux: Duculot, 1970. 117–46. ————. "Les deux noms de Jérusalem dans l'évangile de Luc." *RSR* 69 (1981) 57–70. **Powell, M. A.** *What Are They Saying about Luke?* New York/Mahwah, NJ: Paulist, 1989. ————. "Are the Sands Still Shifting? An Update on Lukan Scholarship." *TrinSemRev* 11 (1989) 15–22. ————. "The Religious Leaders in Luke: A Literary-Critical Study." *JBL* 109 (1990) 93–110. ————. "Salvation in Luke-Acts." *WW* 12 (1992) 5–10. **Praeder, M.** "Jesus-Paul, Peter-Paul, and Jesus-Peter Parallelisms in Luke-Acts: A History of Reader Response." *SBLASP* 23 (1984) 23–39. **Prior, M.** "Revisiting Luke." *ScrB* 10 (1979) 2–11. **Radl, W.** *Das Lukas-Evangelium.* Erträge der Forschung 261. Darmstadt: Wissenschaftliche Buchgesellschaft, 1988. ————. *Paulus und Jesus im lukanischen Doppelwerk.* Bern/Frankfurt: Lang, 1975. **Ramsay, W. M.** *The Bearing of Recent Discovery on the Trustworthiness of the New Testament.* 2nd ed. London: Hodder & Stoughton, 1915. ————. *"Luke the Physician" and Other Studies in the History of Religion.* Grand Rapids: Baker, 1956 = 1908. **Ravens, D. A. S.** "St. Luke and Atonement." *ExpTim* 97 (1986) 291–94. ————. "Luke 9:7–62 and the Prophetic Role of Jesus." *NTS* 36 (1990)

119–29. **Reese, T.** "The Political Theology of Luke-Acts." *BTB* 22 (1972) 62–65. **Refoulé, F.,** ed. *À cause de l'Évangile: Études sur les Synoptiques et les Actes.* FS J. Dupont. LD 123. Paris: Cerf, 1985. **Rehkopf, F.** *Die lukanische Sonderquelle: Ihr Umfang und Sprachgebrauch.* WUNT 5. Tübingen: Mohr (Siebeck), 1959. **Reicke, B.** *The Gospel of Luke.* Richmond: John Knox, 1964. **Reid, B. E.** "The Centerpiece of Salvation History." *BiTod* 29 (1991) 20–24. **Reiling, J.** "The Use and Translation of *kai egeneto,* 'And It Happened,' in the New Testament." *BT* 16 (1965) 153–63. **Reitzel, F. X.** "St. Luke's Use of the Temple Imagery." *RevRel* 38 (1979) 520–39. **Rese, M.** *Alttestamentliche Motive in der Christologie des Lukas.* Gütersloh: Mohn, 1969. ———. "Das Lukas-Evangelium: Eine Forschungsbericht." *ANRW* II/25. 3 (1985) 2259–328. ———. "Neurere Lukas-Arbeiten: Bemerkungen zur gegenwärtigen Forschungslage." *TLZ* 106 (1981) 225–37. **Richard, E.** "Jesus' Passion and Death in Acts." In *Reimaging,* ed. D. D. Sylva. 153–69, 204–10. ———. "The Divine Purpose: The Jews and the Gentile Mission." *SBLASP* 17 (1978) 267–82. ———. "Luke—Writer, Theologian, Historian: Research and Orientation of the 1970's." *BTB* 13 (1983) 3–15. ———, ed. *New Views on Luke and Acts.* Collegeville, MN: Liturgical, 1990. **Richards, K. H.,** ed. *Society of Biblical Literature. 1982 Seminar Papers.* Chico, CA: Scholars, 1982. **Riches, J.** "Parables and the Search for a New Community." In *The Social World of Formative Christianity and Judaism,* ed. J. Neusner et al. 235–63. ———. *The World of Jesus: First-Century Judaism in Crisis.* Understanding Jesus Today. Cambridge: University Press, 1990. **Ricoeur, P.** "Biblical Hermeneutics." *Semeia* 4 (1975) 29–148. **Riddle, D. W.** "The Occasion of Luke-Acts." *JR* 10 (1930) 545–62. **Riesenfeld, H.** *The Gospel Tradition and Its Beginnings.* London: Mowbray, 1957. **Riesner, R.** *Jesus als Lehrer: Eine Untersuchung zum Ursprung der Evangelien-Überlieferung.* WUNT 2/7, 2nd ed. Tübingen: Mohr (Siebeck), 1984. **Rigaux, B.** *Témoignage de l'évangile de Luc.* Pour une histoire de Jésus 4. Bruges/Paris: Brouwer, 1970. **Ringgren, H.** "Luke's Use of the Old Testament." *HTR* 79 (1986) 227–35. **Robbins, V. K.** "Writing as a Rhetorical Act in Plutarch and the Gospels." In *Persuasive Artistry: Studies in New Testament Rhetoric.* FS G. A. Kennedy, ed. D. F. Watson. JSNTSup 50. Sheffield: JSOT, 1991. 142–68. **Robertson, A. T.** *A Grammar of the Greek New Testament in the Light of Historical Research.* 3rd ed. New York: Hodder & Stoughton, 1919. **Robinson, D. W. B.** "The Use of *Parabolē* in the Synoptic Gospels." *EvQ* 21 (1944) 93–108. **Robinson, J. A. T.** *Twelve New Testament Studies.* SBT 34. London: SCM, 1962. ———. *Redating the New Testament.* Philadelphia: Fortress, 1976. ———. "Elijah, John, and Jesus: An Essay in Detection." *NTS* 4 (1957–58) 263–81. **Robinson, J. M.** *The Problem of History in Mark.* SBT 1/21. London: SCM, 1957. ———. "Jesus' Parables as God Happening." In *Jesus and the Historian.* FS E. C. Colwell, ed. F. T. Trotter. Philadelphia: Fortress, 1968. 134–50. **Robinson, W. C., Jr.** *Der Weg des Herrn: Studien zur Geschichte und Eschatologie im Lukas-Evangelium.* TF 36. Hamburg/Bergstedt: Herbert Reich, 1964. **Rohde, J.** *Rediscovering the Teaching of the Evangelists.* NTL. Tr. D. M. Barton. London: SCM, 1968. **Rolland, P.** "L'arrière-fond sémiotique des évangiles synoptiques." *ETL* 60 (1984) 358–62. ———. "L'organisation du Livre des Actes et de l'ensemble de l'oeuvre de Luc." *Bib* 65 (1984) 81–86. **Roloff, J.** *Apostolat—Verkündigung—Kirche: Ursprung, Inhalt und Funktion des kirchlichen Apostelamtes nach Paulus, Lukas und den Pastoralbriefen.* Gütersloh: Mohn, 1985. ———. *Das Kerygma und der irdische Jesus: Historische Motive in den Jesus-Erzählungen der Evangelien.* Göttingen: Vandenhoeck & Ruprecht, 1970. **Rosenblatt, M.-E.** "Landless and Homeless." *BiTod* 29 (1991) 346–50. **Runnalls, D. R.** "The King as Temple Builder: A Messianic Typology." In *Spirit within Structure.* FS G. Johnston, ed. E. J. Furcha. Allison Park, PA: Pickwick, 1983. 15–38. **Russell, H. G.** "Which Was Written First, Luke or Acts?" *HTR* 48 (1955) 167–74. **Russell, W.** "The Anointing with the Holy Spirit in Luke-Acts." *TJ* 7 (1986) 47–63. **Sahlin, H.** *Der Messias und das Gottesvolk: Studien zur protolukanischen Theologie.* ASNU 12. Uppsala: Almqvist & Wiksells, 1945. ———. *Studien zum dritten Kapitel des Lukasevangeliums.* UUÅ 2. Uppsala/Leipzig: Lundeqvistska/Harrassowitz, 1949. **Saldarini, A. J.** "Interpretation of Luke-Acts and Implications for Jewish-Christian Dialogue." *WW* 12 (1992) 37–42. **Sanders, E. P.** "Jesus and the Kingdom: The Restoration of Israel and the New People of God." In *Jesus, the Gospels, and the Church.* FS

W. R. Farmer, ed. E. P. Sanders. Macon, GA: Mercer, 1987. 225-39. ―――. *Jesus and Juda-ism.* Philadelphia: Fortress, 1985. ―――. *Judaism: Practice and Belief 63 B.C.E.–66 C.E.* Lon-don/Philadelphia: SCM/Trinity, 1992. ―――– and **Davies, M.** *Studying the Synoptic Gos-pels.* London/Philadelphia: SCM/Trinity Press International, 1989. **Sanders, J. A.** "Isaiah in Luke." *Int* 36 (1982) 144–55. **Sanders, J. T.** "The Prophetic Use of Scripture in Luke-Acts." In *Early Jewish and Christian Exegesis.* FS W. H. Brownlee, ed. C. A. Evans and W. F. Stinespring. Atlanta, GA: Scholars, 1987. 191–98. ―――. "The Salvation of the Jews in Luke-Acts." In *Luke-Acts: New Perspectives*, ed. C. H. Talbert. 104–28. ―――. *The Jews in Luke-Acts.* Philadelphia: Fortress, 1987. ―――. "Who Is a Jew and Who Is a Gentile in the Book of Acts?" *NTS* 37 (1991) 434–55. **Sato, M.** *Q und Prophetie.* WUNT 2/29. Tübingen: Mohr-Siebeck, 1988. **Saxer, V.** "Le 'Juste Crucifié' de Platon à Théodoret." *RSLR* 19 (1983) 189–215. **Schaberg, J.** "Daniel 7, 12, and the New Testament Passion-Resurrection Predic-tions." *NTS* 31 (1985) 208–22. **Schelkle, K. H.** *Die Passion Jesu in der Verkündigung das Neuen Testaments: Ein Beitrag zur Formgeschichte und zur Theologie des Neuen Testaments.* Heidelberg: F. H. Kerle, 1949. ―――. "Der Zweck der Gleichnisreden." In *Neues Testament und Kirche.* FS R. Schnackenburg, ed. J. Gnilka. Freiburg: Herder, 1974. 71–75. **Schenk, W.** *Evangelium-Evangelien-Evangeliologie: Ein "hermeneutisches" Manifest.* Theologische Existenz heute 216. Munich: Kaiser, 1983. **Schenke, L.** *Die Wundererzählungen des Markusevangeliums.* SBB. Stuttgart: Katholisches Bibelwerk, n.d. [1974]. **Schlatter, A. von.** *Die Evangelien nach Markus und Lukas.* Stuttgart: Calwer, 1947. ―――. *Der Evangelist Matthäus.* 6th ed. Stuttgart: Calwer, 1963 = 1929. **Schlosser, J.** *La règne de Dieu dans les dits de Jésus.* Paris: Gabalda, 1981. **Schmauch, W.** "In der Wüste." In *In Memoriam Ernst Lohmeyer*, ed. W. Schmauch. Stuttgart: Evangelischen Verlagswerk, 1951. 202–23. ―――. *Orte der Offenbarung und der Offenbarungsort im Neuen Testament.* Göttingen: Vandenhoeck & Ruprecht, 1956. **Schmid, J.** *Das Evangelium nach Markus.* RNT 2. Regensburg: Pustet, 1963. **Schmidt, D. D.** "Syntactical Style in the 'We' Sections of Acts: How Lukan Is It?" In *1989 SBL Seminar Papers*, ed. D. J. Lull. 300–308. **Schmidt, K. L.** *Die Rahmen der Geschichte Jesu: Literarkritische Untersuchungen zur ältesten Jesusüberlieferung.* Berlin: Trowitzsch & Sohn, 1919. **Schmidt, T. E.** *Hostility to Wealth in the Synoptic Gospels.* JSNTSup 15. Sheffield: JSOT, 1987. **Schmithals, W.** "Lukas— Evangelist der Armen." *ThViat* 12 (1975–76) 153–67. ―――. "Die Berichte des Apostelgeschichte über die Bekehrung des Paulus und die 'Tendenz' des Lukas." *ThViat* 14 (1977–78) 145–65. **Schnackenburg, R.** "Die lukanische Eschatologie im Lichte von Aussagen der Apostelgeschichte." In *Glaube und Eschatologie*, ed. E. Grässer and O. Merk. Tübingen: Mohr, 1985. 249–65. ―――– et al., eds. *Die Kirche des Anfangs.* FS H. Schürmann. Leipzig: St. Benno, 1977. **Schneider, G.** *Parusiegleichnisse im Lukasevangelium.* Stuttgart: Katholisches Bibelwerk, 1975. ―――. *Die Apostelgeschichte.* HTKNT. 2 vols. Freiburg: Herder, 1980–82. ―――. *Lukas, Theologe der Heilsgeschichte: Aufsätze zum lukanischen Doppelwerk.* BBB 59. Bonn: Hanstein, 1985. ―――. "Der Zweck des lukan-ischen Doppelwerks." *BZ* 21 (1977) 45–66. ―――. "Schrift und Tradition in der theolo-gischen Neuinterpretation der lukanischen Schriften." *BK* 34 (1979) 112–15. ―――. "Jesu überraschende Antworten: Beobachtungen zu den Apophthegmen des dritten Evange-liums." *NTS* 29 (1983) 321–36. ―――. "Neuere Literatur zum dritten Evangelium (1987–1989)." *TRev* 86 (1990) 353–60. **Schnider, F.** *Jesus der Prophet.* OBO 2. Fribourg/ Göttingen: Universitätsverlag/Vandenhoeck & Ruprecht, 1973. **Schottroff, L., and Stegemann, W.** *Jesus von Nazareth: Hoffnung der Armen.* Stuttgart: Kohlhammer, 1978. **Schrage, W., ed.** *Studien zum Text und zur Ethik des Neuen Testaments.* FS H. Greeven. Berlin/ New York: de Gruyter, 1986. **Schramm, T.** *Der Markus-Stoff bei Lukas: Eine literarkritische und redaktionsgeschichtliche Untersuchung.* SNTSMS 14. Cambridge: University Press, 1971. **Schreckenburg, H.** "Flavius Josephus und die lukanischen Schriften." In *Wort in der Zeit: Neutestamentliche Studien.* FS K. H. Rengstorf, ed. W. Haubeck and M. Backmann. Leiden: Brill, 1980. 179–209. **Schroeder, E. H.** "Luke's Gospel through a Systematician's Lens." *CurTM* 3 (1976) 337–46. **Schroeder, H.-H.** "Haben Jesu Worte über Armut und Reichtum Folgen für das soziale Verhalten?" In *Studien zum Text*, ed. W. Schrage. 397–409. **Schulz, S.**

Die Stunde der Botschaft: Einführung in die Theologie der vier Evangelisten. 2nd ed. Hamburg/ Zürich: Furche/Zwingli, 1970. ————. *Q: Die Spruchquelle der Evangelisten.* Zürich: Theologischer Verlag, 1972. ————. "Gottes Vorsehung bei Lukas." *ZNW* 54 (1963) 104–16. **Schürer, E.** *The History of the Jewish People in the Age of Jesus Christ (175 B.C.–A.D. 135),* rev. ed. G. Vermes et al. 4 vols. Edinburgh: Clark, 1973, 1979, 1986, 1987. **Schürmann, H.** *Quellenkritische Untersuchung des lukanischen Abendmahlsberichtes Lk 22,7–38.* NTAbh 19/5, 20/4–5. 3 vols. Münster in W.: Aschendorff, 1953–57. ————. *Traditionsgeschichtliche Untersuchungen zu den synoptischen Evangelien.* Düsseldorf: Patmos, 1968. ————. *Ursprung und Gestalt: Erörterungen und Besinnungen zum Neuen Testament.* Kommentare und Beiträge zum Alten und Neuen Testament. Düsseldorf: Patmos, 1970. ————. *Gottes Reich—Jesus Geschick: Jesus ureiniger Tod im Licht seiner Basileia-Verkündigung (Teildruck).* Die Botschaft Gottes 2/34. Leipzig: St. Benno-Verlag, 1985. ————. "Sprachliche Reminiszenzen an abgeänderte oder ausgelassene Bestandteile der Spruchsammlung im Lukas- und Matthäusevangelium." *NTS* 6 (1960) 193–210. ————. "Das Thomasevangelium und das lukanische Sondergut." *BZ* 7 (1963) 236–60. **Schütz, F.** *Der leidende Christus: Die angefochtene Gemeinde und das Christuskerygma der lukanischen Schriften.* BWANT 9. Stuttgart: Kohlhammer, 1969. **Schwarz, G.** *Jesus und Judas: Aramaische Untersuchungen zur Jesus-Judas-Überlieferung der Evangelien und der Apostelgeschichte.* BWANT 123. Stuttgart/Berlin/Cologne/Mainz: Kohlhammer, 1988. **Schweizer, E.** *Church Order in the New Testament.* SBT 32. London: SCM, 1961. ————. *Luke: A Challenge to Present Theology.* Atlanta: John Knox, 1982. ————. "Zur lukanischen Christologie." In *Verifikation.* FS G. Ebeling, ed. E. Jungel, J. Wallmann, and W. Werbeck. Tübingen: Mohr, 1982. 43–65. ————. "Zur Frage der Quellen-benutzung durch Lukas." In *Neues Testament und Christologie im Werden: Aufsätze.* Göttingen: Vandenhoeck & Ruprecht, 1982. 33–85. ————. "Plädoyer der Verteidigung in Sachen: Moderne Theologie versus Lukas." *TLZ* 105 (1980) 241–52. **Scott, B. B.** *Jesus, Symbol-Maker for the Kingdom.* Philadelphia: Fortress, 1981. ————. "Parables of Growth Revisited: Notes on the Current State of Parable Research." *BTB* 11 (1981) 3–9. ————. "Essaying the Rock: The Authenticity of the Jesus Parable Tradition." *Forum* 2.1 (1986) 3–53. **Scott, J. A.** *Luke: Greek Physician and Historian.* Evanston: Northwestern University, 1930. **Scroggs, R.** "The Sociological Interpretation of the New Testament: The Present State of Research." *NTS* 26 (1980) 164–79. **Seccombe, D. P.** *Possessions and the Poor in Luke-Acts.* SNTU B/6. Linz, 1982. ————. "Luke and Isaiah." *NTS* 27 (1981) 252–59. **Segbroeck, F. van.** *The Gospel of Luke: A Cumulative Bibliography 1973–88.* BETL 88. Leuven: Leuven UP/Peeters, 1989. **Seifrid, M. A.** "Messiah and Mission in Acts: A Brief Response to J. B. Tyson." *JSNT* 36 (1989) 47–50. **Sellin, G.** "Allegorie und 'Gleichnis': Zur Formenlehre der synoptischen Gleichnisse." *ZTK* 75 (1978) 281–335. **Sheeley, S. M.** *Narrative Asides in Luke-Acts.* JSNTSup 72. Sheffield: JSOT, 1992. ————. "Narrative Asides and Narrative Authority in Luke-Acts." *BTB* 18 (1988) 102–7. **Shelton, J. B.** *Mighty in Word and Deed: The Role of the Holy Spirit in Luke-Acts.* Peabody, MA: Hendrickson, 1991. **Sheridan, M.** "Disciples and Discipleship in Matthew and Luke." *BTB* 3 (1973) 235–55. **Shuler, P. L.** *A Genre for the Gospels.* Philadelphia: Fortress, 1982. **Sider, J. W.** "The Meaning of *Parabole* in the Usage of the Synoptic Evangelists." *Bib* 62 (1981) 453–70. ————. "Nurturing Our Nurse: Literary Scholars and Biblical Exegesis." *CLit* 32 (1982) 15–21. ————. "Rediscovering the Parables: The Logic of the Jeremias Tradition." *JBL* 102 (1983) 61–83. ————. "Proportional Analogy in the Gospel Parables." *NTS* 31 (1985) 1–23. **Siegert, F.** "Lukas—ein Historiker, d.h. ein Rhetor? Freundschaftliche Entgegnung auf Erhardt Güttgemanns." *LingBib* 55 (1984) 57–60. **Simson, P.** "The Drama of the City of God: Jerusalem in St. Luke's Gospel." *Scr* 15 (1963) 65–80. **Siotis, M. A.** "Luke the Evangelist as St. Paul's Collaborator." In *Neues Testament und Geschichte: Historisches Geschehen und Deutung im Neuen Testament.* FS O. Cullmann, ed. H. Baltensweiler and B. Reicke. Zürich/Tübingen: Theologischer Verlag/Mohr (Siebeck), 1972. 105–11. **Siverns, L. E.** "A Definition of Parable." *NESTR* 9 (1988) 60–75. **Sloan, R. B.** *The Favorable Year of the Lord: A Study of Jubilary Theology in the Gospel of Luke.* Fort Worth, TX: Schola, 1977. **Smalley, S. S.** "Spirit, Kingdom, and Prayer in Luke-Acts." *NovT* 15 (1973)

59–71. **Smith, B. T. B.** *The Parables of the Synoptic Gospels.* Cambridge: SPCK, 1937. **Smith, D. E.** "The Eschatology of Acts and Contemporary Exegesis." *CTM* 29 (1958) 881–901. ———. "Table Fellowship as a Literary Motif in the Gospel of Luke." *JBL* 106 (1987) 613–38. **Smith, R. H.** "History and Eschatology in Luke-Acts." *CTM* 29 (1958) 881–901. **Snape, H. C.** "The Composition of the Lukan Writings: A Re-assessment." *HTR* 53 (1960) 27–46. **Snodgrass, K. R.** "Streams of Tradition Emerging from Isaiah 40:1–5 and Their Adaption in the New Testament." *JSNT* 8 (1980) 24–45. **Sparks, H. F. D.** "The Semitisms of St. Luke's Gospel." *JTS*, o.s., 44 (1943) 129–38. ———. "St. Luke's Transpositions." *NTS* 3 (1957) 219–23. **Spicq, C.** *Agapè dans le Nouveau Testament: Analyse des textes.* Vol. 1. EBib. Paris: Gabalda, 1958. **Stalder, K.** "Der heilige Geist in der lukanischen Ekklesiologie." *US* 30 (1975) 287–93. **Standaert, B.** "L'art de composer dans l'oeuvre de Luc." In *À cause de l'Évangile,* ed. F. Refoulé. 323–48. **Stegemann, W.** *Zwischen Synagoge und Obrigkeit: Zur historischen Situation der lukanischen Christen.* FRLANT 152. Göttingen: Vandenhoeck & Ruprecht, 1991. **Stein, R. H.** *An Introduction to the Parables of Jesus.* Philadelphia: Westminster, 1981. ———. "The Matthew-Luke Agreements against Mark: Insight from John." *CBQ* 54 (1992) 482–502. **Stendahl, K.** *The School of St. Matthew, and Its Use of the Old Testament.* Philadelphia: Fortress, 1968. **Stenning, J. F.,** ed. *The Targum of Isaiah.* Oxford: Clarendon, 1949. **Sterling, G. E.** "Luke-Acts and Apologetic Historiography." In *1989 SBL Seminar Papers,* ed. D. J. Lull. 326–42. **Stewart, R. A.** "The Parable Form in the Old Testament and the Rabbinic Literature." *EvQ* 36 (1964) 133–47. **Steyn, G. J.** "Intertextual Similarities between Septuagint Pretexts and Luke's Gospel." *Neot* 24 (1990) 229–46. **Stöger, A.** "Armut und Ehelosigkeit: Besitz und Ehe der Jünger nach dem Lukasevangelium." *GuL* 40 (1967) 43–59. ———. "Die Theologie des Lukasevangeliums." *BLit* 46 (1973) 227–36. **Stonehouse, N. B.** *The Witness of Luke to Christ.* London: Tyndale, 1951. **Strauss, D. F.** *The Life of Jesus Critically Examined.* Ed. P. C. Hodgson. Tr. G. Elliot. SCM Press Lives of Jesus. London: SCM, 1973. **Strobel, A.** "Lukas der Antiochener (Bemerkungen zu Act 11, 28D)." *ZNW* 49 (1958) 131–34. **Stronstad, R.** *The Charismatic Theology of St. Luke.* Peabody, MA: Hendrickson, 1984. **Stuhlmacher, P.** *Das paulinische Evangelium.* Vol. 1, *Vorgeschichte.* FRLANT 95. Göttingen: Vandenhoeck & Ruprecht, 1968. ———. "Warum musste Jesus sterben?" *TB* 16 (1985) 273–85. ———, ed. *Das Evangelium und die Evangelien: Vorträger vom Tübinger Symposium 1982.* WUNT 28. Tübingen: Mohr (Siebeck), 1983. ———, ed. *The Gospel and the Gospels.* Grand Rapids: Eerdmans, 1991. **Suggs, M. J.** *Wisdom, Christology, and Law in Matthew's Gospel.* Cambridge, MA: Harvard University, 1970. **Sundwall, J.** *Die Zusammensetzung des Markusevangeliums.* Acta Academiae Aboensis. Humaniore 9/2. Abo: Tilgmanns, 1934. **Sutcliffe, E. F.** "A Note on the Date of St. Luke's Gospel." *Scr* 3 (1948) 45–46. **Swaeles, R.** "Jesus nouvel Élie dans S. Luc." *AsSeign* 69 (1964) 41–66. ———. "L'évangile du salut: Saint Luc." *ComLit* 1 (1977) 45–70. **Sylva, D. D.** "*Ierousalēm* and *Hierosoluma* in Luke-Acts." *ZNW* 74 (1983) 207–21. ———. "Death and Life at the Center of the World." In *Reimaging,* ed. D. D. Sylva. 153–169, 211–17. ———, ed. *Reimaging the Death of the Lukan Jesus.* Athenäums Monografien. BBS 73. Frankfurt am M.: Anton Hain, 1990. **Taeger, J.-W.** *Der Mensch und sein Heil: Studien zum Bild des Menschen und zur Sicht der Bekehrung bei Lukas.* SNT 14. Gütersloh: Mohn, 1982. ———. "Paulus und Lukas über den Menschen." *ZNW* 71 (1980) 96–108. **Talbert, C. H.** *Luke and the Gnostics: An Examination of the Lukan Purpose.* Nashville: Abingdon, 1966. ———. *The Certainty of the Gospel: The Perspective of Luke-Acts.* Deland, FL: Stetson University, 1981. ———. "The Redaction Critical Quest for Luke the Theologian." In *Jesus and Man's Hope: Proceedings of the Pittsburgh Festival on the Gospels,* ed. D. G. Miller. 2 vols. Pittsburgh: Pittsburgh Theological Seminary, 1970. 1:171–222. ———. *Literary Patterns, Theological Themes, and the Genre of Luke-Acts.* SBLMS 20. Missoula, MT: Scholars, 1974. ———. *What Is a Gospel? The Genre of the Canonical Gospels.* Philadelphia: Fortress, 1977. ———. "The Lukan Presentation of Jesus' Ministry in Galilee: Luke 4:31–9:50." *RevExp* 64 (1967) 485–97. ———. "An Anti-Gnostic Tendency in Lukan Christology." *NTS* 14 (1967–68) 259–71. ———. "Shifting Sands: The Recent Study of the Gospel of Luke." *Int* 30 (1976) 381–95. ———, ed. *Perspectives on Luke-Acts.* Perspectives

General Bibliography   lix

in Religious Studies 5. Danville, VA/Edinburgh: Association of Baptist Professors of Religion/T. & T. Clark, 1978. ————, ed. *Luke-Acts: New Perspectives from the Society of Biblical Literature Seminar.* New York: Crossroad, 1984. **Tannehill, R. C.** "A Study in the Theology of Luke-Acts." *ATR* 43 (1961) 195–203. ————. *The Sword of His Mouth.* Philadelphia/Missoula, MT: Fortress/Scholars, 1975. ————. *The Narrative Unity of Luke-Acts: A Literary Interpretation.* Vol. 1, *The Gospel according to Luke.* Foundations and Facets. Philadelphia: Fortress, 1986. ————. "Israel in Luke-Acts: A Tragic Story." *JBL* 104 (1985) 69–85. ————. "What Kind of King? What Kind of Kingdom? A Study of Luke." *WW* 12 (1992) 17–22. **Taylor, V.** *Behind the Third Gospel.* Oxford: Clarendon, 1926. ————. *The Gospel according to St. Mark.* 2nd ed. London/New York: Macmillan/St. Martin's 1966. ————. "Rehkopf's List of Words and Phrases Illustrative of Pre-Lukan Speech Usage." *JTS,* n.s., 15 (1964) 59–62. **Tenney, M. C.** "Historical Verities in the Gospel of Luke." *BSac* 135 (1978) 126–38. **TeSelle, S. M.** *Speaking in Parables.* Philadelphia: Fortress, 1975. ————. "Parable, Metaphor and Theology." *JAAR* 42 (1974) 630–45. **Theissen, G.** *The First Followers of Jesus: A Sociological Analysis of the Earliest Christianity.* Tr. J. Bowden. London: SCM, 1978. ————. *The Miracle Stories of the Early Christian Tradition.* Tr. F. McDonagh. Edinburgh: T. & T. Clark, 1983. ————. *Localkolorit und Zeitgeschichte in den Evangelien: Ein Beitrage zur Geschichte der synoptischen Tradition.* Novum Testamentum et Orbis Antiquus 8. Fribourg: Universitätsverlag, 1989. ————. *The Gospels in Context: Social and Political History in the Synoptic Tradition.* Tr. L. Maloney. Minneapolis, MN: Fortress, 1991. ————. "Jesusbewegung als charismatische Wertrevolution." *NTS* 35 (1989) 343–60. **Theobald, M.** "Die Anfänge der Kirche: Zur Struktur von Lk 5.1–6.19." *NTS* 30 (1984) 91–108. **Thériault, J.-Y.** "Les dimensions sociales, économiques et politiques dans l'oeuvre de Luc." *ScEs* 26 (1974) 205–31. **Thiselton, A. C.** "On Models and Metaphors: A Critical Dialogue with Robert Morgan." In *The Bible in Three Dimensions,* ed. D. J. A. Clines et al. 337–56. ————. "The Parables as Language-Event: Some Comments on Fuchs's Hermeneutics in the Light of Linguistic Philosophy." *SJT* 23 (1970) 437–68. **Thrall, M. E.** *Greek Particles in the New Testament: Linguistic and Exegetical Studies.* NTTS 3. Leiden: Brill, 1962. **Tiede, D. L.** "'Glory to Thy People, Israel': Luke-Acts and the Jews." In *The Social World of Formative Christianity and Judaism,* ed. J. Neusner et al. 327–41. ————. *Prophecy and History in Luke-Acts.* Philadelphia: Fortress, 1980. **Tinsley, E. J.** "Parable, Allegory, and Mysticism." In *Vindications: Essays in the Historical Basis of Christianity,* ed. A. Hanson. London: SCM, 1966. 153–92. ————. "Parable and Allegory: Some Literary Criteria for the Interpretation of the Parables of Christ." *CQ* 3 (1970) 32–39. ————. "Parables and the Self-Awareness of Jesus." *CQ* 4 (1971) 18–27. **Tödt, H. E.** *The Son of Man in the Synoptic Tradition.* NTL. Tr. D. M. Barton. London: SCM, 1965. **Tolbert, M.** "Leading Ideas of the Gospel of Luke." *RevExp* 64 (1967) 441–51. **Tolbert, M. A.** *Perspectives on the Parables: An Approach to Multiple Interpretations.* Philadelphia: Fortress, 1979. **Tooley, W.** "The Shepherd and Sheep Image in the Teaching of Jesus." *NovT* 7 (1964) 15–25. **Torrey, C. C.** "The Translations Made from the Original Aramaic Gospels." In *Studies in the History of Religions.* FS C. H. Toy, ed. D. G. Lyon and G. F. Moore. New York: Macmillan, 1912. 269–317. ————. *Our Translated Gospels: Some of the Evidence.* New York: Harper, 1936. **Trocmé, É.** *Le "Livre des Actes" et l'histoire.* Études d'histoire et de philosophie religieuses 45. Paris: Presses Universitaires de France, 1957. ————. "The Jews as Seen by Paul and Luke." In *"To See Ourselves as Others See Us": Christians, Jews, and "Others" in Late Antiquity,* ed. J. Neusner and E. S. Frerichs. Chico, CA: Scholars, 1985. 145–61. **Tuckett, C. M.** "The Argument from Order and the Synoptic Problem." *TZ* 36 (1980) 338–54. ————. "Q, the Law and Judaism." In *Law and Religion,* ed. B. Lindars. 90–101, 176–80. ————, ed. *Synoptic Studies: The Ampleforth Conferences of 1982 and 1983.* JSOTSup 7. Sheffield: JSOT, 1984. **Turner, M.** "Spirit Endowment in Luke/Acts: Some Linguistic Considerations." *VoxEv* 12 (1981) 45–63. ————. "The Significance of Receiving the Spirit in Luke-Acts: A Survey of Modern Scholarship." *TJ* 2 (1981) 131–58. ————. "The Spirit and the Power of Jesus' Miracles in the Lucan Conception." *NovT* 33 (1991) 124–52. ————. "The Spirit of Prophecy and the Power of Authoritative

Preaching in Luke-Acts: A Question of Origins." *NTS* 38 (1992) 66–88. **Turner, N.** *Grammatical Insights into the New Testament.* Edinburgh: T. & T. Clark, 1965. ————. "The Minor Verbal Agreements of Mt. and Lk. against Mk." *SE* 1 [= TU 73] (1959) 223–34. **Tyson, J. B.** *The Death of Jesus in Luke-Acts.* Columbia: University of South Carolina, 1986. ————. *Luke-Acts and the Jewish People: Eight Critical Perspectives.* Minneapolis: Augsburg, 1988. ————. *Images of Judaism in Luke-Acts.* Columbia, SC: University of South Carolina, 1992. ————. "The Opposition to Jesus in the Gospel of Luke." *PRS* 5 (1978) 144–50. ————. "The Jewish Public in Luke-Acts." *NTS* 30 (1984) 574–83. ————. "The Gentile Mission and the Authority of Scripture in Acts." *NTS* 33 (1987) 619–31. ————. "Scripture, Torah, and Sabbath in Luke-Acts." In *Jesus, the Gospels, and the Church.* FS W. R. Farmer, ed. E. P. Sanders. Macon, GA: Mercer, 1987. 89–104. ————. "Source Criticism of the Gospel of Luke." In *Perspectives on Luke-Acts,* ed. C. H. Talbert. 24–39. ————. "Torah and Prophets in Luke-Acts: Temporary or Permanent?" In *SBL 1992 Seminar Papers,* ed. E. H. Lovering, Jr. 539–48. **Unnik, W. C. van.** "Luke's Second Book and the Rules of Hellenistic Historiography." In *Les Actes des Apôtres,* ed. J. Kremer. 37–60. ————. "The 'Book of Acts' the Confirmation of the Gospel." *NovT* 4 (1960–61) 26–59. ————. "Jesus the Christ." *NTS* 8 (1961–62) 101–16. **Untergassmair, F. G.** *Kreuzweg und Kreuzigung Jesu: Ein Beitrag zur lukanischen Redaktionsgeschichte und zur Frage nach der lukanischen "Kreuzestheologie."* Paderborner theologische Studien 10. Paderborn: Schöningh, 1980. **Vaage, L. E.** "Q1 and the Historical Jesus: Some Peculiar Sayings (7:33–34; 9:57–58, 59–60; 14:26–27)." *Forum* 5.2 (1989) 160–76. **Vermes, G.** *Scripture and Tradition in Judaism: Haggadic Studies.* SPB 4. Leiden: Brill, 1961. **Vesco, J.-L.** *Jérusalem et son prophète: Une lecture de l'Évangile selon saint Luc.* Paris: Cerf, 1988. **Via, D. O., Jr.** *The Parables: Their Literary and Existential Dimension.* Philadelphia: Fortress, 1967. ————. "Parable and Example Story: A Literary-Structuralist Approach." *Semeia* 1 (1974) 105–33. ————. "A Response to Crossan, Funk, and Petersen." *Semeia* 1 (1974) 222–35. **Via, E. J.** "Women in the Gospel of Luke." In *Women in the World's Religions: Past and Present,* ed. U. King. New York: Paragon, 1987. 38–55. ————. "Women, the Discipleship of Service and the Early Christian Ritual Meal in the Gospel of Luke." *SLJT* 29 (1985) 37–60. **Vielhauer, P.** "Zum 'Paulinismus' der Apostelgeschichte." *EvT* 10 (1950–51) 1–15. **Vincent, J. J.** "The Parables of Jesus as Self-Revelation." *SE* 1 [= TU 73] (1959) 79–99. **Vögtle, A.** "Exegetische Erwägungen über das Wissen und Selbstbewusstsein Jesu." In *Gott in Welt.* FS K. Rahner, ed. J. B. Metz et al. Freiburg/Basel/Vienna: Herder, 1964. 608–67. **Völkel, M.** "Der Anfang Jesu in Galiläa: Bemerkungen zum Gebrauch und zur Funktion Galiläas in den lukanischen Schriften." *ZNW* 64 (1973) 222–32. ————. "Zur Deutung des 'Reiches Gottes' bei Lukas." *ZNW* 65 (1974) 57–70. **Voss, G.** *Die Christologie der lukanischen Schriften in Grundzügen.* StudNeot 2. Paris/Bruges: Brouwer, 1965. **Votaw, C. W.** "The Gospels and Contemporary Biographies." *AJT* 19 (1915) 45–73, 217–49. **Vriezen, T. C.** "Leert Lukas de verwerping van Israël?" *KeTh* 13 (1962) 25–31. **Waal, C. van der.** "The Temple in the Gospel according to Luke." *Neot* 7 (1973) 49–59. **Wagner, G.,** ed. *An Exegetical Bibliography of the New Testament:* Vol. 2, *Luke and Acts.* Macon, GA: Mercer University, 1985. **Wainwright, A. W.** "Luke and the Restoration of the Kingdom to Israel." *ExpTim* 89 (1977) 76–79. **Walaskay, P. W.** *"And so we came to Rome": The Political Perspective of St. Luke.* SNTSMS 49. Cambridge: University Press, 1983. ————. "The Trial and Death of Jesus in the Gospel of Luke." *JBL* 94 (1975) 81–93. **Walker, W. O.** "'Nazareth': A Clue to Synoptic Relations." In *Jesus, the Gospels, and the Church.* FS W. R. Farmer, ed. E. P. Sanders. Macon, GA: Mercer, 1987. 105–18. **Wallis, E. E.** "Aristotelian Echoes in Luke's Discourse Structure." *OPTAT* 2 (1988) 81–88. **Wanke, J.** *Beobachtungen zum Eucharistieverständnis des Lukas auf Grund der lukanischen Mahlberichte.* ETS 8. Leipzig: St. Benno, 1973. **Wansbrough, H.,** ed. *Jesus and the Oral Gospel Tradition.* Sheffield: Sheffield Academic Press, 1991. ————. "Poverty in the Gospel Tradition." *ProcIBA* 6 (1982) 47–57. **Watson, F.** "Why Was Jesus Crucified?" *Theology* 88 (1985) 105–12. **Weatherly, J. A.** "The Jews in Luke-Acts." *TynB* 40 (1989) 107–17. **Weder, H.** *Die Gleichnisse Jesu als Metaphern.* Göttingen: Vandenhoeck & Ruprecht, 1978. **Wehnert, J.** *Die Wir-Passagen der*

Apostelgeschichte: Ein lukanisches Stilsmittel aus jüdischer Tradition. GTA 40. Göttingen: Vandenhoeck & Ruprecht, 1989. **Weinert, F. D.** "The Meaning of the Temple in Luke-Acts." *BTB* 11 (1981) 85–89. ————. "Luke, Stephen, and the Temple in Luke-Acts." *BTB* 17 (1987) 88–90. **Weiser, A.** *Die Knechtsgleichnisse der synoptischen Evangelien.* SANT 29. Munich: Kössel, 1971. **Wenham, J.** *Redating Matthew, Mark and Luke: A Fresh Assault on the Synoptic Problem.* London: Hodder and Stoughton, 1991. ————. "The Identification of Luke." *EvQ* 63 (1991) 3–44. **Wernle, P.** *Die synoptische Frage.* Freiburg i. B./Leipzig: Mohr, 1899. **Wescott, B. F.**, and **Hort, F. J. A.** *The New Testament in the Original Greek.* 2 vols. Cambridge/London: Macmillan, 1890, 1896. **Westermann, C.** *The Parables of Jesus in the Light of the Old Testament,* ed. F. W. Golka and A. H. B. Logan. Tr. F. W. Golka and A. H. B. Logan. Minneapolis, MN: Fortress, 1990. **Wettstein, J. J.** *Novum Testamentum Graecum . . . Opera et Studia.* 2 vols. Amsterdam: Officina Dommeriana, 1751–52. **Wilckens, U.** *Die Missionsreden der Apostelgeschichte: Form- und traditionsgeschichtliche Untersuchungen.* WMANT 5. 2nd ed. Neukirchen-Vluyn: Neukirchener, 1963. **Wilcox, M.** *The Semitisms of Acts.* Oxford: Clarendon, 1965. **Wilder, A.** *Early Christian Rhetoric: The Language of the Gospel.* NTL. London: SCM, 1964; rev. ed., Cambridge, MA: Harvard University, 1971. ————. *Jesus' Parables and the War of Myths: Essays in Imagination in Scripture.* Ed. J. Breech. Philadelphia: Fortress, 1982. ————. "Eschatological Images and Earthly Circumstances." *NTS* 5 (1959) 229–45. **Wilkens, W.** "Die theologische Struktur der Komposition des Lukasevangeliums." *TZ* 34 (1978) 1–13. **Williams, C. S. C.** "The Date of Luke-Acts." *ExpTim* 64 (1952–53) 283–84. **Williams, J. G.** "Neither Here nor There." *Forum* 5.2 (1989) 7–30. **Wilshire, L. E.** "Was Canonical Luke Written in the Second Century?—A Continuing Discussion." *NTS* 20 (1974) 246–53. **Wilson, R. M.** "Farrer and Streeter in the Minor Agreements of Mt. and Lk. against Mk." *SE* 1 [= TU 73] (1959) 254–57. **Wilson, S. G.** *The Gentiles and the Gentile Mission in Luke-Acts.* SNTSMS 23. Cambridge: University Press, 1973. ————. *Luke and the Pastoral Epistles.* London: SPCK, 1979. ————. *Luke and the Law.* SNTSMS 50. Cambridge: University Press, 1983. ————. "Lukan Eschatology." *NTS* 15 (1969–70) 330–47. **Wimmer, J. F.** *Fasting in the New Testament: A Study in Biblical Theology.* Theological Inquiries. New York: Paulist, 1982. **Wink, W.** *John the Baptist in the Gospel Tradition.* SNTSMS 7. Cambridge: University Press, 1968. **Wittig, S.** "A Theory of Multiple Meanings." *Semeia* 9 (1977) 75–103. **Wojcik, J.** *The Road to Emmaus: Reading Luke's Gospel.* West Lafayette, IN: Purdue University Press, 1989. **Wolfe, K. R.** "The Chiastic Structure of Luke-Acts and Some Implications for Worship." *SWJT* 22 (1980) 60–71. **Wren, M.** "Sonship in Luke: The Advantage of a Literary Approach." *SJT* 37 (1984) 301–11. **Yadin, Y.** "A Note on Melchizedek and Qumran." *IEJ* 15 (1965) 152–54. **Yarnold, E.** "The Trinitarian Implications of Luke and Acts." *HeyJ* 7 (1966) 18–32. **Yoder, J. H.** *The Politics of Jesus.* Grand Rapids: Eerdmans, 1972. **Zahn, T. von.** *Introduction to the New Testament.* Tr. J. M. Trout et al. 3 vols. Edinburgh: T. & T. Clark, 1909. **Zeilinger, F.** "Die Bewertung der irdischen Güter im lukanischen Doppelwerk und in den Pastoralbriefen." *BK* 58 (1985) 75–80. **Zeller, D.** *Kommentar zum Logienquelle.* Stuttgarter kleiner Kommentar, Neues Testament 21. Stuttgart: Katholisches Bibelwerk, 1984. **Zerwick, M.** *Biblical Greek, Illustrated by Examples.* Ed. and tr. J. Smith. Scripta Pontifici Instituti Biblici 114. Rome: Pontifical Biblical Institute, 1963. **Ziesler, J. A.** "Luke and the Pharisees." *NTS* 25 (1979) 146–57. **Zimmermann, A. F.** *Neutestamentliche Methodenlehre: Darstellung der historischkritischen Methode.* Stuttgart: Katholisches Bibelwerk, 1968. ————. *Der urchristlichen Lehrer: Studien zum Tradentkreis der διδάσκαλος im frühen Urchristentum.* Tübingen: Mohr (Siebeck), 1984. **Zingg, P.** *Das Wachsen der Kirche: Beiträge zur Frage der lukanischen Redaktion und Theologie.* OBO 3. Fribourg/Göttingen: Universitätsverlag/Vandenhoeck & Ruprecht, 1974. ————. "Die Stellung des Lukas zur Heidenmission." *NZM* 29 (1973) 200–209.

Luke 18:35–24:53

Reaching the City of Destiny   (18:35–19:46)

Jesus makes his way to the city as a royal figure, but ultimately as one who must go into a far country to take full possession of his kingly power. Meanwhile he saves the lost and the blind, restores the temple to its sanctity as a place for prayer, and makes it the base for his own teaching ministry to all the People.

"Jesus, Son of David Have Mercy on Me!"   (18:35–43)

Bibliography

Achtemeier, P. J. "'And he followed him': Miracles and Discipleship in Mark 10:46–52." *Semeia* 11 (1978) 115–45. **Betz, H. D.** "The Early Christian Miracle Story: Some Observations on the Form Critical Problem." *Semeia* 11 (1978) 69–81. **Burger, C.** *Jesus als Davidssohn: Eine traditionsgeschichtliche Untersuchung.* FRLANT 98. Göttingen: Vandenhoeck & Ruprecht, 1970. 42–46, 107–12. **Busse, U.** *Wunder.* 227–34. **Dupont, J.** "L'Aveugle de Jéricho recouvre la vue et suit Jésus (Marc 10, 46–52)." *RevAfTh* 8 (1984) 165–81. **Fisher, L. R.** "'Can This Be the Son of David?'" In *Jesus and the Historian.* FS E. C. Colwell, ed. F. T. Trotter. Philadelphia: Westminster, 1968. 82–97. **Fuchs, A.** *Sprachliche Untersuchungen.* 45–170. **Haenchen, E.** *Der Weg Jesu.* 369–72. **Johnson, E. S., Jr.** "Mark 10:46–52: Blind Bartimaeus." *CBQ* 40 (1978) 191–204. **Kertelge, K.** *Die Wunder Jesu.* 179–82. **Ketter, P.** "Zur Lokalizierung der Blindenheilung bei Jericho." *Bib* 15 (1934) 411–18. **Meynet, R.** "Au coeur du texte: Analyse rhétorique de l'aveugle de Jéricho selon saint Luc." *NRT* 103 (1981) 696–710. **Mirro, J. A.** "Bartimaeus: the Miraculous Cure." *BiTod* 20 (1982) 221–25. **Paul, A.** "La guérison de l'aveugle (des aveugles) de Jéricho." *FV* 69 (1970) 44–69. **Robbins, V. K.** "The Healing of Blind Bartimaeus (10:46–52) in the Marcan Theology." *JBL* 92 (1973) 224–43. **Roloff, J.** *Das Kerygma.* 121–26. **Schramm, T.** *Markus-Stoff.* 143–45. **Steinhauser, M. G.** "The Form of the Bartimaeus Narrative (Mark 10.46–52)." *NTS* 32 (1986) 583–95. **Trilling, W.** *Christusverkündigung in den synoptischen Evangelien: Beispiele gattungsgemässer Auslegung.* Biblische Handbibliothek 4. Munich: Kösel, 1969. 146–64.

Translation

[35]*It so happened that as he drew near to Jericho, there was a certain blind person seated by the road, begging.* [36]*As he heard the crowd passing along, he inquired what this might be.* [37]*They informed him that Jesus the Nazorean was passing by.* [38]*So he called out, "Jesus, Son of David, have mercy on me!"* [39]*Those who were in the lead began to rebuke him that he should be quiet;*[a] *but he cried out all the more,*[b] *"Son of David, have mercy on me!"* [40]*Jesus stopped and commanded him to be brought to him. When he had drawn near, he asked him,* [41]*"What do you want me to do for you?" He said, "Lord, that I might see again!"* [42]*Jesus said to him, "See again! Your faith has saved you."* [43]*Then, immediately, he could see again, and he began to follow him glorifying God; and all the People, as they saw [this] gave praise to God.*

Notes

ª Without change of sense, א A Θ ƒ¹·¹³ etc. have here Mark's σιωπήσῃ.
ᵇ א ƒ¹·¹³ etc. supply here the "Jesus" expected on the basis of v 38.

Form/Structure/Setting

The new section runs from 18:35 to 19:46. It has primarily a christological focus to which the "Son of David" of the present unit makes its own contribution.

The linked set of location markers contributes to the identification of the section here (18:35: ἐν τῷ ἐγγίζειν αὐτὸν εἰς Ἰεριχώ, "when he drew near to Jericho";
19:1: εἰσελθὼν διήρχετο τὴν Ἰεριχώ, "he entered and was passing through Jericho"; v 11: διὰ τὸ ἐγγὺς εἶναι Ἰερουσαλήμ, "because he was near Jerusalem"; v
29: ὡς ἤγγισεν εἰς Βηθφαγὴ καὶ Βηθανίαν, "he went ahead going up to Jerusalem
. . . as he drew near to Bethphage and Bethany"; v 37: ἐγγίζοντος . . . τῇ
καταβάσει τοῦ Ὄρους τῶν Ἐλαιῶν, "as he was drawing near to the descent of
the Mount of Olives"; v 41: ὡς ἤγγισεν, ἰδὼν τὴν πόλιν, "as he drew near, seeing
the city"; v 45: εἰσελθὼν εἰς τὸ ἱερόν, "entering the temple").

The inclusio effect around the Journey to Jerusalem narrative noted in the
last several pericopes continues here: "Son of David" here in the first unit beyond the journey reintroduces the messianism that surfaced in the last unit before
the section in which Luke introduced the journey narrative.

Luke passes over the material of Mark 10:35–45, but continues here with the
Markan sequence in a version of Mark 10:46–52. Luke has changed the location
of the episode, significantly abbreviated the account, clarified some of the obscu-
rity of the Markan account, and added a doxological ending (for details see below).

The original unity of the Markan account has been questioned along a number of fronts. (*i*) Names are unusual in Gospel episodes, so both the location on
the outskirts of Jericho and the name Bartimaeus have been seen as marks of
later development. (*ii*) The disciples and the crowd are introduced rather awkwardly in v 46, so the presence of one and/or the other is often thought to be
secondary. (*iii*) Awkwardness has been sensed in the role of the "many" in v 48
and of the unspecified "they" of v 49, and this along with the unusual doubling of
the appeal made by the blind man to Jesus has convinced many that vv 48–49(50)
represent a later development. (*iv*) The final statement about the man following
Jesus in the way is normally considered secondary because it creates a tension
with ὕπαγε, "go off/depart," earlier in the verse. (*v*) Finally, the uses of "Son of
David" in the episode are generally thought to be additions because they are entirely unmotivated within the pericope, and, taken with other types of reference
to Jesus in the pericope, create both a sense of overload and even a measure of
tension (esp. between "Rabbouni" and "Son of David"). Of these, points *ii, iv,*
and *v* are the most persuasive, though there is considerable difference of opinion about when and why "Son of David" was added to the pericope (for a brief
and balanced discussion see Johnson, *CBQ* 40 [1978] 191–98, though I would be
more inclined to retain vv 48–49 in the original [the structural role is parallel to
that of 2:4], and, despite his reservations, to attribute "Son of David" here to
Mark [cf. Robbins, *JBL* 92 (1973) 224–43]; Steinhauser [*NTS* 32 (1986) 583–95;
and cf. Achtemeier, *Semeia* 11 (1978) 115–45] has more recently argued for the

unity of the whole as a call narrative, but the argument for the call form is far from compelling.)

The discussion about the right form-critical category to which one should assign this account has been inconclusive. The persistence of the blind man is too important for a pronouncement story and at least unusual for a miracle story. In the preserved form, the presence of "Son of David" has a confessional significance that moves beyond the normal range of a miracle story. Call narrative has been ruled out above. A modified miracle-story form seems to be best.

This is the only account in Luke of a restoration of sight (but see 7:21–22). Mark has as well 8:22–26, while Matthew has 9:27–31 (which is likely to be a secondary Matthean formulation). On the healing accounts generally, see at 4:38–39, and on their historicity, see further at 7:11–17; 8:22–25. There can be no doubt that Jesus was known as a healer and that people attributed extraordinary restorations to his power.

Comment

Jesus' power to heal is here shown to remain effective, faith is portrayed as persistent action on the conviction that God's help is to be found with Jesus, royal messianic categories are reintroduced with the blind man's "Son of David," and a popularity base for Jesus with all the People of God is brought to the fore.

35 Luke wants this pericope before 19:1–10, but Zacchaeus is more naturally located in the city so, starting from the Markan words at the beginning of 10:46, Luke relocates the encounter with the blind man from the time of exiting from Jericho to that of entry into Jericho. Luke takes the opportunity to introduce ἐγγίζειν, "to draw near," thus providing a root that he will use three more times in the introductory part of pericopes, or major sections of pericopes, in this section (see above; the verb is also introduced in v 40). Luke drops the mention of disciples, the crowd (he will introduce the crowd in v 36), and the (doubly given) name of the blind man and says that the man was begging, rather than that he was a beggar (Matthew has two unnamed blind people). Since Jericho and Jerusalem are linked already in the reader's mind by 10:30, the sense of approach to Jerusalem now begins to be represented geographically (cf. v 11). From 7:21–22, the reader is aware that from Jesus the blind receive their sight.

36–37 Luke elaborates on how the blind man comes to know that Jesus is passing by, in a manner that accentuates the conversational exchange that characterizes the whole account (with different changes he achieved much the same in 18:24–30). Mark's Ναζαρηνός becomes Ναζωραῖος (cf. Acts 2:22; 3:6; 4:10; 6:14; 22:8; 26:9; the form is found also in Matthew 2:23; 26:71; John 18:5, 7; 19:19). Mark's form means unproblematically "a person from Nazareth," but the sense of the Lukan form remains uncertain. The main suggestions are that (*i*) it is merely a spelling variant for the Markan word; (*ii*) it is related to the Hebrew נזיר, nāzîr, which is used in connection with those who take particular vows of consecration to God (see Num 6:1–21; but the Greek OT knows no such form); (*iii*) it is related to the Hebrew נצר, nēṣer, "shoot/sprout," which could develop a messianic sense via Isa 11:1 (cf. Rev 22:16); (*iv*) the usage can be illuminated from the Mandean writings, which have the Aramaic נצוריא, nāṣôrayyā ʾ, said to mean "observers," for a group related to John the Baptist (though this has the problematic long "o" that the other suggestions lack, its relevance seems doubtful; for further discussion of Ναζωραῖος see R. E. Brown, *The Birth of the Messiah* [Garden City, NY: Doubleday, 1977], 209–13, 223–25; Davies and Allison, *Matthew*, 1:275–84 [who both provide extensive bibliography]). At least for Luke, Ναζωραῖος is best taken in the same sense as the Markan term, though it is not at all unlikely that he has inadvertently used a spelling that is the product of Christian reflection on נזיר or possibly נצר (cf. esp. Matt 2:23). Mark's ἐστιν, "is," becomes παρέρχεται, "is passing by," which causes "Jesus the Nazarene" to be taken now as subject (movement toward Jerusalem is again underlined).

38 Luke changes the introduction here, dropping Mark's "he began," subordinating one of the verbs as a participle, and using βοᾶν in place of Mark's κράζειν to speak of the man's crying out. Luke also brings "Jesus" forward to the beginning of the man's appeal. We are clearly meant to take "Son of David" as a royal messianic designation (see *Pss. Sol.* 17:22; and cf. Luke 1:27, 32: 2:4; 9:20). Despite the links between Solomon as son of David and exorcism in strands of Jewish tradition (as drawn attention to by K. Berger, "Die königlichen Messiastraditionen des Neuen Testaments," *NTS* 20 [1973–74] 1–44; D. C. Duling, "Solomon, Exorcism, and the Son of David," *HTR* 68 [1975] 235–52), there is no real basis for identifying a Jewish expectation of a Davidic healer. In connection with the inclusio around the Journey to Jerusalem narrative, some kind of parallelism with 9:20 is likely. Royal categories are to be important throughout this section. Jesus' own practice, experience, and expectations begin to redefine the expectations of royal messianism. We have seen earlier the role played by Isaianic traditions in Luke's redefinition of traditional messianic hopes (e.g., 3:4–6; 4:18–19; 7:22).

The rich man's appeal to Abraham was the same "have mercy on me" (16:24), and, expressed in the plural, the lepers say the same (17:13). Jesus describes the restoration of the demoniac in Mark 5:19 using the same language: "[the Lord] had mercy on you." The call is for compassionate treatment.

39 Mark's vague "many" is clarified as "those who were in the lead." Luke changes Mark's verb for "should be quiet" and adds an emphatic "he" to go with "cried out" (this time Luke keeps the verb he discarded in v 38). The language of rebuke and call to silence is reminiscent of Jesus' words to the demons (see 4:35), but this is a false trail. The role here of the vanguard of the crowd is, rather, comparable to that of the disciples in v 15 (and cf. 19:40). The man's persistence in the face of such opposition is an expression of his faith, which will be commended in v 42.

40 Mark's "he said, 'Call him'" becomes "he commanded him to be brought to him" (Luke's "to be brought" is appropriate for a blind man). The interchange of others with the blind man disappears, and Mark's graphic account of the man's coming is reduced to ἐγγίσαντος δὲ αὐτοῦ, "when he had drawn near." Finally, the introduction to Jesus' question is simplified to "he asked him."

41 Luke does without τυφλός, "[the] blind man," and αὐτῷ, "to him," and replaces the Semitic ῥαββουνί, "rabbouni," with the κύριε, "Lord," which he frequently uses (the term means more than "Sir," but only takes on the full Christian meaning for those who are ready to confess Jesus as Lord; "Lord" sits more easily with "Son of David" than does Mark's "rabbouni" [equivalent to rabbi]). A plural form of the same question is addressed to the sons of Zebedee in Mark 10:35.

There the answer revealed a request for places of glory, a request that Jesus was unable to honor; the request here is to be able to see again.

42 Luke omits Mark's "depart/go off" and compensates with "see again!" This moves the emphasis slightly from the effect of the man's faith onto the power and authority of Jesus' word (cf. 4:36). "Your faith has saved you" has already occurred at 7:50; 8:48: 17:19 (see discussion at those verses and also at 5:20). The faith is to be related to the persistence in the face of the crowd rather than immediately to the Son-of-David confession.

43 Luke prefers παραχρῆμα (Lukan in sixteen of eighteen NT uses, mostly in the Gospel in connection with instantaneous cures) to Mark's εὐθύς for "immediately." In place of Mark's "in the way," Luke adds the wording from "glorifying God" to the end of the verse (this makes for a more typical miracle-story ending). The man now joins the disciple band on its way to Jerusalem (cf. the language of following in 18:22, 28; this man has nothing that he needs to leave!). "Glorifying God" is a refrain that runs through the Gospel account (cf. at 2:20). It is a recognition that God has been marvelously at work. The People's praise is their equivalent to the man's glorifying of God. A cognate role for "all the People" (God's people) comes again in 19:48 at the beginning of the next section and a third time in 21:38 at its end (the first is πᾶς ὁ λαός, the second ὁ λαός . . . ἅπας and third, again, πᾶς ὁ λαός). This beginning of Jesus' activity against a backdrop of broad-based Jewish affirmation is an important Lukan perspective for the passion to come.

Explanation

The new section takes us through to 19:46 and is concerned with Jesus as a royal figure. As well as reintroducing that motif, this unit also challenges to a faith like that of the blind man and shows how Jesus honors such faith. The unit also points to the widespread Jewish recognition that God was mightily at work in and through Jesus.

The blind man would be on the pilgrim route through Jericho to Jerusalem— a good place to beg. The passing of a crowd piqued his curiosity, and his inquiry gained him the news that Jesus the Nazorean (probably meaning "coming from Nazareth") was passing by. Reader expectation is stirred by knowing already that from Jesus the blind receive their sight (7:21–22).

The man cries out to make himself heard and appeals for mercy (here more as compassion than in connection with forgiveness). He addresses Jesus as "Son of David," which must be taken as a messianic designation (see esp. 1:32 with its mention of "the throne of [Jesus'] father David"). Those in the vanguard of the crowd try to shut him up. Whether they think in terms of not delaying Jesus on his journey or of Jesus as too important to be bothered with such a one, or whether they are seeking to exercise some proprietary claim upon Jesus for themselves remains unclear. In any event, it is clear that for them this blind beggar is unimportant. But the man is not to be deterred. His voice simply becomes louder.

Jesus comes to a standstill and asks for the blind man to be brought (he will not be able easily to find his own way). As he reaches Jesus, he is asked what he wants and expresses, naturally enough, his wish to see again. Jesus points to the man's faith, demonstrated in his persistence to establish contact with Jesus despite all opposition. For Jesus this is key to his restoration. But there is a second key as well: Jesus has only to issue the command "see again," and the authority and power of his word are immediately evident.

The man at once joins the disciple band headed for Jerusalem, but unlike the rich man or even the Apostles (18:22, 28), he has nothing that he needs to leave behind. Not just the man himself but all the People (Luke uses this term technically of God's People, the Jews) recognize that God has been marvellously at work in their midst (Luke will reinforce this point at the beginning and the end of the next main section).

"The Son of Man Came to Seek and to Save the Lost"   19:1–10

Bibliography

Ahern, B. M. "The Zacchaeus Incident." *BiTod* 25 (1987) 348–51. **Arens, E.** *The ΗΛΘΟΝ-Sayings in the Synoptic Tradition.* OBO 10. Freiburg/Göttingen: Universit'atsverlag/ Vandenhoeck & Ruprecht, 1976. 161–80. **Bizer, C.** "Geschichte von Zachäus (Lk 19,1–10)—religionsunterrichtlich, religionskundlich und alternativisch buchstabiert: Ein durchaus subjecktiver Versuch." *EvErz* 28 (1976) 217–24. **Cocagnac, A.-M.** "L'Evangile (Lc 19,10): Zachée, l'église et la maison des pécheurs." *AsSeign* o.s. 91 (1964) 39–51. ———. "L'Evangile (Lc 19,10): Zachée, l'église et la maison des pécheurs." *AsSeign* n.s. 62 (1970) 81–91. **Dauvillier, J.** "Le texte évangelique de Zachée et les obligations des Publicains." *RecAcLég* 5/1 (1951) 28–32. **Derrett, J. D. M.** *Law.* 278–85. **Drury, J.** *Tradition and Design.* 72–75. **Dupont, J.** *Béatitudes.* 2:249–54; 3:160–62. ———. "Le riche publicain Zachée est aussi un fils d'Abraham (Luc 19, 1–10)." In *Der Treue Gottes trauen,* ed. C. Bussmann and W. Radl. 265–76. **Ebel, B.** "Das Evangelium der Kirchweihmesse (Lukas 19, 1–10), gedeutet im Geist der Väter." In *Enkainia: Gesammelte Arbeiten zum 800jährigen Weihegedächtnis der Abteikirche Maria Laach am 24. August 1956,* ed. H. Edmonds. Düsseldorf: Patmos, 1956. 110–22. **Fiedler, P.** *Jesus und die Sünder.* 129–35. **Garland, J. M.** "Retrospect." *ExpTim* 95 (1984–85) 371–73. **Grindlay, B. W.** "Zacchaeus und David." *ExpTim* 99 (1987–88) 46–47. **Hahn, F.** *Titles.* 36, 40–41. **Hamm, D.** "Luke 19:8 Once Again: Does Zacchaeus Defend or Resolve?" *JBL* 107 (1988) 431–37. **Hobbie, F. W.** "Luke 19:1–10." *Int* 31 (1977) 285–90. **Hollenweger, W. J.** *Besuch bei Lukas: 4 narrative Exegesen zu 2 Mose 14, Lukas 2,1–14, 2 Kor 6,4–11 und Lukas 19,1–10.* Traktate 64. Munich: Kaiser, 1981. **Kariamadam, P.** *The End of the Travel Narrative (Luke 18,31–19,46): A Redaction-Critical Investigation.* Kerala: Pontifical Institute of Theology and Philosophy, 1985. ———. *The Zacchaeus Story [Lk. 19,1–10]: A Redaction-Critical Investigation.* Pontifical Institute Publications 42. Alwaye, India: Pontifical Institute of Theology and Philosophy, 1985. **Kerr, A. J.** "Zacchaeus' Decision to Make Four-fold Restitution." *ExpTim* 98 (1986–87) 68–71. **Klein, H.** *Barmherzigkeit gegenüber den Elenden und Geächteten: Studien zur Botschaft des lukanischen Sondergutes.* Biblisch-theologische Studien 10. Neukirchen-Vluyn: Neukirchener, 1987. 68–71. **LaVerdiere, E. A.** "Zacchaeus." *Emman* 90 (1984) 461–65. **Löning, K.** "Ein Platz für die Verlorenen: Zur Formkritik zweier neutestamentlicher Legenden (Lk 7, 36–50; 19, 1–10)." *BibLeb* 12 (1971) 198–208. **Loewe, W. P.** "Towards an Interpretation of Lk 19:1–10." *CBQ* 36 (1974) 321–31. **Mitchell, A. C.** "Zacchaus Revisited: Luke 19,8 as a Defense." *Bib* 71 (1990) 53–76. ———. "The Use of συκοφαντεῖν in Luke 19, 8: Further Evidence in Zacchaeus's Defense." *Bib* 72 (1991) 546–47. **O'Hanlon, J.** "The Story of Zacchaeus and the Lukan Ethic." *JSNT* 12 (1981) 2–26. **O'Toole, R. F.** "The Literary Form of Luke 19:1–10." *JBL* 110 (1991) 107–16. **Ravens, D. A. S.** "Zacchaeus: The Final Part of a Lucan Triptych?" *JSNT* 41 (1991) 19–32. **Rouillard, P.** "Zachée, descends vite." *VSpir* 112 (1965) 300–306. **Salom, A. P.** "Was Zacchaeus Really Reforming?" *ExpTim* 78 (1966–67) 87. **Schneider, G.** "'Der Menschensohn' in der lukanischen Christologie." In *Jesus und der Menschensohn*. FS A. Vögtle, ed. R. Pesch and R. Schnackenburg. Freiburg im B.: Herder, 1975. 267–82, esp. 278–79. **Schwank, B.** "Die Frömmigkeit des Zachäus." *EuA* 54 (1978) 64–66. **Schwarz, G.** "ὅτι τῇ ἡλικίᾳ μικρὸς ἦν." *BibNot* 8 (1979) 23–24. **Vogels, W.** "Structural Analysis and Pastoral Work: The Story of Zacchaeus (Luke 19, 1–10)." *LVit* 33 (1978) 482–92. **Watson, N. M.** "Was Zacchaeus Really Reforming?" *ExpTim* 77 (1965–66) 282–85. **Weymann, V.** "Vom Zwiespalt befreit im Zweispalt leben: Biblisch-theologische Beobachtungen zur Erfahrung der Befreiung vom Bösen inmitten des Bösen (Lc 19,1–10; Gen 32,23–33)." *Reformatio* 26 (1977) 333–42. **White, R. C.** "A Good Word for Zacchaeus? Exegetical Comment on Luke 19:1–10." *LexTQ* 14 (1979) 89–96. ———. "Vindication for Zacchaeus?" *ExpTim* 91 (1979–80) 21. **Willcock, J.** "St. Luke xix. 8." *ExpTim* 28 (1916) 236–37.

Translation

[1]*Having entered Jericho, he was on his way through.* [2]*There was a man there called by the name Zacchaeus, and he was a chief tax collector and was wealthy.* [3]*He was trying to see Jesus—who he was—, but because of the crowd he was not able to, as he was small of stature.* [4]*So, running on ahead,[a] he climbed up into a sycamore-fig tree so as to be able to see him, for he was going to pass along that way.* [5]*As he came to the spot, Jesus looked up and said to him, "Hurry and climb down, for today I must stay at your house."* [6]*He hurried and climbed down, and welcomed him, rejoicing.* [7]*Everyone, as they saw [this], began to grumble, saying, "He went in to lodge with a sinful man!"* [8]*Zacchaeus, as he stood [there], said to the Lord, "Look, Lord, the half of my goods I [plan to] give to the poor, and if I have unlawfully exacted anything from anyone I [will] repay fourfold."* [9]*Jesus said to him, "Today, salvation has come to this house! For he too is a son of Abraham.* [10]*For the Son of Man came to seek and to save the lost."*

Notes

[a] There is a pleonasm in the Gr. here not represented in translation: lit. "running ahead into the before." E F G H L T W Ψ etc. smooth this difficulty by reading προσδραμών, "running to." Others solve the problem by omitting the prepositional phrase (D R W Ψ etc.). (Note that W Ψ do both!)

Form/Structure/Setting

The extended "arrival" in Jerusalem, begun in 18:35, and due to climax in 19:41–44, 45–46, continues here with an episode set at the point where Jesus passes through Jericho (near to Jerusalem; cf. v 11). The "Son of David" of 18:35–43 gives way to "Son of Man" in the present unit (but note the Davidic content of the allusion to Ezek 34). To the deliverance in 18:35–43 of a man lost in blindness and poverty corresponds now the deliverance of a man lost in wealth and corruption.

Luke intrudes this unit (and the following) into the Markan sequence he has been following. The story is preserved by him alone. The language of the telling

is extensively Lukan, but the frequent parataxis and occasional non-Lukan elements, as well as indications of Lukan addition, point to a pre-Lukan account
likely to have provided the whole narrative apart from vv 1 and 8 (see below and
cf. Jeremias, *Sprache*, 275–77).

The account as we have it is quite complex (even without vv 1 and 8). This
makes it difficult to assign the pericope form critically and also raises questions
about its development. At its simplest we have a story about the coming of salvation to a particular well-differentiated individual (this bears some relationship to
each of the categories "biographical apophthegms," "personal-legends," and "stories about Jesus" to which the account has been variously assigned). A possible
minimal original account could have embraced only vv 2–6, since all that follows
is in one way or another a development of what is already present *in nuce* in these
verses. If there has been development, then vv 7, 9–10 were added in a single
stage of development, with the addition of v 8 (by Luke) as a second stage. The
addition of vv 9–10, if such there was, moved the form in the direction of a pronouncement story. Such a development would have a firm basis in other traditions
about the historical Jesus, and it remains quite possible that the full account (without vv 1 and 8) has a single point of origin and reflects an actual experience in
the ministry of Jesus.

Comment

Over the grumblings of the crowd, Jesus works a saving transformation on a
man whose situation seemed to be one of double jeopardy: he is both a chief tax
collector and a man of wealth. Jesus' presence brings salvation, since he has come
as the Son of Man to seek and to save the lost (in line with the anticipation in
Ezek 34 of God himself and [a messianic] David coming to the rescue of the lost
sheep of the house of Israel).

1 The episode here has no intrinsic link with Jericho. And as the language
here is quite Lukan (εἰσελθών . . . τὴν Ἰεριχώ, "entering Jericho," is Lukan paraphrase of Mark 10:46a; διέρχεσθαι, "to go through," is used nine times in the
Gospel), the verse is best seen as the Lukan provision of a setting (the name to
come in v 2 might, however, be taken to count in favor of a pre-Lukan localiza-
tion), which continues the motif of the movement to Jerusalem.

2 Though so much naming happens in Luke-Acts, the pleonastic idiom "called
by the name . . ." (ὀνόματι καλούμενος . . .) is not found elsewhere in Luke-Acts
and so may be pre-Lukan. With the same spelling, the name Zacchaeus is found
in 2 Macc 10:19. The Hebrew name that lies behind it uses a root meaning "clean/
innocent," but it is doubtful whether this etymology plays any role in the story
(the name could point to the man's destiny beyond this encounter with Jesus).
ἀρχιτελώνης, "chief tax collector," is, again, not used elsewhere by Luke (only
here in the NT, and according to Fitzmyer, 1223, not attested in any Greek writing up to this period). Presumably an ἀρχιτελώνης is a holder of a taxing contract
(see at 3:12), but the role of "chief" here is not closely related to a precise knowledge of his place in the tax system, rather, as O'Hanlon well expresses it (*JSNT* 12
[1981] 9), "he is a *chief, rich* tax collector, the sinner supreme." The reader comes
to the story with an awareness (*i*) that Jesus is the "friend of tax collectors and

sinners" (7:34; cf. 5:30), but (*ii*) that it is humanly impossible for the rich to enter the kingdom of God (18:25; cf. v 23).

3 Luke was responsible at 9:9 for καὶ ἐζήτει ἰδεῖν αὐτόν [i.e., τὸν Ἰησοῦν] (lit. "and he was seeking to see him"), but that text may be inspired by this. Though there is no reason to think that this man's desire to see Jesus expresses the same sense of need, the crowd here constitutes the same barrier to access to Jesus that they were initially for the blind man (18:39, cf. v 36). Despite this man's wealth and official power, he is quite unable to penetrate the crowd: he is clearly a social outsider, whose "littleness" in the eyes of others is more than physical.

4 Distinctive vocabulary, construction, and word usage combine to suggest that a strong pre-Lukan residue remains in v 4a. εἰς τὸ ἔμπροσθεν (lit. "into the before") is pleonastic, much as καλούμενος, "called," was in v 1. The "sycamore fig" is found only here in the NT. It is a large evergreen, said to be easy to climb. Apart from the initiative of Jesus in v 5, the man's strategy would have produced only a quite anonymous contact with Jesus, with no communication (neither Jesus nor the crowd is meant to see him climbing the tree).

5 Luke's Jesus has an uncanny knowledge of the secret affairs of others (see at 4:23 and note the coming δεῖ [lit. "it is necessary"] that links in the divine plan and purpose). σπεύσας, "hurry," may, for Luke, reflect the eschatological urgency attached to the presence of Jesus (note the use of "today" here and in v 9 [see there]; and cf. at 9:57–62; 12:54–59). For the domestic hospitality to be extended to Jesus here, cf. 5:29 (and at v 30), but here overnight accommodation appears to be specifically involved as well.

6 The language of the command is now repeated in the indicative. The language of welcome evokes that of the mission charges (see esp. 10:8–9), and its import is underlined by the language of joy (cf. at 1:14): for this man the kingdom of God has made its approach, and he has embraced it. This man is no longer the outsider that he was in vv 3–4.

7 "All" is likely to be Lukan hyperbole. In 5:30; 15:2 (see there), a very similar grumble is directed by Pharisees at, in the first instance, the disciples. But Derrett (*Law*, 281–82) rightly points to the widespread nature of (*i*) the view that to accept the hospitality of a man whose wealth is ill gotten is to become a partner with him in his crimes, and (*ii*) the practice of social ostracism as a means of deterrence. Jesus practices a far more creative alternative (cf. the discussion of love of enemy at 6:27–38).

8 The vocabulary of the verse is quite Lukan, and since the fit is slightly awkward (Zacchaeus addresses Jesus, but his words seem to be in some sense a response to the grumbling of the crowd; Jesus in turn addresses him in v 9, but speaks of him in the third person), it may best be taken as a Lukan development (underlining of the point expressed more subtly by the language of receiving and rejoicing in v 6). σταθείς (lit. "standing"; Luke uses the word in 18:40), by giving a public face to the man's statement, is probably meant to provide the link with the grumbling that precedes. On Luke's use of "the Lord" in narrative, see at 7:13. Here it pushes the following vocative use to a stronger sense than "sir" (Luke's blind man also addresses Jesus as "Lord" [18:41]). The "half" here is significant only in (*i*) being less than the "all" of 18:22; and (*ii*) in representing a radical disposal of wealth for the benefit of the poor (the language echoes that of 18:22, but is closer to that of the Markan source).

On ἐσυκοφάντησα, "unlawfully exacted," see at 3:14. The fourfold restitution
is probably not the fulfillment of any legal requirement. In Jewish law restitution
in connection with theft normally required only the addition of a fifth (Lev 6:2–
5); only in the case of sheep and oxen that had been stolen and then disposed of
or slaughtered (Exod 22:1–4; partly reflected in 2 Sam 12:6) is the restitution on
a much greater scale (fourfold and fivefold respectively [twofold if still in the
possession of the thief]). Roman law required fourfold restoration in certain circumstances, particularly in cases of wrongful accusation in the courts (see Kerr,
ExpTim 98 [1986] 70). A Roman influence on Jewish affairs may be evidenced by
Josephus' reference (*Ant.* 16.3) to fourfold restoration (the context shows that
Exod 22:1–4 is in mind, but Josephus assumes a wider relevance of the fourfold
restoration) and also by the early second-century text Mur 19:10, which envisages a fourfold restoration in connection with a Jewish divorce settlement. Against
this general background, Zacchaeus' scale of restoration appears to more than
compensate for any of his misdeeds.

The view that Zacchaeus is describing his regular practice and not his newfound
intention has recently gained a certain popularity (see White, *LexTQ* 14 [1979]
89–96; id., *ExpTim* 91 [1979–80] 21; Fitzmyer, 1220–21). This involves taking the
present tense verbs as iterative, rather than as futuristic. The story then becomes
a vindication story rather than a salvation story. But the whole tone of the story
finally counts against this view, from the image of Zacchaeus that emerges in vv
3–4, via the mission echoes of v 6, through the role of the other statements similar to v 7 in the Gospel account, to the salvation-of-the-lost emphasis of vv 9–10.

9 That Jesus' words here are said to be addressed to Zacchaeus is likely to be
the product of the introduction of v 8. The words "today" and "salvation" have
suggested to some that the first half of v 9 might belong with v 8 as a Lukan
contribution (see esp. Dupont, *Béatitudes* 2:251), and the second half is also at
times considered Lukan (e.g., Marshall, 698). A text without the first statement
of v 9 seems most unsatisfactory in promoting the flow of thought. Either all the
verse is Lukan, or it all reflects an original component of the narrative. At a literary level, v 10 is more effective coming after a strong indication that the salvation
of a lost one has just happened, than as needing to be, by itself, the response to
the grumbling. This, plus a recognition that the language of "today" (with "house")
is already to be found in v 5, while salvation language is in v 10 (based on Ezek
34:22), leads me to the view that while Luke may have had a hand in the particular wording, the content of v 9 should be considered part of the original account.

The mission charge links of v 6 are here carried further, but with the coming
of salvation taking the place of the drawing near of the kingdom of God (10:9).
On "today," see at 4:21. On "salvation," see at 1:69. Contact with Jesus has transformed Zacchaeus. Despite his manner of life up to this point, Zacchaeus is not
to be disenfranchised from the People of God. As one of the "lost sheep of the
house of Israel" (Matt 10:6), he is not beyond the reach of the present saving
outreach of God. For the role of the link to Abraham in being a candidate for the
promised salvation, see 1:55, 73; 13:16. For a counterbalancing motif that pre-
serves God's freedom and stands against presumption, see 3:8.

10 This verse has obvious links with 5:32, but its particular imagery is inspired
by Ezek 34, where God himself and David gather the scattered sheep of Israel. In

Ezek 34 the needy state of the sheep is the outcome of oppression; the needy state of Zacchaeus has a somewhat different complexion. The verse is not to be seen as an originally separate tradition that has been added here, since some such statement is needed to provide closure after the outcry of v 7. Only the self-designation as Son of Man raises questions (see discussion at 7:34). The usage could well be original, but "Son of Man" may have replaced an earlier "I" (Luke would not be responsible for the change). The influence of Ezek 34 here suggests a Davidic role for this Son of Man. Thus the strand of royal messianism begun in 18:35–43 continues here. On "Son of Man," see further in *Form/Structure/Setting* for 6:1–5 and the "Son of Man" excursus.

Explanation

Proximity to Jerusalem distinguishes the units of 18:35–19:46 from the long journey narrative that preceded. Allusion to Ezek 34 in 19:10 continues for this unit the Davidic note reintroduced by the blind man's cry in 18:38, 39. To the deliverance there of a man lost in blindness and poverty corresponds now the deliverance of a man lost in wealth and corruption. The popular support for the former is to be contrasted with the popular dismay at the latter.

If tax collectors were considered to be unsavory characters, then Zacchaeus as a *chief* tax collector can only be considered to be that much worse. From this starting point the reader comes to the story with an awareness (*i*) that Jesus is the "friend of tax collectors and sinners" (7:34; cf. 5:30), but (*ii*) that it is humanly impossible for the rich to enter the kingdom of God (18:25; cf. v 23).

The crowd bars this man's way to Jesus just as the crowd had done in the case of the blind man. Though this man has the power of wealth and official status, he is clearly a social outsider. In the eyes of his Jewish compatriots, his "littleness" is more than physical. He is a nobody. The man's strategy to see Jesus would not change this situation: he would get a private view from the tree, and that is all (neither Jesus nor the crowd are meant to see him climbing the tree).

The true initiative in the story belongs to Jesus. The Lukan Jesus has an uncanny knowledge of the secret affairs of others. Zacchaeus is not hidden from him! He insists that anonymous acquaintance should give way to close encounter. Jesus invites himself home, and this enables Zacchaeus to welcome him in a manner that echoes the proper reception, in Luke 10, of the missioning seventy with their message and accompanying manifest reality of the kingdom of God. For Zacchaeus the kingdom of God has made its approach, and he has embraced it with joy: he is no longer the outsider of vv 3–4.

The accompanying crowd is more impressed by the "traitor" role and lawless excesses of tax collectors. Such types are hardly to be considered as candidates for salvation! The onlookers are scandalized at the social recognition implied by Jesus' initiative (see 5:30; 15:2). But it is Jesus' approach, not theirs, that demonstrates a power to creatively transform the human situation encountered.

Zacchaeus has been inwardly transformed by his encounter with Jesus. His spontaneous response is to dispose of half his fortune toward meeting the needs of the poor and to make generous provision for putting right the injustices of his previous professional life. In the Lukan account the obvious adequacy of this move serves to relativize the earlier call to the rich ruler to dispose of all his wealth. At the same time it leaves the issue of the practical disposition of money high on the agenda of any who would consider what might be an adequate response to the approach of the kingdom of God.

The coming of Jesus is to be equated with the coming of the kingdom of God, which is in turn to be equated with the coming of salvation. Zacchaeus has encountered the "today" of salvation, the same today of which Jesus speaks in 4:21. This is also the salvation anticipated in 1:69. Those who were convinced of their own holiness were inclined to read others out of the People of God, but the promises to the descendants of Abraham (see 1:55, 73) are also to "the lost sheep of the house of Israel" (Matt 10:6). The "Man of Destiny" came not to confirm customary exclusions but precisely to seek out and save the lost sheep of Israel. The wording here echoes Ezek 34, where God himself and David (presumably a new messianic David) would come to the rescue of the scattered sheep.

Going to a Distant Land to Receive Kingly Power   (19:11-28)

Bibliography

Aletti, J.-N. "Lc 19, 11–28: Parabole des mines et/ou parabole du roi: Remarques sur l'écriture parabolique du Luc." In *Les paraboles évangéliques: Perspectives nouvelles. XIIe congrès de l'ACEF,* ed. J. Delorme. Lectio Divina 135. Paris: Cerf, 1989. 309–32. **Bauer, J. B.** "Die Arbeit als Heilsdimension (Lk 19,26 u. 1 Tim 2,14s)." *BLit* 24 (1956–57) 198–201. **Bouwman, G.** *Das dritte Evangelium: Einübung in die formgeschichtliche Methode.* Düsseldorf: Patmos, 1968. 56–61. **Brightman, F. E.** "S. Luke 19, 21: αἴρεις ὃ οὐκ ἔθηκας." *JTS* 29 (1927–28) 158. **Candlish, R.** "The Pounds and the Talents." *ExpTim* 23 (1911–12) 136–37. **Carroll, J. T.** *Response to the End of History.* 97–103. **Conzelmann, H.** *Luke.* 64, 72–73, 82–83, 113, 121, 138–41, 198. **Dauvillier, J.** "La Parabole des mines ou des talents et le 99 du code de Hammourabi." In *Mélanges.* FS J. Magnol. Paris: Recueil Sirey, 1948. 153–65. **Derrett, J. D. M.** "Law in the New Testament: The Parable of the Talents and Two Logia." *ZNW* 56 (1965) 184–95; reprinted, *Law.* 17–31. ———. "A Horrid Passage in Luke Explained (Lk 19:27)." *ExpTim* 97 (1985–86) 136–38. **Didier, M.** "La parabole des talents et des mines." In *De Jésus aux évangiles: Tradition et rédaction dans les évangiles synoptiques.* FS J. Coppens, ed. I. de la Potterie. BETL 25. 2 vols. Gembloux: Duculot, 1967. 248–71. **Dodd, C. H.** *Parables.* 7, 12, 100, 114–21, 127–29. **DuBuit, F. M.** "La parable des Mines ou des Talents." *Evangile* 49 (1968) 19–27. **Dupont, J.** "La parabole des talents (Mat. 25: 14–30) ou des mines (Luc 19: 12–27)." *RTP* 19 (1969) 376–91. ———. "La parabole des talents (Mat. 25: 14–30)." *AsSeign* n.s. 64 (1969) 18–28. **Enslin, M. S.** "Luke and Matthew, Compilers or Authors?" *ANRW* 2/25.3 (1985) 2357–88, esp. 2385–87. **Fiedler, P.** "Die übergebenen Talente: Auslegung von Mt 25,14–20." *BibLeb* 11 (1970) 259–73. **Foerster, W.** "Das Gleichnis von der anvertrauten Pfunden." In *Verbum Dei manet in aeternum.* FS D. O. Schmitz, ed. W. Foerster. Witten: Luther, 1953. 37–56. **Ganne, P.** "La parabole des talents." *BVC* 45 (1962) 44–53. **Grässer, E.** *Parusieverzögerung.* 114–19. **Holdcroft, I. T.** "The Parable of the Pounds and Origen's Doctrine of Grace." *JTS* 24 (1973) 503–4. **Jeremias, J.** *Parables.* 58–63, 67, 86, 95, 99–100, 136, 166. **Johnson, L. T.** "The Lukan Kingship Parable (Lk. 19:11–27)." *NovT* 24 (1982) 139–59. **Joüon, P.** "La parabole des mines (Luc, 19, 13–27) et la parabole des talents (Matthieu, 25, 14–30)." *RSR* 29 (1939) 489–94. **Jülicher, A.** *Gleichnisreden.* 2:472–95. **Kaestli, J.-D.** *L'Eschatologie.* 38–40. **Kamlah, E.** "Kritik und Interpretation der Parabel von den anvertrauten Geldern: Mt. 25,14ff.; Lk. 19,12ff." *KD* 14 (1968) 28–38. **Lambrecht, J.** *Once More Astonished.* 167–95. **Lüthi, W.** "Das Gleichnis vom anvertrauten Pfund: Predigt über Lk. 19,11–27." In *Das Wort sie sollen lassen stahn.* FS D. A. Schädelin, ed. H. Dürr et al. Bern: H. Lang, 1950. 207–14. **Manns, F.** "La parabole des talents: Wirkungsgeschichte et racines juives." *RevScRel* 65 (1991) 343–62. **McCulloch, W.** "The Pounds and the Talents." *ExpTim* 23 (1911–12) 382–83. **McGaughy, L. C.** "The Fear of Yahweh and the Mission of Judaism: A Postexilic Maxim and Its Early Christian Expansion in the Parable of the Talents." *JBL* 94 (1975) 235–45. **Meynet, R.** *Initiation à la rhétorique biblique: 'Qui donc est le plus grand?' I. Initiations.* Paris: Cerf, 1982. 85–131. **Neuhäusler, E.** "Mit welcher Massstab misst Gott die Menschen? Deutung zweier Jesussprüche." *BibLeb* 11 (1970) 104–13. **Panier, L.** "La parabole des mines: Lécture sémiotique (Lc 19, 11–27)." In *Les paraboles évangéliques: Perspectives nouvelles. XIIe congrès de l'ACEF,* ed. J. Delorme. LD 135. Paris: Cerf, 1989. 333–47. **Pesch, W.** *Der Lohngedanke in der Lehre Jesu verglichen mit der religiösen Lohnlehre des Spätjudentums.* MTS 1/1. Munich: Zink, 1955. 30–39. **Potterie, I. de la** "La parabole du prétendant à la royauté (Lc 19,11–28)." In *À cause de l'Évangile.* FS J. Dupont, ed. F. Refoulé. 613–41. **Resenhöfft, W.** "Jesu Gleichnis von den Talenten, ergänzt durch die Lukas-Fassung." *NTS* 26 (1979–80) 318–31. **Sanders, J. T.** "The Parable of the Pounds and Lucan Anti-Semitism." *TS* 42 (1981) 660–68. **Schneider, G.** *Parusiegleichnisse.* 38–42. **Schulz, S.** *Spruchquelle.* 288–98. **Simpson, J. G.** "The Parable of the Pounds." *ExpTim* 37 (1925–26) 299–302. **Spicq, C.** "Le chrétien doit porter du fruit." *VSpir* 84 (1951) 605–15. **Stock, W.** "The Pounds and the Talents." *ExpTim* 22 (1901–11) 424–25. **Tàrrech, A. P., i.** "La parabole des talents (Mt 25, 14–30) ou des mines (Lc 19, 11–28)." In *À cause de l'Évangile.* FS J. Dupont, ed. F. Refoulé. 165–93. **Taylor, C.** "Plato and the New Testament: 1. St Luke XIX, 21." *JTS* 2 (1901) 432. **Thiessen, H. C.** "The Parable of the Nobleman and the Earthly Kingdom: Luke 19:11–27." *BSac* 91 (1934) 180–90. **Thomson, P.** "'Carry on!' (Luke xix. 13)." *ExpTim* 30 (1918–19) 277. **Weder, H.** *Die Gleichnisse Jesu als Metaphern.* 193–210. **Weinert, F. D.** "The Parable of the Throne Claimant (Luke 19:12,14–15a,27) Reconsidered." *CBQ* 39 (1977) 505–14. **Weiser, A.** *Die Knechtsgleichnisse der synoptischen Evangelien.* SANT 29. Munich: Kösel, 1971. 226–72. **Winterbotham, R.** "Christ, or Archelaus?" *Exp* 8/4 (1912) 338–47. **Zerwick, M.** "Die Parabel vom Thronanwärter." *Bib* 40 (1959) 654–74.

Translation

[11] *As they were listening to these things, he went on to tell them a parable, because he was near Jerusalem and they thought that the kingdom of God was going to appear immediately.* [12] *So he said, "A certain well-born man went into a distant land to acquire kingship*[a] *for himself and [then] to return.* [13] *He called ten of his slaves and gave to them ten mnas, and he said to them, 'Conduct business*[b] *[with this] while I am gone.'* [14] *Some of his fellow citizens hated him and sent a delegation after him to say, 'We do not want this person to rule over us.'* [15] *When he came back, having acquired the kingship, he asked for the slaves to whom he had given the money to be summoned to him, so that he might find out what business they had done.*[c] [16] *The first arrived and said, 'Sir, your mna has earned ten mnas.'* [17] *He said to him, 'Well done, good servant! Since you have been faithful in a very small matter, you are to have authority over ten cities.'* [18] *Then the second one came and said, 'Your mna, sir, has made five mnas.'* [19] *He said to this one as well, 'And you are to be over five cities.'* [20] *Then the*[d] *other one came and said, 'Sir, look,*

your mna which I have had stored away in a sweat cloth. [21]*For I was afraid of you, because you are an exacting person: you carry off what you have not deposited; and you harvest what you have not sown.'* [22]*He said to him, 'Wicked servant, I will judge you out of your [own] mouth. You knew, did you, that I am an exacting person, carrying off what I have not deposited and harvesting what I have not sown?* [23]*Then why didn't you place my money with a bank? Then I would have collected it with interest when I came.'* [24]*Then he said to his attendants, 'Take the mna from him and give it to the one who has ten mnas.'* [25]*They said to him, 'Sir, he has ten mnas!'*—[26e]*I tell you, that to everyone who has shall [more] be given; but from the one who does not have, even what he has will be taken away.*[f]—[27]*'But as for these enemies of mine who did not want me to rule over them, bring them here and slay them before me.'"* [28]*Having said these things he went on ahead, going up to Jerusalem.*

Notes

[a] βασιλεία(ν) (lit. "kingdom") as in v 11.
[b] By reading an infinitive here ℵ A D E L W Θ 13 346 etc. mix direct and indirect speech.
[c] "each one had done" (added τις and singular verb) in A (W) Θ *f*[1,13] 33 892 etc.
[d] "The" is missing from A W Ψ *f*[1] 33 1006 etc., no doubt to help with the problem posed by only three of the ten slaves being mentioned.
[e] A D W Θ Ψ *f*[13] etc. link with γάρ, "for," as in Matthew.
[f] ἀπ' αὐτοῦ, "from him," is added in ℵ[2] A D W Θ Ψ *f*[1,13] etc. to align with the Matthean text.

Form/Structure/Setting

The royal motif of the previous units continues, and just as there has been a certain paralleling of the first two units of this section so there will now be of the next two. Both are accounts of royal arrivals: the one a parable designed to deflect expectation away from Jesus' pending arrival in Jerusalem, the other the account of that arrival (for the purposes of this parallelism vv 41–44 belong with 29–40, though they are treated separately below).

Luke's parable here is a variant of that found in Matt 25:14–30, but with those parts of the parable that concern royal rule (opposition to it, reception in a distant land, sharing it with his stewards, executing his opponents) represented only in the Lukan form. Scholarly opinion is divided about whether Luke and Matthew received the parable in the same form. A decision about this is linked in turn to a second about whether the main differences are redactional developments of an original that in all essentials is represented by the Matthean form (an original like the Lukan form is quite unlikely given the difficulties of the Lukan narrative [the roles of the servants entrusted with funds and of the unwilling citizens seem to operate quite independently, and where the royal motif comes into contact with the servant stream it seems to create tensions in the narrative (see further below)]), or whether these differences represent the main part of a second parable, which has, either by Luke or before him, been merged with the main parable.

Two main factors count in favor of identifying a second parable: (*i*) the narrative that emerges, if we extract and fit together those parts of the parable that deal with royal rule, is in its own right a more or less complete and coherent narrative; and (*ii*) the allusions to Archelaeus that are characteristic of these additions (see below) and that give a quite negative tone to the royal figure seem more likely to point to the boldness of Jesus than to Luke or the church tradition before him (see esp. Zerwick, *Bib* 40 [1959] 654–74; and further Jeremias, *Parables*, 58–60; Weinert, *CBQ* 39 [1977] 505–14; Resenhöfft, *NTS* 26 [1979–80] 327–28; Crossan, *In Parables*, 103). In favor of Lukan redaction is the usefulness of this additional material for the presentation of what are clearly Lukan interests, and the help that its presence gives to the literary structuring at this point. Language considerations (there is some non-Lukan phraseology in these verses) and the partial fit with Lukan interests (see below) tip the balance in favor of a non-Lukan origin in a separate parable. (Though naturally seen by later Christians in connection with Jesus' messianic identity, on the lips of the historical Jesus the use of language that would remind of Achelaeus [whose rule was remembered as one of cruelty and tyranny, and who never actually became a king] is likely to have had the effect of distancing the parable from issues of messianism in favor of a concern simply with the confirmation of authority, which is ignored at one's peril [cf. 20:9–18; 9:26].)

The question remains whether the merging of the parables is Lukan or pre-Lukan. Here the usefulness of the transformed version of the parable to Luke counts in favor of the former. There is no true parallel elsewhere in the Gospel for such a Lukan role, though the formation of 12:35–38 may be suggestive (note esp. the introduction of v 37). So finally, there is nothing that counts strongly against the main parable being available to Matthew and Luke in essentially the same form. For the wording of the source form of the parable see *Comment* below.

There is a broad scholarly consensus that v 26 (par. Matt 25:29) represents the addition of a floating logion to the parable. Apart from this there is very little dissent from the view that this parable may be traced to the historical Jesus (but see Fiedler, "Übergebenen Talente," 271; A. Satake, "Zwei Typen von Menschenbildern in den Gleichnissen Jesu," *AJBI* 4 [1978] 45–84; Goulder, *Midrash*, 440–42). In broad framework the parable is not unlike Mark 13:34–36 (see discussion at 12:35–48), and it shares with quite a number of parables the juxtaposition of an appropriate and an inappropriate response.

The use to which the original parable may have been put by the historical Jesus remains much more open to question. The development of the parable focuses much attention on the case of the man who preserved intact the money entrusted to him, but did nothing with it; and it is largely what we make of this feature of the story that determines the sense proposed (along with the decision made about the identity of the original hearers). Do we have here a general commendation of the virtues of fidelity and effort as necessary for the person who would enter the kingdom of God (Jülicher)? Or do we have an attack on the preservers of the Jewish religious tradition, who have preserved it essentially intact, but not, according to Jesus, made profitable use of it for God (Jeremias)? Or is an attack made on the fear-centered, and therefore legalistic, approach to religion of those whom Jesus attacks (Dupont)? Or do we have a challenge to disciples to make fruitful for God what has now come to them from Jesus (whether this is to be seen more generally, or applied to something as focused as the spreading of the message [Weiser; Weder; Didier])? Or does the rule of God as revealed by Jesus seem to the scribes and Pharisees to ask too much, and the parable describes their revolt against it (Lambrecht)? Or is the challenge to respond to the

message of the kingdom with the dynamism of a bold readiness to risk all, and
not to take refuge in a sterile security (Tàrrech)?

Although early Christians likely applied the parable to the good news they believed Jesus had entrusted to them, it seems finally more likely that the parable
initially evoked the historic trust committed to the People of God and that the
returning master was an image of God, rather than of Jesus himself. The accu-
racy of the servant's perception of his master is more than questionable, but there
is no doubt that he felt pressure from his master's expectations and was quite
unwilling to risk responsibility. Though he took custody of his master's money,
he did not take up the task entrusted to him by his master: he preferred to pass.
Rather than any of the suggestions of the paragraph above, it seems more likely
that Jesus is addressing a certain kind of nominalism among some of his contemporaries: quite happy to be in a general way within the orbit of the People of
God, but unwilling to make themselves answerable to God's expectations in any
committed sense. Feeling that God was something of an exacting tyrant, they chose
to avoid the pressures of fulfilling his expectations rather than to run the risk of
doing what they feared might be too little. The parable challenges directly the
perverted logic of this kind of opting out. But more subtly it places in question
the assumptions made about God (how has he in fact dealt with the other servants?) and draws attention to what these abstainers have failed to realize: though
God's mandates to his servants open up a vast sphere of possibility, he is prepared to accept, when there has been any sort of effort to implement the mandate,
what is actually a minimal return on his investment.

A form of the parable is found in the *Gospel of the Nazaraeans* 18. However,
since this form shows influence both from the Matthean and the Lukan form (as
well as of the parable of the Prodigal Son), it is of no value in tracing the origin
of the parable.

Comment

Jesus is about to enter Jerusalem, and he will do so as a royal figure. However,
he enters not as a royal pretender seeking to take the throne but as one about to
journey far away to gain his royal commission to rule. He will leave behind servants who must see themselves as entrusted with resources to be used to gain
profit for their master, and fellow citizens who object to his royal pretensions.
When he returns with his royal authority secured, he will receive his servants and,
in accord with their fidelity, share his rule with them. Upon his return he will
also liquidate those whose response to his royal claims was treasonable: they have
no place in his kingdom.

11 On the basis of vocabulary, style, other Lukan practice, and the way in
which the present introduction seems to produce a secondary application of the
parable(s), the present verse is widely recognized to be a Lukan contribution.
Luke links with the previous unit by means of ἀκουόντων δὲ αὐτῶν ταῦτα προσθείς,
"as they were listening to these things, he went on to." The linking seems mainly
concerned to provide a formal structural link with the previous unit (cf. 14:15).
Luke may want the "today" of salvation to prepare for the expectation of an immediate appearance of the kingdom of God, but if we press the link too literally

it involves a change of plan for Jesus from v 5 (cf. v 28), which is surely not Luke's point.

The language of nearness continues as one of the markers of the sense of progress in the section. The nearness to Jerusalem is only relative, since Jericho was still seventeen miles from Jerusalem and the journey included a rise of 3,300 feet in altitude. The importance of the proximity of Jerusalem comes from its historic role as throne city, from the time when David took it as his royal city to reign over the united tribes of Israel (1 Sam 5). More recently Herod the Great had taken Jerusalem by force to impose his rule upon the Jewish nation (with particular support from Jericho on the eve of his advance upon Jerusalem [Josephus, *War* 1.335–60; *Ant.* 14.459–91 (his successor Archelaus seems to have been able to take up his rule without force, but only because his Roman associates had already put down a series of uprisings [*War* 2.1–112; *Ant.* 17.20–344])]). I have argued elsewhere ("Luke's Readers," 129–240, esp. 144–203), especially in connection with Acts 6:13–14, that Luke is sensitive to a polemical castigation of Christianity as an insurrectionist movement, hostile to the existing Jerusalem religious structures (cf. the Qumran attitudes to Jerusalem and their expectations of the eschatological fate of the "wicked" regime in power there). In this context, the prospect of the immediate coming of the kingdom of God in Jerusalem takes on the coloring of a military takeover by Jesus at the head of a fanatical band of followers. All of Luke's account to follow is at one level a careful distancing of Jesus from any such possibility. Apart from this specific focus, however, the concern here is to insist that the execution, rather than royal instatement, that awaited Jesus in Jerusalem represented no failure but a stage in the implementation of God's purposes for the consummation of the kingdom.

(The standard view, that the parable seeks to explain the delay of the Parousia, does no justice at all to the link between the expectation of immediacy and the arrival of the historical Jesus in Jerusalem. The view of Johnson [*NovT* 24 (1982) 139–59], that the following messianic acclamation of Jesus is in view [and so Jesus will affirm rather than place in question the popular expectation here], is more sensitive to the link to Jerusalem, but [*i*] it requires an impossible reading of ἀναφαίνεσθαι [lit. "to be lit up" and so: "to be caused to appear"] as "to be revealed" in the sense of "to be declared [as a symbolic manifestation]"; [*ii*] it requires a sense for "kingdom of God" unparalleled elsewhere in Luke; and [*iii*] it allows no justice at all to be done to the actual parable. De la Potterie's variant of this view ["La parabole," 613–41], which makes the messianic acclamation a type of the heavenly enthronement to come, is not unattractive, but it only partly overcomes the difficulties of Johnson's view. While it takes up an important Lukan motif, it leaves us finally with a rather fragmented sense.)

12 Probably only ἄνθρωπος, "person/man," survives of the original opening of the main parable. The shared journey motif makes it possible for Luke to fuse the two parables. Perhaps with a significant infusion of Lukan language, we have here the opening of the second parable. In the world of the day, one went to Rome to gain the status of king before taking up one's rule. This is what Herod the Great had done (Josephus, *War* 1.282–85; *Ant.* 14.374–89), and it is what Archelaus had done as well (*War* 2.14–100; *Ant.* 17.224–340), though he had to be content with the title ethnarch until he proved himself (*War* 2.94; *Ant.* 17.318), which he failed to do. (It is interesting that though Archelaus is only ethnarch, Josephus speaks of "the kingdom" in connection with him, much as does our parable, which refrains from actually calling the chief character a king.) The cruelty and tyranny of the Roman-sponsored rulers of the Herodian family would inevitably be called to mind, though it is unlikely that this evocation was operative for Luke.

The "distant land" stands in implicit contrast to the nearness of Jerusalem and the "immediately" of the popular expectation. Luke thinks in terms of Jesus' instatement at the right hand of God and coming in glory (cf. Acts 2:30, 33–36; Luke 24:26; 22:69; 9:51; Acts 3:20; 1:11).

13 Luke's "ten of his slaves" fits the social status of the man of noble birth who is in line for kingly rule. It probably belongs to Luke's efforts to merge the two parables, but he seems to forget about the number as the story unfolds. Luke's one mna per servant is dramatically less than Matthew's figures where the best provided of the servants receives ten talents, which is six hundred times as much. Luke's amount seems clearly to be a token amount, as a kind of trial. Matthew's represents a more serious financial exposure, but in the story it is still meant as a small amount, which will later give way to a much larger fiscal trust (vv 21, 23). It remains uncertain which is the more original. The Matthean allocations graded according to ability are often thought to represent a development over Luke's simpler equal distribution, but Luke's "ten" in v 24, where his number should be "eleven," is an error best seen as based on an original that had "ten" there and that reflected the Matthean pattern of distribution. Luke may well have been concerned that the source form could be (falsely) read as implying that the outcome may be read already out of the starting point abilities (or allocation) of the respective slaves: the more ability, the more likely to succeed with God; the less ability, the less likely. Not so certain is whether the explanation of this distribution as "according to ability" is an original part of the parable. Also uncertain is whether Luke has provided the final clause of the verse, which makes explicit the business responsibilities laid upon the slaves. Luke may be preparing already to clarify the nature of the failure of the third of the slaves (the use of πρός for "to" with a verb of speaking and the fact that a verb cognate to πραγματεύσασθε, "conduct business," is probably introduced by Luke in v 15 may count in favor of Lukan production).

ἐν ᾧ ἔρχομαι is unusual. Beginning with ἐν ᾧ, the phrase is unlikely to mean "until I come" (as RSV, NIV, etc.). De la Potterie's "while I am coming," referring to the continual coming of Jesus to his own in the church period ("La parabole," 632–35), is artificial. Best is Fitzmyer's "while I am gone" (1235), referring to the whole journey. Luke thinks of the disciples' responsibility in the period of Jesus' absence—perhaps particularly the responsibility mirrored in 9:1–6 and 10:1–16. Luke's writing activity will in its own way be an attempt to discharge this responsibility.

14 Luke now continues the thread of the second parable. The text here has no notable Lukan features, though its language and idioms can be found elsewhere in the Gospel. There is little doubt that we have here an allusion to the delegation that sought to oppose the confirmation by Augustus of Archelaus as ruler of Judea (Josephus, *Ant.* 17.299–314). But we cannot be sure that Luke is aware of this. οἱ δὲ πολῖται is best translated "some of his fellow citizens." If Luke had intended all his fellow citizens, he would have made use of his favored πᾶς, "all." Sanders (*TS* 42 [1981] 660–68) is wrong to find anti-Semitism here.

15 Luke has no equivalent to Matt 25:16–18. It is probably a Matthean development designed to fill the gap between the man's departure and return, but it is also possible that it has been displaced by Luke's addition of v 14. V 15 seems to be for the most part a Lukan reformulation of Matt 25:19 in the light of the royal motif of the second parable. As a king he now acts through the agency of others, and so he asks for his slaves to be called. He wants to know the results of their business activities in his absence. (ἀργύριον, "money," as used here may be what stood in the original parable in place of Matthew's τὰ ὑπάρχοντα αὐτοῦ, "his goods," in 25:14.)

16 Apart from the quantities, Luke is likely to be closer to the original here, but παρεγένετο, "came," may be a Lukan contribution. For the scale of the return, see Derrett, *ZNW* 56 (1965) 190. Ancient business knew very high returns, but also spectacular failures.

17 Lukan intervention is more evident here, where the outcome of the faithful servant's endeavors leads to a share in the rule of the newly established monarch (Luke may also be responsible for εὖγε rather than Matthew's εὖ for "well done!"; for the superlative form ἐλαχίστῳ, "a very small matter"; and for the overall syntactical structure). But the form of the parable in Matthew is likely to be considerably Matthean as well (probably "and faithful" and "enter into the joy of your master"). Cf. the language of 22:29–30. That the reward is commensurate with the success is part of the dynamic of the parable, but it is to some degree an allegorizing element, since it makes no allowance for the arbitrary risk factor in ancient business life (but, then, despotic masters may not always have made such allowances!).

18–19 The case of the second servant is dealt with in parallelism with that of the first, but in v 18 Luke varies the introductory verb for the arrival of the second servant, switches word order for the vocative "Sir," and has both a change of verb and of word order in "has made five mnas." In v 19 he links the second time with δέ, "and/but," rather than καί, "and," now using a καί to mean "also." Finally, he abbreviates heavily the reward statement, which now loses both its praise and its explanation (both, however, to be understood). The Matthean parallelism is considerably stricter. This second instance established the proportionality of the rewards.

20 Luke's ὁ ἕτερος, "the other one," for the third slave has now forgotten that in v 13 the number of slaves involved has been set at ten. The third case begins in reasonably close parallelism to the first two, but then departs drastically from the pattern. Luke uses σουδάριον again in Acts 19:12. It is a Latin loanword and refers to a sweat cloth for the face or the neck. Matthew's slave here buried his stake. The difference is probably a reflection of the difference in the stake involved here: a talent weighed around fifty-five pounds and could not easily be wrapped in a sweat cloth to be hidden (Lambrecht, *Once More*, 179–80). Burying has always been a favored method in the preservation of wealth, so the change is a natural one. In Matthew the man's explanation precedes instead of following the revealing of the fate of the one talent. In the Matthean telling, all the slaves bring the money with them; in the Lukan, only the man who has made no use of his stake. In both these cases the Lukan form is to be preferred both in terms of realism and of artistry.

21 Where Matthew's second image of the master's hardness is no more than a paraphrase of the first, Luke has added what is probably a banking image (perhaps

suggested to him by the master's advice in v 23). The image may be almost proverbial; it is paralleled in several ancient writers (Plato, *Leges* 11.913C; Aelian,
Varia hist. 3.46; Josephus, *Ag. Ap.* 2.216; Philo, *Hypo.* 7.6). Luke's αὐστερός, "se-
vere/exacting/strict," is more likely to be original than Matthew's σκληρός (lit.
"hard," with the suggestion of cruelty and lack of mercy), but the difference is
slight. The slave's image of his master is as one who works things to his own advantage in a way that shamelessly exploits others. The master does not disown
this image, but his treatment of the first two slaves hardly supports it.

22   Luke's historic present here (λέγει, "he says") will be original; "I will judge
you out of your [own] mouth" is likely to be a Lukan embellishment (cf. Job
15:6), and he may be responsible for the repetition involved in having here "I am
an exacting person." But it is Matthew who will have added "and slothful" to "wicked
slave." The master will argue that far from being any excuse for inactivity, this
extreme image that the slave has of him should rather have produced action.

23   The reformulation here is likely to be Lukan (Luke introduces διὰ τί for
"why" in other places; τραπεζίτης, "banker," and κομίζειν, "obtain," are found in
Matthew only here). Luke's ἔδωκας in the sense "put/place" is probably
Septuagintal. The word for "bank" is literally "table." The usage is related to that
in Mark 11:15 of the tables of the moneychangers. For the practice of lending at
interest, see discussion at 16:5. The procedure recommended here would have
produced a rather more modest return than that achieved by the other slaves,
but it would have involved the very minimum of effort on the part of this slave
and would have exposed him to minimal financial risk. Though this was not at all
what the master had asked for, it would at least have produced something for the
master for whom, in this slave's image, gaining more was the consuming passion.
As it is, the slave has neither obeyed the directions of his master, nor even minimally acted in accord with his (surely false) image of his master. See in *Form/
Structure/Setting* above for discussion of the original thrust of this feature of the
parable.

24   The Matthean account has nobody identified to whom the command
"Take from him . . ." can be directed. Luke makes good this lack with "He said
τοῖς παρεστῶσιν," where τοῖς παρεστῶσιν may simply be those standing around,
but, given their task and the royal status of the Lukan figure, are more likely to
be "attendants." The man would actually have eleven mnas already, having gained
ten additional mnas from his business efforts; the "ten" here is likely to be a left-
over from the "ten" of the source, which contained the Matthean numbers. To
have an extra mna to trade with cannot be of much significance for one who now
rules the affairs of ten cities. This is a difficulty with the story that flows from
Luke's fusing of the two parables.

25   There is no parallel to this verse in the Matthean account. Its presence
clarifies the application of v 26 to the situation. It is best seen as a Lukan "improvement," though at this point Luke has temporarily lost sight of the fact that
this slave has meanwhile been entrusted with ten cities.

26   Luke has an introductory "I tell you that" not found in the Matthean account. This may be a fresh introduction after the change of speaker caused by
the insertion of v 25, but is perhaps better seen as coming from the shared source.
In any case it should be seen as functioning in the Lukan text as an aside by

Jesus, rather than as part of the narrative progress of the parable. The additional καὶ περισσευθήσεται, "and he will have a great abundance" (also found in the form of the logion at Matt 13:12 [contrast Mark 4:25]), is likely to be a Matthean doubling [as in Matthew's parallel to v 22]). Luke has removed the pendant construction from the Matthean syntax. This verse is unlikely to have been an original element of the parable: that it is also found in a quite different context raises the possibility that it is a floating logion; on the lips of the master it does not fit the narrative world particularly well, but as an aside on the lips of Jesus it is anomalous; in itself it is an appropriate enough proverbial comment on the respective fates of the favored and non-favored slaves, but its presence shifts the center of attention from the parable's natural focus, which is on the slave who failed his trust.

27 Luke concludes by returning to the royal parable. The action here is a natural part of the consolidation of power of the newly instated monarch. This sort of behavior had been part of Archelaus' strategy on gaining possession of his ethnarchy (Josephus, *War* 2.111) and was a notable feature of Herod the Great's accession to power (*War* 1.351–58). It also has its counterpart in OT victory scenes (1 Sam 15:33). In the Lukan use, this will be a picture of eschatological judgment, but since, for Luke, the destruction of Jerusalem is already the first installment of that judgment (see at 17:31 and esp. at chap. 21), the quasi-military imagery here is appropriately to be linked with what is anticipated in chap. 21. The link with chap. 21 is strengthened by the presence in this section of 19:41–44. On the three horizons of judgment with which Luke works, see at 12:5; 13:3. κατασφάζειν, "to slay," is found only here in the NT.

Luke has no equivalent for the Matthean words in 25:30 of judgment in terms of outer darkness, weeping, and gnashing of teeth. Since Matthew has something similar several times (8:12; 13:42, 50; 22:13; 24:51), it is most likely that he is responsible for the presence of this verse (in the original parable the removal of the trust is itself the judgment that falls on this slave who failed to carry through at all on his master's directive).

28 Luke rounds the unit off with the present words that create with v 11 an inclusion around the parable (beyond the recurrence of "Jerusalem" [different Greek forms for "Jerusalem" are used, but this is a byproduct of the borrowing of the phrase εἰς Ἱεροσόλυμα, "[in]to Jerusalem," in v 28 from Mark 11:1], note the paralleling of ἀκουόντων . . . ταῦτα, "hearing these things," with εἰπὼν ταῦτα, "having said these things"; on the treatment of this verse as the conclusion of the present unit rather than as the beginning of the following see esp. de la Potterie, "La parabole," 627–29, who emphasizes the links between vv 27 and 28). The picture here of Jesus moving on ahead of his companions is a motif found in Mark 10:32, which Luke made no use of in his parallel to that verse (18:31). The forward journey to Jerusalem is now to be seen in the light of the parable.

Explanation

The theme of royalty continues now with this parable of a royal pretender whose claim to a throne is sustained. To the present parable, designed to deflect expectation away from the moment of Jesus' impending arrival in Jerusalem, will correspond the immediately following account of that royal arrival. He will arrive as one about to journey far away to gain his royal commission to rule. As he leaves, he entrusts resources to slaves expected to be trustworthy, but he also has to run the gauntlet of fellow citizens who do their best to see that he does not have his rule confirmed. The former are being tried out for a greater destiny; the latter are in line for an unhappy fate. Luke appears to have merged two of Jesus' parables here.

Perhaps Luke thinks of the language of the "today" of salvation in v 9 as fueling the expectations associated with the impending arrival in Jerusalem. Luke is concerned to say that the execution, rather than royal instatement, that awaited Jesus in Jerusalem represented no failure of the Christian movement. But there is an extra note as well. Luke is concerned to distance Christianity from any kind of "arrival" of the kingdom of God that would look like the bloody takeover of a figure like Herod the Great. Luke knew that accusations that Christianity was sectarian and insurrectionist were part of the arsenal of the opponents of early Christianity. He is concerned to show that Christianity has a quite different nature and plays out its destiny on a much larger canvas.

In the world of the day one went to Rome to gain the status of king before taking up one's rule. Herod the Great had done this, and so had Archelaus his son. Allusions to Archelaus are to be found pervasively through the "royal" strand of the parable, though it is unclear whether Luke was clearly aware of them. Before departure this man hands out a modest amount of money (a mna was worth two hundred denarii, and a denarius was a day laborer's wage) to each of ten slaves who are to use it to engage in business. This turns out to be a kind of test. Luke probably thinks particularly, but not exclusively, of the kind of task that the Twelve and the Seventy have undertaken (9:1–6; 10:1–16).

Some of the man's fellow citizens seek to interfere with the confirmation of his status as ruler, but their bid is clearly unsuccessful and the man comes back with full royal authority. Here the opposition to Jesus, perhaps especially that which culminates in his death, is in view. In the larger Lukan picture the journey is a journey through death and to God (see Acts 2:33–36), and the return is the anticipated coming of the Son of Man (see Luke 21:27–28).

The success achieved by the first two slaves may seem extraordinary to us, but in the ancient world huge risks went with huge returns. They have done well in their trial and are given an important share in the rule of their monarch (cf. 22:29–30). The third slave, however (Luke seems to lose sight of the rest of the ten who were entrusted with money), returns the money, carefully preserved, but has made absolutely no use of it. The man explains his action as provoked by fear, based on his understanding of the exacting nature of his master: this man withdraws from the bank what he has not deposited and claims the harvest that represents the effort of somebody else's sowing.

The image of the master that the reader derives from the parable hardly accords with this, but the master deals with his slave on the slave's own terms. There is no doubt that the slave felt pressure from his master's expectations and, though he took custody of his master's money, he would not accept the responsibility that accompanied it. There is a certain kind of nominalism involved here: readiness in a general way to be identified with Jesus, but unwillingness to be answerable in any committed sense to God's expectations that are made known to us in connection with Jesus; a preference for doing nothing rather than running the risk of doing too little.

The master will argue that the extreme image that the slave has of him, far from being any excuse for inactivity, should rather have produced action. To put the money on deposit with a bank would have produced a rather more modest return than that achieved by the other slaves, but it would have involved the very minimum of effort on the part of this slave and would have exposed him to minimal financial risk. Beyond questioning the logic of the slave's position, this suggestion hints that though God's mandates to his servants open up a vast sphere of possibility, he is prepared to accept, when there has been any sort of effort to implement the mandate, what is actually a minimal return on his investment.

In marked contrast to the other two, the third slave loses his stake in his master's affairs precisely when his master has become the undisputed ruler of the realm. Here too the proverb proves true that winners win yet more and losers lose all that they have. But this slave is not the only loser in our story. His loss suddenly appears modest when it can be compared to that of the fellow citizens who opposed the coming to power of this ruler. They are guilty of treason, and they will pay the ultimate penalty.

Making a Royal Approach to Jerusalem (19:29–40)

Bibliography

Baarlink, H. "Friede im Himmel: Die lukanische Redaktion von Lk 19 38 und ihre Deutung." *ZNW* 76 (1985) 170–86. **Bailey, J. A.** *The Traditions Common to the Gospels of Luke and John.* NovTSup 7. Leiden: Brill, 1963. 22–28. **Barnicki, R.** "Das Zitat von Zach 9:9–10 und die Tiere im Bericht von Matthäus über dem Einzug Jesus in Jerusalem (Mt 21: 1–11)." *NovT* 18 (1976) 161–66. **Bauer, W.** "The 'Colt' of Palm Sunday (Der Palmesel)." *JBL* 72 (1953) 220–29. **Bergen, P. van.** "L'Entrée messianique de Jésus à Jérusalem." *QLP* 38 (1957) 9–24. **Bishop, E. F. F.** "Hosanna: The Word of the Joyful Jerusalem Crowds." *ExpTim* 53 (1941–42) 212–14. **Blenkinsopp, J.** "The Oracle of Judah and the Messianic Entry." *JBL* 80 (1961) 55–64. ———. "The Hidden Messiah and His Entry into Jerusalem." *Scr* 13 (1961) 51–56, 81–88. **Bratcher, R. G.** "A Note on Mark 11:3: ὁ κύριος αὐτοῦ χρείαν ἔχει." *ExpTim* 64 (1952–53) 93. ———. "A Note on Mark 11:3: ὁ κύριος αὐτοῦ χρείαν ἔχει." *BT* 4 (1953) 52. **Bromboszcz, T.** "Der Einzug Jesu in Jerusalem bei Mondschein? Ein Beitrag zur Chronologie der Leidensgeschichte." *BZ* 9 (1911) 164–70. **Burger, C.** *Jesus als Davidssohn: Eine traditionsgeschichtliche Untersuchung.* FRLANT 98. Göttingen: Vandenhoeck & Ruprecht, 1970. 112–14. **Buth, R.** "Luke 19:31–34, Mishnaic Hebrew, and Bible Translation: Is κύριοι τοῦ πώλου singular?" *JBL* 104 (1985) 680–85. **Catchpole, D. R.** "The 'triumphal' entry." In *Jesus and the Politics of His Day,* ed. E. Bammel and C. F. D. Moule. 319–34. **Crossan, J. D.** "Redaction and Citation in Mark 11:9–10 and 11:17." *BR* 17 (1972) 33–50. **Davies, T. L.** "Was Jesus Compelled?" *ExpTim* 42 (1930–31) 526–27. **Derrett, J. D. M.** "Law in the New Testament: The Palm Sunday Colt." *NovT* 13 (1971) 241–58. **Doeve, J. W.** "Purification du temple de desséchement du figuier: Sur la structure du 21ème chapitre de

Matthieu et parallèles (Marc xi.1–xii.12, Luc xix.28–xx.19)." *NTS* 1 (1954–55) 297–308. **Duff, P. B.** "The March of the Divine Warrior and the Advent of the Greco-Roman King: Mark's Account of Jesus' Entry into Jerusalem." *JBL* 111 (1992) 53–71. **Dupont, J.** "L'entrée de Jésus à Jérusalem dans le récit de saint Matthieu (XXI,1–17)." *LumVie* 48 (1960) 1–8. ─────. "L'entrée messianique de Jésus à Jérusalem." *AsSeign* 37 (1965) 46–62. **Fahy, T.** "The Triumphal Entry into Jerusalem." In *New Testament Problems*. Dublin/London: Clorimore and Reynolds/Burns and Oates, 1963. 126–39. **Farmer, W. R.** "The Palm Branches in John 12, 13." *JTS* n.s. 3 (1952) 62–66. **Flender, H.** *St Luke.* 61, 92–94, 103–4. **Frayn, R. S.** "Was Jesus Compelled?" *ExpTim* 43 (1931–32) 381–82. **Freed, E. D.** "The Entry into Jerusalem in the Gospel of John." *JBL* 80 (1961) 329–38. **Frenz, A.** "Mt xxi 5.7." *NovT* 13 (1971) 259–60. **George, A.** *Études sur l'oeuvre de Luc.* 274–76. ─────. "Le royauté de Jésus selon l'évangile de Luc." *ScEccl* 14 (1962) 57–69. **Giblin, C. H.** *The Destruction of Jerusalem.* 47–56. **Haenchen, E.** *Der Weg Jesu.* 372–79. **Haeusler, B.** "Zu Mt 21:3b und Parallelen." *BZ* 14 (1917) 153–58. **Hahn, F.** *Titles.* 82–84, 253–56. **Harvey, A. E.** *Jesus and the Constraints of History.* 120–29. **Herklotz, F.** "Zu Mt 21;9, 15." *BZ* 18 (1928–29) 39. **Jack, J. W.** "Was Jesus Compelled?" *ExpTim* 43 (1931–32) 381–82. **Jacob, R.** *Les péricopes de l'entrée à Jérusalem et de la préparation de la cène: Contribution à l'étude du problème synoptique.* Études Bibliques NS. Paris: Gabalda, 1973. **Johnson, C. H.** "The Song of Entry: Matt 21,9; Mark 11,9; Luke 19,38: John 12,13." *BW* 34 (1909) 47. **Johnson, S. L.** "The Triumphal Entry of Christ." *BSac* 124 (1967) 218–29. **Kennard, J. S.** "'Hosanna' and the Purpose of Jesus." *JBL* 67 (1948) 171–76. **Kuhn, H.-W.** "Das Reittier Jesu in der Einzugsgeschichte des Markusevangeliums." *ZNW* 50 (1959) 82–91. **Lohse, E.** "Hosianna." *NovT* 6 (1963) 113–19. **Mackay, W. M.** "The Contrasts of Palm Sunday." *ExpTim* 44 (1932–33) 275–77. **März, C.-P.** *"Siehe, dein König kommt zu dir . . .": Eine traditionsgeschichtliche Untersuchung zur Einzugsperikope.* ETS 43. Leipzig: St. Benno, 1980. **Mariadasan, V.** *Le triomphe messianique de Jésus et son entrée à Jérusalem: Étude critico-littéraire des traditions évangéliques (Mc 11,1–11; Mt 21,1–11; Lc 19,28–38; Jn 12,12–16).* Tindivanam, India: TNBCLC, 1978. **Mastin, B. A.** "The Date of the Triumphal Entry." *NTS* 16 (1969–70) 76–82. **Meikle, J.** "Was Jesus Compelled?" *ExpTim* 43 (1931–32) 288. **Michel, O.** "πῶλος." *TDNT* 6:959–61. ─────"Eine philologische Frage zur Einzugsgeschichte." *NTS* 6 (1959–60) 81–82. **Patsch, H.** "Der Einzug Jesu in Jerusalem: Ein historischer Versuch." *ZTK* 68 (1971) 1–26. **Paul, A.** "L'entrée de Jésus à Jérusalem (Mc 11; Mt 21; Lc 19; Jn 12)." *AsSeign* 19 (1971) 4–26. **Pesch, R.,** and **Kratz, R.** "Jesus zieht ein in Jerusalem." In *So liest man synoptische: Vol. VI. Passionsgeschichte, Teil I.* Frankfurt am M.: Knecht, 1979. 64–72. **Pieper, K.** "Zum Einzug Jesu in Jerusalem." *BZ* 11 (1913) 397–402. **Rese, M.** *Alttestamentliche Motive in der Christologie des Lukas.* SNT 1. Gütersloh: G. Mohn, 1969. 196–99. **Richardson, C. C.** "Blessed is He that Cometh in the Name of the Lord: A Liturgical Note." *ATR* 29 (1947) 96–98. **Rilliet, F.** "La louange des pierres et le tonnerre: Luc 19,40 chez Jacques de Saroug et dans la patristique syriaque." *RHR* 117 (1985) 293–304. **Ross, J. M.** "Names of God: A Comment on Mark 11.3 and Parallels." *BT* 35 (1984) 443. **Samuel, O.** "Die Regierungsgewalt des Wortes Gottes." *EvT* 3 (1936) 1–3. **Schildenberger, J.** "Der Triumphzug ders Palmsonntag." *BenM* 17 (1935) 100–108. **Schniewind, J.** *Die Parallelperikopen bei Lukas und Johannes.* Leipzig/Darmstadt: Hinrichs/Wissenschaftliche Buchgesellschaft, 1914=1970. 26–28. **Schramm, T.** *Markus-Stoff.* 145–49. **Smith, D. M.** "John 12, 12ff and the Question of John's Use of the Synoptics." *JBL* 81 (1965) 58–64. **Souter, A.** "Interpretation of Certain New Testament Passages—Luke xix. 33." *Exp* 8/8 (1914) 94–95. **Spitta, F.** "Der Volksruf beim Einzug Jesu in Jerusalem." *ZWT* 52 (1910) 307–20. **Stanley, D. M.** "Études mathéennes: l'entrée messianique à Jérusalem." *ScEccl* 6 (1954) 93–106. **Trautmann, M.** *Zeichenhafte Handlungen Jesu: Ein Beitrag zur Frage nach dem geschichtlichen Jesus.* FB 37. Würzburg: Echter, 1980. 347–78. **Viard, A.** "L'entrée de Jésus à Jérusalem (Lc. 19:28–40)." *EV* 84 (1974) 170–72. **Vielhauer, P.** "Ein Weg zur neutestamentlichen Christologie?" *Gesammelte Aufsätze zum Neuen Testament.* TB 31. Munich: Kaiser, 1965. 141–98, esp. 153–57. **Visser 't Hooft, W. A.** "Triumphalism in the Gospels." *SJT* 38 (1985) 491–504.

Translation

[29] *It happened that as he drew near to Bethphage and Bethany,*[a] *to the mount called "Of Olives," he sent two of the*[b] *disciples,* [30] *saying, "Go into the village opposite, where, as you enter, you will find a donkey tethered, on which no person has ever sat. Untie it and bring it [here].* [31] *And if someone asks you why you are untying [it], you must say this:*[c] *'Because the Lord has need of it!'"*[d] [32] *Those sent went off and found [things] just as he had said to them.* [33] *As they were untying the donkey, its owners said to them, "Why are you untying the donkey?"* [34] *They said, "Because the Lord has need of it!"* [35] *Then they brought it to Jesus, and, throwing their garments onto the donkey, they put Jesus [onto the mount].* [36] *As he went along, they strewed their garments on the road.* [37] *As he was already drawing near to the descent of the Mount of Olives, the whole multitude of the disciples began to rejoice and to praise God in loud voices*[e] *for all the mighty works they had seen.* [38] *They said,*

"Blessed is the coming one, the king;[f]
[the one who comes] in the name of the Lord!
There is [to be] peace in heaven,
and glory [for God] in highest heaven."

[39] *Some of the Pharisees from the crowd said to him, "Teacher, rebuke your disciples!"* [40] *He replied, "I tell you, if these are silent,*[g] *the stones will cry out!"*[h]

Notes

[a] The texts differ over whether this name should have an indeclinable form.

[b] "His" in A D W Θ Ψ $f^{1,13}$ etc.

[c] Gr. οὕτως (lit. "so/thus"). αὐτῷ, "to him," is added by A W Θ Ψ $f^{1,13}$ etc.

[d] ὅτι at the beginning of this clause could also be a marker of direct speech, but in vv 33–34, where the clause is repeated, the other direct speech is not introduced by ὅτι.

[e] Gr. sing.

[f] A loss of a definite article makes this "the coming king" in ℵ[c] A K L Δ Θ Π Ψ $f^{1,13}$ etc.; ℵ (063) etc. have simply "the king"; (D) W (579) 1216 etc. have only "the coming one."

[g] The ungrammatical future after ἐάν, "if," is corrected in Θ Ψ $f^{1,13}$ etc. to the aorist subjunctive.

[h] A R W Θ Ψ $f^{1,13}$ etc. have a future perfect here, a tense not otherwise found in the NT, but which could just possibly be original in Luke.

Form/Structure/Setting

The royal motif of the section continues here, and Luke would have the present episode read closely with 19:11–28 (see there): this is no bid for present enthronement in Jerusalem. Luke has positioned the materials of vv 41–44 in order to enhance the parallelism between vv 11–28 and vv 29–44 (vv 29–44 are, at least for certain purposes, properly one unit for Luke; he does, however, provide some measure of separation by means of the renewed use of ἐγγίζειν, "to draw near"; and vv 41–44 have, in any case, been separated here for convenience of consideration).

Luke now returns again to the Markan sequence for what, in Mark, comes after the healing of the blind man (Mark 10:46–52; Luke 18:35–43). For the main narrative there is no sufficient reason for thinking that Luke had access to anything other than his Markan source (but John 12:12–15 may well reflect an independent version of this tradition). For vv 39–40, however, Luke does seem to have been able to draw on a separate tradition, one which in a quite different form stands behind Matt 21:14–16. This tradition will have had no original unity with the main episode here, but has been placed here by Luke, at least in part, to enhance the parallelism between 19:11–28 and 29–44.

The basic historicity of the narrative has received severe challenge, most consistently in connection with the fetching of the donkey, but also in connection with the other elements of the account. In a narrative in which biblical allusion plays such a central role, fundamental historicity is that much more difficult to assess. "The Lord has need of it" seems to be more a formal representation of the comprehensive authority of Jesus than an identifiable aspect of the reporting of an actual episode (but his historical ministry was marked by just such a distinctive authority). The tethered state of the donkey, while natural enough in itself, is spoken of for the sake of the link with Gen 49:11. Jesus' apparent knowledge of remote circumstances may well be a genuine reminiscence of the way in which he was experienced as mysteriously other. The account as we now have it, of the enthusiastic affirmation in word and action as Jesus headed towards Jerusalem on the donkey, is heavily marked by a messianic understanding/application of Zech 9:9 and Ps 118(117):26, and allusion to 2 Kgs 9:13. In the search for a historical core behind the narrator's own interpretation, how are we to distinguish the intention of Jesus from the perception of the enthusiasts and, then, what may be a general enthusiastic endorsement of Jesus from an awareness on the part of those involved that they are taking part in the affirmation of a claim to royal identity being made by Jesus?

John may not be too far wrong with his: "His disciples did not understand this at first" (12:16). I have defended the essential historicity of the Petrine confession at 9:18–20, and despite Catchpole's recent skepticism ("The 'triumphal' entry," 328–30) will in chap. 23 defend the historicity of the Gospel view that Jesus died as a messianic pretender. Against this background, if Jesus, who for all his ministry had walked to his destinations, had made a fuss about getting a donkey to ride the last couple of miles into Jerusalem, at a time when he had been speaking in a way that had caused his disciples to believe that his ministry was headed for some kind of crisis or denouement, then with, or perhaps even without, reference to Zech 9:9, there might be good reason to take this as some kind of prophetic symbolic action designed to assert a fundamental orientation of his ministry: whatever his connection with Jewish messianic expectations might have been, it was not such as would contemplate a coming to power through the violence of a coup (see at 19:11–27 on the violent coming to power of Herod, and to a lesser extent Archelaus). It may be that the enigmatic riding on a donkey on the approach to Jerusalem has a historical basis that can be more confidently asserted than the accompanying affirmation. However, there is no sufficient reason for not accepting the latter as well, as long as its scale and overt content are not taken to be such as would attract Roman attention, and so long as it is seen as a celebration on the part of accompanying sympathizers and not as a welcome by the inhabitants of the city (on this last point see Mariadasan, *Triomphe messianique*).

Catchpole ("The 'triumphal' entry," 319–21) offers an attractive case for correlating the entry with a well-known ancient pattern involving what he calls a "celebratory entry to a city by a hero figure who has previously achieved his triumph" (319). Catchpole points to accounts of the welcome given to a whole series of rulers and military commanders as they enter Jerusalem and other cities after some decisive victory. While not wanting to deny some influence from this pattern (this pattern, which frequently involves the victorious figure going to the temple to worship or even to put things to rights there, may have something to do with the way that, in Luke, the goal of Jesus' entry is the temple and not the city as such), I would want to stress the way in which the Markan account is oriented to what is coming rather than to what has already been achieved (Luke has a more significant orientation back to what has been achieved, but even here, not in a way that displaces the forward-looking orientation). In any case it is quite clear from the series of distinctive features in the narrative that the account has not been simply generated out of the pattern.

Comment

A rich vein of biblical allusion here celebrates the royal identity of Jesus and the sense that something decisive in relation to this identity is about to transpire in Jerusalem. At the same time, the story stresses the distance between this royal figure and other competitors for royal dignity and power. The text looks back on the cumulative achievement of Jesus' ministry and forward to his translation into the heavenly sphere.

29 Luke has already used Mark's εἰς Ἱεροσόλυμα, "to Jerusalem," in v 28. For Mark's ὅτε, "when," with the present verb, Luke substitutes ἐγένετο ὡς, "it happened when/as," with the aorist (ἐγένετο ὡς is not infrequent in the LXX, and it may be considered here as Lukan imitation of Septuagintal style; since, however, the only other uses of this construction in the NT [1:23, 41; 2:15] may reflect a Semitic source, the use here has been appealed to as reflecting a second Lukan source). Luke makes it clear that Ἐλαιῶν, "Of Olives," is a name and not a description by adding τὸ καλούμενον, "called" (cf. 6:15; 7:11; 9:10; etc.). Mark's historic present for "sent" (lit. "sends") also becomes for Luke an aorist.

ἤγγισεν, "he drew near," involves a Greek root that Luke uses throughout this section (18:35; 19:11, 37, 41) to highlight the thread of geographical procession. The location of Bethphage is uncertain, though it must have been close enough to Bethany for the villages to be naturally paired. Its name is normally taken as a transliteration of an Aramaic phrase meaning "house of unripe figs," which is then explained in terms of a species of fig that though edible never seems to ripen properly. Bethany is to be located about two miles east of Jerusalem, on the eastern slopes of the Mount of Olives. The name is again Aramaic, but an etymological sense "house of dates" (Marshall, 712) is likely to be based on the Gospel pairing of the two names; "House of (H)ananiah" is more likely (cf. Fitzmyer, 1248). The Mount of Olives is the central of three main summits of a range rising from the Kidron valley, east of the city and running north-south. Jesus is still on the opposite side of the mountain from Jerusalem. While it is not impossible that the Mount of Olives at this point in Mark has a symbolic significance (in 13:3 it does seem to have a symbolic significance, where Ezek 11:23 appears to be echoed), there is no basis for reading Luke in this way (see Nolland, "Luke's Readers," 129–30). "Two disciples" of the Baptist are involved at 7:19 (and see 22:8; cf. Mark 14:13; Luke 10:1). Given the mysterious complexity of the arrangements for finding and fetching the donkey, the number may be related to the theme of legal adequacy for witness (cf. at 7:18).

30 Luke makes a series of minor editorial adjustments to the Markan text here, of which the most notable are the replacement of several of the verbs with participles; the omission of one of Mark's uses of "immediately"; the better choice of ἀγάγετε, "bring/lead," over Mark's φέρετε, "carry/bring," for the leading of an animal; and the touch of elegance gained by Luke's ἐν ᾗ (lit. "in which") for a Markan paratactic καί, "and" (Luke in this way creates a kind of parallelism with the coming ἐφ᾽ ὅν, "upon which"). One minor piece of artistry worth noting is the chiastic parallelism created in the Lukan ordering of εὑρήσετε πῶλον δεδεμένον, "you will find a donkey tethered," and λύσαντες αὐτὸν ἀγάγετε, untie and bring it." The Markan text leaves unclear which of the two villages is intended, and Luke does not clarify (Matthew solves the problem by only mentioning Bethphage in this episode).

πῶλον is capable of a range of meanings, but despite Bauer (*JBL* 72 [1953] 220–29), it will mean "donkey" here (as in LXX) and not "horse" (as would be more natural in secular Greek of the period; cf. Michel, *NTS* 6 [1959–60] 81–82; id., *TDNT* 6:959–61; Kuhn, *ZNW* 50 [1959] 82–91). Jesus demonstrates an unexplained awareness of (*i*) the location of the beast; (*ii*) its tethered state; (*iii*) the fact that it has never been ridden; and he has the perception to provide, as well, (*iv*) a pattern of words that will ensure the release of the animal by its owners (v 31). While this is of a piece with the Lukan portrayal of Jesus' uncanny awareness of what goes on in other people's minds (see at 4:23; for Mark, prior arrangement could be the preferred explanation [cf. 14:13–15, which Luke reproduces in 22:10–12], but this seems less likely for Luke, and is not certain for Mark), more is surely involved here, especially when the anticipated events are substantiated in vv 32–35. Why the extended treatment? Despite the very limited basis of agreement, only an echo of Gen 49:11 can, to my mind, account for the generosity of this narrative investment. This likelihood is strengthened if (*i*) as maintained by a range of scholars, Zech 9:9 (see discussion at v 35 of the present episode's links with that verse) already involves allusion to Gen 49:11 (or if an exegetical tradition linking the two already existed in the first century); and if (*ii*) "upon which no person has ever sat" is to be traced back to the Septuagintal νέου, "new/young/fresh," used to describe the donkey of Zech 9:9. If there is such a link with Gen 49:11, what significance will it have? There is a dramatic contrast between the royal figure of Gen 49:11–12, who in the best traditions of royal excess and self-indulgence, tethers his own beast to the vine in order to satiate himself on the richness of wine and milk, and the figure (no less royal) in Luke of one who must borrow a donkey in order to stage his royal entry into Jerusalem (Luke will drop the Markan assurance that the donkey will be returned at once), and who does so with full anticipation of rejection and execution. If this contrast is intended, then the humility motif of Zech 9:9, which lacks explicit expression in either the Lukan or the Markan form, is nonetheless likely to be in view (at least in Mark, and probably also in Luke who would have been likely to abbreviate heavily if he had not seen the point). That the donkey had not been used as a mount is of a piece with the use of garments in lieu of trappings in v 36 (cf. Catchpole, "The 'triumphal' entry," 324). The thought here is probably to be related to the requirement that unused beasts be used for sacred purposes (that is beasts whose potential has not been already partly used up; Num 19:2; Deut 21:3; 1 Sam 6:7), and then in turn to the point made in 23:53 that it was a previously unused tomb in which the body of Jesus was placed. It befits his royal dignity that he should not have to share with previous users (the thought actually fits a little awkwardly with the fact that the donkey is only a temporarily borrowed one!). Are we to think of an unbroken mount over which Jesus exercises royal mastery, or should we be less literal and think of a beast trained to be a mount, but not yet put to use, or does the framing of such questions already take us outside the intent of the narrative?

31 Luke makes a series of stylistic alterations to Mark's wording here and drops the Markan clause about the prompt return of the donkey. Though found persuasive by several, we should probably not follow Derrett (*NovT* 13 [1971] 241–58) in appealing here to a (royal) right of impressment for which this statement of need would constitute sufficient justification. Authority is rightly discerned, but this authority is the unique christologically determined authority of Jesus, not the culturally determined authority of a class of persons in society. Nor, despite its fit with the allusion to Gen 49:11 supported above, should the Markan text here (and still less the Lukan text) be read as "his lord/master has need of it." To Luke and to his readers "the Lord" here is the "Lord" of the full Christian affirmation (cf. at 7:13), though in Luke's story line, the terminology need mean no more than "the master" (of the disciples), whose authority, nonetheless, comes with his disciples, who speak the words that have been given to them by their master.

32 Both Matthew and Luke feel the need to specify the subject here. Luke's οἱ ἀπεσταλμένοι, "the ones sent," may be chosen because it is cognate with "apostle," and here these disciples will act as Jesus' authorized delegates (see at 6:12–16). Luke brings "just as he had said" forward from its position in Mark 11:6 and applies it, not to the repetition of Jesus' words, but to finding things just as Jesus had forecast (cf. 22:13 par. Mark 14:16). This places additional emphasis on the foreknowlege of Jesus.

33 Luke continues his pattern of purely stylistic improvement here, but also makes one significant change: Mark's "bystanders" become οἱ κύριοι αὐτοῦ (lit. "his masters/lords"). Luke could intend the phrase to mean those who had charge of the beast, but he probably thinks of owners (Buth [*JBL* 104 (1985) 680–85] offers no adequate justification for reading the phrase in terms of a Hebrew idiom, and therefore as singular). The shared ownership of a donkey has attracted comment as an unlikely state of affairs. The question is asked, just as anticipated, and (in v 34) the answer will be given exactly as coached.

34 Having used the "just as" method of reporting in v 32, Luke here spells out with repetition of Jesus' own words. The authority of these words is so decisive that he feels no need to include Mark's "and they let them [take the animal]."

35 Luke changes all Mark's verbs here (the first as in v 30; the second and third use more elegant language, though Luke may, for the third, be influenced by the Septuagintal language of 1 Kgs 1:33 [but Luke uses the verb also at 10:34 and Acts 23:24; the idiom involving the second verb is found in 2 Sam 20:12; 1 Kgs 19:19 (with the singular "garment" rather than Luke's "garments"), but there is no real reason for linking these texts]). Thus far the initiative has been with Jesus, but now it passes to the disciples (Luke's third verb change may be motivated in part by a desire to make this move more clear cut than the Markan text does). The garments on the donkey may well be in lieu of the missing standard trappings, but there is likely to be as well an allusion to the honoring as king of the newly anointed Jehu in 2 Kgs 9:13.

36 Luke uses a genitive absolute to provide a transitional expression: "as he went along" (Mark's "many" is lost in compensation, which leaves the Lukan text vague about who is engaged in these actions); with a change of tense he makes a continuous process out of the strewing of garments; and he deletes mention of the cutting of leafy branches for the same purpose. An extravagant expression of supreme honoring is clearly intended, but no close parallel has been cited.

37 The content of this verse is not paralleled in the Markan account (nor in Matthew or John). Does the verse betray Luke's access to a second source here? The distinctive use of ἐγγίζειν, "to draw near," with πρός, "to," + dative is the strongest element in the case for such a source. But since we have already noted Luke's use of this verb to mark progress throughout this section of the Gospel, it may be possible to treat this usage as a hybrid influenced by the source use with πρός + acc. in v 29, but taking on the dative that Luke normally uses after this verb. δυνάμεις for "might works" is also unusual for Luke (only a source use in 10:13). The clear links with the language of 2:14 in v 38 stand in support of the language here being a deliberate echo of that in 2:13, 20 (see further below).

The explosion of praise comes as Jesus approaches the crest of the mount, beyond which Jerusalem will come into view. Luke wants to depict a crowd action as in Mark, but for him only disciples are in a position to discern the significance of this entry to anything like the level of perception that would warrant the ecstatic praise and affirmation that he here reports. Besides, a general crowd response here would create confusion about the referent of 13:35b, by making it possible to think that what was anticipated there had now already arrived (cf. v 38 below). At this point of anticipation of the fateful arrival in Jerusalem, the praise concerning "the mighty works" represents a retrospective affirmation of the whole of Jesus' ministry, now drawing to a close (the "multitude" of the disciples will also represent symbolically the whole fruit of Jesus' disciple-making activity), but the praise may also reasonably be taken as indicating the view that these mighty works are a precursor of the messianic blessedness to come out of this fateful entry.

38 Luke dispenses with Mark's opening "hosanna" (he frequently dispenses with transliterated Semitic forms); he incorporates his own understanding of Mark's second "blessed" clause into the first with an added appositional "the king" (John also uses "the king," but the differences are striking and both text forms are natural developments of the Markan form); and for Mark's ὡσαννὰ ἐν τοῖς ὑψίστοις, "hosanna in the highest," Luke has ἐν οὐρανῷ εἰρήνη καὶ δόξα ἐν ὑψίστοις, "in heaven peace, and glory in [the] highest."

Without the intruded "the king," "blessed is he who comes in the name of the Lord" is a quotation from Ps 118(117):26 (Mark's opening "hosanna" is a transliterated version of an Aramaic rendering [cf. Fitzmyer, 1250–51] of part of the previous verse). This section of the psalm is clearly a ritualized welcome for pilgrims arriving in Jerusalem to worship at the temple. It is known to have been used in the great pilgrim feasts (Passover, Tabernacles, and perhaps even Pentecost and Dedication). As "the coming one" Jesus is much more than another pilgrim (cf. at 7:19), and Luke makes this quite explicit with his intrusion of "the king." Despite the word order, it will be the coming that is in the name of the Lord. Luke has not previously used "king" of Jesus, though in this section Jesus is consistently a royal figure. The term becomes important in chap. 23. Jesus is now on his way to royal rule, but only in the terms that 19:11–28 has defined this.

Luke's ἐν οὐρανῷ εἰρήνη καὶ δόξα ἐν ὑψίστοις, "in heaven peace, and glory in [the] highest," has an evident relationship to 2:14: δόξα ἐν ὑψίστοις θεῷ καὶ ἐπὶ γῆς εἰρήνη . . . , "glory in [the] highest to God, and on earth peace. . . ." Baarlink (*ZNW* 76 [1985] 170–86) has emphasized this link and understood it in terms of the removal to heaven, and so from availability to the Jewish leaders in their hostility to Jesus, of the peace that came to the earth with Jesus. But, despite the protest of the Pharisees in vv 39–40, this is hardly a natural reading of the text in its immediate context: the tone is celebratory, not threatening. But it is true that what is being celebrated is oriented to heaven and not to the earth. Though my suggestion does not involve the most natural of meanings for εἰρήνη, "peace," I rather think that Luke has in mind what is about to be achieved in heaven by means of Jesus' exaltation through death to the right hand of God: the multitude of the angels had celebrated (2:13–14) what is achieved on the earth in the birth of Jesus; the multitude of the disciples now celebrate what is achieved in heaven by Jesus' journey through death to exaltation. In both cases "there is glory [for God] in highest heaven." In the unfolding of God's saving intervention, peace has come (or is about to) on earth and in heaven. The NT texts with the closest links are Col 1:20; Rev 12:10. The alternative is to take "peace in heaven" as analogous to "treasure in heaven," but this does no real justice to the parallel with 2:14.

39 That Luke has a source for vv 39–40 is made likely by the evident link with Matt 21:14–16, but given the total failure of shared language and the very limited extent of shared content, the Evangelists will hardly have used a shared source here. It remains unclear what of the verses is traditional and what redactional. Pharisees have been regular antagonists for Jesus in Luke, but they have not been mentioned as present since 17:20 (but see 18:9; cf. v 10). This will be their final appearance, and so their protest here should be taken to encapsulate all that has gone on before. They cannot see what God is doing in Jesus; they see in what he does only the fracturing of their piety and therefore the insulting of God. A Pharisee addresses Jesus as "teacher" in 7:40 (see there). Pharisaic opposition to Jesus' royal pretensions here parallels the role of the fellow citizens in 19:14.

40 In the biblical tradition there is a strong sense that nature participates in the witness and celebration of what God is doing (the verbally closest parallel is actually Hab 2:11 where the stones of the walls of the house and its beams cry out in witness against the wickedness that has been perpetrated, but that is hardly what is happening here). The disciples are marking a moment of high destiny; if *their* marking of it were to be silenced, then the stony terrain around them would need to take their place.

Explanation

The present episode needs to be read closely with 19:11–28: Luke has gone to some pains to present them in parallel. The present royal arrival in Jerusalem is no bid for immediate enthronement there. The narrative here is built upon a basis of biblical allusion and quotation that point to the royal dignity of this arriving figure, but also to the gulf that separates him from the normal understanding of the exercise of the prerogatives of royal power.

The action begins about two miles from Jerusalem, when the pilgrim band was still out of sight of Jerusalem on the eastern slopes of the Mount of Olives. It will reach its climax as Jesus approaches the crest and the city comes into view.

It is unclear which of the villages Luke understands the disciples to have been sent to. Jesus' prior knowledge of what would be found there is clearly of great importance in the account. This is part of his mysterious otherness. It may be that the mention of the *two* disciples is precisely to indicate that the truth of this instance of Jesus' prescience can be legally assured, according to the OT requirements for legally valid witness.

What the disciples are told they will find (and do find) is a tethered donkey that has never been used as a mount. Several biblical allusions are involved here. The first is to Gen 49:11–12. But here more contrast than equation is involved. There is a dramatic contrast between the royal figure of Gen 49:11–12, who in the best traditions of royal excess and self-indulgence, tethers his own beast to the vine in order to satiate himself on the richness of wine and milk, and the figure (no less royal) in Luke of one who must borrow a donkey in order to stage his royal entry into Jerusalem, and who makes his entry with clear awareness of coming rejection and execution.

A second allusion is to Zech 9:9, an allusion pervasive in the narrative. The Greek translation of this verse speaks of a new or fresh donkey, and this is probably behind "on which no person has ever sat." We should see this statement in light of the OT requirement that what was given to God not be something that was already secondhand, and therefore partly used up (see Num 19:2; Deut 21:3; 1 Sam 6:7). A similar point will come in Luke 23:53. This is part of the affirmation of Jesus' royal dignity.

As the disciples carry out their task all goes as Jesus has said it would. Of particular note is the way in which his words, which have been shown again and again in the Gospel to be authoritative, are here shown to be no less so when they are spoken by those who have been sent as authorized delegates by Jesus. We have here something similar to the message of the mission charges (Luke 9:1–6; 10:1–16; and note esp. 10:17).

For the strewing of the garments and the putting of Jesus on the donkey, Luke probably thinks of two scenes in which OT figures prepare for a royal role: Solomon on David's donkey in 1 Kgs 1:33, and the newly anointed Jehu in 2 Kgs 9:13. Jesus is treated to an extravagant expression of supreme honoring.

As Jerusalem is about to come into view, there is an explosion of ecstatic praise to God for all that Jesus represents. The praise focuses on the mighty works of Jesus, and, coming here, it represents a retrospective affirmation of the whole of Jesus' ministry, now drawing to a close. But the link of the excitement to the appearance of Jerusalem suggests that these mighty works are also to be viewed as a precursor of the messianic blessedness that is expected to come out of this fateful entry.

V 38 uses some of the wording of Ps 118:26. The quotation is from what is clearly a ritualized welcome for pilgrims arriving in Jerusalem to worship at the temple. It is known to have been used in the great pilgrim feasts, but as "the coming one" of the psalm, Jesus is much more than another pilgrim (cf. at 7:19), and Luke makes this quite explicit with his intrusion of "the king" (which has no place in the wording of the psalm).

Beyond the quotation from Ps 118:26, the language of vv 37–38 involves allusion, not now to further biblical text, but to an earlier part of Luke's own text: chap. 2:13–14, 20. The intention of this link is disputed, but I think it is best understood as recognition of what is about to be achieved in heaven by means of Jesus' exaltation through death to the right hand of God: the multitude of the angels had celebrated (2:13–14) what is achieved on the earth in the birth of Jesus; the multitude of the disciples now celebrate what is to be achieved in heaven by Jesus' journey through death to exaltation.

As counterpart to the adoring praise of the disciples, we have the complaint of the Pharisees. They cannot see what God is doing in Jesus. Instead, they see only the fracturing of their piety and therefore the insulting of God. The respective roles of disciples and Pharisees provide parallels to those of the slaves and the fellow citizens of the preceding parable. To the Pharisees' complaint, Jesus replies that in such a high moment of destiny, if the disciples were silenced, then lifeless stones would take up the refrain: creation must in some shape or form bear its witness to such a momentous occasion.

Lamenting the Coming Fate of Jerusalem (19:41–44)

Bibliography

Dodd, C. H. "The Fall of Jerusalem and the 'Abomination of Desolation.'" *JRS* 37 (1947) 47–54; reprinted in *More New Testament Studies*. Grand Rapids, MI: Eerdmans, 1968. 69–83. **Dupont, J.** "Il n'en sera pas laissé pierre sur pierre (Marc 13,2; Luc 19,44)." *Bib* 52 (1971) 301–20. **Gaston, L.** *No Stone on Another: Studies in the Significance of the Fall of Jerusalem in the Synoptic Gospels.* NovTSup 23. Leiden: Brill, 1970. 12, 61, 244, 355–60. **Gnilka, J.** *Die Verstockung Israel: Isaias 6,9–10 in der Theologie der Synoptiker.* SANT 3. Munich: Kösel, 1961. 137–40. **Reicke, B.** "Synoptic Prophecies on the Destruction of Jerusalem." In *Studies in New Testament and Early Christian Literature.* FS A. P. Wikgren, ed. D. E. Aune. NovTSup 33. Leiden: Brill, 1972. 121–34. **Robinson, W. C., Jr.** *Der Weg des Herrn.* 50–53, 55–56. **Schramm, T.** *Markus-Stoff.* 146–47. **Tiede, D. L.** "Weeping for Jerusalem." In *Prophecy and History.* 65–96, 143–48. **Uhsadel, W.** "Predigt zum Gedächtnistage der Zerstörung Jerusalems." In *Abraham unser Vater: Juden und Christen im Gespräch über die Bibel.* FS O. Michel, ed. O. Betz et al. Leiden: Brill, 1963. 459–66.

Translation

[41]As he drew near and saw the city, he wept over it [42]saying, "Would that [a] you also had recognized on this day what concerns peace; but now this is hidden from your eyes. [43]For days will come upon you when[b] they will set up [c] siege mounds against you, and

encircle you, and press you on every side; [44] *and they will throw down both you and the children within you, and no stone in you will be left upon another, because you did not recognize the time of your visitation.*"

Notes

[a] Expressed with the prodosis of a condition contrary to fact without following apodosis.
[b] Gr. καί (lit. "and").
[c] περιβαλοῦσιν, "encircle with," is read by A B C² W f^{1,13} 892 1006 etc. The reading may result from a desire to bring the text more into line with what actually happened in the siege of Jerusalem.

Form/Structure/Setting

The increasing proximity of Jerusalem, which is an organizing principle of this section (18:35–19:46), is marked here by the coming into sight of the city. However, no use of the royal motif, so notable in the section, is directly made in this unit. In the parallelism that Luke has created between 19:11–28 and 29–44 (see there), there is a correspondence between the coming fate of Jerusalem lamented here and the fate of the unwilling subjects of v 27.

Luke alone has this episode. Vv 41–42 seem to be largely a setting provided by Luke (though the mention of weeping may have a traditional basis). The final clause of v 44, while it may have some basis in tradition (in the judgment statement in 10:13 there is a reason given for the judgment), is to be identified in its present form as Lukan. For the main part of the material (vv 43–44ab) Luke does, however, seem clearly to be dependent on a source. (See *Comment* below for details.) The imagery of no stone left upon another is also to be found in Mark 13:2 (par. Luke 21:6), but Luke will not have drawn it from there for its present use (see esp. Dupont, *Bib* 52 [1971] 313–20). Rather it is likely that Mark 13:2 has been drawn from a version of the tradition preserved here in Luke (and not from a version of Mark 14:58 as has at times been maintained [for this discussion see Dupont, 301–20]).

The material here takes its place with a number of other anticipations in the Jesus tradition of a coming reckoning for Jerusalem (13:34–35; chap. 21; cf. 11:49–50; 17:22–37; Mark 14:58; etc.). As is typical in prophetic words, it takes up the language of God's past actions to speak of what is anticipated, and can hardly be claimed to be a description after the event of the actual destruction of Jerusalem (see *Comment* below for details; the classic protest against reading the words here and in chap. 21 as a description after the event remains that of Dodd, "The Fall of Jerusalem," 69–83). As a historical prediction what we have here is no less plausible than that made by the Qumran community about the fall of the corrupt regime in Jerusalem (1QpHab 9:5–7). Furthermore, its credentals must be considered to be of a higher order than those of "a voice against Jerusalem and its sanctuary" reported by Josephus to have been uttered repeatedly by another Jesus in the years leading up to the destruction of the city (*War* 6.300–309).

Comment

The coming of the city into sight draws from Jesus, as a weeping Jeremiah, an announcement of its pending doom as a city that has failed to recognize in the ministry of Jesus the visitation of God.

41 This verse may be entirely a Lukan contribution (for ὡς ἤγγισεν, "as he drew near," cf. v 29; for ἔκλαυσεν ἐπ᾽, "he wept over," cf. 23:28 [the only other place in the NT where this idiom occurs; but there it is traditional, which could suggest that the idiom here is traditional as well]; Luke is responsible for ἰδών, "seeing," at least in 5:12; 18:43). Jesus' progress to the city takes yet another step. Jesus' lamentation is especially reminiscent of that of Jeremiah (Jer 9:1; 13:17; 14:17), but Tiede ("Weeping for Jerusalem," 78) catches well the wider canvas: "It is finally the sympathy of the suffering prophet, of Deuteronomy's Moses, of Jeremiah, Isaiah, and Hosea, caught up in the rage, anguish, frustration, and sorrow of God for Israel that constitutes the pathos of the story."

42 Luke may still be formulating here his setting for the verses to come (the failure to recognize recurs in v 44; τὰ πρὸς εἰρήνην, "what concerns peace," may be taken up from v 38; this possibility finds support from the καὶ σύ, "also you," if this is read in connection with the perceptiveness in vv 37–38, by contrast, of the "multitude of the disciples"; this in turn suggests that "in this day" is a reference to the day in which the "multitude of the disciples" make their acclamation and/ or the day of Jesus' royal approach to Jerusalem; νῦν, "now," is one of Luke's preferred words; ἐκρύβη ἀπὸ ὀφθαλμῶν σου, "they are hidden from your eyes," echoes language elements of 18:34 and 24:16). The city collectively is in the same place as the Pharisees of v 39. A motif of general inability to understand has been met already at 8:10 (cf. v 12 and 13:33; Acts 28:26–27). This becomes in Luke 23:34; Acts 3:17; 13:27; 17:30 a culpable but forgivable ignorance. Luke uses language of blindness similarly in connection with disciples (9:45; 18:34; 24:16), but their blindness is only a limited blindness. In both cases it may be best in the Lukan frame to attribute this blindness to Satan (see at 9:45). If the reference to peace is Lukan, and not traditional, then it is hardly likely that there is a play here on the name Jerusalem (as, e.g., Fitzmyer, 1256–57).

43 Now, except for the use of συνέχειν, "to press," the language takes on a non-Lukan cast (the paratactic construction is un-Lukan; ἥξουσιν ἡμέραι is not Luke's idiom for "days will come" [see 5:35; 23:29; cf. Acts 2:20]; periods of time do not come *upon* people elsewhere in Luke-Acts; Luke's natural language for the Romans would not be "your enemies"; four of the key words are not found elsewhere in Luke-Acts [three not elsewhere in the NT]). παρεμβάλλειν means literally "to put in between" and so "to insert or interpose." It is used in the LXX in connection with attacks on cities (e.g., 2 Kgdms 12:28). χάραξ should mean a stake or a palisade, but may come to mean an earthen rampart set with palisades (as the Latin *vallum*). In the LXX the word is used to translate סֹלְלָה, *sōlĕlâ*, which, because of the verb always associated with it, which literally means "to pour out," must refer to a mound of earth (the same term is used to translate מֻצָּב, *muṣṣāb;* though this is clearly a military term, its precise sense is unknown). The mound is part of the equipment used in laying siege to a city. The four Roman earthwork embankments set against the walls of Jerusalem by Titus' army (see Josephus, *War* 5.466) could correspond to this, but do not really fit the use of παρεμβαλοῦσιν, and are not likely to be quite what is in view in the OT language reflected here. περικυκλοῦν is used in connection with the military encirclement of a city (this verb is found in 4 Kgdms 6:14). This could be for siege purposes or to cut off avenues of escape. Titus' army built an encircling wall around Jerusalem (Josephus, *War* 5.508). Only συνέχειν, "to press," is not used in the LXX in connection with the siege of a city (it is found in 1 Kgdms 23:8 in connection with the besieging of David by Saul), and this is the one clearly Lukan term in the description. Not in precise language, but as a whole description, what we find here has its closest parallels in Isa 29:3; Ezek 4:1–3.

44 The non-Lukan cast of the language continues here, except perhaps for the final clause. ἐδαφίζειν is used in the LXX normally of the throwing down to the ground of women and children (thought of as destroying them) in the context of the sacking of a city. It is used in Ezek 31:12 (in connection with the imagery of the cutting down of a tree) of the bringing down of a city, and in Isa 3:26 of the bringing down of Zion. The shared fate of city and children comes closest to being reflected by Nah 3:10; Hos 14:1(ET 13:16). The cumulative effect of the evocation in vv 43–44 of the OT descriptions of military conquest is to call to mind strongly the role of these conquests as judgments of God upon the sin of his people (and/or on the sin of their oppressors, but here the former). The striking imagery of no stone upon another is clearly a development of the idea of the throwing down of a city. It is not found in the OT (the imagery in 2 Sam 17:13 is closest, but there the imagery is of the *dispersal* of the stones of a city; Hag 2:15 uses the imagery of stone upon stone in connection with building). Dupont (*Bib* 52 [1971] 310–20) has argued (to my mind convincingly) that the use of this imagery in Mark 13:2 (par. Luke 21:6) is based on a use of the same dominical tradition as reflected here in Luke. Many centuries earlier Micah had anticipated a similar degree of destruction for Jerusalem (3:12), which did not in fact transpire (Jer 26:18–19). In the Jewish war of A.D. 70, while the walls of Jerusalem were for the most part leveled, some of the towers and at least one section of the wall were left standing (Josephus, *War* 7.1–4).

In the final clause of the verse, ἀνθ' ὧν is likely to be Lukan (cf. at 12:3). The Lukan concern with the ignorance motif has been explored at v 42 above. ἐπισκοπή is used in the NT with the sense "visitation" only here and in 1 Pet 2:12, but Luke has the cognate verb for seven of its ten occurrences in the NT (in one of Luke's uses the sense is different). The time of visitation by God is not the entry to Jerusalem as such, but the whole of the ministry of Jesus, now coming to its end. τὸν καιρὸν τῆς ἐπισκοπῆς σου, "the time of your visitation," may reflect the language of Jer 6:15(LXX): ἐν καιρῷ ἐπισκοπῆς αὐτῶν, "in the time of their visitation," which anticipates the same prospect of destruction for the city, but, by contrast with Luke, sees the visitation of God as itself destructive. See further at chap. 21 for how Luke understands this coming judgment upon Jerusalem.

Explanation

Jesus continues to get closer to Jerusalem. The sight of the city draws from him, as a weeping Jeremiah-like figure, a prophetic announcement of the coming destruction of the city, a fate that awaits it precisely because it has failed to see in the ministry of Jesus the visitation of God that was taking place.

The multitude of the disciples had recognized the connection between Jesus and what makes for peace, but the city of Jerusalem, like the Pharisees of v 39, had not. The populace had been subjected to a blinding that is probably to be understood as satanic. Jesus laments their situation, because he sees, prophetically, the future outcome of it.

The description of what awaits the city is a pastiche of OT texts that describe the taking in siege of cities, and especially of Jerusalem. Not in exact language, but as a whole description, what we find here has its closest parallels in Isa 29:3; Ezek 4:1–3. What Jesus anticipates is a replay of the experience of the Babylonian period. Since in precise detail what actually happened when Jerusalem met its doom in A.D. 70 does not agree with this description, we can be reasonably confident that this is no prophecy after the event. In any case this is not the only evidence that Jesus foretold the destruction of Jerusalem.

The judgment comes because the city had not recognized and responded to the visitation of God occurring in and through the ministry of Jesus. But of course this is no more a writing off of the Jews than the Babylonian exile had been centuries before. Though in individual cases judgment may leave no place for restoration, it is, throughout the OT, primarily a matter of chastisement and purgation for the historic People of God.

Symbolic Protest in the Temple (19:45–46)

Bibliography

Barrett, C. K. "The House of Prayer and the Den of Thieves." In *Jesus und Paulus.* FS W. G. Kümmel, ed. E. E. Ellis and E. Grässer. Göttingen: Vandenhoeck & Ruprecht, 1975. 13–20. **Bauckham, R. J.** "Jesus' Demonstration in the Temple." In *Law and Religion: Essays on the Place of the Law in Israel and Early Christianity,* ed. B. Lindars. Cambridge: Clarke, 1988. 72–89, 171–76. **Brandon, S. G. F.** *Jesus and the Zealots: A Study of the Political Factor in Primitive Christianity.* Manchester: University Press, 1967. 255–57, 330–40. **Braun, F.-M.** "L'Expulsion des vendeurs du Temple (Mt., xxi,12–17,23–27; Mc., xi,15–19,27–33; Lc., xix,45–xx,8; Jo., ii,13–22)." *RB* 38 (1929) 178–200. **Buchanan, G. W.** "Symbolic Money-changers in the Temple?" *NTS* 37 (1991) 280–90. **Buse, I.** "The Cleansing of the Temple in the Synoptics and in John." *ExpTim* 70 (1958–59) 22–24. **Bussche, H. van den.** "Le signe du Temple (Jean 2, 13–22)." *BVC* 20 (1957–58) 92–100. **Caldecott, A.** "The Significance of the 'Cleansing' of the Temple.'" *JTS* 24 (1923) 382–86. **Carmichael, J.** "Jésus-Christ et le Temple." *NRF* 12 (1964) 276–95. **Catchpole, D. R.** "The 'triumphal' entry." In *Jesus and the Politics of His Day,* ed. E. Bammel and C. F. D. Moule. 319–34, esp. 330–34. **Cooke, F. A.** "The Cleansing of the Temple." *ExpTim* 63 (1951–52) 321–22. **Dawsey, J. M.** "Confrontation in the Temple: Luke 19.45–20.47." *PRS* 11 (1984) 153–65. ———. "The Origin of Luke's Positive Perception of the Temple." *PRS* 18 (1991) 5–22. ———. "Was Ur-Markus the Source for Lk 19:45–20:47?" *MelT* 42 (1991) 95–110. **Derrett, J. D. M.** "The Zeal of the House and the Cleansing of the Temple." *DR* 95 (1977) 79–94. **Doeve, J. W.** "Purification du Temple et dessèchement du figuier." *NTS* 1 (1954–55) 297–308. **Eppstein, V.** "The Historicity of the Gospel Account of the Cleansing of the Temple." *ZNW* 55 (1964) 42–58. **Evans, C. A.** "Jesus' Action in the Temple and Evidence of Corruption in the First-Century Temple." In *SBL 1989 Seminar Papers,* ed. D. J. Lull. Atlanta, GA: Scholars, 1989. 522–39. ———. "Jesus' Action in the Temple: Cleansing or Portent of Destruction?" *CBQ* 51 (1989) 237–70. **Fredriksen, P.** "Jesus and the Temple, Mark and the War." In *SBL 1990 Seminar Papers,* ed. D. J. Lull. Atlanta, GA: Scholars, 1990. 293–310. **Haenchen, E.** *Der*

Weg Jesu. 382–89. **Hahn, F.** *Titles.* 155–57. **Hamilton, N. Q.** "Temple Cleansing and Temple Bank." *JBL* 83 (1964) 365–72. **Harvey, A. E.** *Jesus and the Constraints of History.* 129–34. **Hiers, R. H.** "Purification of the Temple: Preparation for the Kingdom of God." *JBL* 90 (1971) 82–90. **Jeremias, J.** "Zwei Miszellen: 1. Antik-jüdische Münzdeutungen; 2. Zur Geschichtlichkeit der Tempelreinigung." *NTS* 23 (1976–77) 177–80, esp. 179–80. **Léon-Dufour, X.** "Le signe du Temple selon saint Jean." *RSR* 39 (1951) 155–75. **Lightfoot, R. H.** "Unsolved New Testament Problems—The Cleansing of the Temple in St John's Gospel." *ExpTim* 60 (1948–49) 64–68. **Lohmyer, E.** "Die Reinigung des Tempels." *TBl* 20 (1941) 257–64. **Manson, T. W.** "The Cleansing of the Temple." *BJRL* 33 (1950–51) 271–82. **Matson, M. A.** "The Contribution to the Temple Cleansing by the Fourth Gospel." In *SBL 1992 Seminar Papers,* ed. E. H. Lovering, Jr. 489–506. **Mendner, S.** "Die Tempelreinigung." *ZNW* 47 (1956) 93–112. **Miller, R. J.** "The (A) Historicity of Jesus' Temple Demonstration: A Test Case in Methodology." In *SBL 1991 Seminar Papers,* ed. E. H. Lovering, Jr. 235–52. **Neusner, J.** "Money-changers in the Temple: The Mishnah's Explanation." *NTS* 35 (1989) 287–90. **Pesch, R.** "Der Anspruch Jesu." *Orientierung* 35 (1971) 53–56. **Richardson, P.** "Why Turn the Tables? Jesus' Protest in the Temple Precincts." In *SBL 1992 Seminar Papers,* ed. E. H. Lovering, Jr. 507–23. **Roloff, J.** *Das Kerygma.* 89–110. **Roth, C.** "The Cleansing of the Temple and Zechariah xiv 21." *NovT* 4 (1960) 174–81. **Runnalls, D.** "The King as Temple Builder: A Messianic Typology." In *Spirit within Structure.* FS G. Johnston, ed. E. J. Furcha. Allison Park, Pa.: Pickwick, 1983. 15–37. **Salin, E.** "Jesus und die Wechsler." Appendix in A. Ben-David, *Jerusalem und Tyros: Ein Beitrag zur palästinensischen Münz-und Wirtschaftgeschichte (126 a.C.–57 p.C.).* Kleine Schriften zur Wirtschaftsgeschichte. Basel/Tübingen: Kyklos/Mohr-Siebeck, 1969. 49–55. **Sanders, E. P.** *Jesus and Judaism.* London: SCM, 1985. 61–76, 363–69. **Schnider, F.,** and **Stenger, W.** *Johannes und die Synoptiker: Vergleich ihrer Parallelen.* Biblische Handbibliothek 9. Munich: Kösel, 1971. 26–53. **Schramm, T.** *Markus-Stoff.* 149. **Söding, T.** "Die Tempelaktion Jesu: Redaktionskritik—Überlieferungsgeschichte—historische Rückfrage (Mk 1,15–19; Mt 21,12–17; Lk 19,45–48; Joh 2,12–22)." *TTZ* 101 (1992) 36–64. **Trautmann, M.** *Zeichenhafte Handlungen Jesu: Ein Beitrag zur Frage nach dem geschichtlichen Jesus.* FB 37. Würzburg: Echter, 1980. 96–103. **Trocmé, E.** "Jésus-Christ et le Temple: éloge d'un naif." *RHPR* 44 (1964) 245–51. ———. "L'Expulsion des marchants du Temple." *NTS* 15 (1968–69) 1–22. **Wagner, G.** "The Cleansing of the Temple." In *Survey Bulletin.* Rüschlikon: Baptist Theological Seminary, 1967. 30–42.

Translation

[45] *Having entered the temple, he began to expel those who were selling,* [46] *saying to them, "It has been written, 'My house shall be a house of prayer,' but you have made it 'a den of robbers.'"*

Notes

While the textual witness offers various accommodations to the Markan text here, none of them is likely to be original.

Form/Structure/Setting

The final unit of the section 18:35–19:46 takes us into Jerusalem, to the temple, where Jesus mounts a symbolic protest against aspects of its present use, prior to making the temple precincts the regular setting for his final period of ministry, in Jerusalem (the following section, 19:47–21:38). That the goal of the extended approach is the temple and not the city as such may have something to do with a pattern for arrival in cities of royal figures or military commanders that has been identified by Catchpole (see *Form/Structure/Setting* at 19:29–40). The temple focus of the final chapters of Luke's Gospel, which is here anticipated, corresponds to the temple focus of the opening chapters.

After 19:41–44, Luke returns to his Markan source (11:15–17). However, he strips out the setting in the account of the cursing of the fig that Mark has provided for the temple incident (11:11–14, 20–25), and he makes no use here of the Markan report of the response of the chief priests and scribes (11:18–19). Luke severely abbreviates in a way that draws the emphasis strongly onto the biblical citations in 19:46. Though there are some agreements in omission between Luke's version and the account in Matt 21:10–13, these do not warrant the assumption of a second source. The account in John 2:13–17 is most likely to be independent of that in the synoptic Gospels. It locates the incident in the temple in the early stages of the ministry of Jesus.

There is a general scholarly consensus that the texts used in Mark 11:17 are not likely to be an original part of the episode. They may be from a separate tradition with its own claim to being traceable back to the historical Jesus, as part of his prophetic critique of his own generation, or (perhaps more likely) they may represent a stage in the early church's use and interpretation of the account of the disturbance created by Jesus in the temple.

The historicity of the core account has occasionally been questioned, but the very difficulties of the account tell strongly in its favor; its historicity is generally recognized even by those who have quite a minimalizing approach. Much more difficult is the question of what the event represented in the mind of Jesus and/ or of those who witnessed it.

Among the many ways in which the temple demonstration has been understood, the following suggestions may be taken as representative: (*i*) trade in the temple was a desecration of its spiritual purpose, so Jesus, with or without help from others, shut down the trade in sacrificial animals and the provision for changing other currencies into the Tyrian coinage, which alone was accepted for payment of the temple tax; (*ii*) as above, but with a focus on the market's interference with the use of the outer temple as a place where Gentiles might worship God; (*iii*) the trade and money exchange exploited the people by making excessive charges for the services provided, so Jesus intervened; (*iv*) the priestly class who were responsible for the presence of the market in the temple were abusing their spiritual calling by being involved in business in this way; (*v*) Jesus was caught up in a conflict between the Sanhedrin and the High Priest Caiaphas in A.D. 30, during which Caiaphas permitted markets in the temple as punitive competition to those controlled by the Sanhedrin on the Mount of Olives (Eppstein, *ZNW* 55 [1964] 42–58); (*vi*) Jesus stopped the sale of temple sacrifices because, for him, worship consisted not in the externals of animal sacrifice but in a purely inward and spiritual worship; (*vii*) the tradition comes not in the life of Jesus but in early church controversy with Judaism, as an expression of early church opposition to the temple cultus; (*viii*) however the abuse in the temple is to be understood, (*a*) Jesus, in conscious fulfillment of Mal 3:1–2, is coming as Lord to his temple to purge like a refiner's fire (notably in Luke, Jesus at this point "takes possession" of the temple as the "schoolroom" [perhaps royal chapel] where he teaches); or (*b*) he contributes to the meeting of the conditions for the coming of the kingdom of God by seeing to it that there should "no longer be a trader in the house of the Lord" (Zech 14:21 [the same verse has also been taken as the basis for the Markan point about not carrying a vessel through the temple]); or (*c*) he acts as a royal figure in line with the place that temple cleansing had in connection with the restoration of the Jewish kingdom in earlier phases of the Jewish kingdom (Hezekiah, Josiah, Judas Maccabee); or (*d*) he aligns himself with a tradition of radical action through zeal for the law, which demonstrated his alignment with the ideology of the zealot freedom fighters, or, more likely, caused people, mistakenly, to draw such a link; or (*e*) he was acting out the part of the Lord in Isa 59:14–20 who in anger brings his own right arm to bear to restore the situation (Derrett, *DR* 95 [1977] 79–94); (*ix*) Jesus' act is a piece of prophetic symbolism, intended (*a*) to bring about the repentance and return of Israel in the last days; or (*b*) to symbolize the destruction for which the temple was destined (as a preliminary to its eschatological restoration: the act would signal that "the end was at hand and that the temple would be destroyed, so that the new and perfect temple might arise" [Sanders, *Jesus*, 75]). Most interpreters join together features from more than one of the listed suggestions.

Given this incredible range of options, is there any possibility of knowing what Jesus intended in this episode in the temple? With any certainty it probably is not. But many of the proposals above have been effectively criticized and should be set aside, while aspects of others have commended themselves from a variety of angles. The following points can be made with some confidence: (*i*) whatever the action meant, it probably took place on a fairly modest scale (there was no police intervention), and should be seen as a symbolic action, rather than as a serious attempt to produce a permanent change in market arrangements; (*ii*) Jesus was involved in the disruption of the standing arrangements for temple worship, which, despite Eppstein, should probably be seen as longstanding arrangements and not as some recent innovation; (*iii*) while the disruption may have stemmed in part from a concern about those particular arrangements (as in Mark 11:17), it is even more likely to be intended as a rather general complaint that those who came to the temple were not offering acceptable worship to God in their lives at a more comprehensive level (cf. Jer 7:8–11; Mal 1:10); (*iv*) the symbolism involved is likely to have a connection with Jewish traditions of temple purification, or even of eschatological temple replacement, but probably without the precision that would enable a choice between these as alternatives (Sanders [*Jesus*, 73–75] is wrong to think that to have identified such an eschatological perspective obviates the need to identify a critical stance on the part of Jesus: all the relevant traditions relate the eschatological hoped-for change to a present situation of failure or limitation).

There is no satisfactory basis for seeking to make a choice between the Johannine dating early in the ministry and the Synoptic dating at its end. Indeed both of these datings might have more to do with the narrative structure of the respective Gospels than with historical memory.

Comment

Jesus mounts a symbolic protest against the commercial activity going on in the temple, which interfered with the proper use of the temple as a house of prayer and was itself being carried on in a corrupt manner.

45   The language of approach that has characterized this section now gives way to the language of arrival. Luke reproduces Markan wording here, but with severe abbreviation. Having spoken in v 41 of Jerusalem coming into sight, Luke feels no need for Mark's specific mention of arrival in the city. From the episode in the temple, Luke omits all mention of the purchasers, the sellers of doves, the overturning of the market furniture, and the interference with the carrying of vessels through the temple area. The use of ἤρξατο, "began," which Luke takes over from his Markan source, may signal the symbolic (token) nature of this expulsion of the temple hawkers. While in Mark the action is probably to be interpreted as symbolizing the coming destruction of the temple, in Luke it is difficult to find more than a protest and a token putting of things to rights, though that about which the Lukan Jesus protests makes its own small contribution to the state of affairs that led Jesus to the confident prediction of 21:5–6 (on the likely sense of the episode in the ministry of the historical Jesus see in *Form/Structure/Setting* above). Luke is concerned to minimize any sense in which Jesus might be seen as critical of the Jerusalem temple. It is as a royal figure making a regal entry into Jerusalem that the Lukan Jesus acts to purify the worship of the temple. Luke has little interest in elucidating in description the precise way in which the commercial activity that was going on in the temple posed a problem; the OT citations in v 46 will provide all the precision that interests him.

46   Luke's "saying" makes the present verse part of the interaction with the sellers rather than of the wider teaching activity that Mark's "and he was teaching and saying" suggests. Luke simplifies by not using the question form with which the Markan version begins, as well as by eliminating the Markan reference to πᾶσιν τοῖς ἔθνεσιν, "for all the nations" (Matthew does this as well). The latter, combined with his switch from Mark's κληθήσεται, "will be called," to καὶ ἔσται, "and [it] will be" (Mark has the LXX wording, which follows the MT closely), enables Luke to treat the quotation from Isa 56:7 as a legal stipulation, rather than as the prophetic word that it is in the text of Isaiah (in Mark this move from prophecy to legal statute has probably already begun, in that the use of the present temple is being criticized on the basis of the prophetic anticipation). In a word addressed to the sellers, the immediate contrast is between prayer and commerce (probably in the sense that the commerce distracts others from prayer, but perhaps also in the sense that the sellers engage in commerce rather than in prayer); but this immediate contrast becomes more pointed in the direction of corrupt commercial activity by means of the use of Jer 7:11 (apart from an aorist verb in place of a perfect, the Lukan and Markan wording agree). (So far as any information on the matter survives, there is every reason to believe that the sale of sacrificial animals was well regulated and not corrupt in any obvious manner.) The link with Jeremiah has already been noted at 19:41–44; the quotation of Jer 7:11 here provides a link with the sixth-century malfunction in the nation's temple-worship-life that was the setting for that prophet's announcement of the coming destruction of temple and city. The words in Jeremiah do not refer to activity in the temple as such, but to the lives of the people in general, who nonetheless make a pious show of things in the temple (this may still be true of the Markan use of the text).

Explanation

The goal of Jesus' extended "arrival" in Jerusalem is the temple, where he mounts a protest against the commercial activity going on there, the presence of which interfered with the proper use of the temple as a house of prayer, and which was in any case being carried on in a corrupt manner. In a symbolic manner he puts the problem to rights, and for the whole of the section to follow (19:47–21:38), he will make the temple precincts the setting for his own teaching ministry.

The original incident in the ministry of the historical Jesus is likely to have looked like a modest attempt to disrupt the standing arrangements for temple worship. In line with texts like Jer 7:8–11; Mal 1:10 it is best seen as making a rather general protest about the lives of the people who were coming to worship in the Jerusalem temple. The action probably had a symbolic connection with a whole stream of Jewish traditions about the end-time purification of the temple, or its final replacement by a new and better temple, with all the faults of the old and its worship put to rights.

In early Christian tradition the episode was interpreted in a number of different ways; Luke is content to provide a fairly simplified presentation of the significance of the episode. Luke's Jesus is far more straightforwardly in favor of the temple than was Mark's.

Teaching Daily in the Temple   (19:47–21:38)

Luke organizes his account of Jesus' daily teaching in the temple into two subsections: 19:47–21:4, which emphasizes the conflict and antagonism between Jesus and segments of the Jewish leadership in Jerusalem; and 21:5–38, which presents Jesus' vision of the unfolding future of turmoil, persecution, and acts of judgment, culminating in the coming of the Son of Man and the establishment of the kingdom of God.

Hostility from the Leaders, with Adulation from the People   (19:47–48)

Bibliography

Kodell, J. "Luke's Use of Laos, 'People,' Especially in the Jerusalem Narrative (Lk 19,28–24,53)." *CBQ* 31 (1969) 327–43.

Translation

[47] *He began to teach daily in the temple. The chief priests and the scribes were seeking to destroy him, along with the leaders of the People,* [48] *but they could not work out what they should do, because all the People hung upon his words.*[a]

Notes

[a] Lit. "hung upon hearing him" or "hung upon him as they were listening."

Form/Structure/Setting

Having reached the temple as the climax of his extended approach to Jerusalem, Jesus is now, through this section, to be found there daily, engaged in a ministry of teaching. The section boundaries are marked by an inclusio created by the parallelism between 19:47–48 at the beginning and 21:37–38 at the end (cf. Lambrecht, "Reading and Rereading," 589–90 [in bibliography for 18:31–34]).

For v 47a Luke is likely to be inspired by the wording of Mark 14:49; for the rest of the unit there is a rewording of Mark 11:18, which represents a continuation of the Markan sequence. The resulting generalizing summary is reminiscent of 4:14–15, which summarizes a Galilean ministry.

Comment

As Jesus sets up as "resident" teacher in the temple, Luke notes a sharp cleavage between the Jewish leadership, intent on Jesus' destruction, and the People, who hung on his every word.

47 In the opening clause, both the periphrastic tense and the καθ' ἡμέραν for "daily" are marks of Lukan style (though the opening τό before the latter is unusual; it may be the correct reading also at Acts 17:11). The prominence that Luke gives to the temple location of Jesus' ministry in Jerusalem is part of his contention that Jesus, and therefore Christians (despite anticipating its fall in a divine judgment), had the highest of regards for this central point of Jewish reverence. Luke will make it clear in 24:52–53 and in Acts with the continued Christian orientation to the temple that not even the execution of Jesus at the instigation of those who control the temple can dislodge this Christian loyalty. Luke adds οἱ πρῶτοι τοῦ λαοῦ (lit. "the first [ones] of the People"; Luke uses πρῶτοι of leaders also in Acts 13:50; 25:2; 28:17; cf. 17:4; 28:7) to the Markan leadership groups. On the other two groups, see at 9:21–22; here also Luke probably thinks of the constituent groups of the Sanhedrin, but his phrase is chosen for the sake of the poignancy of contrast between "leaders of the People" and "the People" themselves. Ways in which Luke will refer to the Jerusalem leadership later in the Gospel are "the chief priests and the scribes, with the elders" (20:1); "the scribes and chief priests" (20:19); "chief priests and scribes" (22:2; 23:10); "chief priests, temple officers, and elders" (22:52); "eldership of the People, both chief priests and scribes" (22:66); "the chief priests and the rulers" (23:13); "the rulers" (23:35); "the chief priests and the rulers" (24:20). Luke moves the focus from Mark's how to destroy Jesus onto simply the desire to destroy him (Luke saves the issue of "how" for v 48). For Luke, Pharisees have been regular antagonists to Jesus (and Jesus to them), but they are not part of the leadership group that ultimately sets out to destroy him (see Luke's moderation of Mark at 6:11, but cf. also 11:53–54; this picture of non-involvement of the Pharisees has the general support of the passion narratives preserved by each of the evangelists, but Matthew has 27:62 and John has 18:3).

48 The Markan wording is completely reformulated. Mark's direct link between the temple disturbance and the leaders' plotting of Jesus' destruction is lost; and where for Mark the role of the crowd's positive response to the teaching of Jesus is to provoke the leaders to fear him and therefore to seek to destroy him (and so represents a partial explanation of the leadership response to the temple incident), for Luke the role of this response is to stand, temporarily, in the way of the leaders plan to destroy Jesus. In Luke "the crowd" becomes "all the People," that is God's People: God's People are totally taken up by what Jesus teaches. This spontaneous recognition by the People of God is offered as part of the case that Luke seeks to make for the authenticity of Jesus. Luke works with this distinction between the leaders and the People also in 20:1–6, 19, 26, 45; 22:2; 23:5, 35; 24:19–20 (cf. Kodell, *CBQ* 31 [1969] 327–43). Luke would probably have us understand that the influence of the leaders gradually overwhelms the better sense of the People of God in general (this may account for the apparently divergent use at 23:13, and more importantly for such texts in Acts as 6:12; 12:3, cf. vv 4 and 11; 21:30; 28:26–27), and that it is precisely the unhelpful role of the leaders that has led to the situation in Luke's own day of cleavage between Christianity and Judaism. ἐξεκρέματο αὐτοῦ ἀκούων could either be "hung upon hearing him" or "hung upon him, as they were listening" (the sense is little changed).

After Luke's addition of v 47a, which serves to generalize, Mark's 11:19 is no longer suitable at this point, so Luke reserves it for 21:37, at the end of this section.

Explanation

Having made his protest about the markets in the temple, Jesus establishes himself as a regular daily teacher in the temple. This will be the setting for the material of the whole section from 19:47–21:38, and the section will end as it began on this note of daily teaching in the temple. The Lukan Jesus is strongly affirmative of the place and importance of the temple in Jewish (and Jewish-Christian) piety.

Now the leadership groups that together make up the Sanhedrin, the highest Jewish governing authority, are brought to an extreme state of provocation by this figure who has set himself up as "resident" teacher in their holiest place. They plot his destruction, but their machinations are temporarily blocked by the way in which, in marked contrast to their leaders, all the people—for Luke, the historic People of God—hang on his every word.

"By What Authority Do You Do These Things?" (20:1–8)

Bibliography

Haenchen, E. *Der Weg Jesu.* 392–96. **Kremer, J.** "Jesu Antwort auf die Frage nach seiner Vollmacht: Eine Auslegung von Mk 11,27–33." *BibLeb* 9 (1968) 128–36. **Mussies, G.** "The Sense of συλλογιζέσθαι at Luke XX 5." In *Miscellanea Neotestamentica: Studia ad NT praesertim pertinentia a sociis sodalicii Batavi, cuius nomen Studiosorum NTi Conventus, anno 1976 quintum lustrum complentis suscepta,* ed. T Baarda et al. NovTSup 47–48. Leiden: Brill, 1978. 2:59–76. **Roloff, J.** *Das Kerygma.* 93–95, 101–2. **Schramm, T.** *Markus-Stoff.* 149–50. **Shae, G. S.** "The Question on the Authority of Jesus." *NovT* 16 (1974) 1–29.

Translation

[1]*It happened on one of those days, as he was teaching the People in the temple and announcing the good news, that the chief priests*[a] *and the scribes, with the elders, came up* [2]*and said to him, "Tell us*[b] *by what authority you do these things; who gave you this authority?"* [3]*He answered them, "I will ask you a question*[c] *as well, and you must tell me [the answer]:* [4]*Was the baptism of John [authorized] from heaven or [did it only come] from human beings?"* [5]*They reasoned*[d] *among themselves saying, "If we say, 'From heaven,' [then] he will say, 'Why didn't you believe him?'* [6]*But if we say, 'From human beings,' all the People will stone us, for they are persuaded that John is a prophet."* [7]*They answered that they did not know where it was from.* [8]*Jesus said to them, "Neither will I tell you by what authority I do these things."*

Notes

[a] Despite the support of B. M. Metzger (*The Text of the New Testament* [New York: Oxford University, 1964] 238–39; but see id., *A Textual Commentary on the Greek New Testament*, 170), H. Greeven ("Erwägungen zur synoptischen Textkritik," *NTS* 6 [1959–60] 281–96, esp. 295–96) and Fitzmyer (1271,

1274), the reading ἱερεῖς, "priests," of A E G H K W Γ Δ Π etc. can hardly be original, given the Lukan thought development in this section of the Gospel.

   b "Tell us" is missing from ℵ C sy^s etc., which conforms to the Matthean and Markan texts.

   c Gr. λόγον (lit. "word").

   d ℵ C D W Θ etc. conform the text here to the other synoptists with διελογίζοντο, "they were disputing."

Form/Structure/Setting

The sequence of units from 20:1–47 (and probably to 21:4, with the rich being coordinated with the leaders) takes its point of departure from the antagonism of the Jerusalem Jewish leadership to Jesus, identified in 19:47–48. There is also a measure of reiteration of Jesus' popularity with the People. 20:1–21:4 (with 19:47–48 as introduction to this subsection as well as to the whole) thus constitutes a subsection within the larger section 19:47–21:38.

Passing over the Markan completion of the fig-tree incident, Luke continues with his Markan sequence here and will do so for the remainder of the section, omitting only 12:28–34 (of which he will use only the beginning of v 28 and the end of v 34), having made substantial use of this material at 10:25–28 (see there).

Despite a couple of minor agreements with Matthew, there is no real likelihood of the use of a second source here. In connection with the prehistory of the Markan text, the analysis of Shae of the immediately pre-Markan form seems well based: only the first clause of 11:27, and v 32 from "they were afraid of the crowd" should be considered as Markan contributions (*NovT* 16 [1974] 4–10); in v 27 the use of a leadership set identical to that which Mark uses elsewhere may also be vulnerable, but the location in the temple seems more secure).

Bultmann's attempt (*History*, 20) to identify vv 31–33 as a later development has been well criticized for finding here a belief in the Baptist along the lines of Christian belief in Jesus, but his sense that there is a change between v 30 and vv 31–32 in the way in which human and divine authorization are being contrasted does seem to have merit (Shae's attempt [*NovT* 16 (1974) 10–14] to identify an early dialogue form without the shape of a controversy is an all too speculative attempt to develop Bultmann's insight by postulating a more extensive earliest source on the basis of appeal to a rabbinic pattern of teaching through question and counter question; beyond its merely speculative nature, it is vulnerable at the point of the dating of the rabbinic materials appealed to, and in connection with the difference of senses claimed for the two questions in Mark 11:28).

If we take the account to have terminated originally with v 30, then the thrust of Jesus' response is to question whether John's ministry needed any kind of official sanction to be valid, the implication being that both John's and his own ministry were validated from heaven, not through the official channels of religious authority in Judaism. Vv 31–33 represent an attempt to spell this out against a backdrop of antagonism and in connection with the lack of impact of the ministry of John on official Judaism, contrasted with its extensive impact on popular Judaism. But in the spelling out, the contrast between ἐξ οὐρανοῦ ("from heaven") and ἐξ ἀνθρώπων (lit. "from people") shifts in the sense given to its second member from "authorized at a human level" to "only a human affair and therefore not authentically of God." The original short form is of a piece with other statements of the historical Jesus in affirmation of John and is not likely to be a product of early church reflection.

Comment

In the present interchange, the religious leaders of Jerusalem express their antagonism to Jesus but do not move discernibly closer to their goal of destroying him. Rather, they reveal their own bankruptcy as guides to the truth. At the same time the passage suggests that the authenticity base for Jesus is like and somehow related to the authenticity base for John.

1 Not having used Mark 11:19, Luke has no need for a return to the city here. καὶ ἐγένετο ἐν μιᾷ τῶν ἡμερῶν (lit. "it happened in one of those days") is introduced identically by Luke at 5:17 (and almost so at 8:22). The reference to teaching the People in the temple merely reiterates material from 19:47–48. Its presence encourages us to take the questioning here as concerned with establishing the authority for Jesus' teaching. Luke glosses "teaching" with his favored verb εὐαγγελίζεσθαι, "evangelize/announce good news" (Marshall, 722, is wrong to think that for Luke there is no presentation of the gospel in this section). The Lukan ἐπέστησαν, "they came up/stood by," displaces Mark's ἔρχονται πρὸς αὐτόν, "they come to him." Luke reproduces Mark's leadership groups but subordinates "the elders" ("with the elders"). The three terms here are those of 9:22 (see there), but Luke will intend the same people as in 19:47 (see there).

2 Luke drops a Markan repetition but adds two redundancies of his own (λέγοντες, "saying"; εἰπὸν ἡμῖν, "tell us"); he makes other minor changes. The two questions here are not really different (against Shae, *NovT* 16 [1974] 11): the former is more general, while the second becomes more precise by focusing on the issue of authorization. The authority in question is Jesus' authority to teach as he does. The manifest reality of Jesus' authority, evident in 5:32, 36; 5:24, is not in view here. It may be that the claim of these leadership groups to be able to authorize in various ways sits in the background at this point.

3 Luke as elsewhere with εἶπεν, "he said," adds a redundant ἀποκριθείς (lit. "having answered"), and in compensation he drops Mark's "Jesus"; he reduces Mark's verb for "I will ask" to the simple form; he substitutes "I also" for Mark's "one"; he prefers "tell me" to Mark's "answer me"; and he drops as repetitive Mark's final clause. Jesus trades question for question: as will become clear he will answer if they will answer.

4 Luke's main change here is to drop Mark's repetition of ἀποκρίθητέ μοι, "you must answer me," from v 29. Jesus' question is about the basis for John's baptism. Has it only a human basis? (Perhaps we could gloss this, in part, as "Did John get or need your permission for his teaching?") Or does the authority of God stand behind the challenge that it represents? The relevance of such a question is based upon the significant parallel between the teaching of Jesus and the challenge and eschatological expectations associated with John (on the parallelism between John and Jesus see chaps. 1–2 and 7). On the contrast between a human matter and what comes from God, cf. Acts 5:38. The question puts Jesus' adversaries into a cleft stick.

5 Luke's changes here are only minor, except for the replacement of Mark's διελογίζοντο, "were disputing," with συνελογίσαντο. Mussies ("συλλογίζεσθαι," 59–76) has argued convincingly that the semantic range of this verb does not extend to "dispute/debate"; rather it must mean here something like "to reason" (beyond his thorough survey of the texts in which the verb is used, Mussies points to the way in which Luke has in effect [by comparison with Mark] completed the steps of the syllogism here). The implication is that the leadership groups in Jerusalem had been untouched by the ministry of John.

6 Beyond minor changes, Luke's changes in the verse are in connection with the correction of the broken syntax of the Markan text. This involves recasting an editorial comment into part of one of the steps in the reasoning of these embarrassed leaders. In the change, by talking of the prospect of stoning (Luke speaks of stoning quite a lot of times, but elsewhere with the simple form of the verb or a quite different verb for "to stone"), Luke dispenses with the fear language of Mark (he dispensed with it also in 19:48, but will accept the language at 20:19); and he introduces a use of ὁ λάος ἅπας, "all the People [of God]" (which he introduced in 19:49). Luke's πεπεισμένος, "being convinced/persuaded," makes a better parallel with ἐπιστεύσατε, "did . . . believe," in v 5 than Mark's εἶχον (lit. "had"). The People are considered to be deeply committed to the prophetic status of the now dead John. For John as a prophet, see 1:76; 7:26, 28–30.

7 Luke abbreviates and moves to indirect speech expressed with an infinitive. For the evasion, cf. 22:68. One would not want to look to be guided into the truth by leaders who make their answers on such a basis as that which has been revealed here. The Chrisian movement, by contrast, bases itself on commitments for which one is prepared to die.

8 Apart from the replacement of a historical present with an aorist verb, Luke reproduces the Markan wording here. Jesus' antagonists have failed to answer his question so he refuses to answer theirs. As the parallelism established with John makes quite clear, there is no evasion intended, but Jesus' questioners have by their prevarication forfeited any right to have their question treated as expressing any genuine interest in learning the truth.

Explanation

The hostility of the Jerusalem leaders that surfaced in 19:47–48 is picked up in the present unit and those that follow to 21:4, in a series of scenes in which there are conflict and mutual antagonism between Jesus and segments of the Jewish leadership. In this first incident in the series, the leadership groups take a shared initiative, which, instead of bringing them closer to their goal of destroying Jesus, is tripped up by Jesus' counter-questioning, and in the end reveals these leaders to be blind guides for the People.

The setting is Jesus' teaching of the People and sharing with them his message of good news. Jesus' questioners come from the leadership groups that made up the Sanhedrin, the highest level of Jewish authority. They want to know what gives Jesus the right to teach as he is doing; he has certainly not been authorized to do so by them! If the question had been put to another, he might have answered by giving the name of one who had been his own teacher in matters of the law.

Jesus trades question for question, implicitly suggesting that he will somehow build his answer to their question on their answer to his question. He asks his questioners to answer in connection with the now dead John the Baptist something like the question that they have just put to him (Jesus), except that in Jesus' form of the question the options have been set in a distinctive manner: did John's baptism come from God or was it merely a human matter? If it was from God, then questions of authorization rather lose their point; if it was only a human matter, then authorization through even the best channels of religious authorization could not legitimate what presented itself falsely as a decisive prophetic act.

By asking this question, Jesus suggests, in effect, that the most useful frame of reference for judging his own case is the prophetic framework that was evidently widely recognized as appropriate in the case of John. But Jesus' interlocutors are unprepared to face a question set in such terms. They clearly had not themselves responded in repentance to the ministry of John, so could hardly make a public affirmation of his authority from God. But they were well aware that John had been widely recognized as a prophet among those who made up the bulk of the People of God. Publicly to go against this popular groundswell could be dangerous to life and limb. Political expediency demanded that they should utter neither of the answers that Jesus' question allowed. They equivocated.

Jesus' antagonists failed to answer his question, so he refused to answer theirs. But no evasion is intended. The issue that lies on the table is the question of whether both the ministry of John and the ministry of Jesus have their authorization immediately from God himself. The claims of the institutional framework become irrelevant in the face of such a possibility. In any case, those who represent that institutional framework have, by their equivocation, forfeited any right to have their own question treated as a legitimate quest for truth.

The Fate of the Wicked Tenant Farmers   *(20:9–19)*

Bibliography

Bammel, E. "Das Gleichnis von den bösen Winzern (Mk. 12,1–9) und das jüdische Erbrecht." *RIDA* 3/6 (1959) 11–17. **Black, M.** "The Parable as Allegory." *BJRL* 42 (1959–60) 273–87. ———. "The Christological Use of the Old Testament in the New Testament." *NTS* 18 (1971–72) 1–14, esp. 11–14. **Blank, J.** "Die Sendung des Sohnes: Zur christologischen Bedeutung des Gleichnisses von den bösen Winzern Mk 12,1–12." In *Neues Testament und Kirche.* FS R. Schnackenburg, ed. J. Gnilka. Freiburg im B.: Herder, 1974. 11–41. **Bornkamm, G.** "λικμάω." *TDNT* 4:280–81. **Brown, R. E.** "Parable and Allegory Reconsidered." *NovT* 5 (1962) 36–45; reprinted in *New Testament Essays.* Milwaukee: Bruce, 1965. 254–64. **Bruce, F. F.** "New Wine in Old Wine Skins: III. The Corner Stone." *ExpTim* 84 (1972–73) 231–35. **Burkitt, F. C.** "The Parable of the Wicked Husbandmen." In *Transactions of the Third International Congress for the History of Religions,* 2, ed. P. S. Allen and J. de M. Johnson. Oxford: Clarendon, 1908. 2:321–28. **Carlston, C. E.** *The Parables.* 40–45, 76–81, 178–90. **Crossan, J. D.** "The Parable of the Wicked Husbandmen." *JBL* 90 (1971) 451–65. **Dehandschutter, B.** "La parabole des vignerons homicides (Mc., XII, 1–12) et l'évangile selon Thomas." In *L'Évangile selon Marc: Tradition et redaction,* ed. M. Sabbe. BETL 34. Gembloux: Duculot, 1974. 203–19. **Derrett, J. D. M.** "Fresh Light on the Parable of the Wicked Vinedressers." *RIDA* 3/10 (1963) 11–41; reprinted in *Law.* 286–312. ———. "The Stone That the Builders Rejected." *SE* 4 [=TU 102] (1968) 180–86. ———. "Allegory and the Wicked Vinedressers." *JTS* 25 (1974) 426–32. **Dodd, C. H.** *Parables.* 96–102, 127. **Dombois, H.** "Juristische Bemerkungen zum Gleichnis von den bösen Weingärtnern." *NZSTR* 8 (1966) 361–73. **Doran, R.** "Luke 20:18: A Warrior's Boast?" *CBQ* 45 (1983) 61–67. **Drury, J.** "The

Sower, the Vineyard, and the Place of Allegory in the Interpretation of Mark's Parables."
JTS 24 (1973) 367–79. **Duplantier, J.-P.** "Les vignerons meurtriers: le trail d'une parabole." In
Les paraboles évangéliques: Perspectives nouvelles. XIIe congrès de l'ACFEB, ed. J. Delorme. Lectio
Divina 135. Paris: Cerf, 1989. 259–70. **Eck, E., van,** and **Aarde, A. G., van.** "A Narratological
Analysis of Mark 12:1–12: The Plot of the Gospel of Mark in a Nutshell." *HTS* 45 (1989) 778–
800. **Frankenmölle, H.** "Hat Jesus sich selbst verkündet? Christologische Implikationen in
den vormarkinischen Parabeln." *BibLeb* 13 (1972) 184–207, esp. 196–204 **Giblin, C. H.** *The
Destruction of Jerusalem.* 57–73. **Giroud, J.-C.,** and **Panier, L.** *Sémiotique: Une pratique de lecture et
d'analyse des textes bibliques.* Cahiers Évangile 59. Paris: Cerf, 1987. **Gray, A.** "The Parable of
the Wicked Husbandmen (Matthew xxi. 33–41; Mark xii. 1–9; Luke xx. 9–16)." *HibJ* 19 (1920–
21) 42–52. **Gressman, H.** "Der Eckstein." *Palästinajahrbuch* 6 (1910) 38–46. **Guillet, J.** "Jésus
et la politique." *RSR* 59 (1971) 531–44. **Haenchen, E.** *Der Weg Jesu.* 396–405. **Harnisch, W.** "Der
bezwingende Vorsprung des Guten: Zur Parabel von den bösen Winzern (Markus 12,1ff.
und Parallelen)." In *Die Sprache der Bilder: Gleichnis und Metapher in Literatur und Theologie,* ed.
H. Weder. Zeitzeichen 4, GTB Siebenstern 558. Gütersloh: Mohn, 1989. 22–38. **Hengel, M.**
"Das Gleichnis von den Weingärtnern Mc 12,1–12 im Lichte der Zenonpapyri und der
rabbinischen Gleichnisse." *ZNW* 59 (1968) 1–39. **Hester, J. D.** "Socio-Rhetorical Criticism
and the Parable of the Tenants." *JSNT* 45 (1992) 27–57. **Hezser, C.** *Lohnmetaphorik und
Arbeitswel in Mt 20,1–16: Das Gleichnis von den Arbeitern im Weinberg im Rahmen rabbinischer
Lohngleichnisse.* Novum Testamentum et Orbis Antiquus 15. Fribourg: Universitätsverlag, 1990.
Hubaut, M. *La parabole des vignerons homicides.* Cahiers de la Revue Biblique 16. Paris: Gabalda,
1976. ———. "La parabole des vignerons homicides: son authenticité, sa visée première."
RTL 6 (1975) 51–61. **Iersel, B. M. F. van.** *"Der Sohn" in den synoptischen Jesusworten: Christus-
bezeichnung Jesu?* NovTSup 3. Leiden: Brill, 1964. 124–45. **Jeremias, J.** *Parables.* 31, 41, 70–77, 86,
93, 108, 204. ———. "Κεφαλὴ γωνίας—Ἀκρογωνιαῖος." *ZNW* 29 (1930) 264–80. ———.
"Eckstein-Schussstein." *ZNW* 36 (1937) 154–57. ———. "λίθος, λίθινος." *TDNT* 4:268–80,
esp. 271–77. **Jülicher, A.** *Gleichnisreden.* 2:385–406. **Kaino, K. L.** "The Parable of the Wicked
Tenants in Its Synoptic Tradition." Diss., Regent College, Vancouver, 1983. **Kim, S.** "Jesus—
The Son of God, the Stone, the Son of Man, and the Servant: The Role of Zechariah in
the Self-Understanding of Jesus." In *Tradition and Interpretation in the New Testament.* FS E.
E. Ellis, ed. G. F. Hawthorne and O. Betz. Grand Rapids: Eerdmans, 1987. 134–48. **Klauck,
H.-J.** *Allegorie und Allegorese.* 286–316. ———. "Das Gleichnis vom Mord im Weinberg
(Mk 12,1–12; Mt 21,33–46; Lk 20,9–19)." *BibLeb* 11 (1970) 118–45. **Kümmel, W. G.** "Das
Gleichnis von den bösen Weingärtnern (Mark. 12. 1–9)." In *Aux sources de la tradition
chrétienne.* FS M. Goguel, by P. Benoit et al. Neuchâtel/Paris: Delachaux et Niestlé, 1950.
120–31; reprinted in *Heilsgeschehen und Geschichte: Gesammelte Aufsätze 1933–1964.* Marburg:
Elwert, 1965. 207–17. **Léon-Dufour, X.** "La parabole des vignerons homicides." In *Etudes
d'évangiles.* Parole de Dieu. Paris: Editions du Seuil, 1965. 303–44. ———. "La parabole
des vignerons homicides." *ScEccl* 17 (1965) 365–96; digested *TD* 15 (1967) 30–36. **Lindars, B.**
New Testament Apologetic: The Doctrinal Significance of Old Testament Quotations. London: SCM,
1961. 169–86. **Lohmeyer, E.** "Das Gleichnis von den bösen Wiengärtnern." *ZST* 18 (1941)
243–59. **Lowe, M.** "From the Parable of the Vineyard to a Pre-Synoptic Source." *NTS* 28
(1982) 257–63. **Milavec, A.** "Mark's Parable of the Wicked Husbandman as Reaffirming
God's Predilection for Israel." *JES* 26 (1989) 289–312. ———. "The Identity of 'the Son'
and 'the Others': Mark's Parable of the Wicked Husbandman Reconsidered." *BTB* 20
(1990) 30–37. **Montefiore, H.** "A Comparison of the Parables of the Gospel according to
Thomas and of the Synoptic Gospels." *NTS* 7 (1960–61) 220–48, esp. 236–38. **Mussner, F.**
"Die Bösen Winzer nach Matthäus 21, 33–46." In *Antijudaismus im Neuen Testament? Exegetische
und systematische Beiträge,* ed. P. Eckert et al. Abhandlungen zum christlich-jüdischen Dia-
log 2. Munich: Kaiser, 1967. 129–34. **Nestle, E.** "Lk 20,18." *ZNW* 8 (1907) 321–22. **Newell,
J. E.,** and **R. R.** "The Parable of the Wicked Tenants." *NovT* 14 (1972) 226–37. **Orchard, B.**
"J. A. T. Robinson and the Synoptic Problem." *NTS* 22 (1975–76) 346–52. **Pedersen, S.**
"Zum Problem der vaticinia ex eventu: Eine Analyse von Mt. 21, 33–46 par.; 22, 1–10 par."

ST 19 (1965) 167–88. **Rese, M.** *Alttestamentliche Motive.* 171–73. **Robinson, J. A. T.** "The Parable of the Wicked Husbandmen: A Test of Synoptic Relationships." *NTS* 21 (1974–75) 443–61. **Schoedel, W. R.** "Parables in the Gospel of Thomas: Oral Tradition or Gnostic Exegesis?" *CTM* 43 (1972) 548–60, esp. 557–60. **Schrage, W.** *Das Verhältnis des Thomas-Evangeliums zur synoptischen Tradition und zu den koptischen Evangelienübersetzungen.* BZNW 29. Berlin: Töpelmann, 1964. 137–45. **Schramm, T.** *Markus-Stoff.* 150–67. **Sevrin, J.-M.** "Un groupement de trois paraboles contre les richesses dans l'Évangile selon Thomas: EvTh 63, 64, 65." In *Les paraboles évangéliques: Perspectives nouvelles. XIIe congrès de l'ACFEB,* ed. J. Delorme. LD 135. Paris: Cerf, 1989. 423–39, esp. 433–39. **Snodgrass, K. R.** "The Parable of the Wicked Husbandmen: Is the Gospel of Thomas Version the Original?" *NTS* 21 (1974–75) 142–44. **Trilling, W.** "Le jugement sur le faux Israël (Matthieu 21, 33–46)." In *L'annonce du Christ dans les évangiles synoptiques.* LD 69. Tr. G. Bret and A. Chazelle. Paris: Cerf, 1971. 165–89. ———. "Les vignerons homicides: Mt 21, 33–46." *AsSeign* 58 (1974) 55–65. **Trimaille, M.** "La parabole des vignerons meurtriers (Mc 12, 1–12)." In *Les paraboles évangéliques: Perspectives nouvelles. XIIe congrès de l'ACFEB,* ed. J. Delorme. LD 135. Paris: Cerf, 1989. 247–58. **Weder, H.** *Die Gleichnisse Jesu als Metaphern.* 147–62. **Weiser, A.** *Die Knechtsgleichnisse.* 49–57.

Translation

⁹*Then he began to speak to the People this parable. "A*ᵃ *man planted a vineyard and leased it to farmers and went away for quite a time.* ¹⁰*When the time came, he sent a slave to the farmers so that they might give*ᵇ *him [his share] from the fruit of the vineyard. The farmers beat him and sent him away empty-handed.* ¹¹*He proceeded to send another slave; but they beat and shamed him and sent him away empty-handed.* ¹²*He proceeded to send a third; but they wounded and thrust out this one as well.* ¹³*The master of the vineyard said, 'What shall I do? I shall send my beloved son! Perhaps*ᶜ *they will respect him.'* ¹⁴*When the farmers saw him they reasoned, saying to one another, 'This is the heir!* ᵈ*Let us kill him, so that the inheritance will be ours.'* ¹⁵*So they thrust him out of the vineyard and killed [him]. What then will the master of the vineyard do to them?* ¹⁶*He will come and destroy these farmers and give the vineyard to others."*

When they heard this they said, "Heaven forbid!" ¹⁷*But looking at them he said, "What then is this that stands written, 'A stone which the builders rejected—this became the head of the corner'?* ¹⁸*Everyone who falls on that stone will be crushed; on whomever it falls, it shatters him."*

¹⁹*The scribes and the chief priests*ᵉ *sought to lay their hands upon him at that very hour; but they feared the People. For they realized that he had spoken this parable with reference to them.*

Notes

ᵃ τίς, "a certain," is added by A W Θ *f*¹³ 1241 etc. to conform to other Lukan parable introductions.
ᵇ The future tense here is unusual in a ἵνα purpose clause and is corrected to the subjunctive in C D R W Θ Ψ etc.
ᶜ ἰδόντες, "seeing," is added here by A R W Θ Ψ etc. It has come forward from v 14.
ᵈ Mark's δεῦτε, "come," is found in ℵ C D L R Θ etc.
ᵉ The order is reversed in ℵ D R Ψ etc.

Form/Structure/Setting

Though this parable is told "to the People" (v 9), it is told as a parable about the Jewish leaders (v 19). Thus in Luke's hands, it continues the account of teaching addressed to the People and conflict with the Jerusalem leadership, which was announced in 19:47–48.

Luke is following the Markan sequence here, but whether Mark is his only source remains somewhat less certain. The weight of the case for a possible second source comes from the juxtaposition of three considerations: (*i*) the preserved parable appears to have been somewhat allegorized in the course of transmission, and there is a reasonable scholarly consensus as to what the earliest form of the parable might have been (see further below); (*ii*) the *Gospel of Thomas* (saying 65) has preserved a form of the parable strikingly close to this scholarly reconstruction, which suggests that the form there should be considered as independent and closer to the original than the Synoptic versions; (*iii*) at important points it is the Lukan form that comes closest to this postulated most original form. Taken together these considerations might seem to imply that both the Lukan and *Gospel of Thomas* forms reflect access to a pre-Markan form of the parable.

There are, however, a series of factors that together vitiate the confidence with which we can make such an inference. (*i*) The following saying 66 of the *Gospel of Thomas* is clearly a version of the tradition found in Luke 20:17 and parallels; and it is a version that appears to have been abbreviated and altered in the interests of a "gnostic" understanding (involving the esoteric possession of knowledge). Now, since the addition to the parable of the appeal to Ps 118:22 would seem to belong to a developed stage in the allegorization of the parable, the presence here of saying 66 suggests that the form of parable that ultimately lies behind the *Gospel of Thomas* should have been an allegorized form. (*ii*) The *Gospel of Thomas* form of the parable finishes with the death of the son (followed by a challenge to hear). The narrative tells only of a man's loss of both his vineyard and his son to his wicked tenant farmers. As a picture of how bad the world is, this fits well into the *Gospel of Thomas;* but, as a story, the account lacks closure, without the question at least being raised of how the man will cope, or what he will do (Crossan [*JBL* 90 (1971) 451–65] tries to take the story [in the *Gospel of Thomas* form] as the story of the tenants, but it simply is not told that way). At this point at least the *Gospel of Thomas* version seems to be an abbreviated version. (*iii*) Since the *Gospel of Thomas* has no place for the salvation history that the allegorization of the parable involved, it would seem altogether plausible that, along with the dropping of the ending of the parable, the allegorization that ensured that the parable would be read as a telling of salvation history has been stripped out of it for its present role. (*iv*) The pattern of three (two servants and then the son) found in the *Gospel of Thomas* form is often thought to tell in its favor, but where the final element in the group is in some way to be set over against the preceding elements, then Luke's pattern of three + one is superior dramatically and may be original (one might venture a guess that the reduction in the number of servants to two in the *Gospel of Thomas* is a result of the introduction after the first servant's return of "The master said, 'Perhaps [they] did not recognize [him]'": this explanation could not easily be used a second time, but to offer another would stand in the way of taking up this knowledge motif in "the tenants knew that it was he who was the heir to the vineyard"). (*v*) Finally we have had cause to recognize Luke's fine skills as a story teller. It is not at all unlikely that his own sense of drama and narrative development would take him a long way toward restoring to its original dramatic simplicity a story that had been overlayed with allegorical development (cf. Jeremias, *Parables,* 72, n. 84).

Though certainty is not possible, the weight of probability would seem finally to be on the side of the view that Luke works here only from his Markan source (if the *Gospel of Thomas* version depends here on the synoptic Gospels, then to judge from minor agreements, both Mark and Luke were consulted).

While the basis for deciding between Markan and pre-Markan developments is limited, there is general agreement about the shape of the most original form of the parable. The elaboration of the stages in the preparation of the vineyard takes place under the influence of Isa 5:2 and is likely to be secondary. The generalizing of Mark 12:5b is in the interests of the sequence of OT prophets and will be secondary. Though the text may conceivably have its own independent place in the Jesus tradition, the use of Ps 118:22–23 here is almost certainly a later development as part of the elaboration of a salvation-historical reading of the parable (given the possibility of word-play in Hebrew between "son" and "stone," the connection is likely already to have been made in the pre-Greek phase of the tradition [but note the suggestive proposal of Trimaille ("La parabole," 253–55) who, noting the frequent juxtaposition of planting and building in both OT and NT texts, sees the juxtaposition as based upon the linking of the planting of the parable and the building of the Psalm]). "Beloved" as an epithet for the son is likely to be part of the same development. The transfer of the vineyard to others may be an original feature of the parable, but it is perhaps more likely that the original finished with the question (in terms of the main thrust of the narrative, the difference is slight). It is widely agreed that the original had only individual servants. As indicated above, I favor three single servants; others are influenced by the *Gospel of Thomas* to favor two. It is intrinsically likely that there was some kind of development (probably an intensification) in the treatment from one servant to the next, but in this respect the telling is too overlayed to make any serious attempt at restoration (it is, however, unlikely that any of the servants was killed).

For all its damage to the simplicity of the story, the salvation-historical development of the parable is no more than a particular elaboration of what is intrinsic to the parable. As in other of Jesus' parables, the central character is a God-figure. The distinction in the parable between the vineyard and those who are responsible for it (and for the share of the crop going to the owner) makes it natural to read the parable in connection with the Jewish leadership groups of Jesus' day. The distinction between the slaves and the son corresponds to the sense of eschatological climax that Jesus clearly associated with his own ministry, and the ominous prospect of the next initiative from the father introduces a judgment motif that is at home with other historical Jesus material.

The parable is thus inalienably semi-allegorical. But despite the occasional judgment to the contrary, this should not be taken as counting against its authenticity (see "Modern Parables Research" at the end of the Introduction). Its complaint against the leaders of the People of God is clearly in continuity with the OT prophetic tradition with which the historical Jesus was so aligned. The parable may be taken as involving Jesus' prophetic anticipation of his own death (and, as I have argued at 9:21–22, Jesus did anticipate his own death), but prophetic anticipation is not necessarily involved here. The parable is interested in the rejection by the leaders of the claim of God made upon his People through the ministry of Jesus. The death of the son may, within the parabolic narrative, be no more than a powerful image for this rejection, or it may perhaps be a logical extrapolation from present hostility: the pressure of the claim of God made present through the ministry of Jesus will not go away as long as he lives to continue to exercise his ministry. In the latter case the parable would become a powerful warning against, and a hinting at the consequences of, such a decisive rejection of God's final and decisive emissary. The place of the son in the parable is not christologically determined, except indirectly: the coming of the son is here the ultimate expression of the claim of the owner upon his vineyard.

Comment

The attitude of the leaders to Jesus is exposed as an unwillingness to be accountable to God. They are in the presence of God's final bid to gain their compliance, and their rejection of this ambassador can only lead to disaster for themselves, and to their role as leaders being taken over by others.

9   Luke has intervened in the Markan wording here with πρὸς τὸν λαόν, "to the People" (linking back to 20:1; 19:48—this too is part of teaching the People in the temple); with a change from ἐν παραβολαῖς, "parabolically/in parables," to τὴν παραβολὴν ταύτην, "this parable" (there is only one parable [the same phrase is found at 4:23; 12:41; 15:3; 18:9]); by deleting the Markan account of the preparation of the vineyard (this echoed Isa 5:2, but, whereas in the allegory such language expresses personal involvement, the departure of the man in the present parable does not allow the language to perform a corresponding role; Luke is likely to have restored the parable to its original shape here); by adding χρόνους ἱκανούς, "for quite a time" (the language allows for a sufficient time of absence for the action of the parable, but also for the development of the unexpressed assumption on the part of the tenant farmers that his absence was permanent; cf. 8:27; 23:8; Acts 8:11; 14:3; 27:9); and in other minor ways.

The place of such absentee landlord arrangements in first-century Palestine is documented by Hengel (*ZNW* 59 [1968] 1–39) and Derrett (*Law*, 286–312). Despite attempts to unlock the parable by means of appeal to particulars of this practice and popular attitudes to it, Fitzmyer (1283) is right to maintain that the sense of the parable is in no way dependent on such matters. The landlord is clearly a God-figure, and his absence allows for his dealing with the People of God through intermediaries, and perhaps also for a future "coming." Even without Isa 5:2, the vineyard functions as a figure for Israel (cf. Ps 80:9–14[ET 8–13]; Isa 27:2–5; Jer 2:21; Hos 10:1; Ezek 19:10–14).

10   Luke lightly recasts his Markan source. The main changes are his non-repetition of "the farmers" from the first clause to the second, the related refocusing of the second clause upon the farmers' giving instead of on the slave's receiving, and the dropping of a specific mention of the seizing of the slave (he will do the same in the case of the son in v 15). The nature of the rental agreement is clearly based on a share of the crop. If, as appears to be the case, vines came under the stricture of Lev 19:23–25 (cf. *b. Ber.* 35a), then it would be the fifth year before there would be a claimable share. The owner's representative fails in his task and is beaten up for his troubles. Though there is nothing unrealistic for the first-century Palestinian world in this attempt to take advantage of an absentee landlord, to fill out the narrative in terms of possible justifications for a withholding of the rental share of the crop is to go against the grain of the story-line development. As soon as we seek to move from the story to its meaning, we cannot avoid a link between this slave (and the other two) and the OT prophets (see, e.g., Jer 7:25–26).

11 More extensive Lukan recasting has happened here. Notably Luke accepts only the use of the verb ἀτιμάζειν, "to dishonor," from the Markan description of this second slave's reception. He adds this in participle form to a repetition of the language used of the reception of the first of the slaves. Mark's πάλιν ἀπέστειλεν πρὸς αὐτοὺς ἄλλον, "again he sent to them another," becomes the more Lukan προσέθετο ἕτερον πέμψαι (lit. "he added to send a different").

12 Luke totally recasts the report of the third slave and dispenses with the following generalizing reference to the sending of many slaves (in sequence). Luke repeats the προσέθετο . . . πέμψαι (lit. "he added to send"), which he used in v 11, but introduces the third slave as "third" rather than as "a different" one. Then, for language variation, he describes the fate of this one with the words καὶ τοῦτον τραυματίσαντες ἐξέβαλον, "this one also they wounded and thrust out" ("thrust out" is brought forward from the account of the expulsion of the son). For Luke there is not the escalation from case to case (the use of "also" makes it clear that "wounded" does not have such a role) that the Markan sequence of three manifested (but which is then undermined by the generalizing final statement, with its "some they beat; some they killed"). Escalation is retained exclusively for the case of the son. This gives a greater psychological credibility to the father's decision to send the son, since there has been no question of threat to life up to this point.

13 Here again there is extensive Lukan recasting. Luke extends the brief piece of Markan reported speech into a soliloquy (he is probably responsible for the developed soliloquy at 15:17–19 and 16:3 [and cf. 12:17–19] as well; τί ποιήσω, "what shall I do," could provide a link with Isa 5:4[LXX], but the similarity is probably fortuitous). The owner is identified as "the Lord/master of the vineyard" (Luke has the language from Mark 12:9), perhaps to strengthen the God and Israel reference of the story. Mark's ἕνα . . . υἱὸν ἀγαπητόν, "one beloved son," becomes τὸν υἱόν μου τὸν ἀγαπητόν, "my beloved son," in order deliberately to echo the language of 3:22 (see there and cf. 9:35), and thus Luke's sonship Christology. Since Mark's formulation in 12:6a is clearly related to v 5b, which is almost certainly an addition to the parable, and since "beloved" is in any case at this point in the development of the story a slightly odd element, it is reasonable to think that its inclusion already in Mark (or prior to Mark), and then more so in Luke, is a result of an increasingly christological reading of the parable (cf. the end of *Form/Structure/Setting* above). Unlike God, the owner in the Lukan parable does not realize the extent of the danger into which he is sending his son. Luke's ἴσως, "perhaps," prepares for the outcome in a way that Mark's confident statement does not.

14 Lukan rewording is fairly extensive, but not particularly significant here. ἰδόντες αὐτόν, "seeing him," marks the shift of scene: from the place of the father's deliberations before the departure of the son to the vineyard at the point of the son's arrival (Matthew also used ἰδόντες in a similar way). Luke introduces διελογίζοντο, which must mean here "reasoned" and not "pondered" as elsewhere in Luke's use of the verb. Luke drops Mark's δεῦτε, "come" (and so weakens what may be a borrowing of language from Gen 37:20 in the Markan text [with wider allusion to vv 18–20]) and eliminates the Markan parataxis in favor of a ἵνα purpose clause. The identification as heir is based on this being an only son (explicit in Mark 12:6 and probably implied by the use of ἀγαπητός, "beloved"). The tenant farmers think of the absence of the owner as a permanent state of affairs. It is, therefore, to go beyond the horizon of the story to ask whether they assume they can claim the estate after the murder of the son because they believe the father is already dead or because they think he has already transferred the estate to the son. The point is precisely the shortsightedness of failing to reckon with any subsequent action by the owner himself (is this already quasi-allegorical?). It is finally beside the point to discuss whether, in the legal and political state of affairs that pertained at the time, there was any real likelihood of getting away with such an act.

15 Luke's main change here from Mark (shared by Matthew, but with no exact agreement) is to reverse the sequence of putting to death and expulsion from the vineyard. The Markan parable thinks in terms of an exposed corpse left to be scavenged. Luke and Matthew think in terms of Jesus' execution outside the walls of Jerusalem (cf. Heb 13:12–13; John 19:17).

Despite the limiting "for quite a time" in v 9, the permanence of the owner's absence has increasingly become a credible underlying assumption of the narrative. The denoument is reached with the shattering of this assumption. Is there an allusion to Isa 5:5? If so, one might suggest that the parable is developed in deliberate contrast to the allegory of Isa 5.

16 Luke follows the Markan wording closely but adds the report of a reaction, "hearing [this] they said, 'Heaven forbid!'" The realism of the story somewhat breaks down here, unless we see "destroy those farmers" as simply graphic language for bringing them to justice (though we might appeal to ancient practices of taking justice into one's own hands by family members in cases of homicide). The wording, and perhaps even the presence of this section, is likely to be influenced by Christian use of judgment language.

With the letting of the vineyard to others, there is a return to realism (to take the sense here as involving the giving of the vineyard to others as a gift is not adequately motivated in the story, despite the owner's lack of heir upon the murder of his son), but this is probably still part of the secondary development. The displacement of the Jewish leadership will be understood by Luke in terms of the emergent role of a Christian leadership for the renewed People of God. Despite their enthusiasm for Jesus, the People are reluctant to contemplate such a root and branch displacement of their leadership groups. μὴ γένοιτο, found only here in the Gospels, is used idiomatically to express a strong negative reaction.

17 For Luke the appeal to Ps 118:22 is in response to the protest of v 16b. A series of changes from the Markan source supports this role (ἐμβλέψας αὐτοῖς, "looking at them" [Luke dropped this verb at 18:22, 24, but may have added it at 22:61]; τί οὖν, "what then," as the introduction to the question). Mark's "this scripture" becomes τὸ γεγραμμένον τοῦτο (lit. "this the having been written"; cf. 18:31; 21:22; 22:37; 24:44). The wording of Ps 118:22 is as in Mark (=LXX), but v 23 has been dropped as less relevant (and/or in compensation for the coming addition of v 18).

In Ps 118 "the builders" are part of the imagery and have no specific identity; a proverbial saying is being applied to the fate of the key figure of the psalm, a royal figure who is ultimately exalted after having been previously downtrodden, humiliated, and threatened with death. But in the Gospel usage, because of the connection with the parable, "the builders" are not simply people who handle building stones but those who are the builders of Israel, that is, those who are the leaders of Israel. The judgment made by the builders is juxtaposed with the actual importance of the stone, and the importance of the stone is vindicated by its final place in the building being constructed. In Luke's hands and after the death of the son in the parable, this must point finally to the vindication of Jesus through resurrection (cf. Acts 2:29–36; etc.). The imagery involved in "the head of the corner" is disputed. It may be a foundation stone binding two walls at the corner of a building, or it may be a keystone locking into place the stones of an arch or some similarly constructed feature of a building. There are other suggestions as well. The difference of imagery does not affect the final sense.

Probably Luke sees the resurrection vindication of Jesus as preparatory to the emergence of the new Christian leadership of the People of God (cf. Acts 1–2). In this way, he sees the Psalm quotation as supporting the conclusion of the parable with its transfer of the vineyard to others.

18 Despite the inclusion of this material in most texts of Matt 21:44 (it is omitted by D 33 it sy^s Eus), the verse is normally considered to be secondary there. If it were to be original, the source judgments made above would need to be revised. The material represents an elaboration of the role of the stone of v 17, but with imagery that is quite incompatible with that of the quotation from Ps 118. Doran (*CBQ* 45 [1983] 61–67) offers a not unattractive case for taking the verse as a warrior's boast (taking the uses of πίπτειν, "fall," in the sense of "fall upon in attack"), but the Lukan Jesus is hardly such a warrior. To be preferred is the traditional explanation, which finds allusion here both to Isa 8:14–15 (note the linking of Ps 118:22 and Isa 8:14 also in 1 Pet 2:8) and to Dan 2:34, 44–45. The falling involved is in the former case likely to be that of falling from a height and being crushed upon impact with this unyielding stone, and in the latter case the stone does the falling and shatters the one unlucky enough to be where it lands (the verb λικμᾶν used here originally meant only "winnow," but by metaphorical development it comes to mean "scatter," "flatten," "destroy," "shatter," etc.; this verb is found in the Theodotion text of Dan 2:44). Luke is drawing on Christian tradition to elaborate his stone reference from Ps 118:22. In the context of the Lukan parable, the apparent vulnerability of the son is contrasted with the actual and ultimate vulnerability of all others in relation to his permanence and solidity as the "stone." A somewhat similar saying is found in *Midr. Esth* 3:6: "If a stone falls on a pot, woe to the pot! If the pot falls on the stone, woe to the pot! Either way, woe to the pot!" The challenge is to side with the son in his permanence or to be set aside, with the leaders who think they can do away with the one who threatens their autonomous claim upon the vineyard.

19 Luke drops Mark's departure clause from the end. Otherwise, he builds his more elaborate statement fairly closely upon the Markan wording. Luke introduces here the leadership groups with which he opened this section in 19:47. He makes use of the Septuagintal idiom "to lay hands upon," which he will also use at 21:12 (the same idiom is found in Matt 26:50; cf. Luke 22:53). He adds ἐν αὐτῇ τῇ ὥρᾳ, "in that hour," which he also has (with or without ἐν) at 2:38; 10:21; 13:31; 24:33; cf. 7:21. As already found in the introduction to the section 19:47–48, Jesus' good standing with the People thwarts the destructive purposes of the leaders. The parable has clearly been told with reference to the leaders. But instead of checking their impulses, it only makes them more determined than ever to destroy Jesus.

Explanation

In this episode, Jesus takes the initiative. He tells a parable to the People, clearly a parable about their leaders. The hostility of the leaders to Jesus is portrayed as the culmination of a history of unwillingness to be accountable to God. In this heightened situation of the presence of the owner's son, they are now confronted with their final opportunity for compliance. God's ultimate messenger may seem vulnerable to their destructive impulses, but their response to him represents a final parting of the ways. The "vulnerable" son will prove to be an indestructible rock, and the owner whose absence has been traded upon will return to reassign the vineyard to other tenant farmers (= leaders of God's People).

A certain inspiration for the parable comes from Isa 5:1–7, where the owner of a vineyard is also a God-figure. While in Isaiah the focus is on the vineyard itself, in our parable the focus is on those who have responsibility for the vineyard, that is the leaders of God's People, identified in v 19 as the scribes and the chief priests.

In our parable, the owner is absent and deals with his tenants by means of a series of messengers. At the start of the parable it is clear that his absence is only temporary, but as the action unfolds, the key figures, and even the listeners, lose sight of this fact. This motif has to do with the perceived remoteness and therefore powerlessness of God. In the end, the parable declares any thought of God's powerlessness to be a delusion.

Though we should not think of each of the slaves as representing a particular prophet, the dispatching of a series of slaves to ask for the owner's share of the crop corresponds to the way in which God has throughout Israel's history made known what he requires from his People. The imagery of the parable highlights the leaders' importance for this accountability to God: they must bear the weight of responsibility for seeing that what has been promised to God is in fact delivered to him.

Though the parable has a real correspondence with the story of God's dealings with his People, it is a story in its own right and needs to be read as such. We will miss its power if we see it only as a coded account of the sending of the prophets and then of the Son. There are even parts of the story that are not true of God's dealings (for example the suffering fate of Jesus is not at all uncertain from the start, as might be suggested by v 13).

The tenant farmers in the story do not think beyond the immediate present. They think that the owner can only deal with them from a distance, so that the destruction of the son and heir will release the vineyard for claim by possession. They have sorely miscalculated.

There is no single event with which we can identify the coming of the owner to destroy and reassign. The destruction of Jerusalem in A.D. 70 certainly led to an extensive destruction of the leadership structure of Jerusalem and of Judaism more broadly, but the new leadership that emerged after that war is certainly not in view here. The reassignment is rather that seen in Acts with the development of the Christian leadership of the renewed People of God.

Despite their enthusiasm for Jesus, the People are reluctant to contemplate such a root and branch displacement of their leadership groups. But the Lukan Jesus presses the point by turning to Ps 118:22. "The builders" in that verse are to be identified with the leaders, and contrasted with their negative judgment of a certain stone is that stone's ultimately central role in the building (the actual imagery is in detail uncertain). In Luke's hands, and after the death of the son in the parable, this must point finally to the vindication of Jesus through resurrection (cf. Acts 2:29–36; etc.).

The importance of this stone is elaborated in v 18 with statements that probably find their ultimate basis in Isa 8:14–15 and Dan 2:34, 44–45. Whether the stone is seen as the moving projectile that encounters the individual, or the individual is the moving projectile that encounters the stone, collision will prove disastrous. The immediate vulnerability of the son of the parable is to be contrasted with the ultimate vulnerability of all else in relation to his permanence and solidity as the "stone." The challenge is to side with the son in his permanence or to be set aside, with the leaders, who think they can do away with the one who threatens their autonomous claim upon the vineyard.

The addition of this section on the stone causes us to go back to the parable and to focus rather more on the son. In particular, a renewed interest in the identity of the son highlights the role of the phrase "my beloved son" in v 13. This is the same phrase used by the voice from heaven in 3:22. Clearly we are to find here the same understanding of Jesus as one with a unique relationship to God as father.

The leaders realize that the parable has been told with reference to them, but instead of checking their impulses, it only makes them more determined than ever to destroy Jesus. For the present, Jesus' good standing with the People thwarts their destructive purposes.

"Is It Lawful to Pay Tribute to Caesar?"   (20:20–26)

Bibliography

Abel, E. L. "Jesus and the Cause of Jewish National Independence." *REJ* 128 (1969) 247–52. **Abrahams, I.** "Give unto Caesar." In *Studies in Pharisaism and the Gospels. Series 1.* Cambridge: University Press, 1917. 62–65. **Anon.** "L'impôt à César (Luc, 20, 20–26)." *SémiotBib* 18 (1980) 8–15. **Barrett, C. K.** "The New Testament Doctrine of Church and State." In *New Testament Essays.* London: SPCK, 1972. 1–19. **Bergen, P. van.** "L'Impôt dû à César." *LumVieSup* 50 (1960) 12–18. **Bornkamm, G.** *Jesus of Nazareth.* New York: Harper and Row, 1975. 120–24. **Brandon, S. G. F.** *The Trial of Jesus of Nazareth.* London: Batsford, 1968. 66–68. **Bruce, F. F.** "Render to Caesar." In *Jesus and the Politics of His Day,* ed. E. Bammel and C. F. D. Moule. Cambridge: University Press, 1984. 249–63. **Cassidy, R. J.** *Jesus, Politics and Society: A Study of Luke's Gospel.* Maryknoll, NY: Orbis, 1978. 55–61. **Castelli, E.** "Hermeneutik und Kairos." *TF* 58 (1976) 60–64. **Derrett, J. D. M.** "Luke's Perspective on Tribute to Caesar." In *Political Issues in Luke-Acts,* ed. R. J. Cassidy et al. 38–48. ————. "'Render to Caesar.'" In *Law* 313–38.

Giblin, C. H. "'The Things of God' in the Question Concerning Tribute to Caesar (Lk 20:25; Mk 12:17; Mt 22:21)." *CBQ* 33 (1971) 510–27. **Goppelt, L.** "Die Freiheit zur Kaisersteuer (Zu Mk. 12,17 und Röm 13,1–7)." In *Ecclesia und Res Publica.* FS K. D. Schmidt, ed. G. Kretschmar and B. Lohse. Göttingen: Vandenhoeck & Ruprecht, 1961. 40–50; ET "The Freedom to Pay the Imperial Tax (Mk 12,17)." *SE* 2 [=TU 87] (1964) 183–94. **Haenchen, E.** *Der Weg Jesu.* 406–9. **Hart, H. St. J.** "The Coin of 'Render unto Caesar . . .' (A Note on Some Aspects of Mark 12:13–17; Matt. 22:15–22; Luke 20:20–26)." In *Jesus and the Politics of His Day,* ed. E. Bammel and C. F. D. Moule. Cambridge: University Press, 1984. 241–48. **Kennard, J. S.** *Render to God: A Study of the Tribute Passage.* New York: Oxford University, 1950. **Loewe, H. M. J.** *"Render unto Caesar": Religious and Political Loyalty in Palestine.* Cambridge: University Press, 1940. **Petzke, G.** "Der historische Jesus in der sozialethischen Diskussion." In *Jesus Christus in Historie und Theologie.* FS H. Conzelmann, ed. G. Strecker. Tübingen: Mohr-Siebeck, 1975. 223–35. **Rist, M.** "Caesar or God (Mark 12:13–17)? A Study in Formgeschichte." *JR* 16 (1936) 317–31. **Salin, E.** "Jesus und die Wechsler." Appendix in A. Ben-David, *Jerusalem und Tyros: Ein Beitrag zur palästinensischen Münz- und Wirtschaftsgeschichte (126 a.C.—57 p.C.).* Kleine Schriften zur Wirtschaftsgeschichte. Basel/Tübingen: Kyklos/Mohr-Siebeck, 1969. 49–55. **Schrage, W.** *Die Christen und der Staat nach dem Neuen Testament.* Gütersloh: Mohn, 1971. 30–40. **Schramm, T.** *Markus-Stoff.* 168–70. **Stauffer, E.** *Christ and the Caesars: Historical Sketches.* London: SCM, 1955. 112–37. **Stock, A.** "'Render to Caesar.'" *BiTod* 62 (1972) 929–34. **Tagawa, K.** "Jésus critiquant l'idéologie théocratique: Une étude de Marc 12, 13–17." In *Reconnaissance à S. de Dietrich.* CBFV. Paris: Foi et Vie, 1971. 117–25. **Völkl, R.** *Christ und Welt nach dem Neuen Testament.* Würzburg: Echter, 1961. 113–15.

Translation

[20] *So they watched [him] closely and sent spies who pretended to be righteous so that they might catch him out in his speech, in order to*[a] *hand him over to the jurisdiction and power of the governor.* [21] *They asked him, "Teacher, we know that you speak and teach truthfully and show no partiality, but truly teach the way of God:* [22] *is it lawful for us to give tribute to Caesar or not?"* [23] *He realized their trickery and said to them,* [b] *Show me a denarius.*[c] [24] *Whose image and inscription does it have [on it]?" They*[d] *said, "Caesar's."* [25] *He said to them, "So you should give to Caesar the [things] that are Caesar's, and to God the [things] that are God's."* [26] *They were unable to catch him out in his*[e] *speech in the presence of the People. Marveling at his answer they were reduced to silence.*

Notes

[a] The unusual use of ὥστε here of purpose is "corrected" to εἰς τό by A W Ψ *f* [1,13] etc.

[b] A C D W Θ Ψ etc. conform to Matthew and Mark here with the addition of τί με πειράζετε, "why do you try me?"

[c] ℵ C L 0266[vid] *f* [1,13] etc. add οἱ δὲ ἔδειξαν, "they showed," to provide a completion along the lines of that in Matthew and Mark.

[d] A redundant ἀποκριθέντες, "having answered," is supplied by A C D W Θ Ψ *f* [1,13] etc. and could be original (it does not come from Matthew or Mark).

[e] αὐτοῦ, "his," is not found in ℵ B L 892 etc. and may not be original.

Form/Structure/Setting

After Jesus' initiative in 20:9–19, the scribes and the chief priests again resume the initiative in their altercation with Jesus. In pursuit of their desire to entrap him (19:47–48; 20:19), they adopt a new strategy, and here act secretly by means of agents.

The Markan sequence continues with no indication that Luke has any other source (there are versions of this pericope in the early second-century Egerton Papyrus 2, frg. 2r; *Gos. Thom.* 100; and Justin Martyr, *Apol.* 1.17.2, but these are all clearly secondary). At the beginning and the end, Luke's adaptation of his source is particularly evident (in v 20 there is already a preparation for 23:2; in v 26 some of the Lukan language of v 20 recurs, and Luke introduces "in the presence of the People" to connect with what is a leitmotif for him throughout this section).

The account takes the form of a pronouncement story with the weight falling squarely upon the pronouncement of Jesus in v 25. The pronouncement, however, could not have been transmitted without its narrative context, which, except perhaps for the identification of the senders and the final note of amazement, must be considered to be as old as is the transmission of the pronouncement itself. There has scarcely been any questioning of the historicity of the episode, apart from Petzke's attempt ("Historische Jesus," 223–35; and cf. E. Hirsch, *Frühgeschichte des Evangeliums. Erster Buch: Das Werden des Markusevangeliums,* 2nd ed. [Tübingen, 1951] 131), in the interests of creating a unified sense that fits into the historical ministry of Jesus, to discredit the final part of v 25 as added for the purpose of later Christian apologetic to demonstrate that Christians saw no tension between the demands of the state and those of God (Petzke sees in the original a fundamental criticism by Jesus of the world system with its service to mammon, and of his antagonists who show by their possession of the Roman coin that they have sold their souls to this system [to be logically consistent of course *they* must pay the taxes]). Petzke attributes a radicality to Jesus' views on money that cannot be consistently sustained from the historical Jesus materials. His understanding of the pericope needs to be scrutinized in the light of the considerations adduced in the *Comment* below.

Comment

Under the cover of deceit, spies from the scribes and chief priests try to trap Jesus into compromising himself, either with the Roman authorities or with the nationalist sentiment of the People with whom he is so popular. Though he gives a straightforward answer to their question, Jesus succeeds in turning the spotlight of scrutiny away from himself and back upon the spies themselves.

20 Though he otherwise prefers middle forms, Luke will be responsible for παρατηρήσαντες, "watched closely." Mark's Pharisees and Herodians disappear as distractions in connection with the demarcation that Luke has provided between the opposed antagonists (see v 19). Luke elaborates Mark's "sent . . . in order to entrap" in terms of spies sent to infiltrate the enthusiastic crowds of the People, to whom Jesus was addressing his teaching. In the Infancy Gospel, righteousness is an important quality in connection with openness to the eschatological fulfillment of the divine purpose that begins there. The pretense of righteousness is introduced by Luke also in 16:15; and cf. 10:29; 18:9. The idiomatic use of λαμβάνειν (lit. "to take") of catching someone out in something is without parallel in the NT (apart from its repetition in v 26), but is known elsewhere (see

LUKE 20:20-26

Xenophon, *Anab.* 4.7.12). The desire of the leaders to destroy Jesus is given political contours here by Luke with his addition of the final clause (cf. 23:2–5). As
in 4:29 (and cf. variant readings at 9:52; Acts 20:24), the ὥστε used to introduce
this clause expresses purpose and not simply result.

21 Luke accepts as skeleton for this verse Mark's "teacher, we know that" and
"but truly teach the way of God" (the texts also share a use of "face," but this is
embedded in somewhat different idioms). For the rest, he extensively reformulates but with little change of sense. By introducing "they asked," Luke labels the
preamble as already part of the question. On the address as "teacher," see at 7:40.
λαμβάνεις πρόσωπον is a Lukan Septuagintalism, not documented in classical or
Hellenistic Greek (e.g., Lev 19:15; Ps 82:2; Lam 4:16; cf. Fitzmyer, 115, 1295).
The "way of God" imagery is an extension of the use of the image of walking (in
God's commandments) for the concrete living out of one's life (in obedience to
God). The imagery is found often in the OT (e.g., Deut 8:6; 10:12–13; Isa 30:21).
The preamble is meant to be disarming; it is part of the subterfuge of these spies.

22 The Lukan word order is slightly different from the Markan. Luke uses
the more general φόρον, which could apply to any kind of tribute or tax, in place
of Mark's κῆνσον, which is a loanword from Latin and may be restricted in sense
to a head tax. And he allows a personalizing ἡμᾶς, "us," to take the place of Mark's
continuation with "should we give, or should we not give?" For Luke these spies
hoped to get what is claimed against Jesus at 23:2: they wanted something against
him that would impress a Roman court.

There had clearly been rioting and rebellion at the time when, as a preliminary to incorporating it into the taxing structure of the empire, Quirinius
conducted a major census in Palestine in A.D. 6–7 (see Josephus, *War* 2.118; *Ant.*
18.1–8). Josephus links the role of Judas the Galilean in this revolt with the emergence of the Zealot movement and its leadership in the final revolt that led to
the downfall of Jerusalem in A.D. 70, but there is reason to be cautious about this
connection. Nonetheless, the combination of three things would suggest that the
appropriateness of these foreign levees would be a perennial area of questioning: (*i*) extremely burdensome levels of taxation (the Roman taxes are to be seen
as adding to what was already a quite heavy level of religiously based taxation;
some estimates put the total tax burden as high as 40 percent); (*ii*) a natural
antipathy to foreign domination; and (*iii*) an understandable conviction that as
God's People their proper natural state was as a free nation subject to God alone
(the traditional prophetic view, however, was "that this was Yahweh's judgment
on his people for their unfaithfulness, and must be endured until he lifted it;
until then, the withholding of tribute from a foreign ruler was an act of rebellion
against Yahweh" [Bruce, "Render to Caesar," 255]). The language ἔξεστιν, "is it
lawful," raises the possibility that some kind of failure of loyalty to God and his
law might be involved in making these tax payments.

23 Luke has totally reformulated here, but with only modest change of meaning. Mark's "hypocrisy" has become "trickery," and Luke has nothing
corresponding to Mark's "Why put me to the test?" Does Jesus' awareness of the
motivation of his questioners condition the role and/or meaning of the answer
to come?

24 Luke abbreviates and slightly recasts his Markan source here. The denarius
had an image of the head of the emperor on one side with an inscription bearing

his name and designation (the obverse varied from time to time; see Hart, "The Coin," 241–48, for a discussion of the denarius seen by Jesus). Fitzmyer (1296) suggests that "the image and inscription on an ancient coin would have been understood as a property seal; the coins *belonged* to Caesar." This may be too strong, but we can at least say that his name upon them entitled him to set the terms and conditions of their use. Though the potential for such a sensitivity is clearly there, it is doubtful whether the prohibition of images in Exod 20:4, 23 affected first-century Jewish use of Roman coinage (the coinage used for the temple tax had the image of a god on it; but cf. Hippolytus, *Refutation of All Heresies*, 9.21, who speaks of a sect of Essenes who would not handle coins because of the images they bore; since, however, in other respects his information seems to be confused in this section, the statement must be treated with caution).

25 Luke's alterations here are minor, the most significant being the insertion of the inferential particle τοίνυν meaning "hence/so/indeed." The sense of this statement, which constitutes the heart of the pericope, remains disputed. Major questions are as follows. (*i*) Is the statement of general application, or is its application to be limited in some way? (*a*) Does the answer meet craftiness with craftiness and therefore remain purely ad hominem, at least in its first half? (*b*) Does the answer apply only to Roman coinage users, as those already fatally compromised with the foreign overlords? (*c*) Is the answer to be narrowly related to the leadership groups from whom the questioning comes? (*ii*) Is ἀπόδοτε to be rendered "give" or "give back" (and on the second translation, should we understand that there is a call to withdraw from participation in the Roman economy)? (*iii*) What is the precise sense of the genitives "of Caesar" and "of God"? Is it (*a*) "owned by," (*b*) "owing to," or (*c*) "to which he has a right"? (*iv*) How does the added καὶ τὰ τοῦ θεοῦ τῷ θεῷ (lit."and to God, the [things] of God") fit into the development? (*a*) It lacks a supporting statement comparable to that provided for the Caesar half of the statement: should we provide as understood a parallel supporting statement in terms of the divine image in humanity [as many, but esp. Giblin, *CBQ* 33 (1971) 520–25, who points to Isa 44:5 to parallel the "inscription" on the coin] or should we treat this second element as a pious intrusive addition to the original [as Petzke, "Historische Jesus," 223–35]? (*b*) Are the paralleled elements to receive equal stress (as in a traditional two-kingdoms view, but as is also the case if we refer "the things of God" to the temple tax), or is the second meant totally to overshadow the first (pay the taxes by all means, but they hardly matter—what matters [in the present moment of eschatological urgency] is radical obedience to God), or even to overturn its natural sense (let Caesar have his coins, but he has no rights over the land of Israel, which belongs only to God [as Brandon, *Trial*, 66–68])? (*iv*) Finally does irony play a role here? While not all the nuances will be caught, almost all of the existing views can be mapped in relation to this set of questions (which it must be noted are interlocked and cannot, therefore, be addressed simply in sequence; though it clearly involves irony, a view that defies allocation is that of Tagawa ["Jésus critiquant," 117–25], who finds a sense something like "you who impose the temple tax as 'of God' might as well pay the Roman taxes as 'of Caesar,' since both reflect the same oppressive exploitation of the people").

The role of the coin would seem to exclude any interpretation that does not give considerable weight to the first of the paralleled elements. The irony in the account, such as it is, is the irony of the contrast between ready use of Roman coinage for its commercial advantages, but lack of interest in being so linked to the Romans when a cost rather than an advantage is involved. In the thought development an anchor point for Jesus' introduction of the claim of God is provided by the use of ἔξεστιν, "is it lawful," in v 22: the possibility is envisaged there of defining the requirement of God negatively in terms of withdrawal of taxes from the Romans (and so aligning piety and self-interest); Jesus defines it instead positively in terms of giving God his due (Barrett ["Church and State," 7] notes the link between the owner's share of the crop in the preceding parable and the rendering to God called for here). This allows us to take with full force the first of the paralleled elements, but also to recognize a measure of end-stress. The link via ἔξεστιν precludes the need to introduce the human imaging of God into the thought here. There is finally no reason for limiting the application of the statement in any way (the role of the coin is by contrast more situation specific, designed as it is to preclude the answer being taken in any "unpatriotic" sense).

26 Mark finishes here with a note of the amazement of his hearers. Luke expands upon this in the conclusion that he fashions for this episode (the idiom using λαμβάνειν is repeated from v 20 but this time with ῥήματος for "word" in place of the λόγου of v 20; Luke introduces "the People" yet again into this section [cf. most recently v 19]; σιγᾶν, "to be silent," is Lukan idiom). The mission of the spies has failed. They have gained nothing that can be used to forward their desire to destroy Jesus nor have they been able to discredit him in the eyes of the People: they have themselves been reduced to silence, amazed at Jesus' capacity to deal with their stratagem. As in 20:1–8, an initiative from Jesus' antagonists has been neutralized and turned around.

Explanation

The attempt by the scribes and chief priests to bring Jesus to destruction continues here by means of secret envoys who infiltrate the crowds of Jesus' enthusiastic listeners. Vocally professing their own affirmation of Jesus, they ask him a question they think will either leave him compromised with the Roman authorities or alienated from the nationalistic sympathies of the People.

The spies feign the righteousness that was the setting in the Infancy Gospel for the reception of the beginning of God's present new initiative, but their desire is to have a charge on which to hand him over to the Roman governor. As becomes clear in 23:2, the leaders and their envoys are so far from righteousness that they cheerfully invent a charge before the governor, though Jesus has failed to provide them justification.

What the envoys say about Jesus in pretense is in fact a true description of this temple teacher. The movement that developed from him would at times be known as "the Way" (Acts 24:14, 22; the imagery of the way is related to Jewish imagery of the conduct of life as a walk). Perhaps Jesus' lack of partiality to which his questioners refer is precisely what we should find striking about his answer.

The question was about taxes. And taxes were no more popular in Jesus' day than in our own, indeed less so since they were a heavy burden on a not very affluent people; they were levied by foreign overlords; and they violated the Jewish People's sense of what was proper for the very chosen of God, who should be a free nation subject to God alone. There had been riots in A.D. 6–7 when Palestine first came under the taxing structure of the empire, and various petitions to Rome can be documented from the period, seeking an amelioration of the tax burden. The form of the question seems to suggest that the taxes might not only be a bad thing, but that payment of them might represent some kind of failure of loyalty to God and his law.

Jesus sees through the masquerade and forms his answer accordingly. His answer will have its basis in the facts of life both for the leaders and for the rank and file of the Jewish People. A denarius would not be too hard to produce for visual inspection: such an amount could conceivably be carried by even the poorest laborer, for whom it represented one day's pay. The link between the denarius and Caesar was hard to miss with his portrait and his name and designation stamped clearly into its surface. The Jewish People readily used his coinage to advantage in their commercial life.

The denarius so readily produced and the image and inscription upon it become the starting point for Jesus' answer to the question posed him. The elements of the answer are clear enough, but precisely how Jesus' thinking works here, and just what the implications are have remained somewhat less clear (various questions are identified in *Comment* above and sample views identified). Perhaps we can best unravel Jesus' answer in the following way.

Jesus' reply is based upon noting the contrast between ready use of Roman coinage for its commercial advantages and lack of interest in being so linked to the Romans when a cost rather than an advantage is involved. To get perspective here we must also reach back to v 22, where "is it lawful" envisages the possibility of defining the requirement of God negatively in terms of withdrawal of taxes from the Romans. This represents a convenient alignment of piety and self-interest, which Jesus (in agreement with the attitude of the OT prophets to the subjugation of the nation by foreigners) rejects on the basis of the general participation in the economic structure provided by the Romans (cf. Jer 29:7). In Jesus' view one shows that one is law-abiding and pious, not by withholding the taxes demanded by Caesar, but by actively giving God his due. We should not miss the link between the owner's share of the crop in the preceding parable and the rendering to God called for here.

Though Jesus was dealing only with the specific situation of taxes to Rome in his own day and situation, there is at least a beginning point here for the exhortations of Rom 13:1–7 and 1 Pet 2:13–17 in connection with the Christian response to the role of the state.

"At the Resurrection, Whose Wife Will This Woman Be?" (20:27–40)

Bibliography

Baumbach, G. "Der sadduzäische Konservativismus." In *Literatur und Religion des Frühjudentums,* ed. J. Maier and J. Schreiner. Würzburg: Echter, 1973. 201–13. **Bianchi, U.**

"The Religio-historical Relevance of Luke 20:34–36." In *Studies in Gnosticism and Hellenistic Religions.* FS G. Quispel, ed. R. Van den Broek and M. J. Vermaseren. Leiden: Brill, 1981. 31–37. **Carton, G.** "Comme des anges dans le ciel." *BVC* 28 (1959) 46–52. **Charpentier, E.** "Tous vivent pour lui: Lc 20,27–38." *AsSeign* n.s. 63 (1971) 82–94. **Cohn-Sherbok, D. M.** "Jesus' Defence of the Resurrection of the Dead." *JSNT* 11 (1981) 64–73. **Daalen, D. H. van.** "Some Observations on Mark 12,24–27." *SE* 4 [=TU 102] 241–45. **Downing, F. G.** "The Resurrection of the Dead: Jesus and Philo." *JSNT* 15 (1982) 42–50. **Dreyfus, F.** "L'Argument scripturaire de Jésus en faveur de la résurrection des morts (Marc, XII, 26–27)." *RB* 66 (1959) 213–24. **Ellis, E. E.** "Jesus, the Sadducees and Qumran." *NTS* 10 (1963–64) 274–79. **Gundry, R. H.** *The Use of the Old Testament in St. Matthew's Gospel.* NovTSup 18. Leiden: Brill, 1967. 20–22. **Haenchen, E.** *Der Weg Jesu.* 409–12. **Janzen, J. G.** "Resurrection and Hermeneutics: On Exodus 3.6 in Mark 12.26." *JSNT* 23 (1985) 43–58. **Kilgallen, J. J.** "The Sadducees and Resurrection from the Dead: Luke 20,27–40." *Bib* 67 (1986) 478–95. **Le Moyne, J.** *Les Sadducéens.* EBib. Paris: Gabalda, 1972. 123–27, 129–35. **Manns, F.** "La technique du 'Al Tiqra' dans les évangiles." *RevScRel* 64 (1990) 1–7. **Meyer, R.** "Σαδδουκαῖος." *TDNT* 7:35–54. **Mudíso Mbâ Mundla, J. G.** *Jesus und die Führer Israels: Studien zu den sog. Jerusalemer Streitgesprächen.* NTAbh NF 17. Münster: Aschendorff, 1984. 71–109, 299–305. **Müller, K.** "Jesus und die Sadduzäer." In *Biblische Randbemerkungen.* FS R. Schnackenburg, ed. H. Merklein and J. Lange. Würzburg: Echter, 1974. 3–24. **Rigaux, B.** *Dieu l'a ressuscité: Exégèse et théologie biblique.* Gembloux: Duculot, 1973. 24–39, 46–51. **Schramm, T.** *Markus-Stoff.* 170–71. **Schubert, K.** "Die Entwicklung der Auferstehungslehre von der nachexilischen bis zur frührabbinischen Zeit." *BZ* 6 (1962) 177–214. **Schwankl, O.** *Die Sadduzäerfrage (Mk. 12,18–27 parr): Eine exegetisch-theologische Studie zur Auferstehungserwartung.* BBB 66. Frankfurt/M: Athenäum, 1987. **Strawson, W.** *Jesus and the Future Life: A Study in the Synoptic Gospels.* London: Epworth, 1959. 203–10. **Suhl, A.** *Die Funktion der alttestamentlichen Zitate und Anspielungen im Markusevangelium.* Gütersloh: Mohn, 1965. 67–72. **Trowitzsch, M.** "Gemeinschaft der Lebenden und der Toten: Lk 20,38 als Text der Ekklesiologie." *ZTK* 79 (1982) 221–29. **Weir, T. H.** "Luke xx. 20." *ExpTim* 28 (1916–17) 426. **Wiles, M.** "Studies in Texts: Lk 20.34–36." *Th* 60 (1957) 500–502.

Translation

[27] *Some of the Sadducees, who oppose[a] [the idea that] there is a resurrection, came up to [him] and put a question,* [28] *saying, "Moses wrote for us, 'If someone's brother dies, and he has a wife, but is childless, then his brother must take the woman and raise up offspring for his brother.'* [29] *Now there were[b] seven brothers. The first, having taken a wife, died childless.* [30] *Both the second* [31] *and the third took her, and [the rest of] the seven as well: they did not leave children and they died.* [32] *Later on the woman also died.* [33] *The woman[c] then—in the resurrection—of which of them will she be[d] wife? For the seven [all] had had her as wife."*

[34] *Jesus said to them, "The sons of this age marry and are given in marriage;[e]* [35] *but those who are considered worthy to attain to that age and to the resurrection of the dead neither marry nor are given in marriage.* [36] *For they are no longer able to die, since they are equal to angels, and are sons of God, being sons of the resurrection.* [37] *That the dead are raised, even Moses made known, [in the passage] about the bush, when it speaks about '[the] Lord the God of Abraham and God of Isaac and God of Jacob.'* [38] *He is not God of the dead, but of the living! For, so far as God is concerned all are alive!"*

[39] *Some of the scribes responded, "Teacher, you have spoken well!"* [40] *For they no longer dared to ask him anything.*

Notes

a Gr. *ἀντιλέγοντες*. The simple verb (as in Mark) is read by ℵ B C D L Θ *f* [1] etc.

b ℵ[1] D q sy[s] have the *παρ' ἡμῖν*, "among us," of the Matthean text.

c The pendant construction here is avoided by the omission of *ἡ γυνή*, "the woman," in ℵ A D W Θ Ψ *f* [1,13] etc.

d Gr. *γίνεται*. ℵ D G L Θ Ψ *f* [1] etc. read *ἔσται*, "will be," as in Mark and Matthew. The sense is unchanged.

e D *ff*[2] i q r [1] sy[sc] (and cf. a c e l) read, as well or instead, *γεννῶνται καὶ γεννῶσιν*, "are begotten and beget." Marshall (741) thinks that this poorly attested variant may be original.

Form/Structure/Setting

Though we should probably think of the Sadducees as belonging to the leadership classes set against Jesus, the concern of "the chief priests, scribes, and elders" to see Jesus destroyed, prominent from the beginning of the section (19:47), now fades from sight, only to return with renewed vigor at the beginning of the next section (see 22:1–2). In the remaining units of this "half-section" to 21:4 (cf. at 20:1–8), Jesus will be critical of the opinions or actions of different segments of the leadership classes of Jerusalem. The teaching emphasis of this section continues.

Luke continues here with the Markan sequence. There is some question whether the use of another source is reflected in vv 34b–36. A second source is not impossible, but both the language and the thought are of a sufficiently Lukan hue to make such a suggestion unnecessary, and certainly unprovable. The last clause of v 38b is likely to be part of the same development. Vv 39–40 are Luke's compensation for his failure to include the following Markan episode (12:28–34): v 39 is based on Mark 12:28, while v 40 is a version of Mark 12:34.

The material is in the form of an elaborate pronouncement story (a controversy dialogue), but as in the preceding pericope (20:20–26), the narrative setting must be judged to be as old as the pronouncement. The discussion of whether this episode should be traced to the historical Jesus focuses upon v 37–38 (Mark 12:26–27), which Bultmann (*History*, 26) considered to be an addition to an earlier form. This is less likely in view of Lohmeyer's identification (*Markus*, 256 and n. 5) already in Mark 12:24 of the bipolar structure that is taken up chiastically in v 25 and vv 26–27 ("power of God" in v 25; "Scriptures" in vv 26–27). The main reasons for denying the scriptural argument to the historical Jesus seem to be: (*i*) that the historical Jesus does not quote Scripture very often, but the early church does; (*ii*) that when Jesus does quote Scripture, his way of using it is not what we find here; and (*iii*) that in any case the argument involved here is so weak that it should not be attributed to the historical Jesus. There is a certain validity to points *i* and *ii*, but in an exchange with Sadducees Jesus may well have adopted a strategy that was unusual for him but had particular appropriateness given their starting point. In any case we must be wary of allowing the core in which we have the greatest confidence to be an iron hand limiting what is possible for the historical Jesus. Point *iii* has no proper place in scholarship and is likely to reveal more about the cultural assumptions of our scholarly tradition than about historical probabilities. As discussed below, the argument, while making its own assumptions, is hardly such as to be judged at once to be specious.

Comment

Some Sadducees come and seek to destroy the credibility of Jesus' belief in resurrection beyond death. But it is their own limited capacity to envision the glories of the future that God has for his People that is finally revealed. And it is they who, despite their commitment to the Mosaic books, have failed to plumb the depths of the commitment of God to his People reflected in the traditional Pentateuchal wording "God of Abraham and God of Isaac and God of Jacob."

27 Lukan touches here include δέ for καί as the initial link word; the use of τινες (lit. "certain ones" [Luke appears to have missed the fact that the displacement into the genitive of "Sadducees" produced by the introduction of τινες would require in strict grammar that the following phrase (in the nominative) should now be applied to the τινες and not generally to the Sadducees; this cannot be his intention]); and a reduction of Mark's finite verbs ἔρχονται, "come," and λέγουσιν, "say," to the participles προσελθόντες, "coming to," and ἀντιλέγοντες (lit. "saying against"). Sadducees occur only here in the Gospel, but are to be found also in Acts 4:1; 5:17; 23:6-8 (aside from the Synoptic parallels to this present episode [where Matthew has an additional use in the transition verse at the end of his version], they are found elsewhere in the NT only in a number of Matthean texts where Matthew sets them in parallel to the Pharisees [3:7; 16:1, 6, 11, 12]).

The name "Sadducees" (Hebrew צדוקים, *ṣdwqym*) derives from "Zadok" (Hebrew צדוק, *ṣdwq*) and refers to that Zadok whose descendants became the authorized high-priestly line in the post-exilic period (see esp. Ezek 40:46; 43:19; Sir 51:12[Hebrew]). The Sadducees in the first century seem to have been an aristocratic group of members and supporters of this high-priestly family who had to some extent developed their own distinctive views on matters of faith and practice (see Josephus, *War* 2.165-66; *Ant.* 13.297-98; 18.16-17). They were strongly oriented to the pentateuch (the view of many of the Church Fathers that they entirely rejected the prophets is probably an overstatement; while they certainly had their own traditions of pentateuchal interpretation, they were at odds with the authority given in Pharisaic circles to traditional developments), and of particular interest here is their disbelief in the resurrection of the dead. The approval of Jesus' answer, to be registered in v 39 by some of the scribes, reflects the contrasting Pharisaic affirmation of belief in resurrection (of which Luke will make particular mileage in Acts 22:6-9).

28 A good part of the Markan wording is preserved. The main changes are: "and leaves a wife" becomes "having a wife"; "does not leave a child" becomes "is childless." In v 21 Jesus has also been addressed as teacher with less than full seriousness. These Sadducees point to the Mosaic provision (Deut 25:5-10; cf. Gen 38:8-10; Ruth 3:9-4:10) of levirate marriage, designed in the first instance to provide a son to perpetuate the name of a man who has died before any sons have been born to him. In Deuteronomy the provision is restricted to brothers who live together. Despite the introduction with "Moses wrote," the wording of Deut 25:5 is much abridged and heavily paraphrased, and for the final clause our text is dependent rather on Gen 38:8.

29-32 Luke links with an οὖν, "then/so/therefore"; he has "taking" for Mark's "took . . . and," and "died childless" for Mark's "dying he did not leave any offspring"; he links the second and third cases into a single clause and drops Mark's spelling out of the second case; he keeps Mark's "in the same way" for use in connection with the whole seven cases considered together (the Lukan compression leaves the logic defective: we must supply "took her and" after "in the same way"; and we are obliged to take "also the seven" as in effect "also the rest of the seven" [where for purposes of the understood clause about taking the woman, the phrase will cover cases four to seven, but for the childlessness clause, the phrase must cover cases two to seven]). Mark's οὐκ ἀφῆκαν σπέρμα, "did not leave offspring," becomes οὐ κατέλιπον τέκνα, "did not leave children" (now accepting the verb that was displaced in v 28 in connection with leaving a widow behind, and no longer using the adjective introduced in v 29). Finally Mark's "last of all" becomes "later." The sequence of seven is simply a good story-telling number. The lack of children allows the sequence of weddings to continue unchecked and also allows the marriages to be as close to identical as possible. Le Moyne (*Les Sadducéens*, 126–27) cites for comparison a rabbinic text in which levirate marriage leaves a man with twelve levirate wives.

33 Luke adds an introductory "the woman, then" and replaces Mark's future ἔσται, "will be," with the futuristic γίνεται (lit. "becomes"; but see textual note above). The argument is meant to be a reductio ad absurdum: "granted your belief in resurrection, does not the given scenario produce for you a knot that cannot be untangled?" The popular assumption will have been that marriage relationship continued in the future world much as in this (Str-B 1:888–89).

34 Very little of the Markan wording survives here. In particular the accusation of error is dropped and the reference to the marriage practices of this age introduced. Luke has used "the sons of this age" at 16:8, where it is likely to be Lukan. The sense is slightly different here, but not fundamentally, since there is an implicit contrast here between those who are [only] sons of this age and those who are considered worthy of the age to come. "Marry and are given in marriage" was found at 17:27 (there with γαμίζειν [as in Matthew] rather than γαμίσκειν for the second verb) in connection with the living out of life with an earthbound horizon. Note the way that "sons" is used here to embrace women as well as men (it is women who are given in marriage).

35 After his own beginning, Luke joins his Markan source at "the resurrection from among the dead" (Mark has the idea verbally: "they rise from among the dead"). καταξιοῦσθαι, "to be found/considered worthy," is used by Luke again at Acts 5:41 (and on the thought here, cf. as well Acts 13:46). "That age" is the correlate to "this age" in v 34. This future age is referred to as "the age to come" at 18:30 (see there). Resurrection is here a privilege bestowed by God on a certain number who are on some basis (not here specified) considered worthy. In the resurrection state, marrying and giving in marriage are activities that have now been left behind.

36 Mark's "but they are like angels in heaven" is represented as "for they are equal to angels." Luke has provided the rest of the verse. The logic of resurrection is taken by Luke to imply not only an escape from the arms of death at the point of resurrection but also a permanent invulnerability to death thereafter. In this new situation there can, therefore, be no place for taking steps to provide sons to carry on the family name. Modern scholars are often troubled at the narrow view of marriage that seems to be implied by this argument that the lack of need for procreation demonstrates the lack of need for marriage. Kilgallen (*Bib*

67 [1986] 478–95) seeks to restrict the scope of the argument to levirate marriage, but this is hardly convincing. Perhaps more helpfully Wiles (*Theol* 60 [1957] 500–502) suggests that the unitive function of marriage whereby it "represents the deepest form of personal relationship, the highest form of social experience" does not in resurrection require the exclusivity that is proper for the present age (presumably it will still not be good for man to be alone!).

"Equal to angels" is in support of "not able to die," not of the abandonment of marriage (against Fitzmyer, 1305; but cf. *1 Enoch* 15:6 for the thought that the angelic beings in heaven would not naturally have wives). Though linguistically close, in Philo's ἴσος ἀγγέλοις γεγονώς, "having become equal to the angels" (*De sacrif. Abel* 5), the likeness for Philo is to the angels' "unbodied and blessed souls," which is quite different from what we have here. Much closer are *2 Apoc. Bar.* 51:5, 10, where the risen righteous will be "changed into the splendor of angels" and will be "like the angels." The comparison should not be seen in terms of (a newly gained) intrinsic immortality, but rather in connection with a certain kind of heavenly glory and dignity of form that carries with it freedom from demise through bodily decline, disease, or accident.

"Sons of God" is probably used here in connection with the dignity attaching to membership of the heavenly order (or rather of the age to come, which is here treated as linked with the heavenly order). The phrase is used in some such sense in Gen 6:2; Job 1:6 (where the LXX has "angels of God"; for additional comparison texts see G. Fohrer and E. Schweizer, *TDNT* 8:347–49, 355). The designation "sons of God" finds its explanation in the appended participial phrase: through resurrection they have been transported into the glories of the age to come. This final "son of" is to be reckoned among the Lukan Septuagintalisms.

Having disposed of the conundrum set for him by his Sadducean antagonists, Jesus now turns to the issue of pentateuchal support for belief in resurrection.

37 While the main sequence and content are as in Mark, the wording is significantly different throughout (Luke takes Mark's "concerning the dead" inside the following ὅτι, "that," clause to make "the dead" the subject of the verb; Mark's "have you not read in the book of Moses" becomes "Moses made known/revealed"; "how [πῶς] God said to him saying" is reduced to "when [ὡς] it/he says"; "I [am] the God of . . ." becomes "[the] Lord [in the acc.], the God [acc.] of . . .").

For rabbinic attempts to deduce resurrection of the dead from the Torah see *b. Sanh.* 90b, 91b. "[The passage] about the bush" is Exod 3:1–4:17. The words quoted are, in the Markan text, clearly from 3:6. In the Lukan text we are closer to the wording of 3:15, but in the absence of a following verb, Luke has changed the nominatives to accusatives as kind of objects to λέγει, "it/he says (here: speaks about)." It could be God who "says/speaks about," but, though the words in Exodus are set on the lips of God, the flow is a little simpler if we take the verb impersonally as "it [i.e., the text] says/speaks about." Downing (*JSNT* 15 [1982] 42–50) has drawn attention to Philo's reflections on Exod 3:6, 15 in *De Abrahamo* 50–55, where Philo also is clearly impressed (and even somewhat embarrassed) with how God "integrally joins his name with" (51) the names of the Patriarchs. Philo identifies the Patriarchs in the texts as referring not to human figures but to virtues and comments "for the nature of man is perishable, but that of virtue is imperishable" (55). In what sense, then, can God in the Lukan text be the God of the Patriarchs long after they are dead and gone?

38 Luke brings "God" to the beginning of the sentence and provides a transitional δέ (lit. "and/but"). He drops Mark's "you are greatly in error" and adds "for all live to him." God will not have continued to advertise himself as God of the Patriarchs if he had finished with them and abandoned them to the grave. Dreyfus (*RB* 66 [1959] 213–24) has shown how in the OT and in ongoing Jewish tradition "God of " in connection with the Patriarchs points to God in his role of savior, protector, and deliverer. Dreyfus recognizes that in an earlier OT perception of life there would have been no thought that God's protection had failed if one died in a good old age with a generous supply of offspring. But, Dreyfus argues, by the time of Jesus, to stop there in one's hopes for God's protection would be severely to foreshorten the reach of one's faith in the power of God and his covenant commitment to one's protection and well-being. More recent study has not, in my view, improved on this approach.

How does Luke's added clause continue the thought? Fitzmyer (1301–2) argues strongly that it expresses a view of the immortality of the soul. Josephus clearly thinks in terms of an immortal soul (*War* 3.374) and expresses Pharisaic belief to his Hellenistic readers in just these terms (*War* 2.163; 3.374). Belief in the survival beyond death of the righteous is clearly evident in Wis 1:15; 3:4; 8:13; 15:3; 4 Macc 7:19; 9:8; 14:5; 16:25; 17:18 (though this is hardly to be simply identified with belief in the immortality of the soul, as is frequently assumed). It is also likely that Luke elsewhere reflects a belief in some kind of continuing life beyond death (see at 16:22–23). However, a statement about the immortality of the soul seems out of place in the present Lukan context where the focus is on the issue of resurrection (cf. Ellis, *NTS* 10 [1963–64] 275). It may be best to make a distinction between being alive "as far as God is concerned" (αὐτῷ) and being alive as far as the People themselves are concerned. The shadowy world of the grave has nothing of life about it, if it is to be seen as a perpetual state; but if it is to be seen rather as a place of availability for a future beyond resurrection, made possible by the power of God, then those waiting in the wings, so to speak, are very much alive from the point of view of the purposes of God. We might paraphrase "all (no matter whether they have passed beyond death or not) are available to God's future purposes, and so in that sense still living." But Fitzmyer (1307) has rightly noted that Luke, by adding the final clause to this verse, is probably intending the verse to become an allusion to 4 Macc 7:19. For this reason, in the light of Luke 16:22–23 and the texts from Wisdom and 4 Maccabees listed above, we should probably go further and find here the view that God has taken the righteous dead [alive] to his own realm, where they await their resurrection future (cf. Wis 3:7–8), and perhaps conversely has deposited the unrighteous dead in Sheol in anticipatory suffering, awaiting the day of their final judgment.

39 This verse is based on Mark 12:28. Luke generalizes by moving to the plural, matches "some of the Sadducees" in v 27 with "some of the scribes" here, and makes their involvement not a fresh question based on having been impressed by Jesus' answer, but simply a public acknowledgment of how well he had answered (the address as "teacher" merely repeats that of the Sadducees). While in general terms Luke sees the leadership groups of the Jewish People as all standing opposed to Jesus, the exceptions to this are very important to him as part of the case for the authenticity of the Christian movement as the true fulfillment of the hopes of Judaism.

40   For this verse Luke draws on Mark 12:34b. In changing from Mark's universal "nobody" to an undefined "they," Luke is likely to intend us to restrict the sense to the Sadducees, but we cannot be quite certain. These scribes are, then, impressed that Jesus has silenced the Sadducees.

Explanation

The conspiracy to seek Jesus' destruction temporarily fades from sight to return with a vengeance at the beginning of the next section (22:1). A different kind of critical interaction between Jesus and various segments of the leadership classes occupies the units from here to 21:4. Some Sadducees seek to make Jesus' belief in resurrection look ridiculous, but he points them to a vision of the future, beyond anything they have been able to conceive, and invites them to go deeper in drawing out the implications of the Mosaic scriptures that were so important to them.

The Sadducees in the first century seem to have been an aristocratic group of members and supporters of the Zadokite high-priestly family who had to some extent developed their own distinctive views on matters of faith and practice. Other Jewish groups, and notably the Pharisees, had come to believe in a future resurrection. But this view, which is only marginally to be found in the OT, and not obviously at all in the books of the law, was one that the more skeptical and more conservative Sadducees had not accepted.

Levirate marriage (based on Deut 25:5–10; cf. Gen 38:8–10) was a way of keeping a man's name from dying out. Its provisions seemed to the Sadducees to make it obvious that to think of a resurrection future only landed one in tangles that proved the idea a nonsense. According to their logic there would not be rules like this for the present life, if that life were to go on after death through resurrection.

Jesus has an answer ready for their riddle. Their focus on marriage involved a perspective bounded by the horizons of this world. Marriage is an institution for this world, but for those whom God deems worthy of the resurrection life, there is a glorious new mode of existence. Resurrection existence is in a deathless realm. So there can be no place for taking steps to provide sons to carry on the family name. It would be quite out of place to think in terms of a cycle of the generations. (It is perhaps best to think of the relational function of marriage, removed in the life of the age to come from connection with procreation and eroticism, as no longer needing the exclusivity that is now proper to marriage.)

"Equal to angels" does not mean ethereal. Rather it suggests that resurrection will have a certain kind of heavenly glory and dignity of form that carries with it freedom from demise through physical decline, disease, or accident. "Sons of God" refers here to the way in which resurrected beings in the new age will be as in some sense members of the heavenly order (much as was the case with the angelic figures in Gen 6:2; Job 1:6). The designation "sons of God" is somewhat explained by the following "being sons of the resurrection": through resurrection they have been transformed into that glorious state fitting for the age to come.

Jesus points his questioners to a text from Moses himself (see Exod 3:6, 15). The question is: "In what sense can God be the God of the Patriarchs long after they are supposed to be dead and gone?" God will not have continued to advertise himself as God of the Patriarchs if he had long ago finished with them and abandoned them to the grave! When the OT and Jewish tradition spoke of God as God of the Patriarchs, they regularly did so in connection with God as savior, protector, and deliverer. From a first-century Jewish perspective, was it good enough to say that God had fully acquitted his role as protector by being their protector up to the point of a good long life and offspring? Surely not!

What does the text mean by "So far as God is concerned all are alive"? It might mean that all (whether they have passed to the shadowy world of the grave or not) are available to God's future purposes, and so in that sense still living. Or it might reflect the view gaining ground in Judaism that, rather than being snuffed out at death, people lived on in some form and experienced in a preliminary way what would be their ultimate fate at the day of resurrection and judgment. According to this view, people continue to exist only in relation to God's future purpose, but they do continue to exist.

Since the matter of the resurrection was a standing dispute between Pharisees and Sadducees (see Acts 23:6–9), it is not surprising that Luke reports that some of the (Pharisaic) scribes were impressed by Jesus' answer. Jesus and Christianity after him take up the best from the most enlightened of the Jewish views of the day. Jesus has effectively silenced the Sadducees, and we will hear no more from them.

"How Is It That [People] Say That the Christ Is to Be a Son of David?" (20:41–44)

Bibliography

Burger, C. *Jesus als Davidssohn: Eine traditionsgeschichtliche Untersuchung.* FRLANT 98. Göttingen: Vandenhoeck & Ruprecht, 1970. 52–59, 64–70, 114–16. **Chilton, B.** "Jesus ben David: Reflections on the Davidssohnfrage." *JSNT* 14 (1982) 88–112. **Cullmann, O.** *Christology.* 130–33. **Daube, D.** *The New Testament and Rabbinic Judaism.* London: University of London/Athlone, 1956. 158–69. ———. "Four Types of Questions." *JTS* 2 (1951) 45–48. **Fitzmyer, J. A.** "The Son of David Tradition and Mt 22:41–46 and Parallels." *Concil* 20 (1967) 75–87. ———. "The Contribution of Qumran Aramaic to the Study of the New Testament." *NTS* 20 (1973–74) 382–407, esp. 386–91. **France, R. T.** *Jesus and the Old Testament: His Application of Old Testament Passages to Himself and His Mission.* London: Inter-Varsity, 1971. 100–102, 163–69. **Friedrich, G.** "Messianische Hohepriesterwartung in den Synoptikern." *ZTK* 53 (1956) 265–311, esp. 286–89. **Gagg, R. P.** "Jesus und die Davidssohnfrage: Zur Exegese von Markus 12,35–37." *TZ* 7 (1951) 18–30. **Hahn, F.** *Titles.* 103–15, 191, 251–62. **Hay, D. M.** *Glory at the Right Hand: Psalm 110 in Early Christianity.* SBLMS 18. Nashville: Abingdon, 1973. Esp. 104–21. **Iersel, B. M. F. van.** *"Der Sohn" in den synoptischen Jesusworten: Christusbeichnung Jesu?* NovTSup 3. Leiden: Brill, 1964. 171–73. **Lindars, B.** *New Testament Apologetic: The Doctrinal Significance of Old Testament Quotations.* London: SCM, 1961. 45–51. **Lövestam, E.** "Die Davidssohnfrage." *SEÅ* 27 (1962) 72–82. **Lohse, E.** "υἱὸς Δαυίδ." *TDNT* 8:478–88. ———. "Der König aus Davids Geschlecht: Bemerkungen zur messianischen Erwartung der Synagoge." In *Abraham unser Vater: Juden und Christen im Gespräch über die Bibel.* FS O. Michel, ed. O. Betz et al. AGSU 5. Leiden: Brill, 1963. 337–45. **Michaelis, W.** "Die Davidssohnschaft Jesu als historisches und kerygmatisches Problem."

In *Der historische Jesus und der kerygmatische Christus*, ed. H. Ristow and K. Matthiae. 2nd ed. Berlin: Evangelische Verlagsanstalt, 1962. 317–30. **Neugebauer, F.** "Die Davidssohnfrage (Mark xii. 35–7 Parr.) und der Menschensohn." *NTS* 21 (1974–75) 81–108. **Rese, M.** *Alttestamentliche Motive.* 173–74. **Schneider, G.** "Zur Vorgeschichte des christologischen Prädikats 'Sohn Davids.'" *TTZ* 80 (1971) 247–53. ———. "Die Davidssohnfrage (Mk 12, 35–37)." *Bib* 53 (1972) 65–90. **Suhl, A.** "Der Davidssohn im Matthäus-Evangelium." *ZNW* 59 (1968) 57–81. **Wrede, W.** "Jesus als Davidssohn." In *Vorträge und Studien.* Tübingen: Mohr-Siebeck, 1907. 147–77.

Translation

[41] *He said to them, "How is it that [people] say that the Christ is to be a son of David?* [42] *For David himself says in the book of Psalms, '[The] Lord said to my lord, "Sit at my right hand,* [43] *until I make your enemies a footstool for your feet."'* [44] *David, then, calls him lord; so how is he his son?"*

Notes

There are no important textual variants.

Form/Structure/Setting

After his effective rebuttal of the Sadducean challenge, Luke's Jesus now turns his critical eye upon the view that the Christ is (no more than) David's son. In Mark this is a view of the scribes, but Luke removes the attribution, probably in the interests of allowing vv 41–44 to stand as a buffer between the report of scribes who commend Jesus (v 39) and that of scribes whom Jesus criticizes (vv 45–47). Despite the loss of attribution, we should no doubt understand in the Lukan context that this is a view promoted by some of the leadership groups opposed to Jesus.

Luke skips over Mark 12:28–34 for which he has a substantial parallel in 10:25–28 (see there) and continues here with a parallel to Mark 12:35–37a. Despite some agreement with Matthew in v 38, it is not likely that Luke used anything other than his Markan source; Luke's editing is quite restrained. The form is variously identified as dominical saying or pronouncement story. The implicitly situational nature of what Jesus says makes it probably preferable to classify as a pronouncement story, but little is at stake.

On a number of grounds, the question of whether this episode should be traced back to the historical Jesus is often answered in the negative (e.g., Hahn, *Titles,* 104–5, points to [i] the kind of appeal to Scripture; [ii] the interest in Christology as such; and [iii] the "transference of a real divine predicate" [Lord] to the messiah, as all counting heavily against the historical authenticity of the account; Lindar's argument [*Apologetic,* 47], that in the account the Psalm is taken, on the basis of later Christian perspectives, to speak "of a lordship that was greater than anything that David could claim for himself," mistakes the thrust of the narrative, which stresses that this figure is *David's* lord). An adequate answer to the question of historicity is not possible apart from a careful consideration of the related question of the original function and sense of the account. Inevitably, the answer is also likely to be heavily influenced by one's overall understanding of christological development in the earliest stages of the life of the church.

The main views as to the original function and sense of the account would seem to be the following. (*i*) The necessity of Davidic descent of the messiah is being denied (by Jesus in connection with his messianic pretensions or by Christian groups who were sensitive about their inability to prove the Davidic descent of Jesus?). (*ii*) Not Davidic descent as such, but its importance is being denied here by Jesus (cf. Mark 3:33). (*iii*) Not Davidic descent, but the messianic title "son of David" is being rejected for the messiah (to distance him from the political aspirations associated with this title and to point to a less earthbound and/or more spiritual set of eschatological expectations [perhaps in connection with Son of Man expectations (Friedrich [*ZTK* 53 (1956) 286–89] sees the alternative, instead, as a priestly messiah)], or alternatively to ward off a possible objection to a Son of God Christology). (*iv*) This is part of a fourfold scheme evidenced in rabbinic discussion, and into which the present passage contributes a discussion about (apparent) conflict between different passages of Scripture (for the origin of this view see Daube, *JTS* 2 [1951] 45–48; id., *Rabbinic Judaism*, 158–69). (*v*) Jesus makes no christological point here; his goal is, rather, in controversy with his opponents, to ask a difficult question in order to break off the conversation (Gagg, *TZ* 7 [1951] 18–30). (*vi*) Davidic descent is not denied here, but a much more exalted view of the messiah's origin is called for as well. (*vii*) The account poses a question the key to whose answer may be found in Rom 1:3–4: in earthly life the messiah is son of David, but through resurrection he becomes Lord. (*viii*) Jesus, who accepts the designation "son of David" (with overtones of Solomonic wisdom and especially of exorcistic and therapeutic skill), is here protesting the scribal equation of "son of David" and "messiah" (Chilton, *JSNT* 14 [1982] 88–112). Scholars offer different nuances for some of these views and also combine elements from more than one of them.

It is not possible to provide here a full interaction with this range of views, but a number of main points can be made. (*i*) The suggestions in points *ii, iv, v, vii,* and *viii* above can be set aside as not likely to contribute to an understanding of the original, but some of them may have a bearing on how the pericope should be seen in its present Synoptic contexts. (*ii*) The limited early use of a titular "Son of David," along with the use of "my lord" in the Psalm quotation, and "his son" in Mark 12:37 tip the scales in the direction of reading "son of David" primarily in terms of Davidic descent rather than a titular "Son of David." (*iii*) Nonetheless, the point being protested is likely to be not so much the question of descent as such, but a restricted view of the messianic program that went along with seeing the messiah as a Davidic figure and his activity as strongly in the line of the paradigm of the early united kingdom of Israel, under David and Solomon. (*iv*) That the Synoptists show no embarrassment in combining this episode with an affirmation of Davidic descent must cause us to leave the possibility open that from the beginning no denial of Davidic descent was intended. (*v*) There is no reason to speak of a "divine predicate" in connection with the use of "lord" in the pericope: in the episode, "lord" keeps the royal overtones that are provided for it by the use of "my lord" in the psalm (cf. at 1:43). (*vi*) The quotation of the whole of Ps 110:1, and not just the first line, is probably in the interests of identifying the lord spoken of as the one linked to God's decisive intervention ("sit . . . until I make your enemies . . ."), and therefore as the messiah. (*vii*) Set in the historical ministry of Jesus, the episode would not constitute a messianic claim of any kind, but would be a provocative remark designed to open up the question of the nature of the hoped-for ultimate intervention of God in the affairs of his People (of course in a wider sense this could not be separated from the question of Jesus' own relationship to the fulfillment of the hoped-for kingdom of God).

Does such an original fit into the historical ministry of Jesus? Most of the points that have been raised against the historicity of the account depend upon an understanding of the original different from that which emerges from the points just made above. Neugebauer (*NTS* 21 [1974] 102–3) makes the important point that something altogether larger than a renewal of the Davidic kingdom was expected already by John the Baptist of the eschatological agent. He points further (104–5) to the way that, in line with our present text, John's eschatological expectations focused on the person of God's instrument, something unusual for Jewish eschatology of the day. Given the undoubted links between John and Jesus, these features of John's message make more credible a context in the ministry of Jesus for the christological focus of the present episode. The difficulties that remain are those posed by the way in which Scripture is appealed to here. To many, the use by Jesus of the traditional attribution of the Psalm to David is a problem, but Jesus' concern is with the perspectives of biblical faith, not those of historical reconstruction. Beyond that there is the more general problem of attributing this sort of quoting of Scripture to the historical Jesus. On this, see at 20:27–40 where Scripture is used not dissimilarly. The strongest positive argument in favor of historicity is the very vagueness of the account, well reflected in the multitude of views as to its sense. When the early church used Ps 110:1 in the light of the resurrection, it made its points rather more clearly than is the case here!

Comment

Jesus has no identified antagonists here, but as in the preceding episodes he seeks to challenge the limited perspectives that governed people's views of the working of God and of the requirements of their own response to God. Messianic hope involves for Jesus much more than simply a glorious rerun of the triumphs of the kingdom of David.

41 Luke drops the mention of teaching in the temple (that is the understood setting for the whole of this section) and replaces the Markan response language with εἶπεν δὲ πρὸς αὐτούς, "he said to them." It is unclear who Luke thinks of as being addressed. Most likely, guided by the main drift of the section, we should think of address to the People, but v 45 to come raises the possibility of address to the disciples in the hearing of the People (neither the Sadducees nor the scribes, though nearest at hand, make for good sense and/or account for the Lukan redaction). Unlike Mark, Luke prefers not to treat the view Jesus criticizes as specifically scribal (see *Form/Structure/Setting* above). Luke replaces Mark's ὅτι, "that," clause with an infinitive construction. Davidic descent for the one through whom God would deal with his People in the hoped-for future is frequently attested in the OT. As a messianic title, however, "Son of David" is found prior to the NT only in *Pss. Sol.* 17:21. It comes into its own as a messianic designation in the early rabbinic period. Solomon as son of David is linked to exorcism and healing in some strands of Jewish tradition (see at 18:38). In our present text the use is unlikely to be titular. Rather the reference is to Davidic descent, but with the added implication that, in the view criticized, seeing the messiah as a Davidic descendant implied a messianic future delimited by the pattern provided by the past role of David (see *Form/Structure/Setting* above). The political imagery of Ps 110 from which Jesus will quote should, however, warn us against taking the episode as an anti-political statement (cf. Marshall, 744–45). The point is rather the positive one, that there is something bigger here than can be contained in merely Davidic categories.

42   Mark's "said by (ἐν) the Holy Spirit" becomes "says in the book of Psalms" (see Acts 1:30; cf. Luke 24:44; Acts 13:33). Jesus appeals to the traditional heading of Ps 110: "A psalm of David." Seventy-three of the OT psalms are so identified. It is possible that לדוד, *lĕdāwid*, originally meant something other than or more general than "of/by David," but in Jesus' day that is how the words were understood (cf. the attribution to David in 11QPsᵃ 27:2–11 of several thousand psalms and cultic songs). The argument builds heavily on the fact that these words quoted from Ps 110 are on David's lips. Apart from a definite article lost before "Lord" (which does not affect the sense), the part of the Psalm quoted in this verse is identical to the LXX (as was the Markan text). The first "Lord" is God, and behind it stands the "Yahweh" of the Hebrew OT. The idiom involved with the second "lord" ("my lord") represents a way of speaking to or about the king. The curious fact from Jesus' point of view is that King David should speak of another as his king. This is what he will come back to in v 44. However, the Psalm quote does not stop there but continues with the words of God: "sit at my right hand . . ." The continuation of the quotation shows that, for the one spoken of as "my lord," God will act decisively to establish his rule. This decisive intervention of God is understood eschatologically by Jesus, and therefore justifies for him the application of the text to the messiah, rather than to some other royal figure. There is no good evidence of a messianic understanding of the psalm prior to Jesus, but quite a satisfactory basis, in Jewish terms, for so interpreting it. For the "right hand" as the place of honor/influence, cf. 2 Kgs 2:19; Ps 45:9; Mark 10:37.

For Luke the promise "Sit at my right hand" attains a more precise sense in connection with his understanding of Jesus' journey through death and resurrection to glory at the right hand of God (see esp. the role of Ps 110:1 in the argument at Acts 2:25–36; cf. at Luke 19:12). Jesus will allude to Ps 110:1 in his response to the Sanhedrin in 22:69.

43   Luke conforms Mark's ὑποκάτω, "under," to the ὑποπόδιον, "a stool [for]," that was to be found in his Greek OT. The imagery is of abject submission. Of all the kings of Israel and Judah, only the messiah will rule with such unopposed authority.

44   Luke and Matthew agree against Mark here in the use of οὖν, "then," καλεῖ, "calls," and πῶς, "how," but each of these changes is natural enough for the respective evangelists. So the agreement is probably only coincidental. A messiah who is defined on the basis of his Davidic descent can do no justice to this inversion according to which David as a father calls his (many generations removed) son "lord."

Explanation

Rebuttal of the Sadducees is now balanced by criticism of the messianic understanding of other groups. Luke will think of views current among the leadership groups with whom Jesus is in contention. Jesus continues to challenge the restricted views of groups of his contemporaries, as he seeks to open up a vision of

the depth and breadth of the purposes of God and an understanding of the full
scope of what it means to respond to the present working of God.

The puzzle that Jesus puts in this episode is clear enough, but the answer that
he seeks to evoke is less so. Many views exist as to the original meaning of this
account (see *Form/Structure/Setting* above for a survey of views). The meaning of
the episode in the finished Gospel text can be more certainly determined than
can the meaning of the account in its original use.

It was generally considered that the messiah would be a descendant of David,
and for this there was much OT support. But this idea of Davidic descent also
restricted the scope of people's vision of what God would achieve in the days of
the messiah and their understanding of the role of the messiah himself. The Lukan
Jesus is not concerned to overturn the idea of Davidic descent but rather to overturn its controlling influence on people's messianic understanding.

In Ps 110:1 Jesus finds a text with the potential for opening up the rigid limitations of people's expectations. Working from the traditional ascription of the Psalm
to David, Jesus draws attention to the curious phenomenon of king David speaking of another as his royal lord. The normal pattern would be, of course, that
David's descendants would address him as lord! This inversion needs to be accounted for.

Jesus not only quotes the first line of the psalm but continues with the rest of
the verse. This is probably to show that the psalm is about the messiah. Though
God had certainly promised to be with the royal line of David's descendants, such
a decisive divine intervention can only be expected for the establishment of the
rule of the messiah. "Sit at my right hand" is an image for gaining the supreme
place of honor/influence (see 2 Kgs 2:19; Ps 45:9; Mark 10:37). But for Luke in
his finished Gospel the sense becomes more precise, because Luke can see the
text in the light of Jesus' journey through death and resurrection to glory at the
right hand of God. Ps 110:1 will play an important role in connection with the
resurrection and ascension in the argument at Acts 2:25–36.

The imagery of enemies as footstools is one of abject submission. Luke does not
make it precisely clear how he sees this working out in connection with Jesus, but
undoubtedly the judgment upon Jerusalem anticipated in Luke 21 fits in here, as
does the wider judgment of the nations anticipated there. In the larger Lukan picture, the coming of Jesus as Son of Man lies beyond the humiliation of the enemies.

Criticism of Scribes   (20:45–47)

Bibliography

Derrett, J. D. M. "'Eating Up the Houses of Widows': Jesus's Comment on Lawyers?" *NovT*
14 (1972) 1–9. **Keck, F.** *Die öffentliche Abschiedsrede Jesu in Lk 20,45–21,36: Eine redaktions-
und motivgeschichtliche Untersuchung.* FB 25. Stuttgart: Katholisches Bibelwerk, 1976. 36–46.
Rengstorf, K. H. "Die στολαί der Schriftgelehrten: Eine Erläuterung zu Mark. 12,38." In

Abraham unser Vater: Juden und Christen im Gespräch über die Bibel. FS O. Michel, ed. O. Betz et al. AGSU 5. Leiden: Brill, 1963. 383–404.

Translation

[45]*As all the People were listening, he said to the*[a] *disciples,* [46]*"Beware of those*[b] *scribes who want to walk about in fine garb and love to be greeted*[c] *in the marketplaces and [to have] the prime seats in the synagogues and first places at dinners,* [47]*who devour widows' estates*[d] *and make long prayers in pretense. These will receive a greater condemnation."*

Notes

[a] "His" in אA K L W Θ Ψ $f^{1,13}$ etc.
[b] Lit. "the."
[c] Lit. "greetings."
[d] Lit. "houses."

Form/Structure/Setting

While certain of the scribes appear in a positive light in 20:39, here Jesus, as he continues his critical engagement with views and practices of various of the leadership groups, warns against following the lead of some who belonged to the scribal class. Keck (*Abschiedsrede*, esp. 37, 41–44), identifies the beginning of a new major section here on the basis of the clear definition of audience and the use of προσέχειν, "beware/take care," in 20:45 and 21:34. But the same audience may well be implied already for 20:41–44 (see there), and in any case the role of "the People" picks up on their role in 19:48; 20:1, 6, 9, 19, 26; προσέχειν is used in rather different idioms in 20:45 and 21:34; and 20:45–47; 21:1–4 are singularly ill suited as introductory pericopes for 21:5–36. On the sectioning, see further at 19:47–48 and 20:1–8.

Luke continues to follow the Markan sequence, and, except for v 45, most of the Markan wording. The unit is in the form of a warning: it warns against behaving like the scribes whose practice is described. Reluctance to attribute such sayings to the historical Jesus is based upon the inappropriateness of blanket condemnations of whole classes of people. On such blanket criticism, see at 11:37–54. Blanket class criticism is evidenced in the prophets: it has a rhetorical force and should not be ruled out for the historical Jesus. Here, however, at least in the Markan and Lukan settings, we have criticism only of those scribes who behave as described.

Comment

Jesus' critical eye now turns to some of the scribes whose ostentatious self-importance and publicly demonstrated piety go along with heartless exploitation of the weak.

45 Luke takes up the use of ἀκούειν from his Markan source (where the hearing involved referred to the previous comments of Jesus on the Davidic descent of the messiah), and he brings forward "disciples" from Mark 12:43. Otherwise the verse is a Lukan formulation (cf. esp. 19:48). For the background role of the People, cf. 20:26. "Disciples" have not been specifically mentioned since 19:39.

They become the central audience here as those already committed to being directed by the words of Jesus.

46 Beyond the deletion as redundant of Mark's opening reference to teaching (cf. at v 41), the only significant Lukan interventions are προσέχετε for Mark's βλέπετε for "beware" (Mark's other use of the βλέπετε ἀπό idiom [8:15] is in the large Markan section not reproduced by Luke; a version of Mark 8:15, using προσέχετε ἀπό, is found in 12:1, but as the Matthean form also uses προσέχετε ἀπό, Luke may have it there from a second source) and the addition of φιλούντων, "loving," which eliminates a zeugma in the Markan construction (Luke may be influenced by his source for 11:43). On scribes, see at 5:17. τῶν γραμματέων τῶν θελόντων . . . could be "the scribes, who like . . ." or it could be "those scribes who like. . . ." In view of the positive role of some of the scribes in 20:39, the latter is to be preferred. Rengstorf ("στολαί," 385–95) has shown how στολαί tends to be used of various kinds of distinctive clothing with some sort of functional character (so: of the garb of soldiers, priests, kings, etc.). The context does not allow us to follow Rengstorf further when he argues that a distinctive sabbath dress is referred to here, which some of the scribes had taken to wearing in an attempt to get all people to add this custom to their sabbath-honoring rituals (396–403). We should think, rather, of ostentatious garments denoting the high office that scribes considered themselves to have. Correspondingly the greetings involve recognition of their scribal status, as do the prime seats in the synagogues and seats of honor at feasts. Pharisees are accused of the same preoccupation with greetings and synagogue seats in 11:43 (see there). On love of places of honor at banquets, see at 14:7–11.

47 Luke reproduces the Markan wording except for correcting Mark's grammar with a change from participles to finite verbs for "devour" and "pray." Idioms similar to "devour the houses" are found in Greek literature (see O. Michel, *TDNT* 5:131 and n. 3). Exactly how the scribes were seen as taking advantage of the vulnerability of widows so as to eat away at their estates is not specified. Of the wide range of suggestions put forward, the most plausible are those that think of the scribes as acting improperly in their legal capacity as guardians of estates (cf. *b. Gitt.* 52b; see esp. Derrett [*NovT* 14 (1972) 1–9]) and those who see the offense in terms of abuse of hospitality (cf. *As. Mos.* 7:6; see Jeremias, *Jerusalem*, 114). Other possibilities include (illegally) charging for legal aid to widows, taking property from widows as security against debts that could not be paid, or receiving large sums of money in return for a commitment to pray at length for the widows.

Though the self-important behavior of the scribes is described critically, the overt criticism is clearly focused on the treatment of widows and falsity in prayer (representing duty to neighbor and to God respectively?). πρόφασις is what one asserts, and it normally refers to one's actual motive for doing something or the pretext or ostensible motive that one publicly announces. The dative is used somewhat similarly in Acts 27:30. The best sense here is probably "in pretense." Derrett (*NovT* 14 [1972] 2–3, 7–8), however, argues that the word implies here actual motivation, but that this motivation is intended to establish a reputation for piety that would lead to one being appointed guardian of various estates, which could then be misappropriated: "with such an end in view, indulge in lengthy prayers" (8). The logic is too convoluted to be persuasive.

Gradation of judgments has been met already at Luke 12:47–48 (see there). κρίμα is a neutral term for "decision/judgment/verdict," but can be used (as here) as a synonym for κατακρίμα, "condemnation." Luke does so again in 23:40; 24:20.

Explanation

Jesus continues his critical engagement with segments of the Jerusalem leadership groups. He now criticizes the exploitation of widows by scribes who are full of public self-importance.

The disciples are addressed as those already committed to being directed by the words of Jesus. As regularly through this section, however, the People are there for it all. These scribes (we should not think that these remarks would be true of all scribes in Jesus' day) strut about in their impressive garb and press to be given every mark of public recognition. But behind this display of importance they exploit the weak (the text probably thinks in terms of abuse of the role of guardianship of widows' estates, or of hospitality demands that went far beyond the means of poor widows, but we cannot be sure), and their lengthy prayers are nothing more than a pretense. Neither toward God nor toward neighbor is there genuine goodness.

Those who think themselves important, and then abuse the opportunities that are theirs, can only expect a more severe judgment from God than will be the ordinary lot of humankind.

The Giving of the Rich and the Poor (21:1–4)

Bibliography

Blass, F. "On Mark xii. 42 and xv. 16." *ExpTim* 10 (1898–99) 185–87, 286–87. **Degenhardt, H.-J.** *Lukas, Evangelist der Armen.* 93–97. **LaVerdiere, E.** "The Widow's Mite." *Emman* 92 (1986) 316–21, 341. **Lee, G. M.** "The Story of the Widow's Mite." *ExpTim* 82 (1971) 344. **Malbon, E. S.** "The Poor Widow in Mark and Her Poor Rich Readers." *CBQ* 53 (1991) 589–604. **Murray, G.** "Did Luke Use Mark?" *DR* 104 (1986) 268–71. **Ramsay, W. M.** "On Mark xii. 42." *ExpTim* 10 (1898–99) 232, 336. **Simon, L.** "Le sou de la veuve: Marc 12/41–44." *ETR* 44 (1969) 115–26. **Sperber, D.** "Mark xii 42 and Its Metrological Background: A Study in Ancient Syriac Versions." *NovT* 9 (1967) 178–90. **Sugirtharajah, R. S.** "The Widow's Mite Revalued." *ExpTim* 103 (1991–92) 42–43. **Wright, A. G.** "The Widow's Mites: Praise or Lament?—A Matter of Context." *CBQ* 44 (1982) 256–65.

Translation

[1]*Looking up, he saw the rich putting their gifts into the treasury,* [2]*and he saw a certain poor widow putting in two lepta.* [3]*Then he said, "Truly I say to you, that this poor widow has put in more than all [the rest].* [4]*For these [only] put into the offering[a] out of their leftovers; she, out of what she lacked, has put in all the livelihood that she had."*

Notes

ᵃ τοῦ θεοῦ, "of God," is added by A D W Θ Ψ 063 1012 ᵛⁱᵈ *f*¹,¹³ etc.

Form/Structure/Setting

It seems likely that Luke considers the rich here to have a place among the leaders of the People, and that Jesus' critical engagement with the leadership groupings in Jerusalem, which has marked this section from 19:47 up to this point, should be thought of as continuing here.

Luke continues to follow the Markan sequence. He drops the change of location and the calling of the disciples, but otherwise makes only relatively insignificant changes to his Markan source. The tradition has the form of a pronouncement story but with a unitary composition that would not allow for the pronouncement to be detached from the narrative setting. Occasionally the suggestion has been made that a parable has here become an event, but there is nothing to commend such views. Borrowing has also been suggested (see at v 3 below for the existence of similar stories), but despite the genuine similarities that exist, the present story partakes of the radical vision of the historical Jesus and shares in his demonstrated disregard for practicalities (see further at v 3 below).

Though nothing is verbally close, there may be some inspiration from the feeding of Elijah by the poor widow of Zarephath (1 Kgs 17:8–16).

Comment

Jesus now criticizes the comfortable piety of the rich, whose giving to the temple treasury has nothing about it of the passionate commitment to God demonstrated by the poor widow, whose two lepta represent all that she has.

1 Luke drops the change of location and adds in compensation "looking up." He dispenses with the general picture of a whole crowd of givers and focuses exclusively on the characters upon whom Jesus will make his judgment. Mark's χαλκόν (properly "copper coinage," but also used more generally of money) becomes τὰ δῶρα, "the gifts," which suggests nonobligatory contributions. Luke reduces to a participial phrase Mark's separate clause about making contributions and moves "rich" to an emphatic end position (dropping, however, a reference to there being "many" of them). Luke's rich no longer give πολλά, "large sums." There are other minor changes as well. γαζοφυλάκιον means "treasure room/treasury" and is used in both the singular and plural in connection with the Jerusalem temple (see BAGD, 149, for references). The treasury appears to have been used for safekeeping of legal documents and private wealth, along with accumulated temple wealth and valuable items, as well as for the collection of tithes and gifts. The location is uncertain: Josephus (*War* 5.200) has "the treasury" (pl.) in the inner court of the temple; John 8:20 has Jesus teaching there, while our Lukan text requires access for women. *m. Šeqal.* 2.1; 6.1, 5 refer to a series of thirteen chests marked for various kinds of contributions. The contributions of the rich will have supplied the financial backbone for the maintenance and functioning of the temple.

2 Luke establishes a measure of parallelism between his introductions of the rich givers and of the poor widow (the coming of the widow is dropped; $\epsilon \hat{i} \delta \epsilon \nu$, "he saw," is repeated; the same participial construction is used for her act of contribution [but with a chiastic reversal of word order]). Where the identity of the givers as rich has had the place of emphasis in v 1, here the woman's "two lepta" are in the place of emphasis. Having dropped the "many" in v 1, Luke correspondingly replaces Mark's "one" with "a certain." Mark's $\pi \tau \omega \chi \acute{\eta}$ for "poor" becomes the rather more poetic $\pi \epsilon \nu \iota \chi \rho \acute{a} \nu$; it is not likely that he intends any difference of sense (he reverts to the Markan term in v 3), but possibly Luke prefers the term for one who actually has some minimal resources for livelihood. On the coinage, see at 12:59. Luke drops Mark's explanatory "which is a quadrans" (using a Latin loan word).

3 Luke does not need to have Jesus call the twelve since they have just been addressed by Jesus in 20:45–47 (no doubt he intends to continue the audience arrangement of 20:45). Luke replaces Mark's "amen" here with "truly" (as in 9:27) and drops Mark's elaboration of the "all" as "those who put [their gifts] into the treasury" (the "all" works better in the Markan text with "the crowd" as antecedent). Greek literature, Jewish tradition, and even Buddhist tradition can be quarried for stories or statements that set a higher value on the small gift of the poor than on the extravagant gifts of the rich (Fitzmyer, 1320, provides a useful list of relevant sources; see esp. Josephus, *Ant.* 6.149; *Lev. Rab.* 107a). Given this widespread sentiment, it is difficult to see how we could possibly take Jesus' words in some opposite sense as does Wright (*CBQ* 44 [1982] 256–65; accepted by Fitzmyer, 1320, 1322), for whom Jesus is lamenting that the women has been duped by the religious sentiments instilled by the Jerusalem leaders (the woman thus experiences a different version of the widows' fate of 20:47, and her contribution goes toward a temple that is destined for destruction [21:6]).

The Lukan Jesus is thoroughly in favor of the temple and its worship: as recently as 19:45–46 he has, at least symbolically, put to rights the abuses interfering with temple worship; and for this whole section he is presented as a regular daily temple-teacher. The woman's priorities may be compared with those of Anna (2:36–38). The idea that there is a contradiction with the Corban tradition of Mark 7:9–13 depends upon the assumption that Jesus is a practical teacher, but he is not! He readily isolates a single issue in a way that leaves unaddressed its inevitable interrelatedness with other issues (see at 6:27–38; 10:38–42). He calls for a radical self-abandonment to God in a manner that frequently leaves unanswered questions about the practicalities of life (cf. at 9:59–61; 12:22–34). This woman is storing up treasure for herself in heaven (cf. 12:33–34). Though in practical ethics it may be important to stress that one should treat oneself as one ought to treat others, that particular movement of thought has no place in the teaching of Jesus. Jesus commends the woman's evident passionate commitment to the cause of God. He looks no further.

4 Luke adds $o\hat{\upsilon}\tau o\iota$, "these," for emphasis; completes with $\epsilon\hat{\iota}\varsigma$ $\tau\grave{a}$ $\delta\hat{\omega}\rho a$ (lit. "into the gifts") which must mean something like "into the offering(s)"; replaces Mark's $\hat{\upsilon}\sigma\tau\epsilon\rho\acute{\eta}\sigma\epsilon\omega\varsigma$, "lack," with the more concrete $\hat{\upsilon}\sigma\tau\epsilon\rho\acute{\eta}\mu a\tau o\varsigma$, "that which [she] lacked"; and conflates Mark's appositional construction into $\tau\grave{o}\nu$ $\beta\acute{\iota}o\nu$ $\ddot{o}\nu$ $\epsilon\hat{\iota}\chi\epsilon\nu$, "the livelihood which she had." In the language of paradox, the rich gave only out of their leftovers; the widow gave out of what she did not even have. We should not think that it is impossible for rich people to give appropriately (Zacchaeus does), but in line with Luke's general view of the power of riches to ensnare, the text assumes that the giving of the rich, even if considerable (and Luke seems to think it was not, since he has dropped the indication of large gifts from his source in v 1), was giving at a level that remained token and therefore gave no expression to any deep commitment to God. Jesus is accusing the rich of not being serious with God. For a similar generosity of giving, cf. 2 Cor 8:1–5. The story shows no interest in how it is that Jesus knows that the two lepta represent the woman's whole livelihood.

Explanation

To be rich in ancient societies made one automatically part of the leadership classes, and so Jesus, in the last of the present series of critical engagement with segments of the leadership classes (from 19:47), now turns his gaze upon the rich. He criticizes their comfortable piety, contrasting the minimal demand made upon them by their giving to the temple with the extravagance of the poor widow's commitment to the cause of God.

The Markan text speaks of the large sums given by the rich, but Luke, with his deep sense of the way in which riches tend to entrap, drops this note: he is quite sure that at least in relation to their wealth the amounts involved were not large. There were chests in the temple to receive the various dues and freewill offerings of the People. Here the latter are in view. These would be used to sustain the temple worship. Jesus observes the giving of the rich and the giving of a poor widow, whose gift consists of two of the smallest coins in cirulation in Palestine at the time. The amount she gives would not buy a quarter of an hour of a day laborer's time.

In setting a higher value upon a small gift from a poor person than on a large gift from a rich person, Jesus expresses a sentiment that has clear parallels in Greek, Jewish, and even Buddhist traditions. However, in its "impracticality" regarding the woman's ongoing life, it has the mark of Jesus and his radical teaching about it. And in its identification of commitment to the Jewish temple with commitment to God, it fits in strongly with an emphasis that is important to Luke (cf. Anna in 2:36–38). Jesus contrasts the woman's evident passionate commitment to the cause of God with a notable corresponding lack in the giving of the rich.

To emphasize his point, Jesus makes use of the language of paradox as he describes the situation of the widow. The rich are only giving from their leftovers, expressing no commitment at all. But the poor widow is said to give out of what she does not even have. The language is, of course, hyperbolic, and Jesus goes on to clarify that she gives "all the livelihood that she has." This has to be an expression of a passionate and wholehearted commitment. For a similar generosity of giving, see 2 Cor 8:1–5.

The Coming Destruction of the Temple   (21:5–6)

Bibliography

FOR 21:5–36:

Bacon, B. W. "The Apocalyptic Chapter of the Synoptic Gospels." *JBL* 28 (1909) 1–25. **Barclay, W.** "Great Themes of the New Testament: VI. Matthew xxiv." *ExpTim* 70 (1959) 326–30; 71 (1960) 376–79. **Bartsch, H.-W.** *Wachet aber zu jeder Zeit!* 118–23. **Beasley-Murray, G. R.** *Jesus and the Future: An Examination of the Criticism of the Eschatological Discourse, Mark 13 with Special Reference to the Little Apocalypse Theory.* London/New York: Macmillan/St. Martin's, 1954. ————. *A Commentary on Mark 13.* London/New York: Macmillan/St. Martin's, 1957. ————. *Jesus and the Kingdom of God.* Grand Rapids/Exeter: Eerdmans/Paternoster, 1986. 322–37. ————. "The Rise and Fall of the Little Apocalypse Theory." *ExpTim* 64 (1952–53) 346–49. ————. "The Eschatological Discourse of Jesus." *RevExp* 57 (1960) 153–66. ————. "Second Thoughts on the Composition of Mark 13." *NTS* 29 (1983) 414–20. **Black, C. C.** "An Oration at Olivet: Some Rhetorical Dimensions of Mark 13." In *Persuasive Artistry: Studies in New Testament Rhetoric.* FS G. A. Kennedy, ed. D. F. Watson. Sheffield: JSOT, 1991. 66–92. **Brandenburger, E.** *Markus 13 und die Apokalyptik.* Göttingen: Vandenhoeck & Ruprecht, 1984. **Braumann, G.** "Das Mittel der Zeit: Erwägungen zur theologie des Lukasevangeliums." *ZNW* 54 (1963) 117–45, esp. 140–44. **Bristol, L. O.** "Mark's Little Apocalypse: A Hypothesis." *ExpTim* 51 (1939–40) 301–3. **Busch, F.** *Zum Verständnis der synoptischen Eschatologie: Markus 13 neu untersucht.* Gütersloh: Bertelsmann, 1938. **Carroll, J. T.** *Response to the End of History.* 103–19. **Conzelmann, H.** *Luke.* 125–36. ————. "Geschichte und Eschaton nach Mc. 13." *ZNW* 50 (1959) 210–21. **Cotter, A. C.** "The Eschatological Discourse." *CBQ* 1 (1939) 125–32, 204–13. **Cousar, C. B.** "Eschatology and Mark's 'Theologia Crucis': A Critical Analysis of Mark 13." *Int* 24 (1970) 321–35. **Cranfield, C. E. B.** "St. Mark 13." *SJT* 6 (1953) 189–96, 287–303; 7 (1954) 284–303. **Dewar, F.** "Chapter 13 and the Passion Narrative in St Mark." *Th* 64 (1961) 99–107. **Dupont, J.** "La ruine du Temple et la fin des temps dans le discours de Mc 13." In *Apocalypses et théologies de l'espérance,* ed. L. Monloubou. LD 95. Paris: Cerf, 1977. 207–69. ————. *Les trois apocalypses synoptiques: Marc 13; Matthieu 24–25; Luc 21.* LD 121. Paris: Cerf, 1985. ————. "Les épreuves des chrétiens avant la fin du monde: Lc 21,5–19." *AsSeign* n.s. 64 (1969) 77–86. **Easton, B. S.** "The Little Apocalypse." *BW* 40 (1912) 130–38. **Estes, D. F.** "The Eschatological Discourse of Jesus." *RevExp* 15 (1918) 411–36. **Feuillet, A.** "Le discours de Jésus sur la ruine du Temple d'après Marc XIII et Luc XXI, 5–36." *RB* 55 (1948) 481–502; 56 (1949) 61–92. ————. "La signification fondamentale de Marc XIII: Recherches sur l'eschatologie des Synoptiques." *RevThom* 80 (1980) 181–215. **Flender, H.** *St. Luke.* 107–17. **Flückiger, F.** "Die Redaktion der Zukunftsrede in Mark. 13." *TZ* 26 (1970) 395–409. **Ford, D.** *The Abomination of Desolation in Biblical Eschatology.* Washington: University Press of America, 1979. **France, R. T.** *Jesus and the Old Testament.* 227–39. **Fuller, G. C.** "The Olivet Discourse: An Apocalyptic Timetable." *WTJ* 28 (1966) 157–63. **Gaston, L.** *No Stone on Another: Studies in the Significance of the Fall of Jerusalem in the Synoptic Gospels.* NovTSup 23. Leiden: Brill, 1970. 8–64, 355–69. ————. "Sondergut und Markus-Stoff in Luk. 21." *TZ* 16 (1960) 161–72. **Geddert, T. J.** *Watchwords: Mark 13 in Markan Eschatology.* JSNTSup 26. Sheffield: JSOT, 1989. **Geiger, R.** *Die lukanischen Endzeitsreden: Studien zur Eschatologie des Lukas-Evangeliums.* Europäische Hochschulschriften 23/16. Bern/Frankfurt: H. Lang/P. Lang, 1973. 149–258. **Glasson, T. F.** "Mark xiii and the Greek Old Testament." *ExpTim* 69 (1958) 213–15. **Grässer, E.** *Parusieverzögerung.* 152–70. **Grayston, K.** "The Study of Mark XIII." *BJRL* 56 (1973–74) 371–87. **Hahn, F.** Die Rede von der Parusie des Menschensohnes Markus 13." In *Jesus der*

Menschensohn, FS A. Vögtle, ed. R. Pesch and R. Schnackenburg. Freiburg im B.: Herder, 1975. 240–66. **Hallbäck, G.** "Der anonyme Plan: Analyse von Mk 13, 5–27 im Hinblick auf die Relevance der apokalyptischen Rede für die Problematik der Aussage." *LingBib* 49 (1981) 28–53. **Hanley, E. A.** "The Destruction of Jerusalem: Mark, Chap. 13." *BW* 34 (1909) 45–46. **Harder, G.** "Das eschatologische Geschichtsbild der sogenannten kleinen Apokalypse Markus 13." *ThViat* 4 (1952–53) 71–107. **Hartman, L.** *Prophecy Interpreted: The Formation of Some Jewish Apocalyptic Texts and of the Eschatological Discourse Mark 13 par.* ConB, NT ser. 1. Lund: Gleerup, 1966. Esp. 226–35. **Hölscher, G.** "Der Ursprung der Apokalypse Mk 13." *TBl* 121 (1933) 193–202. **Hooker, M. D.** "Trial and Tribulation in Mark XIII." *BJRL* 65 (1982) 78–99. **Jones, A.** "Did Christ Foretell the End of the World in Mark XIII?" *Scr* 4 (1951) 264–73. **Kaestli, J.-D.** "Luc 21:5–36: L'Apocalypse synoptique." In *L'Eschatologie.* 41–57. **Kallilkuzhuppil, J.** "The Glorification of the Suffering Church (Mk 13.1–37)." *Biblebhashyam* 9 (1983) 247–57. **Keck, F.** *Die öffentliche Abschiedsrede Jesu in Lk 20,45–21,36: Eine redaktions- und motivgeschichtliche Untersuchung.* FB 25. Stuttgart: Katholisches Bibelwerk, 1976. **Kümmel, W. G.** *Promise and Fulfilment: The Eschatological Message of Jesus.* SBT 23. Naperville, IL: Allenson, 1957. 95–104. **Lagrange, M.-J.** "L'Avènement du Fils de l'Homme." *RB* n.s. 3 (1906) 382–411, 561–74. **Lambrecht, J.** "La structure de Mc., XIII." In *De Jésus aux évangiles: Tradition et rédaction dans les évangiles synoptiques.* FS I. Coppens, ed. I. de la Potterie. BETL 25. Gembloux: Duculot, 1967. 2:140–64. ———. *Die Redaktion der Markus-Apokalypse: Literarische Analyse und Strukturuntersuchung.* AnBib 28. Rome: Biblical Institute, 1967. ———. "Die Logia-Quellen von Markus 13." *Bib* 47 (1966) 321–60. ———. "Die 'Midrasch-Quelle' von Mk 13." *Bib* 49 (1968) 254–70. **Maddox, R.** *The Purpose of Luke-Acts.* 115–23. **Manson, T. W.** *The Sayings of Jesus.* 323–37. **Marxsen, W.** *Mark the Evangelist: Studies on the Redaction History of the Gospel.* Nashville, TN: Abingdon, 1969. 151–206, esp. 190–98. **Neirynck, F.** "Marc 13: Examen critique de l'interprétation de R. Pesch." In *Evangelica: Gospel Studies—Études d'évangile. Collected Essays,* ed. F. Van Segbroeck. BETL 60. Leuven: University Press/Peeters, 1982. 565–97. ———. "Le discours anti-apokalyptique de Mc., XIII." In *Evangelica: Gospel Studies—Études d'évangile. Collected Essays,* ed. F. Van Segbroeck. BETL 60. Leuven: University Press/Peeters, 1982. 598–608. ———. "Le discours anti-apokalyptique de Mc., XIII." *ETL* 45 (1969) 154–64. ———. "Marc 13: Examen critique de l'interprétation de R. Pesch." *ETL* 53 (1980) 369–401. **Nicol, W.** "Tradition und Redaction in Luke 21." *Neot* 7 (1973) 61–71. **Nolland, J.** "Luke's Readers." 129–240. **O'Flynn, J. A.** "The Eschatological Discourse." *ITQ* 18 (1951) 277–81. **Parsch, P.** "Un discours de Jésus." In *Apprenons à lire la Bible.* Paris: Desclée de Brouwer, 1956. 166–72. **Perrot, C.** "Essai sur le discours eschatologique (Mc. XIII, 1–37; Mt. XXIV, 1–36; Lc. XXI, 5–36." *RSR* 47 (1959) 481–514. **Pesch, R.** *Naherwartungen: Tradition und Redaktion in Mk 13.* KuBANT. Düsseldorf: Patmos, 1968. ———. "Markus 13." In *L'Apocalypse johannique et l'Apocalyptique dans le Nouveau Testament,* ed. J. Lambrecht. Gembloux: Duculot, 1980. 355–68. **Piganiol, A.** "Observations sur la date de l'apocalypse synoptique." *RHPR* 4 (1924) 245–49. **Rigaux, B.** "La seconde venue du Messie." In *La venue du Messie: messianisme et eschatologie.* RechBib 6. Bruges: Desclée de Brouwer, 1962. 117–216. ———. "ΒΔΕΛΥΓΜΑ ΤΗΣ ΕΡΗΜΩΣΕΩΣ Mc 13,14; Mt 24,15." *Bib* 40 (1959) 675–83. **Roarck, D. M.** "The Great Eschatological Discourse." *NovT* 7 (1964–65) 122–27. **Robinson, W. C., Jr.** *Der Weg des Herrn.* 47–50, 64–66. **Rohr, J.** "Der Sprachgebrauch des Markusevangeliums und die 'Markusapokalypse.'" *TQ* 89 (1907) 507–36. **Rousseau, F.** "La structure de Marc 13." *Bib* 56 (1975) 157–72. **Schramm, T.** *Markus-Stoff.* 171–82. **Shaw, R. H.** "A Conjecture on the Signs of the End." *ATR* 47 (1965) 96–102. **Spitta, F.** "Die grosse eschatologische Rede Jesu." *TSK* 82 (1909) 348–401. **Tagawa, K.** "Marc 13: La tâtonnement d'un homme réaliste éveillé face à la tradition apocalyptique." *FV* 76 (1977) 11–44. **Taylor, V.** "Unsolved New Testament Problems—The Apocalyptic Discourse of Mark 13." *ExpTim* 60 (1948–49) 94–98. **Tiede, D. L.** "Weeping for Jerusalem." In *Prophecy and History.* 65–96, 143–48. **Verheyden, J.** "The Source(s) of Luke 21." In *L'évangile de Luc* (1989), ed. F. Neirynck. 491–516. **Völter, D.** "Die eschatologische Rede Jesu und seine Weissangung von der Zerstörung Jerusalems." *STZ* 31 (1915) 180–202. **Walter, N.**

"Tempelserstörung und synoptische Apokalypse." *ZNW* 57 (1966) 38–49. **Walvoord, J. F.** "Christ's Olivet Discourse on the Time of the End: Prophecies Fulfilled in the Present Age." *BSac* 128 (1971) 206–14. **Wenham, D.** "Paul and the Synoptic Apocalypse." In *Gospel Perspectives: Studies of History and Tradition in the Four Gospels. Vol. 2*, ed. R. T. France and D. Wenham. Sheffield: JSOT, 1981. 345–75. ————. "This generation will not pass. . . ." In *Christ the Lord: Studies in Christology.* FS D. Guthrie, ed. H. H. Rowdon. Leicester: IVP, 1982. 127–50. ————. *The Rediscovery of Jesus' Eschatological Discourse.* Gospel Perspectives 4. Sheffield: JSOT Press, 1984. 175–334. ————. "Recent Studies of Mark 13." *TSFB* 71 (1975) 6–15; 72 (1975) 1–9. **Zmijewski, J.** *Die Eschatologiereden des Lukas-Evangeliums: Eine traditions- und redaktionsgeschichtliche Untersuchung zu Lk 21,5–36 und Lk 17,20–37.* BBB 40. Bonn: Hanstein, 1972. 43–325, 541–72. ————. "Die Eschatologiereden Lk 21 und Lk 17: Überlegungen zum Verständnis und zur Einordnung der lukanischen Eschatologie." *BibLeb* 14 (1973) 30–40.

FOR 21:5–6:

Bihler, J. *Die Stephanusgeschichte im Zusammenhang der Apostelgeschichte.* Münchener theologische Studien, I. Historische Abteil 16. Munich: Hueber, 1963. 13–16. **Dupont, J.** "Il n'en sera pas laissé pierre sur pierre (Marc 13,2; Luc 19,44)." *Bib* 52 (1971) 301–20. **Meyer, R.** *Der Prophet aus Galiläa: Studie zum Jesusbild der drei ersten Evangelien.* Leipzig: Hinrichs, 1940 (= Darmstadt: Wissenschaftliche Buchgesellschaft, 1970). 16–18. **Schlosser, J.** "La parole de Jésus sur le fin du Temple." *NTS* 36 (1990) 398–414. **Vielhauer, P.** *Oikodome: Aufsätze zum Neuen Testament, Band 2*, ed. G. Klein. Theologische Bücherei 65. Munich: C. Kaiser, 1979. 59–66.

Translation

⁵*As some people were talking about the temple, how it was adorned with beautiful stones and offerings, he said,* ⁶*"These things which you see—days will come in which there will not be left stone upon stone*[a] *which will not be thrown down."*

Notes

[a] The Markan and Matthean ὧδε, "here," is added by ℵ B L *f*¹³ 892 etc.

Form/Structure/Setting

The section 19:47–21:38, during which Jesus teaches in the temple, divides between the units up to 21:4, with their depiction of criticism, conflict, and antagonism between Jesus and various segments of the leadership of Jerusalem, and the units from 21:5 to 21:36 in which Jesus anticipates the unfolding of the future to the coming of the kingdom of God and the Son of Man. These two major subsections are set within an inclusio made up of the opening and closing units (19:47–49; 21:37–38).

Since 21:5–36 is largely a single continuous monologue, the division of units is at times a little arbitrary, but wherever possible it does seek to mark the major transitions in the text. For 21:5–36 Luke continues to follow the Markan sequence, but there is less than agreement about whether his Markan source is the main basis upon which he has produced his version of these materials. There is little doubt that Luke had access to additional materials for this eschatological discourse.

What is in dispute, however, is whether, in materials where Luke only partially parallels his Markan source, Luke is editing rather freely or following an alternative source. At the maximal end are those who consider that Luke has had at his disposal an extensive second version of the eschatological discourse covering as much as vv 5-7, 10-15, 18-20, 21b-26a, 28-31, 34-36 (various scholars suggest a somewhat smaller range for the second source here). This view is mostly found linked with a Proto-Luke hypothesis, according to which Luke was first written without access to the Markan materials and then at a second stage of editing the Markan materials were added into the existing framework (mostly in large blocks). At the minimal end are those who would only allow the influence of an additional tradition in the case of the few verses that have echoes in chap. 17 (esp. vv 23, 27 [v 31 is likely to have its source in the Markan eschatological discourse (13:15)]). (V 18 sounds proverbial, and so is likely to be traditional in that sense, but not necessarily as part of any eschatological discourse.)

Given Luke's general level of intervention in the reproduction of sources, it is difficult to have much confidence in proposals that maximize the scope of a single second source: much of the material is better explained as Lukan editing of his Markan source. There are, however, a series of verses of additional material, where the content is not significantly Lukan, and where it would seem in principle reasonable to suspect access to additional tradition. A generous list of such verses might include vv 11, 18, 21b, 22, 23b, 24, 25, 26a, 28, 34-36. A less generous list might exclude vv 11, 21b, 25a, and possibly even vv 22, 28, and 34-36. The real difficulty is in conceiving of any form other than a more elaborate eschatological discourse in which these materials might have been preserved and communicated. A rather distinctive approach, which has its own answer to this problem, is offered by Wenham (*Rediscovery*), who argues at length for the view that there was an original extended eschatological discourse from which the Synoptic evangelists have excerpted and which they have to varying degrees edited. Wenham produces a reasonable unity for his extended discourse and argues his case with considerable care, but the resulting discourse does not commend itself as a primitive unity and (though with all tentativeness) too much of the case moves speculatively from what could have been the case to what was likely to have been the case. An alternative way of accounting for the additional materials may be in terms of overlapping oral traditions, but perhaps best might be the postulation of an additional eschatological discourse of more limited scope with a content embracing something like vv 11b (beginning "there will be terrors"), 18, 20, 21b, 22, 23b, (24), (25a), (25b), 26a, 28 (v 20 is included as a necessary center of coherence; see *Comment* at 21:9 for a basis for thinking that this source may have originally also included an equivalent to v 9a). However, this too is conjectural. Further source discussion will be provided unit by unit.

The question of the source(s), in turn, for Luke's Markan source, as represented by Mark 13, has for a long time been the subject of an intense debate that shows no signs of declining. A long period of popularity has been enjoyed by the view that the core of Mark 13 is based upon a Jewish or Jewish-Christian apocalyptic pamphlet. Much of the cogency of the original nineteenth-century case for denying the materials to the historical Jesus has collapsed with the demise of the accompanying liberal reconstruction of the historical Jesus (see T. Colani, *Jésus Christ et les croyances messianiques de son temps* [Strasbourg: Treuttel et Würz, 1864], who identifies Mark 13 with the oracle spoken of in Eusebius, *H.E.* 3.5.3, as the basis upon which the Christians of Jerusalem fled to Pella at the beginning of the Jewish war; the historicity of this flight to Pella has come under serious attack, but also defense, in more recent scholarship [S. F. G. Brandon, *The Fall of Jerusalem and the Christian Church*, 2nd ed. [London: SPCK, 1957] 168–73; S. F. G. Brandon, *Jesus and the Zealots* [Manchester: University Press, 1967] 208–16; S. Sowers, "The Circumstances and Recollection of the Pella-flight," *TZ* 26 [1970] 305–20; M. Simon, "Le migration à Pella: Légende ou réalité?" *RSR* 60 [1972] 37–54; B. C. Gray, "The Movements of the Jerusalem Church during the First Jewish War," *JEW* 24 [1973] 1–7; J. J. Gunther, "The Fate of the Jerusalem Church," *TZ* 29 (1973) 81–94; C. Koester, "The Origin and Significance of the Flight to Pella Tradition," *CBQ* 51 [1989] 90–106; G. Lüdemann, "The Successors of Pre-70 Jerusalem Christianity: A Critical Evaluation of the Pella-Tradition," in *Jewish and Christian Self-Definition: Volume 1. The Shaping of Christianity in the Second and Third Centuries*, ed. E. P. Sanders [London: SCM, 1980] 161–73, 245–54; Neirynck, *BETL* 53 [1980] 566–71, 577–85; J. Verheyden, "The Flight of the Christians to Pella," *ETL* 66 [1990] 368–84; the apocalyptic pamphlet has at times been linked not to the Jewish war but to the period of crisis in Jerusalem in the time of Caligula [A.D. 40], and at times it has been seen as going through two editions for use in the two periods of crisis respectively [just occasionally the setting up by Pilate of imperial standards in Jerusalem in A.D. 19 is proposed as the point of origin]). However, new arguments have emerged, and the Jewish-Christian apocalyptic-pamphlet view continues to find powerful supporters (it may be fair to say that the version of this that involved the taking over of a Jewish apocalyptic text and Christianizing it [so Bultmann, *History*, 122] never enjoyed the same levels of popularity and seems to have largely dropped from sight).

While Colani attributed the whole of Mark 13:5–31 to the apocalyptic pamphlet, other proponents of the general view have been more inclined to recognize the composite nature of the materials and to identify only a certain proportion of the material as coming from the apocalyptic pamphlet (so variable has been the identification of this core that Beasley-Murray [*Commentary*, 10] can report that every single verse of Mark 13:5–31 has been included and excluded in one or another of the reconstructions of the original document).

Alongside the apocalyptic pamphlet theory need to be set some of the main competing alternatives. Lambrecht ("Structure," 14–64; *Redaktion*) sees Mark 13 as essentially a Markan creation, drawing on a form of Q tradition that he uses rather loosely, and inspired by a series of OT texts. Only vv 2, 5b–6, 9, 11–13, 14b–16, 21–22, 30–36 have any kind of basis in the Jesus tradition, and of these the tradition base for v 32 is extremely modest. Hartmann (*Prophecy Interpreted*) identifies a midrashic nucleus based on Dan 2:31–45; 7:7–27; 8:9–26; 9:24–27; 11:21–12:4, 13. He considers this to have consisted of vv (5a), 5b–8a, (8b), 12–16, 19–22, 24–27, and is quite content to allow that in its earliest form this midrash goes back to the historical Jesus. Flückiger (*TZ* 26 [1970] 395–409) identifies three intermingled sources: an apocalyptic source in the third person consisting of vv 8, 12, 17, 19–20, 24–27; a temple prophecy source in the second person made up of vv 1–4, 14–16, 18, 28–32; a collection of missionary sayings also in the second person and involving vv 5–6, 21–23, 7, 9–11, 13 (minus editorial insertions). Finally we note the view of Grayston (*BJRL* 56 [1974] 371–87) who, guided by the location of four temporal clauses followed by imperatives in Mark 13 and somewhat by the distinction between second and third person elements in the chapter, finds an original consisting of vv 7a, 9a, (9b), 11, 14–16, 18, 21, 23 and expanded largely from general apocalyptic tradition.

Of these, Flückiger and Grayston do not provide a basis for their allocations of materials that is finally convincing, while Lambrecht demands an editorial technique for Mark 13 that does not seem to be true of other sections of the Gospel. As well, Lambrecht seems, at least in the case of his basis for vv 15–16, to have conceived the direction of dependence backwards (cf. at Luke 17:22–37 on v 31). Hartman offers the most promising approach, though he does tend to move from secure links between Daniel and Mark 13 to insecure ones, and he is too ready to eliminate materials that have no possible link with Daniel, where the discipline of such single-mindedness is hardly characteristic of ancient exposition. Nonetheless, a broad link with Daniel does seem to be evident with at least the following connections to be accepted: Mark 13:7 and Dan 2:28; Mark 13:14 and Dan 7:27; 12:11; Mark 13:19 and Dan 12:1; Mark 13:26 and Dan 7:13, 14. What remains uncertain, however, is whether all of these Daniel links belong to the original wording of the material, or whether, rather, the extent of their presence is to be attributed to a rewriting in Danielic idiom (perhaps inspired by an original Danielic link for only Mark 13:26).

There seems to be no reason to deny to the historical Jesus an expectation of impending judgment upon his People, nor to question that he would, as Jeremiah before him, have focused his expectation of the coming judgment upon the city of Jerusalem and/or its holy sanctuary. When Jesus' view that the intervention of God in the world had reached a decisive stage in connection with his own ministry is linked with his experience of the substantial rejection of his ministry, especially by the leadership classes, it becomes difficult not to attribute to him some such expectation of impending judgment. The expectation of a present generation judgment would seem to have a good base of multiple attestation in the Gospel tradition (Luke 9:27; 11:49–50; 13:34–35; 19:41–44; Luke 21 [which I have suggested above fuses Mark 13 and another eschatological discourse, though this is likely to be a separately transmitted variant of the same tradition]).

If such is the case, then there is an adequate basis for claiming a core of Mark 13 for the historical Jesus. Thus, there is finally no need to postulate an apocalyptic pamphlet, which may be a good thing since the present "apocalyptic pamphlet" is so unlike the apocalyptic documents available for comparison (see Grayston, BJRL 56 [1974] 379–81; Feuillet, RevThom 80 [1980] 187). This is not to deny the composite nature of the present form of Mark 13, but it is to claim that, no matter how extensive the developments may have been, both in terms of rewording and in terms of the incorporation of further traditional materials, the chapter is built upon a significant core that is likely to go back to the historical Jesus (it may be that some general guidance as to the scope of this core is available from the scope of the additional form of the eschatological discourse, which, as I have suggested above, Luke is likely to have employed).

The source question will receive further attention unit by unit.

An outline may help to clarify the large shape and main developments in the discourse (naturally the outline reflects the results yet to emerge in the discussion below). Overhearing in the temple the (self-congratulatory) glorying in the temple by some unnamed people, Jesus, speaking to his disciples in the hearing of the

People, predicts the temple's coming destruction. The disciples ask how and when this will be. Jesus cautions them against any enthusiasm for the destruction of the temple and any thought that as Christians they have a role in making it happen. Then he begins to outline the sequence of events within which the destruction of the temple (and the city with it) will take place. Jesus maps an escalating pattern, from reports of wars and uprisings to the involvement of the whole cosmos, as all the nations of the world convulse under the judgment of God.

But even before this pattern of escalation has its beginning a yet more important beginning is located in the persecution, witness, suffering, and deliverance of the disciple community. This prepares for the coming judgment in a way that significantly parallels Jesus' own path of rejection and suffering in preparation for the coming judgment on the Jewish People.

Well along the curve of escalation comes the disaster to befall Jerusalem. Disciples are to flee when they see armies preparing to lay siege to the city: the city is doomed to fall, to fulfill all scriptural expectations about judgment upon God's rebellious People. But after Jerusalem has felt the full brunt of God's anger, the gentile nations too will get their turn: when the times are ripe, localized judgment in Palestine will give way to (escalate to) a time of judgment for each and every nation of the world. This will herald the coming of the Son of Man and the final deliverance that he will bring.

The disciples are encouraged with the parable of the fig tree and all the trees to find sure pointers to the nearness of deliverance in the unfolding sequence of disasters as they happen; and they are referred to the solid and abiding significance of the words of Jesus in the midst of all this sea of change. In light of all this, Jesus ends with a call to vigilance and prayer: a well sign-posted development to the end will strike as a sudden and unexpected snare if the disciples fail in this discipline.

For vv 5–6, Luke describes a different setting from Mark's, uses an imprecise "certain ones" as speakers instead of Mark's "one of the disciples," and otherwise retains little of the precise Markan wording. The changes make good redactional sense, and there is no sufficient reason to consider that Luke has used more than his Markan source. These verses have the form of a pronouncement story, which may have circulated quite independently of the following materials. The agreement with Luke 19:44, however, over the striking image of not one stone being left upon another raises the possibility that Mark 13:1–2 has been composed by Mark as an introduction to the eschatological chapter on the basis of a tradition like 19:41–44 (see Dupont, *Bib* 52 [1971] 301–20). If this is right, then the redundancy involved in having οὐ μὴ καταλυθῇ, "which will not be thrown down/destroyed" (Mark 13:2), to follow "there will not be left here one stone upon another" is probably to be explained in terms of a secondary dependence upon Mark 14:58.

Comment

The grandeur of the temple, resplendent with the tributes offered in honor of its God, should not lull people into feeling that all is well with God and the world. Indeed all is not well, and the temple of which people were so proud is destined for the same fate as befell the temple of Jeremiah's day, a temple that had become a focus of false security before God among those whose lives failed to honor him.

5   Luke reformulates extensively: what in Mark was an interaction between a certain disciple and Jesus becomes in Luke a tableau played out in front of Jesus upon which he comments to his disciples (rather as in 21:1–4); what in Mark need express no more than that disciple's impression of the fortress-like impregnability of the Jerusalem temple becomes in Luke what is probably meant to be a subtle expression of a falsely based claim upon God's favor (God is fitly honored and his commitment to Jerusalem assured by the presence of a temple made splendid by magnificent offerings; cf. Jer 7; and, for the language, 2 Macc 9:16; Philo, *Ad Gaium* 23.157). See Nolland, "Luke's Readers," 135–42. On the stones used in the building of the Herodian temple see Josephus, *Ant.* 15.392; *War* 5.189; and for an exuberant description of the grandeur of the temple see *War* 5.184–226; *Ant.* 15.391–402. The offerings in view here are those used to beautify and enrich the temple (cf. 2 Macc 3:2; 9:16; Josephus, *War* 5.210–12; *Ant.* 15.395).

6   Unlike in Mark, Jesus in Luke no longer responds directly to the representative(s) of the sentiment (the "you" who "see" are not the anonymous speakers of v 5, but rather "the disciples" . . . "[in the hearing of] all the People" who are identified as Jesus' audience in 20:45). Luke introduces a pendant construction ("these things which you see" [using θεωρεῖτε in place of Mark's βλέπεις) for Mark's grammatically complete "Do you see these great buildings?" (different from Mark, Luke has not used "buildings" in v 5 and so cannot take the term up again here). Luke's added ἐλεύσεται ἡμέραι, "days will come" (redactional also in 17:22; found as well in 5:35; with a present tense in 23:29; and with ἥξουσιν in 19:43), is best seen in relation to the prophetic formula, particularly favored by Jeremiah, ἰδοὺ ἔρχονται ἡμέραι, "behold days are coming" (twelve of seventeen uses, including one in chap. 7 [v 32], a chapter that has other links with the present section). The usage heightens the sense of threat or promise (here the former) in what follows. Luke uses "in which" to link this insertion and prefers simple negative futures for Mark's οὐ μή + aorist subjunctives (emphatic negative futures). Luke deletes Mark's ὧδε, "here," and prefers the dative after ἐπί, "upon" (he failed to make a corresponding change at 19:44). Luke retains the redundancy of the final Markan clause. He will have no parallel to Mark 14:58 but will make use of the link that the language provides at Acts 6:13.

A similar utter desolation of the temple was anticipated many centuries earlier by Jeremiah (7:1–14; 22:5; cf. 52:12–13). Josephus linked the two destructions by maintaining that the firing of the temple in A.D. 70 had taken place on the same day of the year as the firing of the temple by the king of Babylon (*War* 6.250). Luke is also keenly aware of the parallelism.

Explanation

The criticism, conflict, and antagonism of the first half of the present section (19:47–21:38) now give way to a series of linked units in which Jesus anticipates the unfolding of the future to the coming of the kingdom of God and the Son of Man. For the People of God, as for the wider world of the Gentiles, the future that leads to the coming of the kingdom of God and the Son of Man involves the pouring out of God's wrath in judgment.

The setting for the discourse about the future is provided by a group of un-named people who are heard to glory in the magnificence of the temple and the splendor of the adornments provided through the votive offerings that had been given there. There is an implicit expression here of claim upon God akin to that found in Jer 7. God must surely be delighted by all the honors he has received!

The conflict between Jesus as God's emissary and the various leadership groups in 19:47–21:4 suggests, however, that God is probably not delighted after all. And Jesus' words to his disciples here confirm this impression. He describes a judgment that will obliterate the very shrine that was considered to symbolize God's commitment to his People and their claim upon God. Jesus speaks much as Jeremiah had in the vanguard of the sixth-century destruction of Jerusalem and temple (see Jer 7). History will replay itself on a yet grander scale.

The Buildup to the Coming Devastation (21:7–11)

Bibliography

Manson, W. "The *ΕΓΩ ΕΙΜΙ* of the Messianic Presence in the New Testament." *JTS* 48 (1947) 137–45.

And see at 21:5–6.

Translation

> [7] *They asked him, "Teacher, when then will these things be and what is the sign, when these things are to happen?"* [8] *He said, "See that you are not led astray! For many will come in my name saying, 'I am [he],' and 'the time has drawn near.' Do not go after them.* [9] *When you hear of wars and uprisings do not be terrified. For it is necessary that these things happen first. However, the fulfillment*[a] *will not occur immediately."* [10] *Then he said to them, "Nation will rise against nation and kingdom against kingdom;* [11] *there will be great earthquakes, and famines and plagues from place to place; there will be dreadful portents and great signs from heaven."*

Notes

[a] Gr. *τέλος* (lit. "end").

Form/Structure/Setting

Jesus' remark in v 6 provokes questioning by the disciples about timing and about what sign might point to the impending disaster. Jesus' answer carries on to v 36, but it begins in vv 8–11 with a warning about being misled and an account of a rising crescendo of tumult in the world.

Luke follows the Markan sequence, and though there are significant differences (once again [as in vv 5–6] a change of location is deleted, specified persons [here the questioners] becomed anonymous, and a reference to Jesus' name is dropped; "the time has drawn near" is added to the false message of v 8; and in v 11 "these [are] the beginnings of the birth pangs" is displaced by "there will be dreadful portents and great signs from heaven"), there is no sufficient reason for postulating an additional source, except perhaps for v 11b (see further at 21:5–6).

The Markan material is itself not unitary. The question of Mark 13:4 is best seen as a Markan formulation, preparing for the discourse to follow (though the tensions within the question itself might argue for a traditional core [as Zmijewski, *Eschatologiereden*, 85–87; etc.], it is perhaps more likely to result from the artificiality of formulating a question that needs to follow v 2 and at the same time anticipate what is to come in vv 5–37). The material of v 5 occurs in another form in Luke 17:23, a form likely to be closer to the original (see discussion there). Vv 7–8 belong together (as well as shared subject matter, there is a parallelism of structure). They form no original unity with what precedes or follows, but it is difficult to see how they could have been transmitted without a larger context. War is "a standard apocalyptic stage prop" (Fitzmyer, 1336), and it is certainly possible that the verses belong to a late stage in the development of this discourse. But war belongs to the OT judgments in history (see Isa 19:2; 2 Chr 15:6) every bit as much as to an apocalyptic climax at the end of history (*4 Ezra* 13:31). An original unity with the materials to come in vv 14–20 is perhaps yet more likely, since v 14 certainly requires some introductory material, and vv 7–8 would provide introductory material of the correct genre.

Comment

How and when will the destruction of the temple take place? Certainly not by violent intervention by Christ or his followers! An escalating pattern of wars and disturbances, along with earthquakes, famines, and plagues and with dreadful portents and signs from heaven, will be part of the divinely appointed process that leads to the demise of the temple.

7 In line with his desire to set the whole of this section in the temple precincts, Luke deletes the Markan setting. The Markan privacy is also removed, and along with it goes the list of names of those privileged to be with Jesus at this point. The Markan "teacher," which was not used in v 5, is used here (on Luke's use of "teacher" in address to Jesus see at 7:40). Luke finds Mark's "all" before "these things" unmotivated and deletes it (it was formulated by Mark more with an eye to what is to come than with reference to what precedes). Similarly, Mark's rather grand συντελεῖσθαι, "to be accomplished," is reduced to γίνεσθαι, "to happen" (in the process obscuring what is likely to have been an allusion to Dan 12:7 [see LXX wording]). In the Lukan question, nothing appears beyond the destruction of the temple as envisaged in v 6. There are other minor changes.

Why should the disciples assume that there will be a sign given before the destruction of the temple? And what might constitute such a sign? I have argued elsewhere ("Luke's Readers," esp. 208–12), in connection with the thesis that Luke writes with an awareness of a Jewish polemical use of the tradition behind Mark 14:58/Acts 6:14 (used to stigmatize Christians as followers of a schismatic pseudo-messiah, unfaithful to central Jewish practices, who planned a revolutionary takeover in Jerusalem involving the destruction of the present temple [see "Luke's Readers," 144–203]), that Luke is served by a deliberate ambiguity in the sign language here. Against the background of this Jewish polemic the σημεῖον could be taken as the "signal" for the assault on Jerusalem and its temple and is thus well motivated in this particular way. But as the discourse unfolds, it becomes quite clear that the answer distances itself from all such assumptions and that the question has after all not been intended in such a sense at all.

The role of the sign here is to be seen against the background of the signs of 2 Kgs 19:29–31 = Isa 37:30–32; Isa 7:11–16 (and cf. Exod 3:12), where the sign is not so much a warning announcement coming immediately prior to the prophesied event but serves rather to provide a time frame for the coming of the heralded future. It is likely, therefore, that we should see "the sign" in a somewhat encompassing way as the increasing turmoil in the world around, culminating in the encirclement of Jerusalem by armies.

8 Luke strips out from his Markan source the fresh introduction of Jesus and the language of beginning. He recasts Mark's μή τις ὑμᾶς πλανήσῃ (lit. "lest someone lead you astray") into the passive, adds "and the time has drawn near" to the language of those who would mislead, and replaces Mark's "and they will lead many astray" with "do not go after them." There are other minor changes.

For Luke, Christians are well warned against those who would mislead and will, therefore, not be led astray. ἐπὶ τῷ ὀνόματί μου (lit. "upon my name") has been taken in quite a number of ways ("as Christians"; "pretending to be me"; "claiming my authority"; "speaking in my name [as OT prophets spoke in the name of Yahweh]"; etc.). But the traditional understanding "claiming to be the Christ, i.e., claiming my office" has the most to commend it (see Nolland, "Luke's Readers," 213–18, 313–23). ἐγώ εἰμι (lit. "I [emphatic] am") has most often been taken to mean "I am the Christ," but by some to mean "[that] I am here" (announcing Jesus' secret presence), or as a mark of prophetic possession in which the speaker becomes the mouthpiece of the deity (see discussion in "Luke's Readers," 213–16). The predominant view is certainly the correct one.

Luke's addition of "the time has drawn near" has often been taken as warning against all preaching of the imminence of the eschaton. But this is to lose sight of the immediate context, in which the time we have been encouraged to focus on is that of the destruction of the temple (and cf. the use of the same verb form in v 20; and the almost identical language in Lam 4:18 in connection with the destruction of Jerusalem). Again, the Jewish polemic may offer insight, with its suggestion (with a certain family likeness to Qumran hostility to the leadership in Jerusalem and dreams of future violent displacement of that leadership) that the Christian messiah had been expected to lead his followers in an attack on Jerusalem, to wreak vengeance on the present regime, to destroy the temple and forcibly to set up a Christian regime. Against this background Luke's rewording "do not follow them" may be taken as forbidding the following into battle of messianic war leaders who declare that the time is ripe for Jerusalem's destruction. Contrast the totally passive role assigned to Christians at the time of the destruction (v 21) and the absence of Jesus in the crucial period and until his later arrival as the Son of Man (v 27, 36). The aim of the verse in Luke's hands is to distance Christianity from the Jewish polemical caricature. In the process, he produces a form of the prophecy that, while it accurately reflects strands within the range of Jewish thinking of the period received historically, so far as we are aware, describes no precise fulfillment.

9 Luke's changes here are ἀκαταστασίας, "uprisings," for Mark's ἀκοὰς πολέμων, "rumors of wars"; πτοηθῆτε, "be terrified," for θροεῖσθε, "be disturbed/frightened"; οὐκ εὐθέως, "not immediately," for οὔπω, "not yet"; and the addition of γὰρ ταῦτα . . . πρῶτον, "for these things [to happen] first" (there may be an allusion to Jer 51:46 in the Markan text that Luke's editing has obscured; if this is so, then a corresponding allusion to v 45 may be better preserved in Luke 21:21b, to v 55 in Luke 21:25b, and, possibly, to v 48 in Luke 21:25–26). Repeatedly in the OT, terror is a natural response to the prospect of war (e.g., Amos 3:6). The encouragement here not to be terrified is the beginning point of a thread through the chapter of indications that there is in the midst of this rising tide of turmoil and distress some kind of protection for the disciple community (cf. vv 18–19, 21, 28 [but contrast v 16]). The specific reason provided for not being terrified is the divine necessity that is in control of this apparently chaotic and out of control unfolding of events (an allusion to Dan 2:28 is claimed but is far from certain). Luke marks here the beginning point of an unfolding development, which will carry through to τὸ τέλος (lit. "the end"), but not at once (Luke's "not immediately" is not really different from Mark's "not yet" when we take into account Mark's "these [are the] beginning of the birth-pangs," which Luke does not use). τὸ τέλος may be deliberately ambiguous, but its most evident reference is to the end of the temple, possibly with the word taking the sense "fulfillment" as it does in 22:37. Alternatively it may function as a synonym for judgment, along the lines of the uses in Ezek 7:2–3, 6–7. In the development of the chapter, we should note the continuity as well as escalation from v 9 to vv 10–11 and to vv 25–26 (Luke's change to "uprisings" [i.e., smaller-scale disturbances] may be in the interests of marking more clearly this escalation).

10 Luke provides a fresh beginning here with "Then he said to them" (Mark linked with "for," but Luke has used that in v 9; cf. the Lukan insertion at 6:5). The language here may allude to 2 Chr 15:6 (for the reference to "nation against nation") and to Isa 19:2 (for "kingdom against kingdom"; these texts share a reference to "city against city" not used here). If this is so, then these preliminary experiences must be seen as already coming within the orbit, in a preliminary way, of that climactic judgment that is to be anticipated later in the chapter.

11 Luke moves the verb "will be" from its Markan opening position and drops Mark's repetition of the verb. He adds "great" to "earthquakes" to replace "from place to place," which he steals to link instead with "famines." With "famines" Luke pairs "plagues" (the Greek terms are λιμοί and λοιμοί, so they form a natural literary pair [see Hesiod, Op. 243; Thucydides, Hist. 2.54; T. Judah 23:3; Sib. Or. 8:175]). For some of these disasters, cf. Ezek 38:19–22; Isa 5:13–14; Hag 2:6; Rev 6:8; 11:13; etc. In place of Mark's "these [are the] beginning of the birth-pangs," Luke continues the list with "there will be dreadful portents and great signs from heaven" (perhaps from a second source). In terms of the escalation, it may be right to distinguish "signs from heaven" = "signs from God" here from the signs in the heavenly bodies of v 25, or alternatively "signs in the sky" from the signs in the heavenly bodies. V 11b has interesting parallels in Josephus' description of events surrounding the destruction of the temple in A.D. 70 (War 6.288–311; cf. also Tacitus Hist. 5.13; 2 Macc 5:2–3; Sib. Or. 3:796–808). The Lukan changes in vv 10–11 make what was in Mark an elaboration of the point of the previous verse into a separate escalating development. There is, however, no reason up to this point for seeing this development as heading toward anything other than the destruction of the temple as introduced in v 6.

Explanation

Jesus' forecast naturally provokes questioning: how and when will the destruction of the temple take place? The answer begins by rejecting any Christian do-it-yourself origination of the divinely ordained future. He then portrays an escalating sequence of human and natural disasters, along with portents from God, that will begin the process leading inexorably to the destruction of the temple.

There is quite an ambiguity in the question about "the sign." It would seem that there was a Jewish caricature of Christianity used in polemic that was based on the traditions behind Mark 14:58; Acts 6:13–14. This represented Christianity as violently opposed to the normal practices of Judaism and as fostering dreams of a violent capture of Jerusalem, involving the destruction of the temple and the imposition of a Christian regime. Against this background "the sign" could be a signal that the time had come to make an attack on Jerusalem. Luke allows for the possibility of the question being (mis-)taken this way in order to show, especially in v 8, how wrong it is to see Christians in any such light.

If the sign is no signal to attack, neither is it likely to be narrowly conceived as a warning announcement, immediately to precede the prophesied event. As in 2 Kgs 19:29–31 and Isa 37:30–32, it is more likely that the sign provides something of a time frame for the anticipated event. It is to be thought of in a rather more encompassing manner as related to the picture Jesus is about to create of increasing turmoil in the world around, culminating in the encirclement of Jerusalem by armies.

The false Christs anticipated in v 8 are those who would encourage their followers to work actively for the destruction of the temple: "the time has come for its destruction; let's go and do it." Christians have been warned to avoid such involvement (see v 21 below) and would not follow any such leader.

Instead, Jesus finds the beginning point of the process that will lead to the temple's destruction in reports of wars and uprisings (events with which disciples have no personal connection). They should not be terrified by what seems to be a chaotic unfolding of events because such are not simply random manifestations threatening to engulf them. Far from it! They represent the necessary unfolding of the divine plan. As the chapter develops, it will become clearer that this unfolding future includes a measure of special protection for the disciple band.

The identified beginning point is subject to escalation, and the escalation is spelled out in vv 10–11. Beyond the human disaster of war there will be earthquakes, famines, and plagues. And beyond these again there will be dreadful portents and signs from heaven. The Jewish historian Josephus reported such portents and signs in the buildup to the destruction of Jerusalem and the temple. There was a widespread belief in the ancient world that such manifestations would anticipate or accompany highly significant happenings. Against such a background, it is hard to be sure, as moderns, how literally to take such language. In any case, we can detect a rising crescendo that has not reached its high point by v 11.

Persecution Comes First of All   (21:12-19)

Bibliography

Barrett, C. K. *The Holy Spirit and the Gospel Tradition.* London: SPCK, 1966. 130-32. **Dupont, J.** "La persécution comme situation missionaire (Marc 13, 9-11)." In *Die Kirche des Anfangs,* ed. R. Schnackenburg et al. 97-114. **Fuchs, A.** *Sprachliche Untersuchungen.* 37-44, 171-91. **Giblet, J.** "Les promesses de l'Esprit et la mission des apôtres dans les évangiles." *Irénikon* 30 (1957) 5-43, esp. 17-19. **Grässer, E.** *Parusieverzögerung.* 158-61. **Hartman, L.** *Testimonium linguae: Participial Constructions in the Synoptic Gospels: A Linguistic Examination of Luke 21,13.* ConNT 19. Lund: Gleerup, 1963. 57-75. **Kilpatrick, G. D.** "Mark xiii. 9-10." *JTS* n.s. 9 (1958) 81-86. **Kühschelm, R.** *Jüngerverfolgung und Geschick Jesu: Eine exegetisch-bibeltheologische Untersuchung der synoptischen Verfolgungsankündigungen Mk 13,9-13 par und Mt 23,29-36 par.* OBS 5. Klosterneuburg: Österreichisches Katholisches Bibelwerk, 1983. **Mahoney, M.** "Luke 21:14-15: Editorial Rewriting or Authenticity?" *ITQ* 47 (1980) 220-38. **Reicke, B.** "A Test of Synoptic Relationships: Matthew 10,17-23 and 24,9-14 with Parallels." In *New Synoptic Studies,* ed. W. R. Farmer. Macon, GA: Mercer, 1983. 209-29.

And see at 21:5-6.

Translation

[12] *"But [even] before all these things, they will lay their hands upon you*[a] *and perse-cute [you], handing you over to synagogues and prisons, [and with you] being brought before kings and governors for the sake of my name.* [13] *This will lead to [an opportunity] for you for witness.* [14] *Determine in your hearts, then, not to prepare beforehand in order to make a defense.* [15] *For I will give you a mouth and wisdom which none of your oppo-nents will be able to withstand or contradict.* [16] *You will be handed over even by parents and brothers, and relatives and friends, and they will have some of you put to death.*[b] [17] *You will be hated by all because of my name.* [18] *But not a hair of your head will perish.* [19] *By your steadfastness secure*[c] *your lives!"*

Notes

[a] ℵ reads "them," which can only be a mechanical transcription error.
[b] Lit. "they will put some of you to death."
[c] A B Θ *f*[13] 33 pc lat sa bo[pt] read κτήσεσθε, "you will secure." The thought flows more easily and consistently with this reading, and it is just possible that it is original.

Form/Structure/Setting

Before the necessary wars and uprisings make their appearance, the persecu-tion of the disciple community begins. Many locate the end of the parenthesis begun in v 12 at v 24, but there are considerable difficulties with such a terminus: (*i*) in this arrangement Jerusalem (and thus the temple) gets destroyed in the parenthesis, which is awkward given the starting point in v 6; (*ii*) there is no con-tinuity between the themes of vv 12-19 and v 20, which makes v 20 a more natural breaking point; (*iii*) the fresh time indication at v 20 points in the same direction;

(*iv*) the war language of vv 9, 10 is good preparation for the role of armies in v 20; (*v*) the measure of parallelism between v 23a and 26a is best respected if the former is not separated into a parenthesis.

Luke continues to follow the Markan sequence, while providing with his chronological parenthesis his own precision of the relationship between events anticipated in this chapter. For the most part, nothing beyond the Markan source is evident, but for vv 14–15 it is likely (against the consensus of scholarship) that Luke has made further use of the second source also reflected in part at 12:11–12 (see there and *Comment* below), and v 18 may be from the second eschatological discourse with which Luke appears to have conflated his Markan source in this chapter (see at 21:5–6).

The materials behind the Markan section do not constitute an original unity. Mark 13:9–11, 12(–13a), and 13(b) are each likely to have independent tradition histories. The tradition behind vv 9–11 (without the last phrase of v 9 and all of v 10) is independently attested by a second source available to Matthew and Luke. On its fundamental historicity, cf. at 12:11–12. The tradition behind Mark 13:12 clearly has some family likeness to that behind Luke 12:51–53. Though it is likely that Jesus anticipated the emergence, in connection with allegiance to himself, of fundamental divisions between even those most intimately related (cf. 14:26), it is not clear whether the specific language here, and in particular the elaboration in terms of allusion to Mic 7:6, goes back to the historical Jesus or not (on the place of Mic 7:6 in the Gospels and Jewish tradition see Grelot [*Bib* 67 (1986) 363–77]). V 13a may still belong to the allusion to Mic 7:6 (see *Comment* below). Though the steadfastness commended in v 13b fits well enough the historical Jesus, the formulation here is likely to be Markan.

Luke retains the large shape of the Markan structure with its move from persecution to "triumph" in 13:9–11 and then again in vv 12–13. He reinforces the positive tone of the outcome in Luke 21:18–19.

Comment

The persecution of the disciples follows in the train of the rejection of Jesus, and is yet more fundamental than the wars and portents in the pattern of events leading to the judgment that is to fall on the Jerusalem temple. The exalted Jesus will himself provide the powerful words of witness needed to confute every foe; and though some will die, Christians who remain steadfast in their confession of faith will experience divine protection to an extraordinary degree.

12 Luke's total reformulation includes the replacement of Mark's opening words of warning by his own "Before all this" through to "persecute [you]" (Dupont [*Trois apocalypses*,114] has drawn attention to the way in which Luke has systematically changed the tone through vv 12–19 from that of warning to that of encouragement and call for confidence; the idiom "to lay hands upon" has been introduced by Luke in 20:19 in connection with Jesus and is used here to link the disciples' coming experience and his; "persecute" is probably for the sake of a link with 11:49); the use of "synagogues" and "prisons" as a pair instead of Mark's "councils [συνέδρια] and synagogues" (Luke does not speak of "councils"; he uses the word only of the Sanhedrin); the loss of Mark's mention of beatings (since beatings are frequent in Acts and also part of the passion account [a fact curiously denied by Kühschelm, *Jüngerfolgung* 200], the loss is likely to be only stylistically motivated); reversal of the order in which governors and kings are introduced (possibly with the order in Ps 2:2 in mind [cf. Acts 4:25–29], but perhaps just to start at the higher level, as is his practice elsewhere); replacement of "for my sake" with "for the sake of my name" (Luke does not use the precise phrase elsewhere, but he uses "the name of" in relation to Jesus many times, predominantly in connection with the actual utterance of Jesus' name; here the sense is probably "because of the confession of me which you make"). Luke creates an awkwardness with his use of ἀπαγομένους, "being brought": this participle forms a kind of parallel to παραδιδόντες, "handing over," where the latter refers back to the persecutors who have been the subject of the preceding verbs, while the former refers back to the use of ὑμᾶς, "you," after the first verb.

Far from being concerned to distance his account of the persecution of Christians from his narrative of the developments to the final crisis, Luke's "before all this" gives to the persecution a fundamental significance for precisely this final crisis (cf. 11:49–51 and discussion there). The persecutors are introduced anonymously, but that both the Jewish and the gentile spheres are involved is signalled by "synagogues" and "governors," respectively. The Acts material provides extensive illustrations of how he saw this to be worked out concretely in the life of the church.

13 Luke amplifies Mark's εἰς μαρτύριον αὐτοῖς, "for a witness to/against them," into the separate statement ἀποβήσεται ὑμῖν εἰς μαρτύριον (translated above as "this will lead to [an opportunity] for you for witness"). The sense of Luke's form has been taken in various ways. Hartman (*Testimonium*, 57–75; cf. Zmijewski, *Eschatologiereden*, 161–69; Dupont, *Trois apocalypses*, 115–16) thinks of a testimony in the disciples' favor at the eschatological judgment, but this makes for a hardly warranted intrusion into the present context. Other unlikely senses include "this will cause you to be shown up in a positive light" and "this will show you how stiff-necked and therefore destined to judgment are the Jews" (for the latter see Keck, *Abschiedsrede*, 205–8). The majority of scholars rightly see that Luke has changed the Markan meaning little here. In question is only whether Luke thinks of the whole response to the courtroom situation as constituting the witness or whether he thinks more narrowly of verbal witness to the Christian faith. Despite the normal distinction between μαρτύριον as the objective testimony and μαρτυρία as the act of testifying (which would favor the latter view), comparison with Acts 4:33 and the role of verbal activity in vv 12 and 14–15 incline me to think that he intends the latter.

Luke lacks an equivalent to Mark 13:10: the verse does not lend itself to Luke's pattern of editing all the materials of this unit to second person plural forms (see Dupont, *Trois apocalypses*, 113); the general point about witnessing to the faith has already been adequately made; Luke avoids the noun form "gospel"; and from his point of view the gospel to the nations is at this point still anachronistic (24:47 may be a Lukan equivalent to the Markan verse).

14 θέτε . . . ἐν ταῖς καρδίαις ὑμῶν (lit. "place in your hearts") is Semitic but is likely to be a Lukan Septuagintalism (cf. at 1:66; see 1 Kgdms 21:13; Mal 2:2; and esp. Hag 2:15). προμελετᾶν, "prepare, rehearse beforehand," which has a technical use in connection with practicing or memorizing a speech (see BAGD, 708), is likely to be a Lukan improvement (this is the only NT occurrence). The use of ἀπολογηθῆναι, "make a defense," is the one clear verbal link (beyond a γάρ, "for") with the form of this tradition given at Luke 12:11–12 (see there).

15 Luke is likely to be responsible for making Jesus himself the dispenser of "mouth and wisdom" (cf. Acts 18:9–10; 4:29). Otherwise Luke probably follows quite closely his second source here (cf. at 12:11–12). The role of the mouth is quite prominent in OT diction, but only Judg 9:38 comes close to the idiom involved here. The gift of wisdom is a widely attested idea within and outside Judaism. In Luke, cf. 2:40, 52; 7:35; 11:49. "Wisdom" and "Spirit" are paired in Acts 6:10 (reverse order in 6:3), "wisdom" and "stature" in Luke 2:52, "grace" and "wisdom" in Acts 7:10. Luke is responsible for some of these pairings but is not likely to have originated the pairing here of "mouth" and "wisdom" (the similar language in Acts 6:10 [note the use there of ἀντιστῆναι, "withstand," as well] is to recall the present verse). ἅπαντες οἱ ἀντικείμενοι (lit. "all the opponents") echoes 13:17 and makes clear that 13:10–17 is a working out in Jesus' own ministry (but not directly in a courtroom context) of what is promised to his disciples here for the future (considering its schematic role there, it is likely that the language in 13:17 has been borrowed from the present verse to make the link).

In v 16 it becomes clear, however, that being able to speak so powerfully is not a guarantee of safe deliverance.

16 Luke changes to a second person verb form and adopts his own approach to the formulation of this prophecy of intimate betrayal: Mark identifies both parties in each of a series of family relationships and deals with children betraying parents in a separate clause; Luke treats all together but specifies in each case only one party, seeing each in terms of the relationship to the "you" of the verb. Luke introduces a general term for relatives and also moves beyond family to include friends. By dropping "to death" from the statement about handing over and by adding "some of you," Luke makes it clear that the prospect of death is not general. In the Lukan rewording, the allusion to Mic 7:6 in Mark 13:12 disappears from sight. The involvement of family and friends is yet more distressing than the anonymous opponents introduced in v 12. The death of some is amply illustrated in Acts, but there is no reported incident of intimate betrayal (the prototype will be betrayal of Jesus by Judas).

17 Mark 13:13a is reproduced without change. The widespread unpopularity of the Christian movement is reflected in Acts 28:22, but Luke is unlikely to think in terms of a necessary profound antagonism between Christians and all others (cf. Acts 19:31; etc.). Perhaps he takes "all" as "all sorts of" rather than universally, or more likely as referring to all (sorts of) family and other intimate links (the LXX of Mic 7:6 has "[the] enemies of a man will be all the men in his house[hold]"). But in the context of the movement toward the eschatological climax, there is a tendency toward dualistic language, and Luke may consider that the extremity of the language is appropriate in such a setting. διὰ τὸ ὄνομά μου, "because of my name," is likely, as for the similar phrase in v 12, to refer to confession of allegiance to Jesus.

18 Luke adds v 18, which may come from a second eschatological discourse (see at 21:5–6). The addition strengthens the positive thrust of v 19 to come. Though 12:7 is based on the Jewish idiom reflected here as well (see at 12:7), that verse is hardly a doublet of 21:18. Luke will echo the present promise in Acts 27:34 (those with Paul participate in his divine protection). Though Luke admits the reality of the prospect of death in v 16, he thinks, nevertheless, very concretely, and more generally, of the reality of divine protection in the midst of extreme difficulty (there is no encouragement at all to spiritualize here). Again the material in Acts provides ample illustration.

19 The threatening edge to Mark's word of encouragement disappears in the Lukan editing: there is no questioning of the disciples' perseverance, only a pointing to steadfastness in the confession of Christ as offering the place of security for the future. Following on v 18, Luke thinks concretely of the saving of life in the midst of danger (he thinks of deliverance in concrete situations and not, as in Mark, of salvation resulting from a steady perseverance to the eschaton/fall of Jerusalem). Luke deliberately uses language that will sound paradoxical in a context where secular wisdom would suggest that renouncing Christ is what will assure life. Of course the assurance of the present verse cannot negate the thrust of v 16, but it is 9:24 and not the present verse that proposes a larger view that can embrace death as a way to retain life.

Explanation

Wars and portents may be important markers, but what begins yet earlier and is of more fundamental importance is the persecution of the disciple community. Luke begins a parenthesis here that he will carry through to v 19 at the end of this unit. The story describes terrible persecution balanced by help from on high that is more than a match for the opposition.

Persecution of Christians follows the opposition mounted to Jesus himself and makes its own contribution to the onset of the divine judgment that is to be the outcome of the rejection of his ministry (see 12:49–53; 11:49–51; 13:34–35; 19:41–44). It is clear from the venues involved that Luke thinks in terms of persecution in both the Jewish and gentile spheres.

For Christians, persecution is to be an opportunity for faithful confession and bearing witness to the Christian faith one has professed. What is called for in these situations of legal answerability is not a well-prepared defense script but simply the readiness to become the mouthpiece of the exalted Jesus. This will produce a powerful witness, which not even the most hardened of opponents will be able to withstand or contradict (cf. Acts 6:10).

Persecution will, however, come from even the closest of quarters: from the bosom of one's family and from one's intimate friends (the prototype for intimate betrayal is Judas' betrayal of Jesus). And persecution will for some of the disciple band lead to loss of life (cf. Acts 7:60; 12:2). Indeed the disciple must look forward to the prospect of universal hatred.

But if this is so, the disciple may also look forward to dramatic and palpable divine protection. Again Acts provides illustrations, of both a miraculous and a non-miraculous nature (e.g., Acts 4:21, 29; 9:23–25; 12:6–11; etc.). Where popular wisdom would see the renunciation of faith in Christ as the way to save one's life, our text maintains exactly the opposite. The key to the preservation of life is precisely steadfastness in the confession of Christ. This will not cover every case (see v 16), and there is a place for backing up to the even more paradoxical teaching of 9:24, but the point here is the reality of the divine protection of life in the midst of the most dangerous of situations into which one has been placed for confessing Christ.

The Devastation of Jerusalem (21:20–24)

Bibliography

Braumann, G. "Die lukanische Interpretation der Zerstörung Jerusalems." *NovT* 6 (1963) 120–27. **Conzelmann, H.** *Luke.* 125–32. **Dodd, C. H.** "The Fall of Jerusalem." *JRS* 37 (1947) 47–54; reprinted in *More New Testament Studies.* Grand Rapids: Eerdmans, 1968. 69–83. **Flückiger, F.** "Luk. 21.20–24 und die Zerstörung Jerusalems." *TZ* 28 (1972) 385–90. **Giblin, C. H.** *The Destruction of Jerusalem according to Luke's Gospel: A Historical-Typological Moral.* AnBib 107. Rome: Biblical Institute Press, 1985. **Holst, R.** "God's Truth in a Kaleidoscope: Using a Synopsis." *CurTM* 3 (1976) 347–54. **Pedersen, S.** "Zum Problem der vaticinia ex eventu (Eine analyse von Mt. 21,33–46 par.; 22,1–10 par.)." *ST* 19 (1965) 167–88. **Reicke, B.** "Synoptic Prophecies on the Destruction of Jerusalem." In *Studies in the New Testament and Early Christian Literature.* FS A. P. Wikgren. NovTSup 33. Leiden: Brill, 1972. 121–34. **Taylor, V.** "A Cry from the Siege: A Suggestion regarding a Non-Marcan Oracle Embedded in Lk. xxi 20–36." *JTS* 26 (1924–25) 136–44. **Wainwright, A. W.** "Luke and the Restoration of the Kingdom to Israel." *ExpTim* 89 (1977–78) 76–79.

And see at 21:5–6.

Translation

[20] *"When you see Jerusalem surrounded by armies,[a] then know that its devastation has drawn near.* [21] *Then let those who are in Judea flee to the mountains, and let[b] those in the midst of the city[c] go out from it, and those out in the fields not enter it.* [22] *For these are days of vengeance to fulfill all that has been written.* [23] *Woe to those who are pregnant and to those who are nursing [infants] in those days. For there will be great calamity upon the land and wrath against this People.* [24] *They will fall by the mouth of the sword and be led captive to all the nations, until the times for the nations have their fulfillment."[d]*

Notes

[a] Or "camps."

[b] D vg[mss] rather curiously have inserted a negative here.

[c] Gr. αὐτοῦ, "her/it."

[d] Gr. πληρωθῶσιν (lit. "are filled/filled").

Form/Structure/Setting

The continuity point for v 20 is v 11, since vv 12–19 have been a chronological parenthesis (see at 21:12–19: vv 12–19 set the background more remotely than do vv 8–11). The pattern of escalation from v 9 to vv 10–11 will continue in vv 25–26. The judgment of God upon Jerusalem takes its place along the curve of this escalation that leads ultimately to worldwide judgment upon the nations and to the coming of the kingdom of God and the Son of Man.

Again we have the Markan sequence, but now only a small amount of close agreement with the Markan wording (in v 20 the opening three words and the use of ἐρήμωσις, "devastation"; in v 21 the opening clause; the whole of v 23). Scholarly opinion is split over whether Luke has extensively rewritten (after the destruction of Jerusalem?) or he is reflecting a second source. A second source view involving vv 20, 21bc, 22, 23b, and possibly also v 24 as part of a larger document including also vv 11b, 18, 26a, 28, and possibly vv 25a, 25b is favored in the survey at 21:5–6 above (see further there). Luke is likely to have intervened in the wording of v 22b. V 24 is something of a pastiche of OT allusion; it is clear that it has reached its present form on the basis of the Septuagint, but it is not really possible to tell what Luke's role might have been in its formation. In any case, none of the description in vv 20–24 warrants the suspicion that it has been formulated in the light of the actual experience of A.D. 66–70.

The elaborate allusion to Scripture that is involved in both the Markan form and the second form available to Luke (esp. if a form of v 24 predates Luke), combined with the fact that the series of allusions is almost entirely different, indicates that we are dealing with highly interpreted accounts. There is every likelihood that a core goes back to the historical Jesus, but this has undergone major transformation, in the context of scriptural meditation. No definite delineation of the underlying words of Jesus is possible (see further at 21:5–6).

Comment

Report of wars, disasters in the wider world setting, and the experience of portents now give way to the concrete threat of surrounding armies. The disciples are to flee the impending doom of the city, aware that this is God's definitive judgment upon a history of disobedience to him. As in a previous time, God's historic People will experience his wrath in death and exile to slavery. But the gentile instruments of God's judgment will themselves experience judgment in turn.

20 The opening "When you see" and the use of ἐρήμωσις, "devastation/desolation," are all that Luke and Mark have in common here. As was the case in 19:41–44, the vocabulary used in connection with the fall of Jerusalem can all be culled from LXX descriptions of earlier threat to Jerusalem (e.g., for the terms used in v 20, see Isa 29:3; Jer 41:1 [MT 34:1]; 51:6, 22 [MT 44:6, 22]). The disciple community will come face to face with the imminent demise of Jerusalem (and thus the temple) in terms of the sight of an attacking army rather than in terms of a warrior messiah who urges them to the attack, saying the "the time has drawn near" (see v 8). In the early stages of the Roman engagement with Jerusalem, the city was in fact effectively isolated, hemmed in by the army on every side (see Josephus, War 4.486–90).

The temple focus of vv 5–6 has given way to a whole Jerusalem focus here. The Markan equivalent (13:14) maintained the temple focus but, with its Danielic allusion ("desolating sacrilege"; see Dan 12:11; cf. 9:27; 11:31), concerned itself with the desecration rather than the destruction of the temple. The possibility is raised at 21:5–6 above that the Danielic allusions of the Markan form might represent a (pre-)Markan apocalyptic encoding rather than the more straightforward Lukan form being a secondary decoding (in light of the actual events of the war). Since for Mark the temple desecration implies disaster for the whole of Judea, the significance of the difference of focus should not be exaggerated.

21 The clearest evidence of Luke's use of a second source in this unit comes from the conflation here between the final clause of Mark 13:14 (reproduced exactly), which has a whole Judean perspective, and the second and third clauses of Luke 21:21 (not paralleled in Mark), in which the perspective returns to the Jerusalem perspective that was operative in v 20 ("in the midst of her" can only be "in the midst of Jerusalem"; for a possible allusion to Jer 51:45 in v 21bc see at 21:9). From time immemorial mountains have been a place of retreat and refuge from a pressing enemy force (cf. Judg 1:34; 6:2; 1 Sam 23:19; 26:1; Jer 16:16; 50:6; Lam 4:19). A fortified city is a normal place of refuge in time of war, but this city is destined to fall, so the normal pattern of advice is reversed for those within and without the walls of the city. Cf. Jeremiah's advice in Jer 21:8–10.

After the earlier isolation of Jerusalem by the Roman forces, the news of Nero's death and its aftermath led to a delay in the prosecution of the war in Judea and of the assault on Jerusalem (*War* 4.497–98, 501–2). This resulted in some relaxation of the stranglehold on the city (the activities of Simon described in *War* 4.503–76 imply that this is the case). Though "wisdom after the event" is frequently claimed as the basis for features of the Gospel account of Jerusalem's fall, the possibility that an opportunity might present itself to slip out of the city after an initial encirclement hardly requires hindsight to present itself. The same had been true of the Babylonian siege (Jer 34:21; 37:11 [Jer 52:7 even reports escape from the city (finally thwarted) while the city was encircled by the Babylonians]) and must have been a standard part of the ebb and flow of war.

The relationship between this directive to flee and the flight of the Jerusalem Christians to Pella as reported by Eusebius (*H.E.* 3.5.3) remains uncertain despite extensive scholarly discussion (for bibliography see *Form/Structure/Setting* at 21:5–6). Did the flight occur at the beginning of the Jewish war, as suggested by Eusebius, or later? Did it occur at all? Did the tradition behind Mark 13/Luke 21 influence the oracle said to be the basis of the departure? The view that Mark 13 and Luke 21 depend upon a Jewish-Christian apocalyptic pamphlet is rejected at 21:5–6 above.

22 Luke has no parallel to Mark 13:15–16. He has used a version of this at 17:31 (taken from his Markan source). In any case, though they make quite different points, there is too much structural similarity between these materials and what Luke has in v 21bc (but with the house in the former taking the place of the city in the latter) to make a good literary sequence. V 22 has no Markan parallel. "Days of vengeance" has its closest Septuagintal parallel in Hos 9:7. Also worth considering is Jer 51:6 (LXX 28:6), "time of vengeance." Though it refers to Babylon rather than to Israel, it uses נקמה, *nĕqāmāh*, which (despite the Septuagintal translators of Hos 9:7) is closer to the Greek ἐκδίκησις than is the שלם, *šillūm* of Hos 9:7, and which follows imagery of fleeing from a doomed city as does Luke 21:22. Jer 51:6 involves inflicting upon Babylon what she had earlier inflicted upon Jerusalem (cf. 50:15), and so an allusion to Jer 51:6 would prepare for the move from judgment upon Jerusalem by the Gentiles to judgment in turn upon the Gentiles, which we find in v 24 (see discussion below) and vv 25–26 (the wider perspective of judgment would seem to be already in view with the "all" of v 22b).

Though Luke introduces πάντα τὰ γεγραμμένα, "everything that is written," at 18:31 and probably at 24:44, he does not elsewhere use the verb πιμπλάναι, "to fill/ fulfill," in connection with the fulfillment of Scripture. We cannot be sure what Luke's source read at this point. The vengeance to be exacted will be the culmination and completion of all God's acts and threats of judgment recorded in Scripture. It will be the final squaring of the accounts of justice for the whole course of history.

23 Luke uses Markan material and wording for v 23a. On οὐαί, "woe," see at 6:24. In the Markan context the difficulty for pregnant and nursing women is likely to be focused on their inability to move with the haste necessitated by the situation. There is less emphasis on haste in the Lukan context, where we should think more generally of women in such situations being less well equipped to handle extreme hardship.

Luke does not reproduce Mark 13:18, "pray that it may not happen in winter." Despite Fitzmyer's confident assertion (1346), the omission probably has nothing to do with the fact that the siege lasted from April to late August: such knowledge would only mean that Luke could have recorded the verse with an awareness that the prayer was duly offered and answered. Rather we should note that in Mark the transition from v 18 to v 19 is not particularly smooth and would be no better with Luke 21:23b, which Luke will use in place of Mark 13:19.

Luke displaces Mark 13:19, with its Danielic language (see Dan 12:1; but also Ezek 5:9; and cf. Jer 30:7), with v 23b, which is likely to be from his other source. Though not in a form that is verbally close, the sentiment expressed in v 23b on a national scale will be repeated on a worldwide scale (and in connection with the gentile nations) in v(v) (25b), 26a. Disaster will befall the land of Judea as God's wrath is poured out upon his People (the parallelism between the phrases of v 23b encourages the reading of τῆς γῆς as "the land [of Judah]" rather than "the earth," as does the appearance later [v 26a] in the wider gentile context of τῇ οἰκουμένῃ, "the [inhabited] world"). "The People" have appeared in a positive sight elsewhere in this section (19:47–21:38), but Luke is aware that "the leaders of the People" (19:47) will eventually take (the most part of) the Jewish People with them into opposition to Jesus and the Christian movement (see esp. 23:13, 18, 23; and developments in Acts).

24 There is no Markan parallel to v 24. "They will fall by the mouth of the sword" is linguistically close to Sir 28:18: "Many have fallen by the mouth of the sword," but if there is any link it is only a matter of borrowed diction. Jer 20:4–6 ("They will fall by the sword of their enemies . . . you will go into captivity") is much closer in general theme and also uses a noun cognate with "will be taken captive" (21:7 has the imagery of "the mouth of the sword"). "To all the nations" is likely to be an allusion to Deut 28:64, which contemplates Israel, as a result of disobedience to the words of the law, being scattered among all the nations (cf. also Ezek 32:9). "Jerusalem will be trampled under foot by the nations" is probably an allusion to the LXX text of Zech 12:3 where the pattern in vv 2–4 is of the nations plundering Jerusalem, only in turn to be smitten by God (MT is much less close; cf. also Dan 8:13; Rev 11:2). Though Josephus confirms that in the war many were put to the sword (*War* 6.271–73, 420 put the figure at 1,100,000, but ancient figures are notoriously unreliable) and many taken captive (*War* 7.118, 138, 154, 420 have Jewish captives involved in Titus' triumphal procession in Rome and put the number at 97,000), there is nothing here to raise suspicion of formulation in the light of the actual experience of A.D. 66–70.

The final clause is normally referred to the time period in which the gentile nations have dominance, or occasionally to the period of the gentile mission (e.g., Zmijewski, *Eschatologiereden*, 217–18; Wiefel, 353). But there is much to be said for taking καιροὶ ἐθνῶν, "times of [the] nations," as referring to the period for a judgment upon the gentile nations (cf. Wellhausen, 118) that corresponds to the judgment upon Jerusalem: after the καιρός, "time," of Jerusalem (v 20; cf. v 8) come the καιροί, "times," of the nations (cf. Conzelmann, *Luke*, 130: "the times of the Gentiles [v 24] have not yet come"). For the sense required for πληρωθῶσιν (lit. "are fulfilled"), cf. the use of the verb at Mark 1:15; some find a similar use of συμπληροῦν at Luke 9:51, but it has not been taken so above. For the general thought, see also Ezek 30:3; Jer 27:7; and, perhaps, Obad 16. The underlying pattern here of judgment upon Jerusalem/Judah/Israel followed by judgment upon the instruments of their judgment may be found in Isa 10; 13–14; 33; 47; Jer 50–51; Dan 9:26–27; and cf. Ezek 38; Hab 1:1–2:3; *2 Apoc. Bar.* 12:3–4. See further Nolland ("Luke's Readers," 227–30). Does the ἄχρι οὗ, "until," contemplate a future restoration of Jerusalem beyond the judgment of the gentile nations (cf. Tiede, "Weeping," 89; Chance, *Jerusalem*, 133–34)?

Luke does not make use of Mark 13:20. Perhaps he does not know what to make of the idea of shortening of the days (it has nothing to do in the first instance with an imminent Parousia). In any case his alternative to Mark 13:19 is not set in such extreme language and so does not require the amelioration offered here. As well, Luke's development in v 24 means that there is no longer a place for Mark 13:20: the action has moved on past that point already.

By the end of v 24 the perspective has already moved beyond that of the destruction of Jerusalem and its temple. Despite the starting point in vv 5–7, the narrative has developed a momentum of its own and would lack closure if it stopped at the point where the question of v 7 had received its answer. It has become clear that the answer to that question opens up a perspective on issues yet larger.

Explanation

V 20 picks up the story from v 11. The escalation from v 9 to vv 10–11 will continue after vv 20–24 in vv 25–26. The judgment of Jerusalem is a staging point along this path of escalation to worldwide judgment and the coming of the kingdom of God and the Son of Man. In the face of the threatening disaster, the disciples are to flee. They know that the gentile instruments of judgment cannot be resisted: this is God's judgment at the climax of a history of rebellion and disobedience. But in their turn the gentile instruments of judgment will themselves be judged.

Not raging wars at some distance but the encircling presence of gentile armies is what finally signals the imminence of the temple's doom (caught up in the wider doom of the city). Disciples in Judea are to flee to the safety of the hills. And contrary to popular wisdom in war, those in the walled city of Jerusalem are to leave, and those in the fields outside the wall are not to return to the protection of the city: this city is doomed; it can offer no protection. While it might seem too late to flee once the city is surrounded, in the ebb and flow of war it was to be anticipated that a siege might be mounted and lifted a number of times before being successfully prosecuted. In the actual event, news of Nero's death and the unsettled times that followed appear to have created the necessary respite.

At various points in the history of Israel, and especially in the Babylonian captivity, God has acted in judgment. All of God's acts of judgment and threats of judgment, as recorded in Scripture, come to their culmination in the prospect of judgment held forth here. There will now be a final squaring of the accounts of justice for the whole course of history (cf. 11:50–51). Pregnant and nursing women are additionally vulnerable and will therefore suffer more in the terrible times to come. There is nothing abstract or spiritualized about the picture of judgment involved here: it is a matter of human disaster in the course of human history.

V 24 is a pastiche of allusions to OT descriptions of judgment upon Jerusalem (see esp. Jer 20:4–6; 28:64; and the Greek text of Zech 12:3). People will be put to the sword or taken captive as slaves to the whole range of gentile nations. Josephus, the Jewish historian of the period, confirms that large numbers met these fates in the war of A.D. 66–70. But this picture of judgment is only a staging post along the way as matters continue to escalate. V 24 finishes with a mention of "the times of the nations" which, I have argued above, should be taken as a reference to the time for a turn of judgment for each one of the nations. Vv 25–26 will take this thought further, but here we can note finally the pervasive OT pattern of judgment upon Jerusalem/Israel/Judah followed by judgment in turn upon the instruments of their judgment (e.g., Isa 10; Jer 50–52).

Judgment of the Nations, and the Coming of the Son of Man   (21:25–28)

Bibliography

Gardiner, J. A. "Studies in Texts: Luke 21.28." *Th* 59 (1956) 460–62. **George, A.** "La venue du Fils de l'Homme: Lc 21,25–28, 34–36." *AsSeign* n.s. 5 (1969) 71–78. **Hartman, L.** "La parousie du Fils de l'homme Mc 13, 24–32." *AsSeign* n.s. 64 (1969) 47–57. **Lauras, A.** "Le commentaire patristique de Lc. 21,25–33." In *Studia patristica* 7. TU 92. Berlin: Akademie, 1966. 503–15. **Varro, R.** "Le Christ est notre avenir (Luc, 21, 25–33)." *AmCl* 78 (1968) 659–62. ————, **Becquet, G.** and **Beauvery, R.** "Le Christ est notre avenir." *EV* 90 (1970) 605–8.

And see at 21:5–6.

Translation

   ²⁵ *"There will be signs in the sun and the moon and the stars; and on the earth distress of nations in anxiety at the roaring and tossing of the sea,* ²⁶*people fainting*[a] *with fear and foreboding at what is coming upon the world. For the powers of heaven will be shaken.* ²⁷ *Then they will see the Son of Man coming on a cloud with power and great glory.* ²⁸ *When these things begin to happen, straighten yourselves up and raise your heads, because your deliverance is drawing near."*

Notes

   [a] Gr. ἀποψυχόντων (lit. "breathing out/stopping breathing" and so: "fainting" or "expiring").

Form/Structure/Setting

Passing over Mark 13:21–23, Luke provides his parallel to Mark's vv 24–27. He is dealing now with "the times of the nations," which provide a worldwide and escalated version of what he has anticipated in 21:20–24 in connection with Jerusalem. This will usher in the coming of the Son of Man who will bring final deliverance.

Luke 21:25a is clearly a version of Mark 13:24–25a, but on balance it seems more likely that Luke has drawn it from a second source (on the view that Luke had a second source for parts of this chapter see at 21:5–6). Luke 21:25b is unparalleled in Mark and is likely to be from the same source that continues in v 26a (which also lacks parallel in Mark). For v 26b Luke takes up the Markan source and continues with it through v 27. But he then drops Mark 13:27 and concludes the unit in v 28 with further material drawn from his second source (material that performs in that source something like the role of Mark 13:26, but in rather more general terms; it is likely that the introduction to v 28 is a Lukan formulation).

As in 21:20–24, the elaborate patterns of scriptural allusion suggest that we have materials that have been heavily interpreted by means of scriptural meditation in the process of transmission.

Comment

Beyond the destruction of Jerusalem comes a time of universal upheaval that will bring upon the nations their own experience of divine judgment. This will usher in the coming of the Son of Man and the final deliverance, which he will bring.

25 Luke makes no use of Mark 13:21–23. It probably seems out of place and repetitive to him after vv 5–6. Luke has not used Mark 13:20, so the repetition here of "the elect" may also have discouraged him from using this piece. As well, Luke has used a version of v 21 already in 17:23. There is an evident relationship between v 25 and v 11 (linked in chiastic pattern by reference to natural disturbance and signs from heaven). While v 25b goes entirely its own way, v 25a is clearly a version of what we find in Mark 13:24–25a. I think it most likely that a version of v 25 stood in Luke's second source, but this remains less than certain (for a possible allusion to Jer 51:55 in v 25b and perhaps to v 48 in Luke 21:25–26, see at 21:9). What Luke has in mind for these signs is clearer from the Markan text, where there is an evident connection with OT texts in which the heavenly bodies provide their own dramatic accompaniment to the execution of God's judgment upon the nations (see Isa 13:10; 34:4; Ezek 32:7; Joel 3:3–4 [*ET* 2:30–31] [Isa 13:10 is particularly echoed in Mark and is instructive for its setting in an oracle against Babylon; Joel 3:3–4 is in the setting of the coming of the "Day of the Lord," which will lead finally to the restoration of God's People and the judgment of the nations who have been the cause of their suffering]).

V 25b may be dependent on the Greek text of Isa 24:19 for "on the earth distress of nations in anxiety" and on Ps 46:3 for "at the roaring of the sea and the waves" (as Fitzmyer, 1349). The picture is of people anticipating in terror the unleashing of the destructive forces of chaos. This sense of a dreaded future is developed further in v 26.

26 V 26a has no counterpart in Mark, but v 26b is clearly a slightly edited rendition of Mark 13:25b. There may be some Lukan language in v 26a (esp. ἐπερχομένων, "coming upon"; possibly οἰκουμένη, "[inhabited] world"), but in the absence of a close relationship with an OT text and in terms of fit, it seems best to think that Luke is following his second source here. We should note the a-b-b-a pattern (heaven-earth-earth-heaven) that Luke has created in vv 25–26.

The same note of dreadful anticipation, but with quite different language, may be found in Rev 6:16. It is likely that from Luke's point of view everything from the wars and uprisings of v 9 participates in a preliminary way in the reality of that judgment of God about to come to full expression (cf. at v 10). The question now comes: how is the final climax of judgment represented in our text? The normal answer given is that the judgment is symbolized by the coming of the Son of Man in v 27. But the picture in vv 34–36 is rather that the climax of the world-wide judgment already in the unfolding of human history precedes the coming of the Son of Man. And Luke's positioning of v 28 tends to the same end. It would seem, then, that Luke has either adopted the same strategy as that found in Rev 11:14–18 where we are taken to the brink of the final disaster ("woe") and then taken beyond to the new and positive situation of the rule of God, with only a glance back. Or, Luke intends the final disaster to be represented by the final clause of v 26: "For the powers of heaven will be shaken." If, as seems likely, v 26b is based upon a conflation of Isa 34:4 and Hag 2:6 (20), then it could function quite successfully as a symbol of the climactic judgment upon the nations, and the latter of our two options may be the preferred one.

27 When this whole process has run its course, the Son of Man will appear as a figure of power and glory. Luke reproduces Mark 13:27 in an only slightly edited form. On "Son of Man," see the "Son of Man" excursus and at 6:1–5. A future coming of the Son of Man is anticipated in 9:26 (see there); 12:40 (cf. v 8); 17:24, 26, 30; 18:8; 21:36. 21:27 is the first Lukan Son of Man saying where the Dan 7:13 link is clear (the combination of "Son of Man," "coming," and "in/on a cloud" make the allusion clear, though Luke changes the Markan "clouds" to singular where Dan 7:13 has the plural ["they will see" could be taken to correspond to "I saw" in Dan 7:13]). The Danielic Son of Man has judgment passed in his favor at the divine assize and receives from God glory and everlasting dominion over the nations. 17:22–37 has set up the expectation that disciples will long for the coming of the Son of Man.

28 Once again Luke drops a verse from Mark that speaks of the elect (Mark 13:27: the gathering of the elect by the angels at the directive of the freshly arrived Son of Man). Instead Luke continues with a verse likely to come from his second source (the opening ἀρχομένων τούτων γίνεσθαι, "when these things begin to happen," is, however, likely to be Lukan, considering its vocabulary, grammatical construction, and structural role in the chapter). Luke is imprecise about how far back one should take the referent of "these things." This may be deliberate, since he will see deliverance as progressively closer the further the process of escalation has developed (of course v 27 is to be excluded, since the coming of the Son of Man is immediately synonymous with the coming of the disciples' deliverance). Again we meet a paradoxical inversion: the sequence of future events Luke describes in the chapter is such as would naturally burden and oppress (despite elements of special divine protection and directives for avoiding the disaster of Jerusalem, the disciples are to be seen as unavoidably caught up in the sufferings of these increasingly turbulent times), but the encouragement is to see the developing pattern of disasters as progressive assurances of the near approach of final deliverance.

Explanation

Luke deals now with "the times of the nations" with its worldwide version of a judgment for which that upon Jerusalem has been a microcosm. This universal judgment will usher in the coming of the Son of Man to whom the disciples look for final deliverance.

The "signs in the sun and the moon and the stars" point us back to OT texts in which the heavenly bodies provide their own dramatic accompaniment to the execution of God's judgment upon the nations (see Isa 13:10; 34:4; Ezek 32:7; Joel 2:30–31). As in v 11 it is difficult to be sure how literally to take this, but there seems to be an escalation from v 11 to v 25. The people seem to be particularly aware of the threat posed by the sea (the sea is an ancient symbol of chaos; the text here may echo Ps 46:3). The picture is of people anticipating in terror the unleashing of the destructive forces of chaos. This sense of a dreaded future is developed further in v 26. The world will be shaken up to such an extent that the very powers of heaven will be shaken (elements of Isa 34:4 and Hag 2:6 seem to be combined here).

When this whole process has run its course, the Son of Man will appear as a figure of power and glory. The language echoes that of Dan 7:13 where a "son of man" figure comes, has judgment passed in his favor at the divine assize, and receives from God glory and everlasting dominion over the nations. This is a coming for which disciples long. So, everything that brings it closer must be a cause of encouragement. Thus, as the disciples begin to witness the unfolding tale of woe that the Lukan Jesus has predicted in this chapter, indeed as they are themselves caught up in the times of turmoil and distress, their reaction should be exactly the opposite to that which would be natural under such burdens: they should stand erect and raise their heads because their final deliverance draws near.

New Leaves Herald the Summer *(21:29–33)*

Bibliography

Berger, K. *Die Amen-Worte Jesu.* BZNW 39. Berlin: de Gruyter, 1970. 68–69. **Dupont, J.** "La parabole du figuier qui bourgeonne (Mc, XIII, 28–29 et par.)." *RB* 75 (1968) 526–48. **Holman, C. L.** "The Idea of an Imminent Parousia in the Synoptic Gospels." *StBibT* 3 (1973) 15–31. **Jeremias, J.** *Parables.* 119–20. **Jülicher, A.** *Gleichnisreden.* 2:3–11. **Klauck, H.-J.** *Allegorie und Allegorese.* 316–25. **Künzi, M.** *Das Naherwartungslogion Mk 9.1 par: Geschichte seiner Auslegung, mit einem Nachwort zur Auslegungsgeschichte von Markus 13, 30 par.* Tübingen: Mohr, 1977. 213–24. **Lövestam, E.** "The ἡ γενεὰ αὕτη Eschatology in Mk 13,30 parr." In *L'Apocalypse johannique et l'Apocalyptique dans le Nouveau Testament,* ed. J. Lambrecht. Gembloux: Duculot, 1980. 403–13. **Löw, I.** "Zum Feigengleichnis." *ZNW* 11 (1910) 167–68. **Meinertz, M.** "Dieses Geschlecht." *BZ* 1 (1957) 283–89. **Schneider, G.** *Parusiegleichnisse.* 55–61, 62–66. **Schütz, R.** "Das Feigengleichnis der Synoptikern." *ZNW* 10 (1909) 333–34. ———. "Zum Feigengleichnis." *ZNW* 12 (1911) 88.

And see at 21:5–6.

Translation

²⁹*He told them a parable: "Look at the fig tree and all the trees.* ³⁰*When they have already put forth their leaves, seeing it for yourselves, you know that summer is already near.* ³¹*In the same way also, you, when you see these [things] happening, will know*ᵃ *that the kingdom of God is near.* ³²*Amen, I say to you, that this generation will not have passed away before all [things] happen.* ³³*Heaven and earth will pass away, but my words will not pass away."*

Notes

ᵃ Gr. present tense. B D W Θ 579 etc. read γινώσκεται, "it is known."

Form/Structure/Setting

Vv 29–33 provide support for v 28, though v 33 may take a further step and speak of the abiding significance of the words of Jesus even beyond the upheaval in heaven and earth that ushers in the kingdom of God. Luke continues to follow the Markan sequence, and there is no evidence of influence from any other source. Luke will make no use of Mark 13:32. As elsewhere in the chapter, the Markan material here seems to be composite.

The parable of the fig tree may not have been originally applied to a warning of future events. The clearly composite nature of the eschatological chapter and the likeness to Luke 12:54–56 raise the possibility that the original application was rather to what was present in the ministry of Jesus, as sign of the presence/nearness of the kingdom of God (see esp. Dupont, *RB* 75 [1968] 536–46; it is not impossible that a word-play between קיץ, *qayiṣ*, "summer," and קץ, *qēṣ*, "end," was involved in the original application of the parable [cf. Amos 8:1–2, which makes use of the secondary meaning for קיץ of "summer fruit"]).

The present formulation of Mark 13:30 is dependent on its place in the chapter ("all these things"), but it is likely that it takes its inspiration from sayings of Jesus that emphasized the significance of his own generation (cf. 7:31–35; 11:29–32, 49–51). Mark 13:31 is likely to have been added as a detached saying. It may represent a church formulation of the reality of the authority experienced in the words of Jesus and evidently claimed by the historical Jesus.

Comment

The disturbing events are to function for the disciples as signs of the near approach of the kingdom of God (just as new growth on the different trees heralds the approach of summer). Jesus' own generation will see it all. In this world in transition only the words of Jesus have permanence.

29   The parable and its explanation will provide support for the thrust of v 28. For Mark's "From the fig tree learn the parable," Luke writes "He told them a parable: Look at the fig tree and all the trees." Luke's generalization here is likely to correspond to his development through the discourse of a parallelism between the Jewish fate and the fate of the gentile nations (I owe the suggestion that the fig tree and all the trees symbolize Israel and all the nations to the late Professor G. W. H. Lampe).

30 For the first half of the verse Luke again provides his own wording: "when they have already put forth their leaves, seeing it for yourselves." For the second half he simply adds a second "already" to what he has from his Markan source. While emphasizing the totally adequate basis for knowing for oneself, the language changes carry no significant change of meaning. The parable may have been inspired by Cant 2:11–13. The fig tree is particularly fitting for making such a point because, unlike many Palestinian trees, it loses its leaves in winter and comes into leaf quite late in the spring.

31 Here Luke changes only the final "at the gates" of Mark 13:29 to "the kingdom of God" (this does, however, requires the grammar of the clause to be somewhat differently construed). Mark has been accused of infelicity in his use of οὕτως καὶ ὑμεῖς (lit. "in the same way also you") to make the transition from parable to application (e.g., Dupont, *RB* 75 [1968] 532–33), but perhaps καί, "also," should be read with οὕτως, "in the same way," and ὑμεῖς, "you," seen not as emphatic but simply as a mechanism for containing the "when" clause within the scope of the principal clause (and perhaps also encouraging the reading of the verb as a futuristic present rather than as an imperative).

From the happening of which things should one deduce the nearness of the kingdom of God? Though the referent is often restricted to vv 25–26, the drift of the Lukan development thus far must surely encourage us to take a comprehensive view of "these things" (but with vv 27–28 excluded, since what they report is equivalent to the coming of the kingdom of God, and with a certain focus on the sequence of the judgment of Jerusalem and the judgment of the nations): through all the anticipated happenings the message is to be heard that the kingdom of God is near and becoming nearer. Zmijewski's understanding (*Eschatologiereden*, 268–72) is that the "nearness" here is not chronological but is making a statement that generalizes to wider dimensions of unfolding history the view that in the ministry of Jesus the kingdom of God was in the process of breaking in (cf. Luke 12:54–56). This involves, however, something of a misunderstanding of Luke's use of kingdom language in connection with the presence of Jesus; it is based on a partial misunderstanding of Luke 12:54–56, a text that, in any case, does not use kingdom of God language (see there); and it hardly does justice to the thoroughly chronological nature of developments in the chapter. As in 11:2; 14:15; 17:20; 19:11, Luke thinks here of the eschatological consummation of the kingdom of God.

32 Luke changes Mark little; most notably Mark's "all these [things]" becomes simply "all [things]" (Luke may have in mind the "all" of v 22). On the opening "amen," see at 4:24. Despite the series of attempts to apply ἡ γενεὰ αὕτη, "this generation," to something other than the generation of Jesus' contemporaries, all the alternatives (the Jewish People; humanity; the generation of the end-time signs) are finally artificial and represent imposition based upon some supposition brought to the text (Luke uses "this generation" also in 7:31; 11:29, 30, 31, 32, 50, 51; Acts 2:40). This verse is a standing embarrassment to all attempts to see the delay of the Parousia as a major Lukan preoccupation. There is, by contrast, no suggestion that the verse is an embarrassment to Luke.

As the prophets before him had regularly done, the Gospel Jesus presents as part of a single development things that belong together in principle but turn out to be separated chronologically in a manner that he did not anticipate. (Caird [*Language and Imagery*, 243–71] has argued forcefully that, at least in part, this involved a deliberate use in a metaphorical manner of end-of-the-world language in connection with what the prophets well knew was not the end of the world. The present and immediately future events were to be seen in the light of and somehow as participating in the reality of what would one day be fully true eschatologically. His insights are pertinent to the present discussion but are not capable in themselves of eliminating the difficulty over timing.) The fundamental driving force for the sentiment expressed in this verse is the conviction that Jesus' Jewish contemporaries in Palestine ("this generation") were to find themselves at a climax point in the purposes of God in judgment (cf. esp. 11:49–51), just as they had been experiencing a climax point of God's saving purposes in the ministry of Jesus. As with the earlier prophets the anticipation of the future was first and formost an interpretation, in the light of a knowledge of God, of the significance of the present and of the nature of its development out of the past.

33   Here Luke reproduces the Markan wording unaltered. Should we correlate the passing away of heaven and earth with the upheavals envisaged in vv 25–26 (as Zmijewski, *Eschatologiereden*, 284)? We have a difficult choice, since to do so obliges us to take "my words" not in connection with the prediction of the future anticipated in Luke 21 but rather in connection with the abiding significance of the teaching of Jesus (cf. 16:17, in connection with the abiding significance of the law). The context does not immediately encourage this sense for "my words." The alternative is to fail to make the correlation with vv 25–27, despite its contextual appropriateness and to gain a more immediate sense for "my words" of "the words of this discourse." The closest OT parallels (Isa 40:8; Pss 102:25–27; 119:89, 160) might be considered to favor the former option.

Luke makes no use of Mark 13:32. Acts 1:7 may be in his eyes some kind of an equivalent. In any case Luke is likely to feel that Mark 13:32 could only detract from the force that he intends for the preceding verse.

Explanation

The parabolic teaching of vv 29–31 reinforces the teaching in v 28 about finding signs of the nearness of deliverance in the unfolding sequence of disasters. V 32 sets a limiting time frame for the whole of the anticipated future. And v 33 points to the solid and abiding nature of the words of Jesus amidst all this sea of change.

The trees, with their cycle of seasonal new beginnings, are used as an illustration by Jesus to underline the point of v 28: as the new growth on the fig tree and the other trees points to the nearness of summer, so the disasters that befall Jerusalem and then the nations of the world surely point to the nearness of the full end-time manifestation of the kingdom of God.

Many try to take "this generation" to mean something different to the generation of Jesus' contemporaries but all the alternatives offered are finally unnatural, and are proposed as ways out of a problem rather than as natural readings of the text. I cannot avoid the conclusion that the Lukan Jesus anticipated that all that he prophesied would run its course in a single generation. This probably should not disturb us unduly, since it is what we find again and again in the OT prophets. The prophets were aware that what they prophesied for their own generations was "of the stuff of" end-time events. They considered that the soon-to-come events needed to be seen in connection with God's ultimate intervention in human affairs. It is often quite unclear what distinction they were able to make between the working out of God's purposes in their own generation and the ultimate working out of God's purposes. They may at times have deliberately used end-of-the-world language in a metaphorical manner in connection with what they well knew was not the end of the world; it is hard to be sure. In any case they put together, as though they would happen together, things that belong together in principle but turn out to be separated chronologically by large spans of time. The Lukan Jesus has done the same.

The turmoil and upheaval through which the kingdom of God is ushered in will inevitably dislodge all the assumptions and securities of ordinary life. Even the fixedness of heaven and earth can no longer be taken for granted. But through all the change there is one point of security: the permanent and abiding significance of the teaching of Jesus.

The Vigilant and Prayerful Will Stand before the Son of Man (21:34–36)

Bibliography

Aejmelaeus, L. *Wachen vor dem Ende: Die traditionsgeschichtlichen Wurzeln von 1 Thess 5:1–11 und Luk 21:34–36.* Schriften der Finnischen Exegetischen Gesellschaft 44. Helsinki: Finnischen Exegetischen Gesellschaft, 1985. vi–157. **Lövestam, E.** *Spiritual Wakefulness in the New Testament.* Lunds universitets årskrift 1/55.3. Lund: Gleerup, 1963. 122–32. **Ott, W.** *Gebet und Heil.* 73–75. **Schneider, G.** "'Der Menschensohn' in der lukanischen Christologie." In *Jesus und der Menschensohn,* ed. R. Pesch and R. Schnackenburg. Freiburg/Basel/Vienna: Herder, 1975. 267–82, esp. 268–71. **Schwarz, G.** "μηποτε βαρηθωσιν υμων αι καρδιαι." *BibNot* 10 (1979) 40. **Stout, J. C.** "Agrypnein—Luke 21:36." *BRev* 3 (1918) 621–23. **Tödt, H. E.** *The Son of Man in the Synoptic Tradition.* New Testament Library. Philadelphia: Westminster, 1965. 94–98.

And see at 21:5–6.

Translation

[34] *"Beware that your minds not be dulled by carousing, drunkenness, and the worries of life, so that*[a] *that day comes upon you suddenly,* [35] *like a snare. For*[b] *it will come upon all those who dwell on the face of all the earth.* [36] *Stay awake at all times, praying that you may have strength to escape all these things which are to happen, and to stand before the Son of Man."*

Notes

[a] Gr. και (lit. "and").

b"For" is placed earlier by A C W Θ Ψ $f^{1,13}$ etc., which enables "like a snare" to be read as part of the following sentence. This appears to be influenced by an awareness of the allusion to Isa 24:17.

Form/Structure/Setting

The discourse finishes in vv 34–36 with an exhortation to the kind of vigilance that will enable the disciples to make their way safely through the coming tumult and then to stand secure before the Son of Man.

Vv 34–36 are a Lukan replacement for Mark 13:33–37. Luke has made use (from a separate source) of a version of Mark 13:33–37 at 12:35–38 and does not wish to be repetitive here. Some find a source behind Luke 21:34–36, but while Luke clearly draws on the tradition and on the parenetic language of his own church environment, it seems most likely that he has himself forged this concluding section to Jesus' words. Elements from Mark 13:33–37 have had some influence.

Comment

Abandonment to the cares and pleasures of life will blind one to the ever nearer approach of the climax of the eschatological development. In order not to be suddenly caught in the snare that this climax will be to all who are not ready, the disciple must be constantly vigilant and pray for strength to make it safely through the exigencies of that time to reach the place of safety before the Son of Man.

34 Luke prefers προσέχετε, "beware," to Mark's βλέπετε, "see." The full Lukan form, προσέχετε ἑαυτοῖς (lit. "beware with respect to yourselves"), is found also at 12:1 (contrast Mark 8:15); 17:3; Acts 5:35; 20:28. βαρηθῶσιν ὑμῶν αἱ καρδίαι (lit. "your hearts be weighed down") could reflect the LXX idiom used in connection with the hardening of the heart of the Pharaoh of Egypt (Exod 7:14 [with the present verb]; Exod 8:32 [LXX v 28]; 1 Kgdms 6:6; etc. [with the related verb, βαρύνειν]), but the wider Hellenistic world spoke of being "heavy with wine" (cf. Schwarz, BibNot 10 [1979] 40), and failure of alertness would seem to be more to the point here than hard-heartedness. Since Luke is about to draw on the imagery of Isa 24:17 (see at v 35), it is not unlikely that the juxtaposition of "carousing" (κραιπάλη) and "drunkenness" (μέθη) is inspired by their juxtaposition in Isa 24:20 (LXX). If so, a metaphorical use there has been displaced by a thoroughly literal one here (since the juxtaposition is a natural one and is evidenced elsewhere, the dependence on Isa 24:20 remains uncertain). μέθη (in the plural) occurs in Pauline ethical exhortation in Rom 13:13; Gal 5:21. For μερίμναις βιωτικαῖς, "worries of life," cf. μεριμνῶν ... τοῦ βίου, "worries of life," in Luke 8:14, where the alternative genitive construction (τοῦ βίου, "of life") allows "of life" to relate to each of a sequence of nouns. Luke frequently warns against preoccupation with, and unwillingness to part from, the goods of this life.

The use of "that day" here finds its closest points of comparison in 10:12; 17:31. Luke probably thinks here of the time of climactic destruction that anticipates and leads to the arrival of the Son of Man. αἰφνίδιος, "suddenly," is used in a similar context in 1 Thess 5:2 (ἐφιστάναι, "come upon," is found in 1 Thess 5:3). The onset of the final period will be sudden and unexpected to those whose minds have been dulled by the way that they live out their lives. For the alert disciples, however, the developments traced in the present chapter will be constant signs of the nearness of the end. There is clearly a tension between the "apocalyptic" program with its unfolding times outlined in Luke 21 and the coming that catches people by surprise, which we find in 12:35–40 and 17:20–21, 22–37. Luke wants to have it both ways, and in as much as he provides any reconciliation it is in terms of what we have here in 21:34. The signs are only signs to those disciples whose life of discipleship makes them alert to the nearness of the kingdom of God.

35 "Like a snare" completes the sense of v 34 but sits at the head of v 35 because of a reading (see *Notes* for the textual variant responsible) based upon the awareness that it begins the allusion to Isa 24:17, which will be carried on by "upon all who dwell upon the face of all the earth" ("the face of the earth" is used by Luke again in Acts 17:26; it is a biblical idiom [Gen 41:56; Deut 7:6; Isa 23:17; etc.]). Isa 24 anticipates the desolation of earth and heaven in the coming judgment. While "that day" will come upon all, it will come as a trap or a snare only upon those who are not ready for it.

36 ἀγρυπνεῖτε, "stay awake," echoes Mark 13:33 (cf. Eph 6:18; Heb 13:17), while "at all times" reflects the uncertain timing of the master's return in the Markan parable (the use of καιρός, "time," perhaps coming also from 13:33). Luke's δεόμενοι, "praying," uses what is almost a distinctive Lukan verb for praying. One is probably to stay awake in order to pray (or at least praying is an important activity of the wakefulness), not by means of praying (as Zmijewski, *Eschatologiereden*, 289 n. 21). Constant prayer is enjoined in 18:1, 7–8; Rom 12:12; 1 Thess 5:17. Prayer for strength to escape contains echoes of the situation of Luke 21:21, 23 and also possibly of the injunction to pray of Mark 13:18, which Luke did not use at that point. Luke does something similar at 17:34 (see there). In both cases there is a question about how precisely Luke intends the imagery of the language to be applied in a larger context. ταῦτα πάντα, "all these [things]," recalls the language of v 12 while [ταῦτα] . . . τὰ μέλλοντα γίνεσθαι, "[these (things)] . . . which are to happen," reaches back further to the initial question in v 7. "To stand before the Son of Man" is probably Luke's own paraphrase and summary of vv 27–28: it denotes the successful negotiation of the trials of the eschatological period and the safe arrival at the place of abiding security (standing before the Son of Man is an image of deliverance, not an image of standing in a judicial dock [cf. *1 Apoc. Enoch* 62:8, 13; 1QH 4:21–22]).

Explanation

The answer of Jesus to the disciples' question in v 7 ends with an exhortation. It is a call to vigilance and prayer. Without a disciplined life of discipleship, what should be for the disciples a well-signposted development pointing to the near approach of the end will come as a sudden and unexpected snare.

Abandonment to the cares and pleasures of life will blind one to the ever nearer approach of the climax of the end-time development. For those so preoccupied, "that day" will come suddenly, and, coming, it will prove to be a snare that entraps. "That day" will be the development to its climax of the time of turmoil and destruction that anticipates the arrival of the Son of Man. The text echoes the language of Isa 24:17 in pointing to the universal embrace of that coming day, which will be the downfall of many.

The alternative approach to life is thought of as constant wakefulness (cf. Eph 6:18; Heb 13:17). And this constant wakefulness is to be used for prayer: prayer for strength to survive the period of strife in order to arrive safely at the place of abiding security with the freshly arrived Son of Man. As the discourse now comes to an end, some of the language of this verse deliberately echoes earlier phrases and ideas (see vv 7, 12, 21, 23, and 27–28).

Days in the Temple and Nights on the Mount of Olives (21:37–38)

Bibliography

See at 21:5–6.

Translation

[37] *By day he was in the temple teaching and by night, going out, he would spend the night on the mount called "Of Olives."* [38] *All the People rose early in the morning [to come] to him in the temple, in order to listen to him.*[a]

Notes

[a] *f*[13] adds at this point John 7:53–8:11.

Form/Structure/Setting

The Lukan section comes to an end with 21:37–38, which recalls the unit 19:47–48 with which the section began. The verses 21:37–38 are entirely a Lukan formulation designed to round off the section and preparing (at one point) for what is to come (see 22:39). The fragment John 7:53–8:11 has a notable similarity in 8:2 to certain features of these Lukan verses, but this is unlikely to tell us anything about Lukan sources.

Comment

A rhythm of daily teaching in the temple and nightly withdrawal out of the city, to the Mount of Olives, was successful in sustaining a high level of interest among the historic People of God.

37 Apart from word order ἦν . . . ἐν τῷ ἱερῷ διδάσκων, "he was in the temple teaching," is repeated exactly from 19:47 (B T [071] etc. align the word orders), which also uses "day." Luke establishes here the custom that he appeals to in 22:39. Though ηὐλίζετο, "would spend the night," does not necessarily imply sleeping out in the open, the narrative in 22:39–53 provides some support for taking it so here. Luke could base his statement about Jesus' activities in the evening on general pilgrim practice and more specifically on Mark 11:11–12, 19; 14:3, 26. Luke introduces the Mount of Olives here as he did in 19:19 (see there).

38 ὁ λαὸς ἅπας, "all the People," of 19:48 recurs here as πᾶς ὁ λαός (same meaning), and the verb ἀκούειν, "hear," recurs as well. Here the mark of enthusiasm is getting up very early to hear him; there the imagery was "hanging upon his words." The use of ὀρθρίζειν, "get up very early," may represent a Lukan Septuagintalism.

Explanation

Luke rounds off the section by returning to the motifs with which it began in 19:47–48. Jesus retained the interest and support of the historic People of God (but not their leaders) throughout his temple teaching. Pilgrims would regularly spend the night outside the city as Jesus did. His customary evening location on the Mount of Olives would later become the scene of his final prayer before his arrest (see 22:39–53).

The Passion Narrative   (22:1–23:56)

The foci of the passion narrative are the final Passover meal (with its intimately linked "farewell discourse"), the arrest and trial of Jesus (prepared for in prayer on the Mount of Olives), and the crucifixion (with its appended burial narrative). At the instigation of Satan, the passion events are precipitated by Judas' move to betray Jesus, but Jesus remains supremely in charge even as he goes to his death. The disciples stumble, but do not entirely fall away. Luke binds the passion narrative and the resurrection narrative very closely together.

Conspiracy to Arrest Jesus   (22:1–2)

Bibliography

GENERAL PASSION NARRATIVE:

Aletti, J. N. "Mort de Jésus et théorie du récit." *RSR* 73 (1985) 147–60. Allison, D. C. *The End of the Ages Has Come: An Early Interpretation of the Passion and Resurrection of Jesus.* Philadelphia: Fortress, 1985. Bammel, E., ed. *The Trial of Jesus.* FS C. F. D. Moule. SBT 2/13. London/ Naperville, IL: SCM/Allenson, 1970. Bartsch, H.-W. "Historische Erwägungen zur Leidensgeschichte." *EvT* 22 (1962) 449–59. ————. "Die Ideologiekritik des Evangeliums dargestellt an der Leidensgeschichte." *EvT* 34 (1974) 176–95. Bastin, M. *Jésus devant sa Passion.* LD 92. Paris: Cerf, 1976. Beauchamp, P. "Narrativité biblique du récit de la passion." *RSR* 73 (1985) 39–59. Bednarz, M. *Les éléments parénetiques dans la description de la Passion chez les synoptiques.* Rome: Pont. Univ. S. Thomae de Urbe, 1973. Benoit, P. *The Passion and Resurrection of Jesus.* Tr. B. Weatherhead. New York: Herder and Herder, 1969. Bertram, G. *Die Leidengeschichte Jesu und der Christuskult: Eine formgeschichtliche Untersuchung.* FRLANT n.s. 15. Göttingen: Vandenhoeck & Ruprecht, 1922. Best, E. *The Temptation and the Passion: The Markan Soteriology.* SNTSMS 2. 2nd ed. Cambridge: University Press, 1990. xxiii–lxxiv. Biser, E. "Die älteste Passionsgeschichte." *GuL* 56 (1983) 111–18. Bligh, J. "Typology in the Passion Narratives: Daniel, Elijah, Melchizedek." *HeyJ* 6 (1965) 302–9. Borgen, P. "John and the Synoptics in the Passion Narrative." *NTS* 5 (1958–59) 246–59. Bornhäuser, K. *The Death and Resurrection of Christ.* Tr. A. Rumpus. London: Independent Press, 1958. Bovon, F. *Les derniers jours de Jésus: Textes et événements.* Collection 'Flèches.' Neuchâtel/Paris: Delachaux et Niestlé, 1974. Brown, R. E. *A Crucified Christ in Holy Week: Essays on the Four Gospel Passion Narratives.* Collegeville, MN: Liturgical Press, 1986. Bruce, F. F. "The Book of Zechariah and the Passion Narrative." *BJRL* 43 (1960–61) 336–53. Buse, I. "St John and the Passion Narratives of St Matthew and St Luke." *NTS* 7 (1960–61) 65–76. Carmichael, J. *The Death of Jesus.* New York: Harper and Row, 1966. Catchpole, D. R. *The Trial of Jesus.* SPB 18. Leiden: Brill, 1971. Chabrol, C. "Analyse des 'Textes' des Passion." In *Erzählende Semiotik nach Berichten der Bibel.* Munich: Kösel, 1973. 123–55. Chordat, J. L. *Jésus devant sa mort.* Lire la Bible. Paris: Cerf, 1970. Conzelmann, H. "Historie und Theologie in den synoptischen Passionsberichten." In *Zur Bedeutung des Todes Jesu: Exegetische Beiträge,* ed. H. Conzelmann et al. 3rd ed. Gütersloh: G. Mohn, 1968. 35–53. ————. "History and Theology in the Passion Narratives of the Synoptic Gospels." *Int* 24 (1970) 178–97. Cousin, H. *Le prophète assassiné: Histoire des textes évangélique de la Passion.* Paris: Delarge, 1976. **Crespy, G.** "Recherche sur le signification politique de la mort du Christ." *LumVie* 20 (1971) 110–21. **Culpepper, A.** "The Passion and Resurrection in Mark." *RevExp* 75 (1978) 483–600. **Czerski, J.** "Die Passion Christi in den synoptischen Evangelien im Lichte der historisch-literarischen Kritik." *CollTheol* 46 (1976 Sonderheft) 81–96. **Danker, F. W.** "The Literary Unity of Mark 14:1–25." *JBL* 85 (1966) 467–72. **Delling, G.** *Der Kreuztod Jesu in der urchristlichen Verkündigung.* Berlin: Evangelische Verlagsanstalt, 1971. **Delorme, J.** "Sémiotique du récit et récit de la passion." *RSR* 73 (1985) 85–109. **Dibelius, M.** "Das historische Problem der Leidensgeschichte." *ZNW* 30 (1931) 193–201. ————. "La signification religieuse des récits évangéliques de la passion." *RHPR* 13 (1933) 30–45. **Dillon, R. J.** "The Psalms of the Suffering Just in the Accounts of Jesus' Passion." *Worship* 61 (1987) 430–40. **Donahue, J. R.** *Are You the Christ? The Trial Narrative in the Gospel of Mark.* SBLDS 10. Missoula: Scholars, 1973. ————. "Introduction: From Passion Traditions to Passion Narrative." In *The Passion in Mark: Studies on Mark 14:16,* ed. W. H. Kelber. Philadelphia: Fortress, 1976. 1–20. **Dormeyer, D.** *Die Passion Jesu als Verhaltensmodell: Literarische und theologische Analyse der Traditions- und Redaktionsgeschichte der Markuspassion.* NTAbh n.s. 11. Münster im W.: Aschendorff, 1974. **Downing, J.** "Jesus and Martyrdom." *JTS* 14 (1963) 279–93. **Dungan, D. L.** "Jesus and Violence." In *Jesus, the Gospels, and the Church.* FS W. R. Farmer, ed. E. P. Sanders. Macon, GA: Mercer, 1987. 135–62. **Evans, C. F.** "The Tradition of the Passion." In *Explorations in Theology.* London: SCM, 1977. 2:3–17. ————. "The Event of the Passion." In *Explorations in Theology.* London: SCM, 1977. 2:18–33. **Feigel, F. K.** *Der Einfluss des Weissagungsbeweises und anderer Motive auf die Leidensgeschichte: Ein Beitrag zur Evangelien Kritik.* Tübingen: Mohr, 1910. **Finegan, J.** *Die Überlieferung der Leidens- und Auferstehungsgeschichte Jesu.* BZNW 15. Giessen: Töpelmann, 1934. ————. "A Quest for the History behind the Passion." *JBT* 16 (1962) 102–4. **Flesseman, E. van Leer.** "Die Interpretation der Passionsgeschichte vom Alten Testament aus." In *Zur Bedeutung des Todes Jesu,* ed. F. Viering. Gütersloh: Mohn, 1967. 79–96. **Flusser, D.** *Die letzten Tage Jesu in Jerusalem: Das Passionsgeschehen aus jüdischer Sicht. Bericht über neueste Forschungsergebnisse.* Lese-Zeichen. Tr. H. Zechner. Stuttgart: Calwer, 1982. **Galvin, J. P.** "Jesus' Approach to Death: An Examination of Some Recent Studies." *TS* 41 (1980) 713–44. **Garland, D. E.** *One Hundred Years of Study on the Passion Narratives.* NABPR Bibliographic Series 3. Macon, GA: Mercer University, 1989. **Geoltrain, P.** "Les récits de la Passion dans les Synoptiques." *FV* 65 (1966) 41–49. **Gese, H.** "Psalm 22 und das Neue Testament: Der älteste Bericht vom Tode Jesus und die Entstehung des Herrenmahles." *ZTK* 65 (1968) 1–22. **Girard, R.** "The Gospel Passion as Victim's Story." *Cross Currents* 36 (1986–87) 28–38. **Goguel, M.** "Juifs et Romains dans l'histoire de la passion." *RHR* 62 (1910) 165–82, 295–322. **Gollwitzer, H.** *The Dying and Living Lord.* London: SCM, 1960. **Grappe, C.** "Essai sur l'arrière-plan pascal des récits de la dernière nuit de Jésus." *RHPR* 65 (1985) 105–25. **Green, J. B.** *The Death of Jesus: Tradition and Interpretation in the Passion Narrative.* WUNT 2/33. Tübingen: Mohr, 1988. **Guillet, J.** "Les récits de la Passion." *LumVie* 23 (1974) 6–17. **Haulotte, E.** "Du récit quadriforme de la Passion au concept de Croix." *RSR* 73 (1985) 187–228. **Hendrickx, H.** *The Passion Narratives of the Synoptic Gospels.* Revised ed. London: Chapman, 1984. **Hillmann, W.** *Aufbau und Deutung der synoptischen Leidensberichte: Ein Beitrag zur Kompositionstechnik und Sinnbedeutung der drei älteren Evangelien.* Freiburg im B.: Herder, 1941. **Horbury, W.** "The Passion Narratives and Historical Criticism." *Th* 75 (1972) 58–71. **Innitzer, T.** *Kommentar zur Leidens- und Verklärungsgeschichte Jesu Christi.* 4th ed. Vienna: Herder, 1948. **Isaac, J.** "Problèmes de la Passion d'aprés deux études récentes." *Revue Historique* 85 (1961) 119–38. **Janssen, F.** "Die synoptischen Passionsberichte: Ihre theologische Konzeption und literarische Komposition." *BibLeb* 14 (1973) 40–57. **Jeremias, J.** *The Eucharistic Words of Jesus.* Philadelphia: Fortress, 1977. 89–96. **Kelber, W. H.** "Conclusion: From Passion Narrative to Gospel." In *The Passion in Mark: Studies on Mark 14–16,* ed. W. H. Kelber. Philadelphia: Fortress, 1976. 153–80. ————, ed. *The Passion in Mark: Studies in Mark 14–16.* Philadelphia: Fortress, 1976. ————, **Koenkow, A.,** and **Scroggs, R.** "Reflections on the Question: Was There a Pre-Markan Passion Narrative?" In *SBL Seminar Papers 1971,* ed. J. White et al. Missoula, MT: Scholars, 1971. 2:503–85. **Kertelge,**

K., ed. *Der Prozess gegen Jesus: Historische Rückfrage und theologische Deutung.* QD 112. Freibourg/Basel/Vienna: Herder, 1988. **Kiehl, E. H.** *The Passion of Our Lord.* Grand Rapids, MI: Baker, 1990. **Kremer, J.** *Das Ärgernis des Kreuzes: Eine Hinführung zum Verstehen der Leidensgeschichte.* Stuttgart: Katholisches Bibelwerk, 1969. **Kümmel, W. G.** "Jesusforschung seit 1965: Der Prozess und der Kreuzestod Jesu." *TRu* 45 (1980) 293–337. **Kurichianil, J.** "Jesus' Consciousness of His Passion and Death according to the Synoptic Gospels." *Biblebhashyam* 9 (1983) 114–25. **Lacomora, A.,** ed. *The Language of the Cross.* Chicago: Franciscan Herald Press, 1977. **Lange, H. D.** "The Relationship between Psalm 22 and the Passion Narrative." *CurTM* 43 (1972) 610–21. **Leenhardt, F. J.** *La mort et le testament de Jésus.* Essais bibliques 6. Geneva: Labor et Fides, 1983. **Lehmann, M.** *Synoptische Quellenanalyse und die Frage nach dem historischen Jesus.* BZNW 38. Berlin: de Gruyter, 1970. **Lentzen-Deis, F.** "Passionsbericht als Handlungsmodell? Überlegungen zu Anstössen aus der 'pragmatischen' Sprachwissenschaft für die exegetischen Methoden." In *Der Prozess gegen Jesus,* ed. K. Kertelge. 191–232. **Léon-Dufour, X.** "Autour des récits de la Passion." *RSR* 48 (1960) 1419–92. **Limbeck, M.,** ed. *Redaktion und Theologie des Passionsberichtes nach den Synoptikern.* WF 481. Darmstadt: Wissenschaftliche Buchgesellschaft, 1981. **Linnemann, E.** *Studien zur Passionsgeschichte.* FRLANT 102. Göttingen: Vandenhoeck & Ruprecht, 1970. **Lohfink, G.** *The Last Days of Jesus: An Enriching Portrayal of the Passion.* Tr. S. Attanasio. Notre Dame: Ave Maria, 1984. **Lohse, E.** *History of the Suffering and Death of Jesus Christ.* Tr. O. Dietrich. Philadelphia: Fortress, 1967. **Marin, L.** *The Semiotics of the Passion Narrative: Topics and Figures.* PTMS 25. Tr. A. M. Johnson. Pittsburgh: Pickwick, 1980. **Marshall, I. H.** "The Death of Jesus in Recent New Testament Study." *WW* 3 (1983) 12–21. **Mays, J. L.** "Prayer and Christology: Psalm 22 as Perspective on the Passion." *TToday* 42 (1985) 322–31. **McCafferey, U. P.** "Psalm Quotations in the Passion Narratives of the Gospels." *Neot* 14 (1981) 73–89. **Michl, J.** "Der Tod Jesu: Ein Beitrag zur Frage nach Schuld und Verantwortung eines Volkes." *MTZ* 1 (1950) 5–15. **Moberly, W.** "Proclaiming Christ Crucified: Some Reflections on the Use and Abuse of the Gospels." *Anvil* 5 (1988) 31–52. **Moo, D. J.** *The Old Testament in the Gospel Passion Narratives.* Sheffield: Almond, 1983. **Navone, J.,** and **Cooper, T.** *The Story of the Passion.* Rome: Pontifica Università Gregoriana, 1986. **Nickelsburg, G. W. E.** "The Genre and Function of the Markan Passion Narrative." *HTR* 73 (1980) 153–84. **O'Collins, G.** *The Calvary Christ.* Philadelphia/London: Westminster/SCM, 1977. **Oswald, J.** "Die Beziehungen zwischen Psalm 22 und dem vormarkinischen Passionsbericht." *ZKT* 101 (1979) 53–66. **Pesch, R.** "Die Überlieferung der Passion Jesu." In *Rückfrage nach Jesus,* ed. K. Kertelge. QD 63. Freiburg: Herder, 1974. 148–73. ——— and **Kratz, R.** *So liest man synoptisch: Anleitung und Kommentar zum Studium der synoptischen Evangelien. VI und VII. Passionsgeschichte: Erster Teil und zweiter Teil.* Frankfurt: Knecht, 1979–80. **Prigent, P.** "Les récits évangéliques de la Passion et l'utilisation des 'Testimonia.'" *RHR* 161 (1962) 130–32. **Radl, W.** "Der Tod Jesu in der Darstellung der Evangelien." *TGl* 72 (1982) 432–46. **Ramsey, A. M.** "The Narratives of the Passion." *SE* 2 [=TU 87] (1964) 122–34. **Ramsey, M.** *The Narratives of the Passion.* Contemporary Studies in Theology 1. London: Mowbray, 1962. **Richardson, P.** "The Israel-Idea in the Passion Narratives." In *The Trial of Jesus,* ed. E. Bammel. SBT 2/13. 1–10. **Ricoeur, P.** "Le récit interprétatif: Exégèse et théologie dans le récit de la passion." *RSR* 73 (1985) 17–38. **Riedl, J.** "Die evangelische Leidensgeschichte und ihre theologische Aussage." *BLit* 41 (1968) 70–111. **Rivken, E.** *What Crucified Jesus? The Political Execution of a Charismatic.* London: SCM, 1986. **Rose, A.** "L'influence des psaumes sur les announces et les récits de la Passion et de la Résurrectin dans les Évangiles." *OBL* 4 (1962) 297–356. **Ruppert, L.** *Jesus als der leidende Gerechte? Der Weg Jesu im Lichte eines alt- und zwischentestaemtlichen Motivs.* SBS 59. Stuttgart: Katholisches Bibelwerk, 1972. **Sanders, E. P.** *Jesus and Judaism.* London: SCM, 1985. 294–318. **Schelkle, K. H.** *Die Passion Jesu in der Verkündigung des Neuen Testaments: Ein Beitrag zur Formgeschichte und zur Theologie des Neuen Testaments.* Heidelberg: Kerle, 1949. **Schenk, W.** *Die Passionsbericht nach Markus: Untersuchungen zur Überlieferungsgeschichte der Passionstradition.* Gütersloh: Mohn, 1974. ———. "Der derzeigte Stand der Auslegung der Passionsgeschichte." *EvErz* 36 (1984) 527–43. **Schenke, L.** *Studien zur Passionsgeschichte des Markus: Tradition und Redaktion in Markus 14,1–42.* FB 4. Würzburg: Echter, 1971. ———.

Der gekreuzigte Christus. SBS 69. Stuttgart: Katholisches Bibelwerk, 1974. **Schille, G.** "Das Leiden des Herrn: Die evangelische Passionstradition und ihr 'Sitz im Leben.'" *ZTK* 52 (1955) 161–205. **Schmid, J.** "Die Darstellung der Passion Jesu in den Evangelien." *GuL* 27 (1954) 6–15. **Schmidt, K. L.** *Der Rahmen der Geschichte Jesu: Literarkritische Untersuchungen zur ältesten Jesusüberlieferung.* Darmstadt: Wissenschaftliche Buchgesellschaft, 1964–1919. ————. "Die literarische Eigenart der Leidengeschichte Jesu." *CW* 32 (1918) 114–16. **Schneider, G.** *Die Passion Jesu nach den drei älteren Evangelien.* Biblische Handbibliothek 4. Munich: Kösel, 1973. ————. "Das Problem einer vorkanonischen Passionserzählung." *BZ* 16 (1972) 222–44. **Sloyan, G. S.** *Jesus on Trial: The Development of the Passion Narratives and Their Historical and Ecumenical Implications.* Philadelphia: Fortress, 1973. **Soards, M. L.** "The Question of a Pre-Markan Passion Narrative." *Biblebhashyam* 11 (1985) 144–69. **Stadelmann, L. I. J.** "The Passion Narrative in the Synoptics as Structured on Ps 22(21)." *PerTeo* 15 (1983) 193–221. **Suggs, M. J.** "The Passion and Resurrection Narratives." In *Jesus and Man's Hope,* ed. D. G. Miller. Pittsburgh: Theological Seminary, 1971. 323–38. **Taylor, V.** *Formation of the Gospel Tradition.* London: Macmillan, 1949. 13, 44–62. **Temple, S.** "The Two Traditions of the Last Supper, Betrayal and Arrest." *NTS* 7 (1960–61) 77–85. **Trilling, W.** "Die Passion Jesu in der Darstellung der synoptischen Evangelien." *Lebendiges Zeugnis* 1 (1966) 28–46. **Trocmé, É.** *The Passion as Liturgy: A Study in the Origin of the Passion Narratives in the Four Gospels.* London: SCM, 1983. **Vanhoye, A.** *Structure and Theology of the Accounts of the Passion in the Synoptic Gospels.* Tr. C. H. Giblin. Collegeville, MN: Liturgical Press, 1967. ————. "Les récits de la Passion dans les évangiles synoptiques." *AsSeign* 19 (1971) 38–67. **Viering, F.,** ed. *Das Kreuz Jesu Christi als Grund des Heils.* Gütersloh: Mohn, 1967. **Weber, H.-R.** *The Cross: Tradition and Interpretation.* Tr. E. Jessett. Grand Rapids: Eerdmans, 1979. **White, J. L.** "The Way of the Cross: Was There a Pre-Markan Passion Narrative?" *Forum* 3.2 (1987) 35–49. **Wilson, W. R.** *The Execution of Jesus: A Judicial, Literary, and Historical Investigation.* New York: Scribner's, 1970. **Wrege, H. T.** "Die Passionsgeschichte." In *Die Gestalt des Evangeliums.* BET 11. Frankfurt/Bern/Las Vegas: Lang, 1978. 49–96. **Zehrer, F.** *Das Leiden Christi nach den vier Evangelien: Die wichtigsten Passionstexte und ihre hauptsachlichen Probleme.* Vienna: Mayer, 1980. ————. "Sinn und Probelematic der Schriftverwendung in der Passion." *TPQ* 121 (1973) 18–25. ————. "Jesus, der leidende Gerechte, in der Passion." *BLit* 47 (1974) 104–11.

LUKAN PASSION NARRATIVE:

Barr, A. "The Use and Disposal of the Marcan Source in Luke's Passion Narrative." *ExpTim* 55 (1943–44) 227–31. **Beck, B.** "'Imitatio Christi' and the Lukan Passion Narrative." In *Suffering and Martyrdom in the New Testament,* ed. W. Horbury and B. McNeil. Cambridge: University Press, 1981. 28–47. **Blevins, J. L.** "The Passion Narrative: Luke 19:28–24:53." *RevExp* 64 (1967) 513–22. **Blinzler, J.** "Passionsgeschehen und Passionsbericht des Lukasevangeliums." *BK* 24 (1969) 1–4. **Brown, R.** "The Passion according to Luke." *Worship* 60 (1986) 1–9. **Büchele, A.** *Der Tod Jesu im Lukasevangelium.* **Carlson, R. P.** "The Role of the Jewish People in Luke's Passion Narrative." In *SBL 1991 Seminar Papers,* ed. E. H. Lovering, Jr. 82–102. **Cassidy, R. J.** "Luke's Audience, the Chief Priests and the Motive for Jesus' Death." In *Political Issues,* ed. R. J. Cassidy and P. J. Scharper. 146–67. **Chance, J. B.** "The Jewish People and the Death of Jesus in Luke-Acts: Some Implications of an Inconsistent Narrative Role." In *SBL 1991 Seminar Papers,* ed. E. H. Lovering, Jr. 50–81. **Creed, J. M.** "The Supposed 'Proto-Luke' Narrative of the Trial before Pilate: A Rejoinder." *ExpTim* 46 (1934–35) 378–79. **Cribbs, F. L.** "A Study of the Contacts That Exist between St. Luke and St. John." In *SBL 1973 Seminar Papers,* ed. G. W. MacRae. Cambridge, MA: Society of Biblical Literature, 1973. 2:1–93. **Fransen, I.** "Le baptême de sang (Luc 22,1–23,56)." *BVC* 25 (1959) 20–28. **Gaston, L.** "Anti-Judaism and the Passion in Luke and Acts." In *Anti-Judaism and Early Christianity: Vol. 1. Paul and the Gospels,* ed. P. Richardson and D. Granskou. Waterloo: Laurier University, 1986. 127–53. **Green, J. B.** "The Death of Jesus, God's Servant." In *Reimaging,* ed. D. D. Sylva. 1–28, 170–73. **Hanson, R. P. C.** "Does *dikaios* in Luke 23:47 Explode the Proto-Luke Hypothesis?" *Hermathena* 60

(1942) 74–78. **Hawkins, J. C.** "St. Luke's Passion Narrative Considered with Reference to the Synoptic Problem." In *Oxford Studies in the Synoptic Problem,* ed. W. Sanday. Oxford: Clarendon, 1911. 76–94. ————. "St. Luke's Passion Narrative Considered with Reference to the Synoptic Problem." *ExpTim* 15 (1903–04) 122–26, 273–76. **Jankowski, G.** "Passah und Passion: Die Einleitung der Passiongeschichte bei Lukas." *Texte und Kontexte* 13 (1982) 40–60. **Kany, R.** "Der lukanische Bericht von Tod und Auferstehung Jesu aus der Sicht eines hellenistischen Romanlesers." *NovT* 28 (1986) 75–90. **Karris, R. J.** *Luke: Artist and Theologian.* **Kiddle, M.** "The Passion Narrative in St Luke's Gospel." *JTS* 36 (1935) 267–80. **Klein, H.** "Die lukanisch-johanneische Passionstradition." *ZNW* 67 (1976) 155–86. **LaVerdiere, E. A.** "The Passion-Resurrection of Jesus according to St. Luke." *ChicStud* 25 (1986) 35–50. **Matera, F.** *Passion Narratives and Gospel Theologies: Interpreting the Synoptists through Their Passion Stories.* Theological Inquiries. New York: Paulist, 1986. Esp. 150–220, 238–44. **Monsarrat, V.** "Le récit de la passion: un enseignement pour le disciple fidèle (Luc 22–23)." *FV* 81 (1982) 40–47. **Mowery, R. L.** "The Divine Hand and the Divine Plan in the Lukan Passion." In *SBL 1991 Seminar Papers,* ed. E. H. Lovering, Jr. 558–75. **Neyrey, J. H.** *The Passion according to Luke: A Redaction Study of Luke's Soteriology.* Theological Inquiries. New York: Paulist, 1985. **Osty, E.** "Les points de contact entre le récit de la Passion dans saint Luc et saint Jean." *RSR* 39 (1951) 146–54. **Perry, A. M.** *The Sources of Luke's Passion Narrative.* Chicago: University of Chicago, 1920. ————. "Some Outstanding New Testament Problems: V. Luke's Disputed Passion-Source." *ExpTim* 46 (1934–35) 256–60. **Schneider, G.** *Verleugnung, Verspottung und Verhör Jesu nach Lukas, 22,54–71: Studien zur lukanischen Darstellung der Passion.* SANT 22. Munich: Kösel, 1969. 11–72, 174–220. **Schramm, T.** *Markus-Stoff.* 182–84. **Soards, M. L.** *The Passion according to Luke: The Special Material of Luke 22.* JSNTSup 14. Sheffield: JSOT, 1987. **Stöger, A.** "Eigenart und Botschaft der lukanischen Passionsgeschichte." *BK* 24 (1969) 4–8. **Sylva, D. D.,** ed. *Reimaging the Death of the Lukan Jesus.* **Taylor, V.** *The Passion Narrative of St Luke: A Critical and Historical Investigation,* ed. O. E. Evans. SNTSMS 19. Cambridge: University Press, 1972. ————. "Sources of the Lukan Passion Narrative." *ExpTim* 68 (1956–57) 95. **Tiede, D.** "The Death of Jesus and the Trial of Israel in Luke-Acts." In *SBL 1990 Seminar Papers,* ed. D. J. Lull. Atlanta, GA: Scholars, 1990. 158–64. **Tyson, J. B.** *The Death of Jesus in Luke-Acts.* Columbia: University of South Carolina, 1986. **Vööbus, A.** *The Prelude to the Lukan Passion Narrative: Tradition-, Redaction-, Cult-, Motif-Historical and Source-Critical Studies.* Papers of the Estonian Theological Society in Exile 17. Stockholm: ETSE, 1968. **Voss, G.** *Christologie.* 99–130. **Winter, P.** "The Treatment of His Sources by the Third Evangelist in Luke xxi–xxiv." *ST* 8 (1954) 138–72. ————. "Sources of the Lucan Passion Narrative." *ExpTim* 68 (1956–57) 95.

SIGNIFICANCE OF THE DEATH OF JESUS:

Aubry, J. "Valeur salvifique de la mort et de la résurrection de Jésus." *AsSeign* 24 (1969) 66–81. **Balentine, G. L.** "Death of Jesus as a New Exodus." *RevExp* 59 (1962) 27–41. **Bartsch, H.-W.** "Die Bedeutung des Sterbens Jesu nach den Synoptikern." *TZ* 20 (1964) 87–102. **Beckmann, J.** "Das Heilsbedeutung des Kreuzes Jesu." In *Freispruch und Freiheit.* FS W. Kreck, ed. H. G. Geijer. Munich: Kösel, 1973. 19–32. **Bleiben, T. E.** "The Synoptists' Interpretation of the Death of Christ." *ExpTim* 54 (1942–43) 145–49. **Büchele, A.** *Der Tod Jesu im Lukasevangelium.* **Conzelmann, H.,** ed. *Zur Bedeutung des Todes Jesu: Exegetische Beiträge.* Gütersloh: G. Mohn, 1967. **Cousin, H.** "Dieu a-t-il sacrifié son fils Jésus?" *LumVie* 29 (1980) 55–67. **Davies, P. E.** "Did Jesus Die as a Martyr-Prophet?" *BR* 2 (1957) 19–30. ————. "Did Jesus Die as a Martyr-Prophet?" *BR* 19 (1974) 34–74. **Delling, G.** *Der Kreuzestod Jesu in der urchristlichen Verkündigung.* Berlin: Evangelische Verlagsanstalt, 1971. 75–97. **Dupont, J.** *Le discours de Milet: Testament pastoral de Saint Paul (Actes 20, 18–36).* LD 32. Paris: Cerf, 1962. 182–98. **Garrett, S. R.** "The Meaning of Jesus' Death in Luke." *WW* 12 (1992) 11–16. **George, A.** "Comment Jésus a-t-il percu sa propre mort?" *LumVie* 20 (1971) 34–59. ————. "Le sens de la mort de Jésus pour Luc." *RB* 80 (1973) 186–217. **Grosch, H.** "'Andere hat er gerettet . . .': Exegetische und didaktische Besinnung über zwei lukanische Passionstexte." *EvErz* 22 (1970) 233–47. **Gubler, M.-L.** *Die Frühesten Deutungen des Todes Jesu.* Fribourg/Göttingen: Universitätsverlag/

Vandenhoeck & Ruprecht, 1977. **Hengel, M.** *The Atonement: The Origins of the Doctrine in the New Testament.* Philadelphia: Fortress, 1981. 65–75. ————. "Der stellvertretende Sühnetod Jesu: Ein Beitrag zur Entstehung des urchristlichen Kerygmas." *IKZCom* 9 (1980) 1–25, 135–47. **Kodell, J.** "Luke's Theology of the Death of Jesus." In *Sin, Salvation and the Spirit,* ed. D. Durken. Collegeville: Liturgical, 1979. 221–30. **Léon-Dufour, X.** *Face à la mort: Jésus et Paul.* Paris: Seuil, 1979. ————. "Jesus' Understanding of His Death." *TD* 24 (1976) 293–300. ————. "How Did Jesus See His Death?" *TD* 29 (1981) 57–60. **Lohse, E.** *Märtyrer und Gottesknecht: Untersuchungen zur christlichen Verkündigung vom Sühntod Jesu Christi.* Göttingen: Vandenhoeck & Ruprecht, 1955. 113–46. **Moessner, D. P.** "'The Christ Must Suffer,' The Church Must Suffer: Rethinking the Theology of the Cross in Luke-Acts." In *SBL 1990 Seminar Papers,* ed. D. J. Lull. Atlanta, GA: Scholars, 1990. 165–95. **Morris, L.** "The Cross in the Lukan Writings." In *The Cross in the New Testament.* Exeter: Paternoster, n.d. 63–143. **Paul, A.** "Pluralité des interpretations théologiques de la mort due Christ dans le Nouveau Testament." *LumVie* 20 (1971) 18–33. **Roloff, J.** "Anfänge der soteriologischen Deutung des Todes Jesu (Mk. x. 45 und Lk. xxii 27)." *NTS* 19 (1972–73) 38–64. **Schneider, G.** *Verleugnung, Verspottung und Verhör Jesu nach Lukas, 22,54–71: Studien zur lukanischen Darstellung der Passion.* SANT 22. Munich: Kösel, 1969. 169–210. ————. "Die theologische Sicht des Todes Jesu in den Kreuzigungsberichten der Evangelien." *TPQ* 126 (1978) 14–22. **Schürmann, H.** *Jesu ureigener Tod.* Freiburg im B.: Herder, 1975. 56–63, 66–96. ————. "Jesu ureigenes Todesverständnis: Bemerkungen zur 'implizierten Soteriologie' Jesu." In *Begegnung mit dem Wort,* ed. J. Zmijewski and E. Nellessen. BBB 53. Bonn: Peter Hanstein, 1980. 272–309. ————. "Jesu Todesverständnis im Verstehenshorizont seiner Umwelt." *TGl* 70 (1980) 141–60. **Schütz, F.** *Der leidende Christus: Die angefochtene Gemeinde und das Christuskerygma der lukanischen Schriften.* BWANT 89. Stuttgart: Kohlhammer, 1969. **Schwager, R.** "Christ's Death and the Prophetic Critique of Sacrifice." *Semeia* 33 (1985) 109–23. **Smith, R. H.** "Paradise Today: Luke's Passion Narrative." *CurTM* 3 (1976) 323–36. **Stalder, K.** "Die Heilsbedeutung des Todes Jesu in den lukanischen Schriften." *IKZ* 52 (1962) 222–42. **Trilling, W.** "Der Tod Jesu, Ende der alten Weltzeit." In *Christusverkündigung in den synoptischen Evangelien.* Munich: Kösel, 1969. 191–211. **Untergassmair, F. G.** *Kreuzweg und Kreuzigung Jesu.* ————. "Thesen zur Sinndeutung des Todes Jesu in der lukanischen Passiongeschichte." *TGl* 70 (1980) 180–93. **Voss, G.** *Christologie.* 99–130. **Williams, S. K.** *Jesus' Death as Saving Event: The Background and Origin of a Concept.* HDR 2. Missoula, MT: Scholars, 1975. **Zehnle, R.** "The Salvific Character of Jesus' Death in Lucan Soteriology." *TS* 30 (1969) 420–44.

DATING OF THE LAST SUPPER/THE CRUCIFIXION:

Benoit, P. "La date de la cène." In *Exégèse et théologie.* Paris: Cerf, 1961. 1:255–61; ET: "The Date of the Last Supper." In *Jesus and the Gospel.* Tr. B. Weatherhead. London: Darton, Longman and Todd, 1973. 1:87–93. **Black, M.** "The Arrest and Trial of Jesus and the Date of the Last Supper." In *New Testament Essays.* FS T. W. Manson, ed. A. J. B. Higgins. Manchester: Manchester University, 1959. 19–33. **Blinzler, J.** "Qumran-Kalender und Passionschronologie." *ZNW* 49 (1958) 238–51. **Braun, H.** *Qumran und das Neue Testament.* Tübingen: Mohr-Siebeck, 1966. 2:29–54. **Brown, R. E.** "The Problem of Historicity in John." In *New Testament Essays.* Milwaukee, WI: Bruce, 1965. 143–67, esp. 160–67. **Carmignac, J.** "Comment Jésus et ses contemporains pouvaient-ils célébrer la Pâque à une date no officielle?" *RevQ* 5 (1964–66) 59–79. **Chwolson, D.** *Das letzte Passamahl Christi und der Tag seines Todes.* Leipzig: H. Haessel, 1908. **Daly, R. J.** "The Eucharist and Redemption: The Last Supper and Jesus' Understanding of His Death." *BTB* 11 (1981) 21–27. **Delorme, J.** "Jesus a-t-il pris la dernière cène le mardi soir?" *AmCl* 67 (1957) 218–23, 229–34. **Dockx, S.** "Le 14 Nisan de l'an 30." In *Chronologies neotestamentaires et vie de L'Église primitive: Recherches exegetiques.* Gembloux: Duculot, 1976. 21–29. ————. "Chronologie du dernier jour de la vie de Jésus." In *Chronologies neotestamentaires et vie de L'Église primitive: Recherches exegetiques.* Gembloux: Duculot, 1976. 31–43. **Dugmore, C. W.** "A Note on the Quartodecimans." In *Studia patristica IV.* TU 79. Berlin: Akademie, 1961. 410–21. **Fitzmyer, J. A.**

The Dead Sea Scrolls: Major Publications and Tools for Study. SBLRBS 8. Atlanta, GA: Scholars, 1990. 180–86. **Fotheringham, J. K.** "The Evidence of Astronomy and Technical Chronology for the Date of the Crucifixion." *JTS* 35 (1934) 146–62. **Hoehner, H. W.** "Jesus' Last Supper." In *Essays.* FS J. D. Pentecost, ed. S. D. Toussaint and C. H. Dyer. Chicago: Moody, 1986. 63–74. ————. "Chronological Aspects of the Life of Christ: Part IV. The Day of Christ's Crucifixion." *BSac* 131 (1974) 241–64. ————. "Chronological Aspects of the Life of Christ: Part V. The Year of Christ's Crucifixion." *BSac* 131 (1974) 332–48. **Hölscher, G.** *Die Hohenpriesterliste bei Josephus und die evangelische Chronologie.* SAH 3. Heidelberg: C. Winters, 1940. **Holzmeister, U.** "Neuere Arbeiten über das Datum der Kreuzigung Christi." *Bib* 13 (1932) 93–103. **Humphreys, C. J.,** and **Waddington, W. G.** "Dating the Crucifixion." *Nature* 306 (1983) 743–46. **Husband, R. W.** "The Year of the Crucifixion." *TAPA* 46 (1915) 5–27. **Jaubert, A.** *The Date of the Last Supper.* Staten Island, NY: Alba House, 1965. ————. "Le calendrier des Jubilés et de la secte de Qumrân: Ses origines bibliques." *VT* 3 (1953) 250–64. ————. "La date de la dernière Cène." *RHR* 146 (1954) 140–73. ————. "Le calendrier des Jubilés et les jours liturgiques de la semaine." *VT* 7 (1957) 35–61. ————. "Le mercredi où Jésus fut livré." *NTS* 14 (1967–68) 145–64. **Maier, P. L.** "Sejanus, Pilate, and the Date of the Crucifixion." *CH* 37 (1968) 3–13. **Mann, C. S.** "The Chronology of the Passion and the Qumran Calendar." *CQR* 160 (1959) 446–56. **Martin, E. L.** *The Year of Christ's Crucifixion.* Foundation for Biblical Research Exposition. Pasadena, CA: The Foundation for Biblical Research, 1983. **Mulder, H.** "John xviii 28 and the Date of the Crucifixion." In *Miscellanea Neotestamentica,* ed. T. Baarda, A. F. J. Klijn, and W. C. Van Unnik. NovTSup 48. Leiden: Brill, 1978. 87–106. **Ogg, G.** "The Chronology of the Last Supper." In *Historicity and Chronology in the New Testament,* ed. D. E. Nineham et al. London: SCM, 1965. 92–96. **Ruckstuhl, E.** *Chronology of the Last Days of Jesus: A Critical Study.* Tr. V. J. Drapela. New York: Desclée, 1965. ————. "Zur Chronologie der Leidensgeschichte Jesu." *SNTU* 10 (1985) 27–61; reprinted in *Jesus im Horizont der Evangelien.* Stuttgarter Biblische Aufsatzbände 3. Stuttgart: Katholisches Bibelwerk, 1988. 101–40. ————. "Zur Chronologie der Leidensgeschichte Jesu (II. Teil)." *SNTU* 11 (1986) 97–129; reprinted in *Jesus im Horizont der Evangelien.* Stuttgarter Biblische Aufsatzbände 3. Stuttgart: Katholisches Bibelwerk, 1988. 141–76, with Nachtrag 177–84. **Schaumberger, J.** "Der 14. Nisan als Kreuzigungstag und die Synoptiker." *Bib* 9 (1928) 57–77. **Skehan, P. W.** "The Date of the Last Supper." *CBQ* 20 (1958) 192–99. **Smith, B. D.** "The Chronology of the Last Supper." *WTJ* 53 (1991) 29–45. **Strobel, A.** *Ursprung und Geschichte des frühchristlichen Osterkalenders.* TU 121. Berlin: Akademie, 1977. 109–21. ————. "Der Termin des Todes Jesu: Überschau und Lösungsverschag unter Einschluss des Qumrankalendars." *ZNW* 51 (1960) 69–101. **Torrey, C. C.** "The Date of the Crucifixion according to the Fourth Gospel." *JBL* 50 (1931) 232–37, 237–50. ————. "In the Fourth Gospel the Last Supper Was the Paschal Meal." *JQR* 42 (1951–52) 237–50. **Turner, H. E. W.** "The Chronological Framework of the Ministry." In *Historicity and Chronology in the New Testament,* ed. D. E. Nineham et al. Theological Collections 6. London: SPCK, 1965. 59–74, esp. 67–74. **Walker, N.** "The Dating of the Last Supper." *JQR* 47 (1957) 293–95. ————. "Pauses in the Passion Story and Their Significance for Chronology." *NovT* 6 (1963) 16–19. ————. "Yet Another Look at the Passion Chronology." *NovT* 6 (1963) 286–89. **Walther, J. A.** "The Chronology of the Passion Week." *JBL* 77 (1958) 116–22. **Zeitlin, S.** "The Date of the Crucifixion according to the Fourth Gospel." *JBL* 51 (1932) 263–71. ————. "I. The Dates of the Birth and the Crucifixion of Jesus." *JQR* 55 (1964) 1–22.

And see also at 22:14–20.

FOR 22:1–2:

Schenke, L. *Studien zur Passionsgeschichte des Markus.* 12–66. **Schwarz, G.** *Jesus und Judas.* 141–48. **Segal, J. B.** *The Hebrew Passover: From the Earliest Times to A.D. 70.* London Oriental Series 12. London/New York: Oxford University, 1963. **Wambacq, B. N.** "Pesah-Massôt." *Bib* 62 (1981) 499–518. **Zerafa, P.** "Passover and Unleavened Bread." *Ang* 41 (1964) 235–50.

Translation

[1] *The feast of Unleavened Bread was drawing near, which is called Passover.* [2] *The chief priests and the scribes were [still] seeking [to work out] how they might do away with him. For they were afraid of the People.*

Notes

There are no significant textual variants.

Form/Structure/Setting

I have followed the traditional sectioning here and separated the passion narrative (22:1–23:56) and the resurrection narrative (24:1–53), but in the Lukan telling there is much to commend treating the final four chapters as a single major section. Note especially the way that 23:56 provides for a tighter continuity of action between the sections than is the case in Mark (where 15:47 to 16:1 already marks continuity); and the way in which the whole of chaps. 22–24 answers to the anticipation of 9:31, 51; 13:32.

22:1–2 is effectively a reiteration of the preceding section 19:47–21:38, which echoes the generalizing summary (19:47–48) that Luke provided at its beginning. The new element here is the approach of Passover. There is broad agreement that Luke uses only his Markan source (Mark 14:1–2). This in turn is best seen as originally belonging in a single unit with the account of Judas' visit to the chief priests (Mark 14:10–11). For further discussion on the Markan source, see at 22:3–6.

For the passion narrative Luke clearly makes use of his Markan source, but there has been considerable debate about whether he had available a second continuous passion narrative (as distinct from access to isolated items of tradition). As will emerge in the analysis of the separate units, I am convinced that Luke did have such a second source available to him. A second Lukan source first becomes visible in 22:15–20, is uncertain for vv 21–23, is clear for vv 24–30, 31–34, 35–38, likely for vv 39–46, 47–54a, 54b–62, clear for vv 63–64, likely for vv 66–71, 23:1–5, quite possible for vv 6–12, uncertain for vv 13–16, likely for vv 18–25, very likely for vv 26–32, likely for vv 33–34, unlikely for vv 35–38, very likely for vv 39–43, quite possible for vv 46–47 in the unit vv 44–49, and possible for vv 50–56. While there is no guarantee that all of this came to Luke from a single source, the sheer quantity makes a second continuous passion narrative almost certain. In many cases the second source would seem to have some link with Johannine tradition, but not in a manner that provides support for literary dependence in one direction or the other.

There has been considerable scholarly dispute over whether there was a pre-Markan passion narrative, or whether Mark is the first creator of such a narrative. If I am at all right about the second Lukan source here, then a pre-Markan passion narrative becomes that much more likely. The question of a pre-Markan passion narrative is addressed most closely at 22:54b–62 below. There I argue for the existence of a such a narrative, but without a great deal of confidence about its scope (it must have included 14:1–2, 10–11 and a version of Peter's denial in connection with a trial before the high priest; it may have included a prediction of the Petrine denial before 14:1–2 [with other materials?]; a trial before Pilate would have been part of the narrative; and once we have this much then a good deal more is necessary to complete the narrative).

As will become clear below, I think that there is a good basis for affirming the fundamental historicity of the passion narratives. Various tendencies are observable in the reporting, and a certain amount of pious imaginative writing has been the vehicle for registering the sense of significance that early Christians attributed to these events. But the main lines are stable among the different strands of tradition, and a whole emerges that has a good measure of historical credibility.

There are a series of dating and timing problems to be raised in connection with the passion narrative. (*i*) Because of the differing chronology of John and the Synoptics, there is the question of whether the Last Supper was in fact a Passover meal. (*ii*) There is the problem of identifying the year in which the crucifixion of Jesus took place. (*iii*) And there are a variety of issues in connection with the sequence and timing of elements of the judicial process mounted against Jesus. Comment will be offered here on the first two of these issues, while discussion on matters connected with the judicial process mounted against Jesus will be found in connection with the units from 22:54.

In contradistinction to the Synoptic picture, a series of verses in John suggest that the final meal of Jesus with his disciples took place before the Passover. The Johannine account gives the impression, further, that Jesus' execution had already taken place on Passover eve and that Jesus was already dying during the time that the Passover lambs were being slaughtered in the temple in preparation for the coming Paschal meal (John 13:1–2; 18:28; 19:14, 31–37 [the recent attempt by B. D. Smith [*WTJ* 53 (1991) 29–45] to demonstrate that the Johannine last Supper is after all a Passover meal underlines the terminological looseness that was already possible in the first century, but fails to convince).

Jeremias (*Eucharistic Words*, 42–55, 81–82) has identified a series of features of the Johannine account that make best sense if the traditions behind the account were, despite the present Johannine chronology, originally traditions about a Passover meal. Some of these features prove no more than that the meal was a special banquet and not simply a regular main meal of the day, but cumulatively Jeremias' case is at least strongly suggestive.

The identification of the currency for some Palestinian Jews of Jesus' period of a solar calendar of 364 days (exactly 52 weeks), differing from the official calendar, which was lunar in orientation and had only 354 days (in fact both calendars required periodic intercalated months [the one much more regularly than the other] to keep the seasons aligned with the calendar; the manner of intercalation is only very imperfectly known) has suggested for some a calendrical solution to the tension between the Johannine and Synoptic accounts. The two calendars, naturally enough, produce different days for the feasts. Could it be that Jesus kept to the solar calendar, which though it had become rather sectarian by the time of Jesus (we know about it mostly from the Qumran documents and *Jubilees*), was evidently the more ancient calendar? According to this view Jesus kept Passover on the Tuesday evening and died on the Friday afternoon, which was the eve of official Passover (the most important advocates of this solution are Jaubert and Ruckstuhl). While by no means an impossible solution, there are significant problems with this suggestion. To mention only two: (*i*) Is it really believable that the temple authorities of Jesus' day permitted sacrifice of Passover lambs in the temple for a separate celebration of "Essene" Passover? (*ii*) Given the sectarian vehemence with which calendrical differences were maintained, is it believable that Jesus' adherence to a sectarian calendar has left no other marks on the Gospel tradition?

There is something of a trail of other earlier calendrical solutions that have been proposed, but of the calendrical solutions offered, that involving the "Essene" calender is by far the least speculative and the best defended.

While I remain unconvinced by the two Passovers solution, something that its proponents focus upon seems to me important to notice. The solar calendar produces a Tuesday evening Passover. Since the tradition is united that Jesus was arrested during the night following the Last Supper and was executed on the Friday, by this reckoning, two whole days are added to the canonical Gospel version of the time that Jesus was kept in custody.

Especially in connection with the Sanhedrin trial, it has long been recognized that there are difficulties in the Markan chronology, which takes us from arrest late on Thursday night to crucifixion at 9 A.M. on Friday morning (John's account involves three more hours). It is not difficult for proponents of the two Passover solution to ease these difficulties by extending the period in custody. Quite apart from the validity of their particular reconstructions, this raises the question of whether the Markan passion day is an artistic and theological day rather than a historical and chronological day.

In 1:21–38, Mark links a series of episodes into a twenty-four-hour chronology, apparently for the purpose of creating something like "a specimen day in the ministry for Jesus," which is then generalized by the travel notice in v 39. There is an even greater deliberateness about the sequence of chronological markers in the Markan passion: 14:1: "two days before the Passover" (needed for the Bethany supper and the Last Supper; and also possibly for the sake of a seven-day scheme for Jesus' time in Jerusalem); v 12: "on the first day of Unleavened Bread, when they sacrificed the Passover lamb"; v 17: "when it was evening"; v 26: "when they had sung a hymn"; v 43: "immediately, while he was still speaking"; v 72: "immediately the cock crowed a second time"; 15:1: "as soon as it was morning"; v 25: "it was the third hour when they crucified him"; v 33: "when the sixth hour had come, there was darkness over the whole land until the ninth hour"; v 42: "when evening had come"; 16:1: "when the sabbath was past."

With only a little filling in, we have at the center of this chronological sequence a twenty-four-hour Jewish day consisting of six hours for the Last Supper (three hours for the Supper with six hours for arrest and Jewish hearing would also be possible), three hours for the Gethsemane prayer (see 14:37 and 41), three hours for arrest and Jewish hearing, three hours for Pilate, three hours on the cross before the darkness, with three further hours to die (so six hours, as, I am suggesting, is the time interval for the Passover meal), three hours dead on the cross before a hurried burial so that he might not be left on the cross on the sabbath. (Schenk, *Passionsbericht*, 144, is mistaken in thinking that Mark presents days as running from morning to evening: the texts he points to show no more than the obvious fact that the beginning point for most public action on a new day could only be after the hours of darkness had passed.) Mark's "passion day" looks suspiciously like a theological and artistic more than a historical and chronological day: the whole sweep of this centrally important unfolding sequence of events has been located on the day of the feast of Passover. It would seem that the sequence of events is portrayed as constituting the new Passover redemption precisely by means of the literary device of containing the events entirely within the time of the actual Passover festival.

If this is at all correct, then the distinction between Mark and John becomes not a disagreement over the nature and sequence of historical events, but rather a difference of strategy about how to portray the connection between the death of Jesus and Passover redemption. John's arrangement creates a powerful connection by means of a timing coincidence (and other coincidences) between the execution of Jesus and the sacrificing of the Passover lamb; Mark has achieved the Passover connection in another way.

When it comes to historical reconstruction, it is likely that the synoptic Gospels are right in their identification of the Last Supper as a Passover meal (see above about the possible traces in the Johannine materials of an original Passover identification for the meal, and see Jeremias [*Eucharistic Words*, 41–55] for features of the Markan account identifying the meal as a Passover meal, not deliberately, but incidentally by reflecting aspects of the customs that regulated Passover at that period [in my judgment, Jeremias' cumulative case has survived the various attempts to discredit his arguments]). However, where John has taken his literary freedom primarily with the timing of the execution of Jesus, Mark has taken his with the number of events that he squeezes into the day of the Passover festival.

We turn now to the question of the year in which these events most likely transpired. Luke seems to date the beginning of the ministry of John the Baptist in A.D. 28–29 (see at 3:1). We can only guess at how long it was before Jesus came to John for baptism; and we do not know for certain the time frame for the development of a separate ministry for Jesus (the timing of the census of 2:2, combined with the "about thirty" of 3:23, adds nothing by way of precision). Uncertainty continues as we try to estimate the length of Jesus' public ministry: the Synoptic ministry *could* have all been in a single year; John reports a series of Jewish festivals that make three years a better estimate. The above discussion, unfortunately, removes one of the few fixed points thought to have been available to determine the date of Jesus' death. If my reconstruction is at all correct, then we can no longer be certain about the day on which Passover fell in that particular year. Jesus died on a Friday, but Passover probably came earlier in the week. Astronomical calculations can identify, at least within a day or so, the day on which Passover is likely to have fallen in any particular year during the relevant period (if, as is normally assumed, observation, and not simply calculation, was the basis for declaring the beginning of the new month [a table of dates for the new moon at the beginning of the month Nisan, for the relevant period, based on astronomical calculations may be consulted in H. H. Goldstine, *New and Full Moons 1001 B.C. to A.D. 1651* (Philadelphia: American Philosophical Society, 1973) 86; this may be compared with dates for Nisan 1 from R. A. Parker and W. H. Dubberstein, *Babylonian Chronology 625 B.C.–A.D. 75* (Providence: Brown University, 1956) 86–87]). But if we do not know the day on which Passover fell that year, then we cannot eliminate years on the basis of astronomical calculation. We may think ourselves justified in eliminating years in which Passover fell on, say, Thursday through Sunday, but given a day or so of uncertainty, this would definitely eliminate only A.D. 30 and 33, and even these eliminations can only be on a sliding scale of probabilities. We have no sufficient basis for estimating how long or short a period Jesus would have needed to be in custody before his execution (A.D. 28 and 32 would both be attractive options, each extending the arrest period by a couple of days). The results of our inquiry must therefore be almost entirely negative: Jesus is likely to have died in the half decade A.D. 30–35, perhaps earlier in this period rather than later, but it does not seem possible to be more precise.

Comment

As Passover approaches there has been no change in the situation of the preceding section, in which the plans of the Jerusalem leadership are held in check by Jesus' popularity with the People.

1 Only πάσχα, "Passover," and a use of τὰ ἄζυμα, "the [feast of] Unleavened Bread," survives of Mark's wording (but Luke spells out "feast of"). Luke introduces the language of approach (ἤγγιζεν), which he made considerable use of in the section 18:35–19:46. Perhaps he intends with this to suggest that Passover represented some kind of climax point in connection with the thus far thwarted machinations of the Jewish authorities. Otherwise, the juxtaposition of vv 1 and 2 remains unmotivated and must be treated as a Markan relic that has lost its Markan motivation. Luke treats Passover and Unleavened Bread as interchangeable names for the Pilgrim feast. This is not strictly correct but can be well paralleled in Jewish usage of the period (cf. B. D. Smith, *WTJ* 51 [1991] 32–39; Fitzmyer, 440). Passover is properly the feast prepared for by the slaughter of the lamb in the late afternoon of 14 Nisan and celebrated in family or wider groupings from after sunset (and thus by the normal Jewish reckoning on 15 Nisan) with an elaborate meal built around the lamb. The Passover liturgy and detailed regulation went through various developments, and it is not always possible to be confident about the state of development already in the lifetime of Jesus. Unleavened Bread is a week-long feast, prepared for with the removal of all leaven on 14 Nisan and continuing for a week in which all bread eaten was to be unleavened (see Exod 12; Lev 23:5–6; Num 28:16–17; Deut 16:1–8).

2 Luke begins his sentence with the Markan wording (as far as "seeking"), but soon moves into fresh formulation, retaining only πῶς, "how," γάρ, "for" (but with a different role), and a use of λαός, "People" (with a different case), of the actual Markan language. Luke does not carry over the Markan emphasis on subterfuge (ἐν δόλῳ) or on the problem of arresting Jesus at the time of the feast (ἐν τῇ ἑορτῇ). For the final clause, Luke echoes language he has used in 20:19. In Luke's hands the whole verse recalls 19:47b–48 (though he does not bother to add, as there, "along with the leaders of the People"). Once again Luke makes the point that the positive attitude of the Jewish People complicated the desired accomplishment of the Jerusalem leadership to effect Jesus' demise (the use of γάρ picks up on the earlier use of πῶς).

Explanation

The whole scope of Jesus' teaching ministry in Jerusalem, with all its conflict between Jesus and the Jewish leadership, had done nothing to resolve the stalemate from which Luke's account begins in 19:47–48. Jesus' popularity with the Jewish People still stands in the way of the Jewish leaders as they seek to have him destroyed. But now Passover is drawing near and matters are due to come to a head.

Luke identifies Passover (with its Passover lamb) and Unleavened Bread (with its week, starting with Passover, in which the Jewish People were required to keep totally separate from leaven and leavened bread). These are technically distinct, but often in loose parlance equated.

Betrayal by Judas   (22:3–6)

Bibliography

Bacon, B. W. "What Did Jesus Betray?" *HibJ* 19 (1920–21) 476–93. **Baumbach, G.** "Judas—Jünger und Verräter Jesu." *ZdZ* 17 (1963) 91–98. **Brown, S.** *Apostasy and Perseverance.* 82–97. **Buchheit, G.** *Judas Iskarioth (Legende—Geschichte—Deutung).* Gütersloh: Rufer, 1954. **Cullmann, O.** "Le douzième apôtre." *RHPR* 42 (1962) 133–40 = "Die zwölfte Apostel." In *Vorträge und Aufsätze 1925 bis 1962,* ed. K. Frölich. Tübingen/Zürich: Mohr, 1966. 214–22. **Enslin, M. S.** "How the Story Grew: Judas in Fact and Fiction." In *Festschrift to Honor F. Wilber Gingrich,* ed. E. H. Barth and E. E. Cocroft. Leiden: Brill, 1972. 123–41. **Gärtner, B.** *Iscariot.* Facet Books. Biblical Series. Tr. V. I. Gruhm. Philadelphia: Fortress, 1971. **Goldschmidt, H. L.** "Das Judasbild im Neuen Testament aus jüdischer Sicht." In *Heilvoller Verrat? Judas im Neuen Testament,* by H. L. Goldschmidt and M. Limbeck. Stuttgart: Katholisches Bibelwerk, 1976. 9–36. **Hein, K.** "Judas Iscariot: Key to the Last-Supper Narratives?" *NTS* 17 (1970–71) 227–32. **Klauck, H.-J.** *Judas—ein Jünger ders Herrn.* QD 111. Freiburg/Basel/Vienna: Herder, 1987. **Lapide, P. E.** "Verräter oder verraten? Judas in evangelischer und jüdischer Sicht." *LM* 16 (1977) 75–79. **Limbeck, M.** "Das Judasbild im Neuen Testament aus christlicher Sicht." In *Heilvoller Verrat? Judas im Neuen Testament,* by H. L. Goldschmidt and M. Limbeck. Stuttgart: Katholisches Bibelwerk, 1976. 37–101. **Lüthi, K.** "Das Problem des Judas Iskarioth—neu untersucht." *EvT* 16 (1956) 98–114. **Morin, J.-A.** "Les deux derniers des Douzes: Simon le Zélote et Judas Iskariôth." *RB* 80 (1973) 332–58. **Plath, M.** "Warum hat die urchristliche Gemeinde auf die Überlieferung der Judas Erzählung Wert gelegt?" *ZNW* 17 (1916) 178–88. **Popkes, W.** *Christus Traditus: Eine Untersuchung zum Begriff der Dahingabe im Neuen Testament.* ATANT 49. Zürich: Zwingli, 1967. 174–81. **Preisker, H.** "Der Verrat des Judas und das Abendmahl." *ZNW* 41 (1942) 151–55. **Roquefort, D.** "Judas: Une figure de la perversion." *ETR* 58 (1983) 501–13. **Schenke, L.** *Studien zur Passionsgeschichte des Markus.* 119–50. **Schläger, G.** "Die Ungeschichtlichkeit des Verräters Judas." *ZNW* 15 (1914) 50–59. **Schwarz, G.** *Jesus und Judas.* Esp. 176–82. **Smith, W. B.** "Judas Iscariot." *HibJ* 9 (1911) 532–35. **Stein-Schneider, H.** "A la recherche du Judas historique." *ETR* 60 (1985) 403–24. **Tarachow, S.** "Judas, der geliebte Henker." In *Psychoanalytische Interpretationen biblischer Texte,* ed. Y. Spiegel. Munich: Kaiser, 1972. 243–56. **Vogler, W.** *Judas Iskarioth: Untersuchung zu Tradition und Redaktion von Textes des Neuen Testaments und ausserkanonischer Schriften.* Theologische Arbeiten 42. Berlin: Evangelische Verlaganstalt, 1983. **Wagner, H.,** ed. *Judas Iskariot: Menschliches oder heilsgeschichtliches Drama?* Frankfurt: Knecht, 1985. **Wrede, W.** "Judas Ischarioth in der urchristlichen Überlieferung." In *Vorträge und Studien.* Tübingen: Mohr-Siebeck, 1907. 127–46.

And see at 22:1–2.

Translation

³ *Satan entered into Judas called Iscariot, who was of the number of the Twelve,* ⁴*and he went and conferred with the chief priests and the officers about how he might deliver Jesus*[a] *up to them.* ⁵*They were glad and decided to give him money.* ⁶*He agreed and began to seek for an opportunity to deliver him up in the absence of a crowd.*

Notes

[a] Gr.: "him."

Form/Structure/Setting

The impasse of 22:1–2 is broken by Judas Iscariot's visit to the appropriate executive leaders of the Jewish establishment.

Luke passes over the anointing in Mark 14:3–9, having used a related scene at 7:36–50 (see there; the omission is not likely to be for the sake of the anointing anticipated in 23:56–24:1). The omission restores what is likely to have been an original unity between Mark 14:1–2 and 10–11. The differences from Mark can for the most part be reckoned to the Lukan pen, but "Satan entered into" is (apart from word order) found identically in John 13:27 and suggests that a further tradition shared between Luke and John has also left its mark.

If it were to have been separately transmitted, the pre-Markan form of Mark 14:1–2, 10–11 would need to have been completed with some account of the actual handing over. Perhaps the near repetition in v 43 of the words used to introduce Judas in v 10 marks the place where the source continues (Mark feels the need to repeat the introduction because of the material intruded between). The present form of v 43 is formulated in connection with the language of v 48, but a simpler form of it may have completed the betrayal account with something like "He came [answering to the 'went' of v 10] with a crowd from the chief priests[, the scribes and the elders]." But this can be no more than a suggestion. An original form is unlikely to have had the "after two days" of v 1 (this timetable probably means no more than that Mark had a narrative need of a chronology that would allow him to report two main meals before the arrest; it may also contribute to a seven-day calendar for Jesus' time in Jerusalem). The final sentence of v 11 is also likely to be for the sake of Mark's incorporation of this tradition into his larger narrative.

If this reconstruction is along the right lines, we have a tradition in which the betrayal by Judas was arranged and executed in the immediate context of Passover. Judas precipitated official action because he provided a way in which Jesus could be arrested during the feast period without the need to deal with a potentially ugly public scene. Though such a narrative would have undoubted pastoral usefulness, its immediate role is to account for Jesus' arrest precisely at Passover, and in this role it is likely to be historical.

The attempts that have been made to rehabilitate Judas (recently notably that of Schwarz [*Jesus und Judas*]) are finally exercises in uncontrolled speculation. Likewise, the many attempts to identify the nature of Judas' motivation in defecting from the inner circle of Jesus' disciples are, for lack of evidence, no more than imaginative exercises.

Comment

Once the circle of confidence is broken through the defection of one of Jesus' closest followers, popularity with the People will no longer be able to protect him from the efforts of the Jewish leadership: the final Satanic attack has begun.

3 Luke begins with a note drawn from another tradition: "Satan entered into Judas" (cf. John 13:27). On the role of Satan here, cf. at 4:1–13. Satan is active in temptation, sin, and spiritual darkness. While he has not been absent during Jesus' public ministry, the passion period is the opportune time for a particular onslaught (cf. 22:31, 53). The idea of Satan entering a person is unusual but should not be confused with demon possession. The language probably results from the application of the category "spirit" to Satan, perhaps along the lines of the "two spirits" (good and evil) of the Qumran documents (e.g., 1QS 3:13–4:25). *Mart. Isa.* 3:11 uses the related language "Beliar dwelt in the heart of." Cf. also Acts 5:3.

τὸν καλούμενον, "called," may be Lukan (cf. 9:10; Acts 1:23; 15:22), but the change from Mark to the declinable form for Iscariot (contrast Luke 6:16), which is the constant Matthean and Johannine usage (Mark has it at 14:43), may suggest that Luke's second tradition is at work. Luke uses "number" quite a few times in Acts, so "of the number" may be his own contribution. For the name "Iscariot," see at 6:16. Schwarz (*Jesus und Judas,* 7) provides a more complete list of the senses that have been proposed for the term (cf. also the listing in Vogler, *Judas Iskarioth,* 18–20) and defends (6–12), on the basis of conjectural emendation, yet another sense: "man of the city (i.e., Jerusalem)."

4   Luke uses the key elements of the Markan vocabulary here but freshly mints the verse. In particular he adds "and officials" (καὶ στρατηγοῖς), of whom only Luke in the NT speaks (apart from here and in v 52, Luke elsewhere uses the plural only of the magistrates of Philippi); and he takes up again the τὸ πῶς + subjunctive form that he used in v 2, perhaps in order to suggest the correspondence between Judas' proposal and that for which the Jewish leadership was seeking. Suggestions about identity of the temple (cf. v 52) officials range from temple police to accountants of the temple treasury. Whoever they were, their importance here is surely related to their ability to set in motion the arrest of Jesus rather than to their access to funds from the temple treasury to pay Judas for his betrayal!

For "deliver him up," see at 9:44. Judas' act of delivering Jesus up takes its place in the much wider theme of the delivering up of Jesus (beyond the passion predictions see 20:20; 23:25; 24:7, 20; Acts 3:13). Though παραδῷ never means "betray" as such, it is hard to avoid such an overtone here. Judas' role unfolds in 22:6, 21–22, 47–48. The Lukan text makes no attempt to explain what motivated Judas—beyond the reference to Satan (v 3) and to the divine necessity (vv 21–22) of the delivering up (if not of the role of Judas the individual in its execution). In John 6:64–71 the connection is made with a failure of faith, and in 12:4–6 Judas' avarice and dishonesty prepare for his role as betrayer.

5   More of Mark's wording survives here. The major changes are Luke's deletion of "hearing" and his use of συνέθεντο, "agreed," for Mark's ἐπηγγείλαντο, "promised." The chief priests and officials sense that here is a way to move beyond their impasse. Matt 26:15 has thirty pieces of silver as the amount that changed hands.

6   Beyond some recasting, Luke adds significantly at the beginning and the end of the verse: ἐξωμολόγησεν, "agreed," at the beginning raises the profile of the financial transaction in the delivering up of Jesus (the money was not simply a reward); ἄτερ ὄχλου αὐτοῖς (lit. "apart from a crowd to them") at the end takes up the substance of the concern expressed by the leaders in Mark 14:1–2 (and passed over in Luke 22:1–2), to act surreptitiously and to keep the action against Jesus out of the view of the throngs of festival pilgrims. It also answers to the Lukan emphasis on the role of Jesus' popularity with the public ("the People"; see at 19:48) in placing a check on the plans of the Jerusalem hierarchy. Luke uses ἄτερ, "apart from," again at v 35; it is not found elsewhere in the NT.

Explanation

At the initiative of Satan, the impasse of 22:1–2, which has been present since the beginning of Jesus' Jerusalem ministry, is broken. The leaders' fear of the People can no longer protect Jesus once the inner circle of confidence is broken by the defection of Judas.

Satan has not been inactive during the ministry of Jesus, but he concentrates his efforts in particularly opportune times (see 4:13). The passion period is such a time of special Satanic onslaught (see also 22:31, 53). Temptation, sin, and spiritual blindness are the particular currencies of Satan, and here Judas falls entirely under Satan's spell.

To the dilemma of the Jewish leadership corresponds the offer of Judas. Naturally they are delighted and quite ready to strike a financial deal with him. Judas' access to knowledge about the private movements of Jesus meant that he was well placed to find an occasion for bringing an arresting party into contact with Jesus at a time when this action could be kept from the public gaze. No doubt the public would find out in time, but the particular flashpoint situation created by the move to take Jesus into custody could be avoided.

Keeping in mind the wider Lukan narrative, one must not forget that this delivering up of Jesus, though a betrayal, at the same time fulfills the divine intention (e.g., Acts 2:23) and is fully anticipated by Jesus himself (Luke 9:44; 22:21–22; etc.).

Arrangements for the Passover Meal (22:7–13)

Bibliography

Arnott, A. G. "'The First Day of Unleavened . . . ,' Mt 26.17, Mk 14.12, Lk 22.7." *BT* 35 (1984) 235–38. **Chenderlin, F.** "Distributed Observance of the Passover: A Preliminary Test of the Hypothesis." *Bib* 57 (1976) 1–24, esp. 13–14. **Foster, J.** "'Go and Make Ready' (Luke xxii.8, John xiv.2)." *ExpTim* 63 (1951–52) 193. **Green, J. B.** "Preparation for Passover (Luke 22:7–13): A Question of Redactional Technique." *NovT* 29 (1987) 305–19. **Jacob, R.** *Les péricopes de l'entrée à Jérusalem et de la préparation de la cène: Contribution à l'étude du problème synoptique.* Études Bibliques NS. Paris: Gabalda, 1973. **MacMillan, H.** "The Man Bearing a Pitcher of Water: Luke xxii. 10." *ExpTim* 3 (1891–92) 58–60. **Robbins, V. K.** "Last Meal: Preparation, Betrayal, and Absence." In *The Passion in Mark*, ed. W. H. Kelber. 21–40, esp. 21–28. **Sabbe, M.** "The Footwashing in Jn 13 and Its Relation to the Synoptic Gospels." *ETL* 58 (1982) 279–308. **Schenke, L.** *Studien zur Passionsgeschichte des Markus.* 152–98. **Schürmann, H.** *Quellenkritische Untersuchung.* 1:75–104. ———. "Der Abendmahlsbericht Lk 22,7–38 als Gottesdienstordnung, Gemeindeordnung, Lebensordnung." In *Ursprung und Gestalt.* 108–50, esp. 145–48. ———. *Le récit de la dernière cène, Luc 22,7–38: Une règle de célébration eucharistique, une règle communautaire, une règle de vie.* Le Puy: X. Mappus, 1966. ———. "Der Dienst des Petrus und Johannes." *TTZ* 60 (1951) 99–101; reprinted in *Ursprung und Gestalt.* 274–76. **Wanke, J.** *Beobachtungen zum Eucharistieverständnis des Lukas auf Grund der lukanischen Mahlberichte.* Erfurter theologische Schriften 8. Leipzig: St. Benno, 1973. 61–62. **Winter, P.** "Luke 22, 7–18." *Vox theologica* 26 (1955–56) 88–91.

And see at 22:1–2.

Translation

⁷ *The day of Unleavened Bread came, in which it was necessary to slaughter the Passover [lamb].* ⁸ *He sent Peter and John saying, "Go and prepare for us the Passover, so that we*

might eat [it together]." [9] *They said to him, "Where do you want us to prepare [it]?"* [10] *He said to them, "Look, as you go into the city someone*[a] *who is carrying a jar of water will meet you. Follow him into the house into which he goes,* [11] *and you are to say to the householder of the house, 'The teacher says to you, "Where is the*[b] *guest room where I am to eat the Passover with my disciples?"'* [12] *He will show you a large upstairs room already set out; prepare there."* [13] *They went off and found [things] just as he had said to them, and they prepared the Passover.*

Notes

a Gr. ἄνθρωπος, "person/man."
b ℵ C etc. have μου, "my," but this is likely intended to conform the text to Mark.

Form/Structure/Setting

The approaching feast day in 22:1 has arrived now, and Jesus initiates the arranging of the Passover meal. V 14 is often included here but is better linked with vv 15–20 since it marks another coming of a time, beyond that specified in v 7. Also it makes a natural introductory setting for vv 15–20, which otherwise begins abruptly.

The Markan sequence continues, and there is no adequate reason for postulating anything beyond a Markan source (see the detailed language analysis by Schürmann in *Untersuchung,* 1:76–104). In the Markan telling there is a conscious paralleling of 14:12–16 and 11:1–6 (see, e.g., Robbins, "Last Meal," 23–24) though clearly not to the point where the one account has created the other. (Luke appears to be conscious of this parallelism, at some points enhancing it [notably in v 13], but at others reducing the level of agreement [in v 8 both processes are evident].) It is not entirely clear whether the Markan account thinks in terms of supernatural prescience or of prior arrangement. In either case, there is an emphasis on making arrangements discretely for the meal, in order, presumably, to ensure that Jesus' whereabouts on that evening should not become publicly and therefore officially known. This latter aspect of the report constitutes its core, which with some credibility we may trace back to the historical Jesus, as part of his strategy for avoiding arrest until after he had been able to share a final Passover celebration with his disciples (cf. Luke 22:15). It is, however, difficult to suggest in form-critical terms what form of this tradition could have been transmitted as an independent unit (Dormeyer [*Passion,* 91–93] argues for a "prophetic prediction of a sign," appealing to 1 Sam 10:1–10; 1 Kgs 17:8–16; 2 Kgs 1:3–4, but his case is stronger for the related Mark 11:1–10 than for Mark 14:12–16).

Comment

Jesus assigns to leading figures among the Twelve the servant task of making arrangements for the Passover meal he plans to share with his disciples. Despite the looming threat to his life, Jesus remains clearly in control of the situation. The Passover arrangements are set in place in such a way that Jesus' location on this crucial evening will not be public knowledge.

7 The Markan content is freshly worded, partly for the sake of being able to speak of the day as having come, after speaking in v 1 of the feast drawing near (cf. Green, *NovT* 29 [1987] 310). Luke's "the day of Unleavened Bread" (without Mark's "first") is misleading in two respects: Unleavened Bread was a seven-day feast, and (here Mark is equally misleading) it began strictly speaking on 15 Nisan, not 14 Nisan,

which must be the date Luke has in mind, because that is when the lambs were sacrificed (see at 22:1). But the basis for loose reference to 14 Nisan as the beginning of Unleavened Bread is already set in Exod 12:18 with its reference to eating unleavened bread on "the fourteenth day of the month at evening," and is natural enough for a feast that required (in anticipation) the removal of all leaven on 14 Nisan. In *War* 5.99, Josephus speaks of the feast beginning on the fourteenth day of the month *and*, just as Luke does, uses "the day of Unleavened Bread" to describe it.

There is some attractiveness in the view that Luke's choice of an idiom using ἔδει, "it was necessary," to speak of the slaughter of the Passover lamb is to be linked to his use of the same verb in the passion predictions (see 9:22; 17:25; 22:37; 24:7, 26; cf. Green, *NovT* 29 [1987] 312). But this is less than certain. [τὸ] πάσχα means, according to context, the Passover festival, the Passover meal, or the Passover lamb (here the last).

Passover practice had evolved through various stages by the time of Jesus. A festival originally based in the home (cf. Exod 12) later became a temple-based festival (cf. Deut 16:7; 2 Chr 35:13–14). The practice of Jesus' own day combined elements of both: the lambs were slaughtered in the temple forecourts during the afternoon of 14 Nisan, but the meal in the evening was held in family or wider groupings throughout the city (see Jeremias, *Eucharistic Words*, 42–43).

8–9 In editing his Markan source, Luke transfers the initiative from the disciples to Jesus: the general reference to the disciples disappears; their question to Jesus is postponed, and its content is partly reassigned to Jesus to become part of his directive (ἐτοιμάζειν, "prepare," is used in both). As well, Luke introduces Peter and John in place of the two anonymous disciples of Mark. Peter and John are significantly paired elsewhere in Luke-Acts (8:51; 9:28; Acts 1:13; 3:1, 3, 4; 4:13, 19; 8:14), and Schürmann ("Dienst," 274–76) has argued forcefully that they are introduced here, from the perspective of a time period after the death of James (cf. Acts 12:2), as the senior leaders of the apostolic group, being directed by Jesus into a service role (cf. Luke 22:24–27). Also notable is Luke's transformation of Mark's "you [sing. (i.e., Jesus)] may eat" to "we may eat" (now on the lips of Jesus). Luke adds emphasis here to the note of meal fellowship with Jesus present in Mark already at 14:14, but in a less emphatic form. Luke adds "for us" to Mark's "prepare," taking the "for us" from Mark 14:15, which has "prepare for us" (having used "for us" here, he will not repeat it in v 12).

10 Mark's "and he says to them" becomes both "saying" in v 8 and "he said to them" in v 10. Luke makes a series of changes of vocabulary and syntax in line with his own preferences. In the move from ὑπάγετε (lit. "depart"; Mark 14:13) to ἰδοὺ εἰσελθόντων ὑμῶν (lit. "behold, as you enter"), Luke not only uses favored words but also recognizes that after his earlier reconstruction an imperative at this point would be out of place. Mark's "follow him and wherever he enters" seems rough to Luke, who smooths the logic of the development with his "follow him into the house into which he goes."

ἄνθρωπος may mean "man" here (as, e.g., 16:19; 18:10) rather than the more general "person." However, the wider sense remains possible since the ἄνθρωπος meets the disciples rather than vice versa, so that we do not strictly need the more unusual sight of a man carrying the water jar. This person turns up in front of the disciples at just the right time. Jesus is presented as in total control of the situation. It is less clear here than in 19:30–31 whether prescience or prior arrangement is intended. The measure of parallelism stands in favor of the former.

11 Unlike Mark, Luke continues the imperatival force with a future verb (ἐρεῖτε, "you will say"). Otherwise, Luke's main changes are to add a pleonastic "of the house" to οἰκοδεσπότῃ, which already means "master of a house" (for other Lukan pleonasms, cf. BDF 484), and to adjust the use of personal pronouns by adding "to you" to Mark's "says" and taking away Mark's "my" from "guest room" (the latter may not have seemed quite appropriate, while the former may simply be a Lukan "compensation" for having removed the latter).

The water carriers' role will be to get the disciples to the right house and there-fore to the master of the right house. As in 19:31, the disciples are given precise words by Jesus to use as they carry out their orders. Here Jesus is to be identified as "the teacher." On Jesus as teacher, see at 7:40. The Lukan nuance, however, may be to point to Jesus as the one who has exercised the teaching ministry of 19:47–21:38: it is almost as if the householder were being expected to help secrete a fugitive. κατάλυμα is a flexible word for any kind of accommodation (see at 2:7 where the word is used of the place where Mary and Joseph failed to find accommodation).

12 The main Lukan change is to drop the Markan ἕτοιμον, "prepared/ready": no doubt it seemed confusing to follow this with a use of the cognate verb in connec-tion with preparations yet to be made. All sorts of available spaces were set up for Passover groups. The ἀνάγαιον here could be a rooftop but, because of the note of secrecy in the narrative, is more likely to be an upstairs room. ἐστρωμένον is literally "spread out," but here "set up for a banquet." The householder will have such a room prepared for Passover use, but still available for Jesus and the disciple band. Given the imminence of the time of the Passover meal and the huge pressure on space generated by the requirement that the meal be eaten within the walls of Jerusa-lem, this can only be by previous arrangement or by supernatural prompting.

The whole procedure has been set up so that nothing will draw public atten-tion to Jesus and the disciple group who will spend the Passover evening at this particular place. Not even the disciple band (and so not Judas) know where they will be meeting. We are probably to understand that the room is not only fur-nished but also provisioned for the feast, so that all the necessary preparation could be achieved without a good deal of coming and going.

13 By simplifying, Luke produces a more comprehensive statement and one that also parallels 19:32 more closely. Jesus' confidence is not at all misplaced: things are exactly as he said they would be. Despite the looming threat to his life, he is totally master of the situation.

Explanation

The feast day, approaching in 22:1, has now come, and arrangements must be made. This Passover meal will be of particular significance to Jesus with his dis-ciples, and Jesus will not have it disturbed. He knows that the hostile Jerusalem leadership is eager for an opportunity to grab him. Violation of the feast though it might be, the time when the pilgrim throng is dispersed into feasting Passover groups could be quite an opportunity. So Jesus supervises arrangements that will reduce to a minimum the number of people who could know his whereabouts on that fateful evening.

Luke speaks about the feast in a rather loose and even confusing way, since Unleavened Bread technically started only after the onset of 15 Nisan in the evening and was a seven-day festival. But the day intended (14 Nisan) is clear. That Peter and John should be chosen for this menial role anticipates the emphasis that will come in 22:25–27. The necessity that took the lambs to slaughter on that day is parallel to the necessity that would take Jesus to death on the feast day to follow.

Luke emphasizes the coming Passover meal as something Jesus and the disciples will share together. The nature of the importance of this final communal meal will emerge in the account to follow.

There is something of a cloak and dagger atmosphere generated by the procedure Jesus outlines. Luke does not make clear whether Jesus is exhibiting prescience and a supernatural ordering of affairs, or whether we should understand that some prior arrangements have been put in place. In either case, Jesus shows that he remains master of the situation despite the mounting threat to his life. The householder is being asked to cooperate in concealing one who had been exercising a provocative teaching ministry in the temple by day, and who was at this stage something of a fugitive by night. Not even the disciple band itself (including Judas) is to know ahead of time where they will be in the evening.

We should probably understand that the room is not only appropriately furnished for the Passover banquet, but that it is also provisioned, so that preparation could be made there quietly without the need for a lot of coming and going. Jesus has seen to it that his final evening with the disciples, spent in Passover celebration, will not be disturbed.

The Last Supper   (22:14–20)

Bibliography

Aalen, S. "Das Abendmahl als Opfermahl im Neuen Testament." *NovT* 6 (1963) 128–52. **Allen, W. C.** "The Last Supper Was a Passover Meal." *ExpTim* 20 (1908–09) 377. **Amphoux, C.-B.** "Le dernier repas de Jésus, Lc 22/15–20 par." *ETR* 56 (1981) 449–54. **Audet, J.-P.** "Esquisse historique du genre littéraire de la 'bénédiction' juive et de l' 'eucharistie' chrétienne." *RB* 65 (1958) 371–99. **Bacon, B. W.** "The Lukan Tradition of the Lord's Supper." *HTR* 5 (1912) 322–48. **Badia, L. F.** *The Dead Sea People's Sacred Meal and Jesus' Last Supper.* Washington, DC: University Press of America, 1979. **Bahr, G. J.** "The Seder of Passover and the Eucharistic Words." *NovT* 12 (1970) 181–202. **Balembo, B.** "Le produit de la vigne et le vin nouveau: Analyse exégétique de Mc 14,25." *RevAfTh* 8 (1984) 5–16. **Bammel, E.** "$p^{64(67)}$ and the Last Supper." *JTS* 24 (1973) 189–90. **Barclay, W.** *The Lord's Supper.* London: SCM, 1967. **Barrett, C. K.** "Luke xxii.15: To Eat the Passover." *JTS* 9 (1958) 305–7. **Barth, M.** *Das Abendmahl: Pasamahl, Bundesmahl und Messiasmahl.* Theologische Studiën 18. Zollikon/Zürich: Evangelischer, 1945. ———. *Das Mahl des Herrn: Gemeinschaft mit Israel, mit Christus und unter den Gästen.* Neukirchen Vluyn: Neukirchener, 1987. **Beck, N. A.** "The Last Supper as an Efficacious Symbolic Act." *JBL* 89 (1970) 192–98. **Benoit, P.** "The Accounts of the Institution and What They Imply." In *The Eucharist in the New Testament,* ed. J. Delorme et al. 71–101. ———. *Jesus and the Gospel.* Tr. B. Weatherhead. London: Darton, Longman and Todd, 1973. 1:95–122. ———. "Le récit de la Cène dans Lc XXII,15–20: Étude de critique textuelle et littéraire." *RB* 48 (1939) 357–93. **Betz, J.** *Die Eucharistie in der Zeit der Griechischen Väter: I/1.* Freiburg: Herder, 1955. ———. *Die Eucharistie in der Zeit der Griechischen Väter. II/1: Die Realpräsenz des Leibes und Blutes Jesu im Abendmahl nach dem Neuen Testament.* Freiburg: Herder, 1961. ———. "Eucharistie als zentrales Mysterium." In *Mysterium salutis 4/2,* ed. J. Feiner and M. Löhrer. Einsiedeln: Benziger, 1973. 186–209. ———. "Die Eucharistie als sakramentale Gegenwart des

Heilsereignisses 'Jesus' nach dem ältesten Abendmahlsberichte." *GuL* 33 (1960) 166–75.
Black, M. "The 'Fulfilment' in the Kingdom of God." *ExpTim* 57 (1945–46) 25–26.
Blakiston, H. E. D. "The Lucan Account of the Institution of the Lord's Supper." *JTS* 4
(1902–03) 548–55. **Blank, J.** "Der 'eschatologische Ausblick' Mk 14,25 und seine
Bedeutung." In *Kontinuität und Einheit.* FS F. Mussner, ed. P. G. Müller and W. Stenger.
Freiburg/Basel/Vienna: Herder, 1981. 500–518. **Bligh, J.** "Scriptural Inquiry: 'Do this in
commemoration of me.'" *The Way* 5 (1965) 154–59. **Bösen, W.** *Jesusmahl, eucharistisches
Mahl, Endzeitmahl: Ein Beitrag zur Theologie des Lukas.* SBS 97. Stuttgart: Katholisches
Bibelwerk, 1980. **Bokser, B. M.** "Was the Last Supper a Passover Seder?" *BRev* 3 (1987) 24–
33. **Bonsirven, J.** "Hoc est corpum meum: Recherches sur l'original araméen." *Bib* 29
(1948) 205–19. **Bornkamm, G.** *Jesus of Nazareth.* Tr. I. and F. McLuskey with J. M. Robinson.
New York: Harper and Row, 1960. 160–62. ———. "Herrenmahl und Kirche bei Paulus."
ZTK 53 (1956) 312–49. **Box, G. H.** "The Jewish Antecedents of the Eucharist." *JTS* 3 (1901–
2) 357–69. ———. "St Luke xxii 15,16." *JTS* 10 (1908–9) 106–7. **Burchard, C.** "The Importance of Joseph and Asenath for the Study of the New Testament: A General Survey and a
Fresh Look at the Lord's Supper." *NTS* 33 (1987) 102–34. **Burkitt, F. C.** "The Last Supper
and the Paschal Meal." *JTS* 17 (1915–16) 291–97. ——— and **Brooke, A. E.** "St Luke xxii
15,16: What Is the General Meaning?" *JTS* 9 (1907–8) 569–72. **Casey, M.** "The Original
Aramaic Form of Jesus' Interpretation of the Cup." *JTS* 41 (1990) 1–12. **Christie, W. M.**
"Did Christ Eat the Passover with His Disciples? or, The Synoptics versus John's Gospel."
ExpTim 43 (1931–32) 515–19. **Cohn-Sherbok, D.** "A Jewish Note on ΤΟ ΠΟΤΗΡΙΟΝ ΤΗΣ
ΕΥΛΟΓΙΑΣ." *NTS* 27 (1980–81) 704–9. **Cooke, B.** "Synoptic Presentation of the Eucharist
as Covenant Sacrifice." *TS* 21 (1960) 1–44. **Coppens, J.** "Les soi-disant analogies juives de
l'Eucharistie." *ETL* 8 (1931) 238–48. **Cullmann, O.** "La signification de la Sainte-Cène dans
le christianisme primitif." *RHPR* 16 (1936) 1–22. ——— and **Leenhardt, F. J.** *Essays on the
Last Supper.* Ecumenical Studies in Worship 1. London: Lutterworth, 1958. **Dalman, G.**
Jesus-Jeshua: Studies in the Gospels. New York: Ktav, 1971=1929. 86–184. **Daly, R.** "The Eucharist and Redemption: The Last Supper and Jesus' Understanding of His Death." *BTB* 11
(1981) 21–27. **David, J.-E.** "Τὸ αἷμά μου τῆς διαθήκης Mt 26,28: Un faux problème." *Bib*
48 (1967) 291–92. **Delling, G.** "Das Abendmahlsgechehen nach Paulus." *KD* 10 (1964)
61–77. **Delorme, J.** "The Last Supper and the Pasch in the New Testament." In *The Eucharist in the New Testament,* J. Delorme et al. 21–67. ——— et al. *The Eucharist in the New Testament.* Tr. E. M. Stewart. Baltimore/Dublin: Helicon, 1964. **Derrett, J. D. M.** "The Upper
Room and the Dish." *HeyJ* 26 (1985) 373–82. **Descamps, A.** "Les origines de l'Eucharistie."
In *Jésus et l'Église: Études d'exégèse et de théologie.* BETL 77. Leuven: University Press/Peeters,
1987. 455–96. **Didier, J. D.** "A l'institution de l'Eucharistie, le Christ a-t-il dit: 'Ce Sang est
verse?' ou 'sera verse'?" *EV* 81 (1971) 564–65. **Dockx, S.** "Le récit du repas pascal Marc
14,17–26." *Bib* 46 (1965) 445–53. **Dupont, J.** "'Ceci est mon corps,' 'Ceci est mon sang.'"
NRT 80 (1958) 1025–41. **Edanad, A.** "Institution of the Eucharist according to the Synoptic Gospels." *Biblebhashyam* 4 (1978) 322–32. **Eisler, R.** "Das letzte Abendmahl [I]." *ZNW*
24 (1925) 161–92. ———. "Das letzte Abendmahl [II]." *ZNW* 25 (1926) 5–37. **Emerton, J.
A.** "The Aramaic Underlying τὸ αἷμά μου τῆς διαθήκης in Mk XIV. 24." *JTS* n.s. 6 (1955)
238–40. ———. "ΤΟ ΑΙΜΑ ΜΟΥ ΤΗΣ ΔΙΑΘΗΚΗΣ: The Evidence of the Syriac Versions." *JTS* n.s. 13 (1962) 111–17. ———. "Mark xiv. 24 and the Targum to the Psalter."
JTS n.s. 15 (1964) 58–59. **Emminghaus, J. H.** "Stammen die Einsetzungsworte der
Eucharistie von Jesus selber?" *BibLeb* 53 (1980) 36–38. **Feeley-Harnik, G.** *The Lord's Table:
Eucharist and Passover in Early Christianity.* Symbol and Culture. Philadelphia: University
of Pennsylvania, 1981. **Feld, H.** *Das Verständnis des Abendmahls.* Darmstadt: Wissenschaftliche Buchgesellschaft, 1976. **Feneberg, R.** *Christliche Passafeier und Abendmahl: Eine
biblisch-hermeneutische Untersuchung der neutestamentlichen Einsetzungsberichte.* SANT 27.
Munich: Kösel, 1971. **Flusser, D.** "The Last Supper and the Essenes." *Immanuel* 2 (1973)
23–27. **Fuller, R. H.** "The Double Origin of the Eucharist." *BR* 8 (1963) 60–72. **Galot, J.**
"Eucharistie et Incarnation." *NRT* 105 (1983) 549–66. **Gaugler, E.** *Das Abendmahl im*

Neuen Testament. ATANT 11. Basel: Zwingli, 1943. **Goetz, K. G.** "Zur Lösung der Abendmahlsfrage." *TSK* 108 (1937–38) 81–107. **Gottlieb, H.** "*ΤΟ ΑΙΜΑ ΜΟΥ ΤΗΣ ΔΙΑΘΗΚΗΣ.*" *ST* 14 (1960) 115–18. **Gregg, D. W. A.** *Anamnesis in the Eucharist.* Grove Liturgical Study 5. Nottingham: Grove Books, 1976. ———. "Hebraic Antecedents to the Eucharistic *Anamenēsis* Formula." *TynB* 30 (1979) 165–68. **Hagemeyer, O.** "'Tut dies zu meinem Gedächtnis!' (1 Kor 11,24f.; Lk 22,19)." In *Praesentia Christi.* FS J. Betz, ed. L. Lies. Düsseldorf: Patmos, 1984. 101–17. **Hahn, F.** "Die alttestamentlichen Motive in der urchristlichen Abendmahlsüberlieferung." *EvT* 27 (1967) 337–74. ———. "Zum Stand der Erforschung des urchristlichen Herrenmahls." *EvT* 35 (1975) 553–63. ———. "Das Abendmahl und Jesu Todesverständnis." *TR* 76 (1980) 265–72. **Heawood, P. J.** "The Time of the Last Supper." *JQR* 42 (1951–52) 37–44. **Higgins, A. J. B.** *The Lord's Supper in the New Testament.* SBT. London: SCM, 1956. ———. "The Origins of the Eucharist." *NTS* 1 (1954–55) 200–209. **Holtzmann, O.** "Zu Lukas 22,20." *ZNW* 3 (1902) 359. **Hook, N.** *The Eucharist in the New Testament.* London: Epworth, 1964. ———. "The Dominical Cup Saying." *Th* 77 (1974) 625–30. **Hruby, K.** "La pâque juive du temps du Christi à la lumière des documents de la littérature rabbinique." *OrSyr* 6 (1961) 81–94. **Hupfeld, R.** *Die Abendmahlfeier.* Gütersloh: Bertelsmann, 1935. **Huser, T.** "Les récits de l'institution de la Cène: Dissemblances et traditions." *Hokhma* 21 (1982) 28–50. **Jeremias, J.** *New Testament Theology: The Proclamation of Jesus.* New York: Scribner's, 1971. 288–92. ———. *The Eucharistic Words of Jesus.* Philadelphia: Fortress, 1977. ———. "Zur Exegese der Abendmahlsworte Jesu." *EvT* 7 (1947–48) 60–63. ———. "This is My Body. . . ." *ExpTim* 83 (1972) 196–203. **Johnson, P. F.** "A Suggested Understanding of the Eucharistic Words." *SE* 7 [= TU 126] (1982) 265–70. **Jones, D. R.** "*ἀνάμνησις* in the LXX and the Interpretation of 1 Cor. XI.25." *JTS* 6 (1955) 183–91. **Käsemann, E.** "Das Abendmahl im Neuen Testament." In *Abendmahlsgemeinschaft?* by H. Asmussen et al. Munich: Kaiser, 1938. 60–93. **Kaestli, J.-D.** *L'Eschatologie.* 58–59. **Kahlefeld, H.** *Das Abschiedsmahl Jesu und die Eucharistie der Kirche.* Frankfurt: Knecht, 1980. **Kennett, R. H.** *The Last Supper.* Cambridge: Heffer, 1921. **Kertelge, K.** "Die soteriologischen Aussagen in der urchristlichen Abendmahlsüberlieferung und ihre Beziehung zum geschichtlichen Jesus." *TTZ* 81 (1972) 193–202. **Kilmartin, E. J.** *The Eucharist in the Primitive Church.* Englewood Cliffs, NJ: Prentice-Hall, 1965. **Kilpatrick, G. D.** "Eucharist as Sacrifice and Sacrament in the New Testament." In *Neues Testament und Kirche.* FS R. Schnackenburg, ed. J. Gnilka. Freiburg: Herder, 1974. 429–33. ———. "Living Issues in Biblical Scholarship: The Last Supper." *ExpTim* 64 (1952–53) 4–8. **Klauck, H.-J.** *Herrenmahl und hellenistischer Kult: Ein religionsgeschichtliche Untersuchung zum ersten Korintherbrief.* NTAbh n.s. 15. Münster: Aschendorff, 1982. **Knoch, O.** "'Tut das zu meinem Gedächtnis!' (Lk 22,30; 1 Kor 11,24f): Die Feier der Eucharistie in den urchristlichen Gemeinden." In *Freude am Gottesdienst.* FS J. G. Plöger, ed. J. Schreiner. Stuttgart: Katholisches Bibelwerk, 1983. 31–42. **Kodell, J.** *The Eucharist in the New Testament.* Zacchaeus Studies: New Testament. Wilmington, DE: Glazier, 1988. **Kollmann, B.** *Ursprung und Gestalten der frühchristlichen Mahlfeier.* GTA 43. Göttingen: Vandenhoeck & Ruprecht, 1990. **Kosmala, H.** "Das tut zu meinem Gedächtnis." *NovT* 4 (1960–61) 81–94. **Kuhn, K. G.** "Die Abendmahlworte." *TLZ* 75 (1950) 399–408. ———. "The Lord's Supper and the Communal Meal at Qumran." In *The Scrolls and the New Testament,* ed. K. Stendahl. New York: Harper and Row, 1957. 65–93. **Kurz, W. S.** *Farewell Addresses in the New Testament.* Collegeville, MN: Liturgical, 1990. 52–70. ———. "Luke 22:14–38 and Greco-Roman and Biblical Farewell Addresses." *JBL* 104 (1985) 251–68. **Lambert, J. C.** "The Passover and the Lord's Supper." *JTS* 4 (1902–3) 184–93. **Lapide, P. E.** "Der mysteriöse Mazzabrocken: Ging der Eucharistiefeier ein Pessachritus voraus?" *LM* 14 (1975) 120–24. **Laurence, J. D.** "The Eucharist as the Imitation of Christ." *TS* 47 (1986) 286–96. **LaVerdiere, E. A.** "A Discourse at the Last Supper." *BiTod* 71 (1974) 1540–48. ———. "The Eucharist in Luke's Gospel." *Emman* 89 (1983) 446–49, 452. ———. "Do This in Remembrance of Me." *Emman* 90 (1984) 365–69. **Léon-Dufour, X.** "Jésus devant sa mort à la lumière des textes de l'institution eucharistique et des discours d'adieu." In *Jésus aux* *origines de la christologie,* ed. J. Dupont. BETL 40. Gembloux/Leuven: Duculot/University Press, 1975. 141–68. ———. *Le partage du pain eucharistique selon le Nouveau Testament.* Parole de Dieu. Paris: Editions du Seuil, 1982. 266–84. ———. *Sharing the Eucharistic Bread: The Witness of the New Testament.* Tr. M. J. O'Connell. New York: Paulist, 1987. Esp. 87–90, 230–47. ———. "'Faites ceci en mémoire de moi': Luc 22,19–1 Corinthiens 11,25." *Christus* 24 (1977) 200–208. ———. "Das letzte Mahl Jesu und die testamentarische Tradition nach Lk 22." *ZKT* 103 (1981) 33–55. ———. "'Prenez! Ceci est mon corps pour vous.'" *NRT* 104 (1982) 223–40. **Leenhardt, F. J.** *Le Sacrement de la sainte Cène.* Neuchâtel/Paris: Delachaux et Niestlé, 1948. **Lietzmann, H.** *Mass and Lord's Supper.* Tr. and rev. R. D. Richardson. Leiden: Brill, 1979. ———. "Jüdische Passahsitten und der ἀφικόμενος: Kritische Randnotizen zu R. Eislers Aufsatz über 'Das letzte Abendmahl.'" *ZNW* 25 (1926) 1–5. **Lindars, B.** "Joseph and Asenath and the Eucharist." In *Scripture: Meaning and Method.* FS A. T. Hanson, ed. B. P. Thompson. Hull: University Press, 1987. 181–99. **Loeschcke, G.** "Zur Frage nach der Einsetzung und Herkunft der Eucharistie." *ZWT* 54 (1912) 193–205. **Loewe, H.** "Die doppelte Wurzel des Abendmahles in Jesu Tischgemeinschaft." In *Abendmahl in der Tischgemeinschaft,* ed. H. Loewe. Kassel: Stauda, 1971. 9–22. **Lohmeyer, E.** "Das Abendmahl in der Urgemeinde." *JBL* 56 (1937) 217–52. ———. "Vom urchristlichen Abendmahl." *TRu* n.s. 9 (1937) 168–227, 273–312; 10 (1938) 81–99. **Loisy, A.** "Les origines de la cène eucharistique." In *Congrès d'histoire du Christianisme.* FS A. Loisy, ed. P.-L. Couchoud. Annales d'histoire du Christianisme 1. Paris: Rieder, 1928. 1:77–95. **Lys, D.** "Mon corps, s'est ceci (Notule sur Mt 26,26–28 et par.)." *ETR* 45 (1970) 389–90. **Maccoby, H.** "Paul and the Eucharist." *NTS* 37 (1991) 247–67. **Macina, M.** "Fonction liturgique et eschatologique de l'anamnèse eucharistique (Lc 22,19; 1Co 11,24.25)." *EL* 102 (1988) 3–25. **Magne, J. M.** "Les Paroles sur la coupe." In *Logia: Les paroles de Jésus—The Sayings of Jesus,* ed. J. Delobel. BETL 59. Leuven: University Press/Peeters, 1982. 485–90. **Margerie, B. de.** "'Hoc facite in meam commemorationem' (Lc 22,19b): Les exégèsis des Pères préchalcédoniens (150–451)." *Divinitas* 28 (1984) 43–69, 137–49. **Marmorstein, A.** "Das letzte Abendmahl und der Sederabend." *ZNW* 25 (1926) 1–5. **Marshall, I. H.** *Last Supper and Lord's Supper.* Exeter/Grand Rapids: Paternoster/Eerdmans, 1981. **Marxsen, W.** *The Beginnings of Christology: Together with the Lord's Supper.* Philadelphia: Fortress, 1979. 87–122. **McCormick, S.** *The Lord's Supper: A Biblical Interpretation.* Philadelphia: Westminster, 1966. **Meding, W. von.** "1 Korinther 11,26: Vom geschichtlichen Grund des Abendmahls." *EvT* 35 (1975) 544–52. **Merklein, H.** "Erwägungen zur Überlieferungsgeschichte der neutestamentlichen Abendmahlstraditionen." *BZ* 21 (1977) 88–101, 235–44. **Meyer, B. F.** "The Expiation Motif in the Eucharistic Words: A Key to the History of Jesus?" *Greg* 69 (1988) 461–87. **Milligan, G.** "The Last Supper Not a Paschal Meal." *ExpTim* 20 (1908–9) 334. **Monks, G. G.** "The Lucan Account of the Last Supper." *JBL* 44 (1925) 228–60. **Nestle, E.** "Zu Lukas 22,20." *ZNW* 3 (1902) 252. ———. "Zu Lc 22,20." *ZNW* 7 (1906) 256–57. **Oesterley, W. O. E.** *The Jewish Background of the Christian Liturgy.* Oxford: Clarendon, 1925. **Patsch, H.** *Abendmahl und historischer Jesus.* CTM 1. Stuttgart: Calwer, 1972. ———. "Abendmahlsterminologie ausserhalb der Einsetzungsberichte: Erwägungen zur Traditionsgeschichte der Abendmahlsworte." *ZNW* 61 (1971) 210–31. **Pesch, R.** "Exkurs: Die Abendmahlsüberleiferung." In *Markusevangelium.* 364–77. ———. *Wie Jesus das Abendmahl hielt: Der Grund der Eucharistie.* Freiburg im B.: Herder, 1977. ———. *Das Abendmahl und Jesu Todesverständnis.* QD 80. Freiburg: Herder, 1978. ———. "Das Evangelium in Jerusalem: 'Mk. 14,12–26 als älteste Überlieferungsgut der Urgemeinde." In *Das Evangelium und die Evangelien,* ed. P. Stuhlmacher. Tübingen: Mohr-Siebeck, 1983. 113–55. ———. "The Last Supper and Jesus' Understanding of His Death." *Biblebhashyam* 3 (1977) 58–75. **Petzer, J. H.** "Luke 22:19b–20 and the Structure of the Passage." *NovT* 26 (1984) 249–52. **Petzer, K.** "Style and Text in the Lucan Narrative of the Institution of the Lord's Supper (Luke 22.19b–20)." *NTS* 37 (1991) 113–29. **Preiss, T.** "Was the Last Supper a Paschal Meal?" In *Life in Christ.* SBT 13. London: SCM, 1954. 81–96. **Quesnell, Q.** "The Women at Luke's Supper." In *Political Issues,* ed. R. J. Cassidy and P. J. Scharper. 59–79. **Reumann, J. H.** "The Last and the Lord's Supper." *LTSB* 62 (1982) 17–39.

———. "The Problem of the Lord's Supper as Matrix for Albert Schweitzer's 'Quest of the Historical Jesus.'" *NTS* 27 (1980–81) 475–87. **Richardson, R. D.** "Supplementary Essay: A Further Inquiry into Eucharistic Origins with Special Reference to New Testament Problems." In *Mass and Lord's Supper,* H. Lietzmann. 219–697. ———. "The Place of Luke in the Eucharistic Tradition." *SU* 1 [=TU 73] (1959) 663–75. **Robinson, D. W. B.** "The Date and Significance of the Last Supper." *EvQ* 23 (1951) 126–33. **Roustang, F.** "La conversion eucharistique." *Christus* 8 (1961) 438–53. **Roy, J.-B. du.** "Le dernier repas de Jésus." *BVC* 26 (1959) 44–52. **Ruckstuhl, E.** "Neue und alte Überlegungen zu den Abendmahlsworten Jesu." *SNTU* 5 (1980) 79–106; reprinted in *Jesus im Horizont der Evangelien.* Stuttgarter Biblische Aufsatzbände 3. Stuttgart: Katholisches Bibelwerk, 1988. 69–100. **Saldarini, A. J.** *Jesus and Passover.* New York: Paulist, 1984. **Sandvik, B.** *Das Kommen des Herrn beim Abendmahl im Neuen Testament.* ATANT 58. Zürich: Zwingli, 1970. **Schelkle, K. H.** "Das Herrenmahl." In *Rechtfertigung.* FS E. Käsemann, ed. J. Friedrich, W. Pöhlmann, and P. Stuhlmacher. Tübingen/Göttingen: Mohr-Siebeck/Vandenhoeck & Ruprecht, 1976. 385–402. **Schenke, L.** *Studien zur Passionsgeschichte des Markus.* 286–347. **Schenker, A.** *Das Abendmahl Jesu als Brennpunkt des Alten Testaments: Begegnung zwischen den beiden Testamenten: Ein bibeltheologische Skizze.* Biblische Beiträge 13. Fribourg: Schweizerisches Katholisches Bibelwerk, 1977. **Schermann, T.** "Das 'Brotbrechen' im Urchristentum." *BZ* 8 (1910) 33–52, 162–83. **Schlosser, J.** *Le Règne de Dieu dans les dits de Jésus.* Études Bibliques 2. Paris: Gabalda, 1980. 373–417. **Schöffel, S.** "Offenbarung Gottes im hl. Abendmahl." *Luthertum* 48 (1937) 340–46, 353–72; 49 (1938) 33–54. **Schürmann, H.** *Quellenkritische Untersuchung: I. Teil.* ———. *Quellenkritische Untersuchung: II. Teil.* ———. "Jesu Abendmahlsworte im Lichte seiner Abendmahlshandlung." *Ursprung und Gestalt.* 100–107. ———. "Die Semitismen im Einsetzungs bericht bei Markus und bei Lukas." *ZKT* 73 (1951) 72–77. ———. "Die Gestalt der urchristlichen Eucharistiefeier." *MTZ* 6 (1955) 107–31; reprinted in *Ursprung und Gestalt,* 77–99. ———. "Abendmahl, letztes A. Jesu." *LTK* 1 (1957) 26–31. **Schwager, R.** "Geht die Eucharistie auf Jesus zurück?" *Orientierung* 39 (1975) 220–23. **Schwank, B.** "Das ist mein Leib, der für euch hingegeben wird (Lk 22,19)." *EuA* 59 (1983) 279–90. **Schweitzer, A.** *The Problem of the Lord's Supper according to the Scholarly Research of the Nineteenth Century and the Historical Accounts: Volume 1. The Lord's Supper in Relationship to the Life of Jesus and the History of the Early Church,* ed. J. Reumann. Tr. A. J. Mattill, Jr. Macon, GA: Mercer University, 1982. **Schweizer, E.** *The Lord's Supper according to the New Testament.* FBBS 18. Philadelphia: Fortress, 1967. ———. "Das Abendmahl eine Vergegewärtigung des Todes Jesu oder ein eschatologisches Freudenmahl?" *TZ* 2 (1946) 81–100. ———. "Das Herrenmahl im Neuen Testament." *TLZ* 79 (1954) 577–92. **Seeberg, R.** *Das Abendmahl im Neuen Testament.* Berlin: Runge, 1905. **Senn, F. C.** "The Lord's Supper, Not the Passover Seder." *Worship* 60 (1986) 362–68. **Smith, M. A.** "The Lukan Last Supper Narrative." *SE* 6 [= TU 112] (1973) 502–9. **Sparks, H. F. D.** "St. Luke's Transpositions." *NTS* 3 (1956–57) 219–23. **Spitta, F.** "Die urchristlichen Traditionen über Ursprung und Sinn des Abendmahls." In *Zur Geschichte und Literatur des Urchristentums.* Göttingen: Vandenhoeck & Ruprecht, 1893. 1:207–337. **Suffrin, A. E.** "The Last Supper and the Passover." *ExpTim* 29 (1917–18) 475–77. **Sweetland, D. M.** "The Lord's Supper and the Lukan Community." *BTB* 13 (1983) 23–27. **Sykes, M. H.** "The Eucharist as 'Anamnesis.'" *ExpTim* 71 (1959–60) 115–18. **Theissen, G.** "Social Integration and Sacramental Activity: An Analysis of 1 Cor. 11:17–34." In *The Social Setting of Pauline Christianity: Essays on Corinth.* Philadelphia: Fortress, 1982. 145–74. **Thiele, E. R.** "The Day and Hour of Passover Observance in New Testament Times." *ATR* 28 (1946) 163–68. **Turner, N.** "The Style of St Mark's Eucharistic Words." *JTS* 8 (1957) 108–11. **Vööbus, A.** "Kritische Beobachtungen über die lukanische Darstellung des Herrenmahls." *ZNW* 62 (1970) 102–10. **Wagner, V.** Der Bedeutungswandel von *bᵉrît hadāšā* bei der Ausgestaltung der Abendmahlworte." *EvT* 35 (1975) 538–44. **Walther, G.** *Jesus, das Passalamm des Neuen Bundes.* Gütersloh: Bertelsmann, 1950. **Wanke, J.** *Beobachtungen zum Eucharistieverständnis des Lukas auf Grund der lukanischen Mahlberichte.* Erfurter theologische Schriften 8. Leipzig: St. Benno, 1973. **Wellhausen, J.** "Ἄρτον ἔκλασεν, Mc 14,22." *ZNW* 7 (1906) 182.

Weren, W. "The Lord's Supper: An Inquiry into the Coherence in Luke 22,14–18." In *Fides Sacramenti.* FS P. Smulders, ed. H. J. Auf der Maur et al. Assen: Van Gorcum, 1981. 9–26. **White, J. L.** "Beware of Leavened Bread: Markan Imagery in the Last Supper." *Forum* 3.4 (1987) 49–63. **Wilkens, H.** "Die Angange des Herrenmahls." *JLH* 28 (1984) 55–65. **Winnert, A. R.** "The Breaking of the Bread: Does It Symbolize the Passion?" *ExpTim* 88 (1977) 181–82. **Wojciechowski, M.** "Le nazireat et la Passion (Mc 14,25a; 15,23)." *Bib* 65 (1984) 94–96. **Wrede, W.** "Miscellen: 2. 'Τὸ αἷμά μου τῆς διαθήκης.'" *ZNW* 1 (1900) 69–74. **Zeitlin, S.** "The Time of the Passover Meal." *JQR* n.s. 42 (1951–52) 45–50. ———. "The Last Supper as an Ordinary Meal in the Fourth Gospel." *JQR* n.s. 42 (1951–52) 251–60. **Ziesler, J. A.** "The Vow of Abstinence: A Note on Mark 15:25 and Parallels." *Colloquium* 5 (1972) 12–14. ———. "The Vow of Abstinence Again." *Colloquium* 6 (1973) 49–50.

FOR TEXT CRITICAL MATTERS IN LUKE 22:19b–20:

Aland, K. "Die Bedeutung des P⁷⁵ für den Text des Neuen Testaments: Ein Beitrag zur Frage der 'Western Non-Interpolations.'" In *Studien zur Überlieferung des Neuen Testaments und seines Textes.* AzNTT 2. Berlin: de Gruyter, 1967. 155–72, esp. 160, 164–65. **Bate, H. N.** "The 'Shorter Text' of St Luke xxii 15–20." *JTS* 28 (1927) 362–68. **Benoit, P.** "Le récit de la cène dans Lc xxii, 15–20: Etude de critique textuelle det littéraire." *RB* 48 (1939) 357–93. ———. "Luc xxii, 19b–20." *JTS* 49 (1948) 145–47. **Burkitt, F. C.** "On Luke xxii 17–20." *JTS* 28 (1926–27) 178–81. **Chadwick, H.** "The Shorter Text of Luke XXII, 15–20." *HTR* 50 (1957) 249–58. **Cooper, J. C.** "The Problem of the Text in Luke 22:19–20." *LQ* 14 (1962) 39–48. **Eagar, A. R.** "St. Luke's Account of the Last Supper: A Critical Note on the Second Sacrament." *Exp* 7.5 (1908) 252–62, 343–61. **Ehrman, B. D.** "The Cup, the Bread, and the Salvific Effect of Jesus' Death in Luke-Acts." In *SBL 1991 Seminar Papers*, ed. E. H. Lovering, Jr. 154–64. **Fitzmyer, J. A.** "Papyrus Bodmer XIV: Some Features of Our Oldest Text of Luke." *CBQ* 24 (1962) 170–79, esp. 177. **Harnack, A. von.** "Probleme im Texte der Leidensgeschichte Jesu." In *Studien zur Geschichte des Neuen Testaments und der alten Kirche: Vol. 1. Zur neutestamentlichen Textkritik.* Berlin/Liepzig: de Gruyter, 1901. 86–104. **Jeremias, J.** *The Eucharistic Words of Jesus.* Philadelphia: Fortress, 1977. 139–59. **Kenyon, F. G.,** and **Legg, S. C. E.** "The Textual Data." In *The Ministry and the Sacraments*, ed. R. Dunkerley. London: Student Christian Movement, 1937. 271–86, esp. 285–86. **Kilpatrick, G. D.** "Luke xxii. 19b–20." *JTS* 47 (1946) 49–56. **Metzger, B. M.** *Textual Commentary.* 173–77. **Parker, P.** "Three Variant Readings in Luke-Acts." *JBL* 83 (1964) 165–70, esp. 165–67. **Rese, M.** "Zur Problematik von Kurz- und Langtext in Luk. xxii. 17ff." *NTS* 22 (1975–76) 15–31. **Schäfer, K. T.** "Zur Textgeschichte von Lk 22,19b.20." *Bib* 33 (1952) 237–39. **Schürmann, H.** "Lk 22,19b–20 als ursprüngliche Textüberlieferung." *Bib* 32 (1951) 364–92, 522–41; reprinted in *Traditionsgeschichtliche Untersuchungen.* 159–92. ———. "Lk 22,42a das älteste Zeugnis für Lk 22,20." *MTZ* 3 (1952) 185–88; reprinted in *Traditionsgeschichtliche Untersuchungen.* 193–97. **Snodgrass, K.** "'Western Non-Interpolations.'" *JBL* 91 (1972) 369–79. **Throckmorton, B. H., Jr.** "The Longer Reading of Luke 22:19b–20." *ATR* 30 (1948) 55–56. **Vööbus, A.** "A New Approach to the Problem of the Shorter and Longer Text in Luke." *NTS* 15 (1968–69) 457–63. **Westcott, B. F.,** and **Hort, F. J. A.** *The New Testament in the Original Greek.* Cambridge/London: Macmillan, 1890, 1896. 2:63–64 (Appendix).

And see at 22:1–2.

Translation

¹⁴*When the hour had come, he reclined [at table], and the Apostles with him.* ¹⁵*Then he said to them, "How I have longed to eat this Passover [lamb] with you before I suffer!* ¹⁶*For I say to you that I shall certainly not*ᵃ *eat it [again] until it is fulfilled in the kingdom of God."* ¹⁷*And receiving a cup and giving thanks he said, "Take this and share [it] out*

among yourselves. [18]*For*[b] *I say to you, from now on, I shall certainly not drink from the fruit of the vine until the kingdom of God comes."* [19]*Then taking bread and giving thanks he broke [it] and gave [it] to them saying, "This is my body,*[c] *which is given for you; do this in remembrance of me."* [20]*And [he did] the same with the cup after the meal, saying, "This [is] the new covenant [sealed] with my blood, which is poured out for you."*

Notes

[a] There is some doubt here whether we should read a double negative (οὐ μή) with P[75 vid] ℵ A B H L Θ, etc., or (as Mark 14:25) a triple negative (οὐκέτι οὐ μή) with C[2] K P W Δ Π Ψ, etc. (this would add "any longer" to the translation). The former is the more likely.

[b] The Greek γάρ is, for the sake of the parallelism, represented by "for" here as in v 16; but here it does not carry the same inferential force, so could have been dropped in translation.

[c] The best texts and the overwhelming number of texts support the full form of vv 19–20 as represented in the translation above. However, D and some of the Old Latin texts (a, d, *ff*[2], i, l) omit the rest of v 19 and all of v 20. Some other Old Latin texts and some Syriac and Coptic MSS reflect various attempts to deal with either the problem of these two versions of the text or of the apparent cup-bread-cup sequence: vv 17–18 are sometimes placed after the short form of v 19; in syr[c], a version of the missing part of v 19 has been added to this; in syr[s], v 17 has been relocated to the middle of v 20, and v 18 has been delayed to the end of v 20; vv 17–18 are missing altogether from l[32] syr[p] cop[bo ms].

Because of the difficulty of offering an adequate explanation for the deletion involved in the reading adopted by D etc. (it overcomes the "problem" of two cups by settling for a reversed order of cup and bread in which there are careful instructions but no interpretation for the cup, and a minimal interpretation of the bread [this last feature has the virtue of reproducing the Markan interpretation of the bread], and it settles for this when the problem could be much better dealt with by the omission of the cup of v 17), the argument of Westcott and Hort (*New Testament*, 2:63–64), that the reading of D here should be preferred as an instance of "Western Non-Interpolation," gained wide support (quite a number of scholars were impressed also by the fit between the short reading and Luke's apparent lack of an atonement theology in connection with the death of Jesus). In the last several decades, however, this support has been increasingly eroded, and a new consensus in favor of the longer reading has been emerging (in large part because of the studies of Schürmann [*Bib* 32 (1951) 364–92, 522–41] and Jeremias [*Eucharistic Words*, 139–59]). Among the many relevant considerations we may note: (*i*) the value of "Western Non-Interpolations" has increasingly been seen to require demonstration case by case; (*ii*) the structural unity of vv 15–18, 19–20 counts strongly against seeing the longer form as resulting from a scribal addition; (*iii*) Acts 20:28 counts against Luke's deliberate omission from his traditions of material giving a soteriological significance to Jesus' death. Perhaps the best explanation of the shorter text is still that of Jeremias: "we have before us in v 19a the abbreviation of a liturgical text" (*Eucharistic Words*, 158). The text belongs to a context where it may be assumed that everybody knows how to complete the missing words. Jeremias' idea, however, that this abbreviation is for esoteric reasons (158–59, cf. 125–37) remains unconvincing.

Form/Structure/Setting

With "when the hour had come," we reach the climax of the development from v 1 to v 7 to v 14. A marked sense of impending destiny hangs over the meal, which Luke presents in two panels: the old Passover meal, characterized in vv 15–18 and destined for fulfillment in the kingdom of God, gives way to the new Supper of the Lord, which is characterized in vv 19–20. Already in vv 14–20 emerges the farewell-discourse quality that will characterize the material from here to v 38.

Luke begins with a heavily recast version of Mark 14:17 (see *Comment* below). Luke transposes the forecast of betrayal, which comes next in the Markan meal account, to a position following the institution (see at 22:21–23; Luke may be influenced by tradition that he shares with John, who seems also to locate his parallel material after the main body of the meal [Judas leaves the meal immediately after]), and so moves at this point to the main meal account with its words of institution. Luke's own institution narrative is strikingly different from that provided by Mark.

A huge scholarly investment has been made in examining the different forms in which the institution has been preserved (Matt 26:26–29; Mark 14:22–25; 1 Cor 11:23–26; and cf. 1 Cor 10:16–17; John 13–17; 6:25–59; *Did.* 9:1–5; Justin Martyr *Apol.* 1.66.3); in seeking to identify their relationships and to trace them to a common earliest source; and in attempting to determine what part of these traditions may with any confidence be attributed to the historical Jesus. While elements of consensus are identifiable, despite the extended scholarly labor, there is no clear consensus in connection with very many of the fundamental questions raised by the institution narratives (the broad, though hardly universal, acceptance of Luke 22:19b–20 as an authentic part of the Lukan text is a happy exception [this matter is discussed in *Notes* above]). No satisfactory review of the scholarly debate can be provided within the constraints of this present work: after identifying the distinctive features of the different accounts, I must be content here to take up briefly some of the main matters in contention and to give my own judgments about the state of the discussion.

John's account of Jesus' final meal with his disciples is immediately distinctive in describing Jesus washing the disciples' feet rather than distributing interpreted food elements to the disciples. The other NT forms agree in the mention of the taking of bread, the saying of grace over it (either εὐλογήσας, "having blessed," or εὐχαριστήσας, "having given thanks"), the tearing apart of the loaf, the distribution, and the equation of bread and body. They also agree in mentioning the (a) cup, the covenant, and "my blood"; in providing a second equation in connection with the cup or its contents; and in identifying a measure of parallelism between the treatment of the cup and that previously of the bread (εὐχαριστήσας ἔδωκεν, "having given thanks he gave," in Matthew and Mark; ὡσαύτως, "in the same way," in Luke and Paul).

The main differences between the accounts may be identified as follows. Only Luke and Paul have Jesus calling for future repetition of this activity (strictly, Luke's account calls only for a repetition of the bread part; Paul has a second call in connection with the cup saying); these two are also alone in mentioning that the cup comes after a meal in between; these two agree further in having for the cup saying "this cup is the new covenant in my blood" whereas the other forms have "this [namely the wine] is my blood of the covenant" (these alternative forms for the main part of the cup saying involve three significant differences that warrant separate identification: one equates the wine with something, the other the cup; in the one case the equation is made with blood, in the other case the equation is with a covenant; one talks about "the covenant" of Exod 24:8, the other about "the new covenant" of Jer 31:31–34); these two—Paul and Luke—also agree in including "for you" after "my body"; Paul does not have "gave to them" ("the disciples" in Matthew) in connection with the bread, nor the "poured out for many" ("for you" in Luke) of the other three accounts; Paul alone offers the explanation "for as often as you eat this bread and drink the cup, you proclaim the death of the Lord until he comes"; Luke is alone in having "given" with the "for you" of the bread saying; only Matthew and Mark have a directive to take the bread; Matthew has for Mark's report "they all drank from it" (which only he has) the directive "drink from it, all of you"; Matthew is also unique in having "for the forgiveness of sins" attached to his wine saying, and, finally, in expanding the "take" of the bread saying with "eat".

If we widen the focus, then we need also to count among the differences the absence from Paul of any parallel to Mark 14:25 (Paul's "until he comes" is hardly a true parallel) and the presence of Luke's equivalent to Mark 14:25 before the giving of the bread and the wine, in the distinctive development in 22:15–18 with which he opens the meal account. Within this distinctive Lukan block, v 17 offers a further cup saying, which begins with a unique δεξάμενος, "receiving," rather than the λαβών, "taking," of Matthew and Mark; has the εὐχαριστήσας, "having given thanks," of the Matthean and Markan cup saying; has a directive to "take" like the Matthean and Markan *bread* saying (but here with an added "this"); but continues with an unparalleled "and divide it among yourselves," which takes the place of the "gave" of the other forms; and finally is most notable for having no statement identifying the cup or its contents with blood or covenant.

Schürmann (*Quellenkritische Untersuchung*, 1:1–74) and Jeremias (*Eucharistic Words*, 160–64) have persuaded many that Luke 22:15–18 reflects an old tradition from Jesus' final Passover meal with his disciples. But the contrary view that Luke has spun vv 15–18 out of Mark 14:25 has also been widely canvassed (recently, e.g., Kollmann, *Ursprung*, 162–64, with the qualification that v 17 may be a remnant of a eucharistic cup saying known to Luke). The detailed linguistic arguments remain indecisive, since they cannot satisfactorily incorporate Luke's frequent practice of reproducing the substance of a source but using a good deal of his own language. The more general arguments about Luke's editorial procedure do, however, clearly favor a more extensive traditional base than that supplied by Mark 14:25.

A satisfactory source for Luke would probably have had the following contours: (*i*) a minimal narrative setting, which has been displaced by Luke's "and he said to them" (v 15); (*ii*) Jesus' statement of v 15, but without the dative intensifier ἐπιθυμίᾳ (lit. "with desire") and without the explanatory "before I suffer"; (*iii*) a statement like v 16, but possibly introducing the prospect of the kingdom of God (or some other form of eschatological language) in some manner other than with πληρωθῇ ἐν, "is fulfilled in"; (*iv*) the opening part of v 17 up to "said" (just possibly without "gave thanks"); (*v*) a form of v 18, but without the opening "for I say to you." The scene painted in this reconstruction of the tradition available to Luke is of the beginning point of the last supper as a Passover meal, where Jesus expresses his satisfaction at the arrival of this Passover mealtime with his disciples, which he declares to be his last before the coming of the kingdom of God. As he opens the actual meal with the first cup of wine, Jesus reiterates his point, now in terms of this being the last occasion on which he will drink wine before the kingdom of God has dawned. The judgments involved in this reconstruction are given a measure of support in *Comment* below, but their full defense goes beyond the possible scope of the present work.

If this reconstruction is at all correct, then we have a tradition in which Jesus expresses the anticipation of his own imminent demise set in the context of a final Passover meal of Jesus with his disciples (see *Comment* on v 16 below for why this should not be taken as expressing an expectation of the imminence of the kingdom of God). The Passover setting is incidental to the reason for the preservation of the material but is integral to its verbal form. Here is a significant supporting evidence for the Paschal nature of Jesus' final meal with his disciples. (See further on the Paschal nature of the Last Supper at 22:1–2.)

Beyond minor expansions and verbal alterations, Luke has (*i*) enhanced the parallelism between Passover saying and wine saying; and (*ii*) he has introduced traditional elements of eucharistic language into v 17. In this way he makes it clear that he wishes vv 15–18 and vv 19–20 to be treated as two parallel panels, with each constructed in turn of two paralleled parts (cf. the formal structuring identified by J. H. Petzer [*NovT* 26 (1984) 249–52]). It is likely, from the Christian Lord's Supper perspective of Luke's own church experience, that Luke uses vv 15–18 to characterize the Passover, after the pattern of the Lord's Supper with its focus on bread and cup, as a meal of lamb and cup (cf. Benoit [*RB* 48 (1939) 379–83]). I suspect he does so because he wants to present the Lord's Supper as now eclipsing the old Passover. On this Passover day, the one that Jesus had so longed to share with his disciples, a decisive turning point takes place. The commemoration of the old redemption out of Egypt prefigured the new redemption to come with the kingdom of God. But with the death of Jesus the central role of redemption out of Egypt is necessarily displaced. From now on it is to the covenant sealed in the blood of Jesus that believers look as they anticipate the future coming of the kingdom of God. Luke's Last Supper narrative, arranged as it is, documents the moment of transition from Passover as central point of commemoration to Lord's Supper as central point of commemoration.

For vv 19–20 Luke clearly draws on a tradition that has a family likeness to that which we find in 1 Cor 11:23–26. Luke may be influenced by the Markan wording for the participial form of λαβών, "taking," and for καὶ ἔδωκεν αὐτοῖς, "and he gave to them," in v 19. This would also be possible for "poured out for" in v 20. But since other differences from the Pauline version stand in favor of the Lukan as the older form (in the case of "my" in v 20, where the development would not be from the Pauline form) or are likely to represent differences developed in liturgical use rather than through Lukan editing (so the paralleling of "given for you" in v 19 with "poured out for you" in v 20 [though it could be said that Luke's paralleled panels of paralleled items is enhanced by this development]), it may be better to trace this commonality with Mark back to an earlier stage as well (if there is Markan influence, it is hard to see why Luke would not have included the Markan "take" as well, to enhance the parallel with v 17). This preference for seeing Luke's editorial intervention here as minimal finds a measure of support from the broad scholarly tendency to see reflected in the variety of wordings in our texts, in almost every case, difference of liturgical practice rather than Gospel redaction. (It is in connection with Matthew that this issue becomes pressing; in each case the variations from Mark make best sense in connection with liturgical practice, and notably in the case of "drink from it all of you" in place of Mark's "they all drank from it.")

With some notable exceptions (e.g., Kollmann, *Ursprung*; Maccoby, *NTS* 37 [1991] 247–67), the main drift of more recent scholarship has been to enhance confidence that in some form the words of institution go back to the historical Jesus. Though not all of its elements are equally persuasive, I find telling the kind of argument mounted by Schürmann in "Jesu Abendmahlsworte." Schürmann stresses the difficulty, given the failure of the proposed history-of-religions analogies, of satisfactorily accounting for the emergence of the Lord's Supper, with its focus on bread and cup/wine, apart from a specific origin with the historical Jesus, and builds from the actions of Jesus at the Last Supper to the necessity from the beginning of interpretive words that fall within certain parameters.

Many proposals have been offered for the most original form for the words of institution. The following are some of the key considerations brought to bear on the task of tracking back to an original form: (*i*) Significant features that are notably absent in one or more of our primary sources have a reduced claim to originality, since it is hard to produce satisfactory reasons for their omission (the meal between bread and cup is the obvious exception to this). (*ii*) Apparently originally separated by a meal (as reflected in Paul and Luke), the bread and cup saying (but especially the former) would need to be independently intelligible. (*iii*) The loss of the intervening meal (no longer found in Mark or Matthew) is likely to have led to a greater conformity of the bread and cup sayings to one another and perhaps even opened up the possibility of interchange of features between the sayings. (*iv*) Imagery of drinking of blood, let alone human blood, comes across in a Jewish context as extremely harsh (cf. John 6:52–60). This concern has been used to argue for guaranteeing originality and conversely as pointing to a post-Jewish development. (*v*) The eschatological link with Jer 31:31–34 has been seen as more original than the cultic link with Exod 24:8. However, since the role of blood in those forms with a clear Jeremiah link (Luke and Paul) points secondarily to Exod 24:8, then the "new" covenant reference is likely to be the secondary development. (*vi*) Since Jesus' words were presumably spoken in Aramaic, the original must be able to be rendered into Aramaic, which is idiomatic for the period. (*vii*) If the Last Supper was a Passover meal, then the patterns of the Passover meal offer themselves both as constraint upon what would have been possible and as source of illumination for the likely sense of Jesus' actions and words. (*viii*) The link in Luke-Acts between Jesus' meals in the Gospel and the "breaking of bread" in Acts (see 2:42, 46; 20:7, 11; 27:35) represents an identifiable contributory stream into developing church communal meal practice. This link raises questions about the origins of the eucharist. In an extreme form, now largely discredited, this link offers itself as an authentic continuation of a practice inaugurated by the historical Jesus onto which has been secondarily grafted a cultic activity derived from mystery religion practice (see Lietzmann, *Mass and Lord's Supper;* the view survives in a moderated form in Klauck, *Herrenmahl und hellenistischer Kult,* who argues for a continuous development from Jesus to Paul, with Mark 10:45 and a bread saying from the historical Jesus, to which has been added, after Easter, a cup saying with covenant martyr and sacrificial motifs, and which is then transformed from being centered in eschatology into a cultic epiphany of the exalted Lord, and finally under mystery religion influence gains a massive sacramental realism). (*ix*) In the name of coherence with what may be confidently assigned to the historical Jesus, the authenticity of covenant language in the words of institution has been placed in question, as indeed has the whole idea of Jesus interpreting his coming death as in any sense a means of atonement.

For those who are prepared to trace a bread saying to the historical Jesus (and most scholars now are), there is a good measure of consensus that, with or without the verb, the original form will have been "This [is] my body, for you [or perhaps for many]." The Lukan "given" would have developed to parallel the "poured out" of some forms of the cup saying, and the bare "This is my body" of the Markan and Matthean form would have resulted from a movement of interpretive elements to the end, at a time when the meal no longer came between bread and cup (the contrary argument postulates a move of "for you" to the bread in connection with the practice of communion in one kind). Though "for many" is clearly more Semitic, "for you" seems to me to be preferable since it fits better the intimacy of the occasion and the restricted number of the actual participants in the bread and wine. The reconstruction favored here, which includes "for you" without Luke's linking participle ("given"), has been often criticized (following Dalman, *Jesus-Jeshua*, 144–45) as involving the linking of the phrase "for you" in a manner scarcely possible in a Semitic original. However, the validity of this stricture has been rightly questioned by Ruckstuhl (*SNTU* 5 [1980] 100 and n. 47), who draws in part on OT and rabbinic parallels assembled by D. Daube (*Wine in the Bible*, St. Paul's Lecture [Oxford, 1974] 16).

There is not the same measure of consensus concerning the Aramaic word most likely to stand behind the Greek σῶμα, "body." The first of the alternatives is גופא, *gupâ*, which received its classic support from Dalman (*Jesus-Jeshua*, 141–43). The term meant originally "corpse" and then "body" as well, able even to connote the whole person. Fitzmyer (1399) has, however, disputed whether a wider meaning for the term was already possible at the time of Jesus. If he is right, then גופא is probably not Jesus' original word, since "this is my corpse" has not been established in the scholarship as a live option for the sense of Jesus' statement (though perhaps it deserves greater consideration).

The other main option is בשרה, *biśrâ*, which is the Aramaic equivalent to the Hebrew בשר, *bāśār*. The literal translation here is "flesh," but, as has been pointed out, the Hebrew term, and therefore presumably also the corresponding Aramaic term, can carry a wide range of connotations including that of "body" (Job 4:15; Ps 63:2[ET v 1]; Ezek 11:19; etc.) and even of "person" (Num 16:22; Isa 40:5–6; Ps 145:21; etc. [it is moot, however, whether this use of בשר to refer to persons could be applied to an individualized single person, rather than collectively or to an individual thought of as a sample member of a collective]). There has been some questioning of the likelihood of σῶμα being used as translation for בשרה in the first century, though to this it must be said that (somewhat surprisingly) σῶμα represents בשר more frequently in the Septuagint than it represents any other Hebrew word. Admittedly, this is largely because of a large block of uses in Leviticus, concentrated in chap. 15; בשר is in any case many times more frequently represented by σάρξ, "flesh." The argument as to the most likely Aramaic term here is not yet resolved.

For the cup saying there is considerably less agreement. Some are only prepared to trace a cup saying of the Mark 14:25 kind back to the historical Jesus. But most want as well to trace some form of equation statement back to the historical Jesus. The "poured out," though not without supporters, is generally considered to be an interpretive development. A few seek to support an original without reference to "my blood," but the reasons offered are hardly sufficient to overturn the uniformity of the tradition at this point. Others would rather dispense with the covenant language, but this is to reverse the likely move to increased parallelism between the sayings. There is strong support both for the Markan "this is my blood of the covenant" and for the Lukan "this cup is the new covenant in my blood," while Ruckstuhl (*SNTU* 5 [1980] 96–105) has mounted a not unattractive argument for a mixed form: "this cup [is] my blood of the covenant." The recent proposal by Casey (*JTS* 41 [1990] 1–12) to retrovert the Markan form into Aramaic as דמי דנה, דקימא הוא, *dmy dnh, dqymʾ hwʾ* (lit. "my blood this, of the covenant it [is]"), has much to commend it (Casey completes his retroversion with שַׂגִּיאָן עַל מִתְאָשֵׁד, *mt'šd 'l šgy'n*, "poured out for many"), though his confidence that the alternative retroversion אָדֶם קַיִמִי, *'dm qymy*, "my covenant blood" (but lit. "blood of my covenant"), would be taken by the Christian translator as referring to the blood of Jesus' covenant rather than God's (5) seems to me to be misplaced. The case for an original based upon the Markan or Ruckstuhl's mixed form, in my judgment, has more to commend it than that based on the Lukan form.

The question of whether the directive to repeat should be traced back to the Last Supper deserves separate attention. Though its origin with the historical Jesus has been defended with considerable erudition, the majority view is rather to question whether this aspect of the Last Supper should be attributed to the historical Jesus. A decision here is linked with the concern to identify the correct context for these words: "Do this in remembrance of me." Despite the explanatory dictum of Benoit that "one doesn't recite a rubric, one executes it" (*RB* 48 [1939] 386), the absence of a corresponding element in Mark and Matthew does count against its place in the historical Last Supper, since the call to do this *in remembrance* is more than simply a call to repeat. On the other hand, the role of remembrance in Passover/Unleavened Bread (cf. Exod 12:14; Deut 16:3) may be thought to count in favor of a possible origin with Jesus. Jeremias' claim, on the basis of Palestinian memorial formulae, that we should understand εἰς τὴν ἐμὴν ἀνάμνησιν as "that God may remember me" is finally unconvincing because this is not the sense in which the Passover was a memorial (Exod 12:14 has לְזִכָּרוֹן, *lzkkrwn*, which translates literally into Greek as εἰς ἀνάμνησιν, "for a memorial"), and Jeremias cannot parallel the τὴν ἐμήν, nor find texts in which the memorial takes the form of a meal. The parallelism with Hellenistic feasts in memory of the dead is much closer (see esp. *Diogenes Laertius* 10.16–22; Cicero, *Fin.* 2.101). However, one hardly needs anything as precise as this by way of background to render intelligible, especially with the Passover memorial connection readily available, the directive to carry out this ritual activity in order to recall Jesus, who, on the threshold of death, gave his disciples bread and wine, which he identified with himself given over to death. On balance, it is most likely that the actual directive is a later development but that it accurately glosses, in the context of the ongoing life of the early church, Jesus' intention to establish his continuing place in the ongoing meal fellowship he had instituted with his disciples. If we prefer to favor an origin with the historical Jesus, then we must say that this clause was displaced from those forms of the eucharistic liturgy that introduced a liturgical directive to take the offered bread: the imperative force of "do this" was transferred to "take."

It would seem that the original Passover meal setting played little role in the ongoing liturgical use of the words of institution. The historical shape of the Passover meal is so little represented in our traditions that we can no longer be quite certain just how the loaf and cup of the institution related to the role of bread and wine in the Passover celebration. Our attempts to map the institution onto the Passover are inevitably hampered as well by the degree to which we must remain uncertain about how much of the later rigid patterns for Passover were already current in Jesus' day. The earliest Jewish texts are *m. Pesaḥ* 10:1–9 and *t. Pesaḥ* 10.1–14. The texts indicate that the meal occurs after dark and the guests must recline to eat it. The basic outline for the meal that emerges is as follows:

a. cup of wine with a benediction over the cup and the day
b. dipping lettuce/green herbs in a sauce as an appetizer
c. sharing an unleavened loaf of bread (probably with its own benediction, but this is not clear in these sources [further bread would be available as required through the course of the meal])
d. cup of wine (with benediction? [some reconstructions place this cup before the distribution of unleavened bread])
e. main meal including the lamb and vegetables (and presumably the bitter herbs)
f. questions and answers about redemption from Egypt, which involved interpeting various distinctive elements of the meal, especially the unleavened bread and the lamb, but perhaps also the bitter herbs and later the fruit purée with the color and consistency of clay, and perhaps later still the sequence of cups (it is unclear whether this was before, during, or after the main meal; it could even have been before the second cup)
g. first part of Hallel
h. cup of wine (with benediction for the meal)
i. further drinking
j. cup of wine with second part of Hallel over it (or perhaps before it)

How do the loaf and cup of the institution relate to this pattern? In a broad way they clearly fit the pattern of elements of the meal interpreted in connection with God's saving intervention in the life of his People. Also, both the Passover practice that, according to Exod 12, reiterated the experience of the night in which the Israelites left Egypt and the Lord's Supper practice that developed out of this Last Supper experience share the same pattern: the originating occasion anticipated the saving event, while the ongoing celebration looked back to the saving event. For a more specific correlation we almost certainly should identify the bread with the opening loaf of unleavened bread (the view that it should be seen as a loaf introduced at the "afters" stage of the meal has difficulty with the natural sense of 1 Cor 11:25: "after the meal," which comes between bread and cup; another "stand alone" loaf is difficult at any other stage of the meal). The cup is more difficult. The first cup is ruled out simply on the basis of sequence with the bread (the cup of Luke 22:17 is likely to be in Luke's source the first cup, but this identification is obscured by Luke in connection with the more complex role he has for the cup). The second cup may suffer the same fate, but this is less certain. The usual identification made is with the third cup, which came to be called "the cup of blessing" in Jewish Passover discussion (cf. 1 Cor 10:16). There has, however, been some questioning regarding the early use of this convention (perhaps the NT evidence tips the scales as to the early currency of this designation for the third cup). The fourth cup also has its supporters and cannot be decisively ruled out. It is reasonable to give preference to the third cup, but there is no place for confidence here. We probably should follow Schürmann (*Quellenkritische Untersuchung*, 1:60–62; cf. Bahr, *NovT* 12 [1970] 191–92) in seeing the shared cup of the Last Supper narrative as distinctive. The Jewish practice for Passover seems to have been the use of individual cups. On occasion the host might send his own cup to a particular guest as a special mark of honor and as a means of bestowing a blessing, but each of the guests would drink from his own cup for the sequence of cups of wine that marked the course of the meal.

A number of studies have highlighted the relationship between Luke 22:14–38 and the testamentary genre that seems to be reflected in both biblical and Greco-Roman sources (see esp. Léon-Dufour, *ZKT* 103 [1981] 33–55; Kurz, *Farewell Addresses*, 52–70; id., *JBL* 104 [1985] 251–68; Nelson, "Leadership and Discipleship," 105–30). The genre is a relatively loose one, but its existence may help to account for the way in which Luke and John have each gathered together material at this point to create a major "farewell speech" for Jesus. It may also throw some light on the degree to which these speeches deal with "transfer arrangements" in the face of Jesus' imminent departure from his disciples.

Comment

Jesus has successfully evaded the grasp of his enemies for long enough to share this fateful farewell meal with his Apostles. The redemption celebrated in Passover also patterns the ultimate redemption to come; this meal will be Jesus' last participation in Passover before it finds fulfillment in the kingdom of God. Alongside this Passover meal of interpreted elements Jesus places a new liturgical pattern in which bread and cup are identified with Jesus himself as given over to death to seal the new covenant. In this liturgical action Jesus assigns to, and indeed in a proleptic manner confers upon, his own the benefits of his coming death. In the early church in the repetition of this same liturgical action, the exalted Lord will continue to make himself known and confer the benefits of his Paschal death.

14 Luke heavily reformulates Mark 14:17 (see the analysis of Schürmann, *Quellenkritische Untersuchung*, 1:104–10; but Jeremias, *Eucharistic Words*, 99 n. 1, thinks that the lack of specific verbal agreement points rather to a second source). ὅτε ἐγένετο ἡ ὥρα, "when the hour had come," completes the sequence from "the feast was drawing near" (v 1) to "the day of Unleavened Bread came" (v 7). Luke conflates the coming with the taking of places at the table, which Mark reports separately in 14:18 (Luke's verb here is also found at 11:37; 14:10; 17:7: in the context of a Passover meal the verb will mean "recline," but it is likely to have been used more broadly of being at table, without regard for the particular posture). Luke prefers "Apostles" (on Apostles, see at 6:12–16), the term he will dominantly use in Acts in connection with the post-resurrection role of the Twelve, to Mark's "the Twelve" (in chaps. 22–24, Luke uses "the Twelve" only in connection with Judas's part in that number). The construction here with σὺν αὐτῷ, "with him," is reminiscent of 8:1, but here "reclined" will apply to the Apostles as well as to Jesus.

15 Lukan intervention in this verse is likely to include (following Schürmann, *Quellenkritische Untersuchung*, 1:3–14) the use of πρός, "to," after a verb of saying, the use of the cognate dative ἐπιθυμίᾳ (lit. "with desire") as an intensifier (following LXX idiom; see esp. Gen 31:30), and the addition of the explanatory πρὸ τοῦ με παθεῖν, "before I suffer" (linking back to the earlier passion predictions). The other language here is not notably un-Lukan but does not always exhibit Luke's favored patterns.

There is no call for taking the desire expressed here, either in Luke's source or in the present Gospel text, as a desire that is destined to remain unfulfilled (as Jeremias, *Eucharistic Words*, 208; and others). The context is rather the threat to Jesus' freedom, which has been building since chap. 19: despite the ugly situation that has been developing, Jesus has successfully made his way to this final Pass-over with his Apostles (cf. esp. at 22:1–2, 3–6, 7–13). τοῦτο τὸ πάσχα here could be either the Passover meal or the Paschal lamb (or the one as the symbolic cen-ter of the other). Because of the way that Luke structures the parallelism between vv 15–18 and 19–20, we should, for Luke's finished text, understand the refer-ence as to the lamb itself. "Before I suffer," while it links back to the passion predictions (9:22; 17:25), now focuses Jesus' suffering narrowly on his fate in Jerusalem, which was not yet the case in the earlier texts (but cf. 24:26, 46). The mention of Jesus' suffering here already prepares for a parallelism between the role of the (sacrificial) blood of the Paschal lamb in Egypt and the new covenant in Jesus' blood of v 20. It is of a piece with this that Jesus will go to his suffering fate before Passover day has run its course (see further in *Form/Structure/Setting* for 22:1–2).

16   The language here is significantly paralleled in v 18 (note the shared "for I say to you;" the paralleling of "eat" and "drink"; the common use of the em-phatic negative future with οὐ μή, ἕως, "until," and "kingdom of God"), which in turn is clearly a version of what is also preserved in Mark 14:25. The most likely Lukan contribution to the language here is πληρωθῇ, "it is fulfilled" (see Schürmann, *Quellenkritische Untersuchung*, 1:14–23), but he may also be respon-sible for the presence here of "in the kingdom of God" (to enhance the parallelism of vv 15–16 and 17–18). Again, the language is nowhere notably un-Lukan, but it does at points involve idiom that cannot be shown to come spontaneously from Luke's pen and that is not paralleled in Mark 14:25.

This is no vow of abstinence (cf. at v 15) but a prophetic anticipation. But exactly what is anticipated as sufficiently near at hand as to make this Jesus' last Passover meal? Since the note of finality seems to apply restrictedly to Jesus, and not to the whole Apostolic group (nor to all the Jewish People), the reference can hardly be to the impending arrival of the kingdom of God (as often and recently Maccoby [*NTS* 37 (1991) 258–60]). The referent may depend on pre-cisely how we should take "fulfilled" in the phrase "fulfilled in the kingdom of God." Does Luke have in mind Jesus' Paschal death, by means of which God will seal the new covenant (cf. the Exodus language at 9:31)? Does he have in mind the Lord's Supper as practiced in Luke's church, which looks back to this last Passover meal and to the death of Jesus prefigured in it (see the schematic rela-tionship between vv 15–18 and 19–20 as discussed in *Form/Structure/Setting* above)? The former of these does not finally do justice to the anticipation of Jesus' future eating (ἕως ὅτου, "until"). The latter only does so if Luke envisages Jesus as an eating participant in the church's eucharistic celebration. But while Luke clearly thinks in terms of Jesus as making himself known to Christians in the Lord's Sup-per (see at 9:16; 24:30–31), there is no indication that he is conceived of as an eating companion. As attractive as these options may appear in the Lukan frame, it seems we must be content to see here simply the anticipation of the eschatological banquet of the kingdom of God (it is likely that already in the time of Jesus, Passover did not only look back to redemption from Egypt but also on to eschatological redemption to come—this is clear enough for the post-NT period).

If, then, the fulfillment of the Passover is understood to be the eschatological banquet of the kingdom of God, but what Jesus anticipates as impending is not the arrival of the kingdom of God (see above), then it must be his own death (and thus removal from the human scene) that he anticipates. This is already the most likely sense for the tradition that Luke incorporates, and in the Lukan frame it is quite clear that Jesus' removal from the human scene subsequent to death plays an important role in the structuring of his thought about the significance of the ministry of Jesus.

17 The Lukan role in the language here is likely to be more significant. In its present wording, v 17 is strongly reminiscent of eucharistic language, and, within that, it must be considered striking that apart from the opening δεξάμενος, "receiving," and the closing διαμερίσατε εἰς ἑαυτούς, "share [it] among yourselves," all the language can be exactly matched from either the bread or the cup section in Mark 14:22–23. Even these novel pieces have a eucharistic tone to them: δεξάμενος, "receiving," is no more than a synonym for the usual λαβών, "taking," of the institution accounts; and διαμερίσατε εἰς ἑαυτούς, "share [it] among yourselves," has much the same sense as the Matthean πίετε ἐξ αὐτοῦ πάντες, "drink from it all of you." It would seem that Luke has wanted to have a statement here that sounds like it comes from a eucharistic liturgy, and that he has created one largely on the basis of Mark 14:22–23 but has introduced as well either other eucharistic language known to him or a paraphrase of such language. Since, however, this verse is the one in vv 15–18 that has been most confidently identified as having pre-Lukan content (beyond the clear relationship of v 18 to Mark 14:25), we should pause before attributing the whole here to Luke. The pre-Lukan unit that I am supporting for vv 15–18 would need to have had something at this point. It may be that it was the eucharistic potential of an original that read "and receiving a cup he said" (perhaps already with εὐχαριστήσας, "giving thanks" [or, better, with εὐλογήσας, "saying a blessing," which Luke changes to εὐχαριστήσας for the sake of the parallelism with vv 19–20 to come]) that provided Luke with his opportunity here.

What is Luke doing? Fashioning a eucharistic cup report, but one that has no message about the link between the cup and Jesus? Its presence certainly enhances the parallelism between vv 15–18 and vv 19–20: a partaking of lamb and cup in one kind of eucharist is set in parallel with a partaking of bread and cup in another kind of eucharist. It has been suggested in *Form/Structure/Setting* above that in vv 15–18 Luke is characterizing the Passover meal from the perspective of the Christian eucharist as an old and now eclipsed version of the Lord's Supper. While the cup reference here was probably originally to the first Passover cup, the Lukan development prevents us from identifying it historically with one of the four standard Passover cups.

18 This is clearly a version of the same tradition as preserved in Mark 14:25. The Markan verse owes its present location to the cup verse that precedes it. There is, however, a certain awkwardness involved in moving from the the contents of the cup as "my blood of the covenant" in v 24 to "the fruit of the vine" in v 25 (cf. Léon-Dufour, "Jésus devant sa mort," 147). V 25 would be better served by a link back to a cup statement uncomplicated by the eucharistic content of v 24. This is what, I have suggested above, was available in Luke's source at this point. For the wording of v 18, Luke would seem to be responsible for ἀπό τοῦ νῦν, "from now on." The Markan "when I drink it new in the kingdom of God" is likely to be more original than Luke's "the kingdom of God comes," but it remains unclear

how much of the relationship of parallelism, chiasm, and assonance with the end
of v 16 is Lukan and how much pre-Lukan. If we assume considerable Lukan
responsibility, then Luke is also likely to be responsible here for the repetition of
"for I say to you" from v 16 (the "amen, I say to you" of Mark 14:25 is probably a
remnant of what in Luke is v 16, perhaps with the "amen" added to make the
saying more freestanding when it was cut down from its extended form; in Luke's
v 18 γάρ, "for," cannot be given a fully satisfactory sense [see below] and is best
taken as present for formal structural reasons rather than to indicate the precise
sense link; the original form of v 17 suggested above requires an earlier form
here without "for I say to you").

In the context narrowly of vv 17–18 in their present form, it would be easy to
use the connecting γάρ (lit. "for," but sometimes with merely connective force)
to make v 18 into a vow of abstinence. But this is unlikely, given the discussion
above of the paralleled vv 15–16. "Fruit of the vine" is Septuagintal idiom (Deut
22:9; Isa 32:12), but it is also found in *m. Ber.* 6:1 in a blessing over wine. "Drink
from" (rather than simply "drink") is not common in either Greek or the Semitic
languages, but it does occur in both. V 18 anticipates Jesus' impending death in
much the same manner as v 16. While the wine in view will be that of Passover,
the saying here actually implies that Jesus' end will come before there is occasion
for him to have another festive meal of any kind. On the coming of the kingdom
of God, see at 11:2.

19 The relationship between the Lukan and other forms of the institution is
discussed in *Form/Structure/Setting* above. On the formulaic nature of the sequence
λαβών . . . εὐχαριστήσας ἔκλασεν καὶ ἔδωκεν, "taking . . . [after] giving thanks he
broke and gave," see at 9:10–17. The piling up of verbs evokes solemn eucharistic
practice. Jesus takes up the unleavened Passover loaf and utters the blessing with
which the Passover meal began. For the use of ἄρτος of the unleavened Passover
loaf, cf. the LXX text of Exod 29:2; Lev 2:4; Num 6:19; etc., as well as Philo, *Spec.
leg.* 2.158; Josephus, *Ant.* 3.142. The εὐλογήσας (lit. "having blessed") of the
Matthean and Markan forms (these have εὐχαριστήσας [lit. "having given thanks"]
in connection with the cup) is a more natural rendering of the blessing of God
that characterized the Jewish saying of grace. But the emphasis on thanksgiving
has its own secure place in Palestinian Judaism and is notable in the language of
the Qumran thanksgiving hymns (1QH). The use here in Luke of εὐχαριστήσας
may reflect a Christian emphasis on partaking of the eucharist with thanksgiving
(cf. 1 Tim 4:4–5 in a wider context). Given the use in the NT of κλᾶν, "break,"
exclusively for the breaking of bread at meals, there is no reason to suspect any
symbolism here of the breaking of the body of Jesus (though admittedly all the
uses are either liturgical or quasi-liturgical; more important is the place of the
tearing apart of the unleavened loaf clearly evidenced in later Jewish Paschal practice [and indeed the place of breaking of bread in other Jewish meals]).

For a discussion of the most likely original wording of the bread saying, see
Form/Structure/Setting above. One of the questions that faces us as we seek to understand the equation of bread and body is that of how close a parallelism at
various stages in the development of the tradition should be drawn between the
"body" of the bread word and the "blood" of the cup word, and in particular
whether a measure of synthetic parallelism between the statements should be
traced back to the historical Jesus. It makes best sense of later developments to

assume that a considerable parallelism was sensed from the beginning and was foundational to the further development of the parallelism, especially as the bread and cup were brought together from the positions at either end of a meal. In particular, it seems unlikely that we can deny to "my body" a link with Jesus' impending encounter with death when the link between the prospect of death and the "blood" of the cup word is evident.

Rather less certain is whether "body" and "blood" in the institution narrative should be read in relation to the fixed pairing of these terms in some way. "Flesh" (Greek: σάρξ) and "blood" are regularly paired as the constituent parts of the human constitution (Sir 14:18; 17:31; *1 Enoch* 15:4; Matt 16:17; 1 Cor 15:50; Gal 1:16; Heb 2:14). The pairing of "body" and "blood" in this way is less common (but see Philo, *Quis rer. div.* 54). Ezek 39:17–18 (cf. 32:5–6) brings us closer to the death-facing context of the Last Supper, where "flesh" and "blood" are the constituent parts of human bodies as consumed by wild creatures. The use of σῶμα, "body," rather than σάρξ, "flesh," in our institution narratives counts against what would otherwise be the considerable attractiveness of this as background. Despite the claim by Jeremias (*Eucharistic Words*, 200, 221–22), though we do get repeated reference to the separation of the "blood" from the sacrificial "flesh," and we do get reference to the disposal of the sacrificial animal having to do with what is done respectively to the "blood" and to the "flesh" (sometimes "body" in Philo), we do not seem to get the actual use of "flesh" and "blood" as paired terms in connection with sacrificial language. If the pairing of the terms was intended to relate to this sort of sacrificial imagery, then it would be far preferable for the "blood" to be mentioned first. I conclude that it is more likely that "body" and "blood" each point independently to the coming death of Jesus, rather than pointing to it as a fixed pair.

We probably should not finally try to escape the cannibalistic imagery of the words of institution (cf. John 6:53–58). It is notable that the Markan pattern for the cup has the words of interpretation coming after the consumption of the wine. This is likely to be an original historical feature, which was understandably modified out of a natural concern that the participants eat with a clear consciousness of the significance of this bread and wine. Though none of the present accounts allow us to read this sequence for the bread statement, there may be some trace remaining of a more original order in parallel to the Markan sequence for the cup: in Mark, Matthew, and Luke, the giving of the bread is mentioned before the words of interpretation (Paul does not specify the giving). Only Luke specifically corrects the time sequence by using a present participle "saying" to introduce the words of interpretation in place of the aorist finite verbs of the other accounts ("and said"). Mark and Matthew achieve the same correction despite the sequence "gave and said" for Mark and "having given, he said" for Matthew; they begin the words with a directive to take the bread. It seems to me most likely that under this cannibalistic imagery Jesus assigns to his disciples the benefit of his coming death; and that he makes known what he is doing only after they have consumed the bread that transmits the assignment to them. Except for Peter's objection and the subsequent need for some explanation, the dynamic is not dissimilar in John 13:1–17. Beyond the language of assignment, it may not be out of place to speak in terms of a proleptic transmission of the benefit.

In the eucharistic practice of the church, the ignorant passivity of the original beneficiaries is no longer appropriate, and so the bread is equated with the body of Jesus prior to consumption. By providing "given" to go with "for you," in conscious parallelism to the "poured out for you" of the coming cup words, the Lukan text makes explicit the connection between "body" and approaching death. In Thucydides, *History* 2.43.2; Libanus, *Declam.* 24.3, "give one's body" is an image of dying in battle for the sake of one's people.

For comment on "do this in remembrance of me," see *Form/Structure/Setting* above. The Lord's Supper of the church's practice provides a setting in which Jesus as present can confer upon his own the benefits of his life and of his death.

20 Luke keeps the reference to the meal that separates the giving of the bread from the giving of the cup. There is some awkwardness in establishing the relationship between the meal here and the Passover description in vv 15–18. Luke's retention of this meal reference despite the difficulties it creates for his structuring of vv 15–20 may indicate that the eucharistic practice he was familiar with had retained this pattern (cf. Theissen's criticism ["Social Integration," 145–74] of the common view that the Corinthian church practice involved a meal prior to the liturgical sharing of bread and wine). The content of ὡσαύτως, "in the same way," needs a certain amount of adjustment as we move from bread to cup. A single cup is no doubt implied, but not as clearly as in Matthew and Mark. We have noted above in *Form/Structure/Setting* how this represents a striking departure from standard Passover practice: Jesus is actually sharing his own personal cup with the disciples present, rather than having them drink from their individual cups, as will have been the case for the other cups of wine in the Passover sequence (though in v 17 Luke has, with his echoing of eucharistic language, also introduced this sharing of the cup).

The move from wine (or cup) as blood to cup as a covenant may point to an emphasis on participation in the eucharistic cup as a new covenant responsibility (cf. the role of circumcision in Gen 17:10 and of sabbath in Exod 31:16). Where in the Last Supper the initiative lay entirely with Jesus (cf. the suggestions made above about the words of interpretation originally following the consumption of the bread and the wine), in the Lord's Supper the believing community also must bear some of the responsibility. New covenant benefits are passed to those who share in the covenant cup. Where in the earlier form the covenant allusion has been to Exod 24:8 ("the blood of the covenant"), now the immediate allusion is to the "new covenant" of Jer 31:31–34, a covenant based on a new activity of God beyond Sinai, in which he will bestow forgiveness and bring inner renewal. The underlying allusion to Exod 24:8 remains since the new covenant is said to be ἐν τῷ αἵματί μου, which presumably means "[sealed] with my blood." τὸ ὑπὲρ ὑμῶν ἐκχυννόμενον (lit. "the for you poured out") is a neat parallel to τὸ ὑπὲρ ὑμῶν διδόμενον (lit. "the for you given") in the bread word, but where there is a suitable grammatically matching immediate antecedent in v 19, here the immediate antecedent is dative. While some have tried to make grammatical sense of this situation, it is perhaps best to see here instead the ungrammatical product of the meeting of liturgical innovation with liturgical conservatism and delight in tight formal parallelism. Despite the grammar, it must be the blood and not the cup that is poured out. While the blood of sacrificial animals (as well as other wild animals to be eaten) was poured out, "pour out the blood" is also an OT way of speaking about the imposition of violent death (Gen 9:6; Ezek 18:10; Isa 59:7), whether judicially or out of evil intent. While it is hard to rule out allusion to the sacrificial practice (ἐν τῷ αἵματί μου, "[sealed] with my blood," ensures the presence of sacrificial imagery), Jesus' blood was not literally poured out as would be that of a sacrificial animal, so the primary imagery may be that of violent death.

In the context of the prospect of Jesus' absence, through the interpreted loaf and cup the Apostolic band is assured that they are not about to lose all that they have gained through their contact with Jesus. On the contrary, as Jesus' ministry reached its culmination in death, that new thing God has been doing in Jesus will become their secure possession in a fresh way. The Lord who is to be exalted beyond death will be present through the receiving of the bread and the cup; he will make himself known there through that medium and will confer the new covenant blessings upon those who belong to him.

Explanation

The climactic hour of Passover celebration now arrives (see vv 1 and 7). Jesus has been concerned to avoid capture before this Passover meal. He will now for the last time take part in the Passover meal which, as it celebrates redemption from Egypt, also anticipates final redemption of his People by God. He will as well institute a new liturgical pattern in which bread and wine are offered as the body of Jesus and the covenant sealed with his blood. With this liturgical pattern, that which was achieved by Jesus' path of obedience to rejection and death in Jerusalem will be conferred, proleptically here for the Apostolic band, and with reference back to the cross in the church's later practice.

Despite a solid shared core, at least in the first three Gospels, there is a surprising variety in the detail from one Gospel to another as to the precise words and actions of Jesus at the Last Supper. Most notable of all is the distinctiveness of the Johannine account, which locates the Last Supper meal twenty-four hours before the Passover meal and has Jesus dead and buried before the Passover meal. John has a footwashing with interpretation, but no action with bread and cup.

There is a strong reminder here that the Gospels use their narrative techniques not only to report historical events but also to interpret the significance of Jesus and his ministry. John has used the idea of Jesus' flesh and blood as food and drink in connection with the discourse after the feeding of the five thousand (John 6) and feels no need to repeat it here. While the other Gospels draw the link between Jesus' death and the Passover by having both the meal and Jesus' death on the festival day of Passover, John stresses just the same link by having Jesus dying on the cross as the lambs for Passover are being slaughtered in the temple.

Historically the Last Supper probably was the Passover meal. The loaf of bread is likely to have been that which opened the main part of the Passover meal. The identity of the cup is less certain. The best choice would seem to be the third cup, which concluded the main part of the meal. But we should not make anything of these identifications in our present Gospel texts, since the Passover identity of these elements is obscured, rather than built upon, in the Gospel narratives.

Though some scholars are skeptical about tracing the saying about bread and wine (or cup) back to the historical Jesus, there has been a growing scholarly

confidence that in some form the words do go back to Jesus. A reasonable guess
as to the most original forms might be: "this is my body, for you"; "this [or this
cup] is my covenant blood" (the verbs may not have been present in the Aramaic
originals). In the transmission and use of these words, interpretation has been
built into the words by expanding and modifying them in various ways. The different forms we have in the synoptic Gospels and in 1 Cor 11 all probably reflect
forms in use in the communion practice of different churches.

Some ancient texts of the Gospel of Luke are missing the part of v 19 that
comes after "this is my body," and all of v 20. Were these part of Luke's original?
Much doubt was expressed in the earlier part of this century about the place of
these verse in Luke's text, but in recent decades there has been growing confidence that they are properly part of Luke's text. An economical scribe probably
stopped after "this is my body" as an abbreviation, because he assumed that his
readers would all know how to supply the missing words.

With the whole of vv 19–20 in the text, a clear structuring of vv 15–18 and 19–
20 is evident. A sequence of lamb and cup is set in parallel with a sequence of
bread and cup. To the definite paralleling of the lamb and cup sections with each
other corresponds the paralleling of the bread and cup sections with each other.
The cup in v 17 is described in a way that, while mostly distinctive from the language of vv 19–20, clearly echoes eucharistic language as do those verses.

As the Passover meal (lamb) is shared, Jesus expresses his gratification at being able to share it with his Apostles. His words are prophetic of his coming death
and removal from his intimate band, but they also point to the coming of the
kingdom of God, which will bring that full redemption only foreshadowed by the
Passover redemption from Egypt. Jesus' point is reiterated as he takes a cup. While
the wine in view will be that drunk at Passover, the saying here actually implies
that Jesus' end will come before there is occasion for him to have another festive
meal of any kind.

Probably, historically, the cup here is the first cup of the Passover meal (or
possibly the second). But in Luke's account, because the cup is given eucharistic
features and lamb and cup in vv 15–18 are set in parallel with bread and cup in vv
19–20, the cup can no longer be meant to identify a particular cup in the Passover sequence. Rather, Passover lamb and cup are meant in vv 15–18 to
characterize the Passover meal, just as bread and cup are meant in vv 19–20 to
characterize the church's eucharistic celebration. This curious way of describing
the Passover meal comes from seeing it through the eyes of the Christian eucharist:
it is viewed as an old and now eclipsed version of the Lord's Supper.

The piling up of verbs in the opening part of v 19 evokes the solemn ritual of
eucharistic practice. The use of "giving thanks" rather than the "blessing (of God),"
which would be more natural for Jewish Passover, may reflect a Christian emphasis on partaking of the eucharist with thanksgiving (cf. Acts 2:46).

The bread is identified with the body of Jesus given up to death for the sake of
Jesus' followers. The imagery is provocatively cannibalistic. Jesus assigns, and even
in a proleptic manner may be said to be transmitting, to his disciples the benefits
of his coming passion. From its location in time on the other side of the cross,
the church will engage in a liturgical repetition of Jesus' action. In this way, that
Jesus who is no longer present in his historical ministry will make himself known
and confer ever afresh to the disciple community the benefits of his passion.

The reiterated action will bring into the present what might otherwise be lost in the mists of the past. The memorial pattern of the Passover is now to be exploited in a new way in connection with the salvation achievement of Jesus.

Although the course of the meal comes between bread and cup, the two are deliberately set in parallel. Though it is clearer in v 17, we should understand that in v 20 as well Jesus departs from the normal Passover practice and shares his own cup with the assembled group. Normally each would have had his own individual cup for the Passover liturgy. This distinctive action can be related to a Jewish practice in which the host might share his cup with a particular guest as a way of honoring and bestowing a blessing on that individual.

The language of cup as covenant may be to emphasize that participation in the eucharistic cup is a new covenant responsibility (cf. the role of circumcision in Gen 17:10 and of sabbath in Exod 31:16). Where in the Markan form the covenant allusion had been to Exod 24:8 ("the blood of the covenant"), now the immediate allusion is to the "new covenant" of Jer 31:31–34, a covenant based on a new activity of God beyond Sinai, in which he will bestow forgiveness and bring inner renewal. Since, however, the new covenant is said to be "[sealed] with my blood," the underlying allusion to Exod 24:8, with its sealing of the Sinai covenant in blood, remains.

"Poured out for you" may point to the way in which the blood of sacrificial animals was poured out. However, because the blood of Jesus was not literally drained, and since to "pour out the blood" is an OT manner of speaking about the causing of violent death (Gen 9:6; Ezek 18:10; Isa 59:7), the imagery may as well, or instead, be that of impending violent death.

Though Jesus may be about to leave the disciple band, they are not about to lose what they have gained through him. Instead, Jesus' death will secure for them in a new way what they have begun to experience through their link with him.

Jesus' Awareness of His Betrayal   *(22:21–23)*

Bibliography

Christensen, J. "Le fils de l'homme s'en va, ainsi qu'il est écrit de lui." *ST* 10 (1956–57) 28–39. **LaVerdiere, E. A.** "A Discourse at the Last Supper." *BiTod* 71 (1974) 1540–48. **Pesch, R.** "Die Passion des Menschensohns: Eine Studie zu den Menschensohnworten der vormarkinischen Passionsgeschichte." In *Jesus und der Menschensohn*. FS A. Vögtle, ed. R. Pesch and R. Schnackenburg. Freiburg/Basel/Vienna: Herder, 1975. 166–95, esp. 181–83. **Rehkopf, F.** *Die Lukanische Sonderquelle: Ihr Umfang und Sprachgebrauch.* WUNT 5. Tübingen: Mohr-Siebeck, 1959. 7–30. **Robbins, V. K.** "Last Meal: Preparation, Betrayal, and Absence." In *The Passion in Mark*, ed. W. H. Kelber. 21–40, esp. 29–34. **Schenk, W.** *Passionsbericht.* 185–89. **Schenke, L.** *Studien zur Passionsgeschichte des Markus.* 199–285. **Schürmann, H.** *Quellenkritische Untersuchung.* 3:3–21. ———. "Der Abendmahlsbericht Lk 22,7–38 als Gottesdienstordnung, Gemeindeordnung, Lebensordnung." In *Ursprung und Gestalt.* 108–50, esp. 140–43. **Schwarz, G.** *Jesus und Judas.* 162–75. **Sellew, P. H.** "The

Last Supper Discourse in Luke 22:21–38." *Forum* 3.3 (1987) 70–95. **Taylor, V.** *The Passion Narrative of St Luke.* 59–61. **Vogler, W.** *Judas Iskarioth.* 43–47, 79–81.

And see at 22:1–2, 22:14–20, and esp. 22:3–6.

Translation

 21 *"But see! The hand of the one who delivers me up [is] on the table with me.* 22*For the Son of Man goes in accord with what has been determined, but woe to that person through whom he is delivered up."* 23 *They began to ask one another which of them it might be who would do this.*

Notes

There are only minor textual variants.

Form/Structure/Setting

Jesus' announcement of his awareness of the presence of his betrayer among his most intimate circle of followers comes with a chilling shock after the tender intimacy of vv 14–20. The discussion that the announcement sets off among the Apostles provides the transition to the dispute to come in v 24.

Luke has delayed this unit from its Markan position before the institution narrative. The Markan equivalent here (Mark 14:18–21) is rather more extensive than the Lukan rendering. Without close verbal agreement, Luke 22:21 has an evident relationship to the tradition reflected in Mark 14:18b, 20. Luke 22:22 is quite close to Mark 14:21, but it has divine determination rather than attestation in Scripture providing the sense of necessity. It also lacks the final statement of the Markan form as well as one of the references to the Son of Man. Luke 22:23, which reports the disciples' response, shares the word ἤρξαντο, "they began," with Mark's version of the same (Mark 14:19) but otherwise has nothing in common with the Markan version. To dispute the consensus view that Luke uses only his Markan source here are the possible coincidence with John in locating the mention of the betrayal after the meal (Judas leaves the table immediately thereafter, and there is no further mention of the meal) and the evident coincidence with John (cf. John 13:22) in locating the immediate response of the disciples in an interaction with one another rather than, as in Mark, in an interaction individually with Jesus (cf. Cribbs, "A Study of the Contacts," 52). Rehkopf's elaborate case (*Die Lukanische Sonderquelle*, 7–30) for a totally separate Lukan source here is accepted by Taylor (*Passion Narrative*, 59–61) for vv 21 and 23 (but not for v 22). Access to additional tradition here for Luke is a real possibility but has not been definitely demonstrated, since the distinctives of the Lukan account can all be given satisfactory redactional explanations.

The Markan redactional contribution to Mark 14:18–21 has been variously judged. The minimal view as to the traditional content is that of Schenke (*Studien*, 199–285), who allows only a reduced version of v 21 to Mark's source (Schenke argues for an original form that parallels that of Luke 17:1–2 [a form that I have argued above is a Lukan creation]). Dormeyer (*Passion Jesu*, 302–17) offers pertinent criticism of Schenke's approach (on Mark 14:18–21, see esp. 308–15). Dormeyer's own view (94–100) *denies* only v 21 to Markan tradition (along with "the one who eats with me" from v 18 and "one of the twelve" from v 20). Dormeyer offers the more satisfying account of vv 18–20, but for v 21 his case is strongest with respect to denying any original unity between vv 18–20 and v 21 (from vv 18–20, Vogler [*Judas*, 43–47] allows to tradition only v 18bc but considers v 21 to have been incorporated as a separate piece of tradition). The case for Markan intervention in v 21 is strongest for "as it is written concerning him." (Schenk [*Passionsbericht*, 188–89] offers the interesting suggestion that only the final statement in v 21 is not redactional and that it linked originally to v 20b; Robbins, "Last Meal," 33–34 would allow the woe clause as well, but no link to v 20b.)

Though Mark 14:18–20 has about it the air of dramatic literary construction (esp. the role of v 19?), there seems to be no adequate reason for denying to the historical Jesus a saying about anticipating denial from among his own intimate band (though allusion to Ps 41:9 is not impossible, this text has certainly not been responsible for the creation of the tradition). There is, however, no denying the fit of such a saying within the concerns of the early church. The case for early church development of v 21 is stronger, but, with the possible exception of the kind of appeal to Scripture involved here, all the elements reflect motifs found in sayings of the historical Jesus.

Comment

This present revelation of a betrayer within the closest circle of Jesus' followers stands in sharp contrast to the preceding scene in which, against a background of a pre-existing intimate link with him, Jesus has intensified the bonds of intimacy by assigning to these his closest followers the benefits of his coming death. And he has done so in a manner that, by speaking of new covenant commitment between God and his People sealed with the blood of Jesus, has placed its own focus on issues of pledged loyalty.

21 Only "with me" and a use of $\pi\alpha\rho\alpha\delta\iota\delta\acute{o}\nu\alpha\iota$ (lit. "to hand over") reflect the language of the Markan parallel. Mark's form requires a meal in progress, but in Luke the eating seems to have concluded. The contrast expressed by $\pi\lambda\acute{\eta}\nu$ (here a strong form of adversative "but") is the stark antithesis between this announcement of betrayal by one of the Twelve and the intimate scene that preceded. For the reader, $\tauo\hat{u}$ $\pi\alpha\rho\alpha\delta\iota\delta\acute{o}\nu\tauo\varsigma$, "the one who delivers up," links back to v 4 (see there and at 9:44). Here there is clearly no sense that God is the one who delivers Jesus up (but cf. at v 22). The phrase $\dot{\epsilon}\pi\grave{\iota}$ $\tau\hat{\eta}\varsigma$ $\tau\rho\alpha\pi\acute{\epsilon}\zeta\eta\varsigma$ (lit. "upon the table") will recur in v 30 in the context of messianic banquet imagery. This link could be to strengthen the sense that the Last Supper is something of a proleptic messianic banquet.

22 Much of the language here is in common with Mark 14:21. Luke has $\pi o\rho\epsilon\acute{u}\epsilon\tau\alpha\iota$, "goes," for Mark's $\dot{u}\pi\acute{\alpha}\gamma\epsilon\iota$ (lit. "departs"). He has $\kappa\alpha\tau\grave{\alpha}$ $\tau\grave{o}$ $\dot{\omega}\rho\iota\sigma\mu\acute{\epsilon}\nuo\varsigma$, "in accord with what has been determined," for Mark's $\kappa\alpha\theta\grave{\omega}\varsigma$ $\gamma\acute{\epsilon}\gamma\rho\alpha\pi\tau\alpha\iota$ $\pi\epsilon\rho\grave{\iota}$ $\alpha\dot{u}\tauo\hat{u}$, "just as it stands written concerning him." Luke links the woe clause with another $\pi\lambda\acute{\eta}\nu$, "but," for Mark's colorless $\delta\acute{\epsilon}$, "and/but" (and thus repeats the $\pi\lambda\acute{\eta}\nu$ $o\dot{u}\alpha\acute{\iota}$, "but woe," that he has used at 6:24; 17:1).

Jesus is Son of Man in his suffering here as in the classic passion predictions (see at 9:21–22). Luke will take up the scriptural necessity for Jesus's death in

24:25–26 and esp. 44–46. Here he will content himself more imprecisely (but more personally) with the determination in the will of God (the same verb is used by Luke in connection with the will of God in Acts 2:23; 10:42; 17:26, 31) that stands behind Jesus' passage through suffering to glory. The human role of betrayer is in no way excused by the fact that his betraying activity forwards the divine purpose. The betrayer retains full responsibility for the enormity of his act. Unless the language is loose, δι᾽ οὗ (lit. "through whom," but normally translated here "by whom") may point to the ambivalent nature of the delivering up of Jesus: Jesus is delivered up by God, by means of Judas.

23 Though Mark also reports a response by the disciples, his comes rather earlier, and the two forms are linked only by a shared use of ἤρξαντο, "they began." The language has a number of Lukan features: especially the use of τό (lit. "the") to introduce an indirect question for which the optative of the verb is used. Albeit in a rather artificial manner, the discussion back and forth here prepares for the dispute of v 24. Christians had to come to terms with and be warned about the possibility of betrayal by one who is intimately linked with Jesus through the eucharistic life of the church.

Explanation

There is a dramatic change of tone from the warm intimacy of vv 14–20 as Jesus reveals his awareness of the presence of his betrayer.

Though in some sense the Last Supper is a brave anticipation by Jesus with his disciples of the coming messianic banquet of the kingdom of God, the presence of the betrayer at the table highlights the need for the future fulfillment, which will be spoken of in v 30. The Son of Man language here reminds us that Jesus has been speaking of a coming time of suffering for himself under this title since 9:21–22. The cryptic language of necessity is now replaced by reference to what has been determined (by God). Later there will be a stress on how the Scriptures foretold this fate (see 24:25–26, 44–46). "Goes" is probably designed to embrace both the suffering fate and its role for Jesus as gateway to glory at the right hand of God.

As much as Jesus' path to the cross might be fixed in the purpose of God, there is no excuse to be made for the betrayer. He bears full responsibility for the breach of trust and intimacy and the total failure of loyalty that his betrayal involves. Human responsibility and divine sovereignty are not to be played off against each other.

The role of betrayer cannot, however, be left comfortably with Judas. The unresolved questioning of the Apostles in v 23 leaves each of us to face the possibility of being one who betrays Jesus, though linked intimately to him through the communion fellowship of the church.

The Great Are to Serve, While Those Who Have Shared Jesus' Trials Will Gain Royal Stature (22:24–30)

Bibliography

Arens, E. *The HΛΘON-Sayings in the Synoptic Tradition.* OBO 10. Freiburg/Göttingen: Universit'atsverlag/Vandenhoeck & Ruprecht, 1976. 117–61. **Bammel, E.** "Das Ende von Q." In *Verborum veritas.* FS G. Stählin, ed. O. Böcher and K. Haacker. Wuppertal: Brockhaus, 1970. 39–50. ———. "Das 'Testament' Jesu (Luk 22.27ff.)." In *Jesus Nachfolger: Nachfolgeüberlieferungen in der Zeit des frühen Christentums.* Studia Delitzschiana 3/1. Heidelberg: Lambert Schneider, 1988. 74–83. **Broer, I.** "Das Ringen der Gemeinde um Israel: Exegetischer Versuch über Mt 19,28." In *Jesus und der Menschensohn,* FS A. Vögtle, ed. R. Pesch and R. Schnackenburg. Freiburg/Basel/Vienna: Herder, 1975. 148–65. **Brown, S.** *Apostasy and Perseverance.* 62–63. **Clark, K. W.** "The meaning of [κατα]κυριεύειν." In *Studies in New Testament Language and Text.* FS G. D. Kilpatrick, ed. J. K. Elliott. NovTSup 44. Leiden: Brill, 1976. 100–105. **Crossan, J. D.** *In Fragments.* 202–4, 285–95. **Danker, F. W.** "The Endangered Benefactor in Luke-Acts." In *SBL Seminar Papers 1981,* ed. K. H. Richards. Chico, CA: Scholars, 1981. 39–48. **Dupont, J.** "Le logion des douze trônes (Mt 19,28; Lc 22,28–30)." *Bib* 45 (1964) 355–92. **Feuillet, A.** "Le logion sur la rançon." *RSPT* 51 (1967) 365–402. ———. "Le triomphe eschatologique de Jésus d'après quelques textes isolés des Évangiles." *NRT* 71 (1949) 701–22; 80 (1958) 6–28, esp. 715–22. **Fleddermann, H.** "The End of Q." In *SBL 1990 Seminar Papers,* ed. D. J. Lull. Atlanta, GA: Scholars, 1990. 1–10. **George, A.** "La royauté de Jésus selon l'évangile de Luc." *ScEccl* 14 (1962) 57–69. **Guillet, J.** "Luc 22,29: Une formule johannique dans l'évangile de Luc?" *RSR* 69 (1981) 113–22. **Hoffmann, P.,** and **Eid, V.** *Jesus von Nazareth und eine christliche Moral: Sittliche Perspektive der Verkündigung Jesu.* QD 66. Freiburg: Herder, 1975. 186–230. **Jeremias, J.** "Das Lösegeld für Viele." In *Abba: Studien zur neutestamentlichen Theologie und Zeitgeschichte.* Göttingen: Vandenhoeck & Ruprecht, 1966. 216–29. **Joüon, P.** "Notes philologiques sur les évangiles." *RSR* 18 (1928) 345–59, esp. 355. **Kertelge, K.** "Der dienende Menschensohn (Mk 10,45)." In *Jesus und der Menschensohn.* FS A. Vögtle, ed. R. Pesch and R. Schnackenburg. Freiburg: Herder, 1975. 225–39. **Kollmann, B.** *Ursprung und Gestalten der frühchristlichen Mahlfeier.* 176–80. **Lohfink, G.** *Die Sammlung Israels.* 79–84. **Lull, D.** "The Servant-Benefactor as a Model of Greatness (Luke 22:24–30)." *NovT* 28 (1986) 289–305. **Moulder, W. J.** "The Old Testament Background and the Interpretation of Mark x. 45." *NTS* 24 (1977–78) 120–27. **Nelson, P. K.** "Leadership and Discipleship." Ph.D. diss., Trinity College, Bristol, 1991. ———. "The Flow of Thought in Luke 22.24–27." *JSNT* 43 (1991) 113–23. **Page, S. H. T.** "The Authenticity of the Ransom Logion (Mark 10:45b)." In *Studies of History and Tradition in the Four Gospels,* ed. R. T. France and D. Wenham. Gospel Perspectives 1. Sheffield: JSOT, 1980. 137–61. **Rasmussen, L.** "Luke 22:24–27." *Int* 37 (1983) 73–76. **Rickards, R. R.** "Luke 22:25: They Are Called 'Friends of the People.'" *BT* 28 (1977) 445–46. **Roloff, J.** *Apostolat.* 184–88. ———. "Anfänge der soteriologischen Deutung des Todes Jesu (Mk. x. 45 und Lk. xxii. 27)." *NTS* 19 (1972–73) 38–64. **Schlosser, J.** "La genèse de Luc, XXII, 25–27." *RB* 89 (1982) 52–70. **Schürmann, H.** "Der Abendmahlsbericht Lk 22,7–38 als Gottesdienstordnung, Gemeindeordnung, Lebensordnung." In *Ursprung und Gestalt.* 108–50, esp. 136–40. ———. *Quellenkritische Untersuchung.* 3:36–99. **Schulz, A.** *Nachfolgen und Nachahmen.* SANT 6. Munich: Kösel, 1962. 119–21. **Schulz, S.** *Q: Die Spruchquelle.* 330–36. **Stuhlmacher, P.** "Existenzstellvertretung für die Vielen: Mk 10,45 (Mt 20,28). In *Werden und Wirken des Alten Testaments,* FS C. Westermann, ed. R. Albertz et al. Göttingen/Neukirchen: Neukirchener, 1980. 412–

27. **Tannehill, R.** "A Study in the Theology of Luke-Acts." *ATR* 43 (1961) 195–203. **Tiede, D. L.** "The Kings of the Gentiles and the Leader Who Serves: Luke 22:24–30." *WW* 12 (1992) 23–28. **Vööbus, A.** *Prelude to the Lukan Passion Narrative.* 29–40.

And see at 22:1–2 and 22:14–20.

Translation

[24]*A contention also*[a] *arose*[b] *among them about which of them would seem to be the greatest.* [25]*He said to them, "The kings of the nations exercise their lordship over them and those in authority over them have themselves called benefactors.* [26]*It is not to be this way with you! Rather let the greatest among you become like the*[c] *youngest and the one who leads like the one who serves.* [27]*For who is greater, the one who reclines [at table] or the one who serves? Is it not the one who reclines? But in your midst I am like the one who serves.* [28]*But you are those who have stuck with me in my trials.* [29]*Just as my father has conferred royal rule upon me, I also confer [it]*[d] *upon you,*[e] [30]*that you may eat and drink at my table in my kingdom and sit upon thrones judging the twelve tribes of Israel."*

Notes

[a] Missing from ℵ it etc.
[b] Gr. ἐγένετο (lit. "happened").
[c] The article is missing from P[75] and some other texts, while D reads μικρότερος, "smallest" (lit. "smaller").
[d] For ease of translation, the Gr. order of clauses is here reversed.
[e] The lack of a specified object is made good here with διαθήκην, "covenant," by A Θ 579 etc. 579 follows this through by displacing βασιλείαν, "royal rule," with a second use of "covenant."

Form/Structure/Setting

The search for the betrayer in their midst gives way to a dispute over the identity of the greatest among them (the sequencing of discussion of betrayal and dispute over greatness mirrors that in 9:43b–45, 46–48). Luke uses this as the setting for Jesus' teaching in which he calls the great to humble service and promises future exaltation to those who have identified themselves with him in the trials of his own humiliation.

The farewell speech continues here, in the meal setting that Luke has provided for it. The material in the other Gospels that most nearly parallels Luke 22:24–27 (Mark 10:41–45; Matt 20:24–28; 23:11) has nothing of Luke's link with Jesus' final meal with his disciples. Only John 13:1–20 suggests that some impulse from the tradition may have spurred Luke to locate the material here (on the links here with John, see Nelson, "Leadership and Discipleship," 175–77).

There can be little doubt that Luke 22:24–27 is a version of the same tradition as Mark 10:41–45 (note especially the degree of structural parallelism). Much more uncertain, however, is whether Luke's Markan source is the basis for his own version. The strongest case for a separate source can be made in the case of v 27 (see, e.g., Schlosser [*RB* 89 (1982) 52–70], who allows a separate source for this verse alone). There is also, however, considerable force in Schürmann's view (*Quellenkritische Untersuchung*, 3:72–78) that Matt 23:11 is the immediate parallel for Luke 22:26: in Matt 23:11 and Luke 22:26 the already great are addressed, while in Mark 10:43–44 a path to greatness is identified for aspirants. If Luke 22:26 and 27 are both traditional, then either Luke has, by displacing Markan elements, incorporated these verses into a Markan structure, or his source here already had the same basic structure as the Markan account. While some Markan influence cannot be ruled out, the latter seems to be altogether more likely. At the same time, there are good reasons for identifying some of the language as Lukan (see *Comment* below).

If there are two basically independent sources, then the question of greater originality at once arises. It is likely that some of the features that are least original represent Lukan editing (esp. in v 25), but that behind this the greater originality is to be shared between the two sources (Mark for v 26, with its alternative vision of greatness; but Luke for v 27, with the Semitism of its *mashal* form and double question). It is likely that v 27 par. Mark 10:45 was not an original unit with the preceding. Whether the "I" form or the "Son of Man" form is more original in v 27 is hard to determine, since developments in the tradition moved in both directions. The originality of Mark 10:45b with its ransom language remains hotly disputed. On the whole, those who see it as a secondary development, elucidating the service of the Son of Man in light of developing church understanding of the passion, seem to have the better part of the argument; but the debate here is not yet finished.

For vv 28–30 Luke uses material that has a partial parallel in Matt 19:28 (mainly parallelling v 30b). Dupont (*Bib* 45 [1964] 359–60) and others argue that Luke's vv 29–30a constitute a separate unit of tradition, secondarily incorporated at this point. The case is not persuasive, however, because a satisfactory thought unity for this tradition has not been established. This view also fails to reckon with the correspondence between Matthew's throne for the Son of Man and thrones for the Twelve and Luke's kingdoms for the one and the other (see below). Schürmann earlier (*Quellenkritische Untersuchung*, 3:36–54) had identified v 30a as a secondary expansion. This seems the more likely option; and while Schürmann considered the expansion pre-Lukan, more probable on the basis of the language is Luke's own intervention (cf. Schulz, *Q: Die Spruchquelle*, 231 n. 67). In v 29 Luke does seem, however, to be reflecting tradition. In particular Guillet (*RSR* 69 [1981] 113–22), drawing on the analysis of the Johannine pattern by O. de Dinechin ("καθώς: La similitude dans l'évangile selon saint Jean," *RSR* 58 [1970] 195–236), has noted the frequent occurrences in the Gospel of John of variants of the pattern here: "as the father . . . to me, so I . . . to you." The same pattern is found in Rev 2:26–27; cf. 3:21. As so often with the Luke-John links, the link is tantalizing but provides nothing precise for source analysis. We must ask, Has Luke inserted a piece of tradition at v 29, or did he receive his form of vv 28–30 with v 29 already included? Coming to our aid here is the recognition that Matthew's attribution of thrones to both the Son of Man and to the disciples has its analogue in Luke's attribution of a kingdom to each. This makes it much more likely that v 29 was already an integral part of what Luke received. V 28 is mostly without parallel in Matthew ("followed me" and "stuck with me" are somewhat equivalent) and is probably best understood as a Lukan displacement of an original introduction rather more like the Matthean form (perhaps without the "amen"). Because of the judgment that Luke has used a source that he does not have in common with Matthew, less precision is possible about the line between

Lukan tradition and redaction. In any case, it seems best to consider the Matthean form as close to the most primitive form ("in the regeneration" would seem to have no precise Semitic equivalent, but equivalent Semitic new-creation language is readily available [cf. the use of הדשה עשות, *ʿśwt ḥdšh*, "renewal"]; there is some possibility of a Matthean contribution to the language in which the Son of Man is introduced here). The issues involved in historical evaluation here are complex, linked as they are to discussion of the historicity of Jesus' call of the Twelve and of his use of various classes of Son of Man language. While the saying certainly could be an early church development, I find the arguments that have been mounted against its historicity far from persuasive.

We must look to Luke for the juxtaposition of vv 24–27 and 28–30.

Comment

Jesus intervenes in the dispute of the Twelve over greatness with his call for the great among the disciple band to give themselves up to serving roles. This "humiliating" posture demanded of the great is not, however, the end of the story: those who have stood by Jesus in the trials of his own humiliation will be given a share in his own coming royal rule.

24 The content here, though little of the exact language, closely parallels 9:46. The slight tension between the nature of the dispute (who is greatest) and the response of Jesus (how the great are to behave) may count in favor of Lukan formulation. The most Lukan features are the opening ἐγένετο δέ, "it happened," and the use of τό (lit. "the") to introduce an indirect question (note τὸ τίς [lit. "the who"] in v 23 as here). The use of δοκεῖ, "seems," may be influenced by the use of the same verb in Mark 10:42. Luke may introduce the language of appearances precisely because the coming directive and attention to the example of Jesus tend toward the confusion of appearances. It is probably unwise to propose a specific psychological development from the inquiry of v 23 to the contention of v 24. Presumably the contention involves personal bids for preeminence, not just differences of opinions about third parties! The translation of μείζων (lit. "greater") here as "greatest" obscures the fact that the same word appears here and in vv 26, 27.

25 The verbal agreement with Mark 10:42 is very slight, but the structural agreement is notable. All the language differences would be consistent with Lukan alteration of his Markan source, but at the same time none of the language is notably Lukan. The more Hellenistic flavor of the language may be attributable to Luke. The point of the first image is that the gentile rulers "make their political power felt" (Fitzmyer, 1416). "Benefactor" was an honorific title in the Greco-Roman world given to princes, to Roman emperors, and to the gods. In the honor culture of that world, public recognition in various forms was a required return for generosity to those who in any sense were clients of the benefactor. (See F. W. Danker, *Benefactor: Epigraphic Study of a Graeco-Roman and New Testament Semantic Field* [St. Louis, MO: Clayton, 1982]; J. H. Elliott, "Patronage and Clientism in Early Christian Society," *Forum* 3.4 [1987] 39–48.) καλοῦνται could be taken in various ways: if passive, "are called"; if middle, "call themselves," "let themselves be called," or "have themselves called." The last probably provides the best fit here.

26 Again there is only modest verbal agreement with Mark, and here the structural parallelism, while still evident, is less close. Where in Mark the concern is about becoming great, in Luke the concern is about the great becoming like much less exalted figures (as in Matt 23:11). ἡγούμενος, "one who leads," may be Lukan. "The youngest" and "the one who serves" are probably to be related chiastically to "exercise lordship" and "have themselves called benefactors." If this is so, then to "become like the youngest" will have to do with the forgoing of status demands, since youngsters have no status that might require any kind of recognition. This sort of status is to be forgone, and "the one who leads" is not to press his authority upon those whom he leads; he is rather to behave as one who serves them (the imagery of service at table here will be reinforced by the use of language in connection with being the table servant in v 27). Though taken literally, the clause about the greatest would apply only to a single person; that about the one who leads indicates clearly that no such limitation is intended. We should note, however, that in the first instance the text is about how the members of the Apostolic band should relate to one another, and not about how they as the great ones and leaders should relate to the Christian community they are to lead.

27 The language overlap with Mark reaches a low point here: γάρ, "for," to link with the preceding and (rather different kinds of) use of the verb διακονεῖν, "to serve." ἀνάκεισθαι, "to recline [at table]," occurs only here in Luke-Acts. μείζων is "greater" here, where it has been "greatest" in vv 24, 26. The development here takes up in terms of literal table service the servant reference of v 26b. In v 26 the behavior commended is such as will confuse appearances (cf. at v 24); that confusion of appearances becomes explicit here with the double question, which insists upon an answer that the Apostles are aware must be wrong if applied to Jesus on the basis of his self-description in the final clause of the verse. ἐν μέσῳ ὑμῶν εἰμι, "I am in the midst of you," puts the focus upon how Jesus behaves in his dealings with the Twelve. In the present context there is likely to be a reference to what has recently taken place in vv 19–20. It is best to carry the comparative force of ὡς forward from the two instances in v 26 and to translate, as there, "like the one who serves" ("as the table servant" not only fails to pick up on the link from v 26; it also plays havoc with the role of Jesus, who clearly presides as head over the Last Supper). An eschatological use of the table-service image is found at 12:37.

28 ὑμεῖς δέ, "but you," is probably meant to take us back to v 24 with its dispute over who was great. Though the desire to appear as great ones has reared its head, this is not the whole story. These people are the same as those who have stuck with Jesus along the lowly road of his trials (though it has had a number of supporters, there is no real credibility to the view of Conzelmann [*Luke*, 80–81, 83] that the perseverance here begins only with the fresh initiative of Satan in 22:3). While perseverance is an important matter in the Lukan frame (cf. at 8:15 and note the way that in the passion narrative Luke softens the Markan emphasis upon the abandonment of Jesus by the Twelve), the emphasis here is likely to fall more upon "in my trials" (ἐν τοῖς πειρασμοῖς: the singular is translated as "temptation" at 4:13, "trial" in 8:13, and "that which is a trial" in 11:3; 22:40, 46), with the language of trials itself understood in close connection with "like a servant" of v 27. (For the link between πειρασμός, "trial," and the commitment in vv 25–27 to being "like a servant" and not like "the kings of the nations," cf. at 4:1–13, where the linking of these ideas [but not the precise language] is set in the context of Satanic temptation of Jesus to depart from the divinely ordained pattern for his ministry.) It would not be inappropriate to comb through the Gospel narrative and point to the adversities experienced by Jesus in company with the Twelve, but these need then to be seen in connection with that orientation of his ministry to which he committed himself against the pressure of Satanic temptation in 4:1–13 and to which he remained true despite the ensuing difficulties. In connection with the movement from trials to royal rule for the disciples, it is also relevant to call to mind Luke's preoccupation with the idea that Jesus can achieve heavenly glory only through suffering (see esp. 24:26; and for a wider application, Acts 14:22; cf. Lohfink, *Sammlung*, 82).

29 For the appointed royal destiny of Jesus, cf. at 1:32–33; 19:11–28, 29–40; 23:42. Since the understanding of this royal destiny of Jesus is oriented to the future, it is hardly appropriate to draw in here, as some wish to, the horizon of Jesus' impending death and to take διατίθεμαι as "I bequeath [as in a will or last testament]." Though the verb can bear such a sense, its parallel use in connection with God here hardly encourages us to move in such a direction. The more general sense "confer" is to be preferred. It seems best to take βασιλείαν (tr. here as "royal rule," but elsewhere as "kingdom" or "kingship") as supplying the object for both acts of conferral (the alternative is to make the eating and drinking along with the sitting and judging that which Jesus confers; however, this is less satisfactory in relation to the use of καθώς, "just as," and it does not fully bring to expression the parallelism of Jesus' situation with that of the Twelve, a feature here whose importance is confirmed by the presence of "throne" and "thrones" in the Matthean form of this tradition). "Royal rule" is preferred as the translation for βασιλείαν here, since v 30 makes clear that what is involved for the Twelve is more a participation in Jesus' rule than any kind of independent regal status or rule. For Jesus' speaking of God as "my Father," cf. 10:22; 24:49. Despite the various attempts that have been made to find here a ruling role for the Twelve in the life of the early church, the eschatological orientation, in this context, of the rule of Jesus requires the same for the rule of the Twelve. 12:32, while not unrelated, is more general and sees the promised βασιλεία, "kingdom/kingship/royal rule," as possession rather than as activity.

30 The opening ἵνα clause here is better taken as explanatory than as expressing purpose (to receive royal rule *for the purpose of* eating and drinking at Jesus' table is hardly intelligible). Luke also pairs eating and drinking at 5:30, 33; 7:33, 34; 10:7; 12:19; etc. The shared use of "table" in vv 21 and 30 establishes a link between the Last Supper and the future meal envisaged here. Note the spatial use of "kingdom" here (contrast v 29). The fundamental imagery is of the eschatological banquet of God's People (cf. 13:29; 14:15; etc.), but the appeal to it here functions more to establish close linkage to Jesus as foundational for the role of the Twelve in v 30b to follow. This is likely to be Luke's main contribution to the traditional materials he works with here.

Luke is likely to be responsible for removing "twelve" from before "thrones" (cf. Matt 19:28). This is better seen as a simple economy of language than as concerned to avoid the idea that Judas will have a throne (Luke will consider that a throne is designated for Judas, or rather for the slot that Judas occupies, which will be later filled by Matthias [Acts 1:15–26]). The mention of "thrones" follows nicely from the bestowal of royal rule, but κρίνοντες, "judging," is less expected. What does Luke have in mind here? And do we need to reckon here with the possibility that the Lukan sense and that of the earlier tradition run in different directions? The verb κρίνειν is capable of a wide range of meanings, all having to do in some way with the exercise of discrimination. Very often it has judicial overtones, and sometimes the implication is that the judgment to be made is one of condemnation. At times the meaning even becomes "to execute the sentence of judgment upon" (this is more common in the case of the cognate noun). In another direction, the meaning may reach "to govern" (this seems likely in 4 Kgdms 15:5; Ps 2:10, where it is based on the broader sense of the Hebrew שׁפט, *špṭ*; it is possible in Wis 3:8 and has been claimed for 1 Macc 9:73; *Pss. Sol.* 17:26, 29). In Matthew it seems clear enough that the Twelve are to function as "assessors for the sovereign Judge" (Dupont, *Bib* 45 [1964] 378), and this is likely to be close to the original sense of the tradition. In Luke, however, a wider sense, though certainly not without a judicial component, seems to be altogether more likely, since in this case the activity takes place as part of "royal rule." We may want to think in terms of the judicial function of OT kings (e.g., 2 Sam 15:1–6; 1 Kgs 3:16–28) or of the broad sense of judging associated with the judges raised up by God (e.g., Judg 3:9, 15; 6:11–18).

That the activity of judging here, for the Twelve, is directed toward the twelve tribes of Israel is to be understood in close connection with Jesus having made them collaborators with himself in the proclamation of the good news (cf. Dupont, *Bib* 45 [1964] 388). The number of the Apostles already signified the claim upon all Israel of the message Jesus had come to proclaim. The singling out of Israel here is in no sense anti-Jewish: it is only a particular expression of the central place of Israel in the purposes of God (cf. Isa 5:1–6; Amos 3:2; etc.).

Explanation

Discussion about the identity of the betrayer moves on to a contention over which of them was the greatest. To this, Jesus responds with his challenge to the great to behave like table servants. Despite the outbreak here of the desire to seem great, Jesus takes the larger view and, commending the Twelve for sticking with him through the "humiliation" of his own trials, promises them a share in his coming royal rule.

The Twelve show here their interest in appearing great in the eyes of others. As in 9:46, concern for greatness follows incongruously from disclosure of betrayal. Jesus' intervention makes no attempt to answer the question. It simply challenges the great to particular patterns of behavior.

Jesus clarifies his intent by pointing first to the way that gentile rulers make their power felt by those over whom they rule, and then to the way that authority figures use generosity to justify their demand for social recognition: they insist on being glorified as public benefactors. Among the Twelve, things are to be quite different. Instead of demanding public honor, the greatest is to behave as though he had the status only of the youngest member of the group (in a culture where age was a status scale); the leader, instead of making his power felt, is to behave as one whose role is to serve the needs of the others.

There is a clear call for reversal here, as v 27 recognizes with its appeal to table imagery: the one reclining at table to be served the meal is self-evidently greater than the one who is his table servant. But Jesus identifies the practice of his ministry as that of being like a table servant. So soon after vv 19–20 we cannot avoid calling to mind here that the extent of Jesus' self-giving service reached to the point of giving up his life for his own. Here is a great one who does not take advantage of his greatness for himself and who thereby confuses the categories by which we are humanly accustomed to measure significance.

Jesus' teaching in vv 25–27 has implicitly been critical of the Apostolic band. But those same men who are caught up in a petty rivalry over stature are the men who have stood by Jesus, not only in his popularity and achievements but also in those buffetings that could have placed in question the path of humility upon which he believed himself called to walk (in 4:1–13 Jesus experienced as Satanic temptation—the same Greek word as used for "trial" here—the attractions offered by a more self-promoting manner of carrying out his ministry). In that sense they have already come with Jesus as he acted the part of the table servant.

The Lukan Jesus does not see the table-servant pattern as the whole story. His own destined path was one of humble service that would take him to death. But death itself would be a gateway to exalted glory (see 24:26). The pattern here is that the great bend low ultimately to be raised by God to even greater heights.

Jesus knows himself to be in line for royal rule (see the parable in 19:11–28). He promises to those who have shared his lowly path a share as well in that future royal rule. The end-time future is pictured as a never-ending banquet, at table with Jesus in his kingdom. It is in connection with being meal companions of Jesus, and not at all as free agents, that the Twelve get to sit upon royal thrones and are given a part in exercising judgment in connection with Israel.

The scope of the judging activity of the Twelve is said to be the twelve tribes of Israel. This fits with Jesus' symbolism in choosing Twelve in the first place, which signified the claim upon all Israel of the message he came to proclaim and in whose proclamation he made the Twelve collaborators. When a worldwide perspective for the gospel emerges, this becomes, in Paul, "Do you not know that the saints will judge the world?" Such promises are designed to strengthen the hand of disciples who need encouragement along the path of lowly service; for they will find themselves at the mercy of those who show no respect for the divinely ordained nature of this following in the footsteps of a Christ who went to his glory through suffering. The lower disciples are called upon to stoop, the higher they can be expected to be raised in the future kingdom of God.

Satanic Sifting and Denial of Jesus   (22:31–34)

Bibliography

Argyle, A. W. "Luke xxii. 31f." *ExpTim* 64 (1952–53) 222. **Botha, F. J.** "'Umâs in Luke xxii. 31." *ExpTim* 64 (1952–53) 125. **Brown, R. E.** et al., eds. *Peter in the New Testament: A Collaborative*

Assessment by Protestant and Roman Catholic Scholars. Minneapolis, MN/New York: Augsburg/ Paulist, 1973. 119–25. **Brunel, G.** "Et aussitôt le coq chanta." *CCER* 108 (1979) 9–12. **Claudel, G.** *La confession de Pierre: Trajectoire d'une péricope évangelique.* Paris: Gabalda, 1988. 409–32. **Cullmann, O.** "L'Apôtre Pierre instrument du diable et instrument de Dieu: La place de Matt. 16:16–19 dans la tradition primitive." In *New Testament Studies.* FS T. W. Manson, ed. A. J. B. Higgins. Manchester: University Press, 1959. 94–105. **Dietrich, W.** *Das Petrusbild der lukanischen Schriften.* BWANT 94. Stuttgart: Kohlhammer, 1972. 116–39, 154–57. **Dreyfus, P.** "La primauté de Pierre à la lumière de la théologie biblique du reste d'Israël." *Istinia* 2 (1955) 338–46, esp. 342–44. **Feldkämper, L.** *Der betende Jesus als Heilsmittler nach Lukas.* Veröffentlichungen des Missionspriesterseminars 29. St. Augustin bei Bonn: Steyler, 1978. 206–23. **Foerster, W.** "Lukas 22,31f." *ZNW* 46 (1955) 129–33. **Fridrichsen, A.** "Scholia in Novum Testamentum: 1. Luk. 22:31." *SEÅ* 12 (1947) 124–31. **Gundry, R. H.** "The Narrative Framework of Mt 16,17–19: A Critique of Cullmann's Hypothesis." *NovT* 7 (1964–65) 1–9. **Klein, G.** "Die Verleugnung des Petrus: Eine traditionsgeschichtliche Untersuchung." *ZTK* 58 (1961) 285–328; reprinted with supplement in *Rekonstruktion und Interpretation: Gesammelte Aufsätze zum Neuen Testament.* BEvT 50. Munich: Kaiser, 1969. 49–98. ———. "Die Berufung des Petrus." *ZNW* 58 (1967) 1–44, esp. 39–44; reprinted with supplement in *Rekonstruktion und Interpretation: Gesammelte Aufsätze zum Neuen Testament.* BEvT 50. Munich: Kaiser, 1969. 11–48. **Lattey, C.** "A Note on Cockcrow." *Scr* 6 (1953) 53–55. **Lee, R. E.** "Luke xxii. 32." *ExpTim* 38 (1926–27) 233–34. **Lehmann, M.** *Synoptische Quellenanalyse.* 103–6. **Linnemann, E.** *Studien.* 70–108. ———. "Die Verleugnung des Petrus." *ZTK* 63 (1966) 1–32. **Ott, W.** *Gebet und Heil.* 75–81. **Refoulé, F.** "Primauté de Pierre dans les évangiles." *RSR* 38 (1964) 1–41, esp. 21–25. **Schneider, G.** "'Stärke deine Bruder!' (Lc 22,32): Die Aufgabe des Petrus nach Lukas." *Catholica* 30 (1976) 200–206. **Schürmann, H.** *Quellenkritische Untersuchung.* 3:21–35, 99–116. ———. "Der Abendmahlsbericht Lk 22,7–38 als Gottesdienstordnung, Gemeindeordnung, Lebensordnung." In *Ursprung und Gestalt.* 108–51, esp. 128–31, 143–45. **Sutcliffe, E. F.** "'Et tu aliquando conversus,' St. Luke 22,32." *CBQ* 15 (1953) 305–10. **Thompson, J.** "The Odyssey of a Disciple (Luke 22,31–34)." *RestQ* 23 (1980) 77–81. **Thompson, P.** "Epistrephō (Luke xxii. 32)." *ExpTim* 38 (1926–27) 468. **Tobin, W. J.** "The Petrine Primacy: Evidence of the Gospels." *LVit* 23 (1968) 27–70. **Walter, N.** "Die Verleugnung des Petrus." *TVers* 8 (1977) 45–61, esp. 50–53. **Wickert, U.** "Und wenn du dermaleinst dich bekehrst, so stärke deine Brüder." *Catholica* 30 (1976) 269–94. **Wilcox, M.** "The Denial Sequence in Mark xiv. 26–31, 66–72." *NTS* 17 (1970–71) 426–36.

And see at 22:1–2.

Translation

31a *"Simon, Simon! Look out! Satan has asked for you all,*[b] *to sift you like wheat.* 32 *But I have prayed for you that your faith might not give out. You, for your part, when you have turned back, strengthen your brothers."* 33 *Peter*[c] *said to him, "Lord, I am ready to go with you to prison and to death." But Jesus*[d] *said, "I tell you, Peter, a cock will not crow this day before you have denied three times that you know me."*

Notes

[a] ℵ A D W Θ Ψ etc. mark a fresh beginning here with εἶπεν δὲ ὁ κύριος, "The Lord said." This could be original.

[b] "All" is added here to indicate that "you" is pl. (it is sing. in v 32).

[c] Gr. ὁ δέ, "he."

[d] Gr. ὁ δέ, "he."

Form/Structure/Setting

Those who have stuck with Jesus through his trials have been promised future exaltation, but there stands before them a difficult time of Satanic sifting, to which Jesus addresses his attention here. The Petrine denial anticipated here is reported in 22:54–62.

The materials of 22:31–32 have no parallel in Mark or Matthew. Luke uses these verses rather than the material in Mark 14:27 to anticipate the coming time of crisis for the disciple band. There is broad scholarly agreement that Luke is not creating freely here but drawing on a distinctive source (or sources). What has proved more difficult, given the considerable level of apparent Lukan intrusion, is to find agreement about the scope of the original tradition. Some have argued for a fusion here of a tradition underlying v 31 (with plural ὑμᾶς, "you") with a separate tradition behind v 32 (with singular συ, "you," and perhaps including "Simon, Simon" from v 31), but this seems to leave v 32 without adequate motivation. Most identify ποτὲ ἐπιστρέψας, "when you have turned back," as a Lukan expansion, introducing an explicit anticipation of the Petrine denials to come. This may indeed be correct, but if the final clause of v 32 reflects tradition (see below), then something is needed at this point to move the time frame on, either into the period of sifting, or beyond. It is actually the preceding ἵνα clause, "that your faith may not give out," that can be more confidently identified as both Lukan in its present form and as not needed for the basic structural logic of the traditional piece Luke has used. This clause may be Luke's own elucidation of the prayer of Jesus. Finally, it is hard to conceive of a form of the tradition that singled Peter out for special prayer but contained no rationale for that in terms of a special role for him. It seems best to conclude then that, while a considerable part of the language and some part of the thought here are likely to be distinctly Lukan, the tradition Luke used already had something in the place occupied by each of the phrases and clauses that mark the unfolding thought sequence of vv 31–32, with the sole exception of the clause that elucidates the content of Jesus' prayer for Peter.

It is doubtful whether we should find here a tradition that would exclude any place for Peter's denial of Jesus (as Bultmann, *History,* 267; and argued at length by Klein, *Rekonstruktion und Interpretation,* 49–98). Not that Linnemann's alternative is convincing (*Studien,* 70–108), when she locates the origin of the tradition in an early church prophecy anticipating a coming time of trial (one could do a little better by taking the alleged prophecy as commenting on a *present* time of trial; then nothing would be needed in the "when you have turned back" slot). Dietrich seeks to save the day here with his claim (*Petrusbild,* 130–33) that the use of ἐκλείπειν, "give out," rather than, say, παύεσθαι, "cease," encourages us to think already in terms of the prospect of a progressive weakening of faith, causing Jesus to pray that the process may not reach a terminus in which no faith remains. This would mean that it is not only ποτὲ ἐπιστρέψας, "when you have turned back," that allows a place for Peter to have experienced difficulty with faith. Dietrich may indeed be right, but since the clause using ἐκλείπειν, "give out," is likely to be a Lukan addition, this is finally of no help. It is actually the probable absence of this clause from the original tradition that destroys the cogency of Klein's position.

Given the difficulty of determining how great Luke's contribution to the sense (as distinct from the wording) of Luke 22:31–32 is, we can only speak quite generally of the thrust of the prior tradition. It does, however, seem reasonable to maintain that Luke's tradition here anticipated, with the imagery of sifting, a time of Satanic trial for Jesus' disciple band, which would be of limited duration. The expectation is that the disciples would by and large make their way successfully through this time, though they would not be unscathed by the experience. Peter's path through the time of difficulty would be helped by the prayer of Jesus, so that he would come out the other side of the experience with inner resources that could be of particular help to others who had been more traumatized by the experience. (Alternatively, and perhaps better, Peter may have been called upon to strengthen the others during the period of trial, so that he, with the help of Jesus' prayer, and they, with his help, will make their way successfully, though not necessarily without difficulty, through this time of trial.)

Schürmann is likely to be right ("Abendmahlsbericht," 130–31) to suggest that the material here was transmitted in the early church in connection with its challenge to church leaders: sustained by the Lord in the midst of trials, they are to lend strength to their fellow Christians.

In connection with the historical Jesus, some have had difficulty with Jesus' confidence here in the power of his prayer, but this seems to me to involve unwarranted caution, given Jesus' confidence of his authority in other respects. Others have difficulty with any kind of prophetic precision, but there is little precision here: one might even suspect that the disciples were much less caught up in the crisis that involved Jesus' death than he here anticipates. Yet others insist on reserving Petrine priority for the post-Easter situation. This is perhaps a more significant cause for reservation, but the Petrine post-resurrection priority is finally best understood as built upon an existing pre-resurrection prominence in the disciple band. Admittedly the textual base for having the historical Jesus reinforce this prominence is very limited, but we might not reasonably have expected more, since only the horizon of Jesus' departure brings to the fore the issue of leadership in the disciple band.

The shared motif of Luke 22:31–32 and Matt 16:18–19, of some kind of primacy for Peter (Refoulé [*RSR* 38 (1964) 22] and others exaggerate the degree of structural parallelism), provides no adequate basis for making a source link between these materials or claiming that they necessarily belong together historically (against Cullmann, "L'Apôtre Pierre"; etc.; but there is much to be said for Cullmann's desire to relocate the material of Matt 16:18–19 to the end of the ministry of Jesus). The passion setting provided by Luke for the tradition is apt, given what appears to be the background assumption that Jesus will no longer be present with the disciples. The passion setting also fits well the sense of impending crisis conveyed by the imagery of sifting.

The materials in Luke 22:33–34 are mostly taken to be a rewriting of Mark 14:29–31. There are, however, just enough coincidences with John 13:37–38 to raise the question of a second source here as well (apart from the content links, there is also the agreement in locating the material at the meal rather than on the Mount of Olives). This material cannot have been transmitted apart from a knowledge of the denial story, but that is not quite the same thing as insisting that it needs to have been linked to it in a connected narrative. (The denial story, however, would be quite a different account without the cockcrow, which in turn probably requires that an account of Jesus' prediction was linked with it from the beginning. (See further at 22:54b–62.) A version of Peter's protestation and Jesus' prediction could have been transmitted independently in the early church in connection with its usefulness as a "cautionary tale."

Comment

Jesus warns of an imminent time of Satanic sifting. Through his prayer for Peter, and through the strengthening role for which it prepares him, the disciple band will, however, make their way beyond the damaging reversals of that period and on into a new place of stability. Nevertheless, despite all his protestations of loyalty to death, even Peter stands on the threshold of shameful acts of denial.

31 None of the language here is notably Lukan. "Simon" is likely to be traditional, since its presence breaks Luke's pattern of using "Simon" before the calling in 6:14 and "Peter" after (the pattern is also broken at 24:34). In the whole Gospel Jesus addresses Simon Peter by name only here (as Simon [repeated]) and in v 34 (as Peter). For the passion period as a time of particular Satanic attack, cf. at v 3. While Simon is addressed, it is clear that Satan has the whole band of disciples in view. "Asked for you all" makes best sense in connection with the kind of image of Satan that is found in Job 1–2: Satan needs God's permission to bring the kind of difficulties upon people that, he (Satan) hopes, will reveal their lack of integrity in their devotion to God. As in Job, God is understood to have given his permission for the trial. The imagery of sieving is used of this trial: the Satanic attack will sort between the wheat and the rubbish (since a double sieving process was used, it is uncertain whether the grain should be pictured as retained by the sieve or as let through). The sifting image may be dependent upon Amos 9:9.

32 Unlike v 31, the language here is quite Lukan (cf. Schürmann, *Quellenkritische Untersuchung,* 3:105–12). Over against Satan's malevolent purpose is set the intervention of Jesus. Jesus addresses himself in two stages to the testing situation to confront all: prayer for Peter, and a directive for Peter to give aid in turn to the others (note the correlation of ἐγὼ δέ, "I," and καὶ σύ, "you, for your part"). The content of Jesus' prayer is that Peter's faith should not be drained away to nothing by the Satanic onslaught (the verb ἐκλείπειν, "to give out/fail," is used of the running out of money in 16:9). The spelling out here is likely to be a Lukan development (the difficulty that Schürmann [*Quellenkritische Untersuchung,* 3:106] and Jeremias [*Sprache,* 58] have with Luke using a non-final ἵνα is unreasonable in light of 21:36 [with the same verb]). The survival of Peter's faith can be contrasted with the unhappy outcome of a time of trial, which is envisaged in 8:13. Presumably, in Luke's understanding, preservation of a residual faith makes possible Peter's return after his denial of Jesus (the presence of ποτέ, "at some time or other," makes it unlikely that ἐπιστρέψας should be taken either as a Semitism to be translated "again" [so: "strengthen your brothers again" (cf. 3 Kgdms 19:6; Neh 9:28; etc.)] or as a transitive use of the verb [so: "convert and strengthen your brothers"]). We are not to understand that the others have suffered a total failure of faith but only that they are likely not to have fared as well as Peter and that they need help and encouragement after the trauma.

"Strengthen your brothers" uses language that has its natural home in the account Luke gives in Acts of the life of the early church (for "brothers," cf. Acts 1:15; 9:30; 15:23; etc.; for "strengthen," cf. 18:23 [but also Luke 9:51; 16:26 for this verb]). Luke probably has no very precise idea about how Peter actually fulfilled this role, beyond its general accord with his sense of the central place of Peter in the disciple band.

33 The language here is certainly not borrowed from Mark (cf. Mark 14:29, 31), but neither is it strikingly Lukan; Lukan language is likely for "Lord" (cf. at 5:12) and possible for "to go to prison and to death" (cf. Schürmann, *Quellenkritische Untersuchung*, 3:31). There is probably a deliberate echo in Acts 21:13, which suggests that though Peter's protestation proves false in the immediate context, Luke considered it valid in connection with the post-Easter Peter. Peter is imprisoned in Acts 5:18; 12:3. His death is not reported. For the sentiment here, cf. Mark 10:38–39; and esp. John 13:37. In the present Lukan sequence, v 33 is motivated either by the announcement of Jesus' prayer or by the clear implication that Peter will fail (and thus need to turn back). This is slightly artificial. In earlier independent transmission of the pericope, the motivation would be the more general sense of threat that characterized the passion period.

34 The language here is much closer to Mark 14:30, and some influence from the Markan source is likely. But the absence of "this very night" and of "twice" and the move from an infinitive construction to the use of a future negative construction for "crow," followed by $\xi\omega\varsigma$, "until," provide suggestive links with John 13:38. Luke will have contributed the vocative "Peter" (to balance the use of Simon in v 31; cf. Claudel, *Pierre*, 423 and n. 203) and the final $\epsilon l\delta\epsilon\nu a l$, "to know" (probably to weaken the correspondence with Luke 12:9 [cf. the Lukan addition in v 32 about Peter's faith not giving out]). According to *m. Bab. Qam.* 7:7, it was forbidden to raise chickens in Jerusalem because of the holy things, but this is likely to be later idealization. Though the first light normally sets the cocks crowing, one might have heard the first cock crow at any time from 2:30 A.M. onward.

Explanation

Despite the promise of future exaltation, a difficult time of Satanic sifting stands before the Apostolic band. Jesus makes provision for this through his prayer for Peter, and through the strengthening role that he prescribes for Peter. In this way, the disciple band will successfully make their way beyond the damaging reversals of that period and on into a new place of stability. Nevertheless, despite his protestations of being ready for anything, even Peter stands on the threshold of shameful acts of denial.

Satan's asking for the Apostles is rather like what happens with Job in Job 1–2. Satan hopes to bring them to destruction by showing their lack of integrity in their devotion to God. The trial by ordeal that he plans is pictured with the imagery of a sieve, probably one that holds back the rubbish and lets through the wheat.

As in Job, Satan is allowed to have his way within the constraints that God imposes. Jesus strengthens Peter's hand in the situation by praying for him and gives him in turn the task of strengthening the others. Peter is not kept from stumbling by Jesus' prayer, but he is kept from having his faith quite disappear.

Peter is able, therefore, to bounce back from his failure. Though Luke does not provide material on how the other Apostles fared, we are probably to understand that they fared no better than Peter, and perhaps worse. Nevertheless, Satan's intentions for them too are thwarted: after Peter had bounced back from his own failure, he was able to help the others.

No doubt Luke believed that there were patterns here with a relevance for Christians in the early church when they were coping with their own periods of intense trial. He uses for Peter's task language that he will later use in Acts in connection with life in the early church.

Peter reacts by protesting his loyalty unto death. In the longer term, this will be true of Peter, but for now the words prove empty. Before the dawn has come, Peter will have insisted, in a threefold denial, that he does not so much as know Jesus. The shock of the coming denial is somewhat softened for us by Jesus' prediction. There is a cautionary tale here for others as well.

New Rules for a Time of Crisis   (22:35–38)

Bibliography

Bartsch, H.-W. "Jesu Schwertwort, Lukas xxii.35–38: Überlieferungsgeschichtliche Studie." *NTS* 20 (1973–74) 190–203. ———. "The Sword Word of Jesus (Luke 22:35–38)." *BLT* 19 (1974) 149–56. **Cullmann, O.** *Jesus and the Revolutionaries.* New York: Harper and Row, 1970. 47–50. **Derrett, J. D. M.** "History and the Two Swords." In *Studies in the New Testament.* Leiden: Brill, 1982. 3:200–214. **Finlayson, S. K.** "The Enigma of the Swords." *ExpTim* 50 (1938–39) 563. **Gillman, J.** "A Temptation to Violence: The Two Swords in Lk 22:35–38." *LS* 9 (1982) 142–53. **Hahn, F.** *Titles.* 153–55. **Hall, S. G.** "Swords of Offence." *SE* 1 [= TU 73] (1959) 499–502. **Hobhouse, S.** "'And He that Hath No Sword, Let Him . . . Buy One' (Luke xxii.35–38)." *ExpTim* 30 (1918–19) 278–80. **Jones, D. L.** "The Title *Pais* in Luke-Acts." In *SBL Seminar Papers 1982*, ed. K. H. Richards. Chico, CA: Scholars, 1982. 217–26. **Lampe, G. W. H.** "The Two Swords." In *Jesus and the Politics of His Day*, ed. E. Bammel and C. F. D. Moule. Cambridge: University Press, 1984. 335–52. **Larkin, W. J.** "Luke's Use of the Old Testament as Key to His Soteriology." *JETS* 20 (1977) 325–35. **Lecler, J.** "L'Argument des deux glaives (Luc xxii,38)." *RSR* 21 (1931) 299–339; 22 (1932) 151–77, 280–303. **Lehmann, M.** *Synoptische Quellenanalyse.* 148–52. **McDowell, E. A.** "Exegetical Notes." *RevExp* 38 (1941) 44–48. **Minear, P. S.** "A Note on Luke xxii 36." *NovT* 7 (1964–65) 128–34. **Napier, T. M.** "The Enigma of the Swords." *ExpTim* 49 (1937–38) 467–70. ———. "'The Enigma of the Two Swords' (Luke xxii. 35–38)." *ExpTim* 51 (1939–40) 204. **Reinach, S.** "Les deux épées." *RevArch* 4/19 (1912) 435. ———. "Encore les deux épées." *RevArch* 5/10 (1919) 370–71. **Schlatter, A.** *Die beiden Schwerter: Lukas 22,35–38: Ein Stück aus der besonderen Quelle des Lukas.* BFCT 20/6. Gütersloh: Bertelsmann, 1916. **Schürmann, H.** "Der Abendmahlsbericht Lk 22,7–38 als Gottesdienstordnung, Gemeindeordnung, Lebensordnung." In *Ursprung und Gestalt.* 108–50, esp. 131–36. ———. *Quellenkritische Untersuchung.* 3:116–39. **Schwarz, G.** "κυριε ιδου μαχαιραι ωδε δυο." *BibNot* 8 (1979) 22. **Western, W.** "The Enigma of the Swords." *ExpTim* 50 (1938–39) 377. ———. "The Enigma of the Swords, St. Luke xxii, 38." *ExpTim* 52 (1940–41) 357. **Wright, R. F.** "Studies in Texts." *Th* 44 (1942) 296–300.

And see at 22:1–2.

Translation

[35] *He said to them, "When I sent you without purse, or bag, or sandals, did you lack anything?" They said, "Nothing!"* [36] *He said to them, "But now let the one who has a purse take it, and the same with a bag. And the one who does not have [a sword], let him sell his cloak and buy one.*[a] [37] *For I tell you that there must be fulfilled in me this that stands written: 'And he was counted with lawless people.' For what concerns me is coming to an end."* [38] *They said, "Lord, look! Here are two swords." He said, "Enough of that!"*

Notes

[a] Gr. μάχαιραν, "sword," which has been used earlier in the translation (see *Comment*).

Form/Structure/Setting

The meal scene in the upstairs room comes to an end with the present anticipation of the time of crisis that is to engulf not only Jesus but also his closest followers.

Luke 22:35–38 is not paralleled in the other Gospels and has been variously judged as coming from his distinctive source material, as being based on fragments of tradition, or as being simply a Lukan creation. Source judgments are tied up in turn with the varying senses that have been given to the pericope, both in its Lukan frame and as an independent piece of tradition. Based on the discussion below, it seems best to attribute to Luke (beyond language touches) only the introduction of the OT quotation. While v 38 is likely to be pre-Lukan, there is a real possibility that it formed no original part of the episode. Instead, it may have been added at some point to make it clear that the disciples prior to the passion had found it impossible to engage seriously with Jesus' anticipation of the passion and the prospect that they might be profoundly caught up in the associated turmoil. The basic material here will have been transmitted partly as a passion prediction of a different kind and partly as teaching relevant to the Christian mission in times of particular crisis (to be set in a dialectical tension with the teaching of Luke 10:4).

Comment

In the time of Satanic sifting about to begin, the comfortable optimism of Luke 10:4 about God's provision for his messengers will no longer be applicable. The cycle of Jesus' ministry is reaching its end, with all that implies about meeting his end in the form of a violent, criminal's death. The Apostles ought not to think that they will be spared some passing through the fire.

35 Of the language, only the use of οὐθείς for "anything" (actually the negative, since Greek negatives do not cancel) and possibly ἄτερ, "without," look Lukan. The terms used here actually echo 10:4 (the sending of the Seventy) rather than the sending out of the Twelve in 9:1–6. This is either Lukan carelessness, or it reflects dependence on a source in which this language had been associated with the sending out of the Twelve (see source discussion at 10:1–16). Though the missioning disciples had by no means found universal acceptance, there had not been lacking those who would give them welcome and provide for their needs.

36　None of the language here is significantly Lukan. Despite the parallelism of form, it is unlikely that we should treat in parallel ὁ ἔχων (lit. "the one having") and ὁ μὴ ἔχων (lit. "the one not having"). Rather we should reach to the end of the sentence for the understood object of μὴ ἔχων, to get the sense "the one not having one (i.e., a sword)." What is this new situation that has arisen, and does it render the earlier mission instructions permanently out of date? It seems hardly likely that these would have received such emphasis in Luke's account, if he saw them as relevant only to two brief rounds of mission endeavor. They also have such links with other of Jesus' teaching about trust in God that it seems unlikely that total abrogation is intended. (The same may be said for the contrast between the role for the sword commended here and Jesus' commendation elsewhere of nonviolence.)

The immediate Lukan frame for this new instruction is surely the sifting by Satan that has been announced in v 35. As with Job, this involved the temporary removal of the accustomed experience of God's care and protection. It is unlikely that the Lukan Jesus expected any literal implementation of the new directive that he offers here. It is rather a symbolic depiction that difficulties of a kind not hitherto experienced were to be the lot of the disciple band in this period of Satanic trial. No doubt Luke believed there would be other periods of Satanic trial in the early church, beyond that associated with the passion of Jesus. And Jesus' words would have a pertinence to these as well. Indeed they would have a pertinence to mission practice in those times. But such trial is episodic, rather than continual. So the earlier mission charges should be understood as still of relevance. Outside the Lukan frame, less certainty is possible, but any tradition here clearly assumes a passion setting and is best taken in something like the Lukan manner.

The directive to buy a sword deserves a measure of separate consideration. Lined up as it is with purse, bag, and sandals, we can eliminate at once any idea that zealot sympathies are coming to expression with the commendation of the sword. The sword is thought of as part of the equipment required for the self-sufficiency of any traveller in the Roman world. Nothing more than protection of one's person is in view. Similarly there can be no thought that the swords might be used to make a defense of Jesus (as Gillmann, *LS* 9 [1982] 142–53) or might be for use in an anticipated eschatological armed struggle (as Bartsch, *NTS* 20 [1973–74] 190–203).

37　The extent of Lukan language becomes rather more notable here (τοῦτο τὸ γεγραμμένον, "this that stands written," and δεῖ τελεσθῆναι ἐν ἐμοί, "must be fulfilled in me," are almost certainly Lukan; τὸ περὶ ἐμοῦ, "what concerns me," may be Lukan, but Luke uses the phrase elsewhere in the plural [τά rather than τό]). The language of necessity of 9:22; etc. is now combined with the fulfillment of Scripture language of 18:31 (cf. there). The introduction of the quotation with τό (lit. "the") may be a Lukan touch: in Luke it only occurs here to introduce a quotation, but Luke is fond of introducing indirect speech (and esp. questions) in this way.

The citation from Isa 53:12 is strikingly brief. It differs from the Septuagint in having μετά, "with" (corresponding more closely with the MT את, 'ṯ, but Qumran MSS read ל, l, so μετά may simply reflect yet another reading current in the early church), in place of ἐν τοῖς (lit. "in the"). Despite the elaborate attempts that have been made to show that the disciples (with their swords) fulfill the part of the "lawless people," or that this role falls to the two thieves, it seems best to take the quotation as concerned only to evoke more generally the prospect of the violent fate anticipated for the figure in Isa 52–53. The level of Lukan language and the fact that in the Gospel tradition this is the only place where Jesus quotes, rather than alludes to, Isa 53 makes it hard to resist the suggestion that Luke is responsible for the material here: he has probably drawn on the early church's growing use of Isa 53, in order to cast light (cf. Lampe, "Two Swords," 340–41) on the rather cryptic "what concerns me is coming to an end" to follow (for the translation of τέλος ἔχει as "is coming to an end," cf. Mark 3:26). The use of τέλος, "end," here should, at least in the Lukan frame, be related to that of τελειοῦμαι, "I am finished," in 13:32. But in the immediate context it is the prospect of Jesus' death that comes to the fore. (It fits the context less well to take τέλος narrowly as "goal"; to link τέλος with the cognate τελεσθῆναι, "fulfilled," and to translate "fulfillment," while initially attractive, makes the text repetitive and does less than justice to the γάρ, "for.") "The reason why the disciples must be ready for the worst is that their Master also faces the worst" (Marshall, 825).

38 οἱ δὲ εἶπαν, "they said," κύριε, "Lord," and ἰδού, "look," ἱκανόν (lit. "sufficient") could all be Lukan, and the question must be raised whether Luke has provided this verse as a bridge to vv 49–51. Against this possibility, however, must be set the unlikelihood of Luke, against his clear tendency, actually creating material here that is critical of the disciples, and also the fact that Luke's intrusion into v 37 (see above) obscures rather than enhances the thought flow on into v 38. The wording of v 36 has assumed that some will already have swords. Here that assumption is seen to have been true. The concern has, however, never really been with the acquiring of swords (or purses or knapsacks), but with the need for the disciples to cope with hitherto unexperienced and therefore yet unexpected difficulty. The Apostles seem to settle for the detail (having swords) without any real readiness to grapple with what the call to have swords means for them. Jesus' reply ἱκανόν ἐστιν (lit. "it is enough") probably means that, because of the obtuseness of the disciples, he has had enough of this conversation. (It would be just possible to take the answer as transitional to the departure in v 39 and relate it to the whole body of "table-talk" that Luke has brought together in the Last Supper setting: "we have talked enough; it is now time to go.") Another suggestion relates to seeing the disciples as fulfilling the role of the "lawless people" ("two swords with us will make us look like brigands"). Several other less likely suggestions have also been offered.)

Explanation

The leave-taking conversation at the Passover meal comes to an end with a warning that the crisis that is about to engulf Jesus will bring hard times for the Apostolic band as well. In the time of Satanic sifting about to begin, the confident assurance about God's provision for his messengers mirrored in Luke 10:4 will no longer be applicable in the same way.

The messengers of the kingdom had experienced God's amazing provision when they had been sent out without resources. But now they must confront a new situation. Now they are told they must take purse and bag, and if they do not have swords already, they should sell their cloaks to buy them. They had known before that they were being sent out as vulnerable sheep in the midst of ferocious wolves (Luke 10:3). But defenseless and resourceless though they were, in the providence of God they found themselves to be in perfect safety and fully provided for. Now, however, they could no longer take for granted such a privileged passage. To take up ideas from the discussion of vv 31–34, in the coming sifting by Satan it will be rather like it had been for Job, when he found himself cruelly buffeted by life as Satan probed for any weak spot. Where the behavior called for earlier had symbolized God's provision of all else when they focused on the kingdom of God (12:31), now they were to behave as people who should expect to make their way in life with considerable difficulty.

In the first instance, the Lukan Jesus is speaking of the situation for the Apostles during the passion period, so it is unlikely that he expected any literal implementation of the new directive that he offered. But Christian mission takes place between the poles of providential provision and protection and Satanic sifting. And so both the challenge of Luke 10:4 and the warning of 22:36 are pertinent to the mission practice of the Christian church. For the same juxtaposition of apparently contradictory views, compare 21:16–19 and the discussion there.

The difficulties to confront the Apostles are in some way an extension of the difficulties that are about to confront Jesus himself. He is to fulfill in his own person the scriptural image of the rejected servant of God. In particular he is to be labeled a criminal and suffer a criminal's violent fate. The role of Jesus is divinely determined, and he will soon have seen it all through to the end—an end that includes his own violent death. The disciples must be ready for the worst because their Master also faces the worst.

As Jesus prepares the Apostles for the way in which they will be affected as he is engulfed by his coming fate, he has little concern with purses, knapsacks, or swords as such. The Apostles, however, with an obtuseness that we have seen before, seem to settle for the detail (having swords) without any real readiness to grapple with what the call to have swords means to them. So Jesus cuts the conversation off at this point and brings to an end the interchange that has marked the time spent together in this last Passover meal.

Praying to Be Spared Trial   (22:39–46)

Bibliography

Ambruster, C. J. "The Messianic Significance of the Agony in the Garden." *Scr* 16 (1964) 111–19. **Aschermann, H.** "Zum Agoniegebet Jesu, Lc. XXII, 43sq." *ThViat* 5 (1953–54) 143–49. **Baarda, T.** "Luke 22:42–47a: The Emperor Julian as a Witness to the Text of Luke." *NovT* 30 (1988) 289–96. **Barbour, R. S.** "Gethsemane in the Tradition of the Passion." *NTS* 16 (1969–70) 231–51. **Bate, H. N.** "Luke xxii 40." *JTS* 36 (1935) 76–77. **Beck, B.** "Gethsemane in the Four Gospels." *EpR* 15 (1988) 57–65. **Benoit, P.** *The Passion and Resurrection of Jesus.* New York: Herder and Herder, 1969. 1–23. **Bishop, E. F. F.** "A Stone's Throw." *ExpTim* 53 (1941–42) 270–71. **Black, M.** "The Cup Metaphor in Mark xiv. 36." *ExpTim* 59 (1947–48)

195. **Blaising, C. A.** "Gethsemane: A Prayer of Faith." *JETS* 22 (1979) 333–43. **Bobichon, M.** "L'agonie, tentation du Seigneur." *BTS* 99 (1968) 2–5. **Boman, T.** "Der Gebetskampf Jesu." *NTS* 10 (1963–64) 261–73. **Braumann, G.** "Leidenskelch und Todestaufe." *ZNW* 56 (1965) 178–83. **Brongers, H. A.** "Der Zornesbecher." *OTS* 15 (1969) 177–92. **Brown, R. E.** "John and the Synoptic Gospels: A Comparison." In *New Testament Essays*. London: Chapman, 1967(= 1965). 192–213, esp. 192–98. ———. "The Lukan Authorship of Luke 22:43–44." In *SBL 1992 Seminar Papers*, ed. E. H. Lovering, Jr. 154–64. **Brun, L.** "Engel und Blutschweiss Lc 22:43–44." *ZNW* 32 (1933) 265–76. **Cranfield, C. E. B.** "The Cup Metaphor in Mark 14:36 and Parallels." *ExpTim* 59 (1947–48) 137–38. **Cullmann, O.** *Immortality of the Soul or Resurrection of the Dead? The Witness of the New Testament*. London: Epworth, 1958. 21–57. **Daube, D.** "Two Incidents after the Last Supper." In *The New Testament and Rabbinic Judaism*. 330–35, esp. 332–35. ———. "A Prayer Pattern in Judaism." *SE* 1 [= TU 73] (1959) 539–45. **Dibelius, M.** "Gethsemane." *CrQ* 12 (1935) 254–65; reprinted in *Botschaft und Geschichte*, ed. G. Bornkamm. Tübingen: Mohr-Siebeck, 1953. 1:258–71. **Dormeyer, D.** *Passion Jesu*. 124–37. **Duplacy, J.** "La préhistoire du texte en Luc 22:43–44." In *New Testament Textual Criticism: Its Significance for Exegesis*. FS B. M. Metzger, ed. E. J. Epp and G. D. Fee. Oxford: Clarendon, 1981. 77–86. **Ehrman, B.,** and **Plunkett, M.** "The Angel of the Agony: The Textual Problem of Luke 22:43–44." *CBQ* 45 (1983) 401–16. **Eltester, W.** "'Freund, wozu du gekommen bist' (Mt. xxvi 50)." In *Neotestamentica et patristica*. FS O. Cullmann, ed. W. C. van Unnik. NovTSup 6. Leiden: Brill, 1962. 70–91. **Feldkämper, L.** *Der betende Jesus als Heilsmittler nach Lukas*. Veröffentlichungen des Missionspriesterseminars 29. St. Augustin bei Bonn: Steyler, 1978. 224–50. **Feldmeier, R.** *Die Krisis des Gottessohnes: Die Gethsemaneerzählung als Schlüssel des Markuspassion*. WUNT 2/21. Tübingen: Mohr, 1987. **Feuillet, A.** *L'Agonie de Gethsémani: Enquête exégétique et théologique suivie d'une étude du 'Mystère de Jésus' de Pascal*. Paris: Gabalda, 1977. 13–141. ———. "Le récit lucanien de l'agonie de Gethsémani (Lc xxii. 39–46)." *NTS* 22 (1975–76) 397–417. **Fitzmyer, J. A.** "Papyrus Bodmer XIV: Some Features of Our Oldest Text of Luke." *CBQ* 24 (1962) 170–79, esp. 177–79. **Green, J. B.** "Jesus on the Mount of Olives (Luke 22,39–46): Tradition and Theology." *JSNT* 26 (1986) 29–48. **Héring, J.** "Zwei exegetische Probleme in der Perikope von Jesus in Gethsemane (Markus XIV 32–42; Matthäus XXVI 36–46; Lukas XXII 40–46)." In *Neotestamentica et patristica*. FS O. Cullmann, ed. W. C. van Unnik. NovTSup 6. Leiden: Brill, 1962. 64–69. ———. "Simples remarques sur la prière à Gethsémané: Matthieu 26.36–46; Marc 14.32–42; Luc 22.40–46." *RHPR* 39 (1959) 97–102. **Holleran, J. W.** *The Synoptic Gethsemane: A Critical Study*. AnGreg 191. Rome: Gregorian University, 1973. **Indemans, J. H. H. A.** "Das Lukas-Evangelium XXII,45." *SO* 32 (1956) 81–83. **Johnson, S. L., Jr.** "The Agony of Christ." *BSac* 124 (1967) 303–13. **Kelber, W. H.** "The Hour of the Son of Man and the Temptation of the Disciples (Mark 14:32–42)." In *The Passion in Mark: Studies on Mark 14–16*, ed. W. H. Kelber. Philadelphia: Fortress, 1976. 41–60. ———. "Mark 14,32–42: Gethsemane: Passion Christology and Discipleship Failure." *ZNW* 63 (1972) 166–87. **Kenny, A.** "The Transfiguration and the Agony in the Garden." *CBQ* 19 (1957) 444–52. **Kiley, M.** "'Lord, Save My Life' (Ps 116:4) as Generative Text for Jesus' Gethsemane Prayer (Mark 14:36a)." *CBQ* 48 (1986) 655–59. **Kuhn, K. G.** "Jesus in Gethsemane." *EvT* 12 (1952–53) 260–85. **Larkin, W. J.** "The Old Testament Background of Luke xxii. 43–44." *NTS* 25 (1978–79) 250–54. **Léon-Dufour, X.** "Jésus face à la mort menaçante." *NRT* 100 (1978) 802–21. ———. "Jésus à Gethsémani: Essai de lecture synchronique." *ScEs* 31 (1979) 251–68. **Lescow, T.** "Jesus in Gethsemane." *EvT* 26 (1966) 141–59. ———. "Jesus in Gethsemane bei Lukas und im Hebräerbrief." *ZNW* 58 (1967) 215–39. **Linnemann, E.** *Studien*. 11–40, 178–79. **Lods, M.** "Climat de bataille à Gethsemane." *ETR* 60 (1985) 425–29. **Lohse, E.** *Suffering and Death*. 55–68. **Mitton, C. L.** "The Will of God: 1. In the Synoptic Tradition of the Words of Jesus." *ExpTim* 72 (1960–61) 68–71. **Moffatt, J.** "Exegetica: Luke xxii. 44." *Exp* 8/7 (1914) 90–92. **Mohn, W.** "Gethsemane (Mk 14,32–42)." *ZNW* 64 (1973) 194–208. **Neyrey, J. H.** "The Absence of Jesus' Emotions: The Lucan Redaction of Lk 22,39–46." *Bib* 61 (1980) 153–71. **Ott, W.** *Gebet und Heil*. 82–90. **Paton, W. R.** "*Agōnia*

(Agony)." *CRev* 27 (1913) 194. **Pelcé, F.** "Jésus à Gethsémani: Remarques comparatives sur les trois récits évangéliques." *FV* 65 (1966) 89–99. **Radl, W.** *Paulus und Jesus.* 159–68. **Robinson, B. P.** "Gethsemane: The Synoptic and the Johannine Viewpoints." *CQR* 167 (1966) 4–11. **Schenk, W.** *Passionsbericht.* 193–206. **Schenke, L.** *Studien zur Passionsgeschichte des Markus.* 461–560. **Schneider, G.** "Engel und Blutschweiss (Lk 22, 43–44): 'Redaktionsgeschichte' im Dienste der Textkritik." *BZ* 20 (1976) 112–16. **Schürmann, H.** "Lk 22,42a das älteste Zeugnis für Lk 22,20?" *MTZ* 3 (1952) 185–88; reprinted in *Traditionsgeschichtliche Untersuchungen.* 193–97. **Schwarz, G.** *Jesus und Judas.* 59–65. **Skard, E.** "Kleine Beiträge zum Corpus hellenisticum NT." *SO* 30 (1953) 100–103. **Smith, H.** "Acts xx. 8 and Luke xxii. 43." *ExpTim* 16 (1904–5) 478. **Söding, T.** "Gebet und Gebetsmahnung Jesu in Getsemani: Eine redaktionskritische Auslegung von Mk 14,32–42." *BZ* 31 (1987) 76–100. **Soards, M. L.** "On Understanding Luke 22.39." *BT* 36 (1985) 336–37. **Stanley, D. M.** *Jesus in Gethsemane: The Early Church Reflects on the Sufferings of Jesus.* Ramsey, NJ: Paulist, 1980. **Strobel, A.** "Die Psalmengrundlage der Gethsemane: Parallel Hbr, V,7ff." *ZNW* 45 (1954) 252–66. **Szarek, G.** "A Critique of Kelber's 'The Hour of the Son of Man and the Temptation of the Disciples.'" In *SBL 1976 Abstracts and Seminar Papers,* ed. G. MacRae. Missoula, MT: Scholars, 1976. 111–18. **Torris, J.** "L'agonie Jésus (Marc 14,32–42): Intention, sources, historicité." *PenHom* 17 (1973) 75–77. **Tostengard, S.** "Luke 22:39–46." *Int* (1980) 283–88. **Trémel, Y.-B.** "L'Agonie de Jésus." *LumVie* 13 (1964) 79–103. **Unnik, W. C. van.** "Alles ist dir möglich (Mk 14,36)." In *Verborum Veritas,* ed. O. Böcher and K. Haacker. 27–36. **Vanhoye, A.** "L'agnoisse du Christ." *Christus* 18 (1971) 382–89.

And see at 22:1–2.

Translation

[39] *Then Jesus went out and made his way, as was [his] custom, to the Mount of Olives; and the disciples too*[a] *followed him.* [40] *Coming to the place, he said to them, "Pray not to enter into [what will be a] trial [to you]."* [41] *Then he withdrew from them about a stone's throw and knelt down and began to pray,*[b] [42] *saying, "Father, if you will, take*[c] *this cup away from me. Yet not my will, but yours be done!"*[d] [45] *When he arose from prayer he came to the disciples and found them sleeping from grief.* [46] *He said to them, "Why are you sleeping? Rise and pray that you may not enter into [what will be a] trial [to you]."*

Notes

[a] Omitted by B 69 983 1342 etc.

[b] Reading the impf.: the aorist is read by $\mathfrak{P}^{75}$ ℵ T 579 892 etc.

[c] An infinitive form (παρενέγκαι or παρενεγκεῖν) is read here by (ℵ) L f^{13} 579 etc.; A W Ψ 1006 etc. The clause would then need to be taken elliptically, and the transition to the following clause becomes difficult.

[d] Vv 43–44 (ὤφθη δὲ αὐτῷ ἄγγελος ἀπ' οὐρανοῦ ἐνισχύων αὐτόν· καὶ γενόμενος ἐν ἀγωνίᾳ ἐκτενέστερον προσηύχετο· καὶ ἐγένετο ὁ ἱδρὼς αὐτοῦ ὡσεὶ θρόμβοι αἵματος καταβαίνοντες ἐπὶ τὴν γῆν, "There appeared to him an angel from heaven, strengthening him. And being in conflict he prayed yet more earnestly; and his perspiration was like drops of blood, falling down upon the ground.") are missing from $\mathfrak{P}^{69\ vid.\ 75}$ ℵ^1 A B T W etc. and are obelisked in other texts. However, the tradition here was certainly known by the time of Justin Martyr (see *Dial.* 103.8). The arguments for and against inclusion are finely balanced. Both addition and removal are explicable in terms of arguments over Christology. Much of the language is quite in line with Lukan use, but at the same time the material has an emotional tone that is otherwise quite absent from the Lukan account of the Gethsemane scene (contrast Mark). The chiasmic structure of the Lukan account (without vv 43–44; see below) counts against the verses, but not absolutely, since Luke appears to have inherited the chiasm and has (slightly) disturbed it in other ways. After an earlier move in critical opinion toward accepting the verses, the more

recent trend has been to question their presence in the original text of Luke. I have excluded them primarily on the basis of the emotional tone of the verses and secondarily on the basis of the chiasm.

Form/Structure/Setting

The coming time of crisis anticipated in vv 35–38 provides the context for Jesus' urging of the disciples to pray that they might be spared great trial and for Jesus' own prayer. But God's own will remains the supremely important consideration.

With the conclusion of the discourse material that he has gathered into his account of the Last Supper, Luke now returns to the Markan sequence (having reported Jesus' anticipation of Peter's denial already in vv 33–34, Luke passes over the material of Mark 14:27–31). Though there is a good level of basic agreement, the Lukan version of this episode is strikingly different from the Markan. Despite detailed discussion, no consensus has emerged as to whether Luke has severely edited his Markan source or is dependent upon another source here (perhaps with some secondary dependence on Mark and certainly with some editing of his own).

Ehrman and Plunkett (*CBQ* 45 [1983] 413; and noted also by M. Galizzi [*Gesù nel Getsemani* (Zurich: Pas, 1972) 137–38] and Stanley [*Jesus*] 206, 213) have drawn attention to the very clearly chiasmic structure of Luke's account (v 39 is introductory; v 40 corresponds to vv 45c–46 [from "and found"]; v 41a [to "stones throw"] corresponds to v 45b ["coming to the disciples"]; v 41b ["and knelt down and prayed"] corresponds to v 45a; v 42 is the centerpiece [I have moved "and prayed" back one place from its position in Ehrman's and Plunkett's version of the chiasm]). Is it possible to determine whether this chiasm is pre-Lukan or a Lukan creation on the basis of Markan material?

There is one place in the structure where the chiasm would be better for staying closer to the Markan material: Mark's "he fell on the ground and prayed" offers a better counterpart to "[he] rose from prayer" in v 45a than does Luke's θεὶς τὰ γόνατα προσηύχετο (lit. "having placed the knees he prayed"). Since θεὶς τὰ γόνατα is clearly Lukan (cf. Acts 7:60; 9:40; 20:36; 21:5), we have here a modest argument in favor of a pre-Lukan chiasm. The same kind of argument may be relevant in connection with Luke's use of ἀπεσπάσθη, "withdrew," in v 41 [cf. Acts 20:30; 21:1], where Mark's προελθών, "went ahead," corresponds better to ἐλθὼν πρός, "came to," in v 45.

There are also a few places where the chiasm would be sharper without either (*i*) Markan language that Luke may have secondarily added into another tradition (so: τί καθεύδετε, "why are you sleeping" [Mark actually has to Simon: "are you asleep?"]; possibly the whole content reported for Jesus' prayer, since it neither aligns Jesus' prayer closely with that which he asks of the disciples nor categorically distinguishes his prayer [but note John 18:11 for evidence of a wider currency for a cup saying]; and another possible minor instance in the use of a ἵνα clause in v 46) or (*ii*) language that has a high likelihood of being Lukan addition or alteration (so: ἀπὸ τῆς λύπης, "from grief" [here Luke is likely to be influenced by the circle of traditions that he shares with John (cf. John 16:6, 20–22), as for "as was his custom" in v 39 (cf. John 18:2)]; and possibly some of the movement between finite verbs and participles).

Though not in large numbers, there are also language features that, while not simply reproduced from Mark, do not represent natural Lukan choice of language (notably the absence of πρός after verbs of saying). (The small number of agreements between Luke and Matthew against Mark, to which Feuillet [*Agonie*, 66–67] makes appeal, does not seem to be sufficient to warrant a source hypothesis.)

Cumulatively these observations make it seem more likely that Luke has a chiastically formed second source here, which he reproduces with minor alterations (except for the possibility that the wording of Jesus' prayer is based on the Markan source). This second source had a developed focus on the need to pray when facing the prospect of severe trial. Luke has preferred this source because of its compactness, coherence, and conformity to his interests.

The Markan parallel here, which has influenced Luke's account in more minor ways (apart from the prayer, if that has been added), has been subject to many attempts at deconstruction. As it stands, it is not a well-unified account (despite the contrary view of Lohmeyer, *Markus*, 313–21; and more recently Feldmeier, *Krisis*, 70–112) and so invites attention to its tradition history. The scholarly discussion has not, however, produced a consensus. The range of opinion is indicated from the following (far from complete) list of views. Kuhn (*EvT* 12 [1952–53] 260–85) has attracted a measure of support for his view that Mark has conflated two Gethsemane stories into one. Linnemann [*Studien*, 11–40, 178–79] defends a three-stage development from a single original source (including vv 32, 35, 37a, 39a, 40ab, 41a, 40c, 41b), with each stage adding a further focus to the developing account. Kelber (*ZNW* 63 [1972] 166–87) has made Mark responsible for everything, except perhaps a tradition of a Gethsemane lament and prayer. More recently Söding (*BZ* 31 [1987] 76–100) has joined the ranks of those who opt for a two-stage development with a substantial pre-Markan source, to which Mark has made considerable additions (Söding's version has vv 32a, 34, 35a, 36–37, 39, 40ab, 41a, 42 as pre-Markan; this is not too different from Schenke's earlier version [*Studien*, 472–540] of the pre-Markan source, which differs in including only part of vv 32a and 41a, in including vv 33b and 38b, and in excluding vv 39 and 40a but is rather more generous than the view of Mohn [*ZNW* 64 (1973) 194–208], who allows only vv 32, 35, 37a, 41b to be pre-Markan). The Lukan source identified above has some modest bearing on the question of Markan sources as well, but the major part of the Markan source question remains beyond the scope of the present work.

The fundamental historicity of the tradition here is supported by the additional, clearly independent, traditions in Heb 5:7 and John 12:27; 18:11. The attempts to generate the fundamental impulse for the account out of reflection on OT lament psalms is not at all convincing (see the arguments of Boman [*NTS* 10 (1963–64) 261–73] against Dibelius [*CrQ* 12 (1935) 254–65]). In particular, what apparently expresses the desire to avoid what Jesus had previously understood to be the distinctive will of God for himself gains high marks in favor of historicity, from application of the criterion of dissimilarity. In fact, it is my impression that scholarship has not to any satisfactory degree come to terms with the difficulty of fitting the cup saying into the Gospel portrayal of Jesus. The difficulty, I would suggest, is such that there may be those who would want to move in exactly the opposite direction and deny historicity on the basis of lack of coherence with what is otherwise known of the historical Jesus.

Comment

While the disciples are challenged to pray that they might be spared the brunt of the troubles to come but cannot rise to the occasion, Jesus wrestles in prayer with a conflict that appears to have opened up between his own will and what he had understood to be his Father's will. He first asks for the removal of the threatening disaster; but then he reaffirms his commitment to God's will as supreme over his own.

39 It is likely that Luke fuses together here part of Mark 14:26 (Mark's "they went out to the Mount of Olives" becomes "going out [singular] . . . to the Mount of Olives"; Luke drops the Markan mention of the singing of the last part of the Hallel) with the introductory piece of his distinctive source ("and his disciples too followed him" would seem to be from this source). The language κατὰ τὸ ἔθος, "as was his custom," is likely to be Lukan (cf. at 1:9) and is to be read in connection with 21:37, but at the same time Luke is reflecting at this point a traditional element (cf. John 18:2). Reflecting a source usage and not his own normal diction, Luke will mean by "disciples" here the Eleven (as with each of the synoptic Gospels, Luke does not report the departure of Judas; that Judas has left the disciple band only becomes evident with his arrival in company with the group who were to arrest Jesus). It is hard to be sure whether we should make anything of the fact that the disciples "followed" Jesus here (cf. at 5:11). Solidarity with Jesus is clearly important in the Markan account, but not so here, despite the measure of parallelism between the prayer of Jesus himself and the prayer to which he calls the disciples.

40 γενόμενος ἐπί, "coming to," may be Lukan (cf. 24:22; Acts 21:35). The use of τοῦ τόπου, "the place," is not fully prepared for by the present form of v 39, which may suggest that Luke has dropped from his source something that may have provided a more adequate antecedent. In line with the understanding of the final clause of the Lord's Prayer proposed at 11:4 (see there), I take the directive here as for prayer that in the coming crisis the disciples may be spared troubles that take them beyond their capacity to cope. Others take εἰσελθεῖν εἰς πειρασμόν as "to succumb to [the power of] temptation." Many leave the issue of the precise sense without comment.

41 The unstressed καὶ αὐτός (lit. "and he") may be Lukan, as are ἀποσπᾶν, "withdraw," and θεὶς τὰ γόνατα, "knelt down" (see *Form/Structure/Setting*). Jesus is to pray and the disciples are to pray, but there is a clear distinction to be made. In Acts, kneeling is identified as the prayer posture only on occasions where the context suggests that there might be a particular intensity to the prayer.

42 The address is πάτερ, "Father," as in Luke 11:2 (see there). If Mark is Luke's source here, he has dropped "Abba" and used the true vocative for "Father" rather than the nominative with article as in Mark. εἰ βούλει, "if you will," may represent a Lukan abbreviation and alteration of Mark 14:35b (the rare Attic form for the second person singular would reflect Luke's literary aspirations; the Markan form has a certain tension between "if it is possible" in v 35b and "all things are possible for you" in v 36). Again, if Mark is the source for the statement about the will of God, Luke has preferred to link with πλήν, "but/only/yet/nevertheless" (as often), and has formulated the clause in a more abstract manner (cf. Acts 21:14; since the wording is so close to that of a clause of the Matthean form of the Lord's Prayer [Matt 6:10], we must also reckon with the possibility that Luke is reflecting the language of his second source here).

It is very difficult to bring together the confidence of Jesus about the nature of the will of God, which is sustained through the Gospel narrative, and the present request for the removal of the cup, if God should will. This difficulty is not much eased by taking εἰ βούλει idiomatically as meaning something like "please" (as, e.g., Fitzmyer, 1436). The words are clearly spoken in relation to a sense of imminent crisis. "This cup" is to be seen in connection with OT language where the drinking of the cup is an image for being overtaken by disaster, a disaster that is understood as flowing from the wrath of God but as at times enveloping the innocent along with the guilty (see Ps 75:9; Isa 51:17, 22; Jer 25:15; 49:12; Lam 4:21; the imagery in Ps 11:6, while still used in connection with the experience of God's judgment, is rather more like a "cup of destiny," which could have positive or negative contents). The "cup" here is not unlike the "baptism" of Luke 12:50. Jesus prays that he might not after all be engulfed by the impending disaster. The text certainly makes it quite clear that Jesus, in setting his face to go to Jerusalem (9:51), was not in any sense motivated by a death wish; it also underlines the enormity of what he was facing.

Whatever we make of the request for the removal of the cup, what stands finally as fundamental for Jesus is the will of God his Father; to this he commits himself. Over against his own will, which has come to expression in the initial request, he sets this more basic commitment.

[43–44   The role of an angel, the use of a striking simile, and a "physical manifestation at [an] extramundane event" (Green, *JSNT* 26 [1986] 36) are all congenial to Luke; ὤφθη δὲ αὐτῷ ἄγγελος, "there appeared to him an angel," appears identically in 1:11 (and cf. Acts 7:30), and the language of vv 43–44 is, while not strikingly Lukan, generally such that Luke could have penned. Nonetheless, as indicated in *Notes* above, I think these verses are a later insertion into the text.

Presumably the angel is strengthening Jesus for the battle in prayer, which is involved in the need to align his own will with that of his Father. The Father's will is clearly not for the cup to be taken away. Jesus' prayer reaches such an intensity as he works this matter through that he drips with perspiration from the exertion and emotional strain.]

45   Jesus returns from prayer to find that the disciples are not at prayer but sleeping. Luke explains and, in part, excuses their sleep, by adding that it was "from grief" (cf. the end of 9:33): the sense of impending tragedy has brought them to emotional exhaustion.

46   The change of verb for "sleep" from v 45 to v 46 may be an indication that Luke is drawing "why are you sleeping?" from his Markan source. Jesus renews his call of v 40 that his disciples should pray that they might not be called to enter into a sphere of such difficulty that it would prove a threatening trial to them.

Explanation

The scene moves from the Upper Room to the Mount of Olives. Against the background of the impending time of crisis that has come into focus in vv 35–38, Jesus' disciples are challenged to pray to be spared the buffeting of the troubles to come. Jesus for his part wrestles in prayer with the question of his own destiny: his desire is that God should withdraw what he (Jesus) has, up to this point, been declaring as necessary in the plan and purpose of God for himself; but what is God's desire? To this Jesus commits himself afresh as paramount.

In line with the pattern identified in 21:37, Jesus and his disciple band now head for the Mount of Olives, to the place where they had in recent days been staying overnight. Though it is not said, Judas must be understood to have slipped off as they made this short journey. On arrival, Jesus challenges the disciples to pray about what will befall them in the coming crisis. In particular, he tells them to pray to be spared trial (much in the manner of the petition in the Lord's Prayer in 11:4 but now in connection with a specific time of anticipated crisis).

Jesus withdraws out of earshot, but not out of sight, and engages in his own prayer struggle. He kneels to pray: in Acts kneeling is identified as the prayer posture only on occasions where the context suggests that a particular intensity of prayer might be appropriate. His prayer begins from his own sense of intimate link to God as Father. A gap seems to have opened up between his own will and what he has thus far understood to be his Father's will. Jesus' prayer is concerned to bridge that gap. First he prays that the looming disaster not fall upon him (the imagery of drinking from a cup is used in the OT for being overtaken by the doom of God's judgment). Whatever we might try to make of this puzzling development, it makes quite clear that no death wish had set Jesus on the path to his fate in Jerusalem, and it underlines the enormity of what Jesus had to face. But Jesus' prayer does not stop here. What stands finally as fundamental for Jesus is the will of God his Father; to this he commits himself afresh. Over against his own will, which has come to expression in the initial request, he sets this more basic commitment. Though the text does not develop the point, it is the will of Jesus that needs to fall into line.

Vv 43 and 44, which are found at this point in some Greek texts, are not likely to be an original part of the Gospel of Luke (for their sense, see *Comment* above).

When Jesus rises from prayer and comes back to the disciples, he finds them not at prayer but sleeping: the sense of impending doom has caused them such grief that they have become emotionally exhausted. Nevertheless, Jesus renews his urgent insistence that the disciples should pray: how much more important it is to pray that they be spared when their human resources are so obviously limited.

The Arrest of Jesus (22:47–54a)

Bibliography

Benoit, P. *The Passion and Resurrection of Jesus.* New York: Herder and Herder, 1969. 25–48. **Black, M.** "The Arrest and Trial of Jesus and the Date of the Last Supper." In *New Testament Essays.* FS T. W. Manson, ed. A. J. B. Higgins. Manchester: Manchester University, 1959. 19–33. **Busse, U.** *Wunder.* 335–36. **Dauer, A.** *Die Passionsgeschichte im Johannesevangelium: Eine traditionsgeschichtliche und theologische Untersuchung zu Joh 18,1–19,30.* SANT 30. Munich: Kösel, 1972. 49–61. **Dibelius, M.** "Judas und der Judaskuss." In *Botschaft und Geschichte,* ed. G. Bornkamm. 1:272–77. Doeve, J. W. "Die Gefangennahme Jesu in Gethsemane: Eine traditionsgeschichtliche Untersuchung." *SE* 1 [= TU 73] (1959) 458–80. **Dormeyer, D.** *Die Passion Jesu.* 138–46. **Hall, S. G.** "Swords of Offence." *SE* 1 [= TU 73] (1959) 499–502. **Joüon, P.** "Luc 22,50–51: τὸ οὖς, τοῦ ὠτίου." *RSR* 24 (1934) 473–74. **Linnemann, E.** *Studien.* 41–69. **Peri, I.** "Der Weggefährte." *ZNW* 78 (1987) 127–31. **Radl, W.** *Paulus und*

Jesus. 169–221. **Rehkopf, F.** *Die lukanische Sonderquelle: Ihr Umfang und Sprachgebrauch.* WUNT 5. Tübingen: Mohr-Siebeck, 1959. 31–82. **Rice, G. E.** "The Role of the Populace in the Passion Narrative of Luke in Codex Bezae." *AUSS* 19 (1981) 147–53. **Rostovtzeff, M.** "οὓς δεξιὸν ἀποτέμνειν." *ZNW* 33 (1934) 196–99. **Sabbe, M.** "The Arrest of Jesus in Jn 18,1–11 and Its Relation to the Synoptic Gospels: A Critical Evaluation of A. Dauer's Hypothesis." In *L'Évangile de Jean: Sources, rédaction, théologie.* BETL 44. Leuven: University Press/Peeters, 1977. 203–34. **Schenk, W.** *Passionsbericht.* 206–15. **Schneider, G.** *Passion Jesu.* 43–55. ————. "Die Verhaftung Jesu: Traditionsgeschichte von Mk 14,43–52." *ZNW* 63 (1972) 188–209. **Schwarz, G.** *Jesus und Judas.* 189–96. **Vogler, W.** *Judas Iskarioth.* 47–51, 81–85.

And see at 22:1–2, 3–6.

Translation

⁴⁷*While he was still speaking, a crowd [appeared]*[a] *and the one called Judas, one of the Twelve, was coming on ahead of them. He drew near to Jesus in order to kiss him.* ⁴⁸*But Jesus said to him, "Judas, would you betray the Son of Man with a kiss?"* ⁴⁹*Those about him, seeing what was going to happen, said, "Lord, shall we strike with the sword?"* ⁵⁰*A certain one of them struck the slave of the high priest and cut off his right ear.* ⁵¹*Jesus responded, "Allow even this!" And touching the ear, he healed it.* ⁵²*Jesus said to the chief priests, temple officers, and elders who had come upon*[b] *him, "Why did you come out with swords and clubs, as against a robber?* ⁵³*Day after day, as I was with you in the temple, you did not stretch out your hands against me. But this is your hour, and [the time for] the power of darkness."* ⁵⁴*Arresting him, they took [him off] and brought [him] into the house of the high priest.*

Notes

a Lit. "behold, a crowd."
b א G H Δ 700 892 etc. read πρός, "to."

Form/Structure/Setting

The crisis for which Jesus has been preparing the disciples (and himself) now breaks even as Jesus continues to urge the necessity to pray to be spared a great ordeal: the betrayer comes with those who will arrest Jesus (the unit is mostly taken as finishing with v 53, but only v 54a provides closure to the scene).

Luke again follows the Markan sequence here, and despite the detailed argumentation of Rehkopf (*Die lukanische Sonderquelle,* 31–82), there is little to stand against the view that Luke is primarily editing his Markan source. There are, however, a number of indications that Luke may have had access to other traditions as well. Luke's account has a series of links with John (some with 18:1–12, and some of a broader kind): in a Johannine manner Jesus is notably in control of the situation; opposed to Jesus stand, at this significant "hour," the powers of "darkness" (cf. Dauer [*Die Passionsgeschichte,* 60]); as in John the ear that is removed is the *right* ear; as in John the arrest is kept back to the end, and there is no flight of the disciples; and note also the link observed with John 18:2 at Luke 22:39. A series of links with Matthew may also have source implications: in both, Jesus is mentioned by name at the approach of Judas, and he responds verbally to the approach (Ἰησοῦς [δέ] εἶπεν αὐτῷ, "Jesus said to him," is common; John also has Jesus mentioned by name at this stage and has Jesus speak, but without a distinguished approach by Judas); both Matthew and Luke use πατάσσειν, "to strike," of the use of the sword; both report negative responses by Jesus to the use of the sword (as does John).

Various studies have pointed to a series of difficulties in the Markan text that seem to point to its composite nature (see, e.g., Schneider, *ZNW* 63 [1972] 191–92; Linnemann, *Studien*, 41–42). There is, however, no real consensus on the source implications of these difficulties (Linnemann, 41–69, identifies vv 43b, 48, 49b as one source, vv 44–46 as the continuation of a source that begins with vv 1–2, 10–11a, and vv 47, 50, 51–52 as fragments of a narrative about armed opposition and the flight of the disciples at the arrest of Jesus; Dormeyer, *Passion Jesu*, 138–46, identifies vv 34b, 46, 50–52 as constituting Mark's source; Schneider, *ZNW* 63 [1972] 188–209, finds the basic source in vv 43bc–46, 53a; Vogler, *Judas*, 47–51, argues for an original with only vv 43bc, 46). Linnemann is surely right to think in terms of conflation of sources, but Schneider offers on the whole a more convincing delimitation of the most extensively preserved of the sources. This will have originally been a continuation from the material of Mark 14:1–2, 10–11 (see at 22:3–6, where there is also a suggestion about the original wording of Mark 14:43, which has been expanded by Mark to make the present account relatively independent; οἱ παραδιδοὺς αὐτόν [lit. "the one who betrays him"] in v 44 is also likely to be a Markan expansion).

The nocturnal betrayal and arrest of Jesus are undoubtedly historical (cf. 1 Cor 11:23), whatever we may make of the particular variations in the accounts that have been preserved. The account of the betrayal and arrest only makes sense in connection with a larger passion tradition, but that is not quite the same thing as saying that it was necessarily formulated as part of a consecutive passion narrative.

Comment

Even as he is betrayed and arrested, Jesus is master of the situation, labeling the perfidy of Judas' action, checking the impulsive behavior of his disciples, and interpreting and even permitting the arrest.

47 Luke creates drama with ἰδού (lit. "behold") rather than with Mark's εὐθύς, "immediately." Luke's crowd simply "turn up," since Luke gives the verb to Judas' position at their head (cf. Acts 1:16) rather than to his (and so their) coming (Mark's verb will be taken up in v 52). Jeremias may be right (*Sprache*, 295, 20) that the use of καί here is a Hebraism and would not appear in a sentence freely penned by Luke. If so, there is a trace here of a second source. Luke adds ὁ λεγόμενος (lit. "the one called") to Mark's reintroduction of "Judas, one of the Twelve," thus making it more of an echo of his own version of v 3 (where he added τὸν καλούμενον, "the one called," to the Markan phrase). Luke drops the mention of weapons here (Mark has it twice), as he does Mark's indication of whom the crowd comes from (he will add a version of this at v 52). He also drops out the report of the prearranged sign (he will represent its substance in Jesus' reply to

Judas' approach). Luke prefers ἤγγισεν, "drew near," for the approach of Judas to Jesus and, contrary to his main tendency with verbs, reduces Mark's verb for "kiss" from a compound to a simple form (perhaps for the sake of the noun form to come in v 48). Luke drops Mark's ῥαββί, "rabbi" (as he does consistently).

The crisis falls even as Jesus continues to reinforce his exhortation to the disciples. The fresh introduction of Judas helps to compensate for the lack of any indication that Judas had left the disciple band. In Luke's text we do not know at this point anything of the composition of the crowd, but from their leader we are in a position to guess their intention. We can contrast Judas' drawing near to Jesus with the very different kinds of drawing near to Jesus of 15:1; 18:40. Luke leaves uncertain whether Judas was allowed to kiss Jesus or was prevented from it, blocked by Jesus' response.

48 This verse has no counterpart in Mark. The image of betrayal that it creates stands as one of the most powerful ever to have gripped the human imagination. It is not unlikely that for the Son of Man language here Luke draws upon Mark 14:41, of which he made no use in the preceding episode.

49 Dropping Mark 14:46, Luke defers the actual arrest to v 54. The present verse is also distinctly Lukan and is likely to be his own creation: it picks up on v 38 and draws on v 50 to come (for οἱ περὶ αὐτόν, "those about him," cf. Acts 21:8; for ἰδόντες, "seeing," cf. Luke 18:15; κύριε, "Lord," is common in Luke as is the direct question introduced by εἰ [lit. "if"]). The superficial understanding exhibited by the disciples in v 38 now becomes a rather pathetic misapplication of his teaching.

50 The question is asked, but only rhetorically, since no time is allowed for an answer. After "those about him" in v 49, Mark's "those standing around" is not needed. Luke drops the drawing of the sword, probably because the "indecent haste" of the action is clearer without it. The verb used for "struck" is different from the Markan choice (but is found at Mark 14:27), and "the ear" has become "the right ear" (different word for ear). The action exhibits courage and dedication to Jesus (cf. Mark 10:39a) but is practically unrealistic and insensitive to Jesus' own views on the matter. It is perhaps best to understand "the slave of the high priest" here as the personal representative of the high priest and, in that capacity, the leader of the band sent with Judas to arrest Jesus (cf. Schneider, *ZNW* 63 [1972] 202).

51 Mark reports no response by Jesus to this development. Matthew, John, and Luke all have responses (with notable common elements between Matthew and John). Luke has the briefest of responses and supplements this by reporting the healing of the ear (which he alone has). ἀποκριθεὶς εἶπεν (lit. "having answered he said") is Lukan (cf. at 1:19, and for the sense here, cf. 7:40; but it is also available at Mark 14:48) as is ἐᾶτε (cf. Jeremias, *Sprache*, 295). For "ear" here, Luke switches to the word used in the Matthean account.

The sense of ἐᾶτε ἕως τούτου (lit. "[you pl.] let [him/it be] up to/as far as/until this") remains uncertain. Is "this" the sword stroke, the imminent arrest, or the whole "disaster" befalling the ministry of Jesus, beginning with the prospect of arrest? Perhaps the last, with the implication that this whole development is to be accepted as the will of God. The healing of the ear fits Luke's image of Jesus as healer (Luke has eleven of the sixteen synoptic Gospel uses of the verb ἰᾶσθαι, "to heal").

52 Having used ἀποκριθείς (lit. "having answered") in v 51, Luke drops it here; he introduces πρός, "to," after a verb of saying; he uses the verb passed over in v 47 to clarify the change from addressing Judas to addressing the arresting crowd as a whole; and he compensates here for his failure to report the composition of the crowd in v 47 (where Mark's crowd came *from* "the chief priests, scribes, and elders," Luke's *consists of* "chief priests, temple officers [cf. v 4], and elders" [this represents more directly the action of the leaders to achieve Jesus' arrest (cf. 19:47; 20:1, 19)]). The wording of Mark 14:48b is reproduced exactly apart from the final συλλαβεῖν με, "to arrest me" (Luke keeps this verb for v 54). As in Luke 10:30, λῃστής is likely to be used here of the kind of robber who would waylay people traveling in a country area. Though the word can mean "revolutionary," it is unlikely to have any political overtones here. Jesus is being sought as though he were a violent fugitive from justice.

53 The main Lukan touches here are the subordination of the first clause by means of a genitive absolute construction, the dropping of "teaching" as the specific content of Jesus' activity in the temple (for Luke this is already more than clear), and the change from Mark's οὐκ ἐκρατήσατέ με, "did not arrest me," to ἐξετείνατε τὰς χεῖρας ἐπ' ἐμέ (lit. "did not stretch out the hands upon me"), with its echo of 20:19 (but with a different verb). Luke's final clause is distinctive (but for "hour," cf. Mark 14:35, 41).

Jesus points to a notable mismatch between his daily public appearances in the temple and this nocturnal pursuit of him now as though he were a dangerous fugitive from justice. This challenges the probity of an arrest that could not be made in the light of day and in the presence of the general populace who at festival time milled in large numbers around the temple area. The darkness of the night is a cloak for the evil of the action. "Darkness," "power" (as used here), and "Satan" (as used in 22:3) are drawn together in Acts 26:18. It is the "hour" of the Jewish leadership precisely because its members have become in this action instruments of Satan against Jesus. In this hour, designated in the purposes of God, the Satanic assault is permitted.

54a The content here is substantially that of Mark 14:53a, but Luke has delayed the arrest to this point and uses Mark's verb from v 48 to refer to it. He expands Mark's ἀπήγαγον . . . πρός, "they took away . . . to," into ἤγαγον καὶ εἰσήγαγον εἰς τὴν οἰκίαν, "they took and brought into the house [of]" ("the house" here is in line with "courtyard" to come in v 55). Jesus submits to arrest because he now knows that it is his Father's will for him at this time to be delivered over to the dark powers.

Explanation

As the call to prayer is still being repeated, the time of crisis Jesus has been anticipating begins to emerge in the form of a well-armed crowd with Judas at its head. But even as he is betrayed and arrested, Jesus maintains his poise and dominates the scene as he dramatically labels the perfidy of Judas' action, checks the impulsive behavior of his disciples, and interprets and even gives permission for his own arrest.

Only now do we realize that at some point Judas has slipped away in order to be able to implement his evil plans. At the head of the crowd, he comes forward to greet Jesus with a kiss. But Jesus sees at once what is happening and points up the poignancy involved in using the greeting of love as the means of betrayal.

The disciples also realize what is afoot, and their response is to try to fight their way out of the situation: they want to defend Jesus from this armed crowd. The superficial understanding exhibited by the disciples in v 38 of Jesus' teaching (vv 35–37) about the new situation that was about to confront them now becomes a rather pathetic misapplication of his teaching. The disciples ask, but do not wait for an answer: they think they know. Their action shows courage and loyalty to Jesus (cf. Mark 10:39a) but is practically unrealistic and contrary to all that he has taught them about the harsh but necessary future that lay ahead. (We are probably to understand that the slave of the high priest was his personal representative and, therefore, the leader of the arresting party. The disciple involved would have been trying to do rather more than slice off an ear.)

Jesus reacts to this impulsive action by directing them not to interfere: they must allow this to happen, because it fulfills the plan and purpose of God. He reverses this misstep by healing the ear: even at this late stage Jesus is still the great healer.

Jesus then turns his attention to the crowd. As Luke tells it, this crowd consists of members of the Jewish leadership: chief priests, temple officials, and elders. These are the people who found themselves so impotent in relation to Jesus as he taught in the temple (see 19:47; 20:1, 19). Jesus points to an obvious contradiction between his daily public appearances in the temple and this nocturnal pursuit of him now as though he were a dangerous fugitive from justice. Is it not an implicit admission that something is wrong with their view of justice when they have to proceed in this way to arrest him?

Thus far the crowd has done nothing. Judas and the disciples have played minor roles, but the action has been dominated by Jesus. Jesus finishes here by interpreting this nocturnal visit as the onset of the divinely ordained hour in which those who have come to arrest Jesus act as representatives of the ultimate darkness, Satan himself.

As the episode reaches its end, Jesus submits to arrest without struggle and is taken off to the house of the high priest.

The Denials of Peter (22:54b–62)

Bibliography

Benoit, P. *The Passion and Resurrection of Jesus.* New York: Herder and Herder, 1969. 49–72. **Birdsall, J. N.** "τὸ ῥῆμα ὡς εἶπεν αὐτῷ ὁ Ἰησοῦς: Mark xiv. 72." *NovT* 2 (1957) 272–75. **Boomershine, T. E.** "Peter's Denial as Polemic or Confession: The Implications of Media Criticism for Biblical Hermeneutics." *Semeia* 39 (1987) 47–68. **Boyd, W. J. P.** "Peter's Denials: Mark xiv.68; Luke xxii.57." *ExpTim* 67 (1955–56) 341. **Braumann, G.** "Markus 5, 2–5 und Markus 14, 55–64." *ZNW* 52 (1961) 273–78. **Brunet, G.** "Et aussitôt le coq chanta." *CCER* 27 (1979) 9–12. **Bussby, F.** "St. Mark 14:72: An Aramaic Mistranslation?" *BJRL* 21

(1937) 273–74. **Catchpole, D.** *The Trial of Jesus.* SPB 18. Leiden: Brill, 1971. 160–74. **Crossan, J. D.** *The Cross That Spoke: The Origins of the Passion Narrative.* San Francisco: Harper and Row, 1988. **Danson, J. M.** "The Fall of St. Peter." *ExpTim* 19 (1907–8) 307–8. **Dassman, E.** "Die Szene Christus: Petrus mit der Hahn." In *Pietas.* FS B. Kotting, ed. E. Dassman and K. S. Frank. JAC 8. Münster: Aschendorffsche Verlagsbuchhandlung, 1980. 510–11. **Daube, D.** "Limitations on Self-Sacrifice in Jewish Law and Tradition." *Th* 72 (1969) 291–304. **Delorme, J.** "Le procès de Jésus ou la parole risquée (Lc 22,54–23,25)." *RSR* 69 (1981) 123–46. **Derrett, J. D. M.** "The Reason for the Cock-Crowings." *NTS* 29 (1983) 142–44. **Dewey, K. E.** "Peter's Curse and Cursed Peter (Mark 14:53–54, 66–72)." In *The Passion in Mark,* ed. W. H. Kelber. 96–114. **Dietrich, W.** *Das Petrusbild der lukanischen Schriften.* 139–57. **Ernst, J.** "Noch einmal: Die Verleugnung Jesu durch Petrus." In *Petrus und Papst,* ed. A. Brandenburg and H. J. Urban. Münster: Aschendorff, 1977. 43–62. ———. "Noch einmal: Die Verleugnung Jesu durch Petrus." *Catholica* 30 (1976) 207–26. **Evans, C. A.** "'Peter Warming Himself': The Problem of an Editorial 'Seam.'" *JBL* 101 (1982) 245–49. **Fortna, R.** "Jesus and Peter at the High Priest's House: A Test Case for the Question of the Relation between Mark's and John's Gospels." *NTS* 24 (1978) 371–83. **Fox, R.** "Peter's Denial in Mark's Gospel." *BiTod* 25 (1987) 298–303. **Gardiner, W. D.** "The Denial of St. Peter." *ExpTim* 26 (1914–15) 424–26. **Garritt, C. E.** "St. Peter's Denials." *ExpTim* 48 (1936–37) 43–44. **Genest, O.** *Le Christ de la passion: Perspective structurale: Analyse de Mc 14,53–15,47, des parallèles bibliques et extra-bibliques.* Recherches 21. Tournai/Montreal: Desclée/Bellarmin, 1978. **Gerhardsson, B.** "Confession and Denial before Men: Observations on Matt. 26:57–27:2." *JSNT* (1981) 46–66. **Gewalt, D.** "Die Verleugnung des Petrus." In *Theologische Versuche,* ed. J. Rogge and G. Schille. Berlin: Evangelische Verlagsanstalt, 1977. 45–62. ———. "Die Verleugnung des Petrus." *LingBib* 43 (1978) 113–44. **Goguel, M.** "Did Peter Deny His Lord? A Conjecture." *HTR* 25 (1932) 1–27. **Guyot, G. H.** "Peter Denies His Lord." *CBQ* 4 (1942) 111–18. **James, J. C.** "The Dialect of Peter's Denial." *ExpTim* 19 (1907–8) 524. **Klein, G.** "Die Verleugnung des Petrus: Eine traditionsgeschichtliche Untersuchung." *ZTK* 58 (1961) 285–328. **Kosmala, H.** "The Time of the Cock-Crow." *ASTI* 2 (1963) 118–20. ———. "The Time of the Cock-Crow (II)." *ASTI* 6 (1967–68) 132–34. **Kosnetter, J.** "Zur Geschichtlichkeit der Verleugnung Petri." In *Dienst an der Lehre: Studien zur heutigen Philosophie und Theologie.* FS F. K. König. Wiener Beiträge zur Theologie 10. Vienna: Herder, 1965. 127–43. **Krieger, N.** "Knecht des Hohenpriesters." *NovT* 2 (1957–58) 73–74. **Lampe, G. W. H.** "St. Peter's Denial." *BJRL* 55 (1972–73) 346–68. **LaVerdiere, E. A.** "Peter Broke Down and Began to Cry." *Emman* 92 (1986) 70–73. **Lee, G. M.** "Mark 14,72: ἐπιβαλὼν ἔκλαιεν." *Bib* 53 (1972) 411–12. **Lehmann, M.** *Synoptische Quellenanalyse.* 106–12. **Linnemann, E.** *Studien.* 70–108. ———. "Die Verleugnung des Petrus." *ZTK* 63 (1966) 1–32. **Masson, C.** "Le reniement de Pierre: Quelques aspects de la formation d'une tradition." *RHPR* 37 (1957) 24–35. **Mayo, C. H.** "St. Peter's Token of the Cock Crow." *JTS* 22 (1921) 367–70. **McEleney, N. J.** "Peter's Denials—How Many? To Whom?" *CBQ* 52 (1990) 467–72. **Merkel, H.** "Peter's Curse." In *The Trial of Jesus.* FS C. F. D. Moule, ed. E. Bammel. SBT 2/13. London: SCM, 66–71. **Murray, G.** "Saint Peter's Denials." *DR* 103 (1985) 296–98. **Pesch, R.** "Die Verleugnung des Petrus: Eine Studie zu Mk 14,54.66–72 (und Mk 14,26–31)." In *Neues Testament und Kirche.* FS R. Schnackenburg, ed. J. Gnilka. Freiburg im B.: Herder, 1974. 42–62. **Ramsay, W. M.** "The Denials of Peter." *ExpTim* 27 (1915–16) 296–301, 360–63, 410–13, 471–72, 540–42; 28 (1916–17) 276–81. **Rothenaicher, F.** "Zu Mk. 14,70 und Mt. 26,73." *BZ* 23 (1935–36) 192–93. **Schneider, G.** *Verleugnung, Verspottung und Verhör Jesu nach Lukas, 22,54–71: Studien zur lukanischen Darstellung der Passion.* SANT 22. Munich: Kösel, 1969. Esp. 73–96. **Schwank, B.** "Petrus verleugnet Jesus." *SeinSend* 29 (1964) 51–65. **Seitz, O. J. F.** "Peter's 'Profanity': Mark xiv. 71 in the Light of Matthew xvi. 22." *SE* 1 [= TU 73] (1959) 516–19. **Smith, P. V.** "St. Peter's Threefold Denial of Our Lord." *Th* 17 (1928) 341–48. **Soards, M. L.** "'And the Lord Turned and Looked Straight at Peter': Understanding Luke 22,61." *Bib* 67 (1986) 518–19. **Thomson, J. R.** "Saint

Peter's Denials." *ExpTim* 47 (1935–36) 381–82. **Walter, N.** "Die Verleugnung des Petrus." *TVers* 8 (1977) 45–61. **Wenham, J. W.** "How Many Cock-Crowings? The Problem of Harmonistic Text-Variants." *NTS* 25 (1978–79) 523–25. **Wilcox, M.** "The Denial Sequence in Mark xiv. 26–31, 66–72." *NTS* 17 (1970–71) 426–36. **Zeck, P. R.** "Fall und Wiederaufstehen eines Jüngers: Passionsbetrachtung zu Mk 14,66–72." *BibLeb* 7 (1966) 51–57.

And see at 22:1–2, 31–34.

Translation

[54b]*Peter was following at a distance.* [55] *[Some people] had lit a fire in the middle of the courtyard and sat together around it; Peter sat down in the midst*[a] *of them.* [56] *Seeing him sitting at the fire, and staring at him, a certain servant girl said, "Surely*[b] *this fellow was with him!"* [57] *But he denied [it], saying, "Woman, I do not know him!"* [58] *After a little while a different person saw him and said, "Surely you are one of them!" But Peter said, "Man, I am not!"* [59] *When about an hour had passed a certain other person kept up the insistence, saying, "In truth, surely this [fellow] was with him! For he is a Galilean."* [60] *But Peter said, "Man, I do not know what you are saying." Immediately, while he was still speaking, a cock crowed.* [61] *Then the Lord turned and looked [intently] at Peter,*[c] *and Peter remembered the word of the Lord, how he had said to him, "Before the cock crows this day, you will deny me three times."* [62] *He went outside and wept bitterly.*[d]

Notes

[a] ℵ A W Θ Ψ *f*[13] etc. have ἐν μέσῳ here as for "in the middle" earlier in the verse, but the alternative construction with μέσος is more likely to be original.

[b] Treating the opening καί as a sentence adverb.

[c] p[69] seems to have αὐτῷ, "at him."

[d] V 62 is missing from 0171[vid] it. If it is not original, then Luke has no equivalent to the final clause of Mark 14:72. Since he uses the verb κλαίειν, "weep," on nine other occasions in the Gospel, it is hard to see why he would want to omit the clause containing it here, especially when the clause offers such a forceful conclusion to the episode.

Form/Structure/Setting

The spotlight moves from Jesus to Peter, who follows from afar but fails to own his link with Jesus when questioned in the courtyard of the high priest's house. Jesus' prophecy is thus fulfilled, and the cock crow and the look from Jesus drive home to Peter the full enormity of his denial.

The sequence continues to parallel Mark, though Luke offers no equivalent to Mark's report of the fleeing of all the disciples or of "a certain young man" whom those who arrested Jesus tried also to take into custody. Also, having introduced Peter, Luke continues immediately with the denials rather than first reporting a hearing before the high priest (Luke's version of this encounter is delayed until daybreak).

It is relatively easy to account for most of the Lukan text as redaction of Mark 14:54, 66–72. There is, however, one good reason for thinking that this solution may be too simple. In *Notes* above, Luke 22:62 is accepted as part of Luke's text. If this is right, then, since the wording is identical to Matt 26:75, the presence of this verse guarantees that Luke (and Matthew) had access to a separate account of the denials of Peter. This raises the possibility that Luke 22:61a is also dependent upon this source. Thus we cannot rule out the possibility that other distinctive features in Luke's version of the individual denials are to be traced back to his second source (Matthew stays rather closer to Mark, so there is no possibility of characterizing the second source on the basis of shared features between Matthew and Luke). A modest commonality between the second denials in Luke and John is worth reporting: καὶ σὺ ἐκ[ἐξ] . . . εἶ . . . οὐκ εἰμι (lit. "also you from among . . . are . . . I am not"). This is too meager a base, taken alone, for speculation on source links between John and Luke here. For further detail favoring a second Lukan source, see *Comment* below.

Pesch ("Verleugnung," 44–52) offers a powerful case for seeing Mark 14:54, 66–72 as a highly integrated part of the passion narrative, with links also to pre-passion features of the Gospel of Mark. But Pesch rather too easily deduces from this the existence of the account in a pre-Markan passion account. Dewey ("Peter's Curse," 96–108), by contrast, envisages largely Markan formulation with a traditional base only in vv 53a, 54, 66b, 67b, 68, 72b,d (Dewey appears to have been unaware of Pesch's study and so offers no response to Pesch's account of the links that even some of these verses have to other texts in Mark).

If we can assume here Johannine independence of Mark (see John 18:15–27; cf. Fortna, *NTS* 24 [1978] 371–83), then both a threefold denial and an intercalation of the account of Peter's denial within that of the high priest's questioning of Jesus must be pre-Markan. Johannine independence of Mark for the intercalation is seen to be more likely from the observations of Evans (*JBL* 101 [1982] 245–49), who shows that John 18:18c and 25a look much more like an artificial seam, resuming a text after an intrusion, than does the corresponding Mark 14:54 and 67a (in other words, dependence, if it exists, should be of Mark on John!).

On the other side of the debate, v 68b would serve very well as a conclusion for a denial tradition (esp. if we include "and a cock crowed"). This would support an analysis of the threefold denial as a Markan development (so Dewey; Masson's attempt [*RHPR* 37 (1957) 27–29] to explain the situation in terms of a conflation of two denial accounts stumbles over the difficulty of requiring of vv 69–72 a sense of completeness and relative independence as a unit of tradition).

Perhaps Mark is responsible for the formulation of the second and third denials but makes his expansion on the basis of a firm tradition that the denial was threefold (cf. Mark 14:30). Thus he sees himself as making good a defect in the account available to him of the actual denial (this would mean that Mark did not receive the traditions that he uses in 14:27–31 and 53–72 from an already unified source). Apart from a use of πάλιν, "again" (in Mark's second and John's third denial), and ἐκ[ἐξ] . . . εἶ (lit. "out of . . . you are"; in Mark's third and John's first and second denials), unless we count a use of "this man" in quite a different way in John 18:17 and Mark 14:71, the shared content between John and Mark here is restricted to material in Mark 14:54, 66–68 (v 72 adds εὐθύς, "immediately," to the shared content, but given Mark's extravagant use of this term, I make nothing of the agreement). Either John could have independently followed the same impulse as we are considering for Mark, or the source that he used already had a triple denial (the Luke-John link noted above, if significant, would favor the latter). Mark may be responsible for the material in v 72 about Peter remembering, but the final clause of v 72 will be traditional (cf. Luke 22:62; Matt 26:75c).

The tradition available to Mark could not sensibly have been transmitted without an account of the arrest of Jesus (which in turn entails a version of Mark 14:1–2, 10–11), and (because the intercalation is pre-Markan) the tradition unit already included an account of a hearing before the high priest. Such a sequence guarantees the existence of a pre-Markan passion narrative, whatever difficulties there may be in ascertaining its exact scope. Did this pre-Markan source already include an account of Jesus' prediction of Peter's denial? The denial account seems to require it, but there seems to be no place for it after Mark 14:1. Perhaps it belonged to a body of material placed before Mark 14:1, which had Jesus anticipating the coming events.

The shared intercalation means that the Johannine and Markan traditions are not from totally independent streams; and though we have another source reflected in Matthew and Luke, so little of it has been preserved that we can know nothing about its ultimate relationship to the Markan stream of tradition. But even if the tradition base is narrow, despite some attempts to discredit the claim to historicity of the Petrine denials (e.g., Klein, *ZTK* 58 [1961] 285–328; Linnemann, *ZTK* 63 [1966] 1–32), the burden of proof remains strongly upon those who would want to deny the historicity of a tradition whose origin and preservation make little sense in the developing church, if not based on a concern with historical memory (cf. Pesch, "Verleugnung," 42–62; Boomershine, *Semeia* 39 [1987] 47–68, is surely right that the portrayal of Peter is sympathetic and not polemical).

Comment

The recently confident Peter cannot, once Jesus has been arrested, maintain his allegiance to his master in the face of even the challenge mounted by a few nameless people of no particular significance who are sitting around a fire in the courtyard of the high priest's house. But a cockcrow and a look from the captive Jesus show up Peter's denial for what it is, and his bitter tears are the turning point for the reassertion of his loyalty.

54b Mark's καί, "and," becomes δέ, "and/but"; the aorist "followed" is changed to the imperfect "was following," and the linked "him" dropped as redundant, as is the redundant ἀπό, "from," in Mark's expression for "at a distance." In "at a distance," there is an ominous anticipation of the coming failure of Peter's "following" of Jesus (cf. 5:11 and at 9:23).

55 "The courtyard" is found a little later in Mark's account (v 66). Otherwise only Luke's use of ἐκάθητο, "he sat" (and he shares this word with Matthew), is all that might count as a language link with Mark (Mark has the periphrastic imperfect of a compound of this verb with σύν, "with"; Luke also uses a σύν compound with a related verb, of those with whom Peter sat). Luke is likely to be influenced by the language of his second source (the Johannine account also reports the making of a fire, but with different language; only John's account has both the making of the fire and Peter's warming of himself at it [Matthew has neither]). Fitzmyer (1464) points to the clumsiness of the language imagery involved in the juxtaposition of περιαψάντων (lit. "light all around," but probably a pregnant construction for "light [and sit] around") and συγκαθισάντων (lit. "sit together," but intended surely to refer to sitting *around the fire*). Apart from the fact that the group includes a servant girl (cf. v 56), Luke provides no clear identity for the group gathered around the courtyard fire. Peter is waiting to see how things will turn out (as Matthew makes explicit).

56 Rather more of the language could be based on Mark here. ἰδοῦσα, "seeing," αὐτῷ, "at him," πρὸς τὸ φῶς, "at the fire," and καί (meaning in this context something like "surely") are exactly the same; "a certain servant girl" is not too far from Mark's "one of the servant girls [of the high priest]"; and only a Lukan verbal preference separates Luke's "staring" from Mark's "looked [intently]." Luke has a third person form for the servant girl's words (as in Mark's second denial) and the simpler "with [σύν] him" for Mark's "with [μετά] Jesus the Nazarene." The penetrating gazes respectively of the servant girl and of Jesus (v 61) provide the first and the last impulses for the main action of this unit. Peter will seek to hide from the exposure implicit in the former, but he has no weapons against the exposure implicit in the latter.

57 Mark's "know or understand" has been reduced to "know"; and in line with Luke's editing at v 34, it is not now "know . . . what you are saying" but rather "know him." "Woman" as a mode of address is added here, just as "man" will be added to the address in the following denials. There is no good reason to think that "woman" here is meant as a belittling mode of address.

58 Luke drops Mark's mention at this point of Peter's retreat to the forecourt, as well as the first cockcrow. The difficulty of these features in the Markan account has been noted in *Form/Structure/Setting* above. The language here, and to a considerable degree the content, is quite different from the Markan text. In common there is only an opening καί, "and," and ἐξ αὐτῶν (lit. "[out of] them"). Luke has a masculine form in place of Mark's feminine for "seeing." As noted above in *Form/Structure/Setting*, there is rather more in common with John 18:25 (and a little of this commonality is also in Matt 26:73). Luke's second source is likely to be visible. "Man" is likely to be a Lukan touch as "woman" was in v 57. This time the accuser addresses Peter directly and "with him" becomes "of them" ("one of them" in the translation above). The arrest pericope suggests that there may not have been at this point any particular threat of arrest attached to being identified as one of Jesus' disciple band. Nonetheless, the possibility of abuse could have been very real, given that these people in the courtyard might be presumed to be identified at some level or other with the present move to have Jesus arrested. Staying there to see what would happen to Jesus was for Peter becoming dependent upon denying the very link to Jesus that caused him to be there in the first place.

59 The language from Mark here is restricted to a linking καί, "and," and καὶ γὰρ Γαλιλαῖος, "for . . . a Galilean." μετ' αὐτοῦ, "with him," is found also in John 18:26 (in v 56 Luke preferred σὺν αὐτοῦ for this). The καὶ οὗτος . . . ἦν, "surely this [fellow] . . . was," form recurs from v 56. If the thrust of καί has been rightly construed there, then ἐπ' ἀληθείας, "truly," looks like a slightly unfortunate importation of a modified form of Mark's ἀληθῶς, "truly," into a context where it is now a little redundant: "in truth, surely." διαστάσης ὡσεὶ ὥρας μιᾶς, "when about an hour had passed," may be a Lukan touch (cf. Schneider, *Verleugnung*, 86–87), as might be the use of διϊσχυρίζετο, "kept up the insistence" (cf. Acts 12:15). There is, then, likely, but not certain, visibility of a second source here. The passage of time probably suggests that the danger for Peter would seem to have passed. διϊσχυρίζετο has been rendered "kept up the insistence" on the basis that the force of its imperfect tense is that the third accuser continues what the others have begun. The pattern of accusation closely follows that of the first accusation, but now there is a supporting clause. Peter's Galilean origins would be evident either from his accent or dialect (as Matt 26:73) or possibly from some detail in the manner of his dress.

60 There is nothing here that takes us beyond Lukan editing of Mark: Luke does not report the cursing; he adds "man" as in v 58; the name "Peter" is probably a delayed use of the name from Mark 14:70; the denial is partly reminiscent of that which Luke fashioned in v 57 but now with "what you say" used from the Markan form (but with the relative ὅ in place of the interrogative τί); Luke prefers παραχρῆμα to Mark's word for "immediately "; and Luke is quite fond of links in which things happen while words are still being uttered (8:48 and 22:47 from Mark, but also Acts 10:44; Luke 24:36; cf. also 11:37; 9:42; 24:41). Taken literally, Peter's answer hardly makes sense after the previous answers, but we should probably take it less literally to mean something more like "I can't imagine why you are saying this." "While he was still speaking" underlines yet more forcefully than "immediately" the inner connection between Peter's words of denial and the cock-crow.

61 Beyond the clause about the Lord turning to stare at Peter, the material here follows Mark quite closely. Differences are best explained as Lukan redaction. Luke and Matthew agree in replacing Mark's τὸ ῥῆμα, "the word," with τοῦ ῥήματος Ἰησοῦ [τοῦ κυρίου], "the word [gen.] of Jesus [of the Lord]," and in dropping Mark's "twice." But the latter is only the consequence of changes earlier at a point where the Markan text created difficulties, and the former comes in connection with a difficult Markan idiom here (lit. "remembered the word how/as Jesus said to him"; on the idiom, see Birdsall, *NovT* 2 [1957] 272–75), which the two evangelists are likely to have independently felt the need to modify (for Luke's wording, cf. Acts 11:16). Luke only partially catches up here with his editing of Jesus' words in v 34 (where the wording was probably also influenced in part by a second source). In the opening clause both στραφείς, "turned" (cf. 7:13; etc.; see Schneider, *Verleugnung*, 91–92), and ὁ κύριος, "the Lord" (Luke's narrative use of "the Lord" for Jesus starts at 7:13), look Lukan, but ἐνέβλεψεν, "looked [intently]," uses a verb that Luke replaced in v 56. The case for the opening clause here coming from a second source depends on the case for a second source elsewhere in the account. But dependence on a second source is not unlikely.

On Jesus' look, see at v 56. The shallowness of Peter's words in v 33 is now revealed and Peter's interaction there with Jesus sharply recalled. The word of Jesus proves true, and the protestation of Peter is not sustained. We have no basis for determining Jesus' position in the scene. This brief appearance allowed to Jesus in an episode otherwise devoted to Peter shows Jesus maintaining his dominant presence following his arrest. Luke no longer reproduces the wording of Jesus' prediction in a manner that muffles the correspondence with 12:9 (as he did in 22:34).

62 The wording is identical to the final clause of Matthew 26:75. This may be Peter's final named appearance in the Gospel. A resurrection appearance to him (as Simon) is mentioned in 24:34, but this happens off-stage. In 24:12, if it is original, Peter goes to the tomb, finds it empty, and goes home puzzled. Is the turning point for Peter (cf. 22:32) already here in 22:62 in the form of his bitter tears of remorse?

Explanation

The spotlight moves from Jesus to Peter, but one brief and wordless appearance by Jesus shows that he maintains the dominating presence he displayed prior to his arrest. Under pressure Peter's following from afar turns into gross denial of his link with Jesus. But a cockcrow and a look from Jesus bring to mind what had transpired in vv 31–34 and set Peter on the road to recovery.

Peter takes up a vantage point near a fire in the courtyard of the high priest's house in order to see what will become of Jesus. His anonymity is disturbed by the sharp gaze of a servant girl who, looking in his direction, asserts to anyone who will listen that Peter had undoubtedly been with Jesus. Peter protects himself by denying that he so much as knows Jesus, and in this way Jesus' words of v 34 come true. Peter seeks to hide himself from the exposure that this penetrating gaze threatens. At the end of the episode he will have no weapons to hide himself from another equally penetrating look, this time from Jesus.

Soon after, one of the men takes up the question. He looks at Peter and addresses him directly. He puts the matter in terms of Peter definitely being "one of them." Peter's "I am not" is equally emphatic. Of what is Peter frightened? There had been no attempt at the arrest of Jesus to take his companions as well. At most, Peter might have expected to be abused or beaten up and expelled from the courtyard. Staying there to see what would happen to Jesus had for Peter become dependent upon denying the very link to Jesus that caused him to be there in the first place.

Time passes and no one else bothers Peter. The danger seems to have passed. But it was only the lull before the final storm. Now yet another man takes up the call. He goes back to wording like the first challenge but strengthens its force. He begins with an emphatic "in truth" and finishes with a reason for thinking that Peter might have been with Jesus: he was obviously a Galilean (by accent or clothing). Peter responds, not with a straight denial but with a statement that suggests puzzlement about being challenged in this way in the first place.

No one had pressed the matter to the point where Peter's true link with Jesus was exposed. But Peter is undone in the situation by the sound of a cock's crow and a look from Jesus. Memory floods in, and he recalls his own brash confidence and Jesus' sad prediction. The logic of his present position is spelled out in Luke 12:9: the natural outcome should be that Jesus will deny Peter before the angels of God.

The look and the cockcrow show Peter how far he has fallen, but they also put him back on the path to recovery. Peter withdraws and weeps bitter tears of remorse. We learn in 24:34 of his subsequent meeting with the resurrected Lord.

Jesus Mocked in Custody (22:63–65)

Bibliography

Schmidt, K. L. " Ἰησοῦς Χριστὸς κολαφιζόμενος und die 'colaphisation' der Juden." In *Aux sources de la tradition chrétienne,* by P. Benoit et al. 218–27. **Benoit, P.** "Les outrages à

Jésus prophète (Mc xiv 65 par.)." In *Neotestamentica et patristica.* FS O. Cullmann, ed. W. C. van Unnik. Leiden: Brill, 1962. 92–110. **Flusser, D.** "Who Is It That Struck You?" *Immanuel* 20 (1986) 27–32. **Gundry, R. H.** "לממלים: 1 Q Isaiah [a] 50,6 and Mark 14,65." *RevQ* 2 (1960) 559–67. **Miller, D. L.** "ἐμπαίζειν: Playing the Mock Game (Luke 22:63–64)." *JBL* 90 (1971) 309–13. **Neirynck, F.** "Τίς ἐστιν ὁ παίσας σε: Mt 26,68/Lk 22,64 diff. Mk 14,65." *ETL* 63 (1987) 5–47. **Rudberg, G.** "Die Verhöhnung Jesu vor dem Hohenpriester." *ZNW* 24 (1925) 307–9. **Soards, M. L.** "A Literary Analysis of the Origin and Purpose of Luke's Account of the Mockery of Jesus." *BZ* 31 (1987) 110–16. **Unnik, W. C. van.** "Jesu Verhöhnung vor dem Synedrium (Mc 14.65 par.)." *ZNW* 29 (1930) 310–11.

And see at 22:1–2, 54b–62, 66–71.

Translation

[63] *The men who were holding Jesus* [a] *in custody began to mock him and beat [him];* [64] *and blindfolding him, they kept asking, "Prophesy! Who is it that struck you?"* [65] *They also said many other things to him of a blasphemous nature.*

Notes

[a] Gr. αὐτόν, "him," but A W Θ Ψ *f* [1,13] etc. have τὸν Ἰησοῦν, "Jesus."

Form/Structure/Setting

Attention moves back to Jesus, who is being held in custody pending an early morning hearing of the Sanhedrin. The mockery of a cruel soldiers' game fills the vacant hours.

Luke has a mocking of Jesus here, before the Sanhedrin hearing begins, and again while Jesus is with Herod (23:11). Mark has Jesus mocked after the nocturnal meeting with the high priest and the Sanhedrin (14:65; this is, however, before the early morning activity of the Sanhedrin in 15:1) and again after Pilate hands Jesus over to be crucified (15:16–20 [Matthew repeats the Markan pattern]). John has Jesus struck during the hearing before Annas (18:22 [the same verb is used in Luke 22:63]) and mocked as royal pretender by Pilate's soldiers during the course of Pilate's investigation (19:1–3). (In each of the synoptic Gospels, there is further mocking of Jesus at the cross.)

There can be little doubt that Luke had access to a second source for 22:63–64. (*i*) Though Peter has been mentioned more recently, αὐτόν, "him," in v 63 must be Jesus. This infelicity reflects not Lukan formulation on the basis of Mark 14:65 but rather the use of a source reproduced here without the antecedent of its source setting (was this material attached to Luke's second source for 22:47–53a?). (*ii*) Since there is good reason to think that καὶ περικαλύπτειν, "and to blindfold," is an addition to the Markan text from the Lukan (following Green, *Death of Jesus,* 67; Catchpole, *Trial,* 175; Benoit, "Outrages," 98–99; etc.), the extent of agreement between the Markan and Lukan accounts is limited to προφήτευσον, "prophecy," and even here the connotation of the term is rather different. (*iii*) Given Luke's general editorial procedures, he is hardly likely to have relocated the mocking to this point without prompting from a second source. (*iv*) The striking agreement with Matthew against Mark in v 64, τίς ἐστιν ὁ παίσας σε;, "who is it who struck you?" suggests that a second source may have been available to Matthew as well (but note Neirynck [*ETL* 63 (1987) 5–47], who argues on redactional grounds that the phrase may be a secondary interpolation into the Matthean text). (*v*) In light of 18:32 it is unlikely that Luke would have edited out a reference to spitting on Jesus (unless to use it in the context of the trial before Pilate, which he does not do). Similarly, he is unlikely to have edited in a reference to mocking, which in the Lukan passion predictions is anticipated only in a gentile context (18:32).

Luke's second source may not have embraced v 65, which could well be a Lukan generalization.

Given the state of our sources, it is not possible to arbitrate with final confidence between the Markan and the Lukan sequence and content, but a number of features of the Markan account could be seen as heightenings: not simply a group of rough guards but presumably members of the Sanhedrin treat Jesus in this contemptuous manner; the call to prophesy is not now part of a rather cruel game but a mockery of the claim to prophetic powers bound up in Jesus' messianic pretensions (Mark 14:62 has a prophetic dimension); the wording used points to fulfillment in Jesus of the servant role of Isa 50:6. In Mark's material the place of the ὑπηρέται, "attendants/guards/servants," in 14:65 is likely to have a role in the linking and contrasting of Jesus' experience and Peter's (cf. Mark's only other use of the word in v 54).

Comment

The arrested Jesus is subject to mockery and abuse from his custodial guards; their cruel jokes are nothing less than blasphemy. There is no reaction from Jesus; in this scene he is cast simply as the victim.

63 The arresting party is identified in v 52 as consisting of "chief priests, temple officials, and elders," but we should not use that text to make more precise Luke's deliberately general identification here of Jesus' custodians (against Soards, *BZ* 31 [1987] 115). Though Luke is quite fond of συνέχειν (here: "hold in custody"), he does not use it elsewhere in the sense required here. The mockery here will have a counterpart in the behavior of Herod and his soldiers (23:11), and again in that of the soldiers at the cross (23:36). Luke-Acts has more than half of the NT uses of δέρειν, "to beat," used otherwise in the Gospel in parabolic discourse and in Acts of mistreatment of Christian leaders by authorities of one kind or another. The behavior of the guards reflects in a general way the rather brutal nature of legal enforcement of the day but should not be understood in any specific connection with the (undoubtedly practiced) use of torture in legal inquiry.

64 Though the exact game involved has not been documented, several ancient games have been identified that have some relationship to the treatment of Jesus here (e.g., in κολλαβισμός a player with eyes covered has to guess which hand another player has used to strike him; in χαλκῆ μῖα a blindfolded player tries to find other players while being struck by them with papyrus husks [cf. Miller, *JBL* 90 (1971) 309–13]). It is impossible to decide whether an existing game is being reflected or the talk about Jesus has inspired in his case a particular variant of their rough play. The guards are whiling away the night hours at

Jesus' expense. In Luke's version, not a night hearing before the high priest, as in Mark, but only this cruel game of the guards fills the time for Jesus from his arrest until the early morning sitting of the Sanhedrin.

65 ἕτερα πολλά, "many other [things]," looks Lukan (see Schneider, *Verleugnung*, 103–4). The presence of βλασφημοῦντες (lit. "blaspheming/insulting") may be due to an inverted use of the charge in Mark 14:64 that Jesus was guilty of blasphemy, of which Luke otherwise makes no use. Is the behavior of the guards merely insulting, or does Luke from his Christian perspective consider their words to be in fact blasphemous?

Explanation

Attention moves from a devastated Peter back to the Master he has disowned. The remaining hours of darkness are whiled away with Jesus as the butt of the cruel attentions of those charged with keeping him in custody.

Jesus is mocked and beaten and made the center of a cruel game. Various soldiers' games helped to pass the time on guard duty. The game here has perhaps been mounted in a specially inspired form, because of the prophetic aspect of the identity attributed to Jesus in the popular mind. For Luke, given his Christian understanding of the person of Jesus, all of this is nothing less than blasphemy.

Jesus Brought before the Sanhedrin (22:66–71)

Bibliography

GENERAL FOR 22:66–71:

Anderson, C. P. "The Trial of Jesus as Jewish-Christian Polarization: Blasphemy and Polemic in Mark's Gospel." In *Anti-Judaism in Early Christianity: Vol. 1. Paul and the Gospels*, ed. P. Richardson. Waterloo, ON: Wilfred Laurier University, 1986. 107–25. **Bammel, E.** "Die Blutgerichtsbarkeit in der römischen Provinz Judäa vor dem ersten jüdischen Aufstand." *JJS* 25 (1974) 35–63. **Bartsch, H.-W.** "Wer verurteilte Jesu zum Tode?" *NovT* 7 (1964–65) 210–16. **Beavis, M. A.** "The Trial before the Sanhedrin (Mark 14:53–65): Reader Response and Greco Roman Readers." *CBQ* 49 (1987) 581–96. **Ben-Chorin, S.** "Wer hat Jesus zum Tode verurteilt?" *ZRGG* 37 (1985) 63–67. **Benoit, P.** *The Passion and Resurrection of Jesus.* New York: Herder and Herder, 1969. 93–114. ———. *Jesus and the Gospel.* Tr. B. Weatherhead. London: Darton, Longman and Todd, 1973. 1:123–88. ———. "Jésus devant le Sanhedrin." *Angelicum* 20 (1943) 143–65. **Betz, O.** "Probleme des Prozesses Jesu." *ANRW* 2/25.1 (1982) 565–647. ———. "The Temple Scroll and the Trial of Jesus." *SWJT* 30 (1988) 5–8. **Bickermann, E.** "Utilitas Crucis." *RHR* 112 (1935) 169–241. **Blinzler, J.** *The Trial of Jesus: The Jewish and Roman Proceedings against Jesus Christ Described and Assessed from the Oldest Accounts.* Tr. I. and F. McHugh. Westminster: Newman, 1959. ———. *Der Prozess Jesu.* 4th ed. Regensburg: Pustet, 1969. ———. "Geschichtlichkeit und Legalität des jüdischen Prozesses gegen Jesus." *Stimmen der Zeit* 147 (1950–51) 345–57. ———. "Das Synedrium von Jerusalem und die Strafprozessordnung der Mischna." *ZNW* 52 (1961) 54–65.

————. "The Trial of Jesus in the Light of History." *Judaism* 20 (1971) 49–55. **Brandon, S. G. F.** *The Trial of Jesus of Nazareth.* London: Batsford, 1968. ————. "The Trial of Jesus." *Judaism* 20 (1971) 43–48. **Büchsel, F.** "Die Blutgerichtsbarkeit des Synedrions." *ZNW* 30 (1931) 202–10. ————. "Noch einmal: Zur Blutgerichtsbarkeit des Synedrions." *ZNW* 33 (1934) 84–87. **Burkill, T. A.** "The Competence of the Sanhedrin." *VC* 10 (1956) 80–96. ————. "The Trial of Jesus." *VC* 12 (1958) 1–18. **Cantinat, J.** "Jésus devant le Sanhédrin." *NRT* 75 (1953) 300–308. **Cassidy, R.** *Jesus, Politics and Society: A Study of Luke's Gospel.* Maryknoll, NY: Orbis, 1978. 63–76. **Catchpole, D. R.** "The Problem of the Historicity of the Sanhedrin Trial." In *The Trial of Jesus,* ed. E. Bammel. 47–65. ————. *The Trial of Jesus.* 153–220. **Cohen, D.,** and **Paulus, C.** "Einige Bemerkungen zum Prozess Jesu bei den Synoptikern." *ZSSR* 102 (1985) 437–45. **Cohn, H.** *The Trial and Death of Jesus.* New York: Harper and Row, 1967. ————. "Reflections on the Trial of Jesus." *Judaism* 20 (1971) 10–23. **Dabrowski, E.** "The Trial of Jesus in Recent Research." *SE* 4 [= TU 102] (1968) 21–27. **Danby, H.** "The Bearing of the Rabbinical Criminal Code on the Jewish Trial Narratives in the Gospels." *JTS* 21 (1919–20) 51–76. **Davies, A. T.** "The Jews and the Death of Jesus: Theological Reflections." *Int* 23 (1969) 207–17. **Delorme, J.** "Le procès de Jésus ou la parole risquée (Lc 22,54–23,25)." *RSR* 69 (1981) 123–46. **Derrett, J. D. M.** "An Oriental Lawyer Looks at the Trial of Jesus and the Doctrine of the Redemption." In *Law.* 389–460. ————. "Midrash in the New Testament: The Origin of Luke XXII 67–68." *ST* 29 (1975) 147–56. **Doerr, F.** "Der Prozess Jesu in rechtsgeschichtlicher Sicht." *Archiv für Strafrecht und Strafprozess* 55 (1908) 12–65. **Donahue, J. R.** "Temple, Trial, and Royal Christology (Mark 14:53–65)." In *The Passion in Mark,* ed. W. H. Kelber. 61–79. ————. *Are You the Christ? The Trial Narrative in the Gospel of Mark.* SBLDS 10. Missoula, MT: Scholars, 1973. **Duplacy, J.** "Une variante méconnue du texte reçu: '. . . Η ΑΠΟΛΥΣΗΤΕ' (Lc 22, 68)." In *Neutestamentliche Aufsätze.* FS J. Schmid, ed. J. Blinzler et al. Regensburg: Pustet, 1963. 42–52. **Ebeling, H. J.** "Zur Frage nach der Kompetenz des Synhedrion." *ZNW* 35 (1936) 290–95. **Enslin, M. S.** "The Trial of Jesus." *JQR* 60 (1970) 353–55. ————. "The Temple and the Cross." *Judaism* 20 (1971) 24–31. **Feuter, K., Schweizer, E.,** and **Winter, P.** "Diskussion um den Prozess Jesu." In *Wer war Jesus von Nazareth? Die Erforschung einer historischen Gestalt,* ed. G. Strube. Munich: Kindler, 1972. 221–40. **Flender, H.** *Luke: Theologian of Redemptive History.* 44–50. **Flusser, D.** "A Literary Approach to the Trial of Jesus." *Judaism* 20 (1971) 32–36. **France, R. T.** "Jésus devant Caïphe." *Hokhma* 15 (1980) 20–35. **Fricke, W.** *The Court-Martial of Jesus: A Christian Defends the Jews against the Charge of Deicide.* Tr. S. Attanasio. New York: Grove Wiedenfeld, 1990. **Gnilka, J.** "Die Verhandlungen vor dem Synhedrion und vor Pilatus nach Markus 14,53–15,5." *EKK Vorarbeiten* 2 (1970) 5–21. **Goguel, M.** "A propos du procès de Jésus." *ZNW* 31 (1932) 289–301. **Grant, F. C.** "On the Trial of Jesus: A Review Article." *JR* 44 (1964) 230–37. **Grant, R. M.** "The Trial of Jesus in the Light of History." *Judaism* 20 (1971) 37–42. **Haufe, G.** "Der Prozess Jesu im Lichte der gegenwärtigen Forschung." *ZdZ* 22 (1968) 93–101. **Heil, J. P.** "Reader-Response and the Irony of Jesus before the Sanhedrin in Luke 22:66–71." *CBQ* 51 (1989) 271–84. **Hill, D.** "Jesus before the Sanhedrin—On What Charge?" *IBS* 7 (1985) 174–86. **Holzmeister, U.** "Zur Frage der Blutgerichtsbarkeit des Synedriums." *Bib* 19 (1938) 43–59. **Horbury, W.** "The Trial of Jesus in Jewish Tradition." In *The Trial of Jesus,* ed. E. Bammel. 103–21. **Husband, R. W.** *The Prosecution of Jesus: Its Date, History and Legality.* Princeton: Princeton University, 1916. **Imbert, J.** *Le procès de Jésus: "Que sais-je?"* Paris: Presses universitaires de France, 1980. ————. "Le procès de Jésus." *RICP* 19 (1986) 53–66. **Jaubert, A.** "Les séances du Sanhédrin et les récits de la passion." *RHR* 166 (1964) 143–69; 167 (1965) 1–33. **Jeremias, J.** "Zur Geschichtlichkeit des Verhörs Jesu vor dem Hohen Rat." *ZNW* 43 (1950–51) 145–50. **Jonge, M. de.** "The Use of Ο ΧΡΙΣΤΟΣ in the Passion Narrative." In *Jésus aux origines de la christologie,* J. Dupont et al. BETL 40. Gembloux: Duculot, 1975. 169–92. **Juel, D.** *Messiah and Temple: The Trial of Jesus in the Gospel of Mark.* SBLDS 31. Missoula, MT: Scholars, 1977. **Juster, J.** *Les Juifs dans l'Empire romain: Leur condition juridique, économique et sociale.* 2 vols. Paris: Geuthner, 1914. Esp. 2:133–42. **Kempthorne, R.** "Anti-Christian Tendency in pre-Marcan Traditions of the Sanhedrin Trial." *SE* 7 [= TU 126]

(1982) 283–86. **Kertelge, K.,** ed. *Der Prozess gegen Jesus.* **Kilpatrick, G. D.** *The Trial of Jesus.* London: Oxford University, 1953. **Koch, W.** *Der Prozess Jesu: Versuch eines Tatsachenberichts.* Cologne: Kiepenheuer und Witsch, 1966. **Kolping, A.** "'Standrectlich gekreuzigt': Neuere überlegungen zum Prozess Jesu." *TRev* 83 (1987) 265–76. **Kosmala, H.** "Der Prozess Jesu." *SaatHof* 69 (1932) 25–39. **Lapide, P. E.** "Jesu Tode durch Römerhand: Zur blasphemischen These von 'Gottesmord' durch die Juden." In *Gottesverächter und Menschenfeinde? Juden zwischen Jesus und frühchristlicher Kirche,* ed. H. Goldstein. Düsseldorf: Patmos, 1979. 239–55. ————. *Wer war schuld an Jesu Tod?* Gütersloh: Mohn, 1987. **Légasse, S.** "Jésus devant le Sanhédrin: Recherche sur les traditions évangéliques." *RTL* 5 (1974) 170–97. **Lengle, J.** "Zum Prozess Jesu." *Hermes* 70 (1935) 312–21. **Lentzen-Deis, F.** "Passionsbericht als Handlungsmodell? Überlegungen zu Anstössen aus der 'pragmatischen' Sprachwissenschaft für die exegetischen Methoden." In *Der Prozess gegen Jesus,* ed. K. Kertelge. 191–232, esp. 221–32. **Lietzmann, H.** "Der Prozess Jesu." In *Kleine Schriften: 2. Studien zum Neuen Testament,* ed. K. Aland. TU 68. Berlin: Akademie-V., 1958. 251–63. ————. "Bemerkungen zum Prozess Jesu." *ZNW* 30 (1931) 211–15; 31 (1932) 78–84. **Lindeskog, G.** "Der Prozess Jesu im jüdisch-christlichen Religionsgespräch." In *Abraham unser Vater: Juden und Christen in Gespräch über die Bibel.* FS O Michel, ed. O. Betz, M. Hengel, and P. Schmidt. Leiden: Brill, 1963. 325–36. **Linnemann, E.** *Studien.* 109–35. **Lohse, E.** "Der Prozess Jesu Christi." In *Ecclesia et Res Publica.* FS K. D. Schmidt, ed. G. Kretschmar and B. Lohse. Göttingen: Vandenhoeck & Ruprecht, 1961. 24–39. **Matera, F. J.** "Luke 22,66–71: Jesus before the ΠΡΕΣΒΥΤΕΡΙΟΝ." In *L'Évangile de Luc* (1989), ed. F. Neirynck. 517–33. ————. "The Trial of Jesus: Problems and Proposals." *Int* 45 (1991) 5–16. **McLaren, J. S.** *Power and Politics in Palestine.* 88–101. **McRuer, J. C.** *The Trial of Jesus.* Toronto: Clark, Irwin, 1964. **Meyer, F. E.** "Einige Bemerkungen zur Bedeutungen des Terminus 'Synhedrion' in den Schriften des Neuen Testaments." *NTS* 14 (1967–68) 545–51. **Müller, K.** "Möglichkeit und Vollzu, jüdischer Kapitalgerichtsbarkeit im Prozess gegen Jesus von Nazaret." In *Der Prozess gegen Jesus,* ed. K. Kertelge. 41–83. **O'Meara, T. F.** "The Trial of Jesus in an Age of Trials." *TToday* 28 (1972) 451–65. **Pawlikowski, J. T.** "The Trial and Death of Jesus. Reflections in Light of a New Understanding of Judaism." *ChicStud* 25 (1986) 79–94. **Pesch, R.** *Der Prozess Jesu geht weiter.* Freiburg/Basel/Vienna: Herder, 1988. **Radl, W.** "Sonderüberlieferungen bei Lukas? Traditionsgeschichtliche Fragen zu Lk 22,67f; 23,2 und 23,6–12." In *Der Prozess gegen Jesus,* ed. K. Kertelge. 131–47. **Ritt, H.** "Wer war schuld am Jesu Tod? Zeitgeschichte, Recht und theologische Deutung." *BZ* 31 (1987) 165–75. **Rosenblatt, S.** "The Crucifixion of Jesus from the Standpoint of the Pharisaic Law." *JBL* 75 (1956) 315–21. **Rudberg, G.** "Die Verhöhnung Jesu vor dem Hohenpriester." *ZNW* 24 (1925) 307–9. **Sandmel, S.** "The Trial of Jesus: Reservations." *Judaism* 20 (1971) 69–74. **Schinzer, R.** "Die Bedeutung des Prozesses Jesu." *NZSTR* 253 (1983) 138–54. **Schneider, G.** *Verleugnung, Verspottung und Verhör Jesu nach Lukas, 22,54–71: Studien zur lukanischen Darstellung der Passion.* SANT 22. Munich: Kösel, 1969. ————. "Das Verfahren gegen Jesus in der Sicht des dritten Evangeliums (Lk 22,54–23,25): Redaktionskritik und historische Rückfrage" In *Der Prozess gegen Jesus,* ed. K. Kertelge. 111–30. ————. "Gab es eine vorsynoptische Szene 'Jesus vor dem Synedrium'?" *NovT* 12 (1970) 22–39. ————. "Jesus vor dem Synedrium." *BibLeb* 11 (1970) 1–15. **Schubert, K.** "Das Verhör Jesu vor dem Hohen Rat." In *Bibel und zeitgemässer Glaube II,* ed. J. Sint. Klosterneuburg: Buch- und Kunstverlag, 1967. 97–130. ————. "Biblical Criticism Criticised: With Reference to the Markan Report of Jesus' Examination before the Sanhedrin." In *Jesus and the Politics of His Day,* ed. E. Bammel and C. F. D. Moule. 385–402. ————. "Die Juden oder die Römer? Der Prozess Jesu und sein geschichtlicher Hintergrund." *WortWahr* 17 (1962) 701–10. ————. "Die Juden und die Römer." *BLit* 36 (1962–63) 235–42. **Schumann, H.** "Bemerkungen zum Prozess Jesu vor dem Synhedrium." *ZSSR* 82 (1965) 315–20. **Sloyan, G. S.** *Jesus on Trial.* Philadelphia: Fortress, 1973. ————. "Recent Literature on the Trial Narratives of the Four Gospels." In *Critical History and Biblical Faith: New Testament Perspectives,* ed. T. J. Ryan. Villanova: College Theological Society, Villanova University, 1979. 136–76. **Söding, T.** "Der Prozess Jesu: Exegetische, historische und theologische Fragestellungen." *HerKor* 41

(1987) 236–40. **Sobosan, J. G.** "The Trial of Jesus." *JES* 10 (1973) 72–91. **Stewart, R. A.** "Judicial Procedure in New Testament Times." *EvQ* 47 (1975) 94–109. **Strobel, A.** *Die Stunde der Wahrheit: Untersuchungen zum Stafverfahrengegen Jesus.* WUNT 21. Tübingen: Mohr, 1980. **Trilling, W.** *Fragen zur Geschichtlichkeit Jesu.* Düsseldorf: Patmos, 1966. 130–41. ———. *Jésus devant l'histoire.* Paris: Cerf, 1968. 175–88. **Tyson, J. B.** "The Lukan Version of the Trial of Jesus." *NovT* 3 (1959) 249–58. **Valentin, P.** "Les comparutions de Jésus devant le Sanhédrin." *RSR* 59 (1971) 230–36. **Via, E. J.** "According to Luke, Who Put Jesus to Death?" In *Political Issues,* ed. R. J. Cassidy and P. J. Scharper. 122–45. **Walaskay, P. W.** "The Trial and Death of Jesus in the Gospel of Luke." *JBL* 94 (1975) 81–93. **Winter, P.** "Luke XXII 66b–71." *ST* 9 (1955) 112–15. ———. "Marginal Notes on the Trial of Jesus." *ZNW* 50 (1959) 14–33, 221–51. ———. "The Markan Account of Jesus' Trial by the Sanhedrin." *JTS* n.s. 14 (1963) 94–102. ———. "The Trial of Jesus and the Competence of the Sanhedrin." *NTS* 10 (1963–64) 494–99. ———. "The Trial of Jesus." *Commentary* 38/3 (1964) 35–41. ———. *On the Trial of Jesus.* Studia judaica 1. 2nd ed. Rev. T. A. Burkill and G. Vermes. Berlin/New York: de Gruyter, 1974. **Zeitlin, S.** *Who Crucified Jesus?* New York: Harper and Row, 1942. ———. "The Trial and Crucifixion of Jesus Reexamined." *JQR* 31 (1941) 327–69; 32 (1941–42) 175–89, 279–301. ———. "The Political Synedrion and the Religious Synedrion." *JQR* 36 (1945) 109–40. ———. "Synedrion in Greek Literature, the Gospels and the Institution of the Sanhedrin." *JQR* 37 (1946) 189–98. ———. "Synedrion in the Judeo-Hellenistic Literature and Sanhedrin in the Tannaitic Literature." *JQR* 37 (1946) 307–15.

And see at 22:1–2, 54–62.

FOR LUKE 22:69:

Bammel, E. "Erwägungen zur Eschatologie Jesu." *SE* 3 [= TU 88] (1964) 3–32, esp. 23–26. **Borsch, F. H.** "Mark XIV.62 and 1 Enoch LXII.5." *NTS* 14 (1967–68) 565–67. **Catchpole, D.** "The Answer of Jesus to Caiaphas (Matt. XXVI. 64)." *NTS* 17 (1970–71) 213–26. **Dupont, J.** "'Assis à la droite de Dieu': L'interpretation du Ps. 110,1 dans le Nouveau Testament." In *Resurrexit: Acts du Symposion sur la résurrection de Jésus,* ed. E. Dhanis. Rome, 1974. 423–36. **Feuillet, A.** "Le triomphe du fils de l'homme d'après la déclaration du Christ aux Sanhédrites (Mc., xiv, 62; Mt., xxvi, 64; Lc., xxii, 69)." In *La venue du Messie.* RechBib 6. Bruges: Desclée de Brouwer, 1962. 149–71. **Flusser, D.** "'At the Right hand of Power.'" *Immanuel* 14 (1982) 42–46. **Glasson, T. F.** "The Reply to Caiaphas (Mark XIV.62)." *NTS* 7 (1960–61) 88–93. **Goldberg, A.** "Sitzend zur Rechten der Kraft." *BZ* 8 (1964) 284–93. **Hay, D. M.** *Glory at the Right Hand: Psalm 110 in Early Christianity.* SBLMS 18. Missoula: Scholars, 1973. **Kempthorne, R.** "The Marcan Text of Jesus' Answer to the High Priest (Mark xiv 62)." *NovT* 19 (1977) 197–208. **Lamarche, P.** "La déclaration de Jésus devant le Sanhédrin." In *Christ vivant: Essai sur la christologie du Nouveau Testament.* LD 43. Paris: Cerf, 1966. 147–63. **Linton, O.** "The Trial of Jesus and the Interpretation of Psalm cx." *NTS* 7 (1960–61) 258–62. **Lührmann, D.** "Markus 14.55–64: Christologie und Zerstörung des Tempels im Markusevangelium." *NTS* 27 (1980–81) 457–74. **Perrin, N.** "The High Priest's Question and Jesus' Answer." In *The Passion in Mark,* ed. W. H. Kelber. 80–95. ———. "Mark xiv. 62: The End Product of a Christian Pesher Tradition?" *NTS* 12 (1965–66) 150–55. ———. "The Christology of Mark: A Study in Methodology." *JR* 51 (1971) 173–87. **Pesch, R.** "Die Passion des Menschensohns: Eine Studie zu den Menschensohnworten der vormarkinischen Passionsgeschichte." In *Jesus und der Menschensohn.* FS A. Vögtle, ed. R. Pesch and R. Schnackenburg. Freiburg/Basel/Vienna: Herder, 1975. 166–95, esp. 184–89. **Plevnik, J.** "Son of Man Seated at the Right Hand of God: Luke 22,69 in Lucan Christology." *Bib* 72 (1991) 331–47. **Rese, M.** *Alttestamentliche Motive.* 199–200. **Sabbe, M.** "The Son of Man Saying in Acts 7,56." In *Les Actes des Apôtres,* ed. J. Kremer. BETL 48. Gembloux/Leuven: Duculot/University Press, 1979. 241–79.

And see at excursus: "Son of Man" in WBC vol. 35B.

Translation

66 *When it became day, the eldership of the People was gathered together, both chief priests and scribes; and they had Jesus brought into their council meeting,*[a] 67 *and said [to him], "If you are the Christ, tell us!" He said to them, "If I tell you, you will not believe;* 68 *if I ask, you will not answer."*[b] 69 *But from now on the Son of Man will be seated at the right hand of the power of God."* 70 *They all said, "Are you, then, the Son of God?" He said to them, "Do you say that I am?"* 71 *They said, "Why do we still have need of testimony? For we have heard [it] ourselves from his own mouth!"*

Notes

[a] Gr. συνέδριον, normally translated "Sanhedrin." "Council meeting place" would also be possible.
[b] A D W Ψ *f*¹³ etc. add μοι ἢ ἀπολύσητε, "me or release [me]." Its claim to originality has been carefully assessed by Duplacy ("Une variante," 42–52), with negative results.

Form/Structure/Setting

From a night in cruel custody Jesus is taken to an early morning meeting of the Sanhedrin. The Jerusalem leaders at last have Jesus at their mercy away from the public eye. Their antagonistic interaction with Jesus now reaches its high point.

On the Lukan order here, see at 22:54b–62 and 63–65. The change of sequence means that the hearings before the Sanhedrin, before Pilate, and before Herod come in a simple sequence.

Radl ("Sonderüberlieferungen," 146–47) has recently placed in question the argument for a second Lukan source based on the similarity between elements of Luke 22:67–68 and John 10:24–25 (that the dependence is less likely to be of John on Luke has been supported from possible Matthean echoes of the source [ἵνα ἡμῖν εἴπῃς, "that you tell us," in Matt 26:63; cf. εἰπὸν ἡμῖν, "tell us," in Luke 22:66; σὺ εἶπας, "you have said," in Matt 26:64; cf. ὑμεῖς λέγετε, "you say," in Luke 22:70; we should note that the Synoptists all have σὺ λέγεις, "you say," in answer to Pilate]). He proposes an alternative redactional origin for features in Luke 22:67–68, based on a Lukan desire to echo 20:1–8. On this basis Radl is able to account not only for εἰπὸν ἡμῖν, "tell us" (cf. 20:2), but also for the opening λέγοντες, "saying," of 22:67 (cf. 20:2), the ἐὰν δέ (lit. "and if") construction of 22:68 (cf. 20:6), and the use of ἐρωτήσω in 22:68 (cf. 20:3). It seems to me that Radl is likely to be right about the link to 20:1–8 (cf. also Pesch, *Markusevangelium,* 408), but this link involves only εἰπὸν ἡμῖν, "tell us," of the materials that, on the basis of commonality with John and/or Matthew, have led to the postulation of a second source for Luke. In particular the conjunction between εἶπον ὑμῖν καὶ οὐ πιστεύετε, "I have told you and you do not believe" (John 10:25), and ἐὰν ὑμῖν εἴπω, οὐ μὴ πιστεύσητε, "if I tell you, you will certainly not believe" (Luke 22:67), remains striking, especially when, as well, John 10:24 has εἰ σὺ εἶ ὁ Χριστός, εἰπὲ ἡμῖν, "if you are the Christ, tell us," which differs from the wording in Luke 22:67 in only a second aorist in place of a first aorist form. For this argument everything depends on whether John should be considered to have had access to Luke. Since elsewhere the nature of the Luke-John links seems to be best accounted for by common tradition, I take that to be the better explanation here as well. Other source arguments are suggestive without being decisive: (*i*) change of sequence in Luke is often an indication of a second source; (*ii*) Luke usually abbreviates dialogue, so the expansion here in connection with the messianic question may point to a source; (*iii*) Luke is not likely to have dropped the role of the high priest (contrast the role of the high priest in Acts 4:6; 5:17, 21, 27; 7:1; 9:1; 22:5; 23:2, 4, 5; 24:1); (*iv*) Luke is not known for creating parallelism, so the parallelism here is likely to be from a source.

The likelihood of a second Lukan source is more confidently to be maintained than is the scope of its presentation in Luke's account. Luke might be responsible for v 66 on the basis of Mark 15:1, but this is not likely; he is likely to be responsible for v 68, as a reiteration from 20:1–8; he could have introduced v 69 on the basis of his Markan source, but the near agreement of Matthew and Luke against Mark (ἀπ' ἄρτι, "from now on"; ἀπὸ τοῦ νῦν, "from now on"; no time phrase) stands in favor of something comparable coming at this point in the second source; and v 71 is quite likely to have been formed by Luke on the basis of Mark 14:63b–64a (what has this displaced of the second source?).

While Mark's source here will be from a pre-Markan passion narrative (see at 22:54b–62), the same level of confidence is not possible in the case of Luke's second source for the Sanhedrin hearing. However, the sheer fact of a second source for so many of the passion pericopes counts in favor of the existence of a second sequential passion source.

Unlike the Markan account, the Lukan account (and even more so the Lukan source, if its scope has been rightly discerned) has none of the marks of a formal trial about it. It might best be described as a pretrial investigation, preparing the ground for a bid to have Jesus tried before the Roman prefect. The hearing confirms the resolve of the Sanhedrin members to see Jesus destroyed (cf. 22:2) and provides them with additional material to lay before Pilate (cf. 23:2). The Markan account is concerned about testimony against Jesus that would justify putting him to death; it calls witnesses, provides opportunity for the defendant to respond to the testimony against him, and reports a unanimous verdict: "condemned as deserving death." But despite the more clearly judicial nature of the proceedings, here too the hearing is preliminary to Jesus' being handed over to Pilate and to a hearing before him in which the chief priests appear in the role of accusers, rather than as representatives of a court seeking to have its verdict formally confirmed by a higher authority. What can we know about what is likely to have happened historically?

Fundamental to an attempt at historical reconstruction is the question of the competence in capital matters of the Sanhedrin as the highest Jewish court (like most others, I am not persuaded by Zeitlin's case [see bibliography above] for the existence of separate religious and political Sanhedrins, nor by the variant of it proposed by Rivkin [*HUCA* 46 (1975) 181–99], according to which the Sanhedrin involved in Jesus' death was simply an ad hoc committee called together by the high priest and used by the Roman governor to advise him in connection with the implementation of Imperial policy with regard to a matter of considerable local sensitivity [for a good "average" view on the Sanhedrin, see Schürer, rev. and ed. Vermes et al., *The History of the Jewish People*, 2:199–226, but this assumes a degree of stability and continuity in Jewish practice that is open to question; the weaknesses in the standard scholarly synthesis are exposed by Sanders, *Judaism*, 472–88 (and cf. McLaren, *Power and Politics*, esp. 210–22), but he offers an unnecessarily minimalist approach]). Though some support can still be found for Lietzmann's view ("Prozess Jesu") that the Sanhedrin in Jesus' day retained the death penalty, this view has a limited following and is surely to be rejected (for a well-argued recent statement of the view that only in connection with violation of the temple was there any concession to Jewish capital law, see Müller, "Kapitalberichtsbarkeit," 41–83 [even in these cases the jurisdiction remains firmly in the hands of the governor, and the most we can speak of is a share in the Roman judicial proceedings]). A decision by the Sanhedrin, sitting as a court, that Jesus was guilty of a capital charge under Jewish law, unless the charge was in connection with the violation of the temple, would pose no threat to his life. Even in connection with such a charge, their decision would not preclude the need for a further trial before the Roman prefect. In these circumstances it would seem better, in the case of Jesus, to speak of a hearing before the Sanhedrin rather than a trial. (This is not to deny that the Sanhedrin believed it had the intrinsic right to deal with capital crime nor that, on occasion, Roman limitations on Jewish autonomy were transgressed, and that Roman authority might not always have considered it expedient to act against such transgression. But there is no reason to think in terms of an act of defiance in the case of Jesus.)

If this is right (that the Sanhedrin was not in fact trying Jesus for his life in connection with an alleged capital offense), then it is a moot point how much we should be concerned about whether the proceedings were conducted in accordance with (later rabbinic and perhaps idealized) standing regulations for the conduct of capital cases by the Sanhedrin (see esp. *m. San.* 4:1). The role of the Sanhedrin is undoubtedly to be seen as judicial in some sense, but there is no basis for pressing the claim of particular regulations dealing with capital cases. There must also be doubt about the appropriateness of seeking to identify with certainty the crime *in Jewish law* for which Jesus was being tried. This is not to deny the pertinence to the Sanhedrin's dealing with Jesus of such texts as Deut 13 on the judgment of a seducer of the people or Deut 17:12–13 on the fate of one who shows contempt for the judge or priest in Jerusalem. It is only to claim that the hearing should not be examined for its formal adequacy in connection either with general Jewish judicial practice or in connection with the establishment of guilt in connection with a particular charge. The gathering was concerned to assure itself that petitioning Pilate to hear a capital case against this man was appropriate and concerned to prepare the groundwork for pressing such a charge. In the Synoptic accounts of the hearing before Pilate, no attempt is made to appeal to any basis in specifically Jewish law for seeking a death penalty (unless Luke's "perverting our nation" [23:2] should be given this sense; John has "We have a law, and according to that law he ought to die, because he claimed to be the Son of God" [19:7], but this is not likely to be a direct historical reminiscence).

What then of the views that see the "trial" before the Sanhedrin as only a product of later tension between Christians and Jews, and perhaps as part of a Christian strategy to maximize Jewish responsibility in order to minimize Roman responsibility, in the context of the need for Christianity to present itself in the best possible light to the Roman world in the later first century? Despite the degree of parallelism between Mark's hearings before the high priest and Pilate, the case for the one being spun out of the other (as Baumann, "Markus 15,2–5 und Markus 14,55–64," *ZNW* 52 [1961] 273–78) is hardly credible. One cannot easily account for the Jesus of the Gospels being tried before the Roman prefect; his ministry was so thoroughly an in-house Jewish affair. His gathering of crowds may have been somewhat disturbing to the sensibilities of the Roman overlords, but precious little else in his ministry would have attracted the attention of the Romans (on the "triumphal entry," see at 19:29–40, and on the "cleansing of the temple," see at 19:45–46). His trial by Rome makes altogether better sense if there was a Jewish bridge to the Romans of precisely the kind that the Gospel accounts offer us.

It is, however, a much more difficult matter to speak with any confidence about the details of the Jewish hearing(s). The main feature of the tentative reconstruction of Luke's second source offered above is Jesus' refusal to deny that he is messiah (but what did this source say would be so from now on?). The Johannine account (18:13–14, 19–24) has a hearing with Annas in which the thrust of Jesus' answer to Annas (whose question is about Jesus' disciples and his teaching, not about Jesus' own identity) is that he has taught everything openly in public, so has nothing to add now (then there is a hearing before Caiaphas for which no content is reported). The Markan account (14:53–66; 15:1) is heavily influenced by the contrast between the confession made by Jesus and the denials by Peter: Jesus emphatically affirms his messiahship and maintains that his hearers will see this worked out in terms of "the Son of Man seated at the right hand of the Power, and coming with the clouds of heaven." Mark also has quite an emphasis on false witness against Jesus and, in particular, on the use against Jesus of a version of the saying about the destruction and renewal of the temple. (Mark 15:1 is sometimes taken as a more original short account of a morning Jewish hearing, but this is based on taking συμβούλιον ποιήσαντες as "held a consultation" [implying that they (freshly) gathered to have a meeting of the Sanhedrin], whereas it is almost certainly to be taken as "reached a decision/decided on a plan of action" [cf. Schneider, *NovT* 12 (1970) 27–28; id., "Verfahren," 117; but see the contrary view of Légasse, *RTL* 5 (1974) 191, appealing to Benoit, *Angelicum* 20 (1943) 146–47]. The misunderstanding is a natural one [possibly going back to Luke], only to be avoided when we see that the separation of 15:1 from the earlier account of the hearing is simply a product of the intercalation into the hearing of the account of Peter's denials.)

The role for Annas provided in John would seem to be unmotivated if not based on historical reminiscence. But for the rest, John's account has become the occasion for making points that are otherwise important in the Johannine narrative. If we read Mark 15:1 as suggested above, then the night setting for the Markan hearing loses all prominence and is best seen as no more than a byproduct of the Markan chronological compression (see at 22:1–2): the hearing simply follows from the arrest, which was certainly made under the cover of darkness. The use in Mark of an alleged threat by Jesus against the temple has significant points in favor of its basic authenticity: (*i*) it fits well with the fact that, in respect to violation of the temple, the Roman authorities were committed to accommodating Jewish sensibilities, even to the extent of executing offenders (see above); (*ii*) John 2:19 and other Gospel materials in connection with the temple suggest that the accusation would have had some basis of plausibility in things the historical Jesus had said and done (see at 19:45–46; 21:5–6). Since it is difficult to account for a move from Mark's bold ἐγώ εἰμι, "I am," to Luke's more cautious "if I tell you, you will not believe" and "[do] you say that I am[?]," we should give priority to the Lukan version in this respect (as the role in Mark of the deliberate contrasting of Jesus and Peter would tend to confirm).

The Son of Man statement, the last component piece on which I will make comment, is the most difficult to assess. Given Mark's interest in a bold confession by Jesus in contrast to Peter's denial, it is not difficult to imagine that the Son of Man statement in 14:62 has been developed out of the tradition found in 12:35–37 and 13:26 (this would involve a more "instant" development than Perrin's "end product of a Christian Pesher tradition" [*NTS* 12 (1966) 150–55]). Against this there is, however, the support from Matthew-Luke agreement for something at this point in Luke's second source (see above), and this something would need to have been such that Luke could consider Mark 14:62 an appropriate replacement (assuming that the Markan text is to be taken as the basis for his own at this point; the differences between Luke and Mark here are easily attributable to Lukan redaction). Also, is Mark likely to be responsible for generating the use of τῆς δυνάμεως, "of Power," as a Jewish periphrasis for "of God"?

The question of origin cannot be separated from that of the role of the text in its present Markan context and possible role in the putative second Lukan source, a role that, in either case, is not immediately clear. The transition from "Christ" to "Son of Man" involved is also to be found in Mark 8:29, 31; 13:21–22, 26. The text has been variously taken (*i*) as having to do with the confirmation of Jesus' messianic identity in the (impending) eschatological denouement (cf. the future confirmatory role of the Son of Man in Mark 8:38 [see discussion at Luke 9:23–27]); (*ii*) as a threat of judgment by Jesus as Son of Man against those who are in the process of judging Jesus himself (e.g., Pesch, "Menschensohnes," 185; this view depends altogether too heavily on the belief that "Son of Man" was already titular in the time of Jesus and as such referred to one who was to be apocalyptic judge [see the excursus: "Son of Man"]); or (*iii*) as a way of giving precision to the sense in which Jesus claims that he is messiah. The third of these provides the smoothest transition in the Markan text, but the first view provides a more believable role for a form of this text in the reconstructed second Lukan source: "if I tell you, you won't believe [that I am the Christ], but the imminent coming of the one who, established in glory at the right hand of the Father, cannot have his identity mistaken will confirm the true nature of my identity."

It seems most likely, then, that Mark found the Son of Man statement already in his tradition at this point and that something cognate was at this position in Luke's second source. Mark may, however, have been responsible for giving a confessional force to the text, whereas in his source (as in Luke's second source), it functioned rather as an appeal to a future confirmation by the glorious Son of Man of the true nature of the identity of Jesus. Now this double pre-Markan attestation does not prove that we are dealing with an original feature of the Jewish hearing. But taken with the concordance established for the second Lukan source and the affinity of this saying with other Gospel materials whose authenticity has been defended in the present commentary (see esp. at 9:23–27 and 20:41–44; as well as more generally the excursus: "Son of Man"), the source judgments help make the case that it is more likely than not that a Son of Man saying was an original feature of the Jewish hearing. Greater uncertainty must remain as to the precise contours of the original Son of Man saying. We are probably to think in terms of some glorious manifestation of the Son of Man, and there is no particular reason to deny the allusion to Dan 7:13 as the means by which this motif comes to expression. The place in the original of the allusion to Ps 110:1 remains much less secure, though (apart from the royal note contributed by the psalm setting) its contribution to the thought has close affinity with what I have taken to be the original form for Luke 9:26 (see at 9:23–27).

Comment

In the privacy of their own council chambers, the members of the Sanhedrin continue their quest for a means by which to destroy Jesus. Jesus neither clearly affirms nor denies the suggestion that he (might think that he) is the Christ. Instead he questions the good faith of those who ask and predicts the glorification of the Son of Man to the right hand of God. For the Sanhedrin, this is a sufficient confession.

66 There is a certain similarity between v 66 and Mark 15:1, especially if 15:1 is (mis-)understood as referring to a morning hearing of the Sanhedrin. We should note, however, the striking lack of shared language (apart from uses of "and," there are only "chief priests," "scribes," and "Sanhedrin"; and of these the last probably means for Luke the Sanhedrin *meeting* or even the place of meeting of the Sanhedrin and not the Sanhedrin *members* as in Mark, while "scribes" is used in a different grammatical construction). Though there are undoubted Lukan touches to the language, it seems most likely that Luke is reflecting his second source here (cf. Green, *Death of Jesus,* 69–70; Schneider, *Verleugnung,* 105–12; Catchpole, *Trial,* 190–93; Matthew's "of the People" and "led [him] away" (ἀπήγαγον) in 27:1 and "were gathered together" in 26:57b may well be language from this second source).

Luke envisages Jesus being held during the (remaining) hours of darkness, pending an early morning gathering of the Sanhedrin. This pattern is found again in Acts (4:3; 5:17–22). For the group gathered here, Luke uses τὸ πρεσβυτέριον τοῦ λαοῦ, "the eldership of the People" (he will use πρεσβυτέριον again in connection with the highest level of Jewish leadership in Acts 22:5), then specifies this eldership as made up both of chief priests and of scribes. On scribes, see at 5:17. For the different ways in which Luke refers to the upper echelons of Jewish political/legal leadership in Jerusalem, see at 9:22. We are probably to understand that the Sanhedrin meets in their regular meeting place and has Jesus brought to them from the high priest's house (ἀπήγαγον [lit. "they led away"] is best taken causatively [the council "had him brought"]). The critical interaction that has led to this point may be tracked from 19:47–49 through 20:1–8, 9–19, 20–26, 45–47, (21:1–4), 22:2, 3–6, 47–53 to the present scene.

67 Where Mark has the high priest interrogating, Luke, more vaguely, makes the whole council the source of the questioning. Instead of Mark's "Christ, the son of the Blessed," Luke has the epithets used separately (but with "Son of God") in questions that are separated by the Son of Man saying in v 69. The results of the source discussion in *Form/Structure/Setting* above make it likely that a double question was already part of Luke's second source. In this respect, the Markan form is likely to be a conflation based upon the loss of role, after the introduction of the emphatic ἐγώ εἰμι, "I am," for the pair of more subtle answers attributed to Jesus in the Lukan source.

For Luke, Jesus clearly is the Christ (see at 2:11; 9:20; 24:26, 46), but the question is asked here in the context of a hostile interrogation. In any case, the Lukan Jesus does not proclaim himself as the Christ prior to the resurrection, and even then only to his closest followers and only in terms of an insistence that the shape of his own destiny conformed with the scriptural view of the career of the messiah (24:26, 46). In the Lukan account, disciples have publicly used royal language of Jesus at 19:38. The political usefulness of a positive answer will emerge pointedly in 23:2. Jesus' equivocal answer resets the question into the context of issues of faith and of the working of God. Jesus wishes to influence positively the faith of his interrogators; they desire only to obtain the power to destroy him. The situation has a certain likeness to that in Jer 38:14–15, but it is unlikely that any allusion is intended.

68 This verse is likely to be Luke's contribution, based on the similarity he perceives between the present scene and the earlier "interrogation" in 20:1–8 (see above in *Form/Structure/Setting*). There, in response to the question addressed to him, Jesus has asked and his interrogators have failed to answer. The inclusion of v 68 reminds the reader that these Jewish leaders who are questioning Jesus have already, by their prevarication, forfeited any right to have their questions treated as expressing a genuine interest in learning the truth. If we punctuate the final clause of v 70 as a question, we have Jesus asking but receiving no answer.

69 ἀπὸ τοῦ νῦν, "from now on," is Lukan idiom, but Matthew's equivalent, ἀπ' ἄρτι (which is Matthean idiom), suggests that a time expression was found in Luke's second source here. The other differences from Mark are best attributed to Luke himself. Luke is particularly interested in the royal enthronement of Jesus in heaven (cf. 9:51; 19:12; 24:26; Acts 1:11; 2:30, 33–36; 3:20). This will be the vindication of Jesus' messianic identity that counts (cf. Acts 2:23–24; 3:13–15). For the role of Ps 110:1, we can look back to 20:41–44 and on to Acts 2:34–35. Luke drops the visibility of the enthronement (it happens in heaven) and the coming with the clouds (he followed Mark in using this motif in 21:27, but here it introduces an unnecessary complication, and *without it* the text straightforwardly equates the Son of Man who suffers [here from the passion context] with the Christ who is to be enthroned [for the relationship for Luke between Son of Man and Christ, see at 6:1–5; what has up to this point only been expressed in Son of Man language is from now on expressed in Christ language]). On Son of Man more broadly, see the excursus: "Son of Man." Luke is responsible for an added "of God" in 8:11; 9:20; 23:35; and possibly 15:10; 12:8, 9, so he may well be responsible for the phrase here (for the dynamic involved, cf. the discussion at 15:10: "power" is an indirect means of speaking of God, which is now oddly coupled with a direct mention of God).

70 Much of the language here could be Lukan or based on Luke's Markan source, but the overall source discussion (see *Form/Structure/Setting* and at v 67) suggests that a second source basis exists (most clearly in Jesus' answer). In v 69 Jesus has stopped short of directly claiming to be the Son of Man who is to be exalted to royal dignity in heaven, but his words are more than suggestive of this possibility. So, his words elicit the question from "all," "Are you, then, the Son of God?" (a statement is also possible ["So you are the Son of God!"]; "of God" is likely to be secondary to the Markan "of the Blessed," despite the fact that "Blessed" as a periphrasis for God has not been exactly paralleled [*m. Ber.* 7:3 (end) comes close]). For Luke, to be "Son of God" is an exalted status and relationship to God experienced by the messiah (cf. at 3:22; 1:26–38), but in the present question the words should be taken as no more than a synonym for "messiah" (see at 3:22 for discussion of a Qumran text that suggests that "Son of God" might already have been in Jewish usage in connection with messianic hope). ὑμεῖς λέγετε ὅτι ἐγώ εἰμι has been variously taken as meaning "the words are yours, but I admit the identification/the words are yours, and I make no comment/I am what you say that I am." But the drift of vv 67–68 suggests that it might be better to punctuate Jesus' answer here as a question: "Do you say/are you saying that I am?" Jesus' antagonists are not prepared to face and answer this question.

71 The form of the question here is close to that in Mark, and the verse is likely to be a free Lukan rendering of the Markan material (Luke has "out of the mouth" also at 4:22; 11:54; 19:22 [but with ἐκ rather than ἀπό for "out of "]). The reference to "testimony" comes slightly oddly into the Lukan narrative, which lacks the Markan calling of witnesses. In fact, in Luke's account the gathered council has not "heard [a confession] from his own lips." Jesus has failed to deny the "charge," and he has added fuel to the speculation that he might consider himself to be the messiah, but he has made no confession as such. This, however, is a nicety that is lost on the hostile interrogators.

Explanation

From custody overnight in the courtyard of the official residence of the high priest, Jesus is taken to an early morning meeting of the high council of the Jewish People, the Sanhedrin. Its members have been in conflict with Jesus since 19:47. Thus far frustrated in their purposes by public support of Jesus, the secret night arrest of Jesus has given them their opportunity. Now they can interrogate him without public answerability.

The accounts that we have in the Gospels are highly theologically colored accounts of how it came to be that Jesus was handed over to the Romans. The differences between them warn us at once that it is likely to be difficult to differentiate clearly between event and interpretation. Despite claims to the contrary, there is, however, no reason to be skeptical about the fundamental historicity of the Gospel account of the role of the political hierarchy in Jerusalem in handing Jesus over to the Roman authority and in pressing for his execution as a criminal.

In his version, Luke treats the chief priests and the scribes as the main constituent groups of what he calls "the eldership of the People." By this he means the members of the Sanhedrin. Recent scholarship has emphasized the need for caution about forming an understanding of this body on the basis of an ideal picture of the Sanhedrin pieced together out of later Jewish documents. Some even doubt that such a standing body even existed (as distinct from an ad hoc council of advice) at the time of Jesus' execution, but this seems to me to involve excessive skepticism. Though we can be less than confident about the makeup of its membership at the time, or its exact mode of functioning, there certainly was such a body, and it combined governing and judicial functions, in accord with the degree of self-government allowed the Jews by their Roman overlords. In the

time of Jesus, the Romans did not allow the Sanhedrin to impose the death penalty. That responsibility resided solely with the Roman prefect. There was, however,
a standing arrangement that the prefect would impose the death penalty in the
case of violations of the Jewish temple. This was the one area of clear concession
to distinctive Jewish understandings of capital crime.

This restriction on the Jewish judiciary means that Jesus was not officially on
trial before the Sanhedrin. They could have tried him and inflicted some lesser
punishment, if they found him guilty of some crime. But in cases where they were
interested in the death penalty, they could do no more than conduct a pretrial
inquiry in order to establish a basis for bringing a case before Pilate. The case
would need to be consistent with his Roman way of thinking (the actual criminal
law of the Roman state was, in the provinces, only strictly applicable to citizens of
Rome) rather than well based in Jewish law, except in the case of violation of the
temple.

Given the preceding conflict in Luke's story, there can be no question at this
hearing of determining the guilt or innocence of Jesus. This hearing was a continuation of the efforts of the Jewish leadership to do away with Jesus. The question
was, What could they take to Pilate? Though Jesus had carefully avoided any claim
to be the messiah, there was much to connect Jesus in the popular mind with
such hopes (see already for John at 3:15; the disciples publicly use royal language
of Jesus at 19:38). Given Roman fears of popular insurrection, this would be the
perfect basis for nailing Jesus: he claims to be a king (see 23:2).

The form of the question in v 67 implies that the questioners want to know the
truth, but the larger story line leaves no doubt that they are only interested in
getting something to use against Jesus. Jesus does not give a straightforward answer. He implies, rather, that he would be quite happy to provide such an answer
if his hearers were open to the possibility that he might be speaking the truth.
Jesus is concerned to influence positively the faith of his interrogators; they wish
only to gain the power to destroy him.

The second part of Jesus' answer echoes his experience with these same leaders in 20:1–8. Their prevarication on that occasion indicates the opportunistic
nature of their engagement with questions about the basis of Jesus' actions and
the nature of his identity. Such people do not deserve to have their questions
answered.

But Jesus does not stop there. His interrogators are interested in matters of
royalty. So, Jesus predicts that in a very short time ("from now on") there will be a
certain mysterious "Son of Man" who will be enthroned in regal splendor at the
right hand of God. Given the use of words from Ps 110:1, a messianic psalm (see
at 20:41–44), there can be no doubt that Jesus refers to a heavenly enthronement
of this figure as messiah. When this happens, there will be no ambiguities as to
messianic identity. But is Jesus right, and will this experience come to him? In the
larger story we are well aware that this is the destiny toward which Jesus has been
headed since 9:51, but for Jesus' hearers all remains ambiguous.

Nonetheless, the questioners seize upon these words of Jesus as tantamount to
a confession: "Are you, then, the Son of God?" For Luke, "Son of God" is an
exalted status and relationship to God experienced by the messiah, but for the
interrogators there is only a heightened repetition of their probe about
messiahship in v 67. The Lukan Jesus turns the question into a challenge to his

questioners: "Do you say that I am?" Jesus' antagonists are not prepared to confront and answer this question.

There is something almost playful about Jesus' responses—playful, but at the same time deadly serious. Jesus has not at all denied the "charge" of claiming to be the messiah. Indeed, he has modestly fueled the fires of any such suspicions about his identity. But he has attempted at each turn to refocus the discussion. The real question, he insists, is about the faith and integrity of his questioners and about whether they are prepared to recognize the work of God.

All this nicety is, however, lost upon Jesus' hostile questioners. They have heard a confession from Jesus' own lips sufficient to their purposes. They have what they want. At the same time, they are revealed to the readers for what they are.

Jesus Brought before Pilate (23:1–5)

Bibliography

Allen, J. E. "Why Pilate?" In *The Trial of Jesus,* ed. E. Bammel. 78–83. **Bailey, J. A.** *Traditions Common to the Gospels of Luke and John.* Leiden: Brill, 1963. 64–77. **Bajsic, A.** "Pilatus, Jesus und Barabbas." *Bib* 48 (1967) 7–28. **Bammel, E.** "The Trial before Pilate." In *Jesus and the Politics of His Day,* ed. E. Bammel and C. F. D. Moule. 403–12. **Becq, J.** "Ponce Pilate et la mort de Jésus." *BTS* 57 (1963) 2–7. **Benoit, P.** *The Passion and Resurrection of Jesus.* 115–51. **Besnier, R.** "Le procès du Christ." *RHD* 18 (1950) 191–209. **Bickermann, E.** "Utilitas crucis: Observations sur les recits du procès de Jésus dans les évangiles canoniques." *RHR* 112 (1935) 169–241. **Blinzler, J.** *Trial of Jesus.* 164–93. ————. *Der Prozess Jesu.* 4th ed. 260–83. ————. "Der Entschied des Pilatus: Exekutions Befehl oder Todesurteil?" *MTZ* 5 (1954) 171–84. **Braumann, G.** "Markus 15,2–5 und Markus 14,55–64." *ZNW* 52 (1961) 273–78. **Büchele, A.** *Der Tod Jesu im Lukasevangelium.* **Burkill, T. A.** "The Condemnation of Jesus: A Critique of Sherwin-White's Thesis." *NovT* 12 (1970) 321–42. **Cantinat, J.** "Jésus devant Pilate." *VSpir* 86 (1952) 227–47. **Colin, J.** "Sur le procès du Christ." *REAnc* 67 (1965) 159–64. **Conzelmann, H.** *Luke.* 86–88. **Creed, J. M.** "The Supposed 'Proto-Lucan' Narrative of the Trial before Pilate: A Rejoinder." *ExpTim* 46 (1934–35) 378–79. **Dekkers, R.** "Jésus et ses disciples devant la loi romaine." *RevUB* 1 (1948–49) 350–52. **Derrett, J. D. M.** "Daniel and Salvation History. (23,1–16)." *DR* 100 (1982) 62–68. **Doyle, A. D.** "Pilate's Career and the Date of the Crucifixion." *JTS* 42 (1941) 190–93. **Finegan, J.** *Die Überlieferung der Leidens- und Auferstehungsgeschichte Jesu.* BZNW 15. Giessen: Töpelmann, 1934. 25–27. **Foulon-Piganiol, C. L.** "Le rôle du peuple dans le procès de Jésus: Une hypothèse juridique et théologique." *NRT* 98 (1976) 627–37. **Garnsey, P.** "The Criminal Jurisdiction of Governors." *JRS* 58 (1968) 51–59. **Harrison, E. F.** "Jesus and Pilate." *BSac* 105 (1948) 307–19. **Heil, J. P.** "Reader-Response and the Irony of the Trial of Jesus in Luke 23:1–25." *ScEs* 43 (1991) 175–86. **Horvath, T.** "Why Was Jesus Brought to Pilate?" *NovT* 11 (1969) 174–84. **Irmscher, J.** "σὺ λέγεις (Mark xv.2—Matt. xxvii.11—Luke xxiii.3)." *StudClas* 2 (1960) 151–58. **Juster, J.** *Les juifs dans l'empire romain: Leur condition juridique, économique et sociale.* Paris: Geuthner, 1914. 2:127–49. **Kastner, K.** *Jesus vor Pilatus: Ein Beitrag zur Leidensgeschichte des Herrn.* NTAbh 4/2–3. Münster in W.: Aschendorff, 1912. 64–78. **Lietzmann, H.** "Der Prozess Jesu." *SPAW phil.-hist.Kl.* 14 (1931) 313–22. **Maier, P. L.** "Sejanus, Pilate, and the Date of the Crucifixion." *CH* 37 (1968) 3–13. **Marin, L.** "Jesus vor Pilatus: Versuch einer Strukturanalyse." In *Erzählende Semiotik nach Berichten der Bibel,* ed. C. Chabrol. Munich,

1973. 87–122. ————. "Jésus devant Pilate: Essai d'analyse structurale." *Langages* 22 (1971) 51–74. **Matera, F. J.** "Luke 23,1–25: Jesus before Pilate, Herod, and Israel." In *L'évangile de Luc* (1989), ed. F. Neirynck. 535–51. **Mayer-Maly, T.** "Das Auftreten der Menge im Prozess Jesu und in den ältesten Christenprozessen." *OAK* 6 (1955) 231–45. **Overstreet, L.** "Roman Law and the Trial of Christ." *BSac* 135 (1978) 323–32. **Radl, W.** "Sonderüberlieferungen bei Lukas? Traditionsgeschichliche Fragen zu Lk 22,67f; 23,2 und 23,6–12." In *Der Prozess gegen Jesus*, ed. K. Kertelge. QD 112. Freiburg: Herder, 1988. 131–47. **Robbins, V. K.** "The Crucifixion and the Speech of Jesus." *Forum* 4.1 (1988) 33–46. **Robinson, W. C., Jr.** *Der Weg des Herrn.* 30–36. **Schmidt, D.** "Luke's 'Innocent' Jesus: A Scriptural Apologetic." In *Political Issues*, ed. R. J. Cassidy and P. J. Scharper. 111–21. **Schneider, G.** "Die politische Anklage gegen Jesus." In *Lukas, Theologe der Heilsgeschichte.* 173–83. ————. *Passion Jesu.* 83–94. ————. "The Political Charge against Jesus (Luke 23:2)." In *Jesus and the Politics of His Day*, ed. E. Bammel and C. F. D. Moule. 403–12. **Sherwin-White, A. N.** "The Trial of Christ." In *Historicity and Chronology in the New Testament*, ed. D. E. Nineham et al. London: SCM, 1965. 97–116. ————. *Roman Society and Roman Law in the New Testament.* Sarum Lectures, 1960–61. Oxford: Clarendon, 1963. 1–47. **Sobosan, J. G.** "The Trial of Jesus." *JES* 10 (1973) 72–91. **Strobel, A.** *Die Stunde der Wahrheit: Untersuchungen zum Strafverfahren gegen Jesus.* WUNT 21. Tübingen: Mohr-Siebeck, 1980. 95–137. **Wansbrough, H.** "Suffered under Pontius Pilate." *Scr* 18 (1966) 84–93. **Winter, P.** *On the Trial of Jesus* (1974). 70–89. ————. "The Trial of Jesus as a Rebel against Rome." *JQ* 16 (1968) 31–37.

And see at 22:1–2, 66–71.

Translation

¹*Then the whole assembly of them rose up and brought him to Pilate.* ²*They began to accuse him, saying, "We found this fellow trying to pervert our nation: forbidding [people] to pay taxes to Caesar, and claiming himself to be Christ, a king."* ³*Pilate asked him, "Are you the king of the Jews?" He replied, "Do you say [so]?"* ⁴*Pilate said to the chief priests and the crowds, "I find no chargeable offense in this man."* ⁵*But they kept insisting, saying, "He stirs up the People,ᵃ teachingᵇ throughout the whole of Judea, beginning from Galilee [and reaching] even to this place."*

Notes

ᵃ ὄχλον, "crowd," is read by ℵ L etc., probably under the influence of the pl. of this word in v 4.
ᵇ Omitted by the original hand of ℵ 1506 it etc.

Form/Structure/Setting

Feeling that they have what they need against Jesus, the Sanhedrin members, en masse, take Jesus off to Pilate. With their repeated allegations, they try to wear down Pilate's initial impression that Jesus is an innocent man.

The sequence is as in Mark 15:1–5. The content of Luke 23:1–5 has a good deal of Lukan language and reflects Lukan concerns, so it could easily be accounted for on the basis of Lukan redaction of the Markan account (see, e.g., Schneider, "Political Charge," 407–14). There is, nevertheless, a significant case to be made for the influence of additional tradition. (*i*) Beyond v 3, where the language is close, there are surprisingly few language contacts between Luke 23:1–5 and Mark 15:1–5. (*ii*) Bailey (*Traditions Common*, 64–65) has identified ten (not equally weighty) features of Luke 23:1–25 in common with the Johannine account, three of which involve vv 1–5. (The link suggested by the language and construction similarities between Luke 23:4 [οὐδὲν εὑρίσκω αἴτιον ἐν τῷ ἀνθρώπῳ τούτῳ, "I find no chargeable offense in this man"] and John 18:38 [ἐγὼ οὐδεμίας εὑρίσκω ἐν αὐτῷ αἰτίαν, "I find no chargeable offense in him"] is reinforced by the shared threefold declaration of innocence [Luke 23:15 can be counted as a fourth, but see there], gains in critical mass from the shared σὺ εἶ ὁ βασιλεὺς τῶν Ἰουδαίων σὺ λέγεις, "Are you the king of the Jews . . . [do] you say [so]" [which is, however, common to all four Gospels], and is supported by the measure of similarity between Luke 23:2, λέγοντα ἑαυτὸν . . . βασιλέα εἶναι, "claiming himself to be . . . a king," and John 19:12, βασιλέα ἑαυτὸν ποιῶν, "making himself a king.") If I am right to think (with most others, but against Bailey [*Traditions Common,* 70]) that John is not dependent upon Luke, then some kind of shared tradition must be involved (a partial verbal agreement against Mark in one word between Matt 27:2 and Luke 23:1 and two words of agreement against Mark between Matt 27:11 and Luke 23:3 are too slight a base to contribute to the source discussion). (*iii*) If Luke is composing on the basis of Mark, then it is hard to account for the loss of παρέδωκαν, "handed over," from Luke 23:1, when this verb plays such a role in the Lukan passion predictions (9:44; 22:22; 24:7; 18:32 [specifically in connection with handing over to the Gentiles]; and cf. 20:20). A second source does seem likely.

Of the five verses of the pericope, only v 5 is not implicated in the case for a second source. Despite the obvious Lukan language in this verse, the drama of the account would seem to require that some renewal of pressure upon Pilate come at this point (if the source had three declarations of innocence as implied above, then we cannot compress the narrative and find the continuation of v 4 in, say, v 16). V 3 requires special attention, because Luke is particularly close to Mark here and, at this point (Mark 15:2), the original unity of the Markan pericope has been questioned (see, e.g., Catchpole, "'Triumphal' entry," in *Jesus and the Politics of His Day,* ed. Bammel and Moule, 328–30). The difficulty with Mark 15:2 is based centrally on two observations. (*i*) V 2 clearly makes a key contribution to the evident literary parallelism between 14:55–64 and 15:1–5 and, therefore, may be suspected of having been generated for the sake of this parallelism. (*ii*) This suspicion may be strengthened when the question is asked, Is there not a tension between the answer given by Jesus in v 2 and the posture of silence in vv 4–5? But these observations do not lead where they have at times been assumed to lead. Two points need to be made. (*i*) There is no real tension between the silence and the conversation: Jesus makes no defense against *accusation,* but he answers *requests for information* (even if his answer is somewhat equivocal). (*ii*) Once we assume that there were hearings both before the Sanhedrin and before Pilate (see at Luke 22:66–71), then it is Mark 15:2 (following 14:61) that (*a*) provides the historically necessary point of continuity between the two hearings and that (*b*) is likely (along with the fact of two hearings) to provide the backbone of intrinsic similarity upon which the literary parallelism has been built (in this connection I would judge that the silence motif has a much less secure basis in one or other of the accounts [perhaps in both]). It seems to me, then, that we should not doubt the original place of v 2 in the Markan account. What of its place in the second Lukan source? In the discussion above, the presence of this material also in John is part of the wider pattern of shared features. This role as part of a pattern favors the presence of Luke 23:3 in Luke's second source (John also could have adopted the material from Mark, but I think it unlikely [as do many others] that John had access to Mark). While the pericope would have a satisfactory literary unity without Luke 23:3, with this element missing, the account portrays a trial in which no attention is paid to the accused, which seems most unlikely. I conclude, then, that the question and answer about Jesus' royal identity were original features of both Mark's source and Luke's second source.

While the fundamental historicity of the trial before Pilate has rarely been questioned, there has been more serious questioning of the particular features of the preserved accounts. The main bases for the questioning of Luke 23:3 have been sufficiently addressed in the source discussion above. The role of Jewish leaders in the trial before Pilate is implied by the Sanhedrin hearing, the fundamental historicity of which has been defended at 22:66-71 (see there; Jewish leaders, in a somewhat analogous way, bring Jesus ben Ananias before the Roman governor Albinus in A.D. 62 [Josephus, *War* 6.300-309]; in the case of the Apostle Paul in Acts 24, Jewish leaders act similarly as prosecutors before the Roman governor Felix).

The remaining feature of 23:1-5 that has been subject to question is the declaration by Pilate of Jesus' innocence (v 4). This clearly had apologetic value for early Christians. Did they devise it to serve such an apologetic role? Such a view, it seems to me, involves excessive skepticism. There are a number of relevant considerations here. (*i*) That Pilate was not convinced of Jesus' guilt is fundamental to the narrative that follows, up to the point at which Jesus is handed over for execution. Christian fabrication would need to have involved fabrication in turn of each of the features of this continuing narrative. (*ii*) Pilate shows a desire to release Jesus in each of the preserved accounts, and there seem to be at least two streams of tradition involved here. (*iii*) We are brought back to the question raised at 22:66-71 (see there): What conceivable basis would Pilate have for feeling that Roman order was threatened by this Jesus? He could simply take the word of the Jewish accusers, but why should he? Realizing that leading Jewish families in Palestine vied for prominence and influence in the Jewish community, where Roman control offered only limited stability (see McLaren, *Power and Politics;* M. Goodman, *The Ruling Class of Judaea: The Origins of the Jewish Revolt against Rome A.D. 66-70* [Cambridge: University Press, 1987] esp. 137-227), Pilate may have perceived this bid to eliminate Jesus as merely an attempt to use his office in the cause of Jewish factionalism. He could reasonably have been expected to have had doubts about what conceivable Roman interest would be served by executing, at the instigation of senior Jewish leadership, a Jewish teacher who had had such obvious grassroots popularity (according to our accounts, it is precisely when this popular support fails to hold up that Pilate agrees to go along with the demands of the Jewish leaders). (*iv*) It is important to recognize that in our accounts Pilate is no noble protector of the innocent (John 19:12 comes closest to this). We see, rather, the actions of a pragmatist, whose central agenda (beyond the protection of his own position) was the promotion of Roman interests in this rather backward province (recent scholarship suggests that the image of Pilate as supremely cruel and unjust that has been formed on the basis of Jewish sources is badly overdrawn [because seen narrowly from the Jewish side]; for Pilate, Roman interests were supreme [he not only served them but had to appear to be serving them], and his proper long-term agenda was the gradual Hellenization of the territory in his charge).

These points are offered in support of the fundamental historicity of Pilate's skepticism about the charges against Jesus laid before him by Jewish leaders. But this is not to say that the threefold declaration of innocence has not been influenced by the interests of dramatic presentation, nor is it to defend the historicity of the specifically Lukan expression (and timing for the expression) of Pilate's viewpoint. If we take the Lukan account too literally as the transcription of a conversational exchange and especially if we set the elements into the context of a formal trial with Pilate as judge, v 4 follows poorly from v 3 (innocence inferred from an [equivocal] confession of "guilt"). This account attributes to Pilate a publicly committed judgment at an early stage in the investigation, putting him in an embarrassingly compromised position when later he gives in to the clamor for Jesus' execution. We do not have a psychologically credible summary of the transcript of formal legal proceedings for at least three very good reasons. (*i*) This was not the trial of a Roman citizen, so in dispensing justice Pilate was not answerable (except in the broadest sense) to either Roman law or fixed procedure. (*ii*) The account is concerned less with providing a coherent sense of development than with identifying major elements in the situation: (*a*) the leaders press a political charge; (*b*) Pilate questions the accused; (*c*) he is skeptical about the accusers; (*d*) the leaders continue to press their charge in the face of Pilate's reluctance to convict. (*iii*) The account we have (particularly in v 4) is undoubtedly colored by a distinctly Christian interest in the innocence of Jesus.

Comment

The Sanhedrin members accuse Jesus of leading the Jewish nation away from its proper loyalty to Caesar. They build credibility for their charges by trading in half-truths. Pilate is skeptical about the charges, but the accusers are insistent.

1 The most Lukan part of the language here is ἅπαν τὸ πλῆθος, "all the assembly/multitude" (see 1:10; 8:37; 19:37; Acts 15:12; 25:24; cf. 23:7), but ἀναστάν, "rose up," and ἤγαγον, "brought," may also be Lukan. Luke is emphasizing the group solidarity involved in bringing Jesus before Pilate. As elsewhere, Luke's "all" is likely to be hyperbolic. The intention in 20:20 now comes to fruition; only with the connivance of Pilate can Jesus be legally destroyed.

2 Apart from a modest echo in John 19:12, this verse is distinctly Lukan. The charges resemble those against Paul in Acts 17:6-7; 24:2-5, which may suggest a Lukan role in their formulation, a view that receives support from a general survey of the language used (see Schneider, "Political Charge," 409-12; Green, *Death of Jesus*, 77-78). κατηγορεῖν, "to accuse," is a technical legal term for bringing charges in court against someone. τοῦτον (lit. "this"), as the opening word of the accusation, is likely to be derogatory and so has been translated "this fellow." διαστρέφειν, "pervert," is used in 9:41 of "this generation" as "perverted." It is used in Acts in connection with the leading of people away from fidelity to the Christian way (13:8, 10; 20:30). In the LXX, using the same verb, Ahab accuses Elijah of being a "perverter" of Israel in 1 Kgs 18:17, 18. The explanation of the "perversion" follows: Jesus is being accused of leading the Jewish nation away from its proper loyalty to Caesar. In 20:20-26 (see there), the Jewish leadership had hoped in vain that Jesus might forbid the paying of tribute to Caesar. As for claiming to be "Christ, a king," he had not done so; he had, however, acted in ways that had led others to make links between himself and various kinds of messianic and eschatological hopes (I have translated "Christ, a king"; "an anointed king" or "a messiah, a king" would also be possible but less in line with other Gospel usage). Jesus had also failed to reject a messianic identity in 22:67–70 (see further there). For Luke, Jesus clearly is the Christ, but by this stage in the Lukan narrative it has become obvious that Jesus does not intend to become a competing focus for political loyalty (see esp. at 19:11–28). Luke portrays the Jewish leadership making opportunistic use of Jesus' links with Jewish messianism (cf. Acts 17:7; Schmidt's attempt ["'Innocent' Jesus," 113–16] to interpret the misinterpretation of the Jewish leaders as an "honest mistake" does not finally succeed).

3 Luke is quite close to the language of Mark 15:2 (he also shares λέγων, "saying," and ἔφη, "said," with Matthew 27:11), but his second source is likely to have included this piece as well. Pilate questions the accused about the charge. While the Jewish rendition of the charge still echoed the religious overtones (with its use of "Christ"), Pilate's rendition, "king of the Jews" (paralleled in Josephus, *Ant.* 15.373, where it is said to have been how a certain Essene hailed the boy Herod), is purely secular. At the same time, the bridging form used in the accusation and the measure of parallelism with 22:67–70 (esp. the similar form of answer from Jesus) make it clear that, from the point of view of Jesus in the story, he is responding to exactly the same suggestion as in 22:67, 69. As in 22:70, I have punctuated the answer as a question, though it is probably not so in the expanded form of John 18:37 (see further at 22:70). One might well think that Pilate would have been rattled by a question coming from the accused about whether he, Pilate, might be of the opinion that Jesus was king of the Jews!

4 This verse is partly paralleled in John 18:38, and as in John there will be a threefold reiteration of Pilate's view that Jesus is innocent. "The chief priests" here stand representatively for the whole Sanhedrin, which, in Luke's account, has come to press the charge against Jesus. The presence of the crowds reflects the public setting in which the prefect dispensed justice (cf. Josephus, *War* 2.301; see Sherwin-White, "Trial," 100). At this stage, there is no reason to identify the crowds with the pressing of the charges, but the situation will apparently change (see at v 13). Pilate's skepticism about the charges is clearly not based in any obvious way on what is reported in v 3 (see discussion in *Form/Structure/Setting*). The failure here to find any cause of culpability in Jesus is of a piece with Luke's stress elsewhere on the politically innocuous nature of the Christian faith (Acts 3:13; 18:14–16; 19:40; 25:18–20, 25; 26:32; etc.). It is part of Luke's concern with the public image of the Christian movement in the larger Greco-Roman world.

5 This verse is unparalleled. καθ᾽ ὅλης τῆς Ἰουδαίας, "throughout the whole of Judea" (cf. Acts 9:31; 10:37), and ἀρξάμενος ἀπὸ [τῆς Γαλιλαίας], "beginning from [Galilee]" (cf. 14:18; 24:27, 47; Acts 1:22; 8:35; 10:37), are likely to be Lukan. ἀνασείειν occurs elsewhere in the NT only at Mark 15:11. Luke could possibly have drawn it in from there (for a possibly analogous phenomenon, see at 22:65). We probably should not include the crowds in the "they" who freshly press the charge (especially given the role of the "People" in this fresh formulation). ἀνασείειν means simply "to stir up," and the Lukan Jesus did create quite a stir, but coming on the heels of v 2, the intended sense is "to incite" against Roman rule. Again the accusers use half-truth to lend credibility to a fundamentally un-true set of accusations: the Lukan Jesus did create quite a stir as he taught throughout the length and breadth of Judea, but his teaching involved nothing that smacked of sedition.

"Judea" is likely to be used here in the broader sense of Jewish Palestine (see at 4:44). The Lukan pattern of Jesus' ministry involves return from baptism and temptation to begin in Galilee (3:23; 4:14–15) a pattern of ministry that is ex-tended through all Jewish Palestine (4:44), and then a decisive turning towards Jerusalem, where he was to be "taken up" (9:51). To this was to correspond a church life which developed from a beginning in Jerusalem (24:47; Acts 1:8, 22) and extended out into the rest of the world. The point here is the simpler one, that Jesus' influence has extended from the periphery to the capital city of Pales-tinian Jewry.

In this section, Luke has painted a scene of conflict in which the issue at stake between Pilate and the Jewish leaders has much less to do with determining the facts of the case than it does with the question of which side would gain the upper hand in the ongoing political struggle in Palestine. As we see in the continuing nar-rative, circumstances and the Jewish leaders' resoluteness of will were to bring them success in this round of the conflict (for a rather more dramatic conflict between Jewish leaders and the Roman governor Florus, see Josephus, *War* 2:301–8).

Explanation

With the ammunition that they think they will need, the Sanhedrin members move as a block to the court of Pilate in order to deliver Jesus into the hands of Roman "justice." By distorting elements of his teaching and presenting a politi-cized version of messiahship, they press their claim that Jesus is seeking to lead the Jewish nation away from its proper loyalty to Caesar. Pilate is skeptical, but they are vehement.

While the preserved accounts of the trial before Pilate have clearly developed on the basis of their significance for the Christian community, their fundamental his-toricity can be well defended. We are witnesses to an episode that fits neatly within the machinations of the fluid world of political power in first-century Palestine.

Only with the cooperation of Pilate can Jesus be legally destroyed. The goal of Jesus' accusers has been to get Jesus to Pilate at least since Luke 20:20. The charge that is laid against Jesus is that of perverting the Jewish nation. This language, otherwise used in the Greek Old Testament and in Luke-Acts in a Jewish or Chris-tian religious context, is quite striking in its connection here with a charge of undermining Roman political authority!

The evidence that Jesus is seeking to pervert the Jewish nation is spelled out in terms of what he is supposed to have said about taxes and about being a claimant to royal power. The former is what the Jewish leaders had hoped he might say in 20:20–26 but did not. The latter is no more true in the literal sense but has a somewhat greater foundation of credibility. Jesus had behaved in a way that had led others to link him with messianic expectations. And he had not rejected a messianic identity for himself at the hearing before the Sanhedrin. The problem with the second strand of accusation is the political context in which Jesus is be-ing linked with royal categories. In Luke's story it has become quite clear by this point that Jesus' messianic identity has nothing to do with his becoming a competing focus of political loyalty (see esp. at 19:11–28). This is opportunistic use of half-truths.

Pilate questions the accused. He takes up the kingship question and expresses it in totally secular language (in the accusation, the juxtaposition of "Christ" and "king" has provided for both religious and political content). Jesus neither affirms nor denies. Instead he asks whether Pilate would himself want to affirm the royal identity of Jesus. What a question from the dock!

Pilate turns his attention back to the accusers. He is skeptical about the charges being pressed. He is well acquainted with the way in which the leading Jewish families vied for prominence and influence. This bid to have Jesus removed from the scene is likely to have appeared to Pilate as an attempt to exploit his office in the cause of Jewish factionalism. What gain would there be for Rome in his execution of a Jewish teacher who had had such obvious grass-roots popularity? Pilate is clearly reluctant to execute Jesus, and our Christian records describe this in terms of his recognition of the innocence of Jesus (in Acts, Luke repeatedly underlines the politically innocuous nature of the Christian faith; this is part of his concern with the public image of the Christian movement). No doubt Pilate does think Jesus not guilty as charged, but his interests are more likely to have been determined by political expediency than by a pure concern for justice.

The Sanhedrin members continue to press their charge against Jesus. As they say, the Lukan Jesus did create quite a stir among the Jewish People as he taught throughout the length and breadth of Jewish Palestine. But the accusers intend to imply that he also incited the People against Roman rule. Again they use half-truth to lend credibility to a fundamentally untrue claim.

Jesus Sent to Appear before Herod (23:6–12)

Bibliography

Blinzler, J. *Der Prozess Jesu.* 4th ed. 284–300. ———. "Herodes und der Tod Jesu." *Klerusblatt* 37 (1957) 118–21. **Bornhäuser, K.** "Die Beteiligung des Herodes am Prozesse Jesu." *NKZ* 40 (1929) 714–18. **Buck, E.** "The Function of the Pericope 'Jesus before Herod' in the Passion Narrative of Luke." In *Wort in der Zeit,* ed. W. Haubeck and M. Bachmann. 165–78. **Corbin, M.** "Jésus devant Hérode: Lecture de Luc 23,6–12." *Christus* 25 (1978) 190–97. **Delbrueck, R.** "Antiquarisches zu den Verspottungen Jesu." *ZNW* 41 (1942) 124–45, esp. 135–37, 140–42. **Dibelius, M.** "Herodes und Pilatus." *ZNW* 16 (1915) 113–26. **Harlow, V. E.** *The Destroyer of Jesus: The Story of Herod Antipas, Tetrarch of Galilee.* 2nd ed. Oklahoma City: Modern Publishers, 1954. **Hoehner, H. W.** "Why Did Pilate Hand Jesus over to Antipas?" In *Trial of Jesus,* ed. E. Bammel. 84–90. ———. *Herod Antipas.* SNTSMS 17. Cambridge: University Press, 1972. 175–76, 224–50. **Joüon, P.** "Luc 23,11: ἐσθῆτα λημπράν." *RSR* 26 (1936) 80–85. **Klein, H.** "Die lukanisch-johanneische Passionstradition." *ZNW* 67 (1976) 155–86, esp. 156–62. **Manus, C. U.** "The Universalism of Luke and the Motif of Reconciliation in Luke 23:6–13." *AJT* 16 (1987) 121–35. **Müller, K.** "Jesus vor Herodes: Eine redaktionsgeschichtliche Untersuchung zu Lk 23,6–12." In *Zur Geschichte* *des Urchristentums*, ed. G. Dautzenberg et al. QD 87. Freiburg: Herder, 1979. 111–41. **Parker, P.** "Herod Antipas and the Death of Jesus." In *Jesus, the Gospels, and the Church.* FS W. R. Farmer, ed. E. P. Sanders. Macon, GA: Mercer, 1987. 197–208. **Radl, W.** "Sonderüberlieferungen bei Lukas? Traditionsgeschichtliche Fragen zu Lk 22,67f; 23,2 und 23,6–12." In *Der Prozess gegen Jesus*, ed. K. Kertelge. 131–47. **Soards, M. L.** "Tradition, Composition, and Theology in Luke's Account of Jesus before Herod Antipas." *Bib* 66 (1985) 344–66. ————. "The Silence of Jesus before Herod: An Interpretative Suggestion." *ABR* 33 (1985) 41–45. ————. "Herod Antipas' Hearing in Luke 23.8." *BT* 37 (1986) 146–47. **Streeter, B. H.** "On the Trial of Our Lord before Herod—A Suggestion." In *Studies in the Synoptic Problem,* ed. W. Sanday. Oxford: Clarendon, 1911. 228–31. **Tyson, J. B.** "Jesus and Herod Antipas." *JBL* 79 (1960) 237–46. **Verrall, A. W.** "Christ before Herod (Luke xxiii 1–16)." *JTS* 10 (1908–9) 321–53.

And see at 22:1–2, 66–71; 23:1–5.

Translation

⁶*When Pilate heard [this] he asked whether the*ᵃ *man was a Galilean.* ⁷*Learning that he was from Herod's jurisdiction, he sent him to Herod, who was also in Jerusalem during those days.* ⁸*Herod, when he saw Jesus, rejoiced greatly, since for a long time he had been wanting to see him, because of what he had heard about him, and he was hoping to see some miracle performed by him.* ⁹*He tried at length to question him, but he would not answer him at all,* ¹⁰*even though the chief priests and the scribes stood by vigorously accusing him.* ¹¹*Then, when*ᵇ *Herod, along with his soldiers, had treated him with contempt and ridiculed him, after putting a splendid garment upon [him], he sent him [back] to Pilate.* ¹²*Herod and Pilate became friends that very day with one another. For previously they had been hostile toward one another.*ᶜ

Notes

ᵃ The definite article is missing from B 700 1241 etc., so ". . . he was a Galilean man."

ᵇ καί, "even," is found here in P⁷⁵ ℵ L T X Ψ *f*¹³ etc. If original, it points to the behavior of Herod and his men as additional opposition to Jesus beyond that of the chief priests and scribes.

ᶜ Vv 10–12 are missing from syˢ.

Form/Structure/Setting

In a situation of impasse between himself and the Jewish leaders, Pilate seizes the Galilean origins of Jesus' ministry as an excuse to "pass the buck" to Herod Antipas. Herod gains fulfillment in this way of a longstanding wish to see Jesus (9:7–9). But Herod, while glad of the opportunity to humiliate an uncooperative Jesus, soon passes the responsibility back to Pilate.

None of the other Gospels offers any parallel to Luke 23:6–12. Scholarly opinion is well divided over the question of Luke's source among (*i*) those who look to a substantial Lukan source (within or apart from a second passion narrative); (*ii*) those who think that Luke had a tradition of Herod Antipas being involved in the trial of Jesus but believe this has been developed into the present narrative on the basis of borrowed Markan motifs and with the introduction of Lukan concerns; and (*iii*) those who consider Luke to be entirely responsible for the pericope. The first opinion seems at first hard to defend in the face of the level of Lukan language and the obvious correlations between the material and "unused" Markan motifs.

The most detailed recent defense of the third option is that of Müller ("Jesus vor Herodes," 111–41). To my mind, his argument becomes overly subtle at a number of points. Throughout, Müller greatly overplays the explanatory power of a Lukan concern to represent correct Roman judicial procedure. More specifically, it is difficult to accept the role for Herod Antipas here as an expert in Jewish affairs in place of the Sanhedrin, which Luke has displaced from that role (no more satisfying is the argument of those who suggest that Antipas has been introduced, in part, for the sake of a parallel with the role of Agrippa in the trial of Paul in Acts 25). The explanations offered for the restored friendship between Antipas and Pilate are also, to my mind, less than convincing.

Soards (*Bib* 66 [1985] 344–66) has recently offered a version of the second option that identifies as the traditional core the involvement of Herod in the trial of Jesus, the former hostility between Pilate and Herod, and the questioning by Herod. The last of these seems to me to be less than secure, but I would want to add the content of v 12a (but without "that very day") to the store of tradition available to Luke. If, however, I am right about this, then the tradition available to Luke will have involved not simply the fact of Herod's involvement but some kind of narrative account of Jesus' being brought before Herod. This in turn raises the need for the narrative to have included some account of Herod's reaction to Jesus (unless we think that to return him to Pilate is response enough). The best candidate for this is the mockery of v 11. No doubt this account of mockery has, ultimately, a common origin with that in Mark 15:16–20, but the setting in Luke may well be more original than that in Mark. So, despite the difficulties, I find myself moving back to the first option. What is more, since it is difficult to see such a narrative as I have proposed as freestanding, it seems best to think of it as being part of Luke's second connected passion source.

If the hearing before Herod Antipas is historical (and I see no reason for denying its historicity; there is little to be said for the older view that the narrative has been spun out of an exegesis of Ps 2:1–2 [cf. Acts 4:24–28]), then how are we to understand his action? Jesus in Jerusalem will not be the political liability to Antipas that, perhaps, Antipas judged him to be when Jesus was in Galilee (13:31). Also, Antipas would need to consider his response in the light of Jesus' popular appeal. Mockery is no statement of innocence; it looks rather more like a measured strategy, designed to undermine the public image of Jesus without creating a direct confrontation. If anyone was to do more, far better to let Pilate bear the responsibility. Pilate's thinking in sending Jesus to Herod in the first place is likely to have had a corresponding motivation. Both seemed to have been of the opinion that, while Jesus himself represented no significant threat, the situation needed to be handled with some delicacy, since strong Jewish feelings and conflicting opinions about Jesus did constitute a potential threat to public order.

Comment

No more than Pilate does Herod want to take the responsibility for dealing with Jesus. Both believe they are dealing with a domestic Jewish power struggle that they would rather avoid, and in this shared perception, they move beyond a longstanding mutual hostility. Herod vents his personal hostility against an uncooperative Jesus but wants no further responsibility for him. Pilate must decide the fate of Jesus.

6 Since the role of Galilee in v 5 was judged to be Lukan, this verse is to be seen as providing a distinctly Lukan linkage with vv 1–5 (for the role of ἀκούσας [lit. "having heard"], cf. 7:29; 14:15; Luke is responsible for seven of the ten uses of "Galilean" in the NT). Peter was picked out as a Galilean in 22:59. Though born in Judea, Jesus was clearly a Galilean by upbringing (cf. 4:16, 24).

7 The most Lukan features of the language here are ἐπιγνοὺς ὅτι, "learning that" (cf. at 1:22), and ἐν ταύταις ταῖς ἡμέραις, "in those days" (cf. at 1:39). ἀνέπεμψεν, "sent," is claimed as Lukan, but apart from Acts 25:21, the Lukan uses of this verb are all dependent on the use here (23:11, 15). ἐξουσία is used here of "jurisdiction" in a manner unparalleled in Luke-Acts (4:6; 22:53 are suggested parallels). Luke's source may have read something like "Since he was from Herod's jurisdiction, he sent him to Herod." On Herod Antipas, see further at 3:1, 19; 9:7–9; 13:31. For Herod in Jerusalem for a Jewish feast, cf. Josephus, *Ant.* 18.122.

Discussions about whether Antipas had inherited his father's rights of extradition (almost certainly not) or about the state of development of Roman law concerning whether a trial should be held in the home province of the accused or in the province where the crime was committed (more likely the latter) are beside the point here. Jesus is understood to have committed the alleged criminal activity as much in Galilee as in Judea and to have begun in Galilee: the problem arose in Galilee, so it was not unreasonable to refer it to the Galilean jurisdiction (Müller's case ["Jesu vor Herodes," 130–32] for seeing Herod's function as only that of an expert adviser to Pilate falls foul of v 7 ["jurisdiction (ἐξούσια) of Herod"] and v 15a ["for he sent him (back) to us"]).

8 Only the use of λίαν, "greatly," gives any pause to the attribution of this verse entirely to Luke (note esp. the periphrastic verb, the use of χρόνος ἱκανός [lit. "sufficient time"], διά + inf. construction, adjectival τις). Herod's desire from 9:9 to see Jesus is now fulfilled (there is a series of verbal links with 9:7–9). The desire is explained as being "because of what he [Herod] had heard about him [Jesus]" (cf. 9:7; the translation adopted is defended by Soards [*BT* 37 (1986) 146–47]). Herod's interest in a σημεῖον (here "miracle," elsewhere "sign") is not the demand that Jesus prove himself with signs, as in 11:16, 29 (though the Lukan text here is likely to have been inspired by these texts), but only the desire to see something spectacular (such as he had heard about at 9:7).

9 Luke uses ἱκανός again after v 8. The verse is generally seen (probably correctly) as a recasting of Mark 15:4–5 (and cf. 14:60–61), for which Luke had no place in his account of the trial before Pilate. Luke introduces here the motif from Mark that Jesus does not stoop to defend himself against slanderous accusations (however, only with v 10 closely connected is the silence adequately motivated: Jesus is questioned by Herod about the accusations leveled at him by the chief priests and scribes [cf. Soards (*Bib* 66 [1985] 352), who shows that vv 9–10 belong closely together and that v 10 should be linked in translation with something like "even though"]). There can be little doubt that Jesus' silence is to be seen as a fulfillment of Isa 53:7 (cf. the citation from 53:12 at Luke 22:37), but in what way is the silence to be understood? It is hardly to be taken as a demonstration of the nobility that bears up under a cruel fate (as Josephus, *Ant.* 15:234–35). Better is the suggestion that Jesus disdains the charges as not deserving of an answer. Certainly the silence makes clear that Jesus is not concerned to placate his accusers. But perhaps best is the idea that Jesus accepts as God's will the suffering to which the charges against him will lead.

10   If v 9 is from Mark, so will v 10 be (Mark 15:3). εἱστήκεισαν, "stood [by]," will recur in v 49. εὐτόνως, "vigorously," replaces Mark's πολλά, "repeatedly" (Luke never accepts Mark's adverbial use of πολλά [cf. Müller, "Jesus vor Herodes," 131 and n. 63]; the only other NT occurrence of εὐτόνως is in Acts 18:28). In 22:2, 66 (cf. 20:19) Luke has the same grouping of only chief priests and scribes; elsewhere they are part of a trio. The reader is meant to carry forward the content provided in vv 2, 5 for the accusation. Luke carries the presence of the accusers forward from the previous scene without explicitly accounting for their presence in this new scene.

11   Only a shared use of ἐμπαίζειν, "ridicule/mock," links the language of v 11 with the related tradition in Mark 15:16–20. Some of the language may be Lukan (note esp. the uses of σύν to mean "along with" and identical wording to describe the garment, as in Acts 10:30), but most of it is not notably so. Luke is not likely to be dependent here on Mark 15:16–20. λαμπρός is literally "bright/shining/radient," but used of a garment it will mean something like "splendid" (cf. Josephus, *Life* 334). Whereas in Mark the clothing is clearly regal, in Luke the dress is that of a dignitary, but without more precise definition. In both cases the garment is meant to mock the pretensions of Jesus. Though Luke's language is unclear, we should probably understand that the mock investiture was the beginning point for the treatment with contempt and the ridicule. Jesus is returned to Pilate in humiliation, but Herod Antipas feels no need to take any further action against Jesus. In v 15 this action on the part of Herod will be taken up as evidence for Jesus' innocence of any major crime. For the Lukan reader, this evidence weighs yet more heavily because of the known hostility of Herod toward Jesus (13:31 and demonstrated here in the mockery of Jesus) and toward his precursor, John (3:19–20).

12   Though friendship language is important to Luke, there is nothing with which to compare the usage here. Pilate and Herod are coupled in Acts 4:27, but not in friendship. There they are agreed in opposition to Jesus, not as here in agreement that Jesus should be released. In Acts 25–26 Festus and Agrippa seem to be in agreement about Paul's political innocence. ἐν αὐτῇ τῇ ἡμέρᾳ, "on that day," is likely to be a Lukan touch (it is used nine times by Luke), as may be προϋπῆρχον (lit. "existed before"; the only other NT use of the verb is in Acts 8:9). Neither the enmity nor its reversal is elsewhere attested (but cf. Philo, *Ad Gaium* 300), but nothing is intrinsically unlikely about either. The correlation between this change of relationship, which would have been publicly visible on a wider canvas, and the shared opinion of Herod and Pilate about what should be done with Jesus, in Luke's eyes, lends credibility to their agreement about Jesus' innocence.

Explanation

The Galilean beginnings of Jesus' ministry seem to offer Pilate a way out of his dilemma: Herod is in Jerusalem for the festival; let him deal with these Jews and their dispute. Herod is glad enough for the opportunity to meet at last this wonder worker, but given the state of public opinion and the fact that the problem is now in Jerusalem and not in Galilee, Herod prefers not to take responsibility. He joins his soldiers in the humiliation of an uncooperative Jesus, but then he sends him back to Pilate. Nonetheless, Herod feels flattered that Pilate chose to involve him, and the perceptions of the two coincide regarding the motivation for the charges leveled by the Jewish leaders. Cooperation in this incident breaks down a longstanding hostility that has stood between them.

Though born in Judea, Jesus considered himself a Galilean and was so considered by others (see 4:16, 24). Since the problem had arisen in Galilee, it could be passed on to the Tetrarch of Galilee, who, conveniently, was in Jerusalem for the Passover festival. A longstanding ambition of Herod's thus comes to fruition (see 9:7–9), so he is delighted. Not that he has any openness to Jesus' message: Jesus was critical enough of those who demanded signs as proof (see 11:16, 29), but Herod was a step further away; he simply hoped he might see a good show. Luke does not even feel the need to tell us that his hopes were thwarted. As for the charges against Jesus, schooled by the accusations of the chief priests and scribes, Herod tries to probe Jesus. But Jesus will not deign so much as to answer his questions. In the description of Jesus' silence, we are meant to find an echo of Isa 53:7: as did the servant there, Jesus accepts the suffering as God's will.

Herod is not prepared to proceed further against Jesus in any judicial way, but he is not above trying to bring Jesus down a peg or two. To mock Jesus' pretensions, Herod and his retinue put a splendid robe upon him and then treat him contemptuously and ridicule him: in this way they point up the contradiction between grand claims and what appears to be powerlessness. Herod sends the humiliated Jesus back to Pilate. A meeting of minds and a measure of cooperation in this incident heal a longstanding rift between Herod and Pilate. Luke is able to point to this more widely evident change of affairs in support of his contention that these two leaders, who otherwise make an unlikely pair, were in agreement about the political innocence of Jesus.

Pilate Declares Jesus Innocent   (23:13–16)

Bibliography

Carroll, J. T. "Luke's Crucifixion Scene." In *Reimaging*, ed. D. D. Sylva. 108–24, 194–203, esp. 108–13. **Cassidy, R. J.** "Luke's Audience, the Chief Priests and the Motive for Jesus' Death." In *Political Issues*, ed. R. J. Cassidy and P. J. Scharper. 146–67, esp. 150–52. **Foulon-Piganiol, C. L.** "Le rôle du peuple dans le procès de Jésus: Une hypothèse juridique et théologique." *NRT* 98 (1976) 627–37. **Kodell, J.** "Luke's Use of *Laos*, 'People,' Especially in the Jerusalem Narrative (Lk 19,28–24,53)." *CBQ* 31 (1969) 327–43. **Mayer-Maly, T.** "Das Auftreten der Menge im Prozess Jesu und in den ältesten Christenprozessen." *OAK* 6 (1955) 231–45. **Rau, G.** "Das Volk in der lukanischen Passionsgeschichte, eine Konjektur zu Lc 23:13." *ZNW* 56 (1965) 41–51.

And see at 22:1–2, 66–71; 23:1–5, 6–12.

Translation

¹³*Pilate called together the chief priests and the rulers and the People* ¹⁴*and said to them, "You brought this man to me as one who was trying to pervert the People. See now, I have examined him in your presence and found in this man no basis*^a *for what you accuse him of.* ¹⁵*What is more,*^b *neither did Herod.* ^c*For he sent him [back] to us.*^c *See, nothing worthy of death has been done by him.* ¹⁶*So I will have him flogged and release him."*

Notes

a Gr. αἴτιον, which, for English idiomatic reasons, is translated in v 4 as "chargeable offense."

b "What is more" represents ἀλλ᾽ (lit. "but").

c-c It is probably the awkwardness of the "us" that has produced the range of readings for this clause. ὑμᾶς," to you," is read by *f* ¹³ 1¹⁸⁵ etc. Many other texts turn the clause around to begin ἀνέπεμψα γάρ, "for I sent." This is completed with ὑμᾶς πρὸς αὐτόν, "you to him," in A D W X Δ Ψ 063 *f*¹ etc.; αὐτὸν πρὸς ὑμᾶς, "him to you," in 71 248 788 1²⁹⁹ etc.; αὐτὸν πρὸς αὐτόν, "him to him," in 274 1¹⁸³. And there are other readings.

Form/Structure/Setting

We move now to a second scene before Pilate, which draws in strands from vv 1–5 and has Pilate appeal to Herod's return of Jesus in support of his own contention that Jesus is innocent. In vv 15–16 there is anticipation of language that we will meet again in vv 22; indeed the unit here is vv 13–25, which has been subdivided only for convenience of presentation. Three times Pilate will address his audience; three times they will press for the execution of Jesus; in the end Pilate will capitulate.

None of the other Gospels has a true parallel to vv 13–16, but as has already been noted (at 23:1–5), Luke and John share a pattern in which Pilate on three occasions declares Jesus innocent. In this pattern, vv 13–16 provide the second declaration. A further tradition link with John may be provided by the flogging that precedes the second Johannine declaration of innocence (John 19:1), and yet another link may be noted in the shared pattern with John of mockery of Jesus in a splendid garment, preceding the second declaration of innocence (John 19:2–3; Luke 23:11). Since the level of Lukan language is quite high, it is not possible to make any confident judgments about the form and scope of Luke's tradition for this pericope.

Comment

After the return of Jesus, Pilate reassembles the Jewish leaders and people ("the crowds of v 4 now become "the People" in preparation for a critical change of role for "the People"). He reiterates his conviction of Jesus' innocence with appeal to Herod's action and proposes a compromise that would involve Jesus' release, but only after an "educative" beating.

13 The uses of συγκαλεσάμενος, "called together," τοὺς ἄρχοντας, "the rulers," and τὸν λαόν, "the People," suggest that this verse is largely Lukan, but the pericope in any form would have needed to reintroduce the protagonists. This is the first time Luke has used "rulers" in connection with those in authority in Jerusalem. He will do so again in v 35; 24:20 (where it is paired again with chief priests; and cf. Acts 3:17; 4:5, 8; 13:27). For a discussion of the various ways in which Luke refers to the Jerusalem leadership in the Gospel, see at 19:47. The conjecture of Rau (*ZNW* 56 [1965] 41–51) that we should, despite the uniform textual witness, read "of the People" rather than "and the People," while initially attractive, fails to do justice to the evidence of Acts. The "People" have been Jesus' protection against the hostile intentions of the Jewish leadership (from 19:47–48). The betrayal was key to the arrest of Jesus because in this way Jesus could be arrested without the knowledge of the People. The reintroduction of the People at this point stirs the reader's expectation. How will they react to the situation in which they now find their hero? This element of the story should probably be understood as continuing in v 18 (see there).

14 πρός with a verb of speaking, καὶ ἰδού (lit. "and behold"), and the use of ἐνώπιον, "in your presence," are all to be noted as Lukan language. The use of ἀνακρίνειν with a forensic nuance is also likely to be Lukan (cf. Green, *Death of Jesus*, 83 and n. 274). The first part of the verse refers back to v 2. Here Luke sets the Jewish language "the People" on the lips of Pilate, where the secular "our nation" was on the lips of Jesus' accusers in v 2. It is likely that Luke intends a double irony here: in the following scene we will witness the way the Jewish leadership has *perverted the People* away from their natural response to Jesus. The second part of the verse is a slightly fuller reiteration of v 4b (see there), with "accuse" taken up from v 2. There will be a third similar declaration in v 22. Though Luke's language is loose, we should not understand that the People are included among those who level the accusation ("perverting the People" makes this clear).

15 πεπραγμένον, "has been done," and καὶ ἰδού (lit. "And behold") are the only clearly Lukan contributions to this verse, but the question must be raised whether Luke has formulated the verse to bind his narrative scenes more closely together. This is the more likely because its presence makes for a fourfold affirmation by Pilate of Jesus' innocence (though this one, indirectly, is Herod's statement and is probably intended by Luke to establish a parallel between Pilate and Herod as witnesses to Jesus' innocence [cf. Schneider, "Verfahren," 128]). On ἀνέπεμψεν, "sent [back]," see at v 7. Unless we take it as a "royal plural," the "us" is slightly awkward in "sent him [back] to us" (according to Luke, those to whom Pilate speaks would not have been there when Herod sent Jesus back; see *Notes* for the textual variants this has produced). The statement of innocence here anticipates some of the language of that in v 22. Innocence of any capital crime allows room for the compromise offered in v 16 in a way that the wording of v 4 does not.

16 This verse will be repeated verbatim in v 22. Only in these two places does Luke use παιδεύειν to mean discipline (by means of a beating). The pre-Lukan character of the verse finds some support in the flogging of John 19:1. In the rough justice meted out to provincials, sufficient justification for such treatment would have been found in the consideration that Jesus *might* have been guilty of some lesser infringement. As a strategy by Pilate, the suggestion is a minor conciliatory gesture.

Explanation

We come now to the second of the three occasions upon which Pilate declares Jesus' innocence. He finds confirmation of his view in that which is implied in Herod's return of the prisoner, but he proposes a concession. He will recognize the concerns of the Jewish leadership to the extent of subjecting Jesus to a corrective beating before releasing him (after all, one can never tell whether Jesus might have been guilty of some lesser offense!).

Up to this point in the passion account, the People have functioned as a buffer between Jesus and the intentions of the Jerusalem leaders. Now they are summoned along with the leadership to hear Pilate pronounce for the second time his conviction that Jesus is innocent of the charges as brought. Will they continue to take Jesus' side now, when it means siding with the occupying power against their own leaders?

In the light of the story development to come, we should probably identify a subtle Lukan irony in the way Luke has Pilate use the phrase "perverting the People" in recalling the earlier charge against Jesus. It is Pilate, not the Jewish leaders (they said "perverting this nation"), who uses the phrase that honors these people as the People of God; and as the story goes on we find that it is the Jewish leadership, not Jesus, that has *perverted the People*, that is, perverted them away from their natural response as the People of God to Jesus.

Under Pressure, Pilate Capitulates to the Will of the Crowd (23:[17]18–25)

Bibliography

Bajsić, A. "Pilatus, Jesus und Barabbas." *Bib* 48 (1967) 7–28. **Bartsch, H.-W.** "Wer verurteilte Jesu zum Tode?" *NovT* 7 (1964–65) 210–16. **Blinzler, J.** *Der Prozess Jesu.* 4th ed. 301–20, 337–46. ———. "Der Entscheid des Pilatus: Exekutionsbefehl oder Todesurteil." *MTZ* 5 (1954) 171–84. **Brandon, S. F. G.** *Jesus and the Zealots.* New York: Scribner's, 1967. 4–5. **Chavel, C. B.** "The Releasing of a Prisoner on the Eve of Passover in Ancient Jerusalem." *JBL* 60 (1941) 273–78. **Cohn, H. H.** *The Trial and Death of Jesus.* New York: Harper and Row, 1967. 162–69. **Colin, J.** *Les villes libres de l'orient gréco-romain et l'envoi au supplice par acclamations populaires.* Collection Latomus 82. Brussels-Berchem: Latomus, 1965. **Davies, S. L.** "Who Is Called Bar Abbas." *NTS* 27 (1980–81) 260–62. **Finegan, J.** *Die Überlieferung der Leidens- und Auferstehungsgeschichte Jesu.* BZNW 15. Giessen: Töpelmann, 1934. 29–30. **Ford, J. M.** "'Crucify Him, Crucify Him' and the Temple Scroll." *ExpTim* 87 (1975–76) 275–78. **Lémonon, J. P.** *Pilate et le gouvernement de la Judée: Textes et monuments.* Études Bibliques. Paris: Gabalda, 1981. 191–95. **Lohfink, G.** *Die Sammlung Israels: Eine Untersuchung zur lukanischen Ekklesiologie.* SANT 39. Munich: Kösel, 1975. 42–43. **Maccoby, H. Z.** "Jesus and Barabbas." *NTS* 16 (1969–70) 55–60. **Merritt, R. L.** "Jesus Barabbas and the Paschal Pardon." *JBL* 104 (1985) 57–68. **Rigg, H. A., Jr.** "Barabbas." *JBL* 64 (1945) 417–56. **Sloyan, G.** *Jesus on Trial.* Philadelphia: Fortress, 1973. 67–68. **Winter, P.** *On the Trial of Jesus* (1974). 131–43.

And see at 22:1–2, 66–71; 23:1–5, 13–16.

Translation

ᵃ ¹⁸*All together, they screamed, "Away with this fellow! Release Barabbas for us!"* ¹⁹(*This was a man who had been imprisoned in connection with a certain riot that had* *occurred in the city, and a murder.)* [20]*Again Pilate called out to them, wanting to release Jesus.* [21]*But they were shouting back, "Crucify, crucify him!"* [22]*A third time he spoke to them, "What evil did this fellow do? I found in him no basis for [a] death [penalty]."* [23]*But they kept pressing [him] with loud shouts, asking for him to be crucified; and their* [b] *voices* [c] *prevailed.* [24]*So Pilate decided that their request should be granted.* [25]*He released the man who had been imprisoned in connection with a riot and a murder, for whom they were asking; and he handed Jesus over to their will.*

Notes

[a] V 17, reading ἀνάγκην δὲ εἶχεν ἀπολύειν αὐτοῖς κατὰ ἑορτὴν ἕνα, "He had to release [some]one for them at the feast," is found in א (D) W X Δ (Θ Ψ) *f*[1,13] etc. It was almost certainly formulated on the basis of the other Gospels to fill a perceived gap in the Lukan text.

[b] καὶ τῶν ἀρχιερέων, "and of the chief priests," has been added in A D K P W X Δ Θ Π Ψ etc.

[c] "Voices" and "shouts" both represent Gr. φωναί.

Form/Structure/Setting

Vv 18–25 continue the scene begun in vv 13–16 and belong properly to the same unit (see there).

Mark's parallel is in 15:6–14. Except in a general sense, however, the two accounts are only close for small stretches of text. Luke 23:18–25 contributes the third of Pilate's declarations to the pattern shared with John, of a threefold declaration of innocence (see at 23:1–5; Luke disturbs this pattern in favor of setting more clearly in parallel Pilate's and Herod's agreement on the innocence of Jesus and of having a threefold interaction between Pilate and his gathered audience). There is also a modest commonality of language between the Lukan and Johannine accounts (use of αἴρειν, "do away with," in Luke 23:18 and John 19:15; the use of direct speech in the call for the release of Barabbas in Luke 23:18 and John 18:40 [John 19:40 also has the τοῦτον, "this [fellow]," of Luke 23:18 and agrees with Luke in having a brief explanation of Barabbas' identity at this point]; a doubled imperative use of σταυροῦν, "crucify," in Luke 23:21 and John 19:6; use of αἴτιον εὑρίσκειν ἐν αὐτῷ, "find evidence of a chargeable offense in him," in Luke 23:22, and εὑρίσκειν ἐν αὐτῷ αἰτίαν, "find a chargeable offense in him," in John 19:6). Several other links with John are noted in *Comment* below. As in the case for Luke 23:13–16, a second Lukan source seems likely, but it is difficult to say anything very definite about its precise scope or content. Luke is likely to have drawn on his Markan source as well and may be responsible himself for the threefold nature of the interaction between Pilate and his audience.

In terms of historicity, the most controversial aspect of this material has been that of the place of Barabbas and the Paschal pardoning of a prisoner. Though all four Gospels are in basic agreement in this matter, such a custom is not otherwise attested in ancient sources, and its historicity is often questioned. However, the methods proposed for the fabrication of such an account, such as the artificial linking of the trial of Jesus with the historical pardoning of an insurrectionist named Barabbas, who was unrelated to either Jesus or to the Jewish Passover, are unsatisfactory and thoroughly speculative (Winter's generation of the episode out of a case of mistaken identity [*Trial,* 142–43] is even less credible and only slightly more credible than views that suggest Jesus is himself the original Barabbas ["Son of the Father" or "Son of the Teacher"]).

There are historical analogies from the period that stand in general favor of the historicity of the Passover pardon. (*i*) There was widespead practice in the Greco-Roman world, as in the Ancient Near Eastern world within which the origins of first-century Judaism are set, of showing clemency at particular religious festivals (some of the evidence is surveyed in Merritt [*JBL* 104 (1985) 58–66]). (*ii*) There is also good evidence for the role of acclamation from the crowd in securing pardon in both Roman and Greek justice (see Mayer-Maly [*OAK* 6 (1955) 231–45; Colin [*Les villes libres*]]). (*iii*) Roman release of prisoners in Judea, who were given amnesty for various political reasons, is reported in Josephus, *Ant.* 20.208–10, 215. (*iv*) From the Jewish side, there is a certain tradition of the public assembly functioning as a court of justice (cf. Jer 26; Sus 28–62) and of the people intervening to redeem a life that was forfeit by judgment of the king (1 Sam 14:43–45).

The historicity of the Passover pardon has also attracted suspicion because of difficulty in agreeing on the procedure adopted or on the strategy of Pilate in involving Jesus in it. Was this a longstanding Jewish custom to which Pilate had accommodated himself (as John 19:39 seems to suggest), or was it more a personal custom (Mark 15:8)? (The attempt to rescue historicity at the expense of treating the matter as not based on custom at all is actually a hindrance when it comes to identifying a credible motivation for Pilate's involvement of Jesus.) Were the people completely free to choose their prisoner (how then do we get a "short list" of Barabbas and Jesus?), or does Mark 15:6 simplify a process that was expected to involve a process of bargaining? The uncertainties are real enough, but hardly basis for questioning fundamental historicity. It is best to see the custom as reflecting an accommodation between the governor and the populace and, in that sense, as both his custom and theirs. We cannot know how long a currency it had. Though some ground rules are intrinsically likely, the texts do not really indicate a limitation upon the people's choice: they have Barabbas in mind, but Jesus is a new candidate upon the scene, and they may want to change their minds in his favor.

The best suggestion to date about the strategy of Pilate is that of Bajsić (*Bib* 48 [1967] 15–20; followed by Strobel, *Stunde*, 127–30; etc.). The central insight of this suggestion is the recognition that Pilate's concern was to avoid, if possible, the need to release Barabbas. The known popularity of Jesus suggested to him that here, in the nick of time, he might have an alternative candidate whom the crowd might be prepared to save by means of the Paschal pardon, at the expense of Barabbas. We have seen at 23:1–5, 6–12 Pilate's reluctance, in the face of popular Jewish support for Jesus, to condemn him at the behest of the Jerusalem leadership. As the pressure from the Jewish leadership is maintained, Pilate sees the possibility of simultaneously playing the crowds against their leaders in connection with Jesus and deflecting the crowds from a choice for Passover amnesty that was troubling to him.

The conclusion to be drawn from the above discussion is that, despite the lack of independent attestation, there is no sufficient reason for denying the historicity of the Paschal pardon.

Comment

Unimpressed by Pilate's conviction of Jesus' innocence and fearing that his release would take the place of a Paschal amnesty for a popular nationalistic villain, the Jewish People gathered before Pilate pressed for Jesus' execution and the release of Barabbas.

18 ἀνέκραγον, "they screamed out," is probably Lukan (cf. 8:28), as may be παμπληθεί, "all together" (only here in the NT). Luke's text leaves the reader to surmise (on a broad Greco-Roman cultural basis) that some kind of Paschal amnesty expectation must be involved. But more seriously, such a custom presumed, it is hard to see how any satisfactory thought sequence can be established from v 16. The unspecified "they" who scream out all together seem at first to be "the chief priests and the rulers and the People" of v 13 and are generally so taken. However, the exclusion of "the People" and the exclusion of "the chief priests and the rulers" have each been canvassed. The former finds some support from the restricted sense for "you" in v 14, but "all together" tends to count against it, as does the crowd scene to which this unit corresponds in the other Gospels (and in the suggested cultural background). Also, we can hardly account for the introduction of "the People" in v 13 on this understanding, and the pattern of uses of "People" in Acts counts against it (see Acts 5:27; 6:12; 12:4, 11; 21:28–30, 36; 26:17; an initially very favorable attitude on the part of the People is transformed into its opposite by misrepresentations to them [esp. 6:11–12; 21:28]), as is the role in the trial before Pilate attributed to the "People of Israel" in general in Acts 3:13.

The latter view (taking "they" as "the People") accounts for the introduction of "the People" in v 13 and provides us with a crowd scene. This leaves us, however, with a strangely unmotivated change of heart toward Jesus on the part of the People (including the leaders as well softens the problem but hardly eliminates it). Whether we opt for a reference to "the People" or a combined group, it seems necessary to draw in the Acts material appealed to above to produce a satisfactory logical transition (in John as well [18:39–40], when the Paschal pardon is introduced, there is no mention of provocation from the leaders to stir the people to animosity [contrast Mark 15:11; Matt 27:20]; this may have source implications]). On balance, it seems best to take the "they" as referring to all those called together by Pilate in v 13.

V 18 seems most naturally to imply that those who screamed out have understood what we find in v 16 as the offer of Jesus as object of the Paschal amnesty, but this makes no sense at all for a group that includes the chief priests and rulers and is not true to the role of v 16 in vv 13–16. The alternative is to separate somewhat the two halves of the demand: "Away with this fellow" adds the People's support to the ongoing demand of the leaders; "release Barabbas for us" represents a dismissal of the issue of Jesus (and Pilate's attempts to release him) in favor of something of much more pressing interest to them. The difficulty here is that in vv 19–24 Barabbas disappears again from sight, and when he surfaces again in v 25 it is in the context of a choice between Jesus and Barabbas. The relationship between the attempt to release Jesus as innocent and the attempt to release him as object of the Paschal amnesty is also difficult to specify in John's account. No real sense can be made of the way that Pilate confuses the question of Jesus' innocence and the possibility of a Paschal pardon for him (in John, Pilate, motivated by his belief in Jesus' innocence, proposes the Paschal pardon to those who have already declared themselves as against Jesus). The commonalities here are likely to reflect a feature of a common source, which has, however, been rather obscured by the respective evangelists, who have each produced texts that seem to have significant defects as narratives at this point.

"Barabbas" is a Grecized form of an Aramaic name ("Son of Abba [= father, as in Jesus' mode of address to God]") attested in fifth- or sixth-century B.C. texts and is the name of a third- or fourth-century A.D. Babylonian rabbi. "Abba" [אבה] has been identified as a personal name on a funerary inscription from near Jerusalem, coming from the period 100 B.C.–A.D. 100 (see further Fitzmyer, 1490).

19　There is probably some influence from Mark 15:7 on the information and language here, but the location is as in John 18:40. Luke does not mention fellow prisoners from the uprising, whereas Mark does so. In their absence, Barabbas becomes more directly linked to the rioting and murder.

20　This verse may well be a Lukan formulation ($\pi\rho\sigma\epsilon\phi\dot\omega\nu\eta\sigma\epsilon\nu$, "called out," in particular is Lukan), contributing to the threefold exchange that Luke fashions between Pilate and those gathered before him. The parallelism between the release of Jesus and of Barabbas is reinforced here.

21　$\dot\epsilon\pi\epsilon\phi\dot\omega\nu\upsilon\nu$, "were shouting back," will be a Lukan contribution. The call for Jesus' crucifixion here is linked by the double use of the imperative to John 19:6 (since Luke is himself capable of doubling imperatives, the link can only be affirmed in the context of the other links with John in this material). Though the basic meaning is rather wider, $\sigma\tau\alpha\upsilon\rho\sigma\dot\upsilon\nu$ in the NT is used exclusively of the Roman means of execution upon a cross. In this context there is no need to discuss the question of possible Jewish practice of crucifixion (cf. J. A. Fitzmyer, "Crucifixion in Ancient Palestine, Qumran Literature, and the New Testament," *CBQ* 40 [1978] 493–513).

22　Luke labels as "third" the attempt here by Pilate to have Jesus released. For the first clause of Pilate's statement, Luke is likely to be drawing on Mark 15:14, while for the second clause he will be drawing on his Johannine source. On this verse, cf. at vv 14b, 15b–16, which are repeated here to a significant degree. The evil that has been done by Barabbas is manifest, but despite accusation, Pilate has been unable to find any evil in Jesus.

23　The formulation here will be Lukan ($\dot\epsilon\pi\dot\epsilon\kappa\epsilon\iota\nu\tau\sigma$, "pressed," $\phi\omega\nu\alpha\hat\iota\varsigma$ $\mu\epsilon\gamma\dot\alpha\lambda\alpha\iota\varsigma$, "loud shouts," $\alpha\dot\iota\tau\sigma\dot\upsilon\mu\epsilon\nu\sigma\iota$, "asking," and possibly $\kappa\alpha\tau\dot\iota\sigma\chi\upsilon\sigma\nu$, "prevailed," are clear Lukan preferences), but the idea that Pilate eventually capitulated to the will of the crowd is clear also in Mark 15:15.

24　Luke now spells out what is involved in "their voices prevailed." $\dot\epsilon\pi\dot\epsilon\kappa\rho\iota\nu\epsilon\nu$, "decided," occurs only here in the NT. It can be used in connection with the delivering of a sentence, but a more general sense is likely here.

25　Luke repeats some of v 19; otherwise the language looks like a Lukan rendering of Mark 15:15bc, though there is a Johannine link at the end. This may account for the loss of Mark's reference to a flogging at this point (in John it comes earlier). Clearly a choice has been made between Barabbas and Jesus. A thread of references to *releasing* runs from v 16 (Jesus), through vv 18 (Barabbas), 20 (Jesus), 22 (Jesus), and to the present verse (Barabbas). Whereas in Luke Jesus is "handed over to the will" of the hostile crowd, this becomes in John "handed over to them" (that is, to those who have sought his crucifixion; Mark uses "handed over" in a more technically legal sense and so provides no indirect object for the verb). John's form reveals the next stage of a development already evident in the Lukan text; Luke still envisages the Roman conduct of the execution, while John (though not consistently) shifts the execution into the hands of the Jews (but see at 23:26 for a discussion of whether Luke too thinks in terms of the Jewish leadership and People as taking Jesus out to execution).

Explanation

The scene before Pilate continues: three times Pilate will suggest the release of Jesus, but three times the crowd will clamor for his execution.

It is clear that the crowd feared that the proposed release of Jesus would take the place of an anticipated Passover clemency for a popular nationalistic villain named Barabbas. What is not clear in Luke's account is how the two matters came to be linked. (For suggestions about the historical sequence of events, see *Form/ Structure/Setting* above.)

The very people who had provided a buffer between Jesus and the hostile intentions of their leaders now join their voices with those leaders in a vigorous popular demand for the execution of their erstwhile hero. What has changed? Luke gives no real explanation, but we can look in a number of directions for some insight. First, it is not unlikely that national solidarity asserted itself in a setting where the choice becomes that between a view sponsored by Pilate and that of their own leaders. Then there is the Barabbas factor. Outside the Gospel accounts, we know nothing of this figure. His popularity can only be explained if we regard him to have in some way represented the nationalistic aspirations of the Jewish people: a morally lax, but instinctive, nationalism wins out over the morally demanding, but less visceral, priorities of Jesus. There are, as well, the clues that come from Acts, where there is the same pattern: Christianity and Christians initially popular with the People, but not with the leadership; then after a time there arises violent hostility. For the rise of hostility, see especially Acts 6:11–12; 21:28. It seems that we should understand that the People have been led astray by their leaders' misrepresentation of Jesus. Finally we should not forget Luke 22:53. In this hour the forces stacked against Jesus, which up to this point have been powerless against him despite all their best efforts, will have their way: in the mystery of God's good purpose, this is the time for the forces of darkness to prevail.

As the story continues, it becomes clear that the People are quite uneasy about what they have done in calling for the execution of Jesus (see vv 27–31, 35).

Pilate was clearly convinced that Jesus was innocent. If his priorities had focused upon justice, he would have had no real difficulty in holding out against the crowd's pressure, now added to the demands of the Jerusalem leadership: he held in his hands the power of Rome. But his priorities were more pragmatic. It was now clear (contrary to his initial understanding) that he would provoke the ire of the wider Jewish public if he gave in to the demands of their leaders. It had also become clear that the crowds were not to be talked into accepting Jesus, in place of Barabbas, as their Passover gift. Given these developments, there was no advantage for Rome, or for Pilate himself, in resisting this pressure. Let them have their way!

On the Way to Execution (23:26–32)

Bibliography

Bailey, J. A. *The Traditions Common to the Gospels of Luke and John.* NovTSup 7. Leiden: Brill, 1963. 78–84. **Benoit, P.** *The Passion and Resurrection of Jesus.* New York: Herder and Herder, 1969. 153–68. **Carroll, J. T.** "Luke's Crucifixion Scene." In *Reimaging,* ed. D. D. Sylva. 108–24, 194–203. **Demel, S.** "Jesu Umgang mit Frauen nach dem Lukasevangelium." *BibNot* 57 (1991) 52–95, esp. 78–82. **Finegan, J.** *Die Überlieferung der Leidens- und Auferstehungsgeschichte Jesu.* BZNW 15. Giessen: Töpelmann, 1934. 30–31. **Flusser, D.** "The Crucified One and the Jews." *Immanuel* 7 (1977) 25–37. **Giblin, C. H.** *The Destruction of Jerusalem.* 93–104. **Käser, W.** "Exegetische und theologische Erwägungen zur Seligpreisung der Kinderlosen Lc 23,29b." *ZNW* 54 (1963) 240–54. **Neyrey, J. H.** "Jesus' Address to the Women of Jerusalem (Lk. 23. 27–31): a Prophetic Judgment Oracle." *NTS* 29 (1983) 74–86. **Schreiber, J.** *Theologie des Vertrauens: Eine redaktionsgeschichtliche Untersuchung des Markusevangeliums.* Hamburg: Furche, 1967. 22–82. ———. *Der Kreuzigungsbericht des Markusevangeliums: Mk 15,20b–41: Eine traditionsgeschichtliche und methodenkritische Untersuchung nach William Wrede (1859–1906).* BZNW 48. Berlin/New York: de Gruyter, 1986. **Soards, M. L.** "Tradition, Composition, and Theology in Jesus' Speech to the 'Daughters of Jerusalem' (Luke 23,26–32)." *Bib* 68 (1987) 221–44. **Untergassmair, F. G.** *Kreuzweg und Kreuzigung Jesu: Ein Beitrag zur lukanischen Redaktionsgeschichte und zur Frage nach der lukanischen "Kreuzestheologie."* PTS 10. Paderborn: Schöningh, 1980.

And see at 22:1–2, 66–71; 23:1–5.

Translation

²⁶*As they led him away*ᵃ *they took hold of* ᵇ*a man named*ᵇ *Simon, a Cyrenian, who was coming [in] from the countryside, and they laid the cross on him so that he might carry it behind Jesus.* ²⁷*A great multitude of the People followed him, and among them were many women*ᶜ *who were beating [their breasts] and wailing for him.* ²⁸*Jesus turned to them and said, "Daughters of Jerusalem, don't weep for me; weep, rather, for yourselves and for your children.* ²⁹*For the days are surely*ᵈ *coming when people*ᵉ *will say, 'How fortunate are the barren, the wombs that have never given birth and the breasts that have never given suck!'* ³⁰*Then people* ᶠ *will begin to say to the mountains, 'Fall on us!' and to the hills, 'Cover us!'* ³¹*For if this is what is done with the* ᵍ *green wood, what will happen to the dry?"* ³²*They led [off], as well, two criminals, to be executed*ʰ *with him.*

Notes

ᵃ B and a few other texts have the verb in the impf.

ᵇ⁻ᵇ Gr. τινα (lit. "a certain").

ᶜ Lit. "a great multitude of the People and women" (shared definite article).

ᵈ "Surely" represents the force of Gr. ἰδού (lit. "behold"), which is, however, missing from P⁷⁵ D *f*¹³ 2542 etc.

ᵉ Unspecified subject in Gr.

ᶠ Unspecified subject in Gr.

ᵍ The definite article is missing from B C 070 etc.

ʰ The verb here is translated "do away with" at 22:2.

Form/Structure/Setting

The scope of the unit is marked out by the statements about being led away/off with which it begins and ends. V 27 also provides links forward to v 35 and v 48. In this way, the three units that make up the crucifixion account proper are linked (the second is subdivided below for convenience of discussion). The present episode marks the movement in time and space from Pilate's court to the place of execution.

Luke passes over Mark's account at this point of the mockery by the soldiers (he has his equivalent for this in vv 11–12). He draws on his Markan source for v 26 (Mark 15:20), and v 32 is likely to be inspired by Mark 15:27. Otherwise, Luke goes his own way here with materials that are not paralleled in any of the other Gospels. There is no scholarly consensus on the tradition history of these materials. Some find a core in vv 27–28, which have been subject to expansion, perhaps in stages. Others are more impressed by the link between vv 28 and 29 as defining the core (with or without v 30). There are those who maintain that Luke has freely created the unit, with minimal use of tradition. Relevant factors toward forming a judgment include the following: (*i*) The way in which the women and the People are welded together in v 27 (see *Comment*) suggests that Luke is adapting traditional material about weeping women for his own purposes. (*ii*) V 29 is not a necessary continuation of v 28 and could have been transmitted apart from its present context. (*iii*) The striking macarism involved in v 29 is not likely to be merely a rewriting of Luke 21:23. (*iv*) The presence of a form of v 29 in *Gos. Thom.* 79 (linked with a form of Luke 11:27–28) may support separate transmission of this saying (but dependence on Luke is possible). (*v*) V 30 is not required by v 29 and is readily understandable as Christian exposition (the likely influence of Semitic idiom counts against Luke being responsible for drawing in Hos 10:8). (*vi*) V 31 is certainly traditional. The question is only whether it is a traditional proverb brought in later because of its appropriateness or it formed an original unity with either vv 27–28 or v 30. Independent transmission as a saying of Jesus is hardly possible. (*vii*) There is little Lukan language in vv 27–31 (see *Comment*). On balance, it would seem best to attribute to Luke only minor redactional changes but to recognize that a complex history of compilation lies behind this material (some part of which may have been at Luke's hands), with (*i*) vv 27–28 providing the original core unit here, (*ii*) to which v 29 has been added as a separately transmitted saying of Jesus, and (*iii*) to which in turn vv 30 and 31 have been added as, respectively, scriptural and proverbial exposition.

There is no way of telling whether Luke's tradition(s) here bears any relationship to the second passion account to which he seems to have had access.

Comment

After their complicity in what has set Jesus on his death march, even as he goes out to the place of execution, the historic People of God (in the persons of women among their number) begin to become distressed about this execution procedure now underway. Their uneasiness is only confirmed by Jesus, who suggests in powerful language that the unhappier plight is theirs rather than his.

26 The agreement with Matthew in having ἀπήγαγον, "led away," in place of Mark's ἐξάγουσιν, "lead out," is likely to be fortuitous. Luke replaces Mark's use of the technical language of Roman impressment (ἀγγαρεύειν) with his favored ἐπιλαμβάνειν, "take," and this brings with it a reformulation of Simon's role (curiously, in the rewording only ἐπέθηκαν, "put/lay on," is obviously Lukan, which leads Green [*Death of Jesus*, 87] to speculate on a possible second source influence here; the natural attractiveness of finding a discipleship pattern reflected is somewhat undermined by the lack of exact vocabulary links to the relevant discipleship sayings [9:23; 14:27]). Simon's family links are omitted, since they will have no significance for Luke's intended audience.

Does Luke want us to understand that Jesus is in Jewish or Roman charge at this point? In strict grammar the "they" who lead Jesus out to execution ought to be those who have called for his execution, and Luke has certainly wanted to emphasize the Jewish desire for this outcome (v 25). But the natural reading of vv 18–25 leaves the crucifixion in Pilate's realm and therefore in Roman hands. Also the continuing Lukan text provides no encouragements for viewing the execution proceedings as in any sense in the hands of the Jewish People or leaders. Since already in vv 14, 18 Luke has shown a certain carelessness about grammatical antecedents, it seems best to retain the consistency of the Lukan picture by assuming the same level of grammatical carelessnes here (easily understandable as a byproduct of the omission of Mark 15:16–20a) and taking the "they" who lead Jesus out to execution as Pilate's soldiers (cf. vv 36, 47, 52).

We do not know whether Simon (though from Cyrene) was now permanently resident in Jerusalem or (perhaps more likely) a pilgrim for the Passover festival (cf. Acts 2:10; a Jewish community in Cyrene is noted by Josephus, *Ag. Ap.* 2.44; *Ant.* 16.160–70). Nor is it clear whether ἀπ' ἀγροῦ means "from [his] field" or "from the countryside [i.e., from outside the city]." Assuming that he is Jewish, on the feast day his activity would be subject to sabbath restriction on activity and travel.

Since the normal practice was for the condemned man to carry his own cross (see at 9:23), one might have expected an explanation for the enlistment of Simon, but none is offered. At the literary level it might be possible to think in terms of a mock enactment of the call to discipleship issued by Jesus, but it is more likely that we have simply a historical reminiscence of an action that was probably made necessary by the weakened state of Jesus due to flagellation (Luke does not report any flagellation).

27 πολὺ πλῆθος τοῦ λαοῦ, "a great multitude of the People," is the most likely Lukan contribution to this verse (cf. at 1:10; ἐκόπτεσθαι, "beat [the breast]," is preferred by Luke at 8:52 and could have replaced some other verb here). For crowds following Jesus in quite different circumstances, cf. 7:9; 9:11. By introducing the People here, Luke is able to use a tradition about weeping women following Jesus to the cross as a means of immediately beginning to distance the People (as distinct from their leaders) from their momentary complicity in the call for the execution of Jesus. He will reinforce this through an inclusio by taking up elements of v 27 in v 48 (v 48 also draws on v 35a). (In this light, we should not mark any clear separation between the People and the women [as, e.g., Neyrey, *NTS* 29 (1983) 75–76]; rather these women are part of the People, and their posture already at this point will become more generally that of the gathered populace as it witnesses the unfolding of the events of the crucifixion [v 48]. Indirectly this literary strategy witnesses to Luke's [here unconscious?] assumption of the intrinsically equal significance of men and

women.) The actions of the women are to be associated with mourning, here able to begin before the death itself, because Jesus is on his death march to the cross (Demel, *BibNot* 57 [1991] 79–80, notes that this motif of the "wailing women" does not recur in connection with the burial). What we have here is more specific than, but not in tension with, the general phenomenon of crowds following a condemned man to his execution (e.g., Lucian, *De morte Pereg.* 34; Ps.-Quintilian, *Declam.* 274). Weeping for one on the way to execution is a motif found in martyr texts (for Classical texts, see Klostermann, 227; for rabbinic materials, see Untergassmair, *Kreuzweg,* 131–36). A link with Zech 12:10–14 is possible but uncertain.

28 Luke is likely to be responsible for στραφεὶς πρὸς αὐτάς, "turning to them" (cf. 7:9; 9:55; 10:23; 22:61 [for the likely force here, cf. at 22:61]), and possibly for the use of πλήν, "but." The phrase "daughters of Jerusalem" is used repeatedly in Canticles (and only there in the OT). The link is probably fortuitous, unless it is meant in an ironic way to suggest that these women function as attendants to the king. Unlike the women, Jesus is not overtaken by a fate for which he is ill prepared: in full obedience to his Father he goes to his appointed destiny, through death and to glory. So one should weep for these women (and their children) rather than for Jesus (the alternatives are presented in a chiastic pattern in the Greek). The Lukan Jesus has already so wept (19:41), and he invites the women to do the same. The future that lies before them has been outlined in 13:34–35; 19:42–44; 21:20–24; cf. 11:49–51 (see at these texts). They will be caught up in a horrendous judgment of God that is to befall the city.

29 None of the language here is notably Lukan. ἰδοὺ ἔρχεται ἡμέραι (lit. "behold, days are coming") is Septuagintal language, notable in Jeremiah (7:32; 16:14; 38:31[= 31:31 in MT]), where it evokes Jeremiah's certainty about the exile and restoration sequence awaiting Judah. The connection is often drawn between Isa 54:1 and this blessing pronounced upon barren and childless women. However, where Isa 54:1 asserts a bright future against a dark present, the Lukan text proposes a dark future in which the natural values of the present will be reversed (though not oriented to the future, 2 *Apoc. Bar.* 10:13–15 is quite similar). The sense is very close to that of Luke 21:23. The choice of the language of blessing in such a context involves an almost bitter irony (it would be truly bitter if εὐλόγηταί, "blessed," had been used rather than μακάριαι, "fortunate"). Fitzmyer (1498) cites a series of classical texts that note the advantage of childlessness when death must be faced (Euripides, *Androm.* 395; *Alces.* 882; Tacitus, *Annales* 2.75; Elder Seneca, *Controv.* 2.3.2; Apuleius, *Apol.* 85.571).

30 The verse is a quotation from Hos 10:8. It differs from the LXX (*i*) in having the pleonastic ἄρξονται λέγειν, "they will begin to say," rather than ἐροῦσιν, "they will say," and (*ii*) in having interchanged πέσετε [LXX has the first aorist ending -ατε, as do some MSS of Luke] ἐφ᾽, "fall upon," and καλύψατε, "cover." Though there is quite a closeness to LXX language (it is the natural and obvious translation of the Hebrew), the first difference could reflect a Semitic paraphrase of the Hosea text (cf. at 13:25 for comment on the singular form of the same expression at 13:26; here the indefinite use of the third person plural active verb is also involved, which may be a further pointer to a Semitic original ["they" are not the privileged women, at least not they alone]). The call is most likely for relief through death from the time of terrible suffering (in the use in Rev 6:16 [cf. 9:6] there is a development from this, adding the idea of the collapsed mountains and

hills possibly acting as a shield from the wrathful gaze of the Lamb). The use of
Hosea provides a link with the apostasy and subsequent exile of Israel.

31 This proverbial-sounding statement remains somewhat obscure. It is not at
once clear whether ἐν in its two occurrences has the thrust of "in the case of" or of
"in the time of." Nor is it clear if "they" of ποιοῦσιν (lit. "they do") is meant to
have a contextually identifiable antecedent or if in Semitic idiom it stands for the
passive. Comparison has been made with Isa 10:16–19; Jer 11:16, 19; Ezek 17:24;
20:47; 24:9–10; Prov 11:31; 1 Pet 4:17–18. From these emerge the use of fire as a
symbol of judgment, an implicit recognition that fire burns the dry more readily
than the green, and a "how much more" comparison between God's judgment upon
righteous and ungodly. But our text is not clearly dependent on any of these.
These texts do, however, create a presumption in favor of ἐν = "in the case of" and
suggest that the imagery of fire is almost certain to be implicitly present. Though
much later, the rabbinic text *Seder Eliyahu Rabbah* 14 (F. 65) suggests that we may
be dealing with an existing proverbial pattern: "When fire consumes the green, what
will the dry do?" (cited after Str-B 2:263; cf. the related saying from *b. Mo^ed Qat.* 25b,
which contrasts the cedar with the hyssop on the wall and continues with other proverbial sayings with a similar thrust). But how is the proverb to be applied?

The active agent(s) for the proverb has been variously taken as God, the Romans, the Jewish leaders, or the Jewish people more generally. "Green wood"
versus "dry" has been applied to the innocence of Jesus versus the guilt of those
who have sent him to his death and to the fullness of life of what Jesus stands for
and brings versus the lack of life of the Judaism that sends him to his death. For
further suggestions, see Evans, 864.

It is likely that each of these suggestions is overly precise in its attempt to de-
code the terms used in the proverb. Jesus does not consider himself to be a natural
object of the disaster that he senses is soon to engulf his people as a judgment
upon their sins, but he goes to the cross at his Father's bidding and as his destined mode of participation in that wider impending disaster (see discussion at
22:42). In relation to this thought, the proverb naturally expresses the inevitability and the scale of the judgment to fall (ποιοῦσιν, "is done," is then best taken as
standing in the place of a passive verb).

32 ἀναιρεθῆναι, "to be done away with," is clearly Lukan, and κακοῦργοι, "criminals," anticipates the distinctively Lukan use of this term in vv 33, 39. As a Lukan
formulation inspired by Mark 15:27, this verse rounds off the unit by forming an
inclusio with v 26. Jesus is now found in the company of "lawless people" (to recall the language of 22:37).

Explanation

Given up to the will of the clamoring crowd, Jesus is led away for execution.
Immediately, the People begin to back away from their complicity in the process
that is now sending Jesus to his death. Jesus suggests to the weeping women among
them that it is they who face a future full of calamity and distress.

Luke's language is loose, but he surely intends us to understand that Roman
soldiers take Jesus to his fate: his fate corresponds to the *will* of the Jewish leaders
and People; the *action* of the Roman authorities implements that will. The Roman military was wont to impress members of the public to do their bidding.

Simon carries the cross (though normally the victim himself would), presumably because Jesus is too weakened by the scourging he has received to be able to do so. However, Luke has not told us about the scourging recorded in the other Gospels.

The attitude of the women from among the historic People of God will become, after the witnessing of the execution itself (v 35) and the manner in which Jesus died, the attitude of the populace as a whole (v 48). The women grieve over the impending death and play the part of mourners ahead of time. The scene here fits with what is elsewhere known of the crowds that followed condemned men to their execution and also with the weeping to be found in Classical and Jewish texts about martyrdom.

Jesus turns and speaks, and suddenly it is clear once more that he is no passive pawn in the grip of larger forces. He suggests that the women should not weep for him but for themselves and their children. Indeed Jesus has himself already wept over the people of this city (19:41). Jesus is not overtaken by a fate for which he is ill prepared: in full obedience to his Father he goes to his appointed destiny, through death and to glory. The future that faces the women has been sketched in 13:34–35; 19:42–44; 21:20–24; and cf. 11:49–51.

The opening clause of v 29 uses language from Jeremiah to evoke Jeremiah's certainty about the exile (and restoration) that he had foretold for his contemporaries: Jesus is foretelling a corresponding fate for the first-century people of Jerusalem. In the midst of this coming calamity the natural values of the present will be reversed, and so, women who have been denied motherhood will consider themselves fortunate.

Language from Hos 10:8 is called upon to evoke the full horror of that future. People will long for death as the only relief from the terrible suffering of that time. In a vein similar to the Jeremiah link noted above, the quotation from Hosea draws a line to the eighth-century apostasy and subsequent exile of Israel.

Finally a proverb is called upon, whose application remains somewhat obscure. It seems best to remind ourselves that Jesus did not consider himself to be a natural object of the disaster that he sensed was soon to engulf his people as a judgment upon their sins. Rather he goes to the cross at his Father's bidding and as his destined mode of participation in that wider impending disaster (see discussion at 22:42). In this light, Jesus sees his own death as the beginning of this disaster; the proverb expresses both the inevitability of the judgment and its scale.

The unit ends with an indication that Jesus is not led out to execution alone: two criminals accompany him. And the reader notes the beginning of a quite specific fulfillment of 22:37.

Jesus Crucified and Mocked (23:33–38)

Bibliography

Benoit, P. *The Passion and Resurrection of Jesus.* New York: Herder and Herder, 1969. 168–80. **Blinzler, J.** *Der Prozess Jesu.* 4th ed. 357–74. **Buhlmann, W.** "Die Kreuzigung Jesu." *HL* 9 (1981) 3–12. **Cantinat, J.** "Le crucifiement de Jésus." *VSpir* 84 (1951) 142–53. **Conzelmann, H.** *Luke.*

88–93. **Crowe, J.** "The LAOS at the Cross: Luke's Crucifixion Scene." In *The Language of the Cross*, ed. A. Lacomara. Chicago: Franciscan Herald, 1978. 77–90. **Dalman, G.** "At the Cross." In *Jesus-Jeshua: Studies in the Gospels*. Tr. P. R. Levertoff. New York: Ktav, 1971–1929. 185–222. **Davison, A.** "The Crucifixion, Burial and Resurrection of Jesus." *PEFQS* 28 (1906) 124–29. **Feldkämper, L.** *Der betende Jesus als Heilsmittler nach Lukas.* Veröffentlichungen des Missionspriesterseminars, 29. St Augustin bei Bonn: Steyler Verlag, 1978. 251–67. **Feuillet, A.** "Souffrance et confiance en Dieu: Commentaire du psaume xxii." *NRT* 70 (1948) 137–49. **Finegan, J.** *Die Überlieferung der Leidens- und Auferstehungsgeschichte Jesu.* BZNW 15. Giessen: Töpelmann, 1934. 31–32. **Jeremias, J.** *Golgotha.* Angelas 1. Leipzig: E. Pfeiffer, 1926. **Lindars, B.** *New Testament Apologetic: The Doctrinal Significance of Old Testament Quotations.* Philadelphia: Westminster, 1961. 88–93. **Linnemann, E.** *Studien zur Passionsgeschichte.* 136–70. **Osborn, G. R.** "Redactional Trajectories in the Crucifixion Narrative." *EvQ* 51 (1979) 80–96. **Paton, W. R.** "Die Kreuzigung Jesu." *ZNW* 2 (1901) 339–41. **Reumann, J. H.** "Psalm 22 at the Cross." *Int* 28 (1974) 39–58. **Robbins, V. K.** "The Crucifixion and the Speech of Jesus." *Forum* 4.1 (1988) 33–46. **Rosenblatt, S.** "The Crucifixion of Jesus from the Standpoint of Pharisaic Law." *JBL* 75 (1956) 315–21. **Schneider, G.** "Die theologische Sicht des Todes Jesu in den Kreuzigungsberichten der Evangelien." *TPQ* 126 (1978) 14–22. **Soards, M. L.** "A Literary Analysis of the Origin and Purpose of Luke's Account of the Mockery of Jesus." *BZ* 31 (1987) 110–16. **Taylor, V.** *The Passion Narrative of St Luke.* 91–99. ———. "The Narrative of the Crucifixion." *NTS* 8 (1961–62) 333–34. **Trilling, W.** "Le Christ, roi crucifié (Lc 23,35–43)." *AsSeign* 65 (1973) 56–67. **Wansbrough, H.** "The Crucifixion of Jesus." *ClerRev* 56 (1971) 251–61. **Weeden, T. J., Sr.** "The Cross as Power in Weakness (Mark 15:20b–41)." In *The Passion in Mark*, ed. W. H. Kelber. 115–34. **Westermann, C.** *Gewendete Klage: Eine Auslegung des 22. Psalms.* BibS(N) 8. 2nd ed. Neukirchen: Neukirchener, 1957. **Winter, P.** *On the Trial of Jesus*, rev. T. A. Burkill and G. Vermes. Studia judaica 1. Berlin/New York: de Gruyter, 1974. 90–96.

ON CRUCIFIXION:

Arnold, M. "La crucifixion dans le droit romain." *BTS* 133 (1971) 4. **Bammel, E.** "Crucifixion as a Punishment in Palestine." In *The Trial of Jesus: Cambridge Studies in Honour of C. F. D. Moule*, ed. E. Bammel. SBT 2/13. London: SCM, 1970. 162–65. **Baumgarten, J. M.** "Does *tlh* in the Temple Scroll refer to Crucifixion?" *JBL* 91 (1972) 472–81. **Buchler, A.** "Die Todesstrafen der Bibel und der jüdisch-nachbiblischen Zeit." *MGWJ* 50 (1906) 542–62, 664–91. **Fischer, H.** *Die offene Kreuzhaltung im Rechtsritual.* FS A. Steinwenter. GRSS 3. Graz/Cologne, 1958. 9–57. **Fitzmyer, J. A.** "Crucifixion in Ancient Palestine, Qumran Literature, and the New Testament." *CBQ* 40 (1978) 493–513; reprinted in *To Advance the Gospel: New Testament Studies.* New York: Crossroads, 1981. 125–46. **Fransen, I.** "L'historien Flavius-Josephe et le supplice de la croix." *BTS* 133 (1971) 5. **Halperin, D. J.** "Crucifixion, the Nahum Pesher, and the Rabbinic Penalty of Strangulation." *JJS* 32 (1981) 32–46. **Harrison, S. J.** "Cicero and 'crurifragium.'" *ClQ* 33 (1983) 453–55. **Hengel, M.** *Crucifixion in the Ancient World and the Folly of the Message of the Cross.* Tr. J. Bowden. Philadelphia: Fortress, 1977. **Hewitt, J. W.** "The Use of Nails in the Crucifixion." *HTR* 25 (1932) 29–46. **Kuhn, H.-W.** "Die Kreuzesstrafe während der frühen Kaiserzeit: Ihre Wirklichkeit und Wertung in der Umwelt des Urchristentums." *ANRW* 2/25.1 (1982) 648–793. **Vogt, J.** "Crucifixion etiam pro nobis: Historische Anmerkungen zum Kreuzestod." *IKZ* 2 (1973) 186–91. **Yadin, Y.** "Pesher Nahum (4QpNahum) Reconsidered." *IEJ* 21 (1971) 1–12. **Zugibe, F. T.** "Two Questions about Crucifixion: Does the Victim Die of Asphyxiation? Would Nails in the Hands Hold the Weight of the Body?" *BRev* 5 (1989) 34–43.

ON GIV꜀AT HA-MIVTAR:

Charlesworth, J. H. "Jesus and Jehohanan: An Archaeological Note on Crucifixion." *ExpTim* 84 (1973) 147–50. **Haas, N.** "Anthropological Observations on the Skeletal Remains from Giv꜀at ha-Mivtar." *IEJ* 20 (1970) 38–59. **Kuhn, H.-W.** "Der Gekreuzigte von

Giv‛at ha-Mivtar: Bilanz einer Entdeckung." In *Theologia Crucis, Signum Crucis.* FS E. Dinkler, ed. C. Andresen and G. Klein. Tübingen, 1979. 303–34. ————. "Zum Gekreuzigten von Giv‛at ha-Mivtar: Korrektur eigenes Versehens in der Erstveröfftlichung." *ZNW* 69 (1978) 118–22. **Möller-Christensen, V.** "Skeletal Remains from Giv‛at ha-Mivtar." *IEJ* 26 (1976) 35–38. **Naveh, J.** "The Ossuary Inscriptions from Giv‛at ha-Mivtar, Jerusalem." *IEJ* 20 (1970) 33–37. **Tzaferis, V.** "Jewish Tombs at and near Giv‛at ha-Mivtar, Jerusalem." *IEJ* 20 (1970) 18–32. ————. "Crucifixion: The Archaeological Evidence." *BAR* 11 (1985) 44–53. **Yadin, Y.** "Epigraphy and Crucifixion." *IEJ* 23 (1973) 19–22. **Zias, J.,** and **Sekeles, E.** "The Crucified Man from Giv‛at ha-Mivtar: A Reappraisal." *IEJ* 35 (1985) 22–27.

On 23:34a:

Dammers, A. H. "Studies in Texts: Luke xxiii, 34a." *Th* 52 (1949) 138–39. **Daube, D.** "'For They Know Not What They Do': Luke 23,34." *StudPat* 4 [= TU 79] (1961) 58–70. **Démann, P.** "'Père pardonnez-leur' (Lc 23,34)." *Cahiers sioniens* 5 (1951) 321–36. **Flusser, D.** "'Sie wissen nicht, was sie tun?' Geschichte eines Herrwortes." In *Kontinuität und Einheit.* FS F. Mussner, ed. P.-G. Müller and W. Stenger. Freiburg/Basel/Vienna: Herder, 1981. 393–410. **Henry, D. M.** "'Father, Forgive Them; for They Know Not What They Do' (Luke xxiii. 34)." *ExpTim* 30 (1918–19) 87. **Moffatt, J.** "Exegetica: Luke xxiii. 34." *Exp* 8/7 (1914) 92–93. **Reid, J.** "The Words from the Cross, I: 'Father, Forgive Them' (Lk. xxiii.34)." *ExpTim* 41 (1929–30) 103–7. **Wilkinson, J.** "The Seven Words from the Cross." *SJT* 17 (1964) 69–82.

On 23:38:

Bammel, E. "The titulus." In *Jesus and the Politics of His Day,* ed. E. Bammel and C. F. D. Moule. Cambridge: University Press, 1984. 353–64. **Lee, G. M.** "The Inscription on the Cross." *PEQ* 100 (1968) 144. **O'Rahilly, A.** "The Title of the Cross." *IER* 65 (1945) 289–97. **Regard, P.-F.** "Le titre de la croix d'après les évangiles." *RevArch* 28 (1928) 95–105.

And see at 22:1–2, 66–71; 23:26–32.

Translation

[33] *When they came to the place called Skull, there they crucified him and the criminals (one on the right and one on the left).* [34] *[a]Jesus was saying, "Father, forgive them; for they do not know what they are doing";[a] they divided up his clothes and cast lots [for them].* [35] *The People stood by, looking on. The leaders[b] sneered [at him], saying, "He saved others; let him save himself, if this is the Christ[c] of God, the Chosen One."* [36] *The soldiers, also, mocked him, coming up and offering him sour wine* [37] *and saying, "If you are the king of the Jews, save yourself!"* [38] *(In fact,[d] there was an inscription[e] above him: "This fellow is the king of the Jews!")*

Notes

a-a This prayer is missing from P75 ℵ1 B D W Θ 070 579 a,d syrs sa bopt etc. Because of this early and widespread negative witness, its authenticity is frequently questioned. Given, however, Luke's conscious paralleling of the deaths of Jesus and Stephen, it is hard to see how Luke could have produced Acts 7:60 without being aware of a tradition like v 34a (since Luke does at times distribute motifs between the Gospel and Acts, we must in the first instance speak in terms of Luke's awareness rather than of confidence that he has reproduced the tradition). And if he was aware of such a tradition, since the language in which it is presented in v 34a makes such a good Lukan fit (see in *Form/ Structure/Setting* below), the best explanation of its presence in many MSS is that Luke put it there.

The deletion of the half verse is likely to reflect a belief that to have executed Jesus was beyond forgiveness (but not so to have executed Stephen).

b The textual tradition shows some confusion about how the relationship between the People and the leaders is to be taken. D drops "the leaders" (compensating with αὐτόν, "him"; thus "They [the People] sneered at him"). A W Θ f¹⁽¹³⁾ 1424 0117 etc. add the People to the leaders with σὺν αὐτοῖς, "with them."

c υἱός, "Son," is added here, or near here, in various ways by P⁷⁵ B D (0124) f¹³ c etc.

d Gr. καί.

e γεγραμμένη, "written" (found in acc. case in Matt 27:37), is added by (A) (D) C³ D R W Θ (Ψ) etc. γράμμασιν ἑλληνικοῖς καὶ ρωμαϊκοῖς καὶ ἑβραϊκοις, "in Greek and Roman and Hebrew letters" (cf. John 19:20), is added by these texts, as well as by א א^c.

Form/Structure/Setting

While divided here for convenience, the Lukan unit probably extends to v 43 ("with the criminals" in the opening verse prepares for the interaction with these criminals with which the unit concludes; the sympathetic but silent witness of the People and the turning of the repentant criminal to Jesus in his need frame the threefold mocking in between). V 35a provides a middle point between v 27 and v 48. That about which Jesus was questioned in the hearings before the Sanhedrin and before Pilate is taken up in the mocking of vv 35b–39.

After going his own way in 23:26–32, Luke returns here to the Markan sequence. The case for a second Lukan source here is fairly weak, but given the extensive evidence for the presence of a second Lukan source for the passion materials up to this point, it is hard not to believe that at least a large part of this second source material has come from a connected passion narrative. In turn, it is impossible that such a narrative lacked an account of the crucifixion. For this reason, even rather modest evidence should be allowed to tip the scales in favor of a second Lukan source here. The points in favor of a second source are: (i) a measure of wording and syntactical similarity between Luke 23:33ab and John 19:17b–18a (Luke: ἦλθον . . . καλούμενον . . . ἐκεῖ ἐσταύρωσαν αὐτόν, "they came . . . called . . . there they crucified him"; John: ἐξῆλθεν . . . λεγόμενον . . . ὅπου αὐτὸν ἐσταύρωσαν, "they came out . . . called . . . where they crucified him"); (ii) agreement with John about introducing the crucifixion of the others immediately after the reference to that of Jesus (v 33; John 19:18; contrast Mark 15:27); (iii) a series of minor agreements of omission with John (omission of drugged wine [v 33; Mark 15:23; John 19:17]; omission of time reference [v 34; Mark 15:25; John 19:18, 24 (Matthew omits this also)]; omission of the cry misunderstood as an appeal to Elijah, but retention of the giving of sour wine [v 36; Mark 15:34–36; John 19:29]); (iv) Jesus' prayer from the cross (if original, and despite its obvious accord with Lukan interests). There is no clear sign of a second Lukan source for the threefold mocking (see at v 35 below).

The unity and antiquity of the Markan source available to Luke here have come under heavy attack. Luke has material in vv 33–38 paralleling Mark 15:22, 24, 26–27, 29a?, 31–32a, 36a. Of this material only vv 22a, 24a (amounting to a bare statement of crucifixion at Golgotha) have not, in the literature, come under repeated suspicion of being later developments in the account (in the case of vv 26–27, normally only one or the other of the verses is considered an addition).

A number of factors contribute to the high level of suspicion about the crucifixion account (only the matters with a bearing on those features of Markan text paralleled in Luke 23:33–38 will be noted here). (i) First there seems to be some repetition in the text that could have source implications: the crucifixion itself is reported in v 24, then repeated in v 25; the contents of v 30a and b are reiterated in other forms in vv 31b and 32ab. (*ii*) Then there is the recognition that elements in the account have been formulated in connection with the wording of OT texts: v 24b repeats the language of Ps 22:18; the shaking of heads in v 29 echoes that in Ps 22:7; the drink of sour wine in v 36 reflects that in Ps 69:21 (the same Greek word for the wine is found in the LXX text [68:22]); the mocking and reviling heaped on Jesus (vv 29–32) correspond to the treatment meted out in Ps 69:7, 9, 12, 19–20 (and cf. Ps 22:7); the presence of the bandits fulfills Isa 53:12. (*iii*) Moreover, there is suspicion about v 31 because the chief priests and the scribes are "typical opponents of Jesus in secondary tradition" (Bultmann, *History*, 273). (*iv*) Finally, difficulties have been sensed in the sequence from any of v 24a, v 24, or v 25 to v 26 or v 27, or both together.

Though the scope of this work does not permit an adequate engagement with Markan source questions, some comment will be offered in each of these areas. (*i*) V 25 is not strictly repetitive once καί (lit. "and") is understood as standing paratactically for "when." But, nonetheless, v 25 is likely to be a Markan addition as suggested at 22:1–2. The reiteration in vv 31b and 32ab is not to be resolved in terms of sources. It points rather to the (Markan or pre-Markan?) artistry in the mockery scene in vv 29–32. (Three groups of mockers are distinguished ["passers by," "the chief priests . . . with the scribes," "the ones crucified with him"], and the activity of each is identified with a different verb ["were blaspheming/reviling," "mocking," "reviled"]. While the third case is not developed, the first two are developed in terms of parallelism and contrast so that [*a*] to the shaking of the heads corresponds the back and forth of πρὸς ἀλλήλους, "to one another"; [*b*] the roles of main verb and participle are interchanged between "were blaspheming . . . saying" and "mocking . . . they were saying"; [*c*] there is address to Jesus in the one case and conversation about him in the other; [*d*] an identifying feature is drawn from the accusation against him before the Sanhedrin in the one case and from the [implied] accusation against him before Pilate in the other case [but with "king of Israel" rather than "king of the Jews"; "the Christ" here comes from the Sanhedrin hearing and, as a break in the pattern, might be a Markan addition]; [*e*] this identification comes before the saving of oneself statement in the one case and after it in the other; and [*f*] each of the statements climaxes with the call to come down from the cross [the latter explaining this call with a final purpose clause]. In the face of such elaborate artistry, there is no place for source deconstruction [unless it is to remove "with the scribes" from v 31 and "the Christ" from v 32 and therefore to label the artistry as pre-Markan].)

(*ii*) It is certainly possible that the account of the division of clothing has been generated out of Ps 22:18, but it remains more likely that it was the custom at executions for clothing to go to the soldiers on duty and that, in Jesus' case, the detail has been preserved for us because of the correspondence with Ps 22:18. It is a little more difficult, though not impossible, to generate the mocking out of the Psalm texts. (If the main point of the mocking was to evoke Ps 69, then the wording could have corresponded more closely to the psalm. Instead the mocking account has its own agenda of concerns.) More difficult yet is it to generate the drink of sour wine out of Ps 69:21. (There are difficulties in the misunderstanding of Jesus' use of Ps 22:1 as referring to Elijah, but that is the setting in which the giving of sour wine falls in Mark's text. It has nothing to do with the malice of

Ps 69:21.) Most unlikely of all is the manufacture of the bandits out of Isa 53:12 (which is not to say that its preservation has nothing to do with Isa 53:12).

(*iii*) I have already suggested that "with the scribes" may be a Markan addition to v 31. There is no reason to dispute the whole verse for the sake of this element. See further above on the role of v 31 in the artistry of vv 29–32.

(*iv*) In connection with the flow of thought through vv 26–27, I wonder whether the critics are insisting upon a standard of narrative unity inappropriate for a passage intended to compile discrete and separately significant points about the crucifixion of Jesus. In any case, without v 25 (see [*i*] above), vv 26–27 do not follow badly from v 24. This is especially true if, noting that the sequence of v 26 and v 27 corresponds to the order of the same information taken up in v 32, we make a paragraph break after v 24 and treat vv 26–27 as an introduction for vv 29–32, providing a wider picture of the crucifixion scene (the account is so thoroughly focused upon Jesus that there is little point in complaining that, after v 26, the introduction of the bandits should have dealt with the inscriptions bearing their charges as well).

From these points it will be clear that I have little confidence in the attempts that have been made to deconstruct the Markan text here. It does not seem to me possible in this case to move back to an earliest core by unraveling a tradition history of the materials. In connection with historical reconstruction, each element will need to be considered on its own merits. For comments in support of the historicity of Jesus' execution with malefactors and of the inscription over his cross, see *Comment* below. The mocking scene, as a piece of artistic literary construction (see above), is the most vulnerable part of the scene in regard to its historicity. Against any simple affirmation of historicity stand (*i*) its nature as an artistic unit, (*ii*) the strong connections between this block and theologically important features of the Markan (and pre-Markan?) text (the use of material from the two hearings is obvious, but there are also links involving the mockery materials between the crucifixion scene and Mark 10:35–45), and (*iii*) the clear elucidation of two contradictory images of the messianic role that this material achieves. Mockery as such is intrinsically likely. The content given to it expresses continuity with credible elements of the trial scenes, but the detail and precise formulation constitute a piece of artistic theological writing.

The only distinctive Lukan element in his rendering of this material is the prayer from the cross in v 34a. While this contains the Lukan motif of ignorance (Acts 3:17; 13:27; 17:30) and also his emphasis on forgiveness (see at 1:77; 24:47), it has a notable boldness, not merely in failing to introduce the necessity of repentance but also in proposing forgiveness precisely in the face of the hostility and expediency that took Jesus to the cross. This goes beyond early Christian sentiment: Stephen, in proposing something similar in Acts 7:60, faces his death in a manner that, at Luke's hands, is concerned to mirror key features of the death of his Lord. The prayer from the cross has good claim to being based upon historical reminiscence. It offers a distinctive and poignant embodiment of Jesus' teaching on love of enemies (cf. at 6:27–28).

Comment

In reporting the actual crucifixion scene, Luke begins to open up again the gap between the People and the Jerusalem leaders. The People are mute and sympathetic witnesses, while the leaders join with the soldiers and one of the criminals in mocking Jesus: What fate is this for a royal figure such as Jesus claimed to be!

33 Luke follows a different source for this verse, a source that has no equivalent to Mark 15:23. Distinctively, he calls the place "Skull," rather than "Place of a Skull," as found in the other Gospels. Distinctively as well, Luke drops the derivation from the Aramaic "Golgotha" (properly גולגלתא, *gûlgultā*), even though "Skull" represents the Aramaic more accurately than does "Place of the Skull." Though normally considered to be near the present Church of the Holy Sepulchre, there is no archaeological certainty about the precise location of Golgotha.

None of the Gospel accounts provides any description of the actual crucifixion of Jesus. For information on the Roman practice of crucifixion, we must rely principally upon ancient literary accounts (a good range of these may be readily consulted in Hengel, *Crucifixion*). These have more recently been supplemented by the discovery of the remains of a Jewish victim of crucifixion in the excavation of ancient cave tombs at Givʿat ha-Mivtar, just north of Jerusalem near Mount Scopus and immediately west of the road to Nablus.

Crucifixion seems to have been designed to be as shocking a means of execution by torture as lent itself to public display. On the whole, the concern seems to have been to prolong the death agony. The sources suggest that there were many different ways in which victims were crucified: various kinds of preliminary torture, different kinds of crosses, different postures on the cross (impaled, cruciform, upside down). The man at Givʿat ha-Mitvar seems to have been supported on the cross in a threefold manner: his forearms were secured to the crossbeam of the cross with iron nails; his buttocks was partially supported on a small shelf; his legs were turned somewhat to the left with the knees rather bent so that a large nail could be driven through a wooden block and then through both heel bones and into the upright of the cross (Yadin, *IEJ* 23 [1973] 19–22, offers a less likely reconstruction, which involves the feet together sandwiched between two blocks of wood and held together by a large nail piercing heels and blocks and the legs spread apart over the upright of the cross to support the body in an upside down position).

We cannot be sure exactly how Jesus was crucified, but it is likely that the nails pierced his forearms rather than, as in the traditional picture, his hands ($\chi\epsilon\hat{\iota}\rho\alpha\varsigma$ in Luke 24:39, 40; John 20:20, 25, 27 can mean "arms" as well as "hands"). Possibly, in connection with Jewish concerns that the body not remain on the cross overnight and especially so on the eve of a sabbath, the use of the buttocks support, which prolonged life and therefore extended the agony, may have been, on occasion, dispensed with for crucifixions in Judea (a crucified man might otherwise survive for days; alternatively, a more rigorous regime of pre-crucifixion flagellation may have been used to abbreviate the death agonies).

The language of "right" and "left" may have come into Luke's account from his Markan source (though Luke has $\dot{\alpha}\rho\iota\sigma\tau\epsilon\rho\hat{\omega}\nu$ [but cf. Mark 10:37] rather than Mark's $\epsilon\dot{\upsilon}\omega\nu\acute{\upsilon}\mu\omega\nu$ for "left"), where it plays a role in the portrayal of the crucifixion as something like an enthronement (cf. Mark 10:35–45). Crucifixion between malefactors seems, however, to have been mentioned in Luke's second source at this particular stage of the narrative (see John 19:18 and source discussion above), where no such role is evident. Does Luke's $\kappa\alpha\kappa o\acute{\upsilon}\rho\gamma o\upsilon\varsigma$, "criminals," in place of Mark's $\lambda\eta\sigma\tau\acute{\alpha}\varsigma$, "bandits," come from his second source, or does it reflect his sensitivity to the political overtones of insurrection that this word could carry?

The use of ληστής in 22:52 (see there) stands in favor of the former. The fabrication of the malefactors out of the need for a fulfillment of Isa 53:12 has already been rejected above. Historical reminiscence is altogether the best explanation of the origin of this feature of the tradition.

34 Luke passes over Mark's time reference in 15:25 and defers the account of the inscription (Mark 15:26) to v 38. V 34a is unique to Luke. On its link with Lukan motifs, but also its distinctiveness, see in *Form/Structure/Setting* above. On Jesus' address to God as Father, see at 10:21; 11:2. While the immediate contrast is between Jesus' concern for his executioners and their disregard of him (as they cast lots to determine claim upon portions of his clothing), the scope of the prayer reaches to all who had a hand in securing Jesus' present position upon the cross. A link with Isa 53:12 has been proposed but is not possible for the LXX and probably involves giving the MT an unintended sense (the servant of Isaiah interposes for the transgressors by bearing their sins rather than by offering a prayer of intercession for them).

Compared to Mark 15:24, Luke has in v 34b interchanged the role of finite verb and participle, preferred the plural for "lots," and provided nothing for Mark's ἐπ᾽ αὐτὰ τίς τί ἄρῃ, "for them: Who should take what?" Given the use of the language of Ps 22:19, it is not possible to determine whether Luke draws directly on Mark here (John has an expanded version of this motif at 19:23–24).

35 As with Mark, Luke has three episodes of mockery; but Mark's mocking passersby in the first position are now "the People" as mute witnesses of it all, so the soldiers have come in to keep the number at three; and Mark's two mocking bandits become one mocker and one who turns to Jesus in his need. As with Mark, there are three different verbs to express the mocking, but now they are ἐξεμυκτήριζον, ἐνέπαιξαν, ἐβλασφήμει, "were sneering," "mocked," "was blaspheming/reviling," rather than Mark's ἐβλασφήμουν, ἐμπαίζοντες, ὠνείδιζον, "were blaspheming/reviling," "mocking," "reviled." The content of the mockery is also significantly different. The Markan call to come down from the cross (15:30, 32) is gone, as is the statement of readiness to "see and believe" (v 32). Consonant with the transfer from the (Jewish) passersby to the (gentile) soldiers, the temple accusation part of Mark's first mockery is displaced by the inscription language "king of the Jews" (also found in the trial before Pilate). In the mockery by the leaders (now called "leaders" in place of Mark's "the chief priests . . . with the scribes"), "he is not able to save himself" becomes "let him save himself," which brings it more closely into line with "save yourself" in the soldiers' mockery; "the Christ, the king of Israel" becomes "the Christ of God, the Chosen One," with evident links to Lukan language (see at 9:20, 35). In the mockery by the leaders and the soldiers, the statements about the disputed identity of Jesus are expressed in "if" clauses ("if you are . . ."). These form a chiasm by coming respectively after and before the main clauses to which they link. Where Mark gave no wording for the mockery by the crucified bandits, Luke takes up again the motif of saving oneself (in the second person form) and adds "and us" in recognition of the shared fate that linked Jesus and the criminals. In place of the "if" clause of the other mockeries, we now have "Are you not the Christ?"

While second source influence cannot be ruled out, all of this can be quite satisfactorily accounted for on the basis of Lukan redaction of his Markan source: Luke sees the artistry of his source, and since his own agenda requires some changes, he creates a comparable piece of artistry to replace that which he needed to disfigure. In the process, Luke rethinks the ways in which Pss 22 and 69 should be echoed in his text (see below).

The People have been following Jesus to the cross (v 27); now they stand silently watching (taking the place of Mark's passersby who blaspheme/revile Jesus). In the Septuagintal text of Ps 22:7–8, the words λαός, "People," θεωρεῖν, "see/look on" (participial use as here: the psalm phrase is "all those who see me"), ἐκμυκτηρίζειν, "sneer," come together as here in Luke. The Lukan wording surely echoes the psalm, which makes it all the more remarkable that Luke differs from the psalm in distributing the seeing and the mocking between People and leaders (cf. at v 27).

The use of καί (lit. "and/even/also") is slightly odd. It should certainly not be taken as implicating the People in the sneering (as Marshall, 869). It may be based on thinking of various groups as playing a role in the scene: "the leaders too played a role; they sneered." Or, possibly, it is forward looking and should be coordinated with the parallel use of καί in v 36: "it is both the case that the leaders sneered *and* that the soldiers mocked." In v 38 there is another rather similar use of καί. Luke has used "rulers" in connection with the Jerusalem leadership in 23:13 and will again in 24:20, but only here does it stand alone in the Gospel (but see Acts 3:17; 13:27). "He saved others" is meant sarcastically. See the discussion at 4:23. The attitude of the Lukan Jesus to the suggestion to "save himself" can be learned from 9:24 (see there). For "the Christ of God," cf. at 9:20, where Luke is responsible for the same formulation. Though not demonstrable, it is certainly possible that ὁ ἐκλεκτός, "the Chosen One," is concerned to echo the use of election language in Wisdom, in connection with the persecution of the righteous at the hands of the wicked (see Wis 3:9; 4:15). Alternatively, since ὁ ἐκλεκτός occurs in the Greek text of Isa 42:1, it might be for the sake of a link with that text, as was ὁ ἐκλελεγμένος, "the Chosen One," in Luke 9:35 (see there). ὁ ἐκλεκτός occurs as a variant reading in John 1:34. An equivalent occurs as a title in *1 Enoch* 45:3; 49:2; 50:5; 51:3, 5; 52:6, 9; 53:6; 55:4; 61:5, 8, 10; but this may be a later development.

36 This is the first mention of soldiers in Luke's passion account since the involvement of Herod's soldiers in a scene of mockery (v 11). The word used here for "soldiers" is found repeatedly in Acts. Luke is not going to use the Elijah misunderstanding in Mark 15:34–36, but the offer of wine here is probably inspired by the Markan giving of wine in v 36 (perhaps conflated with the offer of wine of v 23). At the same time, Luke has an eye on Ps 69:21, where the giving of sour wine comes in the context of scorn and hostility (in Matthew's parallel to Mark 15:23 [27:34], the link to Ps 69:21 is made transparent by the addition of "mixed with gall" with its borrowing from the first half of Ps 69:21). ὄξος is used to designate a rough dry wine, which was the common wine of soldiers.

37 In contrast to the leaders, the soldiers address Jesus directly, but their point is the same (though it is not given to the soldiers to point to the salvific claims of Jesus' ministry). Pilate had used "king of the Jews," as used here by the soldiers, but by locating v 38 at this point, Luke intends to make it clear that in the first instance the soldiers are echoing the language of the inscription.

38 Luke introduces at this point his reference to the inscription reporting the reason for Jesus' execution. Here it functions as a kind of explanatory parenthesis (the force of the καί is probably that the inscription also made the same reference to "king of the Jews" as did the soldiers). Luke shares "was," "inscription," and "the king of the Jews" with his Markan source; otherwise his wording goes its own way.

The practice involved here is not well documented from the earliest period (for a later example, see Eusebius, *Hist. eccl.* 5.1.44). Instead, the early sources point to a custom of having the condemned man or someone in front of him bear the plaque with the inscription (Suetonius, *Calig.* 32.2; *Domit.* 10.1; cf. Dio Cassius 54.8). Mark, however, reports this not as something distinctive done in the case of Jesus (Luke could be taken that way) but as a custom that will be known to his readers. So, it is best to think of the inscription over the cross as one of a number of standard ways of publicizing the cause of execution, for the purpose of deterrence. The wording of the plaque was an exercise in popular communication and, therefore, was not necessarily to be expected to contain a legal description of the crime of which the offender had been found guilty (cf. Bammel, "Titulus," 353–54).

Even if, however, such inscriptions were in use, it is still possible to question the use in the particular case of Jesus. The inscription is sometimes considered to be a secondary development from Mark 15:2, which in turn is seen as a secondary intrusion into the account of the trial before Pilate (the direction of dependence has also been conceived in the reverse direction). At 23:1–5, I have argued against the secondary intrusion view of Mark 15:2. If I am right there, then there seems no real reason for denying a place in the original tradition to the inscription over Jesus' cross. While Christians would value this ironic affirmation of their own conviction about Jesus, this is hardly a basis for considering it a fabrication. The wording provided for the inscription varies slightly from Gospel to Gospel, but all agree on the key phrase "the king of the Jews."

Explanation

Vv 33–38 and 39–43 really belong together: the criminals are there at the start and the end; and the sympathetic People and penitent thief frame the threefold scene of mockery. After coming together for a crucial moment in vv 18–25, the People and their leaders now go separate ways once more. The leaders now have as their partners in mockery the executing soldiers and one of the dying criminals.

All of the Gospel accounts record the actual crucifixion of Jesus in a single Greek word: "they crucified." From ancient literary accounts and more recently from the discovery of the remains near Jerusalem of a man who was crucified at around the time of Jesus, we learn something of what was involved. Crucifixion was a form of execution by torture; it was about as cruel and barbaric as any deterrent dreamed up by humankind. The idea was to prolong the death agony for all to see and be warned. See further in the discussion above on v 33. As Jesus is crucified between the criminals, the prophecy pointed to in 22:37 (Isa 53:12) finds its fulfillment.

In the midst of this dreadful experience, Jesus remains true to his own vision: God is still his Father, and love for his enemies is still his practice, even in this extreme situation. The possibility of forgiveness is a central part of the Lukan understanding of the gospel, and, in Acts, the element of ignorance will be stressed, as forgiveness is offered to any and all, even to those responsible for the execution of Jesus (Acts 3:17; 13:27; 17:20).

The contrast between Jesus and his executioners could not be more extreme: he prays for them, and they cast lots to see who will get which portion of his clothing. The words of Ps 22:19 (from a psalm depicting a suffering righteous person that is frequently applied to Jesus) are used to report this act. Luke will echo language from the Greek version of Ps 22:6–7 at the start of the mocking scene to follow.

The People stand as mute and (as becomes much clearer in v 48) sympathetic witnesses of all this. But there are others who will mock the powerless and dying figure on the cross. "He saved others" is meant sarcastically (see the discussion at 4:23). The attitude of the Lukan Jesus to the suggestion that he "save himself" can be learned from 9:24. The language that the rulers use for Jesus' identity is not exactly that which featured in the hearings. It is more Luke's own wording (see 9:20, 35), but the meaning is not really different. Luke may want "the Chosen One" to remind readers familiar with Jewish writings of the persecution (and ultimate vindication by God) of the righteous in the Jewish writing called the Wisdom of Solomon.

The soldiers' mockery is reported in language that echoes Ps 69:21 (from another psalm reporting the lament of a godly sufferer). In some way, the giving of the wine is seen as insulting. Perhaps the mocking element comes from approaching Jesus as though serving him wine at a banquet.

The soldiers address Jesus as "king of the Jews," the title that was used by Pilate. But their source is the plaque above Jesus' cross, which announced to all the world the reason for his death. Such plaques did not necessarily provide a legal description of the crime but were intended to deter the public from similar behavior. The early Christians valued the irony of this backhanded recognition of their own convictions about Jesus.

Jesus and the Two Criminals   (23:39–43)

Bibliography

Altheim, F., and **Stiehl, R.** "Aramäische Herrenworte." In *Die Araber in der alten Welt.* Vol. 5/2. Berlin: de Gruyter, 1969. 361–67. **Berger, K.** *Die Amen-Worte Jesu.* BZNT 39. Berlin: de Gruyter, 1970. 87. **Blathwayt, T. B.** "The Penitent Thief." *ExpTim* 18 (1906–7) 288. **Boulogne, C.-D.** "La gratitude et la justice depuis Jésus-Christ." *VSpir* 96 (1957) 142–56. **Carroll, J. T.** *Response to the End of History.* 68–70. **Derrett, J. D. M.** "The Two Malefactors (Lk xxiii. 33, 39–43)." In *Studies in the New Testament.* Leiden, Brill, 1982. 3:200–214. **Dupont, J.** *Les Béatitudes.* 3:133–35. **Ellis, E. E.** "Present and Future Eschatology in Luke." *NTS* 12 (1965–66) 27–41. **George, A.** "La royauté de Jésus selon l'évangile de Luc." *ScEccl* 14 (1962) 57–69. **Grelot, P.** "'Aujourd'hui tu seras avec moi dans le Paradis' (Luc, XXIII, 43)." *RB* 74 (1967) 194–214. **Hope, L. P.** "The King's Garden." *ExpTim* 48 (1936–37) 471–73. **Leloir, L.** "Hodie, mecum eris in paradiso (Lc., XXIII, 43)." *RevDiocNamur* 13 (1959) 471–83. **Lewis,**

A. S. "A New Reading of Luke xxiii. 39." *ExpTim* 18 (1906–7) 94–95. **MacGregor, W. M.** "The Words from the Cross, II: The Penitent Thief (Lk. xxiii. 39–43)." *ExpTim* 41 (1929–30) 151–54. **MacRae, G. W.** "With Me in Paradise." *Worship* 35 (1961) 235–40. **Martin, G. C.** "A New Reading of Luke xxiii. 39." *ExpTim* 18 (1906–7) 334–35. **Nestle, E.** "Luke xxiii. 43." *ExpTim* 11 (1899–1900) 429. **Schneider, G.** *Parusiegleichnisse im Lukas-Evangelium.* SBS 74. Stuttgart: Katholisches Bibelwerk, 1975. 81–84. **Smith, R. H.** "Paradise Today: Luke's Passion Narrative." *CurTM* 3 (1976) 323–36. **Strobel, A.** "Der Tod Jesu und das Sterben des Menschen nach Lk 23,39–43." In *Der Tod, ungelöstes Rätsel oder überwundener Feind,* ed. A. Strobel. Stuttgart: Calwer, 1974. 81–102. **Trilling, W.** "L'Evangile (Lc 23,33–43): La promesse de Jésus au bon larron." *AsSeign* o.s. 96 (1967) 31–39. **Weisengoff, J. P.** "Paradise and St. Luke 23:43." *AER* 103 (1940) 163–68. **Wulf, W.** "Jesus, gedenke meiner, wenn du in dein Königtum kommst (Lk 23,42)." *GuL* 37 (1964) 1–3.

And see at 22:1–2; 22:66–71; 23:1–5; 23:33–38.

Translation

   [39] *One of the criminals hanging there reviled him, saying,[a] "Aren't you the Christ? Save yourself and us!"* [40] *The other one responded with a rebuke and said, "Don't you even[b] fear God? For you are under the same sentence!* [41] *And we deserve it.[c] For we are receiving due deserts for what we did; but this [fellow] has done nothing improper."* [42] *Then he said, "Jesus, remember me when you come into[d] your kingdom."* [43] *He said to him, "Amen, I say to you: today you will be with me in paradise."*

Notes

   [a] Omitted by B D L etc.
   [b] Rendering a Gr. οὐδέ at the beginning of the clause. ℵ G etc. have οὐ ("don't you fear . . ."). D has ὅτι οὐ ("[is it the case that] you don't fear . . ."). 69 205 579 983 etc. have οὐδέν ("do you fear . . . not at all").
   [c] Lit. "and we justly."
   [d] ℵ A C² R W Θ Ψ f¹,¹³ etc. read ἐν, "in." The reference would then be to the Parousia. This fits less well into the thought of the passage and into Luke's wider use of kingdom language. These texts also make "Jesus" the indirect object of "said," have the criminal address Jesus as "Lord," and reintroduce Jesus by name in v 43.

Form/Structure/Setting

   In the Lukan structuring, vv 39–43 belong closely with vv 33–38 (see there) and have only been separated for convenience. The material here is distinctive to Luke, though the point in the narrative at which it is found corresponds to that of Mark's notice in 15:32b about the reviling of Jesus by those crucified with him.

   There is too little characteristically Lukan language here (cf. Jeremias, *Sprache,* 306–7) for it to be likely that Luke has spun 23:39–43 entirely out of the brief Markan notice, but the Lukan role in the artistic structuring of vv 33–43 as a whole, and especially in the presentation of the mockery of Jesus (see discussion at v 35), stands in favor of a significant Lukan role. Though special emphasis falls on the saying of Jesus, the preceding interchange is too significant for us to consider this unit a pronouncement story. With Taylor (*Formation,* 56), it is best seen as a story about Jesus.

Despite a degree of genuine parallel between the present account and that of Joseph in prison with the two discredited servants of Pharaoh (Gen 40), as noted by Derrett ("Malefactors," 200–214), the similarities are likely to be fortuitous rather than intentional. More fruitful is Smith's recognition (*CurTM* 3 [1976] 326–27) that this account takes its place with other accounts in which "Luke holds before the eyes of his readers contrasting types serving as positive and negative models" (326).

Comment

One of the criminals adds his mockery to that of the leaders and the soldiers. But the other, more in continuity with the silent sympathy of the People in v 35a, recognizes the innocence of Jesus. In his own unhappy state, he sues Jesus for royal clemency, to be meted out at the time when he will have attained to his royal rule. But Jesus is, ahead of time, already handing out royal clemency, and so he assures this criminal a place in paradise before another day has passed.

39 The clearest Lukan element here is κρεμασθέντων, "hanged" (cf. Acts 5:30; 10:39). Probably κακούργων, "criminals," here is Lukan as well (cf. Luke 23:32), but it could be from a source (cf. 23:33). At v 35 it has been suggested that Luke fashioned his account of the mocking here out of his Markan source (borrowing and adapting elements from the mockery by the Markan passersby and the chief priests and scribes). See further at v 35. The criminal's words are mocking and cynical.

40 ἀποκριθείς . . . ἔφη (lit. "having answered he said") may well be Lukan (cf. 23:3; and Luke's use of ἀποκριθείς εἶπεν), as well as the use of ὁ ἕτερος, "the other." Whereas Fitzmyer (1509) links οὐδέ, "not even," with φοβῇ, "fear," and Marshall (871–72) finds the link with σύ, "you," I think the best sense emerges if the link is with τὸν θεόν, "God": not only has this criminal despised the laws of society and its machinery of justice; now on the brink of death he shows no fear of God (contrast 12:4–5). The second criminal assumes that the present brush with justice, as it takes away the life of the criminal, will have its counterpart in an impending beyond-death answerability to God. Luke no doubt shares this view.

41 The elements most likely to be Lukan here are ἡμεῖς μέν . . . οὗτος δέ, "we . . . this [fellow]," ὧν ἐπράξαμεν, "for what we did," and ἄτοπον, "improper." The logic of the second criminal's rebuke of the first is built upon the *first* deserving his fate, but the relevant statement comes in the plural to indicate that the second criminal is not distancing himself from his companion in this respect. Zealot "freedom fighters" could hardly utter or agree with such a statement. Luke will be interested in offering here a "street-level" confirmation of Pilate's conviction that Jesus was innocent. It is better to think of the second criminal as sensing in the present context Jesus' categorical difference from himself and his fellow criminal, rather than to attribute to him any extensive prior knowledge about Jesus.

42 Luke is unlikely to have formulated the introductory καὶ ἔλεγεν (lit. "and he was saying"; from many occurrences, in singular and plural, in his Markan source, Luke allows this construction to stand only in 6:5). καὶ ἔλεγεν marks the move from words addressed to the fellow thief to words addressed to Jesus. The first criminal had mocked Jesus' royal pretensions. The second criminal also addresses himself to the royal status of Jesus (with God), but he does so with a view to appealing for clemency (cf. Diodorus Siculus 34.2.8–10). In the framework of Lukan thought, Jesus will "come into his kingdom" by means of his passage through death to exaltation at the right hand of God (cf. at 9:51; 19:12; 24:26).

43 Unless σήμερον, "today," can be considered Lukan, none of the language here is notably Lukan (cf. Jeremias, *Sprache*, 307). With different word order and with the plural for the present singular, "amen, I say to you" is found in the other five places where Luke uses "amen" (see at 4:24). It is tempting to find expressed here the view that Jesus came "into this kingdom" on the day of his death. But it is probably better to correlate the use of "today" here with earlier instances in the Gospel and see, instead, a statement that still in the hour of his own death Jesus brings salvation (in the context of the present mocking of his pretensions about saving others, he extends salvation to yet another person). This criminal has no need to wait for Jesus to come into his kingdom; though not yet come to his kingdom, Jesus is already granting royal clemency.

In the NT, "Paradise" is found only here and in 2 Cor 12:4; Rev 2:7. In Greek the word is an early borrowing (attested from the sixth century B.C.) from old Persian, where it meant "an enclosed space." The word also came over into Hebrew. In both Greek and Hebrew the emphasis seems to be upon what grows in a designated space; whether this be fruit trees, timber for the king, or the decorative plantings of a park. In the Septuagint, παράδεισος was used for the garden of Eden (Gen 2:8; 13:10; Ezek 31:8). In Isa 51:3, the promised future restoration involves the wilderness becoming like Eden, the "garden [LXX: παράδεισον] of the Lord." In time this becomes, through reflection on the Genesis account, a hope for an eschatological reversal of the expulsion from the garden (*T. Levi* 18:10–11; Rev 2:7; 22). A further development involved emphasizing the present (hidden) existence of this paradise and, eventually, a peopling of it already with the saints of the past (*1 Enoch* 60:8; 61:12; this last development is encouraged by developments in connection with the understanding of Hades noted at 16:23).

Within the framework of such an understanding of paradise, clearly Jesus will be expected to go immediately after death to paradise (but probably not as an eschatological reopening of paradise, as maintained by Neyrey, *Passion*, 180–84). What is striking is that the criminal who sues for mercy will be there with him! There is no sufficient reason for finding a martyr theology here: though in Jewish thought others may go to a heavenly destiny as a reward for martyrdom (cf. Wis 3:1–9), the word "paradise" is not used in this connection, and it is not on the basis of martyrdom that Jesus gains entry to paradise. Furthermore, the criminal is no martyr.

Explanation

On the unity between vv 33–38 and vv 39–43, see at vv 33–38. Whereas the People and their leaders part company in v 35, here the two criminals part company over their response to Jesus. The silent sympathy of the People and the plea for mercy by the second criminal frame the three occasions of mocking. Though not yet established in his royal rule, Jesus extends royal clemency to this responsive criminal: he will be with Jesus in paradise that very day.

The first dying criminal mocks Jesus in much the same way that the leaders and the soldiers have done. His words are mocking and cynical. The reaction of the second criminal is quite different. He is astonished that his fellow can, under the circumstances, rail in this way: both of them are answering for their crimes by death, removing them from the human system of justice to one in which they must answer to God himself. How far can bravado take one? Does this first criminal not even fear God?

The second criminal senses that Jesus belongs to quite a different category from that to which he and the other criminal belong. Luke will be interested in the way in which this offers a "street-level" recognition of the innocence of Jesus, paralleling Pilate's high-level legal recognition.

The first criminal had mocked Jesus' royal pretensions. The second criminal also addresses himself to the royal status of Jesus (with God), but he does so deferentially, appealing for clemency from Jesus when he has assumed his royal role. In the framework of Lukan thought, Jesus will "come into his kingdom" by means of his passage through death to exaltation at the right hand of God (cf. at 9:51; 19:12; 24:26). But our criminal does not need to wait for this development.

In each "today" in which Jesus was encountered during his ministry, the encounter brought salvation. Even now, in the hour of his own death, Jesus brings salvation. In the context of the mocking of his pretensions about saving others, he extends salvation to yet another person. Though not yet enthroned as king, he already extends royal clemency to those who appeal to him.

In Jewish thought of Jesus' day, the imagery of "paradise" was developed, using an old Persian term, out of reflection about the garden of Eden. In connection with a developing understanding of Hades (see at 16:19–31), paradise came to be understood as the pleasant resting place of some of the privileged dead prior to the great day of resurrection. After death, Jesus would certainly have been expected to be one of those who would go on to paradise. What is striking here is that the criminal who sues for mercy will be there with him!

The Death of Jesus   (23:44–49)

Bibliography

Abramowski, L., and **Goodman, A. E.** "Luke xxiii. 46 παρατίθεμαι in a Rare Syriac Rendering." *NTS* 13 (1966–67) 290–91. **Benoit, P.** *The Passion and Resurrection of Jesus.* New York: Herder and Herder, 1969. 181–204. **Bligh, J.** "Christ's Death Cry." *HeyJ* 1 (1960) 142–46. **Boman, T.** "Das letzte Wort Jesu." *ST* 17 (1963) 103–19. **Bratcher, R. G.** "A Note on υἱὸς θεοῦ (Mark xv. 39)." *ExpTim* 68 (1956) 27–28. **Chronis, H. L.** "The Torn Veil: Cultus and Christology in Mark 15:37–39." *JBL* 101 (1982) 97–114. **Conzelmann, H.** "Historie und Theologie in den synoptischen Passionsberichten." In *Zur Bedeutung des Todes Jesu: Exegetische Beiträge,* ed. H. Conzelmann et al. Gütersloh: Mohn, 1967. 35–53. **Daube, D.** "The Veil of the Temple." In *The New Testament and Rabbinic Judaism.* 23–26. **Demel, S.** "Jesu Umgang mit Frauen nach dem Lukasevangelium." *BibNot* 57 (1991) 52–95, esp. 82–86. **Driver, G. R.** "Two Problems in the New Testament." *JTS* 16 (1965) 327–37, esp. 331–37. **Faessler, M.** "Marc 15,21–39: La Mort de Jésus." *BulCPE* 28 (1976) 28–30. **Feldkämper, L.** *Der betende Jesus als Heilsmittler nach Lukas.* Veröffentlichungen des Missionspriesterseminars, 29. St. Augustin bei Bonn: Steyler Verlag, 1978. 251–84. **Green, J. B.** "The Death of Jesus and the Rending of the Temple Veil (Luke 23:44–49): A Window into Luke's Understanding of Jesus and the Temple." In *SBL 1991 Seminar Papers*, ed. E. H. Lovering, Jr. Atlanta, GA: Scholars, 1991. 543–57. **Hanson, R. P. C.** "Does δίκαιος in Luke xxiii.47 Explode the Proto-Luke Hypothesis." *Hermathena* 60 (1942) 74–78. **Harris, R.** "The Origin of a Famous Lucan Gloss." *ExpTim* 35 (1923–24) 7–10. **Holzmeister, U.** "Die Finsternis beim Tode Jesu." *Bib* 22 (1941) 404–11. **Jonge, M. de.** "Two Interesting Interpretations of the Rending of the Temple-veil in the Testaments of the Twelve Patriarchs." *Bijdragen* 46 (1985) 350–62. **Karris, R. J.** "Luke 23:47 and the Lucan View of Jesus' Death." *JBL* 105 (1986) 65–74. **Killermann, S.** "Die Finsternis beim Tode Jesu." *TGl* 33 (1941) 165–66. **Kilpatrick, G. D.** "A Theme of the Lucan Passion Story and Luke xxiii. 47." *JTS* 43 (1942) 34–36. **Lamarche, P.** "La mort du Christ et la voile du temple: Selon Marc." *NRT* 96 (1974) 583–99. **Lange, J.** "Zur Ausgestaltung der Szene vom Sterben Jesu in den synoptischen Evangelien." In *Biblische Randbemerkungen*. FS R. Schnackenburg, ed. H. Merklein and J. Lange. Würzburg: Echter, 1974. 40–55. **Légasse, S.** "Les voiles du Temple de Jérusalem: Essai de parcours historique." *RB* 87 (1980) 560–89. **Léon-Dufour, X.** "Der Todesschrei Jesu." *TGeg* 21 (1978) 172–78. ———. "Le dernier cri de Jésus." *Études* 348 (1978) 667–82. **Lindeskog, G.** "The Veil of the Temple." In *In honorem A. Fridrichsen sexagenarii*, edenda curavit Seminarium Neotestamenticum Upsaliense. ConNT 11. Lund: Gleerup, 1947. 132–37. **Lowther Clarke, W. K.** "St Luke and the Pseudepigrapha: Two Parallels." *JTS* 15 (1913–14) 597–99. **Mann, C.** "The Centurion at the Cross." *ExpTim* 20 (1908–9) 563–64. **Matera, F.** "The Death of Jesus according to Luke: A Question of Sources." *CBQ* 47 (1985) 469–85. **Michaels, J. R.** "The Centurion's Confession and the Spear Thrust." *CBQ* 29 (1967) 102–9. **Motyer, S.** "The Rending of the Veil: A Markan Pentecost?" *NTS* 33 (1987) 155–57. **Nestle, E.** "Die Sonnenfinsternis bei Jesu Tod." *ZNW* 3 (1902) 246–47. ———. "Matt 27, 51 und Parallelen." *ZNW* 3 (1902) 167–69. **Pelletier, A.** "La tradition synoptique du 'voile déchiré' à la lumière des réalités archéologiques." *RSR* 46 (1958) 161–80. **Pobee, J.** "The Cry of the Centurion—A Cry of Defeat." In *The Trial of Jesus: Cambridge Studies in Honour of C. F. D. Moule*, ed. E. Bammel. SBT 2/13. London: SCM, 1970. 91–102. **Powell, J. E.** "Father, into Thy Hands. . . ." *JTS* 40 (1989) 95–96. **Radl, W.** "Der Tod Jesu in der Darstellung der Evangelien." *TGl* 72 (1982) 432–46. **Rese, M.** *Alttestamentliche Motive.* 200–202. **Sawyer, J. F. A.** "Why Is a Solar Eclipse Mentioned in the Passion Narrative (Luke xxiii. 44–45)?" *JTS* 23 (1972) 124–28. **Schneider, C.** "Der Hauptmann am Kreuz." *ZNW* 33 (1934) 1–17. **Sylva, D.** "The Temple Curtain and Jesus' Death in the Gospel of Luke." *JBL* 105 (1986) 239–50. **Taylor, V.** "The Narrative of the Crucifixion." *NTS* 8 (1961–62) 333–34. **Trilling, W.** "Der Tod Jesu, Ende der alten Weltzeit (Mk 15, 33–41)." In *Christusverkündigung in den synoptischen Evangelien.* Biblische Handbibliothek 4. Munich: Kösel, 1969. 191–211. **Williams, W. H.** "The Veil was Rent." *RevExp* 48 (1951) 275–85. **Yates, T.** "The Words from the Cross, VII: 'And When, Jesus Had Cried with a Loud Voice, He said, Father into Thy Hands I Commend My Spirit' (Luke xxiii. 46)." *ExpTim* 41 (1929–30) 427–29.

And see at 22:1–2, 66–71; 23:1–5, 26–32, 33–38.

Translation

[44]*It was [by] now* [a] *[only] about the sixth hour, but darkness came upon the whole land until the ninth hour;* [45]*for the sun['s light] had failed.* [b] *The curtain of the temple split [down the] middle,* [46]*and Jesus cried out in a loud voice, "Father, into your hands I commit my spirit." When he said this he breathed his last.* [47]*The centurion, seeing what happened, glorified God saying, "Truly this man was righteous!"*

[48]*Then all the crowds who had gathered for this spectacle, seeing what happened, returned home beating their breasts.* [49]*All his acquaintances were standing at a distance, including the* [c]*women who followed from Galilee, looking on.*

Notes

a The awkward ἤδη is omitted by ℵ A C³ D W Θ Ψ *f* ¹,¹³ etc.

b In place of this clause, A C³ (D) W Θ Ψ *f* ¹,¹³ etc. have καὶ ἐσκοτίσθη ὁ ἥλιος, "and the sun was darkened."

c A definite article with the following participle is secure in the text, but a separate article before the noun is found in P⁷⁵ B sa.

Form/Structure/Setting

This unit provides the final climax for three linked units that deal with the crucifixion of Jesus (above, the second is subdivided for convenience of discussion). Beyond the evident continuity of theme, a linking thread is provided by the presence of the observing public (vv 27, 35, 48). This unit is, however, also strongly linked with the following (the women's role is continued in a parallel manner; the parallelism between the crowds and the women is completed in vv 55–56a).

Though Mark provides his climax to the crucifixion account at this same point in his narrative, there are notable differences between Mark and Luke in the order and content of the materials. This has produced conflicting judgments about the relationship of Luke's account to that in his Markan source, though it is generally recognized that "the case for a separate passion narrative used by [Luke] is at its weakest here" (Marshall, 874). The level of Lukan vocabulary is notably high, and all the differences from Mark can be provided with credible redactional motivations (see, e.g., Matera, *CBQ* 47 [1985] 469–85). At the same time, the likelihood that there was a second passion narrative available to Luke makes it possible that elements here have been drawn in from it. If this has happened (which is by no means assured), then the most likely contributions from such a source are the use of Ps 31:6 for Jesus' cry from the cross in v 46 and possibly the different set of words attributed to the centurion after Jesus' death in v 47. Luke is likely to have formed v 48 on the basis of vv 27 and 35a, with a modest influence from Mark 15:40.

Scholars have offered various accounts of the source history of the related Markan materials here. Schreiber considers Mark responsible for incorporating 15:34b–36, 39–41 into a source form that embraced vv 33, 34a, 37–38 (*Markuspassion*, 31). Linnemann agrees about the original source form but maintains that already before Mark the source form had been filled out to encompass vv 33–38 (*Studien*, 168–69). Dormyer offers an original sequence of vv 34ab, 37–38, 40, to which Mark has added vv 34c, 35–36, 39, 41 (*Passion Jesu*, 209). Other suggestions have been made. The desire to deconstruct the Markan text is based in part on: (*i*) the judgment by some that the time indicators are an artificial and later development (thus v 33 is at times seen as an addition); (*ii*) the suspicion that the "loud cry" in both v 34 and v 37 indicates a doublet (Luke has only one); (*iii*) language difficulties in accepting the misunderstanding of the quotation from Ps 22:2 in v 34 as referring to Elijah (Luke does not include this material); (*iv*) the awkwardness of seeking to correlate vv 38 and 39 (Luke has them quite separated); and (*v*) a recognition of the usefulness of v 39 for Markan Christology (the Lukan form would not have suited Mark nearly so well). These matters cannot be addressed in greater detail here.

Whether in its Markan or its Lukan form, the present unit is to be form-critically assigned to the stories about Jesus; but as a unit, it can hardly have circulated independently of a passion narrative.

Comment

The crucifixion scene moves to a climax in the final three hours of Jesus' agony. The Satanic role becomes visible in the unnatural darkness; the temple curtain splits apart for Jesus to encounter afresh, in his final moments, the God of the temple; in words from Ps 31, Jesus, as he faces death, entrusts himself to God; and the centurion recognizes the rightness of Jesus' cause. It has all been witnessed by the gathered crowds, who depart in sorrow, and by Jesus' acquaintances, including the women whose role has been so important from the time in Galilee. Their presence (even if at a distance) as witnesses of the crucifixion prepares them for their future role as witnesses of the resurrection.

44 The parataxic construction (καὶ ἦν ἤδη . . . καί) looks Semitic and seems a strange Lukan substitution for Mark's genitive absolute (but cf. 9:12; perhaps Mark's genitive absolute has been displaced by Luke's following τοῦ ἡλίου ἐκλιπόντος [lit. "the sun failing"]). ὡσεί, "about," is Lukan; the rest of the verse is identical to Mark. Luke passed over Mark's time reference in 15:25 but retains it here: here it seemed the only simple way to refer to a period of darkness that coincided with Jesus' dying hours and to the unnaturalness of darkness at this time (the sixth hour is noon and, so, the time when the sun is normally at the height of its powers). What are we to make of the darkness? For the Lukan sense, surely 22:53 must direct our understanding: Luke thinks of the Satanic onslaught that stands behind the cruel deed that comes now to its fruition. (Though there is a strikingly similar reference in *2 Enoch* 67 to darkness covering the earth as Enoch is translated to heaven, the darkness there functions as a covering for the angelic snatching away of Enoch; so the similarity is only fortuitous. Darkness as a cosmic phenomenon in connection with the coming of the "Day of the Lord" occurs in Joel 2:10; 3:3–4 [ET 2:30–31]; 4:15 [ET 3:15]; Zeph 1:15. The use of Joel 3:1–5 in Acts 2:17–21, linked with Luke's addition here of "for the sun['s light] had failed" [cf. "the sun shall be turned to darkness" in Acts 2:20], suggests that Luke may have an eschatological understanding of this climax to Satan's activity.)

Is the darkness Luke reports literally intended, or is the language purely symbolic? We cannot be absolutely sure. Luke's additional phrase about the sun's light failing has been taken as reference to an eclipse of the sun, and thus as the provision of a naturalistic explanation. But though such language can be used of an eclipse, its meaning is more general. Since a total eclipse is impossible at Passover (i.e., at full moon), a reference to an eclipse is not likely here (note, however, the reference to an eclipse at new moon in Thucydides, *Hist.* 2.28 [as cited by Fitzmyer, 1518]). A more credible natural explanation is a darkening of the sun's light by an intense sand/dust storm (see Driver, *JTS* 16 [1965] 331–35). But is the darkening of the sun to be taken more literally than that which Virgil (*Georgics* 1.466–67) links with the death of Julius Caesar? Or than the turning away of the sun reported in Josephus *Ant.* 14.309? Or than the darkness anticipated by Isa 8:22; Amos 8:9; Zeph 1:5 in connection with God's judgment upon his People? All of these have more of poetry about them than does Luke's text, but Luke does not write without awareness of prophetic imagery, which at times he clearly draws upon. On balance, though for Luke it is the symbolism and not the event as such that has primary significance, we should probably conclude that Luke understood some such event to have literally occurred.

45 "For the sun['s light had failed]" has been commented on at v 44. In Mark the rending of the temple veil comes after the death of Jesus and before the centurion's confession. This was noted above as one of the awkwardnesses of the Markan account, with possible source implications. Has Luke noted the awkwardness, or does he reflect a more original narrative order? Apart from word order and a δέ for a καί, the Lukan wording is the same as the Markan, but with Mark's "into two from above to below" reduced to μέσον, "[down the] middle."

What is the significance of the rending of the temple veil? Quite a range of suggestions has been made. (*i*) Does the rending of the veil express God's distress at what is happening to Jesus, in much the way that people tore their clothing under certain circumstances as an expression of extreme unhappiness? (*ii*) Is the rending of the temple veil symbolic of the destruction of the temple: whether this is seen (*a*) as a further prophesying of its destruction as a judgment of God; (*b*) as a symbolic beginning of the destruction itself; or (*c*) as pointing to the abrogation of the old covenant and its cult? (*iii*) Does the rending of the temple veil symbolize the revealing of the glory of God, hitherto hidden behind the veil of the temple? (*iv*) Are we to think of a new access to God now opened up for all (the veil symbolizing limited priestly access)? (*v*) Does the rent veil symbolize Jesus himself being "destroyed" in death, whether this is (*a*) with the part standing for the whole, and so with Jesus as the "temple" destroyed and to be restored; or (*b*) in what is perhaps the imagery of Heb 10:20, with Jesus' death imaged in this way as the means of access to God; or (*c*) through the rending of his flesh, Jesus unveils his divine identity [closely related to (*iii*) above])? (*vi*) (In the Lukan text only) is the rending of the temple veil, like the opening of heaven in 3:21 and the access to heaven granted to the vision of Stephen in Acts 7:55–56, the means by which close contact is established between the divine and the human sphere? (*vii*) Or should we speak simply of an apocalyptic sign, with significance only to be found in the dramatic nature of the event?

A question that could potentially have a bearing on how we are to find our way through this welter of suggestions is that of whether the reference is to the curtain separating off the most holy part of the temple (where only the high priest was permitted, and he only once a year) or to the outer curtain (which marked off the area restricted to priests)? Of the proposals above, *iii, iv, vi,* and part of *v,* if taken in any close relation to a literal rending of one or the other curtains, have difficulty with the continuing existence of the other curtain, still there as a (partial) hindrance. The other views will work with either curtain. If a choice must be made, the inner curtain should probably be chosen as the more significant barrier (the argument on the other side is the public visibility of the outer curtain).

Of the views listed above, I believe that *iii* has most to commend it in connection with the Markan text (see the arguments of Linnemann, *Studien,* 159–63; *v.c* is really a development of *iii* and has been well argued by Chronis [*JBL* 101 (1982) 97–114], but it is finally an overly precise interpretation). The Lukan order does not, however, favor *iii* (or *v.c*). Sylva (*JBL* 105 [1986] 239–50) has offered the most careful analysis of the Lukan form and significantly, on the basis of the parallelism between the passion accounts of Jesus and of Stephen, has convincingly argued for view *vi* above: the temple veil is parted, and Jesus communes intimately with a God who reveals himself from the temple (for Sylva's case, it is only unfortunate that Luke does not retain in his account of the baptism of Jesus Mark's use of σχίζειν [the verb used for the rending of the temple curtain] for the opening of heaven [3:21; cf. Mark 1:10]).

As with the darkness in v 44, the question of a literal sense needs to be raised here as well. Where the scale seems to me in v 44 to tip in favor of a literal event, here the weighting seems more finely balanced and may even favor pure symbolism.

46 Luke lacks Mark's specific time indication but probably intends the cry to come at the end of the three hours of darkness. Luke has the φωνῇ μεγάλῃ, "with a loud voice," of Mark 15:34, but with the preceding φωνήσας (lit. "having called out") and following εἶπεν, "said," it becomes a Lukan phrase (cf. Acts 16:28, where finite verb and participial forms are interchanged [and the participle is in the present]). Rather than Mark's use of Ps 22:1, Luke has a quotation from Ps 31:6(ET 5; LXX 30:5). The wording is that of the Septuagint, but with present rather than future for the verb and the insertion of "Father." Luke inserts "having said this" (see Acts 7:60) before using ἐξέπνευσεν, "he breathed his last," which Mark has in 15:37 after the second cry.

It remains uncertain whether Luke is the innovator in the use of Ps 31 in place of Ps 22. Matera (*CBQ* 47 [1985] 476) argues in favor of Lukan innovation on the basis of Luke's systematic downplaying of the Markan theme of Jesus' final abandonment by all and total isolation as he dies. But abandonment by God is quite a different matter in Mark from abandonment by humankind (nonetheless, at a more general level, Matera is correct to see that the Ps 31 quotation fits the Lukan development much more comfortably than the Ps 22 quotation would have). ἀφῆκεν τὸ πνεῦμα, "yielded up [his] spirit," in Matt 27:50 and παρέδωκεν τὸ πνεῦμα, "delivered up [his] spirit," in John 19:30, which both have some likelihood of containing allusion to Ps 31:6 (cf. Green, *Death of Jesus*, 97), stand in favor of a pre-Lukan impulse.

Jesus addresses God as Father, as twice before in the passion narrative (22:42; 23:34). Where the psalmist entrusts himself to God in the context of life, Jesus entrusts himself to God in the face of death: through death he will go to God (cf. Acts 7:59), the God with whom he has communed through the parted temple veil. On "spirit," see discussion at 8:55, but see also at 16:23; 23:43. ἐκπνεῖν (lit. "breath out") is a standard Greek way of speaking about dying.

47 Though Luke uses an overall syntactical shape similar to Mark's, the verbal agreement (with slight variation in word order) is restricted to ἰδὼν δὲ ὁ . . . ὁ ἄνθρωπος οὗτος . . . ἦν (lit. "seeing . . . the . . . this man was"). Beyond that, ἑκατοντάρχης for Mark's κεντυρίων is simply a substitution of Luke's preferred term (and Matthew's) for centurion (there is a further agreement with Matthew in the use of "what happened" [sing. in Luke, pl. in Matthew]), and ὄντως is a synonym for Mark's ἀληθῶς, "truly." To glorify God is a Lukan motif (used eight times in the Gospel).

The main source question is whether δίκαιος is Luke's word here or is based on a second source. This question is in turn linked with that of whether the proper sense here is "innocent" or "righteous." Kilpatrick's brief study (*JTS* 43 [1942] 34–36), which documented the possibility of δίκαιος taking the sense "innocent" and pointed to the Lukan thematic interest in the political innocence of Jesus and the movement originating from him, led to a widespread acceptance of this sense. More recent studies, however, noting the fact that Luke never uses the word with this sense elsewhere, indeed uses it soon after of the "righteous" man Joseph, and attending more closely to the detail of the immediate context, which suggests that the statement about Jesus as δίκαιος is something about which God can be glorified, have urged the claims of a wider sense for δίκαιος. (Is God glorified by the discovery that an "innocent" man has just been executed? Normally in Luke people praise God when they recognize that God has been at work in and through Jesus; see esp. Sylva [*JBL* 105 (1986) 239–50; Matera [*CBQ* 47 (1985) 481–84].) This is surely the better approach. In different ways, it seems to me, however, that both Sylva and Matera over-interpret the centurion's statement (for Sylva the thrust is "God's saving justice"; for Matera the point is that Jesus has shown through his righteous behavior that he, and not the religious leaders, is in right relationship with God and that through his unwavering trust in God as Father to the end, Jesus has shown himself to be the Son of God). This over-interpretation comes largely out of a sensitive reading of Lukan thought: it represents the sort of thing that Luke *should have* said at this point. But it is not what he did say. And to my mind their arguments actually stand in favor of Luke being dependent upon a source for the present use of δίκαιος: had Luke been freely composing, he would have said more. (I take the Lukan sense to be something like that element of Matera's view that he expresses in the words "Jesus, and not the religious leaders, stands in the right relationship to God" [483]).

What is it that the centurion is understood to have been seeing? The most obvious thing is the steadfastness of Jesus' commitment to God in the midst of his sufferings. To that we may want to add the darkness, which pointed to the evil of what was transpiring, and possibly even go back to the promise of paradise and the prayer for the forgiveness of those responsible for Jesus being on the cross.

48 This verse is almost certainly a Lukan formulation. The presence of the crowds is based on v 27 (and cf. v 35). Where the multitude in v 27 was developed out of the presence of some weeping women, here it has been developed in relation to the presence of some women followers of Jesus. That the crowds are now gathered is a consequence of their having followed Jesus to the crucifixion scene in v 27. θεωρήσαντες, "seeing," picks up the use of the same verb at v 35 (or possibly comes from the reference to the women in Mark 15:40). τὰ γενόμενα, "what happened," repeats, now in the plural, language from v 47. "Beating their breasts" repeats in substance the action of the women in v 27 (but the language has been borrowed from 18:13). The inclusio effect with v 27 provides assurance that "the crowds" here are the same as "the People" in v 27. "Returned home" parallels what will be said in v 56 of the linked women followers of Jesus.

The gathering of crowds for the spectacle of an execution transcends time and culture, but in a Jewish context, Fitzmyer (1520) notes 3 Macc 5:24. The beating of breasts is best taken as a sign of mourning, which, while something less precise than a specific registration of guilt and contrition, must at least take on overtones of regret in the present context.

49 Luke develops the verse out of Mark 15:40–41 (of which he may already have made significant use at 8:1–3). εἰστήκεισαν, "were standing," repeats the verb used of the People in v 37. From Mark's "women" alone, Luke generalizes to "all his acquaintances" ("all" is repeated from v 48 to enhance the parallelism; "acquaintances" has been used by Luke at 2:44). Luke's συνακολουθοῦσαι, "followed," combines Mark's ἠκολούθουν, "followed," with the συν of Mark's συναναβᾶσαι, "came up" (in Mark the following is "in Galilee" and the coming up is "to Jerusalem"; Luke conflates to get "followed [ἀπό] from Galilee"; in v 55 this will become "having come with [συνεληλυθυῖαι] from [ἐκ] Galilee").

Given the awkwardness of Luke's syntax here, it is difficult to be quite sure what he intends. Probably καί (normally "and") should be translated "including" (cf. the treatment of καί at v 27). If so, all including the women are understood to be "at a distance," but only the women are specifically said to be ὁρῶσαι ταῦτα, "looking on" (lit. "seeing these things"). This should not, however, be taken as excluding the others from "seeing" (as Demel [*BibNot* 57 (1991) 83–84], who also falsely sets over against each other the being at a distance of the acquaintances and the following of the women). Where in Mark "at a distance" is likely to be critical (and even christological), in Luke it may be only a practical precaution (but see at 22:54b for the possibility that Luke also may be sounding a critical note). Luke is likely to see witnessing the crucifixion as a foundation for later being able to function as witnesses to the resurrection, and Luke has both women and men firmly in this role.

Explanation

The crucifixion scene moves to its climax witnessed by all the gathered crowds, all Jesus' acquaintances, and the women who had come with Jesus from Galilee. There is Satanic darkness; Jesus encounters afresh the God of the temple through the split temple curtain and, as he dies, entrusts himself to God; and the centurion recognizes the rightness of Jesus' cause.

When the sun should have been at the height of its powers, instead darkness descended. It was certainly not an eclipse; if a natural explanation is called for, then it is to the intense dust/sand storms of Palestine that we should look. But for Luke, this darkness was important because it pointed to the manifest presence of the dark working of Satan (cf. 22:53). Luke may link this Satanic darkness to OT mentions of darkness as part of the turmoil of the end-time (e.g., Joel 3:1–5 quoted in Acts 2:17–21).

Many suggestions have been made as to the significance of the rending of the temple veil, and it is likely that the significance varies from Gospel to Gospel. For Luke, I think, the best suggestion is that which sees this as opening up the temple as the place where God is to be found enthroned in the Holy of Holies, in much the way that heaven is opened up to Stephen in Acts 7:55–56.

In the encounter with God that results, the Lukan Jesus uses words from Ps 31. However, Jesus adds to the psalm the address to God as Father (cf. 22:42; 23:34), and, where the psalmist entrusts himself to God in the context of life, Jesus entrusts himself to God in the face of death. Indeed, through death he will go to God, as we know well from the Lukan paradigm for Jesus' career and as finds its parallel in the fate of Stephen (cf. Acts 7:59). With these words of commitment on his lips, Jesus breathes his last.

Jesus' last words form a fitting climax to the events that the centurion in charge has witnessed. The impact is profound. He is almost certainly not one who shares the Jewish faith, but it becomes clear to him that, in the deadly conflict between Jesus and the Jewish authorities who have handed him over to Roman justice, it is Jesus, and not these religious authorities, who stands in the right relationship to God. The presence of God with this man has been palpable!

The centurion is not, however, the only witness. The People, introduced to the crucifixion scene in v 27 and mentioned in v 35, are also there. At a fatal moment, they had sided with their leaders against the foreign overlord, Pilate. But this present experience has thoroughly convinced them that this is a sad day for Israel. Their moment of complicity forgotten, these crowds move off beating their breasts in mourning.

Jesus' friends and acquaintances are there as well, including the women who had accompanied him from Galilee (cf. 8:1–3). As a precaution, they stand at a distance, but they witness it all. If they are to be witnesses to the resurrection, then it is important that they can attest, as well, the truth about Jesus' cruel death.

The Burial of Jesus *(23:50–56)*

Bibliography

Bahat, D. "Does the Holy Sepulchre Church Mark the Burial of Jesus?" *BAR* 12.3 (1986) 26–45. **Barkay, G.** "The Garden Tomb: Was Jesus Buried Here?" *BAR* 12.2 (1986) 40–57. **Benoit, P.** *The Passion and Resurrection of Jesus.* New York: Herder and Herder, 1969. 205–30. **Blinzler, J.** *Der Prozess Jesu.* 385–415. ———. "Die Grablegung Christi in historischer Sicht." In *Resurrexit: Actes du symposium international sur la résurrection de Jésus (Rome 1970)*, ed. E. Dhanis. Rome: Editrice vaticana, 1974. 56–107. ———. "Zur Auslegung der Evangelienberichte über Jesu Begräbnis." *MTZ* 3 (1952) 403–14. **Bornhäuser, K.** "Die Kreuzesabnahme und das Begräbnis Jesu." *NKZ* 42 (1931) 38–56. **Brändle, M.** "Die synoptischen Grabeserzählungen." *Orientierung* 31 (1967) 179–84. **Braun, F.-M.** "La sépulture de Jésus." *RB* 45 (1936) 34–52, 184–200, 346–63. **Briend, J.** "La sépulture d'un crucifié." *BTS* 133 (1971) 6–10. **Broer, I.** *Die Urgemeinde und das Grab Jesu: Eine Analyse der Grablegungsgeschichte im Neuen Testament.* SANT 31. Munich: Kösel, 1972. **Brown, R. E.** "The Burial of Jesus (Mark 15:42–47)." *CBQ* 50 (1988) 233–45. **Bulst, W.** "Untersuchungen zum Begräbnis Christi." *MTZ* 3 (1952) 244–55. **Burkitt, F. C.** "A Note on Lk. xxiii 51 in the Dura Fragment." *JTS* 36 (1935) 258–59. **Chafins, T. L.** "Women and Angels . . . When They Speak, It's Time to Listen! A Study of the Structure of Luke 23:50–24:12." *AshTJ* 21 (1990) 11–17. **Cousin, H.** "Sépulture criminelle et sépulture prophétique." *RB* 81 (1974) 375–93. **Cox Evans, L. E.** "The Holy Sepulchre." *PEQ* 100 (1968) 112–36. **Cronin, H. S.** "They Rested the Sabbath Day according to the Commandment: Luke xxiii. 56." *ExpTim* 16 (1904–5) 115–18. **Dhanis, E.** "L'ensevelissement de Jésus et la visite au tombeau dans l'évangile de saint Marc (xv,40–xvi,8)." *Greg* 39 (1958) 367–410. **Finegan, J.** *Die Überlieferung der Leidens- und Auferstehungsgeschichte Jesu.* BZNW 15. Giessen: Töpelmann, 1934. 34–35. **Gaechter, P.** "Zum Begräbnis Jesu." *ZKT* 75 (1953) 220–25. **Goulder, M. D.** "Mark xvi. 1–8 and Parallels." *NTS* 24 (1977–78) 235–40. **Grass, H.** *Ostergeschehen und Osterberichte.* 3rd ed. Göttingen, 1964. 173–83. **Hachlili, R.,** and **Killebrew, A.** "Jewish Funerary Customs during the Second Temple Period, in the Light of the Excavations at the Jericho Necropolis." *PEQ* 115 (1983) 115–26. **Holtzmann, O.** "Das Begräbnis Jesu." *ZNW* 30 (1931) 311–13. **Hynek, R. W.** "Das Grabtuch Christi." *Klerusblatt* 22 (1941) 289–91. **Jackson, C.** "Joseph of Arimathea." *JR* 16 (1936) 332–40. **Kennard, J. S., Jr.** "The Burial of Jesus." *JBL* 74 (1955) 227–38. **Kenyon, K. M.** *Jerusalem: Excavating 3000 Years of History.* London/New York: Thames and Hudson/ McGraw-Hill, 1967. 146–54. **Liebowitz, H.** "Jewish Burial Practices in the Roman Period." *ManQ* 22 (1981–82) 107–17. **Mailhet, J.** "L'ensevelissement de Jésus." *L'Année théologique*

(1948) 21–43. **Masson, C.** "L'ensevelissement de Jésus (Marc xv,42–47)." *RTP* 31 (1943) 192–203. **McBirnie, W. S.** *The Search for the Authentic Tomb of Jesus.* Montrose, CA: Acclaimed Books, 1975. **Mercurio, R.** "A Baptismal Motif in the Gospel Narratives of the Burial." *CBQ* 21 (1959) 39–54. **Michel, O.** "Jüdische Bestattung und urchristliche Östergeschichte." *Jud* 16 (1960) 1–5. **O'Rahilly, A.** "The Burial of Christ." *IER* 58 (1941) 302–16, 493–503; 59 (1942) 150–71. **Pesch, R.** "Der Schluss der vormarkinischen Passionsgeschichte und des Markus-evangeliums: Mk 15,42–16,8." In *L'Evangile selon Marc: Tradition et rédaction,* ed. M. Sabbe. BETL 34. Gembloux: Duculot, 1974. 365–409. **Riesner, R.** "Golgota und die Archaeologie." *BK* 40 (1985) 21–26. **Schreiber, J.** "Die Bestattung Jesu: Redaktionsgeschichtliche Beobachtungen zu Mk 15,42–47 par." *ZNW* 72 (1981) 141–77. **Simons, J.** *Jerusalem in the Old Testament: Researches and Theories.* Leiden, Brill, 1952. 282–343. **Smith, R. H.** "The Tomb of Jesus." *BA* 30 (1967) 74–90. **Vincent, L.-H.** "Garden Tomb: Histoire d'un mythe." *RB* 34 (1925) 401–31. **Winter, P.** "Lucan Sources." *ExpTim* 68 (1957) 285.

And see at 22:1–2, 66–71; 23:1–5, 26–32, 33–38, 44–49.

Translation

⁵⁰*There was a man named Joseph who was a member of the council and a good and righteous man* ⁵¹*(this [man] had not consented to their decision or their action). [He was] from Arimathea, a city of the Jews; and he*ᵃ *was waiting expectantly for the kingdom of God.* ⁵²*This [man] went to Pilate and asked for the body of Jesus;* ⁵³*and taking [it] down he wrapped it in a linen cloth and placed him*ᵇ *in a rock-hewn tomb, where no one had yet been placed.* ⁵⁴*It was the day of preparation, and sabbath was [near to] dawning.*

⁵⁵*The women who had come with Jesus*ᶜ *from Galilee followed along and saw the tomb and how the body was placed.* ⁵⁶*They returned home and prepared [anointing] spices and perfumes.*

On the sabbath, in accord with the commandment, they rested.

Notes

ᵃ "And he" is lit. "who."
ᵇ P⁷⁵ A L W Θ Ψ etc. read αὐτό, "it," referring to the body. But the change from "it" ("wrapped it") to "him" ("placed him") in the preferred reading is both artistically better (see *Comment* below) and prepares for the masculine οὐδείς, "no one," that comes in the next clause.
ᶜ Lit. "him."

Form/Structure/Setting

The present unit is bound to the preceding (vv 44–49) primarily by the continuing role for the Galilean women who were followers of Jesus. They are introduced in v 55 in language reminiscent of v 49 and are said to return home in v 56 in language echoing that used of the crowds returning home in v 48. A forward link as well is provided by the mention of the approaching sabbath in v 54 (cf. v 56b; 24:1). Though included here, v 56b is really a transitional pause between 23:50–56a and 24:1–12.

There is no certain basis for identifing the influence of a second source account, but the measure of agreement between v 53c and Matt 27:60; John 19:41b suggests at least some further shared oral tradition (a judgment that may be nudged in the second-written-source direction by verbal agreements with Matthew in vv 52, 53, 54). This is a story about Jesus that cannot have been transmitted apart from a passion narrative.

The role of the women is often taken to be a secondary element in the Markan tradition, but as Pesch has well demonstrated ("Der Schluss," 365–409), it is unlikely that the materials of Mark 15:40–16:8, or any of its subunits, ever existed without the references to the women. The fundamental historicity of the burial by Joseph of Arimathea is sometimes questioned on the basis of alleged difficulties in the Markan account (see, e.g., the extended study of Broer [*Die Urgemeinde*]), but the suggestions offered for the development of the narrative account for the narrative less effectively than does a basis in historical memory. (The question of whether Pilate would be likely to release the body in this way is addressed below, as is the role of the approaching sabbath as motivation for Joseph's action. Altogether too much has been made of the apparent tension between the unanimous agreement of the Sanhedrin that Jesus deserved death and Joseph's apparently more favorable disposition [the "all" of Mark 14:64 may be just as much a literary flourish as the "all" of 1:5; or Joseph may have been carried along at the time but had second thoughts soon after; or, as is sometimes argued, Joseph's actions may not express a positive view of Jesus at all but only a pious concern for funeral decencies]. There is no documented necessity from the early period for washing and anointing as necessary aspects of burial practice.)

Comment

As at his birth, so at his death, the best of Jewish piety shows itself sensitive to the possibility that in Jesus God was at work. Joseph of Arimathea lends his good offices so that Jesus, though a condemned criminal, might be provided with a decent burial. The female disciples continue to follow along, and, seeing how things are, they make arrangements for a more decent burial preparation of the body after the stipulated sabbath rest was over.

50 Quite a bit here is notably Lukan: ἰδοὺ ἀνήρ (lit. "behold a man"; see at 5:12); ὀνόματι, "by name" (cf. at 10:38); ὑπάρχων (lit. "being"); ἀνὴρ ἀγαθὸς καὶ δίκαιος (cf. Acts 11:24; Luke 1:6; 2:25; Acts 10:22). Luke makes no use of Mark's time reference, but later he will use the reference to the approaching sabbath (v 54; cf. v 56). Luke moves "of Arimathea" into a later position and first develops Mark's εὐσχήμων βουλευτής, "a respected member of the council." He keeps βουλευτής (lit. "councillor," but certainly a member of the Jerusalem Sanhedrin [it is not found elsewhere in the NT]). The Lukan role of Joseph's status as a member of the Sanhedrin is comparable to that of Gamaliel in Acts 5:34 (that at least some highly placed people show respect for Jesus/the Christian movement adds credibility to its claims). Luke expands "respected" into "a good and righteous man" (the role of the upright and the pious lends further credibility to the faith that Luke is commending [cf. 1:6; 2:25]), and, aware of the tension between this affirmation about Joseph and the role of the Sanhedrin in Jesus' downfall, he adds in explanation (v 51), "this [man] had not consented to their decision or their action."

51 The opening clause is a Lukan expansion (see at v 50; the use here of βουλῇ, "decision," is notably Lukan [Luke has ten of thirteen NT occurrences]);

Luke expands Mark's "from Arimathea" with "a city of the Jews" (presumably to distinguish it from gentile cities in Palestine); the final clause is reproduced from Mark, but with the confusing "he also" removed and with Mark's periphrastic verb replaced by a normal imperfect. The location of Arimathea is uncertain. Fitzmyer (1526) provides a convenient list of the various views on offer, but none can be affirmed with any confidence. "Waiting expectantly for the kingdom of God" links Joseph with the piety of Simeon and Anna (cf. at 2:25, 38). Joseph is not a disciple, but he is presented as one who, attentive for the action of God, is open to the possibility that God may be acting in Jesus (cf. Acts 5:35–39). He is a figure not unlike the scribe whom Jesus declared to be "not far from the kingdom of God" (Mark 12:28–34; quotation from v 34; an episode that Luke was unable to incorporate).

52   Luke drops the Markan tribute to Joseph's courage, but, for his report of Joseph's visit to Pilate to ask for the body of Jesus, Luke reproduces with only minor verbal changes the Markan wording (but note the agreement with Matthew for οὗτος προσελθὼν τῷ Πιλάτῳ [lit. "this man having come to Pilate"]). How willing to release the body might Joseph have expected Pilate to be? There is a well-documented Roman reluctance to release to their families and friends the bodies of traitors (see conveniently Brown, *CBQ* 50 [1988] 234–36): there was an understandable fear that such criminals might be imitated as martyr/heroes; the denial of a decent burial was considered likely to reduce the incidence of such imitation. As Joseph made his request, three things counted in his favor: (*i*) in provincial justice administered to those without Roman citizenship, the governor was largely free of formal imperial legal constraint (see at 23:1–5), so Pilate would feel free to follow his own judgment; (*ii*) as a member of the Sanhedrin, and not at all part of Jesus' retinue, Joseph would seem to be a good risk; and, of most importance, (*iii*) Pilate had little fear of unfortunate consequences in a situation where: (*a*) he was not convinced that there ever was any capital culpability; (*b*) the Jewish leadership was firmly against the "offender" and his movement; and (*c*) the volatile public had failed at the crucial moment to support this apparently popular figure. Luke is so confident that he fails to see the need for reporting the granting of Joseph's request (Luke deletes as well Mark's report of Pilate's surprise at death so soon and his confirmation of the fact of death [the Markan surprise is probably uncalled for, if Palestinian crucifixion practice was conformed to Jewish sensibilities as suggested at v 33; it may be no more than a literary device, intended to allow for the reporting of a confirmation of Jesus' certain death]).

53   The Markan purchase of a linen cloth is dropped as an unnecessary detail, as will be the Markan purchase by the women of spices in v 56. Luke and Matthew agree in replacing Mark's ἐνείλησεν, "wrapped," with ἐνετύλιξεν αὐτό, "wrapped it," but this may only be fortuitous (in Luke, the presence of αὐτό allows for rather nice references to the two parts of the phrase "the body of Jesus": *it* is wrapped and *he* is placed [but see textual note above]). Luke prefers μνήματι for "tomb" in place of Mark's μνημείῳ. Luke compresses Mark's "which had been hewn [λελατομημένον] out of the rock" to the adjective "rock-hewn" (λαξευτῷ) and adapts the Markan syntax to make a fresh point: "where no one had yet been placed" (cf. Matt 27:60; John 19:41b).

In Acts 13:29, the removal from the cross and burial are bound up in an undifferentiated manner with the culpable acts of "the residents of Jerusalem and their leaders." σινδών means "fine cloth" but is occasionally used of a burial shroud, as here. (The Shroud of Turin has been proven not to have the requisite antiquity.) The terms used in John 11:44; 19:40; 20:5–7 probably belong to a more elaborate preparation for burial. (On burial customs in the Second Temple period, see Michel, *Jud* 16 [1960] 1–5; Liebowitz, *ManQ* 22 [1981–82] 107–17; Hachlili and Killebrew, *PEQ* 115 [1983] 115–26.) A rock-hewn tomb is likely to have fitted the socio-economic standing of Joseph rather better than that of Jesus himself (cf. Isa 22:16). In and around Jerusalem, tombs hewn out of rock and dating from the first century are quite common, and neither of the two traditional locations for the tomb (the Garden Tomb and the Holy Sepulchre) can confidently be claimed as the place where Jesus' body was laid to rest. Of the two, the historical claims of the Holy Sepulchre site are considerably more weighty (see the accessible reviews in *BAR* 12.2 [1986] 40–57; 12.3 [1986] 26–45). On the unused tomb, see at 19:30.

54 Luke economizes by removing Mark's mention at this point of the closing of the tomb with a stone (he assumes this detail for 24:2). Now he provides an equivalent for the time reference that he passed over at v 50. Luke's language is significantly different from that in Mark, but καί . . . ἦν παρασκευῆ(ς) . . . (προ)σάββατον, "and . . . was . . . day of preparation . . . (day before) sabbath," marks the commonality, and the overall sense is the same. Curiously, ἐπιθώσκειν (lit. "to dawn") is found in the NT only here and in Matt 28:1, a fact that Goulder (*NTS* 24 [1978] 237–40) considers to have source implications, as Matt 28:1 is in a related context. While he may be right that common tradition is involved (in his view, Luke used Matthew), the base is too narrow for any confidence (but see further agreements with Matthew in vv 52, 53).

"The day of preparation" is the day before the sabbath, on which preparations needed to be made so that the sabbath restrictions could be faithfully observed on the following day. Though Luke clearly intends to point to the near arrival of sundown, when sabbath would begin, his particular use of ἐπιθώσκειν has not been paralleled. He could have erred because of a wish to adopt an "elegant" word from his second source (if there was one), or the usage could represent a Greek-speaking Jewish adoption, for use in relation to a Jewish reckoning of the day, of language originating from and better adapted to expressing the dawning of a new day reckoned to begin at first light.

V 54 looks both backward and forward: it explains the need for Joseph's timely action (*m. Šabb.* 23.5 prohibits burial on the sabbath; the same prohibition might normally be expected to apply to the day of Passover as well [cf. *m. Meg.* 1.5], but when a feast day came immediately before or after the sabbath, there is likely to have been a measure of relaxation of sabbath restrictions for the feast day [in the particular case of crucifixion, the stipulation of Deut 21:22–23 would stand in favor of such a relaxation; more generally, see *m. Sanh.* 6.5 for the undesirability of leaving a corpse unburied overnight]), and it establishes a time reference that explains the sequence of actions by the women in vv 55–56 (and 24:1).

55 The verse seems to be a Lukan formulation drawing on the basic information of Mark 15:47 and on Luke 23:49. Mark's ἐθεώρουν, "were seeing," becomes ἐθεάσαντο, "saw" (Luke varies the verbs, having used Mark's verb in v 48, and yet another in v 49); ποῦ τέθειται, "where it was placed," becomes ὡς ἐτέθη, "how it was placed"; Luke uses here the Markan word for "tomb," which he replaced at v 53.

In the Lukan imagery, the women of v 49 are still following Jesus, now to his tomb (perhaps the intensive form κατακολουθήσασαι is chosen because this is the very last piece of following possible for them). On the women and their coming with Jesus from Galilee, see at v 49. In the women's eyes, the body was being dealt with decently, but proper respect required more thorough preparation of the body for burial.

56 V 56 is inspired by Mark 16:1b, but v 56b owes more to Luke himself (cf. the role of Luke in 2:22–24, 39). The return home of the women here corresponds to that of the crowds in v 48. Luke passes over Mark's mention of the purchase of the anointing spices (cf. v 53) and envisages, rather, their preparation. He thinks in terms of there still being time for such preparation before the onset of the sabbath (whereas Mark places the purchase after the sabbath is over). ἀρώματα can refer to anything highly perfumed, whether for use in food (spices), as a perfume, or for embalming a corpse. Luke adds μύρα, which is slightly narrower and is generally translated "ointment" or "perfume." Luke underlines the fidelity to the Jewish law (cf. Exod 20:10; Deut 5:14) of the nascent Christian community, by expanding Mark's "when the sabbath was over" into v 56b. Luke's law-keeping here is stricter than that required in later Jewish tradition (see *m. Šabb.* 23.5).

Explanation

While the part played by Joseph of Arimathea shows the best of Jewish piety as once again sensitive to the possibility that God might be at work in Jesus, the women from Galilee continue here in their important role.

Luke is interested in Joseph's role in much the way that he is interested in that of Gamaliel in Acts 5:34–39: in Luke's eyes, the respect shown by highly placed people for Jesus/the Christian movement adds credibility to the claims of Christianity; at the very least, it shows that this is no fringe phenomenon simply to be ignored.

Luke does not present Joseph as a disciple of Jesus; rather, like Simeon and Anna in the Infancy Gospel (see 2:25, 38), he is a man of authentic Jewish faith, whose expectations regarding God's commitment to his People make him responsive in the present situation.

The bodies of condemned criminals were not always released for burial, especially in cases of treason. But Pilate had never really been convinced of Jesus' guilt, and the body was going here to a respected member of the Sanhedrin, not to Jesus' family or his followers. For the body to have stayed on the cross overnight would have been a violation of Jewish custom (for the most part, the Romans seem to have shown a sensitivity to this). Joseph's offer gave Pilate a convenient way of dealing with this area of Jewish sensibility.

The linen cloth provided a simple but dignified shroud, adequate under the circumstances. While in and around Jerusalem there are still today the remains of many tombs hewn out of the rock, such a burial arrangement is likely to have fit the socio-economic standing of Joseph rather better than that of Jesus himself: Jesus is being dignified in death in a way that he had not been in life; the mention that the tomb had not been previously used is also concerned with the appropriate honoring of the Lord (cf. 19:30). The tomb site within the present

Holy Sepulchre church is, in terms of location and historical tradition, a credible but not certain location for Jesus' burial. The Garden Tomb location is a much less believable alternative.

V 54 both explains the need for this rapid burial and prepares for the women's actions to come. Soon the sun would set, and the sabbath would begin. Anything that urgently needed doing had to be accomplished in the short period remaining before sundown.

Those women who had followed Jesus from Galilee and had witnessed the execution of Jesus now continue their following as they observe the burial arrangements made for Jesus. They see that the body has been dealt with decently. However, from their point of view, for proper respect to be shown, there was still need for more thorough preparation of the body for burial. The crowds had gone home from the crucifixion earlier (v 48); now the women go home. They go home to prepare anointing spices for the body. Their plan is to have things ready so that after the compulsory rest of the sabbath day (as followers of Jesus they faithfully observe the law), they can go at first light on Sunday morning to carry out their intentions.

The Resurrection Narrative   (24:1–53)

Luke's resurrection narrative consists of four parts: the role of the women (plus Peter) in the discovery of the empty tomb and the reception of the angelic message; the experience of the two disciples on the road to Emmaus who meet with a Jesus they cannot recognize, who shows them from the Scriptures the need for the Christ to enter glory through suffering and who becomes known to them in the breaking of the bread; the meeting of the whole group with Jesus, who convinces them that it is he ("flesh and bones"), opens their minds to understand the Scriptures, and directs them regarding their future role; and the closely linked blessing and departure scene in Bethany. Rather schematically, Luke seems to represent all of this as taking place on Easter day.

The Women and Peter Find an Empty Tomb   (24:1–12)

Bibliography

GENERAL ON THE RESURRECTION:

Albertz, M. "Zur Formgeschichte der Auferstehungsberichte." *ZNW* 21 (1922) 259–69. **Allen, D.** "Resurrection Appearances as Evidence." *TToday* 30 (1973) 435–70. **Alsup, J. E.** *The Post-Resurrection Appearance Stories of the Gospel Tradition: A History-of-tradition Analysis with Text-synopsis.* CTM 5. Stuttgart: Calwer, 1975. ———. "Resurrection and Historicity." *ASB* 103 (1988) 5–18. **Althaus, P.** *Die Wahrheit des kirchlichen Osterglaubens: Einspruch Gegen E. Hirsch.* Gütersloh: Bertelsmann, 1940. **Anderson, C.** "The Resurrection of Jesus." In *The Historical Jesus: A Continuing Quest.* Grand Rapids: Eerdmans, 1972. **Anderson, H.** "The Easter Witness of the Evangelists." In *The New Testament in Historical and Contemporary Perspective.* FS G. H. C. MacGregor, ed. H. Anderson and W. Barclay. Oxford: Blackwell, 1965. 156–78. **Barta, K. A.** "Resurrection Narratives: Thresholds of Faith." *BiTod* 27 (1989) 160–65. **Bartsch, H. W.** "Der Ursprung des Osterglaubens." *TZ* 31 (1975) 16–31. **Benoit, P.** *The Passion and Resurrection of Jesus.* 231–342. **Berger, K.** *Die Auferstehung des Propheten.* Esp. 213–35, 608–36. **Broer, I.** "Seid stets bereit, jedem Rede und Antwort zu stehen, der nach der Hoffnung fragt, die euch erfüllt" (1 Petr 3,15): Das leere Grab und die Erscheinungen Jesu im Lichte der historischen Kritik." In *"Der Herr ist wahrhaft auferstanden,"* ed. I. Broer and J. Werbeck. 29–61. ———. "'Der Herr ist wahrhaft auferstanden' (Lk 24,34): Auferstehung Jesu und historisch-kritische Methode. Erwägung zur Entstehung des Osterglaubens." In *Auferstehung Jesu—Auferstehung der Christen: Deutungen des Osterglaubens.* FS A. Vögtle, ed. L. Oberlinner. QD 105. Freiburg: Herder, 1986. 39–62. ———. "'Der Herr ist dem Simon erschienen' (Lk 24,34): Zur Entstehung des Osterglaubens." *SNTU* 13 (1988) 81–100. ——— and **Werbeck, J.,** eds. *"Der Herr ist wahrhaft auferstanden" (Lk 24,34): Biblische und systematische Beiträge zur Enstehung des Osterglaubens.* Stuttgarter Bibelstudien 134. Stuttgart: Katholisches Bibelwerk, 1988. **Brown, R. E.** *The Virginal Conception and Bodily Resurrection of Jesus.* New York: Paulist, 1973. 69–129. ———. *A Risen Christ in Eastertide: Essays on the Gospel Narratives of the Resurrection.* Collegeville, MN: Liturgical, 1991. ———. "The Resurrection and Biblical Criticism." *Commonweal* 87 (1967)

232–36. **Brun, L.** *Die Auferstehung Christi in der urchristliche Überlieferung.* Giessen: Töpelmann, 1925. **Bürgener, K.** *Die Auferstehung Jesu Christi von den Toten.* 3rd ed. Bremen: Selbstverlag des ev.-luth. Pfarramtes an St. Johannes-Soddenmatt, 1976. **Cantinat, J.** *Réflexions sur la résurrection de Jésus (d'après Saint Paul et Saint Marc).* Paris: Gabalda, 1978. **Carnley, P.** *The Structure of Resurrection Belief.* Oxford: Clarendon, 1987. **Clark, W. R.** "Jesus, Lazarus, and Others: Resuscitation or Resurrection?" *RelLif* 49 (1980) 230–41. **Craffert, P. F.** "The Origins of Resurrection Faith: The Challenge of a Social Scientific Approach." *Neot* 23 (1989) 331–48. **Craig, W. L.** "The Bodily Resurrection of Jesus. In *Gospel Perspectives,* ed. R. T. France and D. Wenham. Sheffield: JSOT, 1980. 1:47–74. ————. "Pannenbergs Beweis für die 'Auferstehung Jesu.'" *KD* 34 (1988) 78–104. ————. "On Doubts about the Resurrection." *Modern Theology* 6 (1989) 53–75. **Cranfield, C. E. B.** "The Resurrection of Jesus." *ExpTim* 101 (1990) 167–72. **Crossan, J. D.** "Living Earth and Living Christ: Thoughts on Carol P. Christ's 'Finitude, Death, and Reverence for Life.'" *Semeia* 40 (1987) 109–18. **Daalen, D. H. van.** *The Real Resurrection.* London: Collins, 1972. **Delling, G.** "The Significance of the Resurrection of Jesus for Faith in Jesus Christ." In *The Significance of the Message of the Resurrection for Faith in Jesus Christ,* ed. C. F. D. Moule. SBT 2/8. Naperville, IL: Allenson, 1968. 77–104. **Derrett, J. D. M.** *The Anastasis: The Resurrection of Jesus as an Historical Event.* Shipston-on-Stour, Warwickshire: Drinkwater, 1982. **Descamps, A.** "La structure des récits évangéliques de la Résurrection." *Bib* 40 (1959) 726–41. **Devenisch, P. E.** "The So-Called Resurrection of Jesus and Explicit Christian Faith: Wittgenstein's Philosophy and Marxsen's Exegesis as Linguistic Therapy." *JAAR* 51 (1983) 171–90. **Dhanis, E.,** ed. *Resurrexit: Actes du symposium international sur la résurrection de Jésus (Rome 1970).* Vatican City: Libreria Vaticana, 1974. **Dodd, C. H.** "The Appearances of the Risen Christ: An Essay in Form-Criticism of the Gospels." In *Studies in the Gospels: Essays in Memory of R. H. Lightfoot,* ed. D. E. Nineham. Oxford: Blackwell, 1957. 9–35. **Drane, J. W.** "Some Ideas of Resurrection in the New Testament Period." *TynB* 24 (1973) 99–110. **Dunn, J. D. G.** *Jesus and the Spirit.* 114–34. **Ebert, H.** "Die Krise des Osterglaubens: Zur diskussion über die Auferstehung Jesu." *Hockland* 60 (1968) 305–31. **Eckardt, A. R.** "Why Do You Search among the Dead?" *Encounter* 51 (1990) 1–17. **Eddy, G. T.** "The Resurrection of Jesus Christ: A Consideration of Professor Cranfield's Argument." *ExpTim* 101 (1990) 327–29. **Evans, C. F.** *Resurrection and the New Testament.* SBT 2/12. Naperville, IL: Allenson, 1970. **Fiedler, P.** "Vorösterliche Vorgaben für den Osterglauben." In *"Der Herr ist wahrhaft auferstanden,"* ed. I. Broer and J. Werbeck. 9–28. **Fitzmyer, J. A.** "The Resurrection of Jesus Christ according to the New Testament." *Month* 258 (1987) 402–10. **Freudenberg, W.** *Ist er wirklich auferstanden? Eine Untersuchung der biblischen Aufererstehungsberichte.* Wuppertal: Brockhaus, 1977. **Freyne, S.** "Some Recent Writing on the Resurrection." *ITQ* 38 (1971) 144–63. **Fuller, D. P.** "The Resurrection of Jesus and the Historical Method." *JBR* 34 (1966) 18–24. **Fuller, R. H.** *The Formation of the Resurrection Narratives.* New York: Macmillan, 1971. ————. "The Resurrection of Jesus Christ." *BR* 4 (1960) 8–24. **Galvin, J. P.** "Resurrection als Theologia crucis Jesu: The Foundational Christology of Rudolf Pesch." *TS* 38 (1977) 513–25. ————. "A Recent Jewish View of the Resurrection." *ExpTim* 91 (1978–79) 277–79. ————. "The Origin of Faith in the Resurrection of Jesus: Two Recent Perspectives." *TS* 49 (1988) 25–44. **Gander, G.** "La notion chrétienne primitive de la résurrection." *VCaro* 8 (1954) 33–51. **Gantoy, R.,** ed. *La Bonne Nouvelle de la Résurrection.* Lire la Bible 66. Paris: Cerf, 1981. **Gardner-Smith, P.** *The Narrative of the Resurrection: A Critical Study.* London: Methuen, 1926. **Geering, L.** *Resurrection: A Symbol of Hope.* London/Toronto: Hodder and Stoughton, 1971. **Geisler, N. L.** *The Battle for the Resurrection.* Nashville: Nelson, 1989. ————. "The Significance of Christ's Physical Resurrection." *BSac* 146 (1989) 148–70. **Geyer, H.-G.** "The Resurrection of Jesus Christ: A Survey of the Debate in Present Day Theology." In *The Significance of the Message of the Resurrection for Faith in Jesus Christ,* ed. C. F. D. Moule. SBT 2/8. Naperville, IL: Allenson, 1968. 105–35. **Gibert, P.** *La résurrection du Christ: Le témoignage du Nouveau Testament. De l'histoire à la foi.* Paris/Montreal: Desclée de Brouwer/Bellarmin, 1975. **Goguel, M.** *La Foi à la résurrection de Jésus dans le christianisme primitif.* Bibliothèque de l'Ecole des Hautes Etudes, sc. rel. 57. Paris: Leroux, 1933. **Goppelt, L.** "Die Auferstehung Jesu in der Kritik, ihr Sinn und ihre Glaubwerdigkeit." In *Grundlagen des Glaubens*, ed. P. Rieger and J. Strauss. Tutzinger Texte. Munich: Kösel, 1970. 55–74. **Grass, H.** *Ostergeschehen und Osterberichte.* 2nd ed. Göttingen: Vandenhoeck & Ruprecht, 1962. 15–93. **Grelot, P.** "La résurrection de Jésus et son arrière-plan biblique et juif." In *La résurrection du Christ et l'exégèse moderne*, ed. P. de Surgy. Paris: Cerf, 1969. 17–53. ————. "L'historien devant la Résurrection du Christ." *RHS* 48 (1972) 221–50. ————. "La résurrection de Jésus et l'histoire: Historicité et historialité." *Quatre Fleuves* 15–16 (1982) 145–79. **Guillet, J.** "Les récits évangéliques de la résurrection." *Quatre Fleuves* 15–16 (1982) 7–21. **Gutbrod, K.** *Die Auferstehung Jesu im Neuen Testament.* Stuttgart: Calwer, 1969. **Gutwenger, E.** "The Narration of Jesus' Resurrection." *TD* 16 (1968) 8–13. **Habermas, G. R.** "Jesus' Resurrection and Contemporary Criticism: An Apologetic." *CrisTR* 4 (1989–90) 159–74, 373–85. ———— and **Flew, A. G. N.** *Did Jesus Rise from the Dead? The Resurrection Debate*, ed. T. L. Miethe. San Francisco: Harper and Row, 1987. **Harris, M. J.** *From Grave to Glory: Resurrection in the New Testament. Including a Response to Norman L. Geisler.* Grand Rapids, MI: Zondervan, 1990. **Harvey, N. P.** "Frames of Reference for the Resurrection." *SJT* 42 (1989) 335–39. **Hayes, J. H.** "Resurrection as Enthronement and the Earliest Church Christology." *Int* 22 (1968) 333–45. **Helms, R.** "Resurrection Fictions." *Free Inquiry* Fall (1981) 34–41. **Hempelmann, H.** *Die Auferstehung Jesu Christi—eine historische Tatsache? Eine engagierte Analyse.* Wuppertal: Brockhaus, 1982. **Hendrickx, H.** *The Resurrection Narratives of the Synoptic Gospels.* Rev. ed. London: Chapman, 1984. **Hengel, M.** "Ist der Osterglauben noch zu retten?" *TQ* 153 (1973) 252–69. **Hirsch, E.** *Die Auferstehungsgeschichten und der christliche Glaube.* Tübingen: Mohr, 1940. **Hodges, Z. C.** "Form-Criticism and the Resurrection Accounts." *BSac* 124 (1967) 339–48. **Hooke, S. H.** *The Resurrection of Christ as History and Experience.* London: Darton, Longman and Todd, 1967. **Howe, E. M.** "'But Some Doubted' (Matt. 28:17): A Re-Appraisal of Factors Influencing the Easter Faith of the Early Christian Community." *JETS* 18 (1975) 173–80. **Hübner, H.** "Kreuz und Auferstehung im Neuen Testament." *TRu* 54 (1989) 262–306. **Hughes, G. J.** "Dead Theories, Live Metaphors and the Resurrection." *HeyJ* 29 (1988) 313–28. **Jeremias, J.** "Die älteste Schicht der Osterüberlieferungen." In *Resurrexit*, ed. E. Dhanis. 185–96. **Jones, I. H.** "The Resurrection—a Review Article." *EpR* 15 (1988) 82–89. **Kasper, W.** "Der Glaube an die Auferstehung Jesu vor dem Forum historischer Kritik." *TQ* 153 (1973) 229–41. **Kegel, G.** *Auferstehung Jesu—Auferstehung der Toten: Eine traditionsgeschichtliche Untersuchung zum Neuen Testament.* Gütersloh: Mohn, 1970. **Kendall, D.,** and **O'Collins, G.** "The Uniqueness of the Resurrection Appearances." *CBQ* 54 (1992) 287–307. **Kerr, F.** "Recent Catholic Writing on the Resurrection: (1) The Empty Tomb Story; (2) The Apearance Stories." *NB* 58 (1977) 453–61, 506–15. **Klappert, B.** "Legitmationsformel und Erscheinungsüberlieferung: Zur Formkritik der neutestamentliche Auferstehungstradition. Eine Anfrage an U. Wilckens." *TB* 5 (1974) 67–81. **Koch, G.** *Die Auferstehung Jesu Christi.* Tübingen: Mohr-Siebeck, 1965. **Kolping, A.** "Zur Entstehung des Glaubens an die Auferstehung Jesu." *MTZ* 26 (1975) 56–69. ————. "Um den Realitätscharacter der Ostererscheinungen." *TRev* 73 (1977) 441–50. **Kratz, R.** *Auferweckung als Befreiung: Eine Studie zur Passions- und Auferstehungstheologie des Matthäus.* SBS 65. Stuttgart: Katholisches Bibelwerk, 1973. **Kremer, J.** *Die Osterbotschaft der vier Evangelien: Versuch einer Auslegung der Berichte über das leere Grab und die Erscheinungen des Auferstandenen.* Stuttgarter Bibelstudien. Stuttgart: KBW, 1968. ————. *Das Älteste Zeugnis von der Auferstehung Christi.* SBS 17. 3rd ed. Stuttgart: Katholisches Bibelwerk, 1970. ————. *Die Osterevangelien—Geschichten um Geschichte.* Stuttgart: Katholisches Bibelwerk, 1977. ————. "Die Auferstehung Jesu Christi." In *Handbuch der Fundamentaltheologie: Traktat Religion.* Vol. 2. *Offenbarung.* Freiburg: Herder, 1985. 175–96. ————. "Ist Jesus wirklich von den Toten auferstanden?" *Stimmen der Zeit* 183 (1969) 310–20. ————. "Entstehung und Inhalt des Osterglaubens: Zur neuesten Diskussion." *TRev* 72 (1976) 1–14. ————. "Gibt es keine Auferstehung der Toten?" *Stimmen der Zeit* 204 (1986) 815–28. **Lacoste, J.-Y.** "Du droit de l'histoire au droit de Dieu: sur la résurrection de Jésus." *NRT* 104 (1982) 495–531. **Ladd,**

G. E. *I Believe in the Resurrection of Jesus.* London: Hodder and Stoughton, 1975. **Lake, K.** *The Historical Evidence for the Resurrection of Jesus Christ.* London: William and Norgate, 1907. **Lambrecht, J.** "The Events surrounding the Resurrection of Jesus." *RevAf Th* 5 (1981) 183–95. **Lampe, G.** "The Resurrection." *EpR* 3 (1976) 88–99. ——— and **MacKinnon, D. M.** *The Resurrection: A Dialogue,* ed. W. Purcell. Philadelphia: Westminster, 1966. **Lapide, P.** *The Resurrection of Jesus: A Jewish Perspective.* Tr. W. C. Linss. Minneapolis: Augsburg, 1983. **Legault, A.** "Christophanies et Angélophanies dans les récits évangéliques de la Résurrection." *ScEs* 21 (1969) 443–57. **Legrand, L.** "The Resurrection of Christ." *Biblebhashyam* 1 (1975) 247–55. **Lehmann, K.** "Die Erscheinungen des Herrn: Thesen zur hermeneutisch-theologischen Struktur der Ostererzählungen." In *Theologisches Jahrbuch 1976,* ed. W. Ernst. Leipzig: St. Benno, 1976. 145–58. **Leipoldt, J.** "Zu den Auferstehungsgeschichten." *TLZ* 73 (1948) 737–42. **Léon-Dufour, X.** *Résurrection de Jésus et message pascal.* Parole de Dieu. Paris: Seuil, 1971; ET = *Resurrection and the Message of Easter.* London: Chapman, 1974. **Loewe, W.** "The Appearances of the Risen Lord: Faith, Fact, and Objectivity." *Horizons* 6 (1979) 177–92. **Lohfink, G.** "Die Auferstehung Jesu und die historische Kritik." *BibLeb* 9 (1968) 37–53; digested in "The Resurrection of Jesus and Historical Criticism." *TD* 17 (1969) 110–14. ———. "Der Ablauf der Osterereignisse und die Anfänge der Urgemeinde." *TQ* 160 (1980) 162–76. **Longstaff, T. R. W.** "Empty Tomb and Absent Lord: Mark's Interpretation of Tradition." In *SBL Seminar Papers 1976,* ed. G. MacRae. Missoula, MT: Scholars, 1976. 269–77. **Lorenzen, T.** "Ist der Auferstandene in Galiläa erschienen." *ZNW* 64 (1973) 209–21. **Lunny, W. J.** *The Sociology of the Resurrection.* London: SCM, 1989. **Marxsen, W.** *The Resurrection of Jesus of Nazareth.* Tr. M. Kohl. London: SCM, 1970. ———. "The Resurrection of Jesus as a Historical and Theological Problem." In *The Significance of the Message of the Resurrection for Faith in Jesus Christ,* ed. C. F. D. Moule. SBT 2/8. Naperville, IL: Allenson, 1968. 77–104. ———. *Jesus and Easter: Did God Raise the Historical Jesus from the Dead?* Tr. V. P. Furnish. Nashville, TN: Abingdon, 1990. ——— et al. *Die Bedeutung der Auferstehungsbotschaft für den Glauben an Jesus Christus.* Gütersloh: Mohn, 1966. **McHugh, J.** "The Origin and Growth of the Gospel Traditions: III. The Resurrection." *ClerRev* 58 (1973) 162–75. **Michaelis, W.** *Die Erscheinungen des Auferstandenen.* Basel: Majer, 1944. **Moore, S.** "The Resurrection: A Confusing Paradigm-Shift." *DR* 98 (1980) 257–66. **Moser, J.** "The Resurrection—A New Essay in Biblical Theology." *KTR* 13 (1990) 16–19. **Moule, C. F. D.** "The Post-Resurrection Appearances in the Light of Festival Pilgrimages." *NTS* 4 (1957–58) 58–61. ———, ed. *The Significance of the Message of the Resurrection for Faith in Jesus Christ.* SBT 2/8. Naperville, IL: Allenson, 1968. **Mussner, F.** *Die Auferstehung Jesu.* Biblische Handbibliothek 7. Munich: Kösel, 1969. **Neyrey, J.** *The Resurrection Stories.* Collegeville, MN: Liturgical, 1990. **Nützel, J. M.** "Zum Schicksal der eschatologischen Propheten." *BZ* 20 (1976) 59–92. **O'Collins, G.** *The Easter Jesus.* London: Darton, Longman and Todd, 1973. ———. *What Are They Saying about the Resurrection?* New York: Paulist, 1978. ———. *Jesus Risen: The Resurrection—what actually happened and what does it mean?* London: Dartman, Longman and Todd, 1987. ———. *Interpreting the Resurrection: Examining the Major Problems in the Stories of Jesus' Resurrection.* New York: Paulist, 1988. ———. "Is the Resurrection an 'Historical Event.'" *HeyJ* 8 (1967) 381–87. ——— and **Kendall, D.** "Mary Magdalene as Major Witness to Jesus' Resurrection." *TS* 48 (1987) 631–46. **O'Grady, J. F.** "The Resurrection." *ChicStud* 30 (1991) 220–34. **O'Neill, J. C.** "On the Resurrection as a Historical Question." In *Christ, Faith and History: Cambridge Studies in Christology,* ed. S. W. Sykes and J. P. Clayton. Cambridge: University Press, 1972. 205–19. **Osborne, G. R.** *The Resurrection Narratives: A Redactional Study.* Grand Rapids MI: Baker, 1984. Esp. 99–146. **Osiek, C.** "The Resurrection: Prism of New Testament Faith." *BiTod* 27 (1989) 133–39. **Pamment, M.** Empty Tomb and Resurrection." *NB* 62 (1981) 488–93. **Pannenberg, W.** *Jesus—God and Man.* Tr. L. L. Wilkens and D. A. Priebe. London: SCM, 1968. 53–114. ———. "Did Jesus Really Rise from the Dead?" *Dialog* 4 (1965) 18–35. **Peel, M. L.** "The Resurrection in Recent Scholarly Research." *BRev* 5 (1989) 14–21, 42–43. **Pelletier, A.** "Les apparitions du Ressuscité en termes de la Septante." *Bib* 51 (1970) 76–79. **Perkins, P.** *Resurrection: New Testament Witness* and Contemporary Reflection. Garden City NY: Doubleday, 1984. Esp. 149–69. ———. "'I Have Seen the Lord' (John 20:18): Women Witnesses in the Resurrection." Int 46 (1992) 31–41. **Perret, J.** Ressuscité? Approche historique. Paris: FAC, 1984. **Perrin, N.** The Resurrection according to Matthew, Mark and Luke (British title The Resurrection Narratives: A New Approach). Philadelphia/London: Fortress/SCM, 1977. **Perry, M. C.** The Easter Enigma. London: Faber and Faber, 1959. **Pesch, R.** "Zur Entstehung des Glaubens an die Auferstehung Jesu." TQ 153 (1973) 201–28. ———. "Das 'leere Grab' und der Glaube an Jesu Auferstehung." IKZComm 11 (1982) 6–20. ———. "Zur Entstehung des Glaubens an die Auferstehung Jesu: Ein neuer Versuch." FZPT 30 (1983) 73–98. ———. "Der Schluss der vormarkinischen Passionsgeschichte und des Markusevangeliums: Mk 15,42–16,8." In L'Évangile selon Marc: Tradition et rédaction. 2nd ed. BETL 34. Leuven: University Press/Peeters, 1988. 365–410. **Ponthot, J.** "Gospel Traditions about Christ's Resurrection: Theological Perspectives and Problems of Historicity." LVit 21 (1966) 66–90. **Ramsey, A. M.** The Resurrection of Christ: An Essay in Biblical Theology. Rev. ed. London: G. Bles, 1956. **Rengstorf, K. H.** Die Auferstehung Jesu: Form, Art und Sinn der urchristlichen Osterbotschaft. 4th ed. Witten/Ruhr: Luther, 1960. **Riga, P. J.** "God Allowed Him to Be Seen." BiTod 28 (1990) 220–25. **Rigaux, B.** Dieu l'a ressuscité: Exégèse et théologie biblique. Gembloux: Duculot, 1973. 171–307. **Roberts, J.** "Galilean Resurrection." EpR 15 (1988) 44–46. **Robinson, J. A. T.** "Resurrection in the New Testament." IDB 4:43–53. **Robinson, W. C.** "The Bodily Resurrection of Christ." TZ 13 (1957) 81–101. **Ruckstuhl, E.** "Auferstehung, Erhöhung und Himmelfahrt Jesu." In Jesus im Horizont der Evangelien. Stuttgarter Biblische Aufsatzbände 3. Stuttgart: Katholisches Bibelwerk, 1988. 185–218. **Russel, R.** "Modern Exegesis and the Fact of the Resurrection." DR 76 (1958) 251–64, 329–43. **Schelke, K. H.** "Schöpfung des Glaubens?" TQ 153 (1973) 242–43. **Schillebeeckx, E.** Jesus: An Experiment in Christology. Tr. H. Hoskins. New York: Crossroad, 1979. 320–97. **Schlier, H.** Über die Auferstehung Jesu Christi. Kriterien 10. Einsiedeln: Johannes, 1968. **Schmied, A.** "Auferstehungsglaube ohne Ostererscheinungen?" TGeg 17 (1974) 46–51. ———. "Ostererscheinungen—Ostererfahrung." TGeg 19 (1976) 46–53. ———. "Auferstehungsglaube heute und die ursprüngliche Ostererfahrung." TGeg 20 (1977) 43–50. **Schmitt, J.** "Auferstehung Christi." LTK 1:1028–1035. ———. "Résurrection de Jésus dans le kérygme, la tradition, la catéchèse." DBSup 10:487–582. **Schnell, C. W.** "Tendencies in the Synoptic Resurrection Tradition: Rudolf Bultmann's Legacy and an Important Christian Tradition." Neot 23 (1989) 177–94. **Schnider, F.,** and **Stenger, W.** Die Ostergeschichten der Evangelien. Schriften zur Katechetik 13. Munich: Kösel, 1970. **Schubert, K.** "'Auferstehung Jesu' im Lichte der Religionsgeschichte des Judentums." In Resurrexit, ed. E. Dhanis. 207–29. **Schweizer, E.** "Resurrection in the New Testament." TD 27 (1979) 132–34. ———. "Resurrection—Fact or Illusion?" HBT 1 (1979) 137–59. ———. "Auferstehung—Illusion oder Wirklichkeit?" EvT 41 (1981) 2–19. **Scuka, R. F.** "Resurrection: Critical Reflections on a Doctrine in Search of a Meaning." Modern Theology 6 (1989) 77–95. **Sebastian, T.** "Death and Resurrection in Jewish Apocalyptic." Jeevadhara 9 (1979) 117–27. **Seidensticker, P.** Die Auferstehung Jesu in der Botschaft der Evangelisten: Ein traditionsgeschichtlicher Versuch zum Problem der Sicherung der Osterbotschaft in der apostolischen Zeit. SBS 26. Stuttgart: Katholisches Bibelwerk, 1967. **Selwyn, E. G.** "The Resurrection." In Essays Catholic and Critical, ed. E. G. Selwyn. London: SPCK, 1938. 281–319. **Smit, D. J.** "The Resurrection of Jesus—What Was It? Plurality and Ambiguity in the Christian Resurrection Hope." Neot 23 (1989) 159–75. **Smith, J. J.** "The Resurrection Appearances and the Origin of Easter Faith." Landas 2 (1988) 204–37. **Smith, R. H.** Easter Gospels: The Resurrection of Jesus according to the Four Gospels. Minneapolis: Augsburg, 1983. Esp. 93–143. **Stählin, G.** "'On The Third Day.'" Int 10 (1956) 282–99. **Steinseifer, B.** "Der Ort der Erscheinungen des Auferstandenen: Zur Frage alter Galiläischer Ostertraditionen." ZNW 62 (1972) 232–65. **Stock, A.** "Wirbel um die Auferstehung." Diakonia 6 (1975) 187–92. ———. "Resurrection Appearances and the Disciples' Faith." BiTod 20 (1982) 254–57. **Stuhlmacher, P.** "Kritischer müssen mir die Historisch-Kritischen sein!" TQ 153 (1973) 244–51. **Surgy, P. de,** ed. La résurrection du Christ et l'exégèse moderne. LD 50. Paris: Cerf, 1969. **Swain, L.** "The First Easter: What Really

Happened?" *ClerRev* 59 (1974) 276–83. **Teeple, H. M.** "The Historical Beginnings of the Resurrection Faith." In *Studies in New Testament and Early Christian Literature.* FS A. P. Wikgren, ed. D. E. Aune. NovTSup 33. Leiden: Brill, 1972. 107–20. **Thrall, M. E.** "Resurrection Traditions and Christian Apologetic." *Thomist* 43 (1979) 197–216. **Turner, H. E. W.** "The Resurrection." *ExpTim* 68 (1956–57) 369–71. **Viney, D. W.** "Grave Doubts about the Resurrection." *Encounter* 50 (1989) 125–40. **Vögtle, A.,** and **Pesch, R.** *Wie kam es zum Osterglauben?* Düsseldorf: Patmos, 1975. **Vorster, W. S.** "The Religio-Historical Context of the Resurrection of Jesus and Resurrection Faith in the New Testament." *Neot* 23 (1989) 159–75. **Wansbrough, H.** *Risen from the Dead.* Slough: St Paul Publications, 1978. **Ware, R. C.** "The Resurrection of Jesus." *HeyJ* 16 (1975) 22–35, 174–94. **Watson, F.** "'Historical Evidence' and the Resurrection of Jesus." *Th* 90 (1987) 365–72. **Wengst, K.** *Ostern—Ein wirkliches Gleichnis, eine wahre Geschichte: Zum neutestamentlichen Zeugnis von der Auferweckung Jesu.* Kaiser Taschenbücher 97. Munich: Kaiser, 1991. **Wilckens, U.** "The Tradition-History of the Resurrection of Jesus." In *The Significance of the Message,* ed. C. F. D. Moule. 51–76. ————. "Der Ursprung der Überlieferung der Erscheinungen des Auferstandenen." In *Dogma und Denkstrukturen.* FS E. Schlink, ed. W. Joest and W. Pannenberg. Göttingen: Vandenhoeck & Ruprecht, 1963. 56–95. ————. *Auferstehung: Das biblische Auferstehungszeugnis historisch untersucht und erklärt.* Themen der Theologie 4. Stuttgart/Berlin: Kreuz-V., 1970. Esp. 43–85. ————. *Resurrection: Biblical Testimony to the Resurrection, An Historical Examination and Explanation.* Tr. A. M. Stewart. Atlanta, GA: John Knox, 1978. **Winden, H. W.** *Wie kam und wie kommt es zum Osterglauben? Darstellung, Beurteilung und Weiterführung der durch Rudolf Pesch ausgelösten Diskussion.* Disputationes Theologicae 12. Frankfurt am M./Berne: P. Lang, 1982. **Woschitz, K. M.** "Ostererscheinungen—Grundlage des Glaubens." *Diakonia* 22 (1991) 6–17. **Zehrer, F.** *Die Auferstehung Jesu nach den vier Evangelisten: Die Osterevangelien und ihre hauptsächliche Probleme.* Vienna: Mayer, 1980.

GENERAL FOR LUKE 24:1–53:

Amphoux, C.-B. "Le chapitre 24 de Luc et l'origine de la tradition textuelle du Codex de Bèze (D.05 du NT)." *FilolNT* 4 (1991) 21–49. **Bailey, J. A.** *The Traditions Common to the Gospels of Luke and John.* NovTSup 7. Leiden: Brill, 1963. 85–102. **Brändle, M.** "Auferstehung Jesu nach Lukas." *Orientierung* 24 (1960) 84–89. **Dillon, R. J.** *From Eye-Witnesses to Ministers of the Word: Tradition and Composition in Luke 24.* AnBib 82. Rome: Biblical Institute, 1978. **Dömer, M.** *Das Heil Gottes.* 95–108. **Dupont, J.** "Les discours de Pierre dans les Actes et le chapitre XXIV de l'évangile de Luc." In *L'Évangile de Luc: Problèmes littéraires et théologiques.* FS L. Cerfaux, ed. F. Neirynck. BETL 32. Gembloux/Leuven: Duculot/Leuven University, 1973. 329–74. **Ernst, J.** "Schriftauslegung und Auferstehungsglaube bei Lukas." *TGl* 60 (1970) 360–74. **Gollwitzer, H.** *Jesu Tod und Auferstehung nach dem Bericht des Lukas.* Kaiser Traktate 44. Munich: Kaiser, 1979. **Guillaume, J.-M.** *Luc interprète des anciennes traditions sur la résurrection de Jésus.* EBib. Paris: Gabalda, 1979. **Hebbelthwaite, P.** "Theological Themes in the Lucan Post-Resurrection Narratives." *ClerRev* 50 (1965) 360–69. **Kessler, H.** *Sucht den Lebenden nicht bei den Toten: Die Auferstehung Jesu Christi in biblischer, fundamentalischer und systematischer Sicht.* 2nd ed. Düsseldorf: Patmos, 1987. **LaVerdiere, E. A.** "The Passion and Resurrection of Jesus according to St. Luke." *ChicStud* 25 (1986) 35–50. **Leaney, A. R. C.** "The Resurrection Narratives in Luke (xxiv. 12–53)." *NTS* 2 (1955–56) 110–14. **Lepers, É.** "Témoin d'une expérience (Luc 24)." *Christus* 31 (1984) 445–55. **Lohse, E.** *Die Auferstehung Jesu Christi im Zeugnis des Lukasevangeliums.* BibS(N) 31. Neukirchen: Neukirchener, 1961. **Marshall, I. H.** "The Resurrection in the Acts of the Apostles." In *Apostolic History and the Gospel: Biblical and Historical Essays.* FS F. F. Bruce, ed. W. W. Gasque and R. P. Martin. Exeter/Grand Rapids, MI: Paternoster/Eerdmans, 1970. 92–107. ————. "The Resurrection of Jesus in Luke." *TynB* 24 (1973) 55–98. **Nützel, J. M.** "Vom Hören zum Glauben: Der Weg zum Osterglauben in der Sicht des Lukas." In *Praesentia Christi.* FS J. Betz, ed. L. Lies. Düsseldorf: Patmos, 1984. 37–49. **O'Toole, R. F.** "Luke's Understanding of Jesus' Resurrection—Ascension—Exaltation." *BTB* 9 (1979) 106–14. ————. "Activity of the Risen

Jesus in Luke-Acts." *Bib* 62 (1981) 471-98. **Parsons, M. C.** "A Christological Tendency in P[75]." *JBL* 105 (1986) 463-79. **Plevnik, J.** "The Origin of Easter Faith according to Luke." *Bib* 61 (1980) 492-508. ————. "The Eyewitnesses of the Risen Jesus in Luke 24." *CBQ* 49 (1987) 90-103. **Ponthot, J.** "Vers l'historicisation lucanienne de la séquence pascale." In *À cause de l'Évangile,* ed. F. Refoulé. 643-54. **Rice, G.** "Western Non-interpolations: A Defense of the Apostolate." In *Luke-Acts: New Perspectives,* ed. C. H. Talbert. 1-16. **Rigaux, B.** *Dieu l'a ressuscité: Exégèse et théologie biblique.* Gembloux: Duculot, 1973. 204-9, 220-22. **Schmitt, J.** "Le récit de la résurrection dans l'évangile de Luc: Etude de critique littéraire." *RSR* 25 (1951) 119-37, 219-42. **Schubert, P.** "The Structure and Significance of Luke 24." In *Neutestamentliche Studien.* FS R. Bultmann, ed. W. Eltester. BZNW 21. Berlin: Töpelmann, 1954. 165-86. **Talbert, C. H.** "The Place of the Resurrection in the Theology of Luke." *Int* 46 (1992) 19-30. **Weir, T. H.** "The Stone Rolled Away (Lc XXIV, 2)." *ExpTim* 24 (1912-13) 284. **Wilder, A. N.** "Variant Traditions of the Resurrection in Luke-Acts." *JBL* 62 (1943) 307-18. **Wilkens, W.** "Die theologische Struktur der Komposition des Lukasevangeliums." *TZ* 34 (1978) 1-13.

FOR 24:1-12:

Baird, W. "Luke's Use of Matthew: Griesbach Revisited." *PSTJ* 40 (1987) 35-38. **Baldensperger, G.** "Le tombeau vide." *RHPR* 12 (1932) 413-43; 13 (1933) 105-44; 14 (1937) 97-125. **Bater, R. R.** "Towards a More Biblical View of the Resurrection." *Int* 23 (1969) 47-65. **Benoit, P.** "Marie-Madeleine et les disciples au tombeau selon John 20, 1-18." In *Judentum, Urchristentum, Kirche.* FS J. Jeremias, ed. W. Eltester. Berlin: Töpelmann, 1960. 141-52. ————. *The Passion and Resurrection of Jesus.* New York: Herder and Herder, 1969. 231-61. **Bickermann, E.** "Das leere Grab." *ZNW* 23 (1924) 281-92. **Bode, E. L.** *The First Easter Morning: The Gospel Accounts of the Women's Visit to the Tomb of Jesus.* AnBib 45. Rome: Biblical Institute, 1970. 59-71, 105-26. ————. "A Liturgical *Sitz im Leben* for the Gospel Tradition of the Women's Easter Visit to the Tomb of Jesus?" *CBQ* 32 (1970) 237-42. **Brändle, M.** "Narratives of the Synoptics about the Tomb." *TD* 16 (1968) 22-26. ————. "Did Jesus' Tomb Have to Be Empty?" *TD* 16 (1968) 18-21. **Broer, I.** "Zur heutigen Diskussion der Grabesgeschichte." *BibLeb* 10 (1969) 40-52. **Campenhausen, H. von.** "Der Ablauf der Osterereignisse und das leere Grab." In *Sitzungsberichte der heidelberger Akademie der Wissenschaften 2.* 2nd ed. Heidelberg, 1958; ET = "The Events of Easter and the Empty Tomb." In *Tradition and Life in the Church.* Philadelphia: Fortress, 1968. 42-89. **Claudel, G.** *La confession de Pierre: Trajectoire d'une péricope évangélique.* Études bibliques NS 10. Paris: Gabalda, 1988. 51-91. **Craig, W. L.** "The Empty Tomb of Jesus." In *Gospel Perspectives: Studies of History and Tradition in the Four Gospels,* ed. R. T. France and D. Wenham. Sheffield: JSOT, 1981. 2:173-200. **Crossan, J. D.** "Empty Tomb and Absent Lord." In *The Passion in Mark: Studies on Mark 14-16,* ed. W. H. Kelber. Philadelphia: Fortress, 1976. 135-52. **Curtis, K. P. G.** "Luke xxiv. 12 and John xx. 3-10." *JTS* 22 (1971) 512-15. ————. "Linguistic Support for Three Western Readings in Luke 24." *ExpTim* 83 (1971-72) 344-45. **Delorme, J.** "The Resurrection and Jesus' Tomb: Mark 16,1-8 in the Gospel Tradition." In *The Resurrection and Modern Biblical Thought,* ed. P. de Surgy. New York: Corpus Books, 1970. 74-106. **Dhanis, E.** "L'ensevelissement de Jésus et la visite au tombeau dans l'évangile de Marc (Mc XV, 40-XVI, 8)." *Greg* 39 (1958) 367-410. **Dillon, R. J.** *From Eye-Witnesses to Ministers of the Word: Tradition and Composition in Luke 24.* AnBib 82. Rome: Biblical Institute, 1978. 1-68. **Dussaut, L.** "Le triptyque des apparitions en Luc 24 (Analyse structurelle)." *RB* 94 (1987) 161-213. **Ellicott, C. J.** "The Testimony of the Tomb." *ExpTim* 14 (1902-3) 508-11. **Engelbrecht, J.** "The Empty Tomb (Lk 24:1-12) in Historical Perspective." *Neot* 23 (1989) 235-49. **Farmer, W. R.** "Notes for a Compositional Analysis on the Griesbach Hypothesis of the Empty Tomb Stories in the Synoptic Gospels." In *Occasional Notes on Some Points of Interest in New Testament Studies.* Dallas, TX: Perkins School of Theology, SMU, 1980. 7-14. **Feuillet, A.** "La découverte du tombeau vide en Jean 20,3-10 et la foi au Christ ressuscité."

EV 87 (1977) 257–66, 277–84. **Gaecher, P.** "Die Engelerscheinungen in den Auferstehungsberichten." *ZKT* 89 (1967) 191–202. **Gerits, H.** "Le message pascal au tombeau (Lc 24,1–12): La résurrection selon la présentation théologique de Lc." *EstTeol* 8/15 (1981) 3–63. **Goulder, M. D.** "The Empty Tomb." *Th* 79 (1976) 206–14. ———. "Mark XVI.1–8 and Parallels." *NTS* 24 (1977–78) 235–40. **Grayston, K.** "The Empty Tomb." *ExpTim* 92 (1980–81) 263–67. **Güttgemanns, E.** "Linguistische Analyse vom Mk 16,1–8." *LingBib* 11–12 (1972) 13–53. **Guillaume, J.-M.** *Luc interprète des anciennes traditions sur la résurrection de Jésus.* EBib. Paris: Gabalda, 1979. 15–66. **Hamilton, N. Q.** "Resurrection Tradition and the Composition of Mark." *JBL* 84 (1965) 415–21. **Hebblethwaite, P.** "Theological Themes in the Lucan Post-Resurrection Narratives." *ClerRev* 50 (1965) 360–69. **Hengel, M.** "Maria Magdalena und die Frauen als Zeugen." In *Abraham unser Vater.* FS O. Michel, ed. O. Betz et al. Leiden: Brill, 1963. 243–56. **Hodges, Z. C.** "The Women and the Empty Tomb." *BSac* 123 (1966) 301–9. **Johnson, L. T.** "Luke 24:1–11." *CBQ* 46 (1992) 57–61. **Kremer, J.** "Die Überlieferung vom leeren Grab." In . . . *denn sie werden leben: Sechs Kapitel über Tod, Auferstehung, Neues Leben.* Stuttgart: Katholisches Bibelwerk, 1972. 72–75. ———. "Zur Diskussion über 'das leere Grab.'" In *Resurrexit: Actes du symposium international sur la résurrection de Jésus (Rome 1970),* ed. E. Dhanis. Rome: Editrice vaticana, 1974. 137–68. ———. "Auferstanden—auferweckt." *BZ* 23 (1979) 97–98. **Lacy, J. A.** "*Ēgerthē*—He Has Risen." *BiTod* 36 (1968) 2532–35. **Mahoney, R. P.** *Two Disciples at the Tomb: The Background and Message of John 20,1–10.* Theologie und Wirklichkeit 6. Bern/Frankfurt am M.: Herbert/P. Lang, 1974. **Mangatt, G.** "At the Tomb of Jesus." *Biblebhashyam* 3 (1977) 91–96. **Meynet, R.** "Comment établir un chiasme: À propos des 'pèlerins d'Emmaüs.'" *NRT* 100 (1978) 233–49. **Mildenberger, F.** "Auferstandenen am dritten Tage nach der Schrift." *EvT* 23 (1963) 265–80. **Muddiman, J.** "A Note on Reading Luke xxiv.12." *ETL* 48 (1972) 542–48. **Nauck, W.** "Die Bedeutung des leeren Grabes für den Glauben an den Auferstandenen." *ZNW* 47 (1956) 243–67. **Neirynck, F.** "*anateilantos*." In *Evangelica.* 181–214. ———. "Le récit du tombeau vide dans l'évangile de Luc (24,1–12)." In *Miscellanea.* FS J. Vergote, ed. P. Naster et al. OLP 6/7. Louvain: Departement oriëntalistiek, 1975–76. 427–41. ———. "Lc. xxiv 12: Les témoins du texte occidental." In *Miscellanea neotestamentica: Studia ad Novum Testamentum praesertim pertinentia* . . . , ed. T. Baarda et al. NovTSup 47–48. Leiden: Brill, 1978. 1:45–60. ———. "Les Femmes au Tombeau: Étude de la Rédaction Matthéenne (Matt. XXVIII:1–10)." *NTS* 15 (1969) 168–90. ———. "The Uncorrected Historic Present in Lk. xxiv. 12." *ETL* 48 (1972) 548–53. ———. "*parakupsas blepei*: Lc 24,12 et Jn 20,5." *ETL* 53 (1977) 113–52. ———. "Jn 20,1–10 et les Synoptiques." *ETL* 53 (1977) 430–45. ———. "*apēlthen pros heauton*: Lc 24,12 et Jn 20,10." *ETL* 54 (1978) 104–18. ———. "Marc 16, 1–8: Tradition et Rédaction." *ETL* 56 (1980) 56–88. ———. "John and the Synoptics: The Empty Tomb Stories." *NTS* 30 (1984) 161–87, esp. 172–79. **Niemann, F.-J.** "Die Erzählung vom leeren Grab bei Markus." *ZKT* 101 (1979) 188–99. **Oberlinner, L.** "Die Verkündigung der Auferweckung Jesu im geöfneten und leeren Grab." *ZNW* 73 (1982) 159–82. **Oppermann, R.** "Eine Beobachtung in bezug auf das Problem des Markusschluss." *BibNot* 40 (1987) 24–29. **Paulsen, H.** "Mk. XVI. 1–8." *NovT* 22 (1980) 138–75. **Perrin, N.** "The use of (*para*) *didonai* in Connection with the Passion of Jesus in the New Testament." In *Der Ruf Jesu und die Antwort der Gemeinde: Exegetische Untersuchungen.* FS J. Jeremias, ed. E. Lohse et al. Göttingen: Vandenhoeck & Ruprecht, 1970. 204–12. **Plevnik, J.** "'The Eleven and Those with Them' according to Luke." *CBQ* 40 (1978) 205–11. **Reibl, M.** "Die Erzählung vom leeren Grab: Exegetisch-bibeltheologische Hinführung und Ausblick auf die Lesung der Texte in der Osternacht." *BibLit* 59 (1986) 36–46. **Ritt, H.** "Die Frauen und die Osterbotschaft Synopse der Grabesgeschichten (Mk 16,1–8; Mt 27,62–28,15; Lk 24,1–12; Joh 20,1–18)." In *Die Frau im Urchristentum,* ed. G. Dautzenberg, H. Merklein, and D. Müller. QD 95. Freiburg: Herder, 1983. 117–33. **Ross, J. M.** "The Genuineness of Luke 24:12." *ExpTim* 98 (1986–87) 107–8. **Schenke, L.** *Auferstehungsverkündigung und leeres Grab: Eine traditionsgeschichtliche Untersuchung von Mk 16,1–8.* SBS 33. Stuttgart: Katholisches Bibelwerk, 1968. **Scroggs, R.,** and **Groff, K. I.** "Baptism in Mark: Dying and Rising with Christ." *JBL*

92 (1973) 531–48. **Smith, J. J.** "The Resurrection and the Empty Tomb." *Landas* 1 (1987) 143–64. **Smith, R. H.** "New and Old in Mark 16:1–8." *CTMonth* 43 (1972) 518–27. **Stauffer, E.** "Der Auferstehungsglaube und das leere Grab." *ZRGG* 6 (1954) 146–48. **Stein, R. H.** "Was the Tomb Really Empty?" *JETS* 20 (1977) 23–29. **Stoldt, H.-H.** *Geschichte und Kritik der Markushypothese.* 2nd ed. Giesen/Basel: Brunnen, 1986. 239–64. **Walker, D. A.** "Resurrection, Empty Tomb and Easter Faith." *ExpTim* 101 (1990) 172–75. **Wallace, R. W.** "ὄρθρος." *TAPA* 119 (1989) 201–7. **Wilckens, U.** "Die Perikope vom leeren Grabe Jesu in der nachmarkinischen Traditionsgeschichte." In *Festschrift für Friedrich Smend.* Berlin: Merseburger, 1963. 30–41. **Whitaker, D.** "What Happened to the Body of Jesus?" *ExpTim* 81 (1969–70) 307–11.

Translation

[1] *On the first day of the week very early in the morning, they came to the tomb[a] carrying the [anointing] spices[b] which they had prepared.* [2] [c] *They found the stone rolled away from the tomb,* [3] *and going inside they did not find the body of the Lord Jesus.[d]* [4] *It happened that, while they were puzzling about this,[e] two men appeared to them in gleaming garments.* [5] *As they [the women] became fearful and bowed their faces to the ground,[f] they [the men] said to them, "Why do you seek the living one among the dead?* [6] *He is not here, but he has been raised![g] Remember how he spoke to you while he was still in Galilee,* [7] *saying[h] that it was necessary for the Son of Man to be delivered up into the hands of sinful[i] men and crucified and to rise on the third day."* [8] *Then they remembered his words.* [9] *They returned from the tomb[j] and announced all these things to the Eleven and all those with them.*

[10] *It was[k] Mary Magdalene and Joanna and Mary [the mother] of James, and the rest with them.[l] They kept on saying these things to the the Apostles,* [11] *but[m] these words seemed to them [only] to be nonsense, and they would not believe them.* [12] *But Peter got up and ran to the tomb and, peering in, he saw only[n] the linen cloths, and he went off to his home wondering about what had happened.[o]*

Notes

[a] There is uncertainty about whether the word for "tomb" here is μνῆμα (A B D G H L W Θ Ψ *f*[1,13] etc.) or μνημεῖον (𝔭[75] ℵ C F Δ X etc.). The latter is probably the correct reading for Mark. Luke may conform the Markan term for "tomb" here to that which he used in 23:53; the Markan term is used in v 56, as in 24:2, 9, 12, 22, 24.

[b] ἀρώματα, "[anointing] spices," is omitted by D it sy[s,c]. (For chap. 24 all significant Western readings will be reported because of the importance Western readings have had at a number of key points in the Lukan text of chap. 24.)

[c] D 070 c sa begins with ἐλθοῦσαι, "having come."

[d] "Of the Lord Jesus" is missing from D it.

[e] ἰδού (lit. "behold") has not been rendered in the translation.

[f] D c r[1] restructure the syntax here: coordinated gen. absolutes become a nominative participle and a finite verb, and a linking οἱ δέ is provided to the following clause about the angels.

[g] D it omit this pair of clauses.

[h] Omitted by D c etc.

[i] Omitted by D it.

[j] "From the tomb" is omitted by D it.

[k] Gr. ἦσαν δέ. Omitted by A D W etc.

[l] Many texts (ℵ[2] Θ Ψ 33 69 etc.) respond to the syntax difficulty at this point by adding αἱ, "who." 157 provides καί, "and," as a connective.

[m] Gr. καί.

[n] κείμενα, "lying," is intruded from John 20:6 in the text of A L Θ Ψ 0114 0299 etc. The sense becomes "lying by themselves."

° V 12 is omitted by D it but is found in all other texts, including P^{75}. The Johannine link has in the past been thought to count against the authenticity of the verse. The reading in P^{75} has led to a reevaluation, and there seems now to be a broad consensus that the verse is original (see esp. the considerations adduced by Muddiman [*ETL* 48 (1972) 542–48]). (In chap. 24 the Western text seems to have been concerned to be as short as possible. Quite a bit that did not strike the scribe as essential seems to have been deleted [see textual notes throughout the chapter]).

Form/Structure/Setting

For the close linking of the passion narrative and the resurrection narrative, see at 22:1–2 (the women now set out to complete what they had begun in 23:55–56). For the opening unit, the relationship with the Markan account is close (Mark 16:1–8), but for the remainder of the resurrection narrative, Luke will go his own way. The recurring links with the Johannine tradition that have marked the passion narrative are also to be found in the resurrection narrative.

There is evidence of a high degree of attention to structure in the materials of chap. 24 and especially in those of the Emmaus account. There is elaborate cross-referencing through the repetition of motifs and sets of words, sometimes with an inverted order at the point of repetition (see *Comment* on particular texts for additional details). A number of attempts have been made to identify a chiastic macro-structure in this, either for the Emmaus account or for a larger portion of the chapter (see Léon-Dufour, *Résurrection*, 212–13 [ET 161–62]; Schnider and Stenger, *BZ* 16 [1972] 94–114; D'Arc, *NRT* 99 [1977] 62–76; id., *Les pèlerins*; Meynet, *NRT* 100 [1978] 233–49; Guillaume, *Luc intèrprète*, 75–76; Dussaut, *RB* 94 [1987] 161–213; Rousseau, *SR* 18 [1989] 67–79; and cf. Dupont, "Les disciples," 167–95 [see *Bibliography* for 24:13–35 for items not found in *Bibliography* above]). Uncontroversial is the chiastic (concentric) pattern linking the beginning and the end (finishing with v 33a) of the Emmaus account: parallels are to be noted between vv 13, 33a (from and to Jerusalem); vv 14, 32 (conversations between the two travelers); vv 15, 31b (Jesus joins and leaves them); vv 16, 31a (not able, then able, to recognize him).

To my mind, the most persuasive attempt to outline and defend a chiastic structuring for the whole chapter is that of Meynet, building upon the work of D'Arc (to be precise, the main chiasm proposed by Meynet formally covers only vv 4–46[48], leaving the framing verses as introduction and conclusion outside the chiasm).

Meynet, noting the clear parallelism between v 22–23 (without the final clause) and v 24 and the suitability of the final clause of v 23 ("who say that he is alive") for an emphatic center point for the chiasm, filled in the remainder of the structuring of the Emmaus account by setting "concerning Jesus of Nazareth" of v 19 in parallel with the final phrase of v 27 ("the things concerning himself") and vv 19b–21 in parallel with vv 25–27 (in each of which the things *concerning Jesus* are elaborated). That leaves only vv 17–19a and 28–30, and here I think Meynet goes wrong: he leaves vv 17–19a out of the structure altogether and combines vv 28–30 with v 31, in order to set this in parallel with vv 15 and 16 combined. If the structure is to succeed, it is surely necessary to establish some equivalence between vv 17–19a and vv 28–30 (Dussaut [*RB* 94 (1987) 192–93] does so, but a little artificially, in his development of Meynet's structure). What are the possible links? In both, the idea of staying somewhere surfaces; these two small blocks of text embrace all the interactive dialogue with Jesus in the account (as distinct from the more extended statements in vv 19b–24 and 25–27); in both Jesus deliberately misleads (in v 18 the disciples think Jesus does not know, and in v 28 they are made to think that Jesus intends to travel on further); in as much as v 30 alludes to the Last Supper, it contains an echo of part of "what has happened in [Jerusalem] in these days" (v 18). There is probably enough here to allow the structure to succeed, but this is the least transparent part of the structure.

Meynet also takes into the structure the text before and after the main body of the Emmaus account. Vv 33b–34 share with vv 9c–12 the roles of the Eleven and those with them (in v 9: "all the rest") and of Simon/Peter. (While Meynet identifies a separate parallelism between v 35 and the announcement statement in v 9b, I think it best to include these, so that the parallel includes the contrast between the women being disbelieved and the Emmaus disciples being [by implication] believed, which is to be linked to the progress in the experience of Peter from the former to the latter. It would also be possible to give the statements about Peter their own place in the chiasm [as Dussaut does]). Finally, Meynet identifies the rather large units vv 4b–7(8) and vv 36–46(48) as providing the opening and closing elements of the chiastic structure. Though the links are strong (including an impressive amount of sequential parallelism), the units are rather large, and vv 39–43 make no contribution to the links. Consequently, this may be the least satisfactory part of the structure (while Dussaut's alternative, which breaks up these units and carries the chiasm back to v 1 and on to v 53, allows for a nice paralleling of the arrival of the angels and the departure of Jesus to heaven, it is less convincing in the end).

Meynet also identifies two "themes" as having structural importance. The first asserts that Jesus is alive. It is found as the center point of the chiasm and earlier in v 5 and again in v 34 (related statements in predictive form are found at vv 7, 26, 46). The second deals with the pre-announcement of the passion and resurrection by Jesus and the Scriptures. This theme also occurs three times: straightforwardly in vv 6–7 (foretold by Jesus) and vv 44–48 (foretold by Jesus and the Scriptures) and in a rather more complex manner in the combined effect of vv 19b–21 and 25–27 (foretold by Scriptures [the parts here are bracketed by "the things concerning," while the parallelism between vv 25–27 and vv 44–48 is underlined by the way vv 25–27 are referred to in v 32 (cf. v 45)]). There may also be significance in the way that the failure to find the body is mentioned and then reiterated in the first half of the chiasm (vv 5, 23), while in the second half (vv 30, 35), the breaking of bread is mentioned and then reiterated (the equation of body and bread in 22:19 and the fact that Jesus is made known in the breaking of the bread in 24:30–31 and v 35 suggest that the similarity is more than fortuitous). We should also notice the element of parallelism involved in the way in which the echoes of the feeding of the five thousand (9:10–117) in 24:29–30 are enhanced by the role of the fish in vv 41–43. Finally, there is probably significance in the way that return statements (with the same verb and, in each case, in the penultimate position in the pericope) are provided for (*i*) the women (v 9a); (*ii*) the Emmaus disciples (v 33a); and (*iii*) the disciples returning from the ascension (v 52).

A number of scholars have noted parallels between Luke 24 and Luke 1–2. While some have tried to establish precise correspondences, it seems to me best simply to note that a series of features should ensure that the reader will have his attention returned to the first major section of the Gospel as he reads the last major section (shared focus on Jerusalem; role of Gabriel, other angels, and inspired speakers paralleled by that of angels and the resurrected Jesus [the human reactions are also parallel]; one recounts the origins of the human life of Jesus, the other his departure to heaven; both have an initially vain search for Jesus [or his body]; both are highly structured pieces of writing, with a more problematical relationship to the reporting of historical events than is the case with the chapters between; in both there is a major emphasis on things being [in various ways] in accord with the Scriptures; the Infancy Gospel begins with worship in the temple, while chap. 24 ends with worship in the temple; only in these two sections is there blessing of God; both sections are marked by joy; the hopes of 24:21 strongly echo those expressed in chaps. 1–2).

None of the Gospels attempts to give any account of the actual resurrection (*Gospel of Peter* 35–42 fills this gap). The four Gospels all report the discovery of the empty tomb (by women, with some variation as to which; but John and Luke, if 24:12 is original, have Peter [and John adds "the beloved disciple"] also going to visit the empty tomb). Apart from Mark (who only *anticipates* a meeting with the risen Jesus in Galilee), all of the Gospels also report encounters with the risen Jesus. But although there are any number of common motifs between accounts, no two of the accounts of an encounter with the risen Lord are straightforwardly versions of the same episode. I will discuss the appearances first and then turn to the tradition of the discovery of the empty tomb.

Each of the Gospels with resurrection appearances has "informal" encounters with Jesus prior to any meeting with the Twelve (Eleven). Matthew and John agree in having Mary Magdalene be the first to encounter the risen Lord (in Matthew not alone), but the circumstances and content of the encounter are quite different, except for the agreement that a message is to be conveyed to "my brothers."

Matthew reports a decisive encounter of the Eleven with Jesus on a mountain in Galilee, which has significant correspondences with Luke's report of an encounter in Jerusalem of the Eleven and "those who were with them" (Luke's "disbelieved" corresponds to Matthew's "doubted"; both are commissioning accounts that point to a mission to "all nations"; the assurance of Jesus' perpetual presence corresponds to the sending of the promised "power from on high"; if "worshiped him" is original in Luke 24:52 and if we include the departure scene in vv 50–53 in the comparison, then there is a further shared motif; if we cast the net rather wider, then a correspondence between the "glory" of v 26 [to be reported to the Eleven] and Matthew's "all authority" may be possible). Luke's account in Acts 1:6–11(12) is in some sense a reiteration of the Luke 24 account. It adds a mountain setting to the motifs shared with Matthew; in the place of Matthew's promise of the abiding presence of Jesus there is now, along with the promise of power, the promise of Jesus' future return.

John agrees with Luke in having Jesus (first) meet the disciples in Jerusalem on Easter day, and the respective accounts have further significant correspondences (if original at Luke 24:36, both have "peace to you" as initial greeting; the role of the arms [or hands] and feet in Luke 24:39 corresponds to the role of the arms [or hands] and side in John 20:20 [more so if Luke 24:40 is original, since then there are seven sequential words in common]; in both Luke and John, the sight is received with joy; both Luke and John have commissioning scenes; both anticipate roles involving the forgiveness of sins; the promised "power from on high" corresponds to the giving of the Holy Spirit (Holy Spirit language is used in the Acts 1 version); if the scope is extended to include the meeting a week later at which Thomas was present, then we may want to compare John's "faithless" with Luke's "disbelieved."

John's account of the miraculous catch and the beach breakfast is quite distinct from Luke's account of the road-to-Emmaus encounter, but both involve a meal with Jesus (which probably in each case echoes the feeding of the five thousand) and some kind of initial uncertainty about the identity of Jesus (John's account seems also to involve some kind of commissioning of Peter, which may be compared to the other commissioning accounts). John's account of the appearance to Mary Magdalene also includes the initial inability to recognize Jesus. Both John's beach breakfast and Luke's meeting with the Eleven and those with them use ἔστη ("stood") to introduce Jesus into the episode and have Jesus asking "Do you have anything to eat?" (different Greek for "eat").

The bare list of resurrection appearances in 1 Cor 15:5–8 offers no motifs for comparison. But we should note that it fails to include a first appearance to the women; that it reports an appearance to Peter prior to any appearance to the Twelve (Paul presumably means the remaining eleven of the original twelve), which has a correspondence only in Luke 24:34 (but cf. the curious pattern in John 20:4–8); that it distinguishes an appearance to the Twelve from one "to more than five hundred brothers [and sisters]," which cannot be correlated with the Gospel accounts; that it notes an appearance to James that has left no mark on the Gospel accounts; that (apart from Paul's addition of himself to the list) it finishes with an appearance to "all the apostles" (which seems to indicate a broader group than the Twelve), which again cannot be correlated with the Gospel accounts.

How are we to interpret such a tangled pattern? It is clearly important both for Paul and for the Gospels (Mark excepted for lack of relevant materials) that the risen Jesus appeared on more than one occasion and to different people. Paul shows considerable interest in the order of the appearances, the Gospels less so. Paul provides no location, timing, or content for the meetings; the Gospels provide all three, but with such variations as to make the use of their materials problematic for precise historical reconstruction. While a harmonization allowing a separate identity to each of the many different appearances is by no means impossible, the pattern of shared motifs identified above makes it quite unlikely that this is the best way to proceed. Differences between the respective Gospel accounts seem more likely to reflect, to some extent, different streams of parallel tradition but sometimes as much, or even more so, different redactional strategies on the part of the different evangelists.

Various attempts have been made to classify formally the resurrection appearances. Dodd ("Appearances," 9–25) distinguished two main types: concise narratives constructed according to a fixed pattern and leading up to a saying of the Lord, and circumstantial narratives that do not follow a pattern and are concerned with details and circumstances. Léon-Dufour (*Resurrection*, 80–104) distinguishes a "Jerusalem type" and a "Galilean type." The Jerusalem type is structured by the "unexpected presence" of Jesus, a recognition motif, and the entrusting of a mission and is to be found not only in Luke 24:34–53 and John 20:19–29 but also in Matt 28:9–10 par. John 20:16–17 and in John 21:1–17. A meal setting was also normally part of the pattern, which suggests that the form may have arisen in a eucharistic context. The single exemplar of the Galilean type is Matt 28:18–20. It lacks both the unexpected presence and the recognition motif of the Jerusalem type and has a more developed form of the entrusting with a mission. Léon-Dufour maintains that this second type is modeled upon OT vocation stories, comparing them in particular with Exod 3:6–12 and Jer 1:5–8 (self-presentation, mission, promise). Alsup (*Post-Resurrection Appearance*) labors at length to reduce the Gospel resurrection appearance accounts to a single traditional "Gattung," which, he argues, is based upon the anthropomorphic strand of OT theophany representation (see Gen 18; Exod 3–4; Judg 6; 13; 1 Sam 3). Each of these attempts is insightful, up to a point (and especially that of Léon-Dufour, but he exaggerates the distinctiveness of Matt 28:16–20; this can be seen especially when distinctive features of Matt 28:18–20 are correlated with parallel distinctives in his presentation of the pre-resurrection Jesus: it is rather a "heavenly" Jesus who appears in Matthew, but Matthew's historical Jesus has also been somewhat heavenly), but none of them carries full conviction.

The variation in the Gospel versions of the terms in which the risen Lord commissioned the disciples shows that no fixed form of words was remembered in the tradition; rather, in each case, the shared conviction that the impetus and authority for the early church mission had come from the risen Lord was given expression by the evangelists in terms of their own theological understanding (and drawing on strands within the tradition). It is also unlikely that the commissioning was correlated in the tradition exclusively with one particular appearance of Jesus: the decision by Matthew and Luke (and to a lesser extent John) to tell the story in this way is no more than a sensible presentation strategy.

The question of the relationship between appearances in Jerusalem and Galilee requires a little more discussion. On the face of it, the angelic message in 16:7 would leave no room for initial Jerusalem appearances (but Matthew manages to squeeze one in: 28:9–10), while Luke 24:49 would leave no room for subsequent Galilean appearances. Probably the best harmonization would be achieved by locating the decisive initial appearance(s) in Galilee (perhaps following an appearance to one or more of the women on Easter morning, and even an appearance to the Emmaus disciples, and just possibly an appearance to Peter [do the Gospel records fail to narrate an initial appearance to Peter precisely because, in the aftermath of Peter's denial of Jesus, it gained no credence prior to other appearances (Luke 24:34 to the contrary)?]), with a subsequent set of appearances in Jerusalem, to which the disciple band had returned for the feast of Pentecost (cf. Moule, *NTS* 4 [1957–58] 58–61). Would the tradition manifest the confidence that it does in an *Easter Day* rising simply on the basis of a tradition about the discovery on that day of the empty tomb and without the support of specifically Easter Day appearances? While both Galilee and Jerusalem function symbolically (return to Galilee marks a fresh beginning [on a new footing] for the mission of Jesus; remaining in Jerusalem allows the Christian mission to emerge from the very heart of Jewish faith), it seems to me quite unlikely that either of the locations for resurrection appearances has been generated solely out of the needs of such a symbolism.

There has been an extensive and increasingly sophisticated discussion about what precisely was the nature of the experience of these early disciples of the risen Jesus. This is a discussion that must be largely left to one side here. Only a few comments can be offered.

It can hardly be doubted that some powerful and life-transforming experience overtook the early disciples. The beginnings of the early Christian movement cannot credibly be built on a fraudulent claim on their part, or on a delusion built up solely upon the disappearance of the body of Jesus, or upon a Jesus who only nearly died, or upon a merely theoretical conviction that Jesus must have been vindicated by God beyond his tragic death.

While one can understand and commend scholarly caution about using the Gospel appearance accounts naively to seek to gain access to the appearance experiences of the earliest disciple, the strong tendency in the scholarship to seek to elucidate these earliest experiences almost solely out of Paul's account of his own experience seems to me to be fundamentally flawed. Paul admits in 1 Cor 15:8–9 that his own experience was *sui generis* (while claiming that it, nevertheless, "counted"). For Paul, his experience was not to be correlated with any relationship with the pre-resurrection Jesus. That Paul's experience took place not in the aftermath of the crucifixion but years later offers its own strong warning against too readily identifying the experiences. It seems to me that we must approach the appearance experiences of the earliest Christians primarily through the Gospel accounts, albeit with all necessary caution. (See further at 9:28–36.)

What are the core elements of the Gospel reports? We should probably include the following: only those who were associated with the disciple community experienced appearances of the risen Jesus (too much should not be made of this in connection with the question of the "objectivity" or not of the appearances, since in 1 Cor 15:5–8 the presence of James in the list takes us beyond the disciple band, as does, in a distinctive but notable manner, the case of Paul); Jesus turns up unexpectedly; his identity is not immediately obvious but can be confidently affirmed as the encounter progresses (sometimes in terms of his being the same person as the crucified one); the experience confirms to the disciples that Jesus had come through death and moved beyond (this is clearly viewed as part of Jesus' life story and not simply as an experience of the disciples); though Jesus is experienced as alive once more, there is no expectation of resumption of his previous ministry nor of his availability to the disciples in the way he had been previously (he is implicitly assumed to have moved into some other sphere of existence; apart from Luke 24:51, the accounts either end with Jesus disappearing [exceptionally in Matt 28:10 par. John 20:17, where it is Jesus who is left behind], or they assume a limited time frame for his presence [Matt 28:28 assumes a continuing presence of another kind], without specifying any terminus); the encounter produces a transformation of perspective in the disciples and is generally linked with a sense of being commissioned for a mission task. Of these elements, the identity of the risen one as the crucified one is most vulnerable to being considered part of a reflective interpretive framework rather than part of the core (but this is not the case for the move from uncertainty to certainty about the identity of the one being encountered). Otherwise, these core elements seem to be more primitive than any formulated Christian understanding of the resurrection of Jesus. Beyond these elements, the significance of meals in the pre-Easter ministry could point in the direction of including in the core the meal setting of a number of the appearances; on the other hand, that in the developing church the living Christ was made known to his people in the breaking of the eucharistic bread may count in the opposite direction (of the general commissioning accounts only Acts 1:4 offers a meal setting, and then only if συναλιζόμενος is to be given the sense "eating" [but cf. also Luke 24:41–43]).

The question is often raised concerning whether the risen Jesus appeared to his disciples from heaven or from earth. But to answer such a question calls for a level of interpretation of the experience that goes beyond what is available in the core elements, and it may ultimately set the alternatives inappropriately. The resurrection appearances would seem to have constituted some kind of transitional phenomenon. The resurrected Jesus could no longer be thought of as having a continuous history in the spatio-temporal sphere, but neither had he decisively withdrawn to a heavenly sphere as would later be the case. His proper realm at this stage was in a resurrection sphere of existence not immediately identified with either the heavenly or the earthly; from this resurrection sphere, he would appear to have had access back to the spatio-temporal sphere and on into the heavenly sphere. The Jesus who was being encountered was the Jesus whom the disciples had known, rather than an alien, transcendent Jesus, but there was, nonetheless, a certain resurrection otherness to him.

How close are the history-of-religion analogies for the kind of picture that emerges from the core elements of the Gospel accounts? Relevant traditions might be (*i*) the calling up of Samuel in 1 Sam 28 (visible only to the medium and appearing as "a god coming up out of the earth" [Luke 24:37–39 seems concerned to eliminate such an understanding of the appearances of Jesus; and cf. Philostratus, *Life of Apollonius* 8.12]); (*ii*) the prospect of the return of Elijah in Mal 4:5 (MT 3:23; underlying his return is his translation to heaven in 2 Kgs 2:11, where, in the logic of Malachi, he stands available for some future role); (*iii*) the hoped-for eschatological resurrection of Dan 12:2 (this represents, for those already dead, an anticipation in the deliverance at that time of God's People or recall at that time for shaming and judgment); (*iv*) the restoration to life of the widow's son by Elijah in 1 Kgs 17:17–24 and of the Shunamite's son by Elisha in 2 Kgs 4:18–37 (these exalt the significance of the prophet; the role of the son in each case is quite passive [cf. 2 Kgs 13:21]; the role of such resuscitation in the ministry of Jesus is not dissimilar and has further parallels in Jewish and Greco-Roman sources [see at 7:11–17]); (*v*) the view held by some that Jesus was one of the old prophets come back again (see at Luke 9:7–9; this view would seem to have involved the belief that these prophets had been translated to heaven after death [see discussion at 16:22; 23:43 (in the case of Lazarus this is perhaps seen as involving the taking of the body, but in the case of Jesus and the penitent criminal this would seem not to be the case)]; the role of Moses and Elijah in 9:30–31 may fit in here, but the appearances there may have a proleptic character [see at 9:30]); (*vi*) the view that Jesus was John returned to life (Mark 6:14); (*vii*) the tradition that Philostratus (*Life of Apollonius* 8.31–32) knows of Apollonius being translated to heaven and of a dream appearance (continuing upon waking?) that convinces a skeptical young man about the immortality of the (disembodied) soul (only here do we come at all close to a parallel to the Gospel motif of demonstration of [unexpected] aliveness [an appearance linked to the question of the survival of the souls is also found in Lucian, *Philopseudes* 27–28]; *Life of Apollonius* 7.41–8.13 makes a somewhat different use of the motif of unexpected aliveness in the context of Apollonius' unexpected appearance to friends after they had all but given him up for dead after he had gone on trial for his life before the emperor); (*viii*) apotheosis traditions involving the disappearance of the person (or the body) and the confirmation of apotheosis by means of an appearance (Romulus, Aristeas of Proconnesus, Cleomedes of Astpaleia, Alcmene, Peregrinus Proteus [see Alsup, *Appearance Stories*, 224–29, for texts and convenient outlines]).

Clearly there are some points of genuine similarity in these traditions, but there is no question of subsuming the Gospel tradition under any of these headings or of deriving it from an amalgam of a number of these strands of tradition (Ehrhardt, ["The Disciples of Emmaus," *NTS* 10 (1964) 195–201] argues not unreasonably that, given the relative datings and the historical circumstances, similarities between Philostratus' account of the life of Apollonius and the Gospel tradition about Jesus involve dependence of the former upon the latter).

The Lukan understanding of the significance of the resurrection of Jesus will emerge as the passages of chap. 24 are analyzed. At this point, a number of features of his understanding that emerge more clearly in Acts than in the Gospel will be noted. For Luke, the resurrection is a divine overturning of a faulty human verdict upon Jesus (2:23–24; 3:13–15; 5:30; 13:29–30). The resurrection makes clear the divine affirmation of Jesus as both Lord and Christ (2:36). The resurrection was a necessity because of the impossibility of death keeping this particular person in its grip (2:24); because of who he was, "his flesh" could not be left to "see corruption" (2:31). The resurrection means that there is a living Jesus in whose name (and it is a power to be reckoned with) the disciples are able to proclaim and heal (3:15–16; 4:10). The resurrection is the public assurance that Jesus is the man appointed by God to judge the world in the name of God (17:31; cf. 10:40–42). Though in many ways unique, the resurrection of Jesus is nonetheless the kind of resurrection that, according to Pharisaic piety, was the prospect for all (23:6–9; 24:15, 21; 26:8). Possibly in 4:2 the resurrection of Jesus is made the basis for the resurrection hope of others (cf. 26:23).

We turn our attention now to 24:1–12 and the discovery of the empty tomb, addressing first the question of Lukan source(s). For vv 1–9, there is broad scholarly agreement that Luke's text is primarily his editing of Mark 16:1–8 but no agreement about whether Luke's text also reflects a second source or at least further elements of oral tradition.

There is a series of minor agreements with Matthew that can be quite satisfactorily accounted for as independent redaction by Matthew and Luke, but a couple of places are suggestive of more: the possible echo of Matt 28:1 in Luke 23:54 has been discussed there; Matthew's καθὼς εἶπεν, "just as he said," would offer an excellent anchor point for the development that Luke begins μνήσθητε ὡς ἐλάλησεν, "remember how he said"; Matthew and Luke agree in having the women report what they had seen to the (other) disciples (there is a shared use of ἀπαγγέλλειν τοῖς, "announce to the," and the use of τρέχειν, "run," for Peter's visit to the tomb may echo Matthew's for the women's departure from the tomb [τρέχειν is used of the woman's departure by John as well]).

When the Johannine account is added to the picture, some other suggestive contacts may be noticed: the name of Mary Magdalene is introduced at the same point by Matthew and John; Matthew, Luke, and John seem to agree against Mark (but without coincidence of language) that the arrival at the tomb was earlier than sunrise; the three agree against Mark in reporting nothing of the women's concern over how to remove the stone; John's βλέπει τὸν λίθον ἠρμένον ἐκ τοῦ μνημείου, "sees the stone having been removed from the tomb," parallels in structure Luke's εὗρον τὸ λίθον ἀποκεκυλισμένον ἀπὸ τοῦ μνημείου, "found the stone having been rolled away from the tomb"; Luke and John both have two men/angels; it is just possible that Jesus' question in John to Mary Magdalene, τίνα ζητεῖς, "whom do you seek," and the τί ζητεῖτε, "why do you seek," of the Lukan men echo a common source. (There may be yet another John/Matthew link: an argument has been mounted for Johannine dependence upon Mark on the basis of the similarity between ὅπου ἔκειτο τὸ σῶμα τοῦ Ἰησοῦ, "where the body of Jesus lay [in context "had lain"]," in John 20:12 [location of angels] and ὅπου ἔθηκαν αὐτόν, "where they placed him," in Mark 16:6 [angel's words about empty grave place], but the link is closer to the Matt 28:6 parallel, which has ὅπου ἔκειτο.)

The Johannine links gain in significance because of the strong link between Luke 24:12 and the Johannine account (see discussion below). The likelihood that we are right to accumulate hints from a Matthew/Luke comparison and a John/Luke comparison is made greater by the tradition of an appearance of Jesus to women/a woman at the tomb shared between Matthew and John. Against this background, other agreements that could be accounted for on redactional grounds may after all reflect source selection instead. The case for more than a single source is not decisive, but it does seem more likely than not that a second source was involved (of course, for those who think John used Matthew and Luke and Luke used Matthew, there is no case).

Luke 24:12 is defended as an original part of Luke's text in *Notes* above. There is solid scholarly agreement that there is a source link between 24:12 and John 20:3–10. While there is little modern support for the view that Luke used John here, a number are convinced that John had access to the Lukan text here. Neirynck (*NTS* 30 [1984] 161–87; *ETL* 48 [1972] 548–53; 53 [1977] 113–52; 54 [1978] 104–18) has sought to strengthen the case for this view by arguing that Luke 24:12 is a piece of free Lukan composition and was therefore inaccessible to John apart from the text of the Gospel of Luke. Neirynck is probably right that Luke sets in parallel the experience of the women and that of Peter, but he fails to demonstrate free Lukan composition (his explanation for Luke's use of the [surprising in Luke] historic present βλέπει, "sees" [with παρακύψας, "having bent down/having glanced"], is forced [but his view that παρακύψας is likely to have a different sense in each of the respective Gospels has much to commend it]; it is hard to believe that in free composition Luke would not have provided more obvious vocabulary overlap between his paralleled episodes). Since nothing that is Lukan is carried over to John's rendering, I think it altogether more likely that the two accounts draw upon a common tradition (closer to the Lukan form, but possibly with company for Peter [note Luke's tendency to accentuate the role of Peter, and cf. Luke 24:24 (but note Muddiman's explanation of the plural as a vague plural of anonymity to parallel that for the women [*ETL* 48 (1972) 547]). Claudel (*La confession*, 80–81) offers significant arguments for believing that the tradition of the Petrine visit to the tomb has always existed in connection with that of the women's visit to the tomb.

There is great divergence among the analyses of the tradition history of Mark
16:1–8. At one extreme, there are those who are confident that Mark had no
source materials and is responsible for the free composition of vv 1–8 (e.g.,
Crossan, "Empty Tomb," 135–52), and at the other extreme, it is maintained that
all or almost all of the text is pre-Markan (e.g., Pesch, "Der Schluss," 365–410, for
whom only possibly the list of names in v 1 is redactional). If I am right to think
that the other evangelists drew at this point upon a second source, then we can
eliminate free composition by Mark (in any case, almost all those who have addressed the Markan source question find tensions in the account that suggest the
combination of tradition and redaction).

The main lines along which scholars have argued in seeking to isolate the pre-
Markan (or most original) tradition are (*i*) to identify those elements that disturb
the inner unity of the Markan account; (*ii*) to eliminate those elements that may
have been introduced to unite the tradition in Mark 16:1–8 to the burial tradition;
(*iii*) to determine the relationship of the present Markan account to characteristic Markan vocabulary and theological motifs (with particular attention to possible
deliberate cross-reference); (*iv*) to fashion a lowest-common-denominator account
out of the present Gospel accounts; (*v*) to remove any elements that may have
arisen in the context of early Christian apologetic; (*vi*) to reconstruct an account
that could stand up to historical scrutiny (i.e., removal of obvious miraculous or
supernatural elements); and (*vii*) to bring to bear form-critical considerations in
order to identify those Markan elements that disturb the identified form. No report can be made here of this considerable labor, beyond indicating that,
unfortunately, nothing like a consensus has emerged. I simply offer the following
as my own view.

Beyond what are primarily linguistic changes, I think it most likely that Mark
has introduced (repeated) the names of the women; that he is responsible for
the buildup for the mysterious removal of the stone (so: v 3 and the last clause of
v 4); and that he is responsible for v 7 from or after "and to Peter" (the content of
the women's messenger role). Beyond that, Mark may have played some role in
modifying the time statements, and, just possibly, he is responsible for the women's
silence in v 8. It seems to me most likely that the characteristic features of an
"apocalyptic revelation" belong to the most primitive form of the account. There
is, however, a second approach to source reconstruction that deserves serious
consideration.

It is just possible that Mark is combining a tradition of a meeting with an angelic figure at the tomb, by one or more of the women, with a separate tradition
of the discovery of the empty tomb. If this is the case, it is likely that the tradition
of an angelic encounter was only minimally spelled out (cf. John 20:11–13, where
much of what is present is secondary development; in John an angelic declaration that Jesus has been raised [perhaps: "Whom do you seek? Jesus (or he?) has
been raised"] was probably lost in the juxtaposition of the encounter with the
angels and the encounter with Jesus). Mark will have built up his account of the
encounter out of standard apocalyptic imagery, the tradition of 14:28 (perhaps
with a touch of influence from 14:51–52), and material in his empty tomb tradition that originally related to the women's own observations (perhaps something
like: "they saw the place where they had placed [standing for the passive] him
and Jesus [or the body or he?] was not there").

How confidently can we affirm the historicity of the empty tomb? There is no need here to consider the alternatives that have been considered in popular apologetics (wrong tomb; body removed and hidden by the disciples; body removed by Joseph of Arimathea without the knowledge of the disciples; etc.). The serious alternative to historicity is that the empty tomb tradition is actually a secondary reflection of a theological conviction that Jesus had been raised from the dead. How are we to decide between an origin in historical experience and an origin in theological conviction? While no full discussion can be offered, here are some of the relevant considerations.

Though the two underlying sources identified above take us back beyond the Markan account, there is not the range of primitive attestation for the empty tomb that there is for the resurrection appearances (despite the confident claims made on both sides, one cannot confidently place Paul on one side or the other of this argument [though almost certainly his belief in the resurrection would have assumed an empty tomb]). The second source cannot be sufficiently reconstructed for a decision to be made about whether its origin as a narrative is totally independent of the Markan form.

On balance, it seems likely that the earliest disciples did know the location of the tomb of Jesus (the possibility that his body was not released to Joseph of Arimathea but, rather, buried in a common grave by the Romans is dismissed at 23:50–56 above; a flight by the disciples to Galilee immediately upon the arrest of Jesus is a scholarly construct with no real supporting evidence; some, but only modest, weight can be placed upon the line of tradition that claimed a continuous memory of the location of Jesus' tomb through the early Christian centuries [cf. at 23:53; this line of argumentation would be considerably strengthened if the Markan account does reflect a liturgy used at the tomb site (see esp. Schenke, *Auferstehungsverkündigung*; Delorme, "Resurrection," 85–93; Nauck, *ZNW* 47 [1956] 243–67)]).

The force of the argument that a claim to an empty tomb, if not historical, would have soon been refuted by observation depends for its cogency upon a series of assumptions and has often been overplayed (the resurrection, not the empty tomb, was the focus of Christian proclamation, and some [but I believe wrongly] have questioned whether even resurrection is the most primitive category [see the paragraph above on history of religions comparison for alternative forms in which post-Easter encounters with Jesus could have been understood apart from a physically understood resurrection from the dead]; the argument is only as strong as the case for public knowledge of the location of the tomb [see above]; those for whom the resurrection appearances were "obviously" a nonsense would not bother to seek out refuting evidence [but they might well if significant numbers of the Jewish People were being "led astray" by such claims]; those for whom the tomb was "obviously" empty, because they had met with the risen Christ, would not dream of opening the tomb to check).

While there does not seem to have been any Jewish polemic in which the tomb was claimed not to have been empty, there certainly was a Jewish claim that the body was taken by "Judah the gardener," who later produced it, to the confusion of the early Christians. Though the polemic is preserved only in late sources, the role in Jewish polemic of a gardener who removed the body may go back to early times (see Tertullian, *De Spectaculis* 30; cf. John 20:17). This state of affairs does not count strongly on either side of the argument.

Although in a late Hellenistic context alternative explanations have been offered regarding why a woman/women is/are given the significant role of being prime witness(es) to the emptiness of the tomb and recipient(s) of the angelic proclamation, by far the best explanation for this slightly embarrassing state of affairs (from the point of view of early Christian apologetics) remains that of historical memory (attribution to the women on the basis that only the women were left in Jerusalem after the disciples' flight to Galilee fails if there was no such flight to Galilee; attribution on the basis that only the presence of *women* at the tomb could be readily accounted for [because of their role in Jewish mourning practice] involves a misuse of the evidence concerning Jewish mourning practice; attribution on the basis of the tradition that the women were in close proximity to the crucifixion and involved in the burial has slightly more to commend it; however, as these traditions gain in historical credibility from their capacity to embarrass the early Christian leadership, so does the one under consideration here).

The evidence does seem to favor the historicity of the empty tomb stories, but not with the decisiveness that might be considered desirable. But such is the nature of historical reconstruction! The fact, if not the discovery of, an empty tomb would be very much of a piece with the picture that has emerged above from the core elements of the earliest Gospel tradition of encounter with the risen Jesus.

Despite the focus of our discussion here upon the discovery of the empty tomb, it is important to recognize that the account's own focus is not on the empty tomb but on the encounter with the heavenly messenger(s) who explain(s) the emptiness of the tomb in terms of the announcement of the resurrection of Jesus.

Comment

The attempt by the women to complete the burial niceties for their beloved leader turns out to be not only belated but totally out of keeping with developments that have taken place that morning before they reached the tomb. The body is gone, and heavenly messengers suggest that the women are looking in quite the wrong place for Jesus—reminding them of Jesus' predictions of the passion and resurrection of the Son of Man. The other disciples cannot believe the report, and Peter makes his own vain attempt to locate Jesus (a dead Jesus) at the tomb.

1 While agreeing on "the first day of the week" (lit. "one of the sabbaths"), each of the Gospels has a different time expression. The sense of each would, however, be satisfied by a time of around first light (but Mark has, along with λίαν πρωΐ, "very early," an unexpected ἀνατείλαντος τοῦ ἡλίου, "the sun having risen," which has been suspected of expressing an Easter symbolism). The early morning setting may be reported in conscious connection with the OT tradition of the early morning being the time in which the action of God during the hours of darkness comes to light (cf. Exod 14:24, 37; 2 Kgs 19:35; Pss 30:5; 90:14; 143:8; Isa 37:36; cf. Claudel, *La confession*, 83). Because Luke has the spices prepared before the sabbath, he inadvertently opens up a piece of unfilled time after sunset when the sabbath had ended. The role of the spices in 23:56 is resumed with "carrying the [anointing] spices which they had prepared."

2 As is the case with Matthew and John, Luke has no equivalent to the concern of the Markan women about who will remove the stone (he has not even noted to this point that the tomb was sealed with a stone). It remains uncertain whether we should think in terms of a stone disc flush against the cliff face and rolled in front of the tomb or (perhaps more likely) of something more like a spherical stone plug that was pushed into the tomb opening. The similarity of the Lukan and Johannine syntax suggests that Luke is following a second source here (though the general sense is much the same, only "the stone" and a use of the verb ἀποκυλίζειν, "roll away," are in common with Mark). In John's account, an opened tomb seems to imply a tomb robbed of its body (though no doubt we are to assume that Mary Magalene looked before making her report to Peter and his companion); the Lukan women seem also to find a tomb that has been disturbed. Subsequent experience will require the revision of this opinion: the stone closing the tomb has been supernaturally removed (for the risen Lord? by the risen Lord? by the angels? for the women?).

3 Only "going in" is in common with Mark. In Mark the divine messenger draws attention to the absence of the body, but Luke has the women observe this fact first for themselves. Though Luke quite often in the Gospel speaks of Jesus as "the Lord," only here do we find "the Lord Jesus." This terminology is more prevalent in Acts, occurring seventeen times. The language of failure to find the body will be echoed in v 22; in substance, Peter will have the same experience in v 12. Luke sets in verbal opposition the finding of the stone rolled away and the failure now to find the body.

4 The syntax represented in καὶ ἐγένετο ἐν τῷ . . . καὶ ἰδού (lit. "and it happened while . . . and behold") is thoroughly Lukan (cf. esp. 5:12). The women are perplexed; later, when he has made his own confirmation that the tomb is bodiless, Peter will depart "wondering." Luke's "two" is in common with John 20:12, while ἀστραπτούσῃ, "gleaming," is cognate to Matthew's ἀστραπή, "light[ning]" (but Luke has used the verb in connection with lightning at 17:24). Something of the splendor of God attaches itself to these heavenly visitors. The duality may have to do with legal adequacy as witness (cf. at 10:1). Luke has angelic figures called "men" in Acts 1:10; 10:30. On the Lukan use of ἐφιστάναι, "to appear," cf. at Luke 2:9. Luke is fond of ἐσθής for fine clothing (23:11; Acts 1:10; 10:30; 12:21). Luke may have literary reasons for linking the "two men" of Luke 9:30; 24:4 and Acts 1:10 (each pair comments on decisive steps in the career of Jesus).

5 Only ζητεῖτε, "you [do you] seek[?]," survives of the Markan language. The differences here are all likely to be Lukan (except possibly the question form, which may come from the second source): the Lukan women turn their faces down to avoid the fearsome brightness of the angelic garb (and perhaps in submission); with the question "Why do you seek the living one among the dead?" Luke calls attention to the anomaly of the women coming to anoint a dead Jesus, when he has already risen. (Luke also emphasizes elsewhere the "aliveness" of the risen Jesus [cf. 24:23; Acts 1:3; 25:19]). The reassuring "do not be terrified" has gone (contrast Luke 1:13, 30), and the tone has become rather accusing. The women's ill-advised search has some likeness to that of the search for the ascended Elijah (2 Kgs 2:17–18).

6 The Markan order of the opening clauses is reversed to achieve a more satisfying sequence (as in Matthew; for Luke this creates, as well, a chiasm with

"Why do you seek the living one among the dead?"), and Luke links the clauses with an adversative use of ἀλλά, "but." There is no place any longer for Mark's appeal to (the emptiness of) the place where Jesus' body had lain. Luke replaces Mark's material in which the young man directs the women to take a message to the disciples. Instead, Luke has an angelic appeal to the women to remember something Jesus had said while they were still in Galilee (note that Matthew as well points to Jesus as having spoken earlier of his resurrection).

That "he is not here" is self-evident. That "he has been raised" is both proclamation of the Easter message and explanation of the empty tomb. As in Luke 1, the true state of affairs is elucidated by (a) heavenly messenger(s). Though ἠγέρθη can mean "he has risen" (cf. 11:8; 13:25), in the Lukan frame the more normal passive sense "he has been raised [by God]" is altogether more likely. The angels bear the same witness to the resurrection of Jesus that is to be found in the early Christian preaching (cf. Acts 3:15; 4:10; 5:30; 10:40–42; 13:30–31). For Luke, the call to remember is important because for him the significance of the resurrection is inseparable from Jesus' prior announcement of the necessity of both his suffering and his vindication as Son of Man. Since there is no particular Lukan emphasis upon Galilee as the place of passion prediction, the reference to Galilee here is best seen as prompted by a desire to keep something of the otherwise displaced Markan material (beyond his own positive desire to give emphasis to the passion predictions, Luke needs to delete the Markan material here in order to preserve his schematic concentration in Jerusalem [and environs] of the resurrection experiences and all else that leads into the early life of the Christian church). That Luke wants it to be understood here that the women were recipients of the passion predictions underlines the importance of 8:1–3 in Luke's structuring of his Gospel.

7   The passion prediction of the historical Jesus displaces Mark's angelic message for the disciples (which, however, had its own basis in what Jesus had earlier said). "The Son of Man" is, for emphasis, brought forward, ahead of its clause (cf. Acts 1:2; 13:32–33). For his wording here, Luke draws upon all of his main passion predictions (ὅτι δεῖ τὸν υἱὸν τοῦ ἀνθρώπου, "that the Son of Man must," and καὶ τῇ τρίτῃ ἡμέρᾳ, "and on the third day," are in common with 9:22; 9:44 contributes εἰς χεῖρας ἀνθρώπων, "into the hands of men/people," and a use of the verb παραδιδόναι, "deliver up"; 18:31–32 also uses παραδιδόναι and contributes the use of the verb ἀνιστάναι, "rise" [though this last could have been contributed more exactly by the Markan form of the first passion prediction (8:31)]. For ἁμαρτωλῶν, "sinful/sinners," Luke even draws upon the unused Markan prediction in 14:41. σταυρωθῆναι, "to be crucified," is probably a relic of τὸν ἐσταυρωμένον, "the crucified one," omitted from Luke's version of Mark 16:6. It is now the third day, so the women should have been expecting Jesus to be alive again (Luke achieves prominence for the third day motif by repeating it in vv 21 and 47 and by locating all the action of chap. 24 on the one day).

8   Prompted by the angels, the women remember. Are we to understand that their faith has progressed any further than when these predictions were first given? Dillon (From Eye-Witnesses, 51–52) has argued that the answer is basically no. But in Acts 11:16 a similar remembering provides the key to Peter's understanding of his preceding experience (the imparting of the Holy Spirit [and cf. Luke 22:61]). This suggests that, with memory thus restored and with the assistance of the angelic

revelation, the women are now ready to explain the empty tomb in terms of the gospel message of the resurrection.

9 Luke does not see the purpose of repeating fear language at this point (as Mark does): it is the angels' appearance, not their message, that is terrifying. He takes up again the "return" language that he has already used in connection with the women at 23:56 (displacing Mark's "going out they fled"; "returned" here answers to "came" in v 1 [there will be a *return* of the Emmaus disciples in v 33 and of the disciple band in v 52]). Instead of the Markan silence, Luke (in agreement with Matthew over the use of an aorist form of ἀπαγγέλλειν, "announce") has the women "announce all these things to the Eleven and all the rest" (the other language is Lukan [cf. v 33; Acts 1:26; 2:14; Luke 8:3; 24:10; Acts 2:37]). The Twelve have become Eleven with the defection of Judas; their number will be restored in Acts 1:15–26; cf. 6:2.

10 Luke has delayed until this point his identification of the women involved, having passed over Mark's names in 15:40, 47; 16:1. The women were named at the point where they began their role (8:1–3) and are now named again in connection with the culmination of their role. Luke's names involve some sort of compromise between the Markan set and those whom Luke has himself mentioned at 8:3 (on the Lukan tradition, see further at 8:1–3; the lists agree on Mary Magdalene in first position; Luke continues with his own list for the second name [Joanna] but allows his third name to be displaced by Mark's second [Mary the mother of James]; Mark's third name is dropped; Luke covers the omissions with "and the rest with them").

We should not separate "the rest with them" from the list of names in order to deal with the difficulty in the Lukan syntax (as, e.g., Dillon, *From Eye-Witnesses*, 57–58: the others reinforce the message of the named women). The difficulty is best taken as an indication that "Luke has failed to revise his text correctly" (Marshall, 887). Either Luke forgets the opening "it was" as he continues with "they went on saying," or (perhaps better) there is an asyndeton at this point (Luke may well have been taken up with the playful little chiasm he creates here, which organizes the words from "all these things" in v 9 to "these things" at the end of v 10 (without the verbs) into a chiasm centering on "Joanna" [cf. Dussaut, *RB* 94 (1987) 168]). Best sense is achieved by reading the final clause closely with the following clause in v 11. "Apostles" is probably used here specifically in connection with the early church role of the Apostles as witnesses to the resurrection.

11 Only Luke reports the Apostles' reaction to the report of the women. The formulation is likely to be Lukan, but some traditional basis may be suggested by the use of a similar motif in John 20:25, 27. In the end, the effect of the women's reporting is little different from the Markan silence of the women. Though Luke cannot commend the disregard of this witness by the women to the resurrection of Jesus, it has for him a positive side: the later testimony of the Apostles is that much more impressive because they have been so hard to convince. Though Luke has a high view of women, he reflects here his awareness of the widespread tendency to discount the word of a woman (cf. Josephus, *Ant.* 4.219 on the non-acceptance of legal witness from women [ostensibly as stipulated by the law of God]).

12 Luke draws here on a tradition he shares with John (the two texts agree exactly on ὁ Πέτρος, τὸ μνημεῖον καὶ παρακύψας βλέπει τὰ ὀθόνια, ἀπῆλθεν[ον] πρὸς ἑαυτόν [αὐτούς], "Peter," "the tomb and peered in/looked/bent over and sees the linen cloths," "he[they] departed to his[their] home"). ἔδραμον, "he ran," is found in Matt 28:8, while John 20:2 has the present and v 3 the imperfect of the same verb. ἀναστάς, "got up," and θαυμάζων τὸ γεγονός, "wondering about what had happened" (acc. with θαυμάζων) are likely to be Lukan touches.

Peter, in effect, repeats the discovery of the women (note the minor chiasm linking the coming to the tomb in v 1 and that in v 12) that the tomb is empty. But his spying of the "linen cloths" takes things one step further: anyone who wanted to remove the body would have kept it wrapped in the grave clothes. Like the women, he departs again (but Luke does not conform his source verb here to that used with the women). Peter's wondering corresponds to the puzzlement of the women: as with the women, Peter is not quite sure what has happened.

Luke does not seem to be aware of any tension between his use of σινδών, "a linen cloth," in Luke 23:53 and ὀθόνια, "linen cloths," here. Though the use of both terms is documented for grave clothes, we do not know whether the plural term would necessarily have pointed to a different manner of preparation of the body for burial (ὀθόνια was certainly used in connection with the Egyptian wrapping of mummies, but this practice was not known in Palestine). μόνα can mean "alone" or "only." In a source, the former would best suit the development in John 20:6–7, but in Luke, the latter provides the best fit.

Explanation

From the passion narrative, we move without any sense of break on into the resurrection narrative: the women seek to carry out what we know already they have planned and prepared for. But with the body gone and the angels saying Jesus has been raised, their line of action comes to a dead end. Prompted by the angels, they remember Jesus' predictions and go off to proclaim the resurrection to the Eleven and those with them. They are not believed, but Peter repeats their discovery of the empty tomb.

A puzzling picture emerges from a comparison of the reports in the four Gospels of what happened on Easter morning and beyond. Clearly, each writer has been selective in his own way and has taken up important aspects of the Easter experience and represented them somewhat schematically in connection with his own theological convictions. A basic core of agreement can be identified, but it is probably not wise to attempt to piece the reports together as though they were straightforward accounts of particular episodes. It is clear that there were quite a lot of appearances of the risen Lord, and Gospel writers have felt quite free to transfer features between appearances or to concentrate into one episode what was probably originally shared among a number of episodes.

It seems most likely that, after one or more Easter day appearances, the decisive encounter(s) with the risen Lord took place in Galilee, after the disciples had returned home from the Passover festivities. A subsequent set of appearances took place back in Jerusalem when the disciple band returned for the Feast of Pentecost. Gospel writers tend to concentrate on the one or the other for symbolic reasons: going back to Galilee marks a fresh beginning (on a new footing) for the mission of Jesus; remaining in Jerusalem allows the Christian mission to emerge from the very heartland of Jewish faith.

Core features of the experience of meeting the risen Lord would include: only those associated with the disciple community had the experience; Jesus turned up unexpectedly; his identity was not at once obvious but could be confidently affirmed by the end; the experience convinced them that Jesus had come through death and moved beyond; it seemed that the resurrection sphere into which he had moved was not such that he could be expected to take up where he had left off; rather, Jesus was showing himself to them, and then he would disappear; the encounter transformed them and left them with a powerful sense of commission for a mission task.

Biblical scholars have expressed much skepticism about the historicity of the discovery of the empty tomb by the women. This is understandable when extremely high levels of proof are demanded from narratives that have not been designed to supply such proof. Christian apologists sometimes write as though the evidence for the empty tomb were overwhelming. In fact, the evidence for the resurrection is a good deal stronger. But an empty tomb discovered by the women is still what makes best sense of the evidence on offer.

The early morning arrival at the tomb may be mentioned in order to link with the OT motif of the early morning as the time in which the action of God comes to light following the hours of darkness (cf. Exod 14:24, 37; 2 Kgs 19:35; Ps 30:5; etc.). However, for the women in the story, the stone rolled away would have suggested the interference of parties unknown rather than the action of God.

The discovery that the body was gone would have done nothing to change this perspective. It was all quite puzzling. But two rather splendid-looking male figures suddenly appear in front of them, casting an entirely new light on the matter (in Luke 9:30 and Acts 1:10 as well, a pair of resplendent men comment on decisive steps in the career of Jesus). These figures have about them the splendor of God, and the women are, quite appropriately, fearful and cowed.

The angelic figures accuse the women of coming to anoint a dead Jesus, when they should have known that he was to have risen from the dead. The angels stress the "aliveness" of Jesus in contrast with the sphere of the dead in which the women seek him. The angels proclaim the Easter message that will dominate the early church's preaching: "He has been raised." The women have come on a wild goose chase.

The messengers point the women back to the passion predictions of Jesus, making use of wording that picks up elements from all the main passion predictions (see 9:22, 44; 18:31–32). For Luke, the call for the women to remember is important because for him the significance of the resurrection is inseparable from Jesus' prior announcement of the necessity of both his suffering and his vindication as Son of Man.

The women remember. The empty tomb, the remembered predictions, and the proclamation of the angels assure the women of the reality of the resurrection of Jesus. They go off to proclaim it to their fellow disciples ("the Eleven and all the rest"). At this high point, Luke identifies the women by name. The women were named at the point where they began their role (8:1–3) and are named again in connection with the culmination of their role.

In the cultural stereotypes of the day, however, these are "only women," not to be believed in matters of deep importance. Their report is passed off as hysteria—except that it does prompt Peter to make his own investigation of the tomb.

The response of the Apostles is unconscionable so far as it expresses their attitude toward the women. But Luke is able to turn this to good effect. When the
Apostles are finally found proclaiming the resurrection, one can feel more assurance in the truth of their proclamation when one considers how difficult they
found it to be convinced.

Peter repeats the role of the women. He finds one more clue (the linen cloths),
but he sees no angels. The linen cloths do not fit with the body having been
taken away. What do they mean? Peter goes off wondering, still some considerable distance from having an Easter faith.

Jesus Appears on the Road to Emmaus   *(24:13–35)*

Bibliography

GENERAL FOR 24:13–35:

Adams, J. E. "The Emmaus Story, Lk. xxiv. 13–35: A Suggestion." *ExpTim* 17 (1905–6)
333–35. **Aletti, J.-N.** "Luc 24,13–33: Signes accomplissement et temps." *RSR* 75 (1987) 305–
20. **Allen, W. C.** "Difficulties in the Text of the Gospel Explained from Aramaic." *JTS* 2
(1900–1901) 298–300. **Annand, R.** "'He was seen of Cephas': A Suggestion about the First
Resurrection Appearance to Peter." *SJT* 11 (1958) 180–87. **Arndt, W.** "*Agei*, Luke 24:21."
CurTM 14 (1943) 61. **Benoit, P.** *The Passion and Resurrection of Jesus.* 263–87. **Betz, H. D.**
"The Origin and Nature of Christian Faith according to the Emmaus Legend (Luke 24:13–
32)." *Int* 23 (1969) 32–46. **Bokel, P.** "Luc 24, 25: il leur ouvrit l'esprit à l'intelligence des
Écritures." *BTS* 36 (1961) 2–3. **Bonus, A.** "Emmaus Mistaken for a Person." *ExpTim* 13
(1901–2) 561–62. **Borse, U.** "Der Evangelist als Verfasser der Emmauserzählung." *SNTU*
12 (1987) 35–67. **Bowen, C. R.** "The Emmaus Disciples and the Purposes of Luke." *BW* 35
(1910) 234–45. **Brunk, G. R.** "Journey to Emmaus: A Study in Critical Methodology." In
Essays on Biblical Interpretation, ed. W. M. Swartley. Elkhart, IN: Institute of Mennonite Studies, 1984. 203–22. **Brunot, A.** "Emmaüs, cité pascale de la fraction du pain." *BTS* 36 (1961)
4–11. **Burn, A. E.** "The Unnamed Companion of Cleopas." *ExpTim* 34 (1922–23) 428–29.
Certeau, M. de. "Les pèlerins d'Emmaüs." *Christus* 13 (1957) 56–63. **Charlesworth, C. E.**
"The Unnamed Companion of Cleopas." *ExpTim* 34 (1922–23) 233–34. **Charpentier, E.**
"L'officier éthiopien (Ac 8,26–40) et les disciples d'Emmaüs (Lc 24,13–35)." In *La Pâque
du Christ: Mystère du salut.* FS F.-X. Durrwell, ed. M. Benzerath et al. Paris: Cerf, 1982. 197–
201. **Claudel, G.** *La confession de Pierre.* 133–63. **Crehan, J. H.** "St. Peter's Journey to
Emmaus." *CBQ* 15 (1953) 418–26. **Cummings, C.** "A Tale of Two Travellers." *BiTod* 21
(1983) 116–20. **Dahl, N. A.** "The Crucified Messiah and the Endangered Promises." *WW* 3
(1983) 251–62. **D'Arc, J.** *Les pèlerins d'Emmaüs.* Lire la Bible 47. Paris: Cerf, 1977. ———.
"Le partage du pain à Emmaüs (Luc 24,28–32)." *VSpir* 130 (1976) 896–909. ———.
"Catechesis on the Road to Emmaus." *LVit* 32 (1977) 143–56. ———. "Un grand jeu
d'inclusions dans 'les pèlerins d'Emmaüs.'" *NRT* 99 (1977) 62–76. **DeLeers, S. V.** "The
Road to Emmaus." *BiTod* 24 (1986) 100–107. **Delzant, A.** "Les disciples d'Emmaüs (Luc
24,13–35)." *RSR* 73 (1985) 177–85. **Desremaux, J.** "Les disciples d'Emmaüs: Luc 24,13–
32." *BVC* 56 (1964) 45–46. **Dillon, R. J.** *From Eye-Witnesses to Ministers of the Word: Tradition
and Composition in Luke 24.* AnBib 82. Rome: Biblical Institute, 1978. 69–155. **Dömer, M.**
Das Heil Gottes. 70–79. **Dupont, J.** "Les pèlerins d'Emmaüs (Luc xxiv, 13–35)." In *Miscellanea
biblica B. Ubach,* ed. R. M. Diaz. Scripta et documenta 1. Montserrat: Benedictine Abbey,

1953. 349–74. ————. "The Meal at Emmaus." In *The Eucharist in the New Testament: A Symposium*, ed. J. Delorme. Baltimore/London: Helicon/Chapman, 1964. 105–21. ————. "Les disciples d'Emmaüs (Lc 24,13–35)." In *La Pâque du Christ: Mystère de salut*. FS F.-X. Durrwell, ed. M. Benzerath et al. LD 112. Paris: Cerf, 1982. 167–95; reprinted in *Études*. 2:1153–81. **Ehrhardt, A.** "Emmaus, Romulus and Apollonius." In *Mullus*. FS T. Klauser, ed. A. Stuiber and A. Hermann. JAC Ergänzungsband 1. Münster in W.: Aschendorff, 1964. 93–99. ————. "The Disciples of Emmaus." *NTS* 10 (1963–64) 182–201. **Feuillet, A.** "La recherche du Christ dans la Nouvelle Alliance d'après la christophanie de Jo. 20,11–18: Comparaison avec Cant. 3,1–4 et L'épisode des pèlerins d'Emmaüs." In *L'Homme devant Dieu*. FS H. de Lubac. Théologie 56. Paris: Aubier, 1963. 1:93–112. ————. "Les pèlerins d'Emmaüs (Lc 24, 13–35)." *NovVet* 47 (1972) 89–98. ————. "L'Apparition du Christ à Marie Madeleine Jean 20,11–18: Comparaison avec l'apparition aux disciples d'Emmaüs Luc 24,13–35." *EV* 88 (1978) 193–204, 209–23. **Fichtner, J. A.** "Christ Humiliated and Exalted." *Worship* 36 (1961–62) 308–13. **Fiedler, P.** "Die Gegenwart als österliche Zeit, erfahrbar im Gottesdienst: Die 'Emmausgeschichte' Lk 24,13–35." In *Auferstehung Jesu—Auferstehung der Christen*. FS A. Vögtle, ed. L. Oberlinner. QD 105. Freiburg: Herder, 1986. 124–44. **Gaide, G.** "Les apparitions du Christ ressuscité d'après S. Luc, Luc 24,13–48." *AsSeign* n.s. 24 (1969) 38–56. **Gibbs, J. M.** "Luke 24:13–33 and Acts 8:26–39: The Emmaus Incident and the Eunuch's Baptism as Parallel Stories." *BangTF* 7 (1975) 17–30. **Gillièron, B.** *Le repas d'Emmaüs, quand les yeux s'ouvrent sur le Christ ressuscité*. Aubonne: Moulin, 1984. **Gils, F.** "Pierre et la foi au Christ ressuscité." *ETL* 38 (1962) 5–43. **Grassi, J. A.** "Emmaus Revisited (Luke 24,13–35 and Acts 8,26–40)." *CBQ* 26 (1964) 463–67. **Guillaume, J.-M.** *Luc interprète des anciennes traditions sur la résurrection de Jésus*. EBib. Paris: Gabalda, 1979. 67–159. **Gulielmo, A. de.** "Emmaus." *CBQ* 3 (1941) 293–301. **Hahn, F.** *Mission in the New Testament*. SBT 47. Naperville, IL: Allenson, 1965. 376–82. **Hilkert, M. C.** "Retelling the Gospel Story: Preaching and Narrative." *EglT* 21 (1990) 147–67. **Hoppe, R.** "Da gingen ihnen die Augen auf . . .": Die Emmausgeschichte als Schlüssel zur lukanischen Osterbotschaft." In *Das Zeugnis des Lukas*, ed. P.-G. Müller. 1985. 84–89. **Huffman, N.** "Emmaus among the Resurrection Narratives." *JBL* 64 (1945) 205–26. **Karris, R. J.** "Luke 24:13–35." *Int* 41 (1987) 57–61. **Koet. B.-J.** "Some Traces of a Semantic Field of Interpretation in Luke 24,13–35." *Bijdragen* 46 (1985) 59–73; reprinted in *Five Studies on Interpretation of Scripture in Luke-Acts*. Studiorum Novi Testamenti Auxilia 14. Leuven: University Press/Peeters, 1989. 56–72. **Kremer, J.** "'Der Herr ist wahrhaft auferstanden': Zur Überlieferung und Form von Lk 24,34." *LitMönch* 42 (1968) 33–41. ————. "Die Bezeugung der Auferstehung Christi in Form von Geschichten: Zu Schwierigkeiten und Chancen heutigen Verstehens von Lk 24,13–53." *GuL* 61 (1988) 172–87. **LaVerdiere, E. A.** "When Prophets Break Bread." *Emman* 91 (1985) 77–81. **Leaney, A. R. C.** "The Resurrection Narratives in Luke (xxiv.12–53)." *NTS* 2 (1955–56) 110–14. **Lee, G. M.** "The Walk to Emmaus." *ExpTim* 77 (1965–66) 380–81. **Legrand, L.** "Deux voyages: Lc 2, 41–50; 24, 13–33." *À cause de l'Évangile*, ed. F. Refoulé. 409–30. ————. "Christ the Fellow Traveller: The Emmaus Story in Luke 24:13–35." *ITS* 19 (1982) 33–44. **Lehmann, K.** "Zugang zum Ostergeschehen heute: Am Beispiel der Emmaüserzählung." *IKZComm* 11 (1982) 42–50. **Liefeld, W. L.** "Exegetical Notes: Luke 24:13–35." *TJ* 2 (1981) 223–29. **Lindijer, C. H.** "Two Creative Encounters in the Work of Luke: Luke xxiv 13–35 and Acts viii 26–40." In *Miscellanea Neotestamentica: Studia ad NT praesertim pertinentia a sociis sodalicii Batavi, cuius nomen Studiosorum NTi Conventus, anno 1976 quintum lustrum complentis suscepta*, ed. T Baarda et al. NovTSup 48. Leiden: Brill, 1978. 2:77–85. **Lipiński, E.** "Les disciples d'Emmaüs." *RELiège* 54 (1967) 220–26. **Magne, J. M.** "L'épisode des disciples d' Emmaüs et le récit du paradis terrestre." *CCER* 18 (1971) 29–32. ————. "Le pain de la multiplication des pains et des disciples d'Emmaüs comme preuve de l'origine gnostique des sacrements, de l'Église et du Sauveur." *SE* 6 [= TU 112] (1973) 341–47. **Manns, F.** "Luc 24,32 et son contexte juif." *Anton* 60 (1985) 225–32. **Meissner, S. R. de.** "The Journey to Emmaus." *BSac* 84 (1927) 158–66. **Menoud, P.-H.** "Les Actes des Apôtres et l'eucharistie." *RHPR* 33 (1953) 21–36.

Meynet, R. "Comment établir un chiasme: À propos des 'pèlerins d'Emmaüs.'" *NRT* 100 (1978) 233–49. **Michael, J. H.** "The Text of Luke xxiv. 34." *ExpTim* 60 (1948–49) 292. **Mouson, J.** "Présence du Ressuscité." *CollMech* 54 (1969) 183–204. **Murphy, R. G.** "The Gospel for Easter Monday: The Story of Emmaus." *CBQ* 6 (1944) 131–41. **Nestle, E.** "'Emmaus' Mistaken for a Person." *ExpTim* 13 (1901–2) 477. **Orlett, R.** "The Influence of the Early Liturgy upon the Emmaus Account." *CBQ* 21 (1959) 212–19. **Perrot, C.** "Emmaus oder die Begegnung mit dem Herrn." *TGeg* 26 (1983) 19–25. **Potin, J.** "Les repas avec le Christ ressuscité et l'institution de l'Eucharistie." *BTS* 36 (1961) 12–13. **Radcliffe, T.** "The Emmaus Story: Necessity and Freedom." *NB* 64 (1983) 483–93. **Reid, J.** "Luke XXIV, 35." *ExpTim* 49 (1937–38) 186–89. **Riedl, J.** "'Wirklich, der Herr ist auferweckt worden und dem Simon erschienen' (Lk 24,34): Entstehung und Inhalt des neutestamentlichen Osterglaubens." *BLit* 40 (1967) 81–110. **Rigaux, B.** *Dieu l'a ressuscité: Exégèse et théologie biblique.* Gembloux: Duculot, 1973. 223–32, 245–46. **Robinson, B. P.** "The Place of the Emmaus Story in Luke-Acts." *NTS* 30 (1984) 481–97. **Rosica, T. M.** "In Search of Jesus: The Emmaus Lesson." *Church* 8 (1992) 21–25. **Rousseau, F.** "Un phénomène particulier d'inclusions dans Luc 24.13–35." *SR* 18 (1989) 67–97. **Rusche, H.** "Gastfreundschaft in Emmaus." *BK* 42 (1987) 65–67. **Sawyer, R. D.** "Was Peter the Companion of Cleopas on Easter Afternoon?" *ExpTim* 61 (1949–50) 191–93. **Scheffler, E. H.** "Emmaus: A Historical Perspective." *Neot* 23 (1989) 251–67. **Schnider, F.,** and **Stenger, W.** "Beobachtungen zur Struktur der Emmausperikope (Lk 24,13–35)." *BZ* 16 (1972) 94–114. **Schwarz, G.** "*OI ΔE OΦΘΑΛΜΟI ΑΥΤΩΝ ΕΚΡΑΤΟΥΝΤΟ?* (Lukas 24:16a)." *BibNot* 55 (1990) 16–17. **Smith, R. F.** "Did Not Our Hearts Burn within Us? (24,13–35)." *CurTM* 15 (1988) 187–93. **Souter, A.** "'Emmaus' Mistaken for a Person." *ExpTim* 13 (1901–2) 429–30. **Stöger, A.** "L'Esprit synodal." *Christus* 18 (1971) 406–19. ⸻. "Weggefährten (σύνοδοι) der Auferstandenen." *BLit* 44 (1971) 155–64. **Stravinskas, P. M. J.** "The Emmaus Pericope: Its Sources, Theology and Meaning for Today." *Biblebhashyam* 3 (1977) 97–115. **Swanston, H.** "The Road of Emmaus." *ClerRev* 50 (1965) 506–23. **Thévenot, X.** "Emmaüs, une nouvelle Genèse? Une lecture psychanalytique de Genèse 2–3 et Luc 24, 13–35." *MScRel* 37 (1980) 3–18. **Walker, W. O., Jr.** "Postcrucifixion Appearances and Christian Origins." *JBL* 88 (1969) 157–65. **Walther, O. K.** "A Solemn One Way Trip Becomes a Joyous Roundtrip! A Study of the Structure of Luke 24:13–35." *AshTJ* 14 (1981) 60–67. **Wanke, J.** *Die Emmauserzählung: Eine redaktionsgeschichtliche Untersuchung zu Lk 24,13–35.* ETS 31. Leipzig: St Benno, 1973. ⸻. ". . . wie sie ihm beim Brotbrechen erkannten': Zur Auslegung der Emmauserzählung Lk 24,13–35." *BZ* 18 (1974) 180–92. **Widengren, G.** "Was Not Then Our Heart Burning within Us? (24,32)." In *Essays in Memory of Karl Keréni,* ed. E. C. Polomé. Journal of Indo-European Studies, Monographs 4. Washington: Institute for the Study of Man, 1984. 116–22. **Wulf, F.** "Sie erkannten ihn beim Brechen des Brotes (Lk 24,35)." *GuL* 37 (1964) 81–83.

On the Location of Emmaus:

Bishop, E. F. F. "Where Was Emmaus? Why Not 'Imwas?" *ExpTim* 55 (1943–44) 152–53. **Crowfoot, J. W.** *Early Churches in Palestine.* Schweich Lectures 1937. London: British Academy, 1941. 71. **Duvignau, P.** *Emmaüs: Le site—le mystère.* Paris: Leroux, 1937. **Mackowski, R. M.** "Where Is Biblical Emmaus?" *ScEs* 32 (1980) 93–103. **Sandoli, S. de.** *Emmaus-El Qubeibeh.* 2nd ed. Jerusalem: Franciscan Press, 1980. **Vincent, L.-H.** "La chronologie du groupe monumentale d' 'Amwas." *RB* 55 (1948) 348–75. ⸻. "L'Année archéologique 1924–1925 en Palestine: I.-1. Fouilles de l'Ecole à la basilique d' 'Amwas." *RB* 35 (1926) 117–21.

And see at 24:1–12.

Translation

[13a]*On that same day two of them were going to a village sixty* [b] *stadia from Jerusalem, which [had the] name Emmaus.* [c] [14]*They were talking to one another about all these*

things that had taken place. [15]And[d] as they were talking and discussing, Jesus himself drew near and started to travel along with them, [16]but their eyes were kept from recognizing him.

[17]He said to them, "What are the matters which you are talking about with one another as you walk along?" They stopped[e] [walking and looked] downcast. [18]One of them (named Cleopas) responded,[f] "Are you the only visitor to Jerusalem who does not know what has happened there in these days?" [19]He said [g]to them, "What?" They said[g] to him, "The things concerning Jesus of Nazareth, who was a prophet, mighty in deed and word in the eyes of God and all the People: [20]that our chief priests and rulers delivered him up to be sentenced to death and had him crucified. [21]It was our hope[h] that it is he who was to redeem Israel. Indeed, besides all this, this day is the third since these things happened. [22][i]Some women[j] from among us[j] astonished us: going early to the tomb [23]and not finding his body; they came saying that they had even seen a vision of angels, who say that he is alive. [24]And some of those with us went off to the tomb and found [things] just as the women had said; him they[k] did not see."

[25]He said to them, "You foolish [men], slow of heart to believe[l] in all that the prophets have said! [26]Was it not necessary for the Christ to suffer these things and to enter into his glory?"[m] [27]Then, beginning with Moses and all the prophets, he interpreted to them in all the Scriptures the things concerning himself.

[28]When they drew near[n] to the village to which they were going, he made as if to go on further, [29]but they pressed him [to stay], saying, "Stay with us, because it is[o] towards evening and the day is already[p] far spent. So he went in to stay with them. [30]What happened next[q] was that when he sat down at table with them,[r] as he took the bread, said a blessing, broke[s] [it] and gave[t] it to them, [31][u]their eyes were opened and they recognized him. Then he vanished from their [sight]. [32]Then they said to one another, "Were not our hearts on fire[v] within us as he spoke to us on the way, when he opened [up] the Scriptures for us?" [33]They rose in the same hour[w] and returned to Jerusalem.

They found the Eleven and those with them gathered together [and] [34]saying,[x] "The Lord has indeed been raised and has appeared to Simon!" [35]So they explained what had happened on the way, and how he had been made known to them in the breaking of the bread.

Notes

[a] An opening καὶ ἰδού (lit. "and behold") is left untranslated. It is dropped by D e (with change of word order).

[b] The number is "one hundered and sixty" in ℵ Θ 079[vid] etc. See *Comment* for difficulties about the location of Emmaus.

[c] D has Οὐλαμμαούς, which is a variant reading in the LXX for the old name of Bethel in Gen 28:19.

[d] An idiom using ἐγένετο (lit. "it happened") is not represented in translation.

[e] The compactness of expression here has led to omission in D and replacement by καὶ ἐστέ, "and you are," in A[c] W Θ Ψ f[1,13] etc.

[f] Lit. "having answered, said to him."

[gg] D shortens by dropping these words.

[h] Lit. "we were hoping." A more natural tense sequence to the following ἐστίν, "is," is achieved by using the present tense in ℵ Δ Θ etc. and the perfect in P[75]. D corrects in the other direction by reading ἦν, "was," for ἐστίν, "is."

[i] The opening ἀλλὰ καί (lit. "but also/even") is not represented in translation.

[jj] These words are missing from D and a few other texts.

[k] D e have "we."

[l] Missing from D.
[m] P[75] reads βασιλείαν, "kingdom."
[n] Perfect tense rather than aorist in P[75] B.
[o] D it economize by dropping ἐστὶν καί (lit. "it is . . . and").
[p] Omitted by D and a range of other texts.
[q] Gr. καὶ ἐγένετο (lit. "and it happened").
[r] D e economize by dropping "with them."
[s] Missing from D.
[t] The syntax and tense sequence of the set of verbs here is lit. "having taken he blessed and having broken he was giving."
[u] D c e make the connection between the giving of the bread and the opening of the eyes by adding λαβόντων αὐτῶν τὸν ἄρτον ἀπ' αὐτοῦ, "when they took the bread from him."
[v] D has difficulty with the idiom here and reads κεκαλύμμενη (dropping the following "within us" as do P[75] B c e etc.). So: "Were not our hearts veiled."
[w] D c e sa add λυποῦμενοι, "grieving."
[x] D has the Emmaus disciples doing the "saying."

Form/Structure/Setting

Luke emphasizes the Easter Day timing, as well, of this new episode now to be reported. In vv 22–24, the travelers will recapitulate the events of vv 1–12, just as in v 35 they will recapitulate their own experience in the transition to the following episode. For the elaborate chiastic structuring that Luke gives to chap. 24 (centering on the Emmaus account), see at 24:1–12.

Only Luke provides an account of the experience of the two disciples on the road to Emmaus. Some of the motifs here are, however, present in other resurrection appearance accounts, notably in John (delayed recognition: John 20:14–16 [cf. 21:7, 12]; meal: John 21:12–13 [cf. Luke 24:41–43; Acts 10:41]; the idea that Jesus would disappear is not explicit elsewhere, but the temporary duration of each of the appearances is regularly assumed; interpretation of Scripture recurs in Luke 24:44–48 and is also to be related to the Johannine motif of post-resurrection understanding of the way that Scripture applied to Jesus [John 2:17–22; 12:14–16: 20:9; and cf. 14:26]).

There has been extensive scholarly discussion of the question of Lukan source(s) here, with no consensus in sight. Four main views are regularly canvassed: (*i*) Luke has reproduced the story as he received it with only minor change of substance but with significant verbal alteration (earlier views that saw most of the wording as completely pre-Lukan cannot survive the careful analysis of the Lukan language in the pericope; the combination of Lukan language and overloaded account makes even the modification of this represented in the first view a difficult option); (*ii*) Luke received from tradition a version that focused on the risen Christ's interpretation of the OT, to which he has added the motif of Jesus being made known in the breaking of the bread; (*iii*) reversing the preceding view, the interpretation of Scripture is Luke's addition to the story; and (*iv*) Luke has only scraps of tradition, and the story is to be seen as essentially his own free creation.

To proceed from this situation, one might ask whether Luke is entirely responsible for the chiastic structuring of the materials of chap. 24 (see at 24:1–12), or whether he may have developed an existing chiasm. Since vv 22–24 are clearly designed to link the Emmaus account with the empty tomb account, these verses are best taken as Lukan resumé. Their removal does not, however, destroy the chiasm: without them, vv 19b–21 and vv 25–27 become the paralleled pieces in the center of the chiasm, and probably v 21 should be separated as the more original center piece ("this is the third day").

It would seem highly likely that Luke will be responsible for the outer reaches of the chiasm (vv 36–46[48] set in parallel to vv 4b–7[8]; vv 33b–34 set in parallel with vv 9c–12). Luke has been content to mark these parallels in such a way as to leave considerable latitude for preserving existing traditions or developing redactional interests of importance to himself. Perhaps the same is true for developments within the heart of the chiasm. The parallelism between vv 17–19a and 28–30 has been identified above (see at 24:1–12) as the least transparent part of the structure. Does this mean that it is a Lukan development? Certainly vv 17–19a make very little contribution to the account and could have been formulated to make a space for the introduction of vv 28–30 (an earlier form might have had vv 15b–16 set in parallel to vv 28a, 31; 19b–21 will always have needed some brief introduction [perhaps something like "he said, 'What are you discussing?' The one named Cleopas said, 'Do you not know about Jesus of Nazareth, that . . .'"], and this is probably reflected in expanded form in vv 17–19a). This possibility finds further support from the way in which vv 41–43 (where there is fish after the bread of v 30, which contributes to the link between v 29–30 and 9:10–17) seem to overload vv 36–43. Discussion at 9:10–17 suggests the redactional importance for Luke of a link between the identity of Jesus and the feeding of the five thousand (as set in parallel with the eucharistic breaking of bread).

It would seem, then, that a credible account can be offered of an Emmaus story with a chiastic structure, which Luke has incorporated into his chapter by extending the chiasm in both directions, and which he has expanded both for the sake of tying the account into his own story line and in order to recenter the chiasm on the Christian proclamation of the fact of Jesus' resurrection.

Apart from considerations arising from the chiastic structure, perhaps the strongest argument against free Lukan formulation is provided by the impression created in vv 36–43 that the experience of vv 34–35 has made not a scrap of difference to the gathered disciples (cf. Fiedler, "Gegenwart," 125). The contribution of detailed language scrutiny to the case against free Lukan composition will be noted in *Comment* below. Such free composition would also be quite different from the pattern of Lukan compositional procedures that has emerged through the course of the commentary. So far as the choice between focus on the breaking of bread and on the interpretation of Scripture is concerned, it must be admitted that the latter is just as much a Lukan motif as the former. But Luke is rarely an innovator, and most of his motifs are given to him from the tradition (though I am arguing that vv 28b–30 are a Lukan expansion, the measure of similarity to the beach breakfast in John 21 shows that Luke will have had to some degree a traditional basis for his development [it is also likely that Acts 1:4 and esp. 10:41 are more than echoes of Luke's expansion in Luke 24:28b–30]). The view that takes the breaking of bread motif as original is left still with some overload from the tension between the eucharistic emphasis of vv 30–31 and the "entertaining angels unawares" emphasis in vv 28–29; however, if the interpretation of Scripture motif is what Luke intended, vv 28–29 provide Luke with an attractive way of splicing the domestic meal scene (needed for the breaking of bread) into the journey narrative that he inherited.

The range of the resurrection accounts suggests that the tradition set a certain value on accounts that provided contrasting settings for Jesus' appearances. The present account will have contributed an appearance of Jesus to people who were on a journey. The account reflects the early Christian conviction that it was only through encounter with the risen Lord that the key was given for understanding that the passion and resurrection/exaltation were already witnessed to by the Scriptures. From the beginning, the Emmaus story was probably told in connection with a Christian community that located its center of origin in Jerusalem (the return to Jerusalem in the story will have implied from the beginning the reporting of the experience to the mother community). The account was never designed with any apologetic concern to "prove" the resurrection.

The account in Acts 8 of the meeting of Philip with the Ethiopian eunuch has been deliberately modeled quite closely on the Emmaus account (noted by many, but see esp. Gibbs, *BangTF* 7 [1975] 17–30; Lindijer, "Creative Encounters," 2:77–85), but this tells us more about Luke's view that the life of Jesus was to be mirrored in the life of the early church than it does about how to handle the Emmaus account itself (though the parallelism is to be located both in similarity of substance and in redactional detail, it would seem that at points the similarity is closer for Luke's source than for the present text of Luke 24:13–35 [this judgment depends upon *not* finding a genuine parallel between the breaking of bread in the one and the baptism in the other]).

Comment

The camera moves from a musing Peter to unnamed traveling disciples. Jesus meets them incognito and elicits from them a brief career statement for the historical Jesus, which ends by balancing the terrible bruising of their hopes in connection with Jesus against the puzzling state of affairs that had been reached by v 12. Jesus rebukes the disciples' unbelief in the prophets and explains from the Scriptures the path through suffering to glory that the Christ was destined to take. As the journey comes to its end, the disciples press hospitality on the incognito Jesus and discover in the breaking of the bread that they have, unawares, entertained their risen Lord. Now they have the clue to the power of his biblical exposition! They rush back to Jerusalem with the news, only to be greeted by news of an appearance to Peter.

13 Various idioms here look Lukan (καὶ ἰδού [lit. "and behold"], ἐν αὐτῇ τῇ ἡμέρᾳ, "in that very hour," ᾗ ὄνομα [lit. "to which a name"], and the periphrastic tense). Though ἐν αὐτῇ τῇ ἡμέρᾳ is a Lukan linkage, the story will always have been set on the third day (see v 21b and discussion in *Form/Structure/Setting* above). See at v 18 below for the view that "two" here is a Lukan touch: the original would have envisaged a larger group. The presence of "two" may link with the theme of legal witness, as in v 4 (cf. at 10:1). For the antecedent of "of them" we must reach back to v 9b, since Cleopas is not one of the Apostles of vv 10–11. The text offers no motivation for the journey. As normally understood, it is a puzzling journey on Easter day for people aware of the happenings reported in vv 22–24, who would need some very specific motivation for leaving the scene before every attempt had been made to unravel the mystery (the level of credibility becomes less the farther Emmaus is believed to be from Jerusalem), but vv 22–24 are probably not an original part of the story. In any case, see below for the possibility that the journey to Emmaus was simply for overnight accommodation for the remaining days of Unleavened Bread.

There have been three sites identified as Emmaus. (*i*) There was an Emmaus about twenty miles west-northwest of Jerusalem, which is mentioned in 1 Macc 3:40, 57; 4:3; etc. and also referred to by Josephus (*War* 2.63; *Ant.* 17.282; etc.). Its name later became Nicopolis, but the modern name of the village is ʿAmwas, which is an Arabic rendering of the Greek for Emmaus. (*ii*) Another Emmaus was also known to Josephus (*War* 7.217). This one was about three and a half miles northwest of Jerusalem. Its modern name is Kuoniyeh. It lay on the site of ancient Mozah (Josh 18:26). (*iii*) The Crusaders identified the village of el-Qubeibeh as the Gospel Emmaus. It is about 7.1 miles from Jerusalem, on the road to Lydda. Though modern Arabs refer to the place as ʿAmwas, this practice would seem to have no antiquity. (For further details on the sites, see Fitzmyer, 1561–62.) Luke's "sixty stadia" fits the third option (a stadion is 607 feet), but for lack of ancient support, this option must be judged a Crusader identification of convenience. The second site seems the most likely, with Luke's text to be explained either as intending to mean "sixty stadia round trip" or as reflecting a confusion between the round-trip distance and the actual distance. It is possible that some of those who were crammed into (greater-)Jerusalem to meet the Passover requirement that they reside there for Passover moved away from the crowding for the remaining days of Unleavened Bread.

14 Most of the language here has a Lukan cast (unstressed καὶ αὐτοί [lit. "and they"]; πρός with a verb of speaking; ὁμιλεῖν, "talk"; and generalizing use of πᾶς ὁ, "all the"). In Luke's finished version, the scope of what they are discussing is represented in vv 19–24.

15 Again the language here is strongly Lukan (καὶ ἐγένετο ἐν τῷ . . . καὶ αὐτός [lit. "and it happened in the . . . and he"]; ὁμιλεῖν again; ἐγγίζειν, "draw near" [but see at v 28 for the likelihood that this verb is pre-Lukan here]). The opening clause is a storyteller's repetition. Presumably, Jesus is assumed either to be moving away from Jerusalem, as were the disciples, or (as v 28b might suggest) to be already on his way home after Passover.

16 Luke is fond of the articular infinitive and has most of those NT uses of ἐπιγινώσκειν for which the sense is "recognize." The failure to recognize Jesus here is normally attributed to divine intention but also occasionally to the state of heart of the disciples. I think it more likely that this is a Satanic blinding (but not without link to the state of mind of the disciples), which will be overcome by the victorious Jesus (cf. at 18:34). There is no reason to think of Jesus being in "another form," as in the later ending of Mark (16:12), but there is a motif link with other resurrection accounts in which the identity of Jesus was not obvious at once (see *Form/Structure/Setting* at 24:1–12). Connections are often drawn between Jesus' appearance here and Greco-Roman stories of gods turning up in human form and not being immediately recognizable (see, e.g., Bultmann, *History*, 286 n. 1; also note Homer, *Odyssey* 1.320; and for the Jewish side, see Tob 5:4–5; cf. also at v 29), but the stories have only a quite limited similarity to Luke's narrative. More to the point might be Dodd's comparison with ἀναγνώρισις, "the term applied by ancient literary critics to the recognition-scene which was so often the crucial point of a Greek drama" ("Appearances," 14).

17 Though only the uses of πρός with a verb of saying are notably Lukan, the whole verse could well have been penned by Luke (cf. Jeremias, *Sprache*, 314). This third mention of the conversational exchange should probably be judged to overload the narrative. The gloom of the disciples corresponds to the bruising of their hopes caused by the turn of events that they will report in v 20. Neither the empty tomb nor the women's report of the angels' message has been able to lighten the gloom (vv 22–24).

18 The most notable elements of Lukan language here are ὀνόματι, "by name," πρός with a verb of speaking, τὰ γενόμενα, "what had happened," and ἐν ταῖς ἡμέραις ταύταις, "in these days." Only Κλεοπᾶς, "Cleopas," and οὐκ ἔγνως, "did [here: do] you not know" (possibly, but not necessarily, with the preceding paratactic καί [lit. "and"]), are likely to stem from Luke's source. Though it can mean either, here παροικεῖς almost certainly means "you are a visitor to" and not "you are a resident of." There is a nice irony in the disciples accusing Jesus of being one who *does not know* when it is they who *do not know* who is talking with them or that the resurrection has taken place (cf. D'Arc, *LVit* 32 [1977] 148). Note Luke's interest elsewhere in making the point that the events concerning Jesus are well known and therefore available for public scrutiny (cf., e.g., at 4:14b). Why is Cleopas singled out for mention by name? The point has been made that it would be more natural if Cleopas were to be singled out from a larger group than from a group of only two, and on this basis, Luke's "two" in v 13 falls under suspicion of being redactional. This is certainly possible, but one cannot rule out the highlighting of Cleopas because he had some particular importance for those who shaped and repeated the account (an importance no longer evident to Luke, for whom the name only enhances the value of this testimony to the resurrection).

19 Lukan language is evident in τὰ περί, "the things concerning," ἀνὴρ προφήτης (lit. "a man a prophet"), δυνατὸς ἐν, "mighty in" ("mighty in deed and word" is echoed in Stephen's description of Moses as "mighty in [his] words and works" [Acts 7:22]), ἐναντίον, "before," and παντὸς τοῦ λαοῦ, "all the People" (cf. Jeremias, *Sprache*, 315). Ναζαρηνοῦ, "of Nazareth," is the only clearly traditional element (cf. at 18:37). The opening τὰ περί, to be matched by a closing use of the expression in v 27, will be a Lukan enhancement of the chiastic structure. Luke's source probably only identified Jesus at this point as "Jesus of Nazareth." On Luke's treatment of the prophetic identity of Jesus, see at 4:24; 7:16; 9:19. The affirmation of Jesus as a prophet is in Luke's eyes correct (here even God sees it that way) but in need of supplementation. For the affirmative attitude of "all the People" to Jesus, cf. 7:29; 18:43; 19:48; 21:38. For comparable brief description of the career of Jesus, cf. Acts 2:22; 10:37–38.

20 Only οἱ ἄρχοντες, "the rulers," and the use of τε . . . καί to link clauses seem Lukan here (even "*our* rulers" might be traditional, but with the juxtaposition of "chief priests and rulers," it could be Lukan [cf. 23:13]). The failure to mention any role for Pilate and the Romans is often taken as anti-Semitic, but the passage emphasizes the role of the Jewish leadership because of its significance both for theology and for apologetics. In the Lukan organization of the chapter, there is an intended echo here (with v 21b) of v 7.

21 σὺν πᾶσιν τούτοις, "besides all this," and, possibly, ἄγει (lit. "it leads") are the features most likely to be Lukan. Luke has a certain appreciation for traditional phraseology like that used in "the one who is to redeem Israel" (cf. 2:25, 38; 23:51; Acts 1:6) but should not for that reason be made responsible for the language here. ἀλλά γε καί, "indeed," is not found elsewhere in Luke's writings, nor is ἀφ' οὗ, "since" (cf. the use of ἀφ' ἧς, "since" in Luke 7:45; Acts 20:18; 24:11).

For "redeem," see discussion at 1:68; 2:38. God is redeemer in Isa 41:14; 43:14; 44:22–24; *Pss. Sol.* 9:1; and cf. 1 Macc 4:11: "will know that there is one who redeems . . . Israel." The disciples' hopes would appear to have been dashed by the tragic outcome of Jesus' ministry. Luke has probably obscured an original double sense for the reference to the third day: the speaker intends to indicate that the stranger should have heard about the execution of Jesus in this length of time; in the earlier form of the chiastic structure of the story, the third-day reference is the center point, which affirms the possibility of encountering the risen Jesus. The disciples will become aware of their participation in such an encounter as the story unfolds. Luke's added "besides all this" underlines the allusion to resurrection hope (cf. vv 7, 46).

What seems to be an impersonal use of ἄγει here has not been paralleled (Luke has the only other NT use of ἄγειν in a time expression in Acts 19:38), but the alternative, to translate "he [Jesus] spends this third day," makes for a logical transition that is too awkward to be likely.

22 The language here is all quite naturally seen as Lukan, with the possible exception of ἀλλὰ καί (lit. "but even"; cf. Jeremias, *Sprache*, 316). As a Lukan resumé of vv 1–11, vv 22–23 help to link the Emmaus account with its Lukan setting and, with v 24, provide a new centerpiece with a surrounding set of paralleled elements to place at the heart of the chiastic structure. Probably, in Luke's mind, vv 22–24 also function to bring the summary of vv 19–20 up to date, but in doing so they confuse the question of the state of mind of Cleopas and his associate: what are we to understand that they make of these reports? Though "astonished us" makes a much more positive impression (for the idiom, cf. Acts 8:9, 11), it is Luke's counterpart to v 11.

23 Again, the language here would all be quite natural for Luke (for ὀπτασίαν ἑωρακέναι, "to have seen a vision," see 1:22; cf. Acts 26:19; for ζῆν, "that he is alive," see at v 5; "men" in v 4 become "angels" here, as happens inversely in Acts 10:3, 7, 22, cf. v 30). To say that Jesus is alive is to proclaim the Easter gospel. This centerpiece of Luke's chiasm picks up a motif from v 5–6a, the other half of which will be picked up in v 34.

24 Once more the language is best considered as a Lukan reiteration of v 12. The only question is whether the plural here is simply an indefinite form influenced by the plural form for the action of the women in v 22–23 or reflects a tradition that this visit involved more than Peter. The first aorist form εἶπον, "said," may support a tradition being involved here, since Luke elsewhere (forty-nine times in Luke-Acts) uses the second aorist form εἶπαν. On the other hand, the careful parallelism (for the sake of the chiasm) between v 24 and vv 22–23 counts in the other direction. The sequence of key words is:

| women | - certain - us - to the tomb - found [negated]- | came | - saying - seen |

| went | - certain - us - to the tomb - found - | women | - said - saw [negated]. |

The lack of any actual sighting of Jesus leaves the disciples uncertain about what has really happened.

25 Unstressed καὶ αὐτός (lit. "and he"), the use of πρός with a verb of saying, and πᾶσιν, "all," will all be Lukan, but πιστεύειν ἐπί + dative, "believe (in)," is not Lukan idiom (cf. Acts 9:42; 11:17; 16:31; 22:19), nor is the way that the dative τῇ καρδίᾳ (lit. "with respect to the heart") is used. The point of this statement only becomes fully clear in what follows, but already we can see that the view is being expressed that the devastation felt by the disciples, as well as their unreadiness to go anywhere with the reports of the empty tomb and the vision of angels, reflects an unbelieving attitude. In particular, it shows that things would have been different if their starting point had been a thoroughgoing belief in all the evidence of the Scriptures. In 18:31–33, Luke has already claimed a scriptural witness to the passion and resurrection of Jesus, and he will come back to the point in vv 44–47.

26 Closest to "to suffer these things" is "to suffer many things" in 9:22; 17:25. These also share the language of necessity of the present verse (a particular Lukan preoccupation [cf. at 9:21–22]). Closest to "enter into his glory" here are the uses of "glory" in 9:31–32; cf. also 9:26; 21:27; Acts 22:11. Despite the Lukan links, the wording is probably more traditional than Lukan, since (*i*) the thought development of the account requires something equivalent at this stage (after v 25, vv 26–27 need to mention the suffering of the redemptive figure [the actual word "Christ" may be Lukan] and the outcome of the suffering, as well as the interpretation of Scripture); and (*ii*) "glory" is not the word that Luke would most naturally have penned at this point.

See discussion at 6:1–5 on the relationship between the use of "Son of Man" and "Christ" in connection with the suffering of Jesus: from this point on, Luke will use "Christ" when referring to the suffering of Jesus. Is "glory" here a reference to the resurrection, as is sometimes suggested, and not to exaltation to heaven? Certainly the closest parallels to 24:26 as a whole all refer to the resurrection, and such a reference here would be quite convenient for systematizing Luke's teaching. But Luke's other uses of "glory" hardly support such a sense, and no external parallels have been offered to lend support to such an understanding of "glory." In the Lukan frame, "glory" can only be the glory of exaltation to the right hand of God.

A second question here is whether the text reflects a view in which Jesus is understood as being raised from death immediately to heaven. Since it is only in Luke and John that there is any clear chronological distinction between resurrection and ascension (John 20:17), one cannot entirely eliminate the possibility that, in the earlier tradition, the use of glory here reflected a view that Jesus was raised from death immediately to heaven. It is, however, doubtful that the appearance to the Emmaus disciples should be viewed as an appearance from heaven, as opposed to the common picture that emerges from the Gospel resurrection appearances (cf. at 24:1–12 [apart from the case of Paul, there is nothing in the appearances tradition that encourages a reading in terms of appearances from heaven]). And the way in which resurrection might seem to be resurrection to heaven in Acts 2:24–35 (but surely is not!) should remind us that once one moves outside a concern about resurrection appearances the NT interest in resurrection is largely in connection with the exaltation of Jesus (Paul has additional interests, but these are not relevant here).

A third question is, Are we to understand that Jesus here has already entered into his glory (as, e.g., Fitzmyer, 1538–39, 1566)? In light of the discussion of resurrection appearances at 24:1–12, I think not. The passion is here the gateway to glory, as implicitly in 9:51, but this does not necessarily affirm that the whole process has already been completed. Again, the common picture appealed to above is relevant, and Luke's ascension accounts have a more satisfactory logic to them if Jesus has not been appearing from heaven for the resurrection appearances.

The *entering into his glory* here has its counterpart in the *coming of the Son of Man in his glory* anticipated in 9:26 (cf. going away to receive kingly power and then returning of 19:12).

27 Most of the language here is likely to be Lukan (cf. Jeremias, *Sprache*, 317), but probably διηρμήνευσεν, "interpreted," is traditional (Luke uses διανοίγειν, "open," in related contexts [vv 31, 32, 45; Acts 17:3]). The phrase "Moses and all the prophets" reflects a traditional coupling of the law and the prophets (cf. 1QS 1:3; 4QDibHam 3:12; Matt 11:13; John 1:45), but in the NT it is a notably Lukan linkage (cf. Luke 16:31; Acts 26:22; 28:23). Presumably after beginning with Moses and the prophets, Jesus goes on to the Writings, which form the other traditional section of the Scriptures (or possibly we should complete the set with the Psalms, as in Luke 24:44). The text reflects an early Christian conviction that the Scriptures witness pervasively to the Christ and, in particular, to the way in which the career of Jesus had unfolded. Such a view has not been generated inductively from a detailed study of the OT. It is a more global phenomenon and involves a particular hermeneutical approach. As we see from OT texts appealed to in Acts, the view is supported by exegesis of chosen texts that were seen to anticipate the shape of Jesus' career (and in particular his death and resurrection/exaltation).

28 Despite being a word favored by Luke, the use of ἐγγίζειν, "draw near," probably originally echoed that in v 15 as part of the chiastic structuring (supported by the use of [συν]πορεύεσθαι, "go [with]"), but it no longer plays this role for Luke, for whom the departure of Jesus (now well separated) has this role. The final clause is likely to be a Lukan expansion, which will continue in vv 29–30. For Jesus' making as if to go on further, cf. Gen 18:3; 19:2. This prepares for the hospitality motif in v 29.

29 All of the language here can well have come from Luke's pen, and quite a bit is strikingly Lukan (see Jeremias, *Sprache*, 318; but Luke's preference for μένειν παρά for "remain with" is hardly clear in the manner claimed by Jeremias). For "they urged," cf. Acts 16:15 (a cognate verb is used in Gen 19:3). κέκλικεν ἤδη ἡ ἡμέρα (lit. "already the day has declined") echoes ἡ δὲ ἡμέρα ἤρξατο κλίνειν (lit. "the day began to decline") of 9:12, preparing for the echoing of the feeding of the five thousand to come in v 30. The A text of Judg 19:9, where it is also a matter of overnight hospitality, is very close to Luke's language here, with εἰς ἑσπέραν κέκλικεν ἡ ἡμέρα (lit. "the day has declined into evening") for Luke's πρὸς ἑσπέραν ἐστὶν καὶ κέκλικεν ἤδη ἡ ἡμέρα (lit. "it is towards evening and the day is already far spent"). In Jewish custom, the main meal of the day seems to have been in the late afternoon (see Jeremias, *Eucharistic Words*, 44–45 [*Bibliography* for 22:15–20]). In the ancient world, hospitality to strangers ranked high as a religious virtue. Both the Jewish and Greco-Roman worlds affirmed this virtue with stories about hospitality extended to incognito gods or angels (see Ovid, *Metamorphoses*, 8.618–724; Heb 13:2; note the comments on Gen 18 in Philo, *Concerning Abraham* 107–13; Josephus, *Ant.* 1.196; *b. Quidd.* 32b). Since the invitation pressed upon Jesus happens in the setting of the "entertaining angels unawares" motif, there is no basis for making a connection with an invocation for the risen Lord to be present in the eucharistic celebration.

30   The stronger language links here are with 9:15–16 rather than with 22:19, but since 9:16 was itself concerned to evoke the Last Supper, and via that, the eucharistic practice of the early church (see at 9:10–17), one should not make too sharp a distinction. Note the way in which Jesus, though the guest, takes upon himself the role of host. The relevant elements of v 30 are taken up in chiastic manner in the reiteration in v 35. There is no sense in which Luke is claiming that Jesus celebrated the eucharist with these disciples; rather, Luke wants to make the point that the Christians of his day were able to have the living Lord made known to them in the eucharist celebration in a manner that was at least analogous to the experience of the Emmaus disciples. There is a measure of parallelism between the bread here and the fish in vv 42–43; the two together take up the bread and fish of the feeding of the five thousand (cf. Dussaut, *RB* 94 [1987] 210–11).

31   Much of the language here seems Lukan (cf. Jeremias, *Sprache*, 318–19), but the main content will be traditional, being the necessary counterpart to v 16. The exposition of Scripture and the breaking of the bread together create the appropriate conditions for Jesus to break through the Satanic blinding that has kept the disciples from perceiving that it was Jesus who was with them. The temporary nature of the presence of Jesus with the disciples may have been implied rather than stated in an earlier form (see discussion of resurrection appearances at 24:1–12). For Luke, the disappearance is the counterpart to the arrival in v 15. Luke marks comparable departures in 1:38; 2:15; 9:33; Acts 10:7; 12:10; cf. 1:9; Luke 4:13. Of particular note is the removal of Philip in Acts 8:39: "the Spirit of the Lord caught up Philip; and the eunuch saw him no more."

32   The chiasm requires a conversation between the disciples at this point, but since the language here is notably Lukan (cf. Jeremias, *Sprache*, 319), there is no way of telling whether Luke has displaced or simply reworded an original. Though long considered unidiomatic Greek, the imagery of a *burning heart* has been paralleled in *PGM* 7.472 (see BAGD 396). In the Lukan text, this verse keeps the focus on the exposition of Scripture being lost once the new emphasis on the breaking of bread has been added. Note in Acts 17:2–3 the coming together of the opening of the Scriptures (as here) and the necessity of Jesus' suffering (as in v 26). It is hard to be sure what "on the way" is meant to evoke (repeated in v 35); it is unlikely to have anything to do with the path of discipleship as a "way"; perhaps it is meant to echo Jesus' teaching activity "on the way" to Jerusalem (cf. 9:57).

33   This verse represents a high concentration of Lukan language (cf. Jeremias, *Sprache*, 319), but there needs to be a return to Jerusalem to balance the departure from Jerusalem in v 13. Perhaps the original had a bare return statement (see the end of *Form/Structure/Setting* above). The present departure statement corresponds to those of vv 9 and 52. The departure is made more urgent by Luke's desire to contain the action of Luke 24 within the scope of Easter Day. The mention of the Eleven and their associates and the reporting in vv 34–35 to follow form the counterpart (in Luke's version of the chiastic structure) to vv 9b–12. For Luke, the Apostolic band and those with them function to guarantee the transfer of the knowledge and significance of all that pertains to Jesus into the life of the church.

34 For the sake of the priority of Peter (cf. at 5:1–11; 22:31–34), Luke needs to interrupt what would be the natural flow on to v 35 (cf. in Acts the placing of the Cornelius episode prior to 11:19–21; cf. 8:4–8). Though the appearance to Peter had kerygmatic importance in the early church (1 Cor 15:5), apparently no narrative account of it had been preserved. To cover this lack, Luke rather cleverly makes use of a narrative setting in which resumé reporting is the appropriate form.

Claudel (*Confession*, 142–43) has suggested with some plausibility that Luke is responsible for the change from "Cephas" to "Simon" here: according to Claudel, Luke 6:14 sets up a language pattern in which "Simon" will be the appropriate word when "the Twelve" are being talked about (and so, correspondingly, when "the Eleven" are spoken of), while "Peter" will be the term to use when the related expression is "the Apostles" (this fits 24:9–12, where "Apostles" is found in v 10). The place of Peter in the chiastic pairing of vv 33b–35 and vv 9b–12 may be highlighted by a minor chiasm between v 34b and v 12 (cf. Dussaut, *RB* 94 [1987] 210). Luke may also be responsible for "the Lord."

35 This verse is a straightforward Lukan resumé of the preceding narrative. Luke is concerned to sustain a twin focus: the scriptural exposition "on the way" and "the breaking of the bread." This latter phrase will recur in Acts 2:42 and in a related verbal form in Acts 2:46; 20:7, 11; and cf. 27:35. If it is not already clear from Acts itself, then the present verse, with its links back through v 30 to the Last Supper and the feeding of the five thousand, makes it quite clear that Luke uses this language to speak of the eucharistic practice of the early church.

Explanation

Still on Easter Day, the focus moves from a musing Peter to two disciples setting off for the village of Emmaus. In an elaborate structuring of the chapter, which is built around the Emmaus account, Luke organizes everything in a concentric pattern of paralleled elements. Luke's telling of the whole story centers on the words of v 23: "who said that he is alive." (For the disciples who make this report, there is no such emphasis, because they do not yet know the truth of this central affirmation.) The risen Jesus who meets them incognito explains to them his path through suffering and to glory from the Scriptures. Invited to stay the night, he acts the host and breaks bread for them. Both activities make a deep impression that results in the disciples' recognition of Jesus. They take the news back to Jerusalem, where already the report of an appearance to Peter has been circulated.

Sixty stadia should probably be taken as the round-trip distance, making Emmaus about three and a half miles away. The disciples might be intending to lodge there for the rest of the Feast of Unleavened Bread, now that the main Passover celebration was over. They are leaving Jerusalem, but their thoughts are dominated by what has so recently transpired in the city.

Jesus joins the disciples as they walk along, but they do not realize that it is he. What keeps them from recognizing him? Quite a number of suggestions have been offered, but in Luke's Gospel, the blinding effect of Satan probably provides the best explanation (see at 18:34). With a two-pronged strategy, Jesus will break through this blindness.

As Jesus converses with the disciples, a nice irony emerges: the disciples point to the apparent ignorance of this man about Jesus, being quite ignorant themselves that they are speaking to none other than this same Jesus. Jesus gets the disciples to tell their story. The elements of their story echo the way in which the early preachers of the gospel outlined the career of Jesus. In their story we should note the emphasis on the public nature of the events, which are therefore well known and open to public scrutiny, and the focus on the responsibility of the Jewish leadership (and not the Jewish People, who consider Jesus to be a prophet) for the execution of Jesus. The disciples, however, cannot yet tell the whole story. The execution of Jesus has cast them into deep gloom, with all their hopes shattered, and the reports of the women and men who had visited the tomb have done no more than suspend them in a state of confusion and uncertainty.

How does Jesus respond to such a scenario? He starts with a rebuke. There is a guilty element to the blindness of these disciples. In particular, the disciples have not responded in a believing manner to the witness of the OT Scriptures. From the prophets, they should have learned that it was necessary for the Christ to reach his glorious destiny by way of suffering. This glorious destiny has been in view since 9:51. Jesus will reach it in 24:53. So endowed with glory, he will be able to return as the glorious Son of Man (see 9:26 and 19:12).

(No doubt the disciples should have known all this, but it is not so obviously found in the OT. Easter faith gives a particular focus to the reading of the OT, and from this perspective one can see how the OT interprets and anticipates what was to be the destiny of Jesus.)

Jesus proceeds to make good the deficit in the disciples' understanding of the Scriptures (how the early church used the Scriptures to point to the resurrection/glorification of Jesus is well illustrated in Acts). From v 32, we learn that not only were their minds informed, but their hearts were also touched. Perhaps now they would be ready for faith in the scriptural witness to the destiny of Jesus as the Christ.

The disciples press hospitality upon Jesus in a way that reminds one of the hospitality extended to angels in Gen 18:3; 19:2. In the logic of their urging, we already get an echo from the feeding of the five thousand (9:10–17; see v 12), which is to be an important background for v 30. In Jewish custom, apart from special occasions, the main meal of the day seems to have been in the late afternoon. In the ancient world, hospitality to strangers ranked high as a religious virtue, and there were various stories, Jewish and otherwise, about "entertaining angels [or gods] unawares" (Heb 13:2). In this case, the disciples will find their hospitality well rewarded!

Though the guest, Jesus plays host. As he breaks the bread, he is recognized. What he does with the bread is reported in words that echo Luke 9:16 and then secondarily 22:19. There is no sense in which Luke is claiming that Jesus celebrated a communion service with these disciples; rather, Luke wants to make the point that the Christians of his day were able to have the living Lord made known to them in their "breaking of bread" in a manner that was at least analogous to the experience of the Emmaus disciples. Earlier in the Gospel, the feeding miracle had had much the same effect for Peter and the others (see at 9:10–17 and then vv 18–20; the link of the bread with the feeding miracle is strengthened by the mention of fish in vv 42–43). As with the other encounters with the risen Lord, this one soon comes to an end, but its effect is permanent.

The disciples thought they had gone home for the evening, but their previous plans no longer seemed appropriate. They must return to Jerusalem and share the good news! But they find that the good news has run ahead of them. Peter, too, has met with the risen Lord (curiously, the Gospels have no actual account of a private meeting with Peter, though Paul puts this at the head of his list in 1 Cor 15:5). Because of the foundational role of Peter, Luke feels that it is important to make clear that the gathered disciples receive Peter's report before they receive the report from the Emmaus disciples. The foundations for the early church's preaching of the resurrection are being gradually developed.

Jesus Appears to the Disciples in Jerusalem (24:36–43)

Bibliography

Bishop, E. F. F. "With Saint Luke in Jerusalem from Easter Day till Pentecost." *ExpTim* 56 (1944–45) 192–94, 220–23. **Boismard, M.-E.** "Le réalisme des récits évangéliques." *LumVie* 107 (1972) 31–41. **Chevallier, M.-A.** "'Pentecôtes' lucaniennes et 'pentecôtes' johanniques. (24,36–49)." *RSR* 69 (1981) 301–13. **Dauer, A.** *Johannes und Lukas: Untersuchungen zu den johanneisch-lukanischen Parallel-Perikopen Joh 4,46–54/Lk 7,1–10; Joh 12,1–8/Lk 7,36–50, 10,38–42; Joh 20,19–29/Lk 24,36–49.* FB 50. Würzburg: Echter, 1984. 207–88. **Dillon, R. J.** *From Eye-Witnesses to Ministers of the Word: Tradition and Composition in Luke 24.* AnBib 82. Rome: Biblical Institute, 1978. 157–203. **George, A.** "Les récits d'apparitions aux Onze à partir de Luc 24, 36–53." In *La résurrection du Christ et l'exégèse moderne,* ed. P. de Surgy et al. LD 50. Paris: Cerf, 1969. 75–104. **Guillaume, J.-M.** *Luc interprète des anciennes traditions sur la résurrection de Jésus.* EBib. Paris: Gabalda, 1979. 163–201. **Kilpatrick, G. D.** "Luke 24:42–43." *NovT* 28 (1986) 306–8. **Neirynck, F.** "Lc 24,36–43: Un récit lucanien." In *À cause de l'Évangile,* ed. F. Refoulé. 655–80. **Nestle, E.** "The Honeycomb in Luke xxiv." *ExpTim* 22 (1910–11) 567–68. **O'Collins, G.** "Did Jesus Eat the Fish (Luke 24:42–43)?" *Greg* 69 (1988) 65–76. **Rigaux, B.** *Dieu l'a ressuscité: Exégèse et théologie biblique.* Gembloux: Duculot, 1973. 258–63, 274–76. **Varro, R.** "Présence du Ressuscité et mission de l'Église (Lc 24,39,47)." *AmCl* 80 (1970) 196–200.

And see at 24:1–12.

Translation

[36]*While they were [still] saying these things, Jesus himself stood in their midst* [a]*and said to them, "Peace to you."* [a] [37]*Startled* [b] *and frightened, they thought they were seeing a spirit.* [c] [38]*So he said to them, "Why are you disturbed and why do doubts arise in your hearts?* [d] [39]*See my hands and my* [e] *feet: that it is I myself. Touch me* [f] *and see. For a spirit does not have flesh* [g] *and bones as you see that I have."* [40h]*When he had said this, he showed them [his] hands and [his] feet.* [41]*While they still disbelieved from joy and [continued] to wonder, he said to them,* [i] *"Have you anything here to eat?"* [42]*They gave him a piece of broiled fish,* [j] [43]*and he took it and ate it in front of them.* [k]

Notes

a-a Omitted by D it, and often considered secondary by earlier scholarship because of the verbal identity with John 20:19. But the Johannine links are still notable without all the disputed pieces; P^{75} supports the otherwise solid testimony in favor of the longer reading; the greeting plays a part in the pattern of encounter with angels that is probably otherwise reflected in the account. The recent consensus favors the originality of the longer reading. The addition of ἐγώ εἰμι, μὴ φοβεῖσθε, "It is I; do not be afraid," in G P (W 579) and some of the versions represents an exploitation of the Johannine link in connection with a recognition of a certain similarity between the encounter with Jesus here and in the walking on the water of John 6:16–21 (see v 20).

b Reading πτοηθέντες. P^{75} B etc. read θροηθέντες and ℵ W read φοβηθέντες, but there is no significant change of sense.

c D has φάντασμα, "apparition/ghost."

d The original here is likely to have the idiomatic use of the sing., which has been "corrected" to the pl. by ℵ A L W Θ Ψ etc.

e There is no second "my" in P^{75} L W Θ etc.

f "Me" is missing from D W Θ etc.

g In a rather unusual usage, the pl. is read here by P^{75} ℵ (D), to match the pl. "bones."

h D it sy^{s,c} omit the verse. Considerations from Note a are pertinent here as well, and see discussion at Dillon (Eye-Witnesses, 183–84).

i "To them" is omitted by D lat.

j The addition here of καὶ ἀπὸ μελισσίου κηρίου, "and some honeycomb," in Θ Ψ $f^{1,13}$ etc. finds some echo in some later eucharistic practice. Kilpatrick (NovT 28 [1986] 306–7) has recently defended the longer text here on the basis of the role of honeycomb in Joseph and Asenath.

k A few MSS complete the meal fellowship here by having Jesus give the rest of the fish to the gathered disciples (K Θ Π f^{13} etc. and versions).

Form/Structure/Setting

After the bridging piece provided by vv 33b–35, Luke continues to emphasize the tight interconnectedness of the units of this section by having the new development reported here break into the reporting of v 35. For the chiastic structuring of the whole chapter, see at 24:1–12 (in this structure, vv 36–46[48] stand parallel to vv 4b–7[8]).

The appearance scene (vv 36–53) clearly has a relationship to the tradition behind Matt 28:16–20 and John 20:19–23 (not to mention Acts 1:6–8). General discussion about the nature of the tradition is provided at 24:1–12. The immediate source question here is that posed by the evidently rather closer relationship between Luke 24:36–41 and John 20:19–20 (the link between Luke 24:47–49 and John 20:21–23 will be discussed with the next unit). The closeness of the link can be seen by setting in parallel the relevant parts of the respective Greek texts (John and then Luke):

ὁ Ἰησοῦς ἔστη εἰς τὸ μέσον καὶ λέγει αὐτοῖς·
      αὐτὸς ἔστη ἐν   μέσῳ καὶ λέγει αὐτοῖς·

εἰρήνη ὑμῖν· καὶ τοῦτο εἰπὼν ἔδειξεν   τὰς
εἰρήνη ὑμῖν· καὶ τοῦτο εἰπὼν ἔδειξεν αὐτοῖς τὰς

χεῖρας καὶ τὴν πλευρὰν αὐτοῖς· ἐχάρησαν
χεῖρας καὶ τοὺς πόδας·   ἀπὸ τῆς χαρᾶς

While there has been no significant modern support for the view that Luke had access to the Johannine text, there has been recent strong support from Dauer

(*Johannes und Lukas*, 207–88) and Neirynck ("Lc 24,36–43," 655–80) for the view that John is here dependent (directly or indirectly) upon the Lukan text. The nub of the argument is that features that are identifiably redactional in the Lukan text are also to be found in the Johannine rendering. Neirynck argues that, in fact, all of the shared features in the respective narratives result from Lukan redaction. In the examination of the Lukan language reported below, it becomes clear that, while there is evidence of considerable Lukan redaction, it is not demonstrable that any of the features shared between the Lukan and Johannine text form part of Luke's development of the text. There is a certain amount that *could* be Lukan (the first three words of v 40 and the greeting in v 36—if it were a deliberate *Lukan* echo of Luke 10:5), and to that degree it cannot be demonstrated that John did not use Luke. But a shared earlier source seems to me altogether more likely.

What can we say about the nature of Luke's source? Naturally, more than language analysis is required for source judgments here. The text does seem to have some relationship to the OT patterns used for reporting encounters with angelic figures (see at vv 36, 37 below). Though this is a pattern that Luke makes use of elsewhere, he does not seem to be responsible for its presence here. Apart from a certain amount of Lukan reformulation, the bridging supplied by v 36a and the probable Lukan expansion in the final clause of v 39 (possibly along with "touch me and see" from the middle of that verse) seem to be the only places in vv 36–40 where Luke is not more or less reproducing tradition. Major intervention begins in v 41, where the joy is likely to echo tradition, while the unbelief and the wondering are used to hold back until later a full response to Jesus' self-revelation.

The joint role of vv 30 and 42–43 in alluding to the feeding miracle have already been discussed (see at v 30). The link between vv 42–43 and 9:10–17 is confirmed in the *Comment* below by the considerable range of correspondences noted there. That 24:28b–30 was seen above to be a Lukan expansion does not require that the same judgment be made for vv 41b–43, but it does oblige us to consider this possibility. Since it is hard to see a significance for the links with the feeding miracle outside the connection with v 30, and since nothing viable is left of vv 41b–43 if we try to subtract the allusions to 9:10–17, we are, I think, forced to identify 24:41b–43 as a Lukan expansion. (As we saw with vv 28b–30, this does not necessarily mean that Luke had no basis in the tradition for the development. The fish breakfast in John 21 can hardly be taken as a development from Luke 24:41b–43, yet it shares with Luke 24:41b–43 the eating of fish while the risen Jesus is with the disciples [judging from the charcoal fire of John 21:9, the fish is broiled as in Luke 24:42], as well as the allusion to the feeding of the five thousand [John 21:9, 13]. Despite considerable imaginative development, there seems to be some common core of tradition involved here.)

It is suggested in the *Comment* below that there has been some pre-Lukan development in the pericope, to reinforce its effectiveness in apologetic defense of the resurrection of Jesus. Luke may have carried this tendency a step further, but his major intervention has been in connection with his concern about how the living Christ may continue to be known in the ongoing life of the church.

There are a number of similarities between the present pericope and the walking on the water in Mark 6:45–51 (unexpected appearance, fear [using ταράσσειν], the idea on the part of the disciples that they might be seeing a ghost, use of ἐγώ εἰμι, "it is I"), a pericope that Luke has not reproduced. While these similarities are striking, all but the idea of a ghost and the use of ἐγώ εἰμι are common to "supernatural" appearances. Moreover, the explanation of inexplicable phenomena in terms of ghosts is a universal phenomenon, as is the role for self-identification. Despite the notable similarity, there is not likely to be any tradition link between the accounts.

Comment

The conviction of vv 34–35 is now provided with fresh foundations as Jesus appears to the gathered disciples, demonstrates that he is not a ghost, and eats some fish before them in an act that echoes the place of the fish in the feeding of the five thousand.

36 The transitional ταῦτα δὲ αὐτῶν λαλούντων, "while they were [still] saying these things," is clearly Lukan (cf. at 22:60); its role is to encourage the reader to see vv 36–43 as further confirming the Easter conviction of vv 33–35. ἔστη, "stood," may have a link with the use of this verb in connection with the appearance of angels in the LXX (see Gen 18:2; Dan 8:15; 12:5; 1 Chr 21:15–16; Tob 5:4[S]; cf. Num 22:22–24; the link could be made more confidently if there were an associated verb of seeing or appearing, but the link is found in Acts 10:30 without such a verb, and possibly also in Luke 1:11). Luke is not likely to be responsible for the historic present: λέγει (lit. "he says"). There may be a link between εἰρήνη ὑμῖν, "peace to you," and the directive to the itinerant missionary in Luke 10:5 to impart peace to the house that he enters (see there [the language is traditional rather than Lukan]). Dillon (Eye-Witnesses, 186–93) argues the case at length, pointing to the additional shared motifs of eating the food set before one and proclamation. The linkages suggested by Dillon are both attractive and suggestive but, beyond the greeting of peace, remain too imprecise to carry conviction. The greeting of peace itself is questionable as a key identifying link because it is a standard Jewish greeting and is also a greeting used in OT encounters with angelic figures (see Dan 10:19; cf. Judg 6:23).

37 πτοηθέντες δὲ καὶ ἔμφοβοι (lit. "having been terrified and [being] fearful") is Lukan language (cf. Dauer, Johannes und Lukas, 262–63). However, the difficulty of such a reaction after vv 34–35 makes it unlikely that Luke has introduced the fear motif here. The fear language could be a further link with the pattern of an angelic visitation (cf. Luke 1:12, 30; 2:9; 24:5; Acts 10:4; Dan 8:17; Tob 12:16), but the continuation of the verse takes us in a rather different direction. Perhaps we have here an adaptation of the "angelophany" form to the needs of an account whose central concern must be with the identification of the one appearing as the risen Jesus. The use of the angelic visitation pattern could lend a certain sense of the supernatural to the account. In vv 44–49, the pattern will be suitably carried forward with the words of Jesus (which have their counterpart in the messages brought by angelic figures). The words ἔμφοβοι γενόμενοι (lit. "becoming fearful") will be intended to echo ἐμφόβων γενομένων (lit. "becoming fearful") in v 5, reinforcing the natural parallelism between the two episodes (in this light, the fact that ἔστη, "stood," in v 36 is cognate with ἐπέστησαν, "appeared," gains a significance not previously evident, as does the similarity between εἶπαν πρὸς αὐτάς, "said to them," and λέγει αὐτοῖς, "says to them," in the same verses and the question form shared between vv 5 and 38).

What does Luke mean here by πνεῦμα, "spirit"? Probably we need to go to the world of mediums and the consulting of the dead to understand the role of "spirit" here (cf. 1 Sam 28:3–19; Isa 8:19; 19:3; 29:4). Though the dead were essentially tied to their graves, it was considered possible at times to call up the dead in the form of ghostly apparitions. One ought, however, not to think of these apparitions as being in any proper sense the person: it was more like some sort of residue of what had been the life of the person. This was possible, but strictly forbidden in the law (Lev 19:31; 20:6; Deut 18:11). The defilement of the grave attached to these specters and calling them up involved meddling in things with which the living have no right to be involved. Calling up the spirits of the dead represented an attempt to reinstate a past upon which God in his inscrutable purposes had closed the door. In (later?) popular thought it became possible to imagine these disembodied specters as occasionally loose about the earth (see *b. Ber.* 18b; already in *4 Ezra* 7:80 there is quite a Hellenistic separation of the body and the spirit, with the attribution of a separate existence to the spirit in the intermediate state; and cf. *Jub.* 23:31). A second but rather less likely possibility is to see the "spirit" as a demon mimicking the form of Jesus.

38 εἶπεν αὐτοῖς, "said to them," lacks the Lukan use of πρός. Only in 1:12 does Luke have ταράσσειν, "trouble," with a comparable sense, and even there its role is different (see at v 37). Luke may be partly responsible for the diction in διὰ τί διαλογισμοὶ ἀναβαίνουσιν ἐν τῇ καρδίᾳ ὑμῶν, "why do doubts arise in your hearts" (as Dauer, *Johannes und Lukas*, 264–66). However, Luke does not use διαλογισμός elsewhere to mean "doubt," and only one of his twenty-eight uses of ἀναβαίνειν (here: "arise") is comparable to the use here; at most Luke will have modified the wording of a source. The disciples here are just as "foolish [and] slow of heart to believe" (v 25) as ever the Emmaus disciples were.

39 If anything is Lukan here, it is likely to be the final clause, "as you see that I have" (for the traditional nature of the content of v 39, see Dauer, *Johannes und Lukas*, 266–68; but for the opposite view, see Neirynck, "Lc 24,36–43," 668). The verse may, however, show the marks of earlier development. The opening part of the verse (to "It is I") could sustain the thought development by itself. "A spirit does not have flesh and bones" would be an accurate and understandable explanatory development (cf. "spirits have no hair" in *Midr. Ruth* 3:9). Finally, "touch me and see" (slightly awkward after the earlier use of "see") could represent a development designed to provide assurance that no "visual deception" was involved. This last development could possibly be set to the account of Luke, who does have another (rather different) use of ψηλαφᾶν, "touch," in Acts 17:27.

Given the loose and rather full clothing characteristic of ancient Palestine, apart from the face, the hands/forearms (χεῖρας could be either) and the feet are the visible parts of a human body (John's "hands/forearms" and "side," with their concern for the wound marks, are likely to represent a later use of this tradition). So it is here that the proper solidity ("flesh") and rigidity ("bones") of the human body become evident. There is really no sign here of anti-gnostic or anti-docetic polemic. The central affirmation is "It is I myself." Everything else is designed to support this affirmation. The point is not to affirm a particular kind of resurrection: in the logic of the account, a spectral appearance would be no resurrection at all! In this context, there is an incidental (but not unintended) affirmation of the inalienable materiality of the human body (resurrected or not).

I cannot avoid the impression that the extensive scholarly difficulty with this particular resurrection account betrays an underlying tendency to be scandalized by materiality. Ancient Hellenistic dualism lives on!

40 καὶ τοῦτο εἰπών, "and saying this," is a thoroughly Lukan turn of phrase (cf. Dauer, *Johannes und Lukas*, 269; but only in Acts does a Lukan use of this idiom actually emerge), but it is even more obviously a Johannine idiom (9:6; 11:28; 13:21; 18:1, 22, 38; 20:14, 20, 22; 21:19). δεικνύναι, "show," is clearly Lukan only in 20:24, which is an insufficient basis for declaring it Lukan here. It is quite possible that v 40 formed no part of the most original form of this account. The verse simply adds additional emphasis by making the inspection of hands/forearms and feet a matter of deliberate display by Jesus.

41 The dative after εἶπεν, "said," and the NT *hapax* βρώσιμον (lit. "[something] eatable") are insufficient to provide assurance of a source form behind the heavy concentration of Lukan language here (see Jeremias, *Sprache*, 321; Dauer, *Johannes und Lukas*, 271–74). However, there will have needed to be a response statement at this point in Luke's source. ἀπιστούντων αὐτῶν ἀπὸ τῆς χαρᾶς (lit. "they being unbelieving from joy") is notably parallel to the Lukan formulation in 22:45: κοιμωμένους αὐτοὺς ἀπὸ τῆς λύπης (lit. "them being asleep from grief"). From the remarkable juxtaposition of unbelief and joy, one might already suspect that some kind of conflation is involved. Since the unbelief and the wondering both echo the state of mind of the disciple band as reported by Luke in vv 11–12, and since these open up the space for the development to follow (which is under suspicion of being a Lukan development), we should probably identify the note of joy as the original element preserved by Luke here (this element is also found in the Johannine text at this point). There is a certain (inverse) correspondence between the request for food here and the offer of hospitality (including food) in v 29. βρώσιμον is cognate with the word used for "food" at 9:13 (βρώματα).

42 ἐπιδιδόναι, "give," is a verb favored by Luke, and it is the verb used at v 30 in the meal scene recalls the feeding miracle in 9:10–17. It has already been suggested that "fish" here has its counterpart in the "bread" of v 30, and so together they correspond to the bread and fish of 9:13, 16 (see at 24:30). ὀπτός, "broiled," is not found elsewhere in NT or LXX. μέρος is found only here in the NT with the sense "piece"; though the Greek word is quite different, in light of the other links, an echo of κλασμάτων, "fragments/pieces," in 9:17 may be intended.

43 ἐνώπιον, "before," is a favored Lukan word, while λαβών (lit. "having taken") and ἔφαγεν, "he ate," are likely here to echo Luke 9:16–17.

The role that we should ascribe to vv 41b–43 depends partly upon where in the account Luke would have us understand that the disciples were able to move on to a full belief in the resurrected Lord. Is it after v 43? This view gives weight to the ἔτι, "still," at the beginning of v 41 and to the participial construction to which it is linked: the eating resolves the residual doubt. But without denying the importance of the eating, two factors count in favor of an alternative view. (*i*) In the Lukan Emmaus account, the combined effect of the exposition of Scripture and the breaking of bread creates an awareness of the reality of the presence of the risen Lord. Vv 44–49 contain strong echoes of the scriptural exposition of vv 25–27, which suggests that here too the exposition of Scripture contributes to the disciples' moving on from their state of (partial) doubt in v 41. (*ii*) In v 52, the (qualified) joy of v 41 is taken up again as an unqualified "great joy" (and note that here the disciples are said for the first time to worship Jesus). In light of these considerations, it seems better to see that Luke is reiterating and expanding the Emmaus pattern: beyond the partial belief achieved by v 41 through the display of hands and feet, here the combined effect of the meal, the teaching/ scriptural exposition, and the experience of the ascension of Jesus brings to maturity faith in the resurrection of Jesus.

If the role of vv 41b–43 is to be seen primarily in this framework, then we ought not to provide any strong link between the eating and the concern about whether the appearance is that of a specter. Eating cannot of itself "prove" Jesus' genuine material humanity (the angelic figures representing the presence of the Lord in Gen 18 manage quite a substantial meal [and. cf. 19:3], while in Tobit the angel Raphael gave every appearance of eating and drinking [see Tob 12:19]). Rather, as in the feeding of the five thousand and as for the Emmaus disciples, Jesus is made known for who he is in the meal setting. Since there is no specific way in which the eating of a piece of broiled fish could achieve such a revelation, we should allow the account to function symbolically. Through it, Luke expresses a eucharistic theology.

Explanation

To the empty tomb, the angelic witness, the experience of the Emmaus disciples, and the report of the experience of Peter, Luke now adds an encounter by the gathered disciples with the risen Lord. Jesus demonstrates that he is no specter and, by eating some fish, provides for Luke's narrative the other half (with verse 30) of the link back to the feeding of the five thousand, that event in his earthly ministry through which the disciple band came to recognize (up to a point) Jesus' true identity.

Occurring while the reporting is still going on, this new development is meant to be taken as further confirmation of the truth of the Easter conviction. Luke will tell this story of Jesus' appearance in language that occasionally evokes OT accounts of the appearance of angelic figures. In this way, Luke probably underlines the "supernatural" nature of what is being experienced and perhaps encourages us to see Jesus speaking as the mouthpiece of God in much the way the angel Gabriel did in chap. 1. In the larger Lukan structuring, there is a deliberate paralleling of the women's experience with the angels at the tomb with this present encounter with the risen Lord.

Jesus' greeting is one of peace, but the disciples feel anything but peaceful about the encounter. They are thoroughly rattled and quite unprepared to see this figure as the risen Lord Jesus. They think rather of the sort of apparitions and voices associated with the calling up of the dead by mediums. The disciples are just as "foolish [and] slow of heart to believe" as ever the Emmaus disciples (v 25) had been. Jesus challenges the disciples about this and moves to overcome their doubts.

Jesus begins by affirming his own identity: "It is I myself." But this is not enough. The disciples have seen Jesus' face. Given the loose and rather full clothing characteristic of ancient Palestine, the lower arms and the feet are the other visible parts of a human body. An examination of these parts should show that Jesus is no specter but has the solidity ("flesh") and the rigidity ("bones") of a proper human body. (No doubt in the interests of Christian apologetics, the account is fashioned to underline heavily the visual and tactile evidence for this appearance not being a mere specter.)

Jesus' efforts are partly successful: joy replaces fear; but there is still unbelief and wondering. The risen Lord is not yet fully known for who he is. As for the Emmaus disciples, Luke tells us that it was in the breaking of bread that things finally came together. The eating of the fish here is the other half of the allusion to the feeding of the five thousand that was noted in the discussion of the Emmaus meal. (Note the vocabulary links through vv 41–43.) In a rather more indirect way than was the case in the Emmaus account, Luke is pointing to the way in which, for the early church, the risen Lord continued to be made known for who he really was in the communion practice of the church.

In vv 36–53, Luke is concerned to reiterate and expand the Emmaus pattern: partial belief is achieved through the display of hands and feet in v 39 and by Jesus' participation in the meal in vv 40–47. Yet to come is the place given to teaching/scriptural exposition in verses 44–49; finally, the disciples experience the ascension of Jesus in vv 50–53. Only then is faith in the resurrection of Jesus brought to its maturity.

Though the disciples' disbelief is reprehensible, for Luke there is clearly an apologetic value in the disciples' difficulty to reach a secure knowledge of the resurrected Lord. The difficulties involved may point as well to the immensity and the mystery being encountered here for the first time in human history.

Jesus Instructs and Expounds Scripture   (24:44–49)

Bibliography

Basset, J.-C. "Dernières paroles du ressuscité et mission de l'Église aujourd'hui (A propos de Mt 28,18–20 et parallèles). *RTP* 114 (1982) 349–67. **Benoit, P.** *The Passion and Resurrection of Jesus.* 313–42. **Bockel, P.** "Luc 24,45: 'Il leur ouvrit l'esprit à l'intelligence des écritures.'" *BTS* 36 (1961) 2–3. **Dillon, R. J.** *From Eye-Witnesses to Ministers of the Word: Tradition and Composition in Luke 24.* AnBib 82. Rome: Biblical Institute, 1978. 203–20. ————. "Easter Revelation and Mission Program in Luke 24:46–48." In *Sin, Salvation, and the Spirit: Commemorating the Fiftieth Year of the Liturgical Press,* ed. D. Durken. Collegeville, MN: Liturgical Press, 1979. 240–70. **Dömer, M.** *Das Heil Gottes.* 99–106. **Duesberg, H.** "He Opened Their Minds to Understand the Scriptures." *Concil* 30 (1968) 111–21. **Dumm, D. R.** "Luke 24:44–49 and Hospitality." In *Sin, Salvation, and the Spirit: Commemorating the Fiftieth Year of the Liturgical Press,* ed. D. Durken. Collegeville MN: Liturgical Press, 1979. 231–39. **Dupont, J.** "La portée christologique de l'évangélisation des nations d'après Luc 24,47." In *Neues Testament und Kirche.* FS R. Schnackenburg, ed. J. Gnilka. Freiburg im B.: Herder, 1974. 125–43. ————. "La mission de Paul d'après Actes 26.16–23 et la mission des apôtres d'après Luc 24.44–49 et Actes 1.8." In *Paul and Paulinism.* FS C. K. Barrett, ed. M. D. Hooker and S. G. Wilson. London: SPCK, 1982. 290–301. **Ernst, J.** "Schriftauslegung und Auferstehungsglaube bei Lukas." *TGl* 60 (1970) 360–74; reprinted in *Schriftauslegung,* ed. J. Ernst. Munich: Schöningh, 1972. 177–92. **George, A.** "L'Intelligence des écritures (Luc 24,44–53)." *BVC* 18 (1957) 65–71. **Hubbard, B. J.** "Commissioning Stories in Luke-Acts: A Study of Their Antecedents, Form and Content." *Semeia* 8 (1977) 103–26. **Kingsbury, J. D.** "Luke 24:44–49." *Int* 35 (1981) 170–74. **Kümmel, W. G.** *Promise and Fulfilment.* 105. **Legrand, L.** "The Missionary Command of the Risen Christ: I. Mission and Resurrection." *ITS* 23 (1986) 290–309. **Prast, F.** *Presbyter und Evangelium in nachapostolischer Zeit: Die Abschiedsrede des Paulus in Milet (Apg. 20,17–38) im Rahmen der lukanischen Konzeption der Evangeliumsverkündigung.* FB 29. Stuttgart: Katholisches Bibelwerk, 1979. 281–84. **Schneider, G.** "Der Missionsauftrag Jesu in der Darstellung der Evangelien." In *Lukas, Theologe der Heilsgeschichte.* 184–205. **Sieber, J. H.** "The Spirit as the 'Promise of My Father' in Luke 24:49." In *Sin, Salvation, and the Spirit: Commemorating the Fiftieth Year of the Liturgical Press,* ed. D. Durken. Collegeville MN: Liturgical Press, 1979. 271–78.

And see at 24:1–12, 36–43.

Translation

[44] *He said to them, "These are my*[a] *words which I spoke to you while I was still with you: 'It is necessary for everything written in the law of Moses and the prophets and the psalms concerning me to be fulfilled.'"* [45] *Then he opened their minds to understand the Scriptures:* [46] *he said to them, "This is what stands written: the Christ is to suffer, and to rise from the dead*[b] *on the third day;* [47] *and repentance for the forgiveness of sins is to be proclaimed in his name to all the nations, beginning*[c] *from Jerusalem.* [48] *You [are]*[d] *witnesses of these things.* [49][e] *I am sending the promise of my Father*[f] *upon you: you are to wait in the city until you are clothed with power from heaven."*

Notes

[a] "My" is missing from ℵ W Θ *f*[1,13] etc.

[b] "From the dead" is missing from D sa.

[c] In P[75] A C[3] W *f*[1,13] etc., the hanging nominative participle ἀρξάμενοι, "beginning," becomes ἀρξάμενον, to agree with ἔθνη, "nations." The genitive form in D Δ[c] etc. is more difficult to explain, as is the masc. nominative sing. in Θ Ψ 565 etc.

[d] The verb ἐστέ, "are," is supplied by ℵ A C L W Θ Ψ etc.

[e] ἰδού (lit. "behold") is left untranslated. It is missing from P[75] ℵ D L 33 lat etc. and may not be original.

[f] "The Father" is missing from D e (so: "my promise").

Form/Structure/Setting

The encounter with the risen Lord continues here, with final teaching and instruction. Vv 44–46 take us again over terrain familiar to us from vv 6–7 and 26–27, but vv 47–49 move into new territory with their mission emphasis. See further at 24:1–12 on the larger structure of the chapter.

There is quite a broadly based consensus that for this unit we are very much in Luke's hands (see Dauer, *Johannes und Lukas,* 275–83; Guillaume, *Luc interprète,* 181–87). Not that this means that Luke lacked a significant foundation in the tradition for what he attributes to the risen Lord here. Luke could draw on the tradition in the Emmaus account at vv 26–27 (see there). Luke had the passion predictions to draw upon. The idea that the pre-passion Jesus had seen his destiny being governed, at least in part, by the need to fulfill Scripture, although distinctly important for Luke, is not unique to him (Luke introduced it into a passion prediction at 18:31, but Mark before him has such an idea at 9:12; 14:21, 49; the early church's use of Scripture was strongly marked by this idea). Luke had available the material of Mark 13:10, which he passed over in chap. 21. Beyond these obvious sources, there is the evident relationship between materials here and in appearance accounts in Matthew and John (see at 24:1–12 for a listing of the shared features).

The uniquely Lukan content (as distinct from formulation and differences at the level of detail) may be reduced to (*i*) the idea that the preaching to all nations was anticipated in the Scriptures and (*ii*) the call *to sit tight in Jerusalem* until the promised power from on high should arrive (I have subsumed here "beginning from Jerusalem" from v 48). Point *i* is a pervasively present conviction through the pages of Acts, which comes into particular focus in Acts 15:15–18 (and cf. esp. 13:47). One might suspect that if the mission to the Gentiles had been as patently obvious to the earliest disciple group as this instruction from the risen Lord should have made it, then the problems leading up to the meeting of Acts 15 would not have occurred in the way they did. There can be little doubt that Luke's version of the risen Lord's teaching here compresses together things that only over a period of time were clearly recognized to be the will of the risen Christ. Point *ii* is a feature of Luke's particular schematic way of linking the mission of Jesus and that of the early church.

The sense that Jesus is no longer to be with the disciples hovers over these verses. When this is seen in connection with the links between the blessing of v 50 and the farewell blessings of Abraham and Moses (see below at vv 50–53), it becomes evident that Luke has shaped these verses with the testamentary genre in mind: this is to be seen as comparable to the final discourse before death of a great man with his family/followers (Tob 12 probably exhibits an adaptation of this genre in connection with the return of the angel Raphael to heaven; Tob 12 also shares with Luke 24 the motif of the revelation of the unknown identity of the central figure).

Comment

Jesus' final conversation with his disciples before his departure to heaven reiterates the conviction that the pattern of his destiny is preset by the testimony of Scripture. Set there, too, is the need for the coming mission of the church, as the disciples bear their witness to what they have seen and heard. For this they will be empowered by the Spirit of God, to be sent to them by the exalted Jesus.

44 All the language here fits Lukan diction. Luke puts down a marker at 18:31 (and cf. 22:37), which prepares for the present reference back to "while I was still with you." The risen Lord repeats the message of the pre-passion Jesus, but now his message strikes home. The incognito risen Lord had delivered much the same message to the Emmaus disciples (cf. 24:27 and see there). Note the deliberate language links between vv 25–27 and v 44 ("he said to them . . . spoke . . . it is [was] necessary . . . Moses . . . all . . . the prophets . . . the Scriptures, ταῖς γραφαῖς [the things having been written, τὰ γεγραμμένα] . . . concerning himself [me] "). Except for the position of "all" (actually multiple present in vv 25–27) and "the Scriptures," even the word order is the same (in v 44, "all" comes before

"Moses," and the participial equivalent for "the Scriptures" comes in between—Luke will use "the Scriptures" in v 45; if we take this as the equivalent, then the verbal sequence will have the inversion of two pairs in what is otherwise a parallel sequence [including v 45 draws in the similarity of idea between "interpreted to them" in v 27 and "opened their minds" in v 45]). There is also a verbal linkage here with vv 6–7. In common is "spoke to you yet being . . . it is necessary," which can be supplemented from v 46 with "to rise on the third day." In the Lukan chiasmic structuring of the chapter, this contributes to the parallelism between vv 4b–7(8) and 36–46(8).

45 The language is Lukan, echoing v 32 in both thought and language (see there). The idiom (to open the heart) in Acts 16:14 is notably similar to the opening of the mind here, but the sense is rather different. The activity involved will be the same as that in v 27.

46 οὕτως γέγραπται (lit. "thus it has been written") is found only here, but Luke uses καθώς or ὡς γέγραπται, "just as" or "as it has been written," in 2:23; 3:4; Acts 7:42; 13:33; 15:15. παθεῖν τὸν Χριστόν (lit. "the Christ to suffer") is repeated from v 26. καὶ ἀναστῆναι . . . τῇ τρίτῃ ἡμέρᾳ, "to rise on the third day," repeats the wording of v 7 (but with the verb brought forward). Luke has not previously used ἐκ νεκρῶν (lit. "out of dead [ones]") in connection with the resurrection of Jesus. He has used the phrase of the possibility of Jesus being John the Baptist raised from the dead (9:7) and in other discussions of resurrection (16:31; 20:35). In the Acts preaching, the phrase will be regularly used with reference to the resurrection of Jesus; it was clearly part of the standard kerygmatic language of the early church.

47 Though various attempts have been made to take it in other ways, the only natural way to take the infinitive κηρυχθῆναι, "to be preached," is in parallel with the previous infinitives: this activity too has been anticipated in the Scriptures (cf. Acts 13:47; 15:15–18). There is much to be said for the well-canvassed view that Luke is making use here of the content of Mark 13:10, which he passed over in chap. 21 (Mark 13:10 has κηρυχθῆναι, "to be preached," and εἰς πάντα τὰ ἔθνη, "to all the nations"; Luke has preferred over Mark's τὸ εὐαγγέλιον, "the gospel" [which Luke never uses in the Gospel (twice in Acts)] his own summary of the gospel message ["repentance for the forgiveness of sins"; the phrase is found in 3:3 (see discussion there) in connection with John's preaching, and Acts 5:31 is closely related]). Though Mark 13:10 is likely to be the immediate source, Matt 28:19 suggests that, in taking Mark 13:10 into a post-resurrection appearance setting, Luke was responding to an impulse already available to him in the tradition. Luke's interest in the universality of the Christian message was marked as early as 2:32 (see there). Of the senses that ἐπὶ τῷ ὀνόματι αὐτοῦ, "in his name," can take (cf. at 9:48a), best here is "by people acting as my representatives" (this finds support from Acts 26:22–23 [which is notably parallel to Luke 24:44–47], where the resurrected Christ proclaims "to the People and to the nations"); also just possible would be a sense based on comparison with Acts 10:43 (where, however, διὰ τοῦ ὀνόματος, "*through* his name" is used): "in my name" would link with "forgiveness of sins," the point being that forgiveness of sins through Jesus is being offered.

The Jerusalem beginning will be reinforced in v 49b (cf. the Galilean beginning for Jesus' ministry in 23:5). It will be elaborated at Acts 1:8 (on the role of this Jerusalem beginning, see discussion at 24:1–12 on Luke's location of the resurrection appearances in Jerusalem).

48   The language here is cryptic. From the immediate context, we can infer that the disciples are directed to witness because they have experienced and are therefore in a position to testify about (*i*) the pre-passion teaching of Jesus with its emphasis on the fulfillment of Scripture with reference to himself; (*ii*) the post-resurrection illumination of the Scriptures by the risen Lord; (*iii*) the passion events themselves; (*iv*) the reality of Jesus' resurrected state; (*v*) the need for universal proclamation of the message of forgiveness in Jesus' name (though to include it technically transcends the logic of the language, it is difficult to see how engagement in proclamation can be excluded from the witness intended); and (*vi*) the need to begin this proclamation in Jerusalem. In the Acts 1:8 parallel (and cf. v 22), the Apostles are to be "my [Jesus'] witnesses," but the wider group in view in Luke 24 makes it clear that the role of the Apostles, though central, is in no way meant to exclude or excuse the wider disciple community from the witnessing task (cf. the relationship between 9:1–6 and 10:1–20; the view of Plevnick [*CBQ* 49 (1987) 90–103], that the role of those with the Eleven in Luke 24 is to be a pool out of which Judas' replacement can be chosen, is much too restricted). As the witnessing takes place in Acts, its central focus is on the resurrection, but also included are the passion events and even the pre-passion ministry of Jesus (1:22; 2:32; 3:15; 5:32; 10:39, 41; 13:31).

49   It is likely that Luke intends a certain echoing here of the infancy materials (esp. chap. 1) with which he began his Gospel ("I send," as the angel Gabriel had been sent in 1:26; anticipation of "the promise," as the infancy events themselves had been in fulfillment of the covenant promise [1:54–55; 70, 72–73]; an outworking of the father/son relationship, as in 1:32, 35; action focused in the holy city, Jerusalem; endowment with "power," as in 1:17 [and cf. v 35]; "from heaven," as was the sunrise of 1:78 [cf. the cognate term "most high" in 1:32, 35, 76; 2:14]). Here we stand on a major threshold, as was the case in the anticipatory aspects of chaps. 1–2. This echoing of the beginning at the end will also be noted at 24:50–53 (see at v 50).

Luke will use the striking idiom "promise of my/the Father" again in Acts 1:4 (even more striking when prefaced with "*I* [*Jesus*] am sending"). There (v 5) it is explained in terms of the Spirit, with reference to the contrast between the baptism John was able to offer and baptism with the Spirit of God (cf. Luke 3:16). The logic of the wait in Jerusalem (which takes us past the ascension) is clarified in Acts 2:33: Jesus sends the Spirit from his place of exaltation at the right hand of God. The language of promise is applied to the Spirit also in Gal 3:14; Eph 1:13. In mind are texts like Isa 32:15; 44:3; Ezek 39:29; Joel 2:28 (quoted in Acts 2:17). In the context of Luke 24:44–49, the Spirit is anticipated distinctly as empowerment for the witnessing task that lies ahead. This prospect of empowerment has its counterpart in the power of the Spirit that undergirded Jesus' own ministry (cf. 4:14; 5:17). The Pentecostal empowering of the disciple band has been prefigured in the "power" given in 9:1 (as the preaching to come has in 9:2): in an anticipatory manner, the disciples have already participated in the ministry of Jesus (9:1–6; 10:1–20); they will in the future carry his ministry forward when he sits exalted at the right hand of God. The directive given here already implies Jesus' imminent departure, to be reported in vv 50–53. Though this is clearer in

Acts 1, in light of the translation to heaven to follow, we should probably see a link here with the transmission of the Spirit from Elijah to Elisha in 2 Kgs 2:9–10.

Explanation

Much of this unit has a familiar ring, as the risen Lord uses his final opportunity for instruction to reiterate the conviction that the passion and resurrection fulfilled the mandate of Scripture. But there is also a less familiar theme, as vv 47–49 open up what will be the preoccupation of the Book of Acts.

The risen Lord points to the identity between his pre-passion teaching and the events of the passion and resurrection and what he now as the risen Lord still wants to affirm. Much of this content has already appeared in a post-resurrection setting in discussion with the Emmaus disciples (vv 25–27), and the angels at the tomb (vv 6–7) have shown some of the same preoccupation.

The scriptural need for the preaching of the gospel to all nations is a note that has not been clearly sounded before, though Luke has shown his interest in the universal claim of the gospel from as early as 2:32. Where do the Scriptures predict this preaching to the nations? Acts 13:47 and 15:15–18 provide some clue to the identity of these Scriptures. Preaching to the nations is indicated as the next stage of the career of the Christ: it is to be carried on by people representing the Christ and, as we will see in a moment, empowered by him. The close identification between the Christ and those who speak in his name is evident from the language of Acts 26:22–23 (cf. 9:4–5).

The message can be summarized as a call for repentance with a view to the forgiveness of sins. In Luke's account, this was already John the Baptist's message (see 3:3), but the story of salvation has developed since then: distinct to the present call to repentance and offer of forgiveness is the foundation in the death and resurrection of Jesus (the offer of the Spirit will also emerge as a new development).

A Jerusalem beginning is important in the Lukan symbolism: though it is for all the world, the gospel emerges from the very heartland of Jewish faith. The pattern will be elaborated at Acts 1:8.

The wording here introduces the witness role of the disciples in a very cryptic manner. We must draw its content first out of the immediate context (vv 36–47), then out of the earlier Gospel material where the disciples experienced the pre-passion ministry of Jesus, and finally out of the Acts story to come, in which we see this witnessing role actually worked out. As will become clear in Acts 1, the Apostles have a central role in witness, but witnessing is a task they share with many others in the Christian community. The logic of witness in the Christian life is that each witnesses to his or her own gift.

Supportive of the witnessing task is the promise of the Holy Spirit in v 49. Various OT texts anticipated an end-time outpouring of the Spirit of God; Jesus goes to exaltation in heaven to send this promised outpouring of the Spirit (see Acts 2:33). As in John 16:7, Jesus must go to his exalted destiny before the Spirit can be given.

However, though the giving of the Spirit needs to wait for Jesus' exaltation, the promise of power here has not lacked anticipations in the time of the ministry of Jesus. Jesus has himself been empowered by the Spirit for his ministry (see 4:14; 5:17); and Jesus has in turn given power to his disciple band, who have been sent out to speak and act in his name (see 9:1–6; 10:1–20).

On the threshold of the post-Easter mission of the church, Luke chooses language for v 49 that has quite a number of echoes from chap. 1, where, at a previous threshold, the imminent coming of the Christ as a human baby was anticipated.

Jesus Ascends to Heaven   (24:50–53)

Bibliography

GENERAL ON THE ASCENSION:

Argyle, A. W. "The Ascension." *ExpTim* 66 (1954–55) 240–42. **Baird, W.** "Ascension and Resurrection: An Intersection of Luke and Paul." In *Texts and Testaments: Critical Essays on the Bible and Early Church Fathers.* San Antonio: Trinity University, 1980. 3–18. **Belser, J. E.** *History of the Passion, Death, and Glorification of Our Saviour, Jesus Christ.* Adapted by F. A. Merks. St. Louis: B. Herder, 1929. 644–58. **Benoit, P.** "The Ascension." In *Jesus and the Gospel.* New York: Herder and Herder, 1973. 1:209–53. **Bertram, G.** "Die Himmelfahrt Jesu vom Kreuz aus und der Glaube an seine Auferstehung." In *Festgabe für Adolf Deissmann zum 60. Geburtstag 7. November 1926.* Tübingen: Mohr-Siebeck, 1927. 187–217. ————. "Der religionsgeschichtliche Hintergrung des Begriffs der 'Erhöhung' in der Septuaginta." *ZAW* 68 (1956) 57–71. **Bock, E.** "Von der Himmelfahrt im Alten und Neuen Testament." *Christengemeinschaft* 4 (1927) 45–50. **Bouwman, G.** "Die Erhöhung Jesu in der lukanischen Theologie." *BZ* 14 (1970) 257–63. **Davies, J. G.** *He Ascended into Heaven: A Study in the History of Doctrine.* London: Lutterworth, 1958. **Devor, R. C.** "The Ascension of Christ and the Dissension of the Church." *Encounter* 33 (1972) 340–58. **Donne, B. K.** *Christ Ascended.* Exeter: Paternoster, 1983. **Flicoteaux, E.** "La glorieuse ascension." *VSpir* 76 (1947) 664–75. **Haroutunian, J.** "The Doctrine of the Ascension: A Study of the New Testament Teaching." *Int* 10 (1956) 270–81. **Holzmeister, U.** "Der Tag der Himmelfahrt des Herrn" *ZKT* 55 (1931) 44–82. **Jansen, J. F.** "The Ascension, the Church, and Theology." *TToday* 16 (1959) 17–29. **Kern, W.** "Das Fortgehen Jesu und das Kommen des Geistes oder Christi Himmelfahrt." *GuL* 41 (1968) 85–90. **Kretschmar, G.** "Himmelfahrt und Pfingsten." *ZKG* 66 (1954–55) 209–53. **Lake, K.** "Note III: The Ascension." In *Beginnings of Christianity,* ed. F. J. Foakes-Jackson and K. Lake. Reprinted. Grand Rapids: Baker, 1979. 5:16–22. **Larrañaga, V.** *L'Ascension de Notre-Seigneur dans le Nouveau Testament.* Scripti pontificii instituti biblici. Rome: Biblical Institute, 1938. **Léon-Dufour, X.** *Resurrection and the Message of Easter.* New York: Holt, Rinehart and Winston, 1974. 80–94. **Lohfink, G.** "Der historische Ansatz der Himmelfahrt Christi." *Catholica* 17 (1963) 44–84. **Mann, C. S.** "The New Testament and the Lord's Ascension." *CQR* 158 (1957) 452–65. **McNamara, M.** "The Ascension and the Exaltation of Christ in the Fourth Gospel." *Scr* 19 (1967) 65–73. **Metzger, B. M.** "The Ascension of Jesus Christ." In *Historical and Literary Studies: Pagan, Jewish, and Christian.* NTTS 8. Grand Rapids, MI: Eerdmans, 1968. 77–87. ————. "The Meaning of Christ's Ascension." In *Search the Scriptures: New Testament Studies.* FS R. T. Stamm, ed. J. M. Meyers et al. Gettysburg Theological Studies 3. Leiden: Brill, 1969. 118–28. **Milligan, W.** *The Ascension and Heavenly Priesthood of Our Lord.* London: Macmillan, 1901. 1–60. **Miquel, P.** "Le mystère de L'Ascension." *QLP* 40 (1959) 105–26. **Moule, C. F. D.** "The Ascension—Acts i.9." *ExpTim* 68 (1957) 205–9. **Ramsey, A. M.** "What Was the Ascension?" In *Historicity and Chronology in the New Testament,* ed. D. E. Nineham. London: SPCK, 1965. 135–44. **Ruckstuhl, E.** "Auferstehung, Erhöhung und Himmelfahrt Jesu." In *Jesus im Horizont der*

Evangelien. Stuttgarter Biblische Aufsatzbände 3. Stuttgart: Katholisches Bibelwerk, 1988. 185–218. **Schelkle, K. H.** "Christi Himmelfahrt." *GuL* 41 (1968) 81–85. **Schillebeeckx, E.** "Ascension and Pentecost." *Worship* 35 (1960–61) 336–63. **Schmitt, A.** *Entrückung— Aufnahme—Himmelfahrt: Untersuchungen zu einem Vorstellungsbereich im Alten Testament.* FB 10. Stuttgart: Katholisches Bibelwerk, 1974. **Seidensticker, P.,** ed. *Zeitgenössische Texte zur Osterbotschaft der Evangelien.* SBS 27. Stuttgart: Katholisches Bibelwerk, 1967. 65–68. **Selwyn, E. G.** "Our Lord's Ascension." *Th* 12 (1926) 241–44. **Toon, P.** *The Ascension of Our Lord.* New York: Nelson, 1984. **Vögtle, A.** "'Erhöht zur Rechten Gottes': Braucht der Osterglaube die Krücken des antiken Weltbildes?" *Orientierung* 45 (1981) 78–80. **Wilson, S. G.** "The Ascension: A Critique and an Interpretation." *ZNW* 59 (1968) 269–81.

FOR 24:50–53:

Bacon, B. W. "The Ascension in Luke and Acts." *Exp* 7/7 (1909) 245–61. **Bouwman, G.** "Die Erhöhung Jesu in der lukanischen Theologie." *BZ* 14 (1970) 257–63. **Creed, J. M.** "The Text and Interpretation of Acts 1:1–2." *JTS* 35 (1934) 176–82. **Davies, J. G.** "The Prefigurement of the Ascension in the Third Gospel." *JTS* 6 (1955) 229–33. **Dillon, R. J.** *From Eye-Witnesses to Ministers of the Word: Tradition and Composition in Luke 24.* AnBib 82. Rome: Biblical Institute, 1978. 170–82, 184, 220–25. **Enslin, M. S.** "The Ascension Story." *JBL* 47 (1928) 60–73. **Epp, E. J.** "The Ascension in the Textual Tradition of Luke-Acts." In *New Testament Textual Criticism: Its Significance for Exegesis.* FS B. M. Metzger, ed. E. J. Epp and G. D. Fee. Oxford: Clarendon, 1981. 131–45. **Fitzmyer, J. A.** "The Ascension of Christ and Pentecost." *TS* 45 (1984) 409–40. **Franklin, E.** "The Ascension and the Eschatology of Luke-Acts." *SJT* 23 (1970) 191–200. **Fridrichsen, A.** "Die Himmelfahrt bei Lukas." *TBl* 6 (1927) 337–41. **Guillaume, J.-M.** *Luc interprète des anciennes traditions sur la résurrection de Jésus.* EBib. Paris: Gabalda, 1979. 203–74. **Hahn, F.** "Die Himmelfahrt Jesu: Ein Gespräch mit Gerhard Lohfink." *Bib* 55 (1974) 418–26. **Houlden, L.** "Beyond Belief: Preaching the Ascension (II)." *Th* 94 (1991) 173–80. **LaVerdiere, E. A.** "The Ascension of the Risen Lord." *BiTod* 95 (1978) 1553–59. **Leaney, A. R. C.** "Why There Were Forty Days between the Resurrection and the Ascension in Acts 1,3." *SE* 4 [= TU 102] (1968) 417–19. **Lohfink, G.** *Die Himmelfahrt Jesu: Untersuchungen zu den Himmelfahrts- und Erhöhungstexten bei Lukas.* SANT 26. Munich: Kösel, 1971. Esp. 147–76. ⸺. "'Was steht ihr da und schauet' (Apg 1,11): Die Himmelfahrts- und lukanischen Geschichtswerk." *BK* 20 (1965) 43–48. **Lowther Clarke, W. K.** "St Luke and the Pseudepigrapha: Two Parallels." *JTS* 15 (1914) 597–99. **MacRae, G. W.** "Whom Heaven Must Receive until the Time." *Int* 27 (1973) 151–65. **Maile, J. F.** "The Ascension in Luke-Acts." *TynB* 37 (1986) 29–59. **Menoud, P.-H.** "Pendant quarante jours (Actes 1:3)." In *Neotestamentica et Patristica.* FS O. Cullmann, ed. W. C. van Unnik. NovTSup 6. Leiden: Brill, 1962. 148–56. ⸺. "Remarques sur les textes de l'ascension dans Luc-Actes." In *Neutestamentliche Studien.* FS R. Bultmann, ed. W. Eltester. BZNW 21. Berlin: Töpelmann, 1954. 148–56; ET = "Observations on the Ascension Narratives in Luke-Acts." In *Jesus Christ and the Faith: A Collection of Studies by P. H. Menoud.* PTMS 18. Tr. E. M. Paul. Pittsburgh: Pickwick, 1978. 107–20. **Michaelis, W.** *Die Erscheinungen des Auferstandenen.* Basel: Majer, 1944. 89–91. ⸺. "Zur Überlieferung der Himmelfahrtsgeschichte." *TBl* 4 (1925) 101–9. **Palatty, P.** "The Ascension of Christ in Lk-Acts: A Study of the Texts." *Biblebhashyam* 12 (1986) 166–81. ⸺. "The Ascension of Christ in Lk-Acts (An exegetical critical study of Lk 24, 50–53 and Acts 1, 2–3, 9–11." *Biblebhashyam* 12 (1986) 100–117. **Parsons, M. C.** "Narrative Closure and Openness in the Plot of the Third Gospel: The Sense of an Ending in Luke 24:50–53." In *SBL 1986 Seminar Papers,* ed. K. H. Richards. Atlanta, GA: Scholars, 1986. 201–23. ⸺. *The Departure of Jesus in Luke-Acts: The Ascension Narratives in Context.* JSNTSup 21. Sheffield: JSOT, 1987. ⸺. "The Text of Acts 1:2 Reconsidered." *CBQ* 50 (1988) 58–71. **Plooij, D.** *The Ascension in the 'Western' Textual Tradition.* Mededelingen der koninklijke Akademie van Wetenschappen, Afd. Letterkunde, Deel 67, ser. A/2. Amsterdam: Noord-Hollandische

Uitg., 1929. 39–60. **Schille, G.** "Die Himmelfahrt." *ZNW* 57 (1966) 183–99. **Schlier, H.** "Jesu Himmelfahrt nach den lukanischen Schriften." *GuL* 34 (1961) 91–99; reprinted in *Besinnung auf das Neue Testament: Exegetische Aufsätze und Vorträge II.* Freiburg: Herder, 1964. 227–41; French version *Essais sur le Nouveau Testament.* LD 46. Paris: Cerf, 1968. 263–78. **Schnider, F.** "Die Himmelfahrt Jesu: Ende oder Anfang? Zum Verständnis des lukanischen Doppelwerkes." In *Kontinuität und Einheit.* FS F. Mussner, ed. P.-G. Müller and W. Stenger. Freiburg: Herder, 1981. 158–72. **Stempvoort, P. A. van.** "The Interpretation of the Ascension in Luke and Acts." *NTS* 5 (1958–59) 30–42. **Weinert, F. D.** "The Meaning of the Temple in Luke-Acts." *BTB* 11 (1981) 85–89. **Woolsey, T. D.** "The End of Luke's Gospel and the Beginning of the Acts: Two Studies." *BSac* 39 (1882) 593–619. **Wulf, F.** "'Und sie kehrten mit grosser Freude nach Jerusalem zurück' (Lk 24,52)." *GuL* 27 (1954) 81–83.

And see at 24:1–12, 13–35, 36–43, 44–49.

Translation

⁵⁰ *He led them out to near Bethany and he lifted up his*[a] *hands and blessed them.* ⁵¹ *What happened was that as he was blessing them he was parted from them and was carried up into heaven.*[b] ⁵² *They worshiped him*[c] *and [then] returned to Jerusalem with great*[d] *joy.* ⁵³ *They spent their time continually in the temple*[e] *blessing God.*[f]

Notes

[a] "His" is missing from D W *ff*².

[b] καὶ ἀνεφέρετο εἰς τὸν οὐρανόν, "and was carried up into heaven," is missing from ℵ D it syˢ. This and the corresponding lack in D it syˢ of προσκυνήσαντες αὐτόν, "worshiped him," from v 52 has attracted a great deal of discussion. With the exception of the study by Parsons (*Departure*, 29–52), the consensus of more recent scholarship is strongly in favor of the authenticity of these phrases (after an earlier tendency to follow the shorter Western readings here). Parsons makes his attempt to identify the christological *tendenz* of P⁷⁵ carry rather too much of the argument. His case is actually undermined by his own exegetical analysis of the verses, in which he has to make a virtue out of Luke's failure to mention specifically the ascension to heaven that the earlier development of the Gospel would have led the reader to expect (see esp. 106–10). The shorter readings are best seen (*i*) as smoothing out the tension between an Easter Day ascension in Luke and one forty days later in Acts (the Gospel scene is reduced to a temporary departure) and (*ii*) as a continuation of the policy of the Western text to abbreviate where possible in chap. 24 (the features that mark the account as an ascension are not needed here because there is a very clear ascension account in Acts 1).

[c] See *Note* b.

[d] "Great" is missing from B.

[e] The temple location has been dropped by A.

[f] A concluding ἀμήν, "amen," is provided by A B C² Θ Ψ *f*¹³ etc.

Form/Structure/Setting

By means of the change of location, the final verses of the Gospel are marked off a little from the earlier parts of the appearance account (vv 36–49) for which they provide the conclusion. This final unit is both the conclusion of the resurrection appearance account and the conclusion of the Gospel as a whole. As already with v 49, links are drawn between vv 50–53 and the infancy materials with which Luke began his Gospel.

Luke will provide another more elaborate account of the ascension in Acts 1:9–12, which he locates on the Mount of Olives, not on Easter day but forty days after the resurrection. Though there is not the slightest external evidence (but note the odd transition to Acts 1:6, both in the way that back reference to the first volume gives way to the beginning of Luke's narrative sequence for volume two and in the way that the location of the scene in vv 6–11 turns out in v 12 to have been the Mount of Olives and not Jerusalem itself, as would have been naturally assumed), there was a period of popularity for the view that there had been considerable later interpolation involved at the end of the Gospel and/or at the beginning of Acts in the formation of our present texts. The most extreme form of this view suggested that both Luke 24:50–53 and Acts 1:1–5 were later insertions, probably to provide a termination for the Gospel and a beginning for Acts when what was said to have been originally one continuous work was split into two. None of the interpolation theories has received any significant recent support. More sophisticated analyses of Lukan redaction have shown that there is no reason to suggest that the texts as we now have them are artificially dislocated in any way.

Just as an artistic and theological logic completes the Gospel story on Easter Day (Grass [*Ostergeschehen*, 44] is quite right to ask what more could be said by the risen Lord after v 49), so in Acts the forty days is likely to have a symbolic rather than a chronological significance. Luke is concerned to affirm the risen Lord's confirmation of the teaching of the historical Jesus (now intelligible to the disciples in a new way). He also has a period of time (fifty days) to fill before the feast of Pentecost to which the giving of the Spirit is tied in his traditions (Wilson, *ZNW* 59 [1968] 270–72). The number forty has an illustrious history: the flood lasted forty days (Gen 7:17); Moses was on Mount Sinai for forty days (Exod 24:18; 34:28); Israel wandered for forty years (Exod 16:35), as Elijah did for forty days (1 Kgs 19:8); Ezra's dictation to restore the destroyed Scriptures took forty days (*4 Ezra* 14:23, 36, 42–45); Jesus spent forty days in the wilderness (Luke 4:2); closest of all, Baruch was given forty days for the instruction of the people before his translation to heaven (*2 Apoc. Bar.* 76:1–5).

It is very difficult to decide what Luke might have had in the way of sources for the formation of his ascension accounts. In the NT, Luke is quite alone in providing such an account (the longer ending of Mark [16:19] has an ascension, but the text does not specify the presence of the disciples; *Gos. Pet.* 55–56 has an unwitnessed ascension reported to the women by the angel at the empty tomb). The language is heavily Lukan in both of his accounts, and a good proportion of the content flows directly out of Luke's use of the pattern for reporting translations to heaven (particularly those of Enoch and Elijah, but with some relationship to the corresponding Hellenistic genre). When the dependence on Sir 50:20–22 is added, and the deliberate links with Luke 2, precious little remains to be drawn from an ascension tradition for Luke 50:50–53.

On the other hand, there are very definite links with Matt 28:16–20, which remind us of the way in which Luke roots even his most creative writing in the tradition. Luke has certainly not invented the idea of Jesus' ascension to heaven (see John 20:17; Eph 4:10; 1 Tim 3:16; 1 Pet 3:22; Heb 4:14; 6:19: 9:24), nor is he alone in drawing a distinction between resurrection and ascension (John 20:17). The idea that there was some kind of withdrawal of the resurrected Jesus would seem to be involved in the time-limited period of resurrection appearances implied in 1 Cor 15:8. But Luke is unique in providing an ascension narrative in which disciples experience the final departure of Jesus for heaven. Since the resurrection appearances are all experiences of a limited time of encounter with the risen Lord, it may be that in order to provide a narrative that brings to expression the shared Christian conviction of Jesus' ascension to heaven, Luke has developed this feature (arrival and departure) in connection with a knowledge that the appearances were all within a strictly limited period of time. For the account in Acts, Luke may have had more from the tradition; we cannot tell.

The texts that speak of the ascension of Jesus normally imply that this ascension is an exaltation. There are other NT texts that deal with the exaltation without any ascension language (notably Phil 2:9–11), but when the contexts are taken into account, an ascension is always implied (e.g., Acts 2:33; 5:31). What, however, of the possibility that we might have an ascension that was not an exaltation? This possibility has been proposed as representing Luke's understanding of the ascension, and it has gained considerable support (e.g., Benoit, "Ascension," 1:243–55; Ruckstuhl, "Auferstehung," 205–9; Fitzmyer, *TS* 45 [1984] 421–25; Maile, *TynB* 37 [1986] 38–58). According to this view, the appearances of Jesus have all been from heaven, and the ascension is simply the end-point of the sequence of appearances (which provides additional assurance to the disciples that Jesus had been translated to heaven at the time of the resurrection, where he now goes at the end of this final appearance). In the discussion at 24:1–12, it was argued that the case of Paul has had an inappropriate influence on the scholarly attempt to reconstruct the earliest traditions of resurrection appearances. In my judgment, the understanding of Lukan ascension being considered here is ultimately under the control of the same methodological error (see also at v 26). To make the ascension the assurance of Jesus' exaltation, but not the event of exaltation, has the appearance of being a contrived solution.

(There is, of course, no doubt that for Paul the resurrection of Jesus entails his exaltation, and even his ascension to heaven [1 Thess 1:10; Rom 1:4; cf. Eph 1:20; Phil 3:20–21]. Indeed, the same is true for Luke, if we may judge from Acts 2:32–33; 5:30–32; and 13:30–37, where "raised" [ἐγείρειν in v 30, but ἀνιστάναι in both vv 33 and 34] seems to do double duty for resurrection and exaltation. But it is quite another matter whether even for Paul this entailment meant that resurrection was resurrection to heavenly exaltation. Paul appears not to have ever had cause to reflect on this matter, but those aspects of his theology of resurrection that draw strong links between the resurrection of Jesus and either the present life or the future resurrection of the believer would seem, in my judgment, to be better served if Paul did not take Jesus' resurrection as resurrection to heavenly exaltation. As divine affirmation, the resurrection inevitably draws a measure of exaltation to itself, but this is in the first instance a visible-in-this-world exaltation and not an exaltation to heaven [see esp. Rom 1:4].)

Comment

The ascension of Jesus to heaven brings to a culmination that sequence of experiences through which the risen Jesus brings his disciples to a clear and definite faith in himself as the resurrected Lord, one who is due nothing less than the reverence of worship. Secure in the blessing of Christ and with great joy, the disciples obediently return to Jerusalem. As they await the promise, they give themselves to fervent worship of God in the temple.

50 ἐξήγαγεν, "he led them out," is likely to be Lukan diction (it may go back to προάγει, "he will go before," in Mark 16:7; there is likely, as well, to be a tradition link to Matt 28:16, where Jesus is also responsible for the location). ἕως, "until," with a following preposition is Lukan (cf. Acts 17:14; 21:5; 26:11). ἕως πρός is best taken to mean "to near Bethany" (cf. Lohfink, *Himmelfahrt*, 166–67). Bethany is on the southeastern slopes of the Mount of Olives. In Acts 1:12, the ascension will be located on the Mount of Olives. The two names are linked already at Luke 19:29. While the Mount of Olives location could be symbolic (see Matt 28:16; Mark 13:3; cf. 1 Sam 15:30, 32; Ezek 11:23; Zech 14:4), the (near) Bethany location would seem to require some basis in tradition (though there are some points of genuine likeness, it is eisegesis to make a "triumphal exit" out of the similarities with 19:28–29, 37–38, as Parsons does [*Departure*, 104]).

Many writers have drawn attention to the close parallelism between a series of elements in vv 50–53 and in Sir 50:20–22. In Ben Sirach the blessing of the People by the high priest Simon comes at the end of a panegyric that lists in historical sequence the exploits of the great ones of Israel's history. The blessing scene, as used by Ben Sirach, has a concluding function in his book, as the parallel scene does in Luke's (cf. Lohfink, *Himmelfahrt*, 169). The two texts exhibit the following parallels (Luke, then Ben Sirach):

ἐπάρος τὰς χεῖρας αὐτοῦ   εὐλόγησεν . . .
ἐπῆρεν   χεῖρας αὐτοῦ . . . δοῦναι εὐλογίαν . . .

προσκυνήσαντες . . . εὐλογοῦντες τὸν θεόν
προσκυνήσει . . .   εὐλογήσατε τὸν θεόν

having lifted up his hands   he blessed . . .
he lifted up his hands . . . to give a blessing . . .

having worshiped . . .   blessing God
[in] worship . . .   bless   God

This degree of parallelism can hardly be accidental, especially when the whole OT can yield only one text that can parallel the raising of hands here for blessing (Lev 9:22 has καὶ ἐξάρας . . . τὰς χεῖρας . . . εὐλόγησεν αὐτούς, "and having lifted up the hands . . . he blessed them"; this is probably the model for Ben Sirach and may have been recognized as such by Luke, since the Lukan text is at a couple of points closer to the LXX text of Lev 9:22). Luke is likely to have found further encouragement from the final blessings of Abraham (Gen 49) and Moses (Deut 33; in *2 Enoch* 56:1; 57:2; 64:4 the pattern of final blessing before death has been secondarily adapted to the situation of the translation of Enoch to heaven; something very similar is happening here in Luke, but there is not likely to be any direct link). Luke passed over the blessing of children from Mark 10:16; he may have wanted to save this motif for the present climactic point.

Luke has no interest in a priestly Christology: the link with Ben Sirach emphasizes the stature of Jesus in Luke's eyes and allows Luke to formulate an effective climax and conclusion; it also allows Luke to exploit the link with the farewell blessings of Abraham and Moses; finally (as we will see in the following paragraph), it allows Luke to forge a link with chap. 2. Luke likely intends a link

between Jesus' capacity to bless here and the achievement of his passion and resurrection, but this is not made precise in any way (but cf. Acts 3:26).

It is likely that the series of links with chap. 1 noted for v 49 (see there) has its
counterpart in a series of links for vv 50–53 with chap. 2 (the threshold is crossed
from anticipation to fulfillment). Here there is "he blessed them," which is found
in 2:34 of Simeon's blessing of Mary and Joseph; in v 51 there will be the language shared with 2:15: καὶ ἐγένετο ... διέστη[ἀπῆλθον] ἀπ' αὐτῶν ... εἰς τὸν
οὐρανόν (lit. "and it happened ... he parted [they departed] from them ... into
heaven"); in v 52 and 2:45, "they returned to Jerusalem" is common, while "great
joy" is shared between v 52 and the message of the angels in 2:10; in v 53, "in the
temple blessing God" has its counterpart with Simeon, who came "into the temple"
and "blessed God" (2:27–28; "continually" in v 53 may have its counterpart in
2:37 in Anna, "who did not leave the temple"). This series of correspondences
makes it more likely in any particular case that the formulation is Lukan.

51 The ἐγένετο (lit. "it happened") construction is typically Lukan. διέστη,
"he parted/departed/went away," is likely to be Lukan (see Lohfink, *Himmelfahrt*,
170: Luke has the other NT uses of the verb; he uses the related ἐπέστη, "he
appeared/turned up/approached/stood near or by," for the beginning of appearances of supernatural figures). ἀναφέρειν, "take up," is found frequently in
Hellenistic accounts of journeys to heaven and translation accounts (Lohfink,
Himmelfahrt, 42, 171).

Though briefly expressed, the translation to heaven here is the goal toward
which the Gospel account has been heading since 9:51 (cf. 9:26, 32; 19:12; 22:69;
24:26; and discussion there). This departure to heaven will be presented in a
more elaborate manner in Acts 1:9–11 (as there are strong links between the
Acts version and the translation of Elijah in 2 Kgs 2 [cf. Sir 48:9, 12; 1 Macc 2:58],
there is something to be said for seeing a link here with the much more briefly
reported accounts of the translation of Enoch in Gen 5:24; Sir 44:16; 49:14 [the
LXX verbs here are, however, ἀναλαμβάνειν, "to be take up," and μετατιθέναι,
"to transpose/translate"; cf. Heb 11:5]).

52 The worship of Jesus here is one of a number of links between Matt 28:16–
20 and Luke 24:36–53 (with Acts 1:6–11), which suggest some shared underlying
tradition (see further at 24:1–12). Unlike his Markan source, Luke has not used
προσκυνεῖν, "worship," earlier for response to Jesus (see Lohfink, *Himmelfahrt*,
171–72). This and the link with Sir 50:21 (where the worship is obviously directed
to God) suggest that Luke intends to suggest that Jesus is at this point the object
of religious reverence in a manner that was not previously the case. The departure of the angel of the Lord in Judg 13:20 also leads to worship ("fell on their
faces to the ground"). The same pattern, and with use of προσκυνεῖν, is found in
accounts of translations to heaven from the Greco-Roman sphere (Sophocles,
Oedipus Coloneus 1654; Plutarch, *Romulus* 27.8–9; Lucian, *De morte Peregrini* 39
[sometimes apotheosis takes place at the moment of translation; sometimes the
translation makes clear that it is a god who has been encountered]).

The return of the disciples here has its counterpart in the return of the women
in v 9 and of the Emmaus disciples in v 33. The return here marks obedience to
the directive of v 49. See discussion at 24:43 for the role of the worship and great
joy in marking the emergence of a clear and unqualified faith in the resurrection
of Jesus. With the coming of the Spirit, all will be in place for the beginning of

the mission task outlined in vv 47–48. The ascension to heaven concludes the earthly work of Jesus; the sending of the Spirit will begin his work from heaven (cf. Lohfink, *Himmelfahrt*, 252; Schnider, "Himmelfahrt," 168–69).

53 The paraphrastic tense, the use of διὰ παντός, "continually," and the temple focus are thoroughly Lukan (cf. Acts 2:46; 3:1; 5:42). The temple focus of the infancy narrative will be repeated for the beginning of the Christian mission to all nations.

Explanation

Luke's second and final resurrection appearance comes to an end with Jesus' ascension to heaven. The change of scene to near Bethany marks off the final verses as a fitting conclusion and climax for the whole book. The self-identification, the showing of limbs, the eating of fish, the reiteration of pre-passion teaching, the exposition of Scriptures, and now the experience of the ascension have worked together to build a firm foundation for resurrection faith. Now the disciples can wait in the temple in joy and confidence, in an attitude of worship, for the fulfillment of the Father's promise.

For the telling of this little episode, Luke draws on a number of patterns. Most extensively he draws upon a description in Sir 50:20–22 of a scene in which the high priest Simon blesses the People of God. The writer of Ben Sirach had used it to bring to a climax and conclusion his account of great heros of the faith; but Luke has a greater hero to put in this climactic spot, whose blessing means much more than that of the Jewish high priest ever could!

Luke has also been inspired by the OT scenes in which Abraham and Moses (Gen 49; Deut 33) provide final instruction and blessing before their deaths. Of course, Jesus' departure is of quite a different kind, and that takes us on to the third pattern upon which Luke is dependent. This is the pattern used to describe the translations to heaven of figures like Enoch and Elijah. The translation of Enoch is reported in Gen 5:24 and that of Elijah in 2 Kgs 2. Other early Jewish texts had accounts of the same translations and added other figures to the list of those so translated. Though this translation clearly had its own unique features, this is the kind of experience that Luke understood Jesus to have undergone at the ascension.

In addition to following these models, Luke desires to have his readers find echoes of chap. 2 of the infancy narrative in this final episode of the Gospel (see *Comment* for details).

Luke will provide a second account of the ascension of Jesus with rather more elaboration in Acts 1. It is notable that Luke sets the Gospel version on the eve of Easter Day, while the Acts version comes forty days after the day of the resurrection. In both cases it would seem that Luke is motivated by symbolic rather than chronological concerns. In the Gospel, he is making clear that the resurrection already entails the glory of ascension to the right hand of God. In Acts, he is concerned to affirm the risen Lord's confirmation of the teaching of the historical Jesus (now intelligible to the disciples in a new way). Forty is an important biblical number, one that finds fresh use in Jewish tradition. As a round number, it suits quite well Luke's narrative need to bridge between the resurrection and the coming of the Spirit at Pentecost (fifty days after Passover).

Though briefly expressed, the translation to heaven is the goal toward which the Gospel account has been heading since 9:51. It leads to the full possession of the glory glimpsed in 9:32 (cf. 24:26), the same glory with which he will come as Son of Man (9:26). It is the departure to a far country to receive kingly power that was spoken of in a parable at 19:12. It is the destiny Jesus announced for himself at 22:69.

After all the doubts and uncertainties, the disciples reach a mature faith in the resurrected one at the point where he is parted from them by ascension. The disciples are filled with joy, and Jesus is treated as an appropriate object of religious reverence for the first time in the Gospel of Luke. The disciples now know what they need to know to carry forward the mission entrusted to them as witnesses.

The disciples' return to Jerusalem marks their obedience to the directive of v 49. More deeply than ever committed to their ancestral faith, they worship fervently in the temple while they await the promise of the Father, which will trigger the next stage of their activity. The ascension of Jesus to heaven has concluded his earthly work; the sending of the Spirit will begin his work from heaven, to be carried out through his disciples.

Bibliographical Addenda for Volume 35A

FOR 1:1–4:

Creech, R. R. "The Most Excellent Narratee: The Significance of Theophilus in Luke-Acts." In *With Steadfast Purpose: Essays on Acts.* FS H. J. Flanders, Jr., ed. N. H. Keathley. Waco, TX: Baylor University, 1990. 107–26. **Kurz, W. S.** "Narrative Approaches to Luke-Acts." *Bib* 68 (1987) 195–220. **Ó Fearghail, F.** *A Study of the Role of Lk 1:1–4:44 in the Composition of Luke's Two-Volume Work.* AnBib 126. Rome: Pontificio Istituto Biblico, 1991. **Omanson, R. L.** "A Note on Luke 1.1–4." *BT* 30 (1979) 446–47. **Plessis, I. J. du.** "Once More: The Purpose of Luke's Prologue." *NovT* (1974) 259–71.

GENERAL FOR 1:5–2:52:

Beauduin, A. "The Infancy Narratives, a Confession of Faith: Texts from Luke 1." *LVit* 39 (1984) 167–77. **Benoit, P.** *Les récits évangéliques de l'enfance de Jésus.* Exégèse et Théologie IV. Paris: Cerf, 1982. 63–94. **Bovon, F.** "Die Geburt und die Kindheit Jesu." *BK* 42 (1987) 162–70. **Busse, U.** "Das 'Evangelium' des Lukas: Die Funktion der Vorgeschichte im lukanischen Doppelwerk." In *Der Treue Gottes trauen,* ed. C. Bussmann and W. Radl. 161–79. **Carroll, J. T.** *Response to the End of History.* 37–53. **Crouch, J. E.** "How Early Christians Viewed the Birth of Jesus." *BRev* 7 (1991) 34–38. **Drewermann, E.** *Dein Name ist wie der Geschmack des Lebens: Tiefenpsychologische Deutung der Kindsheitsgeschichte nach dem Lukas-evangelium.* Freiburg: Herder, 1987. **Ernst, J.** "Lukanische Kindheitserzählung." In *Johannes der Täufer: Interpetation, Geschichte, Wirkungsgeschichten.* Beihefte ZNW 53. Berlin/New York: de Gruyter, 1989. 113–39. **Fiedler, P.** "Geschichten als Theologie und Verkündigung: Die Prologe des Matthäus und Lukas-Evangeluims." In *Zur Theologie der Kindheitsgeschichten: Der heutige Stand der Exegese,* ed. R. Pesch. Munich: Schnell, 1981. 11–26. **Göllner, R.** "Die lukanische Kindheitsgeschichte im Religionsunterricht." *LebSeel* 34 (1980) 270–75. **Gueuret, A.** "Luc 1–2, analyse sémiotique." *SémiotBib* 25 (1982) 35–42. **Higgins, A. J. B.** "Luke 1–2 in Tatian's Diatessaron." *JBL* 103 (1984) 193–222. **Horsley, R. A.** *The Liberation of Christmas: The Infancy Narratives in Social Context.* New York: Crossroad, 1989. **Irigoin, J.** "La composition rythmique des cantiques de Luc." *RB* 98 (1991) 5–50. **Jankowski, G.** "In jenen Tagen: Der politische Kontext zu Lukas 1–2." *TK* 12 (1981) 5–17. **Kassel, M.** "Weibliche Aspekte im lukanischen Kindheitsevangelium." *Diakonia* 15 (1984) 391–97. **Kaut, T.** *Befreier und befreites Volk: Traditions- und redaktionsgeschichtliche Untersuchung zu Magnifikat und Benediktus im Kontext der vorlukanischen Kindheitsgeschichte.* Athenäums Monografien, Theologie: BBB 77. Frankfurt: Hain, 1990. **Mather, P. B.** "The Search for the Living Text of the Lukan Infancy Narrative." In *The Living Text.* FS E. W. Saunders, ed. D. E. Groh and R. Jewett. Washington: University Press of America, 1985. 123–40. **McHugh, J.** "A New Approach to the Infancy Narratives." *Marianum* 40 (1978) 277–87. **Moloney, F. J.** *The Living Voice of the Gospel: The Gospels Today.* New York/Mahwah, NJ: Paulist, 1986. 93–113. **Mülhaupt, E. D.** *Martin Luthers Evangelien-Auslegung: I. Die Weihnachts- und Vorgeschichten bei Matthäus und Lukas.* Göttingen: Vandenhoeck & Ruprecht, 1984. **Neumann, J.** "The Child in the First Two Chapters of the Gospel of Luke." In *Proceedings of the Second International Symposium on Medicine in Bible and Talmud,* ed. S. S. Kottek. Jerusalem: Israel Institute of Medical History, 1985. 164–72. **Panier, L.** "La nomination du Fils de Dieu." *SémiotBib* 59 (1990) 35–41. **Pesch, R.,** ed. *Zur Theologie der Kindheitsgeschichten: Der heutige Stand der Exegese.* Munich: Schnell, 1981. **Resenhöfft, W.** *Die Apostelgeschichte im Wortlaut ihrer beiden Urquellen: Rekonstruktion des Büchleins von der Geburt Johannes des Täufers Lk 1–2.* Europäische

Hochschulschriften XXIII/39. Bern/Frankfurt am M.: Lang, 1974. **Reuss, J.** "Ein unbekannter Kommentar zum 1. Kapitel des Lukasevangeliums." *Bib* 58 (1977) 224–30. **Ryckmans, J.** "Un parallèle sud-arabe à l'imposition du nom de Jean-Baptiste et de Jésus." In *Al-Hudhud*. FS M. Höfner, ed. R. G. Stiegmer. Graz: Franzens-Univ., 1981. 283–94. **Sabourin, L.** "Recent Views on Luke's Infancy Narratives." *RSB* 1 (1981) 18–25. **Schaberg, J.** *The Illegitimacy of Jesus: A Feminist Theological Interpretation of the Infancy Narratives.* New York: Crossroad/Continuum, 1990. **Shuler, P.** "Luke 1–2." In *SBL 1992 Seminar Papers*, ed. E. H. Lovering, Jr. 82–97. **Stählin, W.** "Die Bedeutung der Kindheitsgeschichten Jesu." In *Wissen und Weisheit*. Stuttgart: Evang. Verlagswerk, 1973. 65–73. **Tyson, J. B.** "The Birth Narratives and the Beginning of Luke's Gospel." *Semeia* 52 (1990) 103–20.

FOR 1:5–25:

Brown, R. E. "The Annunciation to Zechariah, the Birth of the Baptist, and the Benedictus (Luke 1:5–25, 57–80)." *Worship* 62 (1988) 482–96. **Buth, R.** "What Is the Priest Doing? Common Sense and Culture." *JerPersp* 4 (1991) 12–13. **Ó Fearghail, F.** "The Imitation of the Septuagint in Luke's Infancy Narrative." *ProcIBA* 12 (1989) 58–78. ————. "The Literary Forms of Lk 1,5–25 and 1,26–38." *Marianum* 43 (1981) 321–44. **Schwarz, G.** "*EΞ EΦHMEPIAΣ ABIA*? (Lukas 1,5)." *BibNot* 53 (1990) 30–31.

FOR 1:26–38:

Bacinoni, V. "Jésus et sa mère d'après les récits lucaniens de l'enfance et d'aprè S. Jean." *AuCoeurAfr* 15 (1975) 175–81. **Benson, G. P.** "Virgin Birth, Virgin Conception." *ExpTim* 98 (1986–87) 139–40. **Bostock, G.** "Virgin Birth or Human Conception?" *ExpTim* 97 (1985–86) 260–63. ————. "Divine Birth, Human Conception." *ExpTim* 98 (1986–87) 331–33. **Brown, R. E.** *The Virginal Conception and Bodily Resurrection of Jesus.* London/Dublin: Chapman, 1973. ————. "The Annunciation to Mary, the Visitation and the Magnificat (Luke 1,26–56)." *Worship* 62 (1988) 249–59. **Butting, K.** "Eine Freundin Gottes: Luk. 1,26–56." *TK* 21 (1984) 42–49. **Buzzetti, C.** "*Κεχαριτωμένη* 'favoured' (Lk 1:28), and the Italian Common Language New Testament ('Parola del Signore')." *BT* 33 (1982) 243. **Conrad, E. W.** "The Annunciation of Birth and the Birth of the Messiah." *CBQ* 47 (1985) 656–63. **Della Corte, E.** "*Κεχαριτωμένη* (Lc 1,28): Crux interpretum." *Marianum* 52 (1990) 101–48. **Faber van der Meulen, H. E.** "Zum jüdischen und hellenistischen Hintergrund von Lukas 1,31." In *Wort in der Zeit*. FS K. H. Rengstorf, ed. W. Haubeck and M. Bachmann. Leiden: Brill, 1980. 108–22. **Fuller, R. H.** "A Note on Luke 1:28 and 38." In *The New Testament Age*. FS B. Reicke, ed. W. C. Weinrich. Macon, GA: Mercer, 1984. 201–6. **Grelot, P.** *Évangiles et histoire.* Introduction à la Bible. Nouvelle édition. Le Nouveau Testament 6. Paris: Desclée, 1986. 187–224. **Laurentin, R.** "Analyse sémiotique des évangiles de Marie [1–2]." *EphMar* 32 (1982) 53–80. **Legrand, L.** *L'annonce à Marie (Lc 1,26–38): Une apocalypse aux origines de l'évangile.* LD 106. Paris: Cerf, 1981. ————. "The Angel Gabriel and Politics: Messianism and Christology." *ITS* 26 (1989) 1–21. **Meynet, R.** "Dieu donne son Nom à Jésus: Analyse rhétorique de Lc 1,26–55 et de 1 Sam 2,1–10." *Bib* 66 (1985) 39–72. **Middleton, D. F.** "The Story of Mary: Luke's Version." *NB* 70 (1989) 555–64. **Miranda, J. P.** "Empfängnis und Geburt Christi." *TK* 8 (1980) 45–61. **Ó Fearghail, F.** "The Literary Forms of Lk 1:5–25 and 1:26–38." *Marianum* 43 (1981) 321–44. **Potterie, I. de la.** "La mère de Jésus et la conception virginale du Fils de Dieu." *Marianum* 40 (1978) 41–90. ————. "L'annonce à Marie." In *Marie dans le mystère de l'alliance.* Collection "Jésus-Christ" 34. Paris: Desclée, 1988. 39–69. **Ryckmans, J.** "Un parallèle sud-arabe à l'imposition du nom de Jean-Baptiste et de Jésus." In *Al-Hudhud*. FS M. Höfner, ed. R. G. Stiegmer. Graz: Franzens-Univ., 1981. 283–94. **Sabourin, L.** "Two Lukan Texts (1:35; 3:22)." *RSB* 1 (1981) 29–33. **Stock, K.** "Von Gott berufen und von den Menschen seliggepriesen: Die Gestalt Marias in Lukas 1,26–56." *GuL* 64 (1991) 52–63. **Wilckens, U.**

"Empfangen vom Heiligen Geist aus der Jungfrau Maria, Lk 1,26–38." In *Zur Theologie der Kindheitsgeschichten: Der heutige Stand der Exegese,* ed. R. Pesch. Munich: Schnell, 1981. 49–73. **Zeller, D.** "Die Ankündigung der Geburt: Wandlungen einer Gattung." In *Zur Theologie der Kindheitsgeschichten: Der heutige Stand der Exegese,* ed. R. Pesch. Munich: Schnell, 1981. 27–48.

FOR 1:46–55:

Bemile, P. *The Magnificat within the Context and Framework of Lukan Theology: An Exegetical Theological Study of Luke 1:46–55.* Regensburger Studien zur Theologie 34. Frankfurt: Peter Lang, 1986. **Brown, R. E.** "The Annunciation to Mary, the Visitation and the Magnificat (Luke 1,26–56)." *Worship* 62 (1988) 249–59. **Coste, R.** *Le Magnificat ou la révolution de Dieu.* Paris: Nouvelle Cité, 1987. **Delorme, J.** "Le Magnificat: La forme et le sens." In *La vie de la parole.* FS P. Grelot, ed. H. Cazelles. Paris: Desclée, 1987. 175–94. ————. "Le monde, la logique et le sens du Magnificat." *SémiotBib* 53 (1989) 1–17. **Gueuret, A.** "Sur Luc 1,46–55: Comment peut-on être amené à penser qu'Elisabeth est 'sémiotiquement' celle qui a prononcé le Cantique en Lc 1,46?" *BulCPE, Supplement* April (1977) 3–11. **Kirchschläger, W.** *Der Lobgesang Mariens: Das Magnifikat.* Freiburg/Switzerland: Kanisius, 1984. **Lohfink, G.** "Der Lobpreis als Antwort auf Gottes Taten." In *Gottes Taten gehen weiter.* Freiburg: Herder, 1985. 79–90. **Marshall, I. H.** "The Interpretation of the Magnificat." In *Der Treue Gottes trauen,* ed. C. Bussmann and W. Radl. 181–96. **Morry, M. F.** "The Magnificat: Reflections." *MarStud* 38 (1987) 63–77. **Müller, G.** "Evangelische Marienverehrung: Luthers Auslegung des Magnifikat." *Luther* 59 (1988) 2–13. **Obbard, E. R.** *Magnificat: The Journey and the Song.* New York/Mahwah, NJ: Paulist, 1985. **Reiterer, F. V.** "Die Funktion des alttestamentlichen Hintergrundes für das Verständnis der Theologie des Magnificat." *HD* 41 (1987) 129–54. **Robinson, B. P.** "Musings on the Magnificat." *Priests and People* 1 (1987–88) 332–35. **Rouillard, P.** "'Magnificat.'" *Catholicisme* 8 (1977) 163–64. **Schlosser, J.** "Marie et la prière de l'Église d'après Lc 1,48 et Ac 1,14." *Mariales* 39 (1982) 13–22. **Scholer, D. M.** "The Magnificat (Luke 1:46–55): Reflections on Its Hermeneutical History." In *Conflict and Context: Hermeneutics in the Americas,* ed. M. L. Branson and C. R. Padilla. Grand Rapids, MI: Eerdmans, 1986. 210–19. **Trèves, M.** "La Magnificat et le Benedictus." *CCER* 27 (1979) 105–10. **Zorrilla, C. H.** "The Magnificat: Song of Justice." In *Conflict and Context: Hermeneutics in the Americas,* ed. M. L. Branson and C. R. Padilla. Grand Rapids, MI: Eerdmans, 1986. 220–37.

FOR 1:67–80:

Carter, W. "Zechariah and the Benedictus (Luke 1,68–79): Practising What He Preaches." *Bib* 69 (1988) 239–47. **Schwartz, D. R.** "On Quirinius, John the Baptist, the Benedictus, Melchizedek, Qumran and Ephesus." *RevQ* 13 (1988) 635–46. **Trèves, M.** "Le Magnificat et le Benedictus (Lc 1.46–55,68–79)." *CCER* 27 (1979) 105–10.

GENERAL FOR 2:1–21:

Aus, R. D. "Die Wiehnachtsgeschichte im Lichte jüdischer Traditionen vom Mose-Kind und Hirten-Messias (Lukas 2,1–20)." In *Wiehnachtsgeschichte, Barmherziger Samariter, Verloren Sohn: Studien zu ihrem jüdischen Hintergrund.* ANTZ 2. Berlin: Institut Kirche und Judentum, 1988. 11–58. **Brenner, A.** "Female Social Behaviour: Two Descriptive Patterns within the 'Birth of the Hero' Paradigm [1,8–2,7]." *VT* 36 (1986) 257–73. **Buby, B.** "The Biblical Prayer of Mary (Lk 2:19,51)." *RevRel* 39 (1980) 577–81. **Chevallier, M.-A.** "L'analyse littéraire des textes du Nouveau Testament." *RHPR* 57 (1977) 367–78. **Conrad, E. W.** "The Annunciation of Birth and the Birth of the Messiah." *CBQ* 47 (1985) 656–63. **Globe, A.** "Some Doctrinal Variants in Matthew 1 and Luke 2, and the Authority of the Neutral Text." *CBQ* 42 (1980) 52–72. **Hollenweger, W. J.** *Besuch bei Lukas: 4 narrative Exegesen zu 2 Mose 14,*

Lukas 2,1–14, 2 Kor 6,4–11 und Lukas 19,1–10. Traktate 64. Munich: Kaiser, 1981. **Kellermann, U.** *Gottes neuer Mensch: Exegetische Meditation der Weihnachtsgeschichte Lk 2,1–20.* Neukirchen-Vluyn: Neukirchener, 1978. **Kerr, A. J.** "No room in the kataluma." *ExpTim* 103 (1991) 15–16. **Kilpatrick, G. D.** "Luke 2:4–5 and Leviticus 25:10." *ZNW* 80 (1989) 264–65. **Lambrecht, J.** "The Child in the Manger: A Meditation on Luke 2:1–20." *LS* 5 (1974–75) 331–35. **Lauverjat, M.** "Luc 2: Une simple approche." *SémiotBib* 27 (1982) 31–47. **Merklein, H.** "Ereignis und Legende: Zur theologischen Aussage der lukanischen Weihnachtsgeschichte Lk 2,1–20." *LebSeel* 31 (1980) 258–64. **Morris, R. L. B.** "Why Αὔγουστος? A Note to Luke 2.1." *NTS* 38 (1992) 142–44. **Must, H.** "A Diatessaric Rendering in Luke 2.7." *NTS* 32 (1986) 136–43. **Nelson, R. D.** "David: A Model for Mary in Luke?" *BTB* 18 (1988) 138–42. **Olley, J. W.** "God on the Move: A Further Look at *Kataluma* in Luke." *ExpTim* 103 (1992) 300–301. **Pesch, R.** "Das Weihnachtsevangelium (Lk 2,1–21): Literarische Kunst. Politische Implikationen." In *Zur Theologie der Kindheitsgeschichten: Der heutige Stand der Exegese*, ed. R. Pesch. Munich: Schnell, 1981. **Richards, H. J.** *The First Christmas: What Really Happened?* Mystic, CT: Twenty-Third Publications, 1986. **Safrai, S.** "No Room in the Inn?" *JerPersp* 4 (1991) 8. **Schüngel-Straumann, H.** "Cäsar oder Christus? Christologische und politische Anliegen im Weihnachtsevangelium des Lukas [2,1–20]." *KatBl* 101 (1976) 796–803. **Steffen, U.** *Die Weihnachtsgeschichte des Lukas.* ARH-Taschenbuch 43. Hamburg: Agentur des Rauhen Hauses, 1978. **Temme, J. M.** "The Shepherds' Role." *BiTod* 29 (1991) 376–78. **Thorley, J.** "When Was Jesus Born?" *GR* 28 (1981) 81–89. **Trudinger, L. P.** "'No Room in the Inn': A Note on Luke 2:7." *ExpTim* 102 (1991) 172–73. **Wolff, A. M.** "Der Kaiser und das Kind: Ein Auslegung von Luk 2,1–10." *TK* 12 (1981) 18–31.

FOR 2:1–21 (ON THE CENSUS):

Buchheit, V. *Hippolyt, Origenes und Ambrosius über den Census Augusti.* FS T. Klauser. Jahrbuch für Antike und Christentum. Ergänzungsband 11. Münster: Aschendorff, 1984. 50–56. **Daoust, J.** "Le recensement de Quirinius." *EV* 94 (1984) 366–67. **Schwartz, D. R.** "On Quirinius, John the Baptist, the Benedictus, Melchizedek, Qumran and Ephesus." *RevQ* 13 (1988) 635–46.

FOR 2:1–21 (ON THE GLORIA [2:14]):

Dodd, C. H. "New Testament Translation Problems." *BT* 28 (1977) 101–16. **Kilpatrick, R. S.** "The Greek Syntax of Luke 2.14." *NTS* 34 (1988) 472–75. **Müller, T.** "Observations on Some New Testament Texts Based on Generative-transformational Grammar." *BT* 29 (1978) 117–20.

GENERAL FOR 2:22–40:

Coackley, J. T. "The Old Man Simeon (Lk 2.25) in Syriac Tradition." *OCP* 47 (1981) 189–212. **Elliot, J. K.** "Anna's Age (Luke 2:36–37)." *NovT* 30 (1988) 100–102. **Meuser, E., Feneberg, W., Knoch, O.,** and **Pesch, R.** "Beiträge zu einem Text des Neuen Testaments (Lk 2,35)." *GuL* 57 (1984) 214–20. **Poirot, D.** "Le rencontre dans le Temple (Luc 2,22–38)." *Carmel* 30 (1983) 83–92. **Quesnel, M.** "Jésus prophète révélé par les prophètes." *Cahiers Évangile* 50 (1984) 6–9. **Robert, R.** "Commet comprendre 'leur purification' en Luc II,22?" *RevThom* 90 (1990) 449–55. **Sudbrack, J.** "Gesetz und Geist: Jesu Darstellung im Tempel." *GuL* 48 (1975) 462–66.

LUKE 2:22–40 (ON THE NUNC DIMITTIS)

Buth, R. "What Kind of Blessing Is That?" *JerPersp* 3 (1990) 7–10. **Jörgensen, P. H.** "Das alte und das neue Israel: Der Lobgesang Simeons—Lk 2,25–35." *FriedIsr* 59 (1976) 147–59.

Radl, W. *Paulus und Jesus im lukanischen Doppelwerk: Untersuchungen zu Parallelmotiven im Lukasevangelium und in der Apostelgeschichte.* Europäische Hochschulschriften XXIII/49. Bern/Frankfurt am M.: Lang, 1975. 69–81. **Rouillard, P.** "'Nunc dimittis.'" *Catholicisme* 9 (1982) 1446–47.

FOR 2:41–52:

Buby, B. "The Biblical Prayer of Mary (Lk 2:19,51)." *RevRel* 39 (1980) 477–81. **Delebecque, É.** "Note sur Lc 2,41–52." *BBudé* (1973) 75–83. **Harris, S. M.** "My Father's House." *ExpTim* 94 (1982–83) 84–85. **Legrand, L.** "Deux voyages: Lc 2, 41–50; 24, 13–33." *À cause de l'Évangile,* ed. F. Refoulé. 409–30. **Ostier, E. L.** "Luc 2,41–52: Le peuple juif, famille de Jésus." *Sens* 34 (1983) 121–23. **Vales, F.** "'Go for Yourself.'" *BiTod* 29 (1991) 310–11.

FOR 3:1–6:

Bachmann, M. "Johannes der Täufer bei Lukas: Nachzügler oder Vorläufer." In *Wort in der Zeit.* FS K. H. Rengstorf, ed. W. Haubeck and M. Bachmann. Leiden: Brill, 1980. 123–55. **Barth, G.** *Die Taufe in frühchristlicher Zeit.* Neukirchen: Neukirchener, 1981. 17–43. **Dobbeler, S. von.** *Das Gericht und das Erbarmen Gottes: Die Botschaft Johannes des Täufers und ihre Rezeption bei den Johannesjüngern im Rahmen der Theologiegeschichte des Frühjudentums.* Anthenäum Monografien BBB 70. Frankfurt am M.: Athenäum, 1988. **Ernst, J.** *Johannes der Taufer, Interpretation— Geschichte—Wirkungsgeschichte.* BZNW 53. Berlin/New York: de Gruyter, 1989. ⸻. "Öffnet die Türen zum Erlöser: Johannes der Taufer—seine Rolle in der Heilgeschichte." *TGl* 74 (1984) 137–65. **Fuchs, A.** "Die Überschneidung von Mk und 'Q' nach B. H. Streeter und E. P. Sanders uns ihre wahre Bedeutung (Mk 1,1–8 par.)." In *Wort in der Zeit.* FS K. H. Rengstorf, ed. W. Haubeck and M. Bachmann. Leiden: Brill, 1980. 28–81. **Luz, U.** "Q 3– 4." In *SBL Seminar Papers 1984,* ed. K. H. Richards. Atlanta, GA: Scholars, 1984. 375–76. **Murphy-O'Connor, J.** "John the Baptist and Jesus: History and Hypothesis." *NTS* 36 (1990) 359–74. **Neirynck, F.** "Une nouvelle théorie synoptique (À propos de Mc.,I,2–6 et par.): Notes critiques." In *Jean et les Synoptiques: Examen critique de l'exégèse de M.-E. Boismard,* in collaboration with J. Delobel et al. BETL 49. Leuven: University Press, 1979. 294–311. **Reicke, B.** "The Historical Setting of John's Baptism." In *Jesus, the Gospels, and the Church.* FS W. R. Farmer, ed. E. P. Sanders. Macon, GA: Mercer, 1987. 209–24. **Robinson, J. M.** "The Preaching of John: Work Sheets for the Reconstruction of Q." In *SBL Seminar Papers 1984,* ed. K. H. Richards. Atlanta, GA: Scholars, 1984. 305–46. **Webb, R. L.** *John the Baptizer.* JSNTSup 62. Sheffield: Sheffield Academic, 1991.

FOR 3:7–18:

Charles, J. D. "The 'Coming One'/'Stronger One' and His Baptism: Matt 3:11–12, Mark 1:8, Luke 3:16–17." *Pneuma* 11 (1989) 37–50. **Chevalier, M.-A.** "L'Apologie du Baptême d'Eau à la Fin du Premier Siècle: Introduction Secondaire de l'Etiologie dans les Récits du Baptême de Jésus." *NTS* 32 (1986) 528–43. **Fleddermann, H.** "John and the Coming One (Matt 3:11–12//Luke 3:16–17)." In *SBL Seminar Papers 1984,* ed. K. H. Richards. Atlanta, GA: Scholars, 1984. 377–84. ⸻. "The Beginning of Q [3,7–9.16–17]." In *SBL Seminar Papers 1985,* ed. K. H. Richards. Atlanta, GA: Scholars, 1985. 153–59. **Hollenbach, P.** "Social Aspects of John the Baptizer's Preaching Mission in the Context of Palestinian Judaism." *ANRW* 2.19.1 (1979) 850–75. **Kazmierski, C. R.** "The Stones of Abraham: John the Baptist and the End of Torah (Matt 3,7–10 par. Luke 3,7–9)." *Bib* 68 (1987) 22–40. **Scheffler, E. H.** "The Social Ethics of the Lukan Baptist (Lk 3:10–14)." *Neot* 24 (1990) 21–36. **Webb, R. L.** "The Activity of John the Baptist's Expected Figure at the Threshing Floor (Matthew 3.2 = Luke 3.17)." *JSNT* 43 (1991) 103–11.

FOR 3:21–22:

Allison, D. C. "The Baptism of Jesus and a New Dead Sea Scroll." *BAR* 18 (1992) 58–60.
Busse, I. "The Markan Account of the Baptism of Jesus and Isa. 63." *JTS* 7 (1956) 74–75.
Chevallier, M.-A. "L'analyse littéraire des textes du Nouveau Testament." *RHPR* 57 (1977)
367–78. Cranfield, C. E. B. "The Baptism of Our Lord: A Study of St. Mark 1:9–11." *SJT* 8
(1955) 53–63. Feldkämper, L. *Der betende Jesus als Heilsmittler nach Lukas*. Veröffentlichungen
des Missionspriesterseminars 29. St. Augustin bei Bonn: Steyler Verlag, 1978. 31–50. Grelot,
P. *Évangiles et histoire*. Introduction à la Bible. Nouvelle édition. Le Nouveau Testament 6.
Paris: Desclée, 1986. 225–58. Jankowski, G. "Messiastaufe: Markus 1, Matthäus 3, Lukas 3:
Die Taufe des Messias im Jordan." *TK* 35 (1987) 17–44. Marchadour, A. "Au commence-
ment, le baptême, les tentations." *Cahier Évangile* 50 (1984) 10–17. Porsch, F. "Erwählt
und erprobt: Die Taufe und Versuchung Jesu." In *Das Zeugnis des Lukas: Impulse für das
Lesejahr C*, ed. P.-G. Müller. Stuttgart: Katholisches Bibelwerk, 1985. 36–43. Ruckstuhl, R.
"Jesus als Gottesohn im Spiegel des markinischen Taufberichts." In *Jesus im Horizont der
Evangelien*. Stuttgarter Biblische Aufsatzbände 3. Stuttgart: Katholisches Bibelwerk, 1988.
9–47. Sabourin, L. "Two Lukan Texts (1:35; 3:2)." *RSB* 1 (1981) 29–33. Telfer, W. "The
Form of the Dove." *JTS* 29 (1926) 238–42.

FOR 3:23–38:

Bauckham, R. "More on Kainam the Son of Arpachshad in Luke's Genealogy." *ETL* 67
(1991) 95–103. Birdsall, J. N. "Some Names in the Lukan Genealogy of Jesus in the Armenian Biblical Tradition." In *Armenian and Biblical Studies*, ed. M. E. Stone. Jerusalem: St.
James, 1976. 13–16. Feuillet, A. "Observations sur les deux généalogies de Jésus-Christ de
saint Matthieu (1,1–17) et de saint Luc (3,23–28)." *EV* 98 (1988) 605–8. Johnson, M. D.
*The Purpose of the Biblical Genealogies with Special Reference to the Setting of the Genealogies of
Jesus*. SNTSMS 8. 2nd ed. Cambridge: University Press, 1989. Nettelhorst, R. P. "The Genealogy of Jesus." *JETS* 31 (1988) 169–72. Plum, K. F. "Genealogy as Theology." *Scandina-
vian Journal of the OT* no. 1 (1989) 66–92. Steyn, G. J. "The Occurrence of 'Kainam' in
Luke's Genealogy: Evidence of Septuagintal Influence?" *ETL* 65 (1989) 409–11.

FOR 4:1–13:

Brawley, R. L. "Canon and Community: Intertextuality, Canon, Interpretation, Christology,
Theology, and Persuasive Rhetoric in Luke 4:1–13." In *SBL 1992 Seminar Papers*, ed. E. H.
Lovering, Jr. 419–34. Davidson, J. A. "The Testing of Jesus." *ExpTim* 94 (1982–83) 113–15.
Eitrem, S. E. *Die Versuchung Christi*. Oslo: Gröndahl, 1924. Fuchs, A. "Versuchung Jesu."
SNTU 9 (1984) 95–159. Garrett, S. R. *The Demise of the Devil*. 38–43. Hester, D. C. "Luke
4:1–13." *Int* 31 (1977) 53–59. Lovreglio, J. "Un désaccord entre les Synoptiques dû à une
erreur de traduction." *BBudé* 4/34 (1975) 549–54. Marchadour, A. "Au commencement,
le baptême, les tentations." *Cahier Évangile* 50 (1984) 10–17. Porsch, R. "Erwählt und
erprobt: Die Taufe und Versuchung Jesu." In *Das Zeugnis des Lukas: Impulse für das Lesejahr
C*, ed. P.-G. Müller. Stuttgart: Katholisches Bibelwerk, 1985. 36–43. Stegner, W. R. "The
Temptation Narrative: A Study in the Use of Scripture by Early Jewish Christians." *BR* 35
(1990) 5–17. Wimmer, J. F. *Fasting in the New Testament*. 31–51. Yates, R. "Jesus and the
Demonic in the Synoptic Gospels." *ITQ* 44 (1977) 39–57. Zeller, D. "Die Versuchungen
Jesu in der Logienquelle." *TTZ* 89 (1980) 61–73.

FOR 4:14–15:

Samain, É. "L'évangile de Luc: Un témoignage ecclésial et missionnaire—Lc 1,1–4; 4,14–
15." *AsSeign* 34 (1973) 60–73.

FOR 4:16–30:

Abraham, M. V. "Good News to the Poor in Luke's Gospel." *Biblebhashyam* 14 (1988) 65–77, esp. 70–73. **Aletti, J.-N.** "Jésus à Nazareth (Lc 4, 16–30): Prophétie, Écriture et typologie." In *À cause de l'Évangile*, ed. R. Refoulé. 431–52. ————. *L'art de raconter Jésus Christ: L'écriture narrative de l'évangile de Luc.* Paris: Seuil, 1989. Esp. 39–61. **Baarda, T.** "'The Flying Jesus': Luke 4:29–30 in the Syriac Datessaron." *VC* 40 (1986) 313–41. **Bauer, D.** "Das fängt ja gut an! Die Ablehnung Jesu in seiner Heimat (Lk 4,16–30)." In *Das Zeugnis des Lukas: Impulse für das Lesejahr C*, ed. P.-G. Müller. Stuttgart: Katholisches Bibelwerk, 1985. 46–53. **Bock, D. L.** *Proclamation from Prophecy and Pattern.* Esp. 105–11. **Bostock, G.** "Jesus as the New Elisha." *ExpTim* 92 (1980–81) 39–41. **Brawley, R. L.** *Luke-Acts and the Jews.* Esp. 6–27. **Casalis, G.** "Un nouvel an. Luc 4/16–21." *ETR* 56 (1981) 148–58. **Chevalon, M.** "À propos de Nazareth." *CCER* 32 (1984) 75–76. **Derrett, J. D. M.** "The 'Nazarenes' in Luke (Luke 4:16–30)." In *New Resolutions.* 111–22. **Dietrich, W.** "'. . . den Armen das Evangelium zu verkünden': Vom befreieneden Sinn biblischer Gesetze." *TZ* 41 (1985) 31–43. **Dupont, J.** "Jésus annonce la bonne nouvelle aux pauvres." In *Associazione biblica italiana, Evangelizare pauperibus.* Atti della XXIV settimana biblica. Brescia: Paideia, 1978. 127–89; reprinted in *Études.* 2:23–85. **Finkel, A.** "La prédication de Jésus à la synagogue un jour de Shabbat: Luc 4,16–28." *SIDJC* 17/3 (1984) 4–12. **Frankemölle, H.** *Evangelium: Begriff und Gattung—Ein Forschungsbericht.* SBB 15. Stuttgart: Katholisches Bibelwerk, 1988. 46–49. **Glöckner, R.** *Die Verkündigung des Heils beim Evangelisten Lukas.* Walberberger Studien 9. Mainz: Grünewald, 1975. 124–32. **Hamm, D.** "Sight to the Blind: Vision as Metaphor in Luke." *Bib* 67 (1986) 457–77. **Johnson, L. T.** *The Literary Function of Possessions in Luke-Acts.* SBLDS 39. Missoula, MT: Scholars, 1977. 91–96. **Kavunkal, J.** "Jubilee the Framework of Evangelization." *Vidyajyoti* 52 (1988) 181–90. **Kehnscherper, G.** *Von Jeremia zu Jesus von Nazareth: Die Ausrufung des Halljahres und das Kommen des Reiches Gottes: Eine sozialethische Untersuchung zu Lk 4,16–30.* Greifswald, 1973. **Kilgallen, J. J.** "Provocation in Luke 4:23–24." *Bib* 70 (1989) 511–16. **Kingsbury, J. D.** *Jesus Christ in Matthew, Mark, and Luke.* Proclamation Commentaries. Philadelphia: Fortress, 1981. 109–13. **Kliesch, K.** "'Den Armen eine gute Nachricht': Die Botschaft des Lukas." In *Das Zeugnis des Lukas*, ed. P.-G. Müller. Stuttgart: Katholisches Bibelwerk, 1985. 10–17. **Koet, B. J.** "'Today this Scripture has been fulfilled in your ears': Jesus' Explanation of Scripture in Luke 4,16–30." In *Five Studies.* 24–55. **Kolasny, J.** "An Example of Rhetorical Criticism: Luke 4:16–30." In *New Views on Luke and Acts*, ed. E. Richard. 67–77. **Lee, G. M.** "Πάντως 'Perhaps.'" *ZNW* 64 (1973) 152. ————. "Further on Πάντως 'Perhaps.'" *NovT* 19 (1977) 240. **Miller, D. G.** "Luke 4:22–30." *Int* 40 (1986) 53–58. **Monshouwer, D.** "The Reading of the Prophet in the Synagogue at Nazareth." *Bib* 72 (1991) 90–99. **Muhlack, G.** *Die Parallelen von Lukas-Evangelium und Apostelgeschichte.* Theologie und Wirklichkeit 8. Bern/Frankfurt am M.: Lang, 1979. 117–25. **Prast, F.** *Presbyter und Evangelium in nachapostolischer Zeit: Die Abschiedsrede des Paulus in Milet (Apg. 20,17–38) im Rahmen der lukanischen Konzeption der Evangeliumsverkündigung.* FB 29. Stuttgart: Katholisches Bibelwerk, 1979. 265–78. **Radl, W.** *Paulus und Jesus im lukanischen Doppelwerk: Untersuchungen zu Parallelmotiven im Lukasevangelium und in der Apostelgeschichte.* Europäische Hochschulschriften XXIII/49. Bern/Frankfurt am M.: Lang, 1975. 82–100. **Reicke, B.** "Jesus in Nazareth: Lk 4,16–30." In *Das Wort und die Wörter.* FS G. Friedrich, ed. H. Balz and S. Schulz. Stuttgart: Kohlhammer, 1973. 47–55. **Reid, D. P.** "Jesus' Return to Nazareth." *BiTod* 23 (1985) 39–43. **Ringe, S. H.** *Jesus, Liberation and the Biblical Jubilee: Images for Ethics and Christology.* Overtures to Biblical Theology 19. Philadelphia: Fortress, 1985. Esp. 36–45, 103–9. ————. "Luke 4:16–44: A Portrait of Jesus as Herald of God's Jubilee." *ProcGLBS* 1 (1981) 73–84. **Sabourin, L.** "'Evangelize the Poor' (Lk 4:18)." *RSB* 1 (1981) 101–9. **Sanders, J. T.** "The Jewish People in Luke-Acts." In *SBL Seminar Papers 1982*, ed. K. H. Richards. Atlanta, GA: Scholars, 1982. 164–68. **Schmitt, J.** "L'oracle d'*is* 61:1ss et sa relecture par Jésus." *RSR* 54 (1980) 97–108. **Schreck, C. J.** "The Nazareth Pericope: Luke 4,16–30 in

Recent Study." In *L'Évangile de Luc* (1989), ed. F. Neirynck. 399–471. **Schwarz, G.** "Versuch einer Wiederherstellung des geistigen Eigentums Jesu." *BibNot* 53 (1990) 32–37. **Shin, G. K.-S.** *Die Ausrufung des endgültigen Jubeljahres durch Jesus in Nazaret: Eine historisch-kritische Studie zu Lk 4, 16–30.* Europäische Hochschulschriften, Reihe 23. Theologie 378. Bern/Frankfurt/ New York/Paris: Lang, 1989. **Siker, J. S.** "'First to the Gentiles': A Literary Analysis of Luke 4:16–30." *JBL* 111 (1982) 73–90. **Walker, T. V.** "Luke 4:16–30." *RevExp* 85 (1988) 321–24.

FOR 4:31–37:

Arens, E. *The HΛΘON-Sayings in the Synoptic Tradition.* OBO 10. Freiburg/Göttingen: Universit'atsverlag/Vandenhoeck & Ruprecht, 1976. 209–21. **Busse, U.** "Metaphorik in neutestamentlichen Wundergeschichten Mk 1,21–28; Joh 9,1–41." In *Metaphorik und Mythos im Neuen Testament,* ed. K. Kertelge. QD 126. Freiburg/Basel/Vienna: Herder, 1990. 110–34. **Rice, G. E.** "Luke 4:31–44: Release for the Captives." *AUSS* 20 (1982) 23–28.

FOR 4:42–44:

Arens, E. *The HΛΘON-Sayings in the Synoptic Tradition.* OBO 10. Freiburg/Göttingen: Universit'atsverlag/Vandenhoeck & Ruprecht, 1976. 194–209. **Murray, G.** "Did Luke Use Mark?" *DR* 104 (1986) 268–71.

FOR 5:1–11:

Albrecht, E. *Zeugnis durch Wort und Verhalten, untersucht an ausgewählten Texten des Neuen Testaments.* Theologische Dissertationen 13. Basel: Reinhardt, 1977. 67–90. **Claudel, G.** *La confession de Pierre: Trajectoire d'une péricope évangelique.* Paris: Gabalda, 1988. 111–32. **Coulot, C.** *Jésus et le disciple: Étude sur l'autorité messianique de Jésus.* Études bibliques NS 8. Paris: Gabalda, 1987. 168–93. **Pope, A.** "More on Luke 5.8." *BT* 41 (1990) 442–43. **Rice, G. E.** "Luke's Thematic Use of the Call to Discipleship." *AUSS* 19 (1981) 51–58. **Rollin, B.** "'Quittant tout, ils le suivirent' (Lc 5,11)." *Via consacrée* 53 (1981) 104–15. **Schlichting, W.** "'Auf dein Wort hin' (Lukas 5,1–11)." *TB* 17 (1986) 113–17.

FOR 5:12–16:

Busse, U. *Wunder.* 103–14. **Elliott, J. K.** "The Healing of the Leper in the Synoptic Parallels." *TZ* 34 (1978) 175–76. **Feldkämper, L.** *Der betende Jesus als Heilsmittler nach Lukas.* Veröffentlichungen des Missionspriesterseminars 29. St. Augustin bei Bonn: Steyler Verlag, 1978. 51–83. **Hulse, E. V.** "The Nature of Biblical 'Leprosy' and the Use of Alternative Medical Terms in Modern Translations of the Bible." *PEQ* 107 (1975) 87–105. **Kazmierski, C. R.** "Evangelist and Leper: A Socio-Cultural Study of Mark 1, 40–45." *NTS* 38 (1992) 37–50.

FOR 5:17–26:

Bock, D. L. "The Son of Man in Luke 5:24." *BulBR* 1 (1991) 109–21. **Busse, U.** *Wunder.* 115–34. **Fiedler, P.** *Jesus und die Sünder.* 107–12. **Fuchs, A.** "Offene Probleme der Synoptikerforschung: Zur Geschichte der Perikope Mk 2,1–8 par Mt 9,1–8 par Lk 5,17–26." *SNTU* 15 (1990) 73–99. **Meynet, R.** "'Crie de joie, stérile!'" *Christus* 33 (1986) 481–89. **Schwarz, G.** "ΑΠΕΣΤΕΓΑΣΑΝ ΤΗΝ ΣΤΕΓΗΝ? (Markus 2,4c)." *BibNot* 54 (1990) 41. **Stegemann, E.** "From Criticism to Enmity: An Interpretation of Mark 2:1–3:6." In *God of the Lowly: Socio-Historical Interpretation of the Bible,* ed. W. Schottroff and W. Stegemann. Tr. M. J. O'Connell. Maryknoll, NY: Orbis, 1984. 104–17. **Trautmann, M.** *Zeichenhafte*

Handlungen Jesu: Ein Beitrag zur Frage nach dem geschichtlichen Jesus. FB 37. Würzburg: Echter, 1980. 234–57.

FOR 5:27–32:

Arens, E. *The HΛΘON-Sayings in the Synoptic Tradition.* OBO 10 Freiburg/Göttingen: Universit'atsverlag/Vandenhoeck & Ruprecht, 1976. 28–63. **Cousar, C. B.** "Luke 5:29–35." *Int* 40 (1986) 58–63. **Fiedler, P.** *Jesus und die Sünder.* 119–29. **Trautmann, M.** *Zeichenhafte Handlungen Jesu: Ein Beitrag zur Frage nach dem geschichtlichen Jesus.* FB 37. Würzburg: Echter, 1980. 132–66.

FOR 5:33–39:

Mead, A. H. "Old and New Wine: St. Luke 5:39." *ExpTim* 99 (1987–88) 234–35. **Wimmer, J. F.** *Fasting in the New Testament.* 85–101.

FOR 6:1–5:

Delobel, J. "Luke 6, 5 in Codex Bezae: The Man Who Worked on Sabbath." *À cause de l'Évangile,* ed. R. Refoulé. 453–78. **Isaac, E.** "Another Note on Luke 6:1." *JBL* 100 (1981) 96–97. **Klinghardt, M.** *Gesetz und Volk Gottes.* 225–29. **Robbins, V. K.** "Plucking Grain on the Sabbath." In *Patterns of Persuasion in the Gospels.* B. L. Mack and V. K. Robbins. Sonoma, CA: Polebridge, 1989. **Safrai, S.** "Sabbath Breakers?" *JerPersp* 3 (1990) 3–5. **Schottroff, L.,** and **Stegemann, W.** "The Sabbath Was Made for Man: The Interpretation of Mark 2:23–28." In *God of the Lowly: Socio-Historical Interpretation of the Bible,* ed. W. Schottroff and W. Stegemann. Tr. M. J. O'Connell. Maryknoll, NY: Orbis, 1984. 118–28. **Skeat, T. C.** "The 'Second-First' Sabbath (Luke 6:1): The Final Solution." *NovT* 30 (1988) 103–6. **Vouga, F.** "Jésus et la loi selon la tradition synoptique." In *Le monde de la Bible.* Genève: Labor et fides, 1988. 49–52.

FOR 6:6–11:

Busse, U. *Wunder.* 135–41. **Klinghardt, M.** *Gesetz und Volk Gottes.* 229–332. **Lee, J. A. L.** "A Non-Aramaism in Luke 6:7." *NovT* 33 (1991) 28–34. **Trautmann, M.** *Zeichenhafte Handlungen Jesu: Ein Beitrag zur Frage nach dem geschichtlichen Jesus.* FB 37. Würzburg: Echter, 1980. 278–318. **Vouga, F.** "Jésus et la loi selon la tradition synoptique." In *Le monde de la Bible.* Genève: Labor et fides, 1988. 64–67.

FOR 6:12–16:

Beutler, J. "Lk 6,16: Punkt oder Komma?" *BZ* 35 (1991) 231–33. **Feldkämper, L.** *Der betende Jesus als Heilsmittler nach Lukas.* Veröffentlichungen des Missionspriesterseminars 29. St. Augustin bei Bonn: Steyler Verlag, 1978. 84–104. **Haacker, K.** "Verwendung und Vermeidung des Apostelbegriffs im lukanischen Werk." *NovT* 30 (1988) 9–38. **Kirchschläger, W.** *Jesu exorzistisches Wirken.* 221–27. **Schwarz, G.** "Φίλιππον καὶ Βαρθολομαῖον?" *BibNot* 56 (1991) 26–30. **Trautmann, M.** *Zeichenhafte Handlungen Jesu: Ein Beitrag zur Frage nach dem geschichtlichen Jesus.* FB 37. Würzburg: Echter, 1980. 167–233.

GENERAL FOR 6:17–49:

Berner, U. *Die Bergpredigt: Rezeption und Auslegung im 20. Jahrhundert.* Göttinger theologische Arbeiten 12. Göttingen: Vandenhoeck & Ruprecht, 1979. **Egger, W.** "Faktoren der

Textkonstitution in der Bergpredigt." *Laurentianum* 19 (1978) 177–98. **Hartin, P. J.** "James and the Q Sermon on the Mount/Plain." In *SBL 1989 Seminar Papers,* ed. D. J. Lull. 440–57. **Hendrickx, H.** *Sermon on the Mount.* Rev. ed. London/San Francisco: Chapman/Harper and Row, 1984. **Lambrecht, J.** *The Sermon on the Mount: Proclamation and Exhortation.* Good News Studies 14. Wilmington, DE: Glazier, 1985. **Luz, U.** "Sermon on the Mount/Plain: Reconstruction of Q(Mt) and Q(Lk)." In *SBL Seminar Papers 1984,* ed. K. H. Richards. Atlanta, GA: Scholars, 1984. 473–79. **Robinson, J. M.** "The Sermon on the Mount/Plain: Work Sheets for the Reconstruction of Q." In *SBL Seminar Papers 1983,* ed. K. H. Richards. Atlanta, GA: Scholars, 1983. 451–54. **Schweizer, E.** *Die Bergpredigt.* Kleine Vandenhoeck-Reihe 1481. Göttingen: Vandenhoeck & Ruprecht, 1982. **Strecker, G.** *The Sermon on the Mount: An Exegetical Commentary.* Nashville, TN: Abingdon, 1988. **Vaage, L. E.** "Composite Texts and Oral Myths: The Case of the 'Sermon' (6:20b–49)." In *SBL 1989 Seminar Papers,* ed. D. J. Lull. 424–39. **Worden, R. D.** "The Q Sermon on the Mount/Plain: Variants and Reconstruction." In *SBL Seminar Papers 1983,* ed. K. H. Richards. Atlanta, GA: Scholars, 1983. 455–71.

FOR 6:20–26:

Boring, M. E. "The Historical-Critical Method's 'Criteria of Authenticity': The Beatitudes in Q and Thomas as a Test Case." *Semeia* 44 (1988) 9–44 (revised version of Forum 1.4 [1985] 3–38). **Broer, I.** *Die Seligpreisungen der Bergpredigt: Studien zu ihren Überlieferung und Interpretation.* BBB 61. Königstein-Bonn: Hanstein, 1986. **Brooke, G. J.** "The Wisdom of Matthew's Beatitudes (4Q Beat and Mt. 5:3–12)." *ScrB* 19 (1989) 35–41. **Cousin, H.** "Les yeux levés sur ses disciples, Jésus disait . . ." *VSpir* 147 (1992) 5–18. **Dupont, J.** *Le message des béatitudes.* Cahiers Évangile 24. Paris: Service biblique Évangile, Cerf, 1978. ————. "Les béatitudes, le coeur du message de Jésus." In *Jésus aujourd'hui: Historiens et exégètes à Radio-Canada II.* Vie, Message et personnalité. Montréal/Paris: Bellarmin/Fleurus, 1980. 75–84. ————. "Heureux les pauvres." *Enjeux* 2 (1979) 3–8. **Hamm, M. D.** *The Beatitudes in Context: What Luke and Matthew Meant.* Zacchaeus Studies: New Testament. Wilmington, DE: Glazier, 1990. **Jacob, G.** "Die Proclamation der messianischen Gemeinde: Zur Auslegung der Makarismen in der Bergpredigt." *TVers* 12 (1981) 47–75. **Kähler, G. C.** "Studien zur Form- und Traditionsgeschichte der biblischen Makarismen." *TLZ* 101 (1976) 77–80. **Kieffer, R.** "Wisdom and Blessing in the Beatitudes of St Matthew and St Luke." *SE* 6 [= TU 112] (1973) 291–95. **Meadors, G. T.** "The 'Poor' in the Beatitudes of Matthew and Luke." *GTJ* 6 (1985) 305–14. **Schlosser, J.** *Le règne de Dieu.* 2:423–50. **Schmitt, J.** "L'oracle d'*is* 61:1ss et sa relecture par Jésus." *RSR* 54 (1980) 97–108. **Stenger, W.** "Die Seligpreisungen der Geschmähten (Mt 5,11–12; Lk 6,22–23)." *Kairos* 28 (1986) 33–60. **Vaage, L. E.** "The Woes in Q (and Matthew and Luke)." In *SBL Seminar Papers 1988,* ed. D. J. Lull. Atlanta, GA: Scholars, 1988. 582–607.

FOR 6:27–38:

Bivin, D. "A Measure of Humility." *JerPersp* 4 (1991) 13–14. **Dupont, J.** "La transmission des paroles de Jésus sur la lampe et la lampe et la mesure dans Marc 4,21–25 et dans la tradition Q. In *Logia,* ed. J. Delobel. 201–36. **Fee, G. D.** "A Text-critical Look at the Synoptic Problem." *NovT* 22 (1980) 12–28. **Feidler, P.** *Jesus und die Sünder.* 185–95. **Fuchs, J.** "Die schwierige Goldene Regel." *StimmZeit* 209 (1991) 773–81. **Gill, D.** "Socrates and Jesus on Non-Retaliation and Love of Enemies." *Horizons* 18 (1991) 246–62. **Hoffmann, P.** "Tradition und Situation: Zur 'Verbindlichkeit' des Gebots der Feindesliebe in der synoptischen Überlieferung und in der gegenwärtigen Friedensdiskussion." In *Ethik im Neuen Testament,* ed. K. Kertelge. QD 102. Freiburg: Herder, 1984. 50–118. **Horsley, R.** "Ethics and Exegesis: Love Your Enemies and the Doctrine of Non-Violence." *JAAR* 54 (1985) 3–31. **Huber, W.**

"Feindschaft und Feindesliebe: Notizen zum Problem des 'Feindes' in der Theologie."
ZEE 26 (1982) 128–58. **Jahnke, V. J.** "'Love Your Enemies': The Value of New Perspectives." *CurTM* 15 (1988) 267–73. **Klassen, W.** *Love of Enemies.* Philadelphia: Fortress, 1984.
Kosch, D. *Die eschatologische Tora des Menschensohnes: Untersuchungen zur Rezeption der Stellung Jesu zur Tora in Q.* Novum Testamentum et Orbis Antiquus 12. Fribourg/Göttingen: Universitätsverlag/Vandenhoeck & Ruprecht, 1989. 213–426. **Légasse, S.** *'Et qui est mon prochain?' Étude sur l'objet de l'agapè dans le Nouveau Testament.* LD 136. Paris: Cerf, 1989.
Lohfink, G. "Der ekklesiale Sitz im Leben der Aufforderung Jesu zum Gewaltverzicht (Mt 5,39b–42/Lk 6,29f)." *TQ* 162 (1982) 236–53. **Merkelbach, R.** "Über eine Stelle im Evangelium des Lukas." *GBZKA* 1 (1973) 171–75. **Neirynck, R.** "Paul and the Sayings of Jesus." In *L'apôtre Paul: Personnalité, style et conception du ministère,* ed. A. Vanhoye. BETL 73. Leuven: University Press/Peeters, 1986. 295–303. **Ricoeur, P.** "The Golden Rule: Exegetical and Theological Perplexities." *NTS* 36 (1990) 392–97. **Schmidt, T. E.** "Burden, Barrier, Blasphemy: Wealth in Matt 6:33, Luke 14:33, and Luke 16:15." *TJ* 9 (1988) 171–89. **Schwarz, G.** "αγαπατε τους εχθρους υμων: Mt 5,44a/Lk 6,27a (35a)." *BibNot* 12 (1980) 32–34.
Strecker, G. "Die Antithesen der Bergpredigt (Mt 5,21–48 par)." *ZNW* 69 (1978) 36–72.
Theissen, G. "Gewaltverzicht und Feindesliebe (Mt 5,38–48/Lk 6,27–38) und deren sozialgeschichtlichen Hintergrund." In *Studien zur Soziologie des Urchristentums.* WUNT 19. Tubingen: Mohr, 1979. 160–97.

For 6:39–49:

Meynet, R. "Histoire de l'analyse rhétorique en exégèse biblique." *Rhetorica* 8 (1990) 291–320.

For 7:1–10:

Brodie, T. "Not Q but Elijah: The Saving of the Centurion's Servant (Luke 77:1–10) as an Internalization of the Saving of the Widow and Her Child (1 Kgs 17:1–16)." *IBS* 14 (1992) 54–71. **Busse, U.** *Wunder.* 141–60. **Gatzweiler, K.** "L'exégèse historico-critique: Une guérison à Capharnaum—Mt 8,5–13; Lc 7,1–10; Jn 4,46–54." *FoiTemps* 9 (1979) 297–315.
Haapa, E. "Zur Selbsteinschätzung des Hauptmanns von Kapharnaum im Lukasevangelium." In *Glaube und Gerechtigkeit.* FS R. Gyllenberg, ed. J. Kiilunen et al. Helsinki: Vammalan Kirjapaino, 1983. 69–76. **Judge, P. J.** "Luke 7,1–10: Sources and Redaction." In *L'Évangile de Luc* (1989), ed. F. Neirynck. 473–89. **Muhlack, G.** *Die Parallelen von Lukas-Evangelium und Apostelgeschichte.* Theologie und Wirklichkeit 8. Bern/Frankfurt am M.: Lang, 1979. 39–54. **Neirynck, F.** "John 4,46–54: Signs Source and/or Synoptic Gospels." *ETL* 60 (1984) 25–44. **Ravens, D. A. S.** "The Setting of Luke's Account of the Anointing: Luke 7.2–8.3." *NTS* 34 (1988) 282–92. **Weiser, A.** *Eine Heilung und ihr dreifacher Bericht (Matthäus 8,5–13; Lukas 7,1–10; Johannes 4,43–54).* Werkstatt Bibelauslegung. Bilder, Interpretationen, Texte. Stuttgart: Katholisches Bibelwerk, 1976. 64–69.

For 7:11–17:

Busse, U. *Wunder.* 161–75. **Demel, S.** "Jesu Umgang mit Frauen nach dem Lukasevangelium." *BibNot* 57 (1991) 52–95, esp. 52–59. **Harris, M. J.** *'The Dead Are Restored to Life': Miracles of Revivification in the Gospels,* ed. D. Wenham and C. Blomberg. Gospel Perspectives VI. Sheffield: JSOT Press, 1986. 295–326. **Klein, H.** *Barmherzigkeit gegenüber den Elenden und Geächteten: Studien zur Botschaft des lukanischen Sondergutes.* Biblisch-theologische Studien 10. Neukirchen-Vluyn: Neukirchener Verlag, 1987. 33–38. **Kluge, J.** *'Die Auferstehung des Jünglings zu Nain' oder 'Der Auferstehungsglaube und die Frage nach Leben und Tod': Zwei Unterrichtsmodelle zu Lk 7,11–17,* ed. R. Kakuschke. Auferstehung—Tod und Leben.

Göttingen: Vandenhoeck & Ruprecht, 1978. 202–20. **Muhlack, G.** *Die Parallelen von Lukas-Evangelium und Apostelgeschichte.* Theologie und Wirklichkeit 8. Bern/Frankfurt am M.: Lang, 1979. 55–71. **Petzke, G.** "Historizität und Bedeutsamkeit von Wunderberichten: Möglichkeiten und Grenzen des religionsgeschichtlichen Vergleichs." In *Neues Testament und christliche Existenz.* FS H. Braun, ed. H. D. Betz. Tübingen: Mohr, 1973. 367–85. **Rochais, G.** *Les récits de résurrection des morts dans le Nouveau Testament.* SNTSMS 40. Cambridge: University Press, 1981. 18–38. **Schnyder, C.** "Zum Leben befreit: Jesus erweckt den einzigen Sohn einer Witwe vom Tode (Lukas 7,11–17)—Eine Totenerweckung." In *Wunder Jesu,* ed. A. Steiner. Basel: Reinhardt, 1978. 78–88.

FOR 7:18–23:

Busse, U. *Wunder.* 176–85. **Cameron, R.** "'What Have You Come Out to See?' Characterization of John and Jesus in the Gospels." *Semeia* 49 (1990) 35–69. **Edwards, R. A.** "Matthew's Use of Q in Chapter Eleven." In *Logia,* ed. J. Delobel. 263–69. **George, A.** "Paroles de Jésus sur ses miracles (Mt 11,5.21; 12,27.28 et par.)." In *Jésus aux origines de la chirstologie,* ed. J. Dupont et al. Gembloux: Duculot, 1975. 283–302. **Habandi, P.** "Eine wieder aktuelle Frage: Zu Lukas 7,18ff.: 'Bist du es, der kommen soll, oder sollen wir auf einen andern warten?'" *ZMR* 6 (1980) 195–98. **Kirchschläger, W.** *Jesu exorzistisches Wirken.* 229–36. **Mearns, C.** "Realized Eschatology in Q? A Consideration of the Sayings in Luke 7.22, 11.20 and 16.16." *SJT* 40 (1987) 189–210. **Neilsen, H. K.** *Heilung und Verkündigung.* 57–65. **Wink, W.** "Jesus' Reply to John: Matt 11:2–6//Luke 7:18–23." *Forum* 5.1 (1989) 121–28. **Witherington, B. III.** "Jesus and the Baptist: Two of a Kind?" In *SBL Seminar Papers 1988,* ed. D. J. Lull. Atlanta, GA: Scholars, 1988. 225–44.

FOR 7:24–28:

Schlosser, J. *Le règne de Dieu dans les dits de Jésus.* Études Bibliques. Paris: Gabalda, 1980. 2:155–78.

FOR 7:29–35:

Cotter, W. J. "The Parable of the Children in the Marketplace, Q (Lk) 7:31–35: An Examination of the Parable's Images and Significance." *NovT* 29 (1987) 289–304. ———. "Children Sitting in the Agora: Q (Luke) 7:31–35." *Forum* 5.2 (1989) 63–82. **Dömer, M.** *Das Heil Gottes: Studien zur Theologie des lukanischen Doppelwerkes.* BBB 51. Köln/Bonn: Hanstein, 1978. 15–18. **Ernst, J.** "Der Spruch von den 'frommen' Sündern und den 'unfrommen' Gerichten (Lk 7,29f): Geschichte der Deutung eines umstrittenen Logions." In *Der Treue Gottes trauen,* ed. C. Bussmann and W. Radl. 197–228. **Fiedler, P.** *Jesus und die Sünder.* 136–47. **Franzmann, M.** "Of Food, Bodies and the Boundless Reign of God in the Synoptic Gospels." *Pacifica* 5 (1992) 17–31. **Magass, W.** "Zum Verständnis des Gleichnisses von den spielenden Kindern (Mt 11, 16–19)." *LingBib* 45 (1979) 59–70. **Noorda, S. J.** "Who Is Who? Lukas 7,29–35." *Segmenten* (Amsterdam) (October 1981) 35–63. **Plessis, I. J. du.** "Contextual Aid for an Identity Crisis: An Attempt to Interpret Luke 7:35." In *A South African Perspective on the New Testament.* FS B. M. Metzger, ed. J. H. Petzer and P. J. Hartin. Leiden: Brill, 1986. 112–27. **Siburt, C.** "The Game of Rejecting God, Luke 7:31–35." *RestQ* 19 (1976) 207–10. **Wimmer, J. F.** *Fasting in the New Testament.* 102–10.

FOR 7:36–50:

Bailey, K. E. *Through Peasant Eyes.* 1–21. **Coakley, J. T.** "The Anointing at Bethany and the Priority of John." *JBL* 107 (1988) 241–56. **Demel, S.** "Jesu Umgang mit Frauen nach dem

Lukasevangelium." *BibNot* 57 (1991) 52–95, esp. 60–67. **Dupont, J.** "Jésus et la pécheresse (Lc 7,36–50)." *ComLit* 65 (1983) 11–17. **Ferry, B.-M.** "La pécheresse pardonnée (Lc 7, 36–50): Pourquoi verse-t-elle des pleurs?" *EV* 99 (1989) 174–76. **Fiedler, P.** *Jesus und die Sünder.* 112–16, 241–48. **Guillet, J.** "'Tes péchés sont pardonnés' (Mc 2,5 et Lc 7,48)." In *De la Tôrah au Messie.* FS H. Cazelles, ed. M. Carrez, J. Doré, and P. Grelot. Paris: Desclée, 1981. 425–29. **Heininger, B.** *Metaphorik, Erzählstruktur und szenisch-dramatische Gestaltung in den Sondergutgleichnissen bei Lukas.* NTAbh n.s. 24. Münster: Aschendorff, 1991. 83–98. **Hofius, O.** "Fusswaschung als Erweis der Liebe: Sprachliche und sachliche Anmerkungen zu Lk 7,44b." *ZNW* 81 (1990) 171–77. **Kilgallen, J. J.** "A Proposal for Interpreting Luke 7,36–50." *Bib* 72 (1991) 305–30. **Leroy, H.** "Vergebung und Gemeinde nach Lk 7,36–50." In *Wort Gottes in der Zeit.* FS K. H. Schelkle, ed. H. Feld and J. Nolte. Düsseldorf: Patmos, 1973. 85–94. **Resseguie, J. L.** "Automatization and Defamiliarization in Luke 7:36–50." *LitTheol* 5 (1991) 137–50. **Robbins, V. K.** "Using a Socio-Rhetorical Poetics to Develop a Unified Method: The Woman Who Anointed Jesus as a Test Case." In *SBL 1992 Seminar Papers,* ed. E. H. Lovering, Jr. 302–19. **Sabbe, M.** "The Footwashing in Jn 13 and Its Relation to the Synoptic Gospels." *ETL* 58 (1982) 279–308. **Salingardes, P.-M.** "'Tu vois cette femme?' Jésus et la pécheresse pardonné (Luc 7,36–50)." *Carmel* 30 (1983) 106–11. **Schäfer, K.** *Zu Gast bei Simon: Eine biblische Geschichte langsam gelesen [7,36–50].* Düsseldorf: Patmos, 1973. **Schulz, F.** "'Discubuit' Jesus.'" *JLH* 25 (1981) 27–48.

FOR 8:1–3:

Demel, S. "Jesu Umgang mit Frauen nach dem Lukasevangelium." *BibNot* 57 (1991) 52–95, esp. 67–73. **Sim, D. C.** "The Women Followers of Jesus: The Implications of Luke 8:1–3." *HeyJ* 30 (1989) 51–62.

FOR 8:4–8:

Dumezil, G. *La parabole du semeur et la parabole de l'allumeur de feu.* FS A.-J. Festugière, ed. E. Lucchesi and H. D. Saffrey. Cahiers d'orientalisme 10. Genève: Cramer, 1984. 107–12. **Garnet, P.** "The Parable of the Sower: How the Multitudes Understood It." In *Spirit within Structure.* FS G. Johnston, ed. E. J. Furcha. Allison Park, PA: Pickwick, 1983. 39–54. **Lindemann, A.** "Die Erzählung von Sämann und der Saat (Mk 4,3–8) und ihre Auslegung als allegorisches Gleichnis." *WD* 21 (1991) 115–31. **Ramaroson, L.** "'Parole-semence' ou 'Peuple-semance' dans la parabole du Semeur?" *ScEs* 40 (1988) 91–101. **Smith, M. H.** "Kinship Is Relative: Mark 3:31–35 and Parallels." *Forum* 6.1 (1990) 80–94.

FOR 8:22–25:

Busse, U. *Wunder.* 196–205. **Fuchs, A.** "Die 'Seesturmperikope' Mk 4:35–41 parr im Wandel der urkirchlichen Verkündigung." *SNTU* 15 (1990) 101–33. **Klauck, H.-J.** *Allegorie und Allegorese in synoptischen Gleichnistexten.* NTAbh 13. 2nd ed. Münster: Aschendorff, 1986. 200–209.

FOR 8:26–39:

Annen, F. "Die Dämonenaustreibungen Jesu in den synoptischen Evangelien." In *Theologisches Jahrbuch 1981,* ed. W. Ernst. Leipzig: St. Benno, 1981. 94–123. **Busse, U.** *Wunder.* 205–19. **Karris, R. J.** "Luke 8:26–39: Jesus, the Pigs, and Human Transformation." *NTR* 4 (1991) 39–51.

FOR 8:40–56:

Busse, U. *Wunder.* 219–31. **Dambrine, L.** "Guérison de la femme hémorroïsse et résurrection de la fille de Jaïre: Un aspect de la lecture d'un texte—Marc 5, 21–43;

Matthieu 9, 18–26; Luc 8, 40–56." In *Reconnaissance à Suzanne de Dietrich.* CBFV. Paris: Foi et Vie, 1971. 75–81. **Genest, O.** "De la fille à la femme à la fille (Luc 8,40–56)." In *De Jésus et des femmes: Lectures sémiotiques.* Recherches NS 14. Montréal, Bellarmin; Paris: Cerf, 1987. 105–20. **Muhlack, G.** *Die Parallelen von Lukas-Evangelium und Apostelgeschichte.* Theologie und Wirklichkeit 8. Bern/Frankfurt am M.: Lang, 1979. 55–71. **Reiser, M.** "Die blutflüssige Frau: Weisen der Vergegenwärtigung biblischer Texte am Beispiel von Mk 5,25–34." *EuA* 68 (1992) 48–56. **Rochais, G.** *Les récits de résurrection des morts dans le Nouveau Testament.* SNTSMS 40. Cambridge: University Press, 1981. 48–50, 74–87. **Suhl, A.** "Die Wunder Jesu: Ereignis und Überlieferung." In *Der Wunderbegriff im Neuen Testament,* ed. A. Suhl. WF 295. Darmstadt: Wissenschaftliche Buchgesellschaft, 1980. 464–509. **Trummer, P.** *Die blutende Frau: Wunderheilung im Neuen Testament.* Fribourg/Basel/Vienna: Herder, 1991.

FOR 9:1–6:

Tuckett, C. M. "Paul and the Synoptic Mission Discourse." *ETL* 60 (1984) 375–81.

FOR 9:7–9:

Neirynck, F. "Marc 6,14–16 et par." *ETL* 65 (1989) 105–9. **Ravens, D. A. S.** "Luke 9.7–62 and the Prophetic Role of Jesus." *NTS* 36 (1990) 119–29.

FOR 9:10–17:

Bammel, E. "The Feeding of the Multitude." In *Jesus and the Politics of His Day,* ed. E. Bammel and C. F. D. Moule. Cambridge: University Press, 1984. 211–40. **Boismard, M.-E.** "The Two-Source Theory at an Impasse." *NTS* 26 (1979–80) 1–17. **Busse, U.** *Wunder.* 232–48. **Cangh, J.-M. van.** *La multiplication des pains et l'eucharistie.* LD 86. Paris: Cerf, 1975. **Grelot, P.** *Évangiles et histoire.* Introduction à la Bible. Nouvelle édition. Le Nouveau Testament 6. Paris: Desclée, 1986. 160–86. **Magne, J. M.** "Le pain de la multiplication des pains et des disciples d'Emmaüs comme preuve de l'origine gnostique des sacrements, de l'Église et du Sauveur." *SE* 6 [= TU 112] (1973) 341–47. ————. "Le processus de judaïsation au témoignage des réécritures du récit de la multiplication des pains." *AugR* 28 (1988) 273–83. **Muhlack, G.** *Die Parallelen von Lukas-Evangelium und Apostelgeschichte.* Theologie und Wirklichkeit 8. Bern/Frankfurt am M.: Lang, 1979. 75–88. **Potterie, I. de la.** "The Multiplication of the Loaves in the Life of Jesus." Tr. E. G. Mathews, Jr. *Communio/IntCathRe* 16 (1989) 499–516. **Seethaler, A.** "Die Brotvermehrung—ein Kirchenspiegel?" *BZ* 34 (1990) 108–12.

FOR 9:18–20:

Claudel, G. *La confession de Pierre: Trajectoire d'une péricope évangélique.* Études bibliques NS 10. Paris: Gabalda, 1988. 167–246. **Feldkämper, L.** *Der betende Jesus als Heilsmittler nach Lukas.* Veröffentlichungen des Missionspriesterseminars 29. St. Augustin bei Bonn: Steyler Verlag, 1978. 105–24.

Index of Authors

Index of Principal Topics

Index of Biblical and Other Ancient Sources

The Old Testament

13:25	605	51:45	1001	32:9	1002
15:15	86	51:46	992	33:11	773
16:5	108	52:7	1001	33:13	875
16:14	1137			34	642, 644, 694, 903, 908
16:16	223, 1001	*Lamentations*		34:14–16	701, 771, 773
17:7–8	374			34:15–16	282
17:8	148	1:1	867	34:16	31
17:11	72	1:13	90	34:22	906
18:1–4	678	4:16	958	34:23–24	91
19:2	678	4:18	991	34:25–31	108
19:10–13	678	4:19	1001	34:28	282
19:13	108	4:20	107	36:9	375
20:4–6	1002, 1004	4:21	50, 1084	36:17	419
21:8–10	1001	5:9	616	36:23	613, 619
21:8	732	5:21	31	36:25–27	610
22:1–8	742, 43			36:25–26	141
22:3–4	580	*Ezekiel*		36:25	236
22:24–30	170–74			36:27	152
23:5	90	1:1–3	140, 144	36:33	141
23:19	153	1:1–2:3	222	37:1–14	45
25:15	1084	1:1	160	37:14	152
25:30–31	550	1:4	498	37:23	141
25:33 (LXX 32:33)	859	1:7	498	37:25	52
26	1130	1:25	162	38	1005
26:17	28	1:28	162, 222	38:19–22	992
26:18–19	932	2:1	469	38:22	708
26:20–24	667	2:2	610	39:6	708
26:21 (LXX)	785	2:3	222	39:29	152, 1220
26:27–28	73	2:9–10	563–64	44:25–27	593
27:7	1003	3:18	668	47	141
27:34 (LXX)	868	3:24	610		
28:36 (LXX)	868	4	223	*Daniel*	
28:64	1004	4:1–3	932–33		
29:7	961	4:6	178	1:5	616
30:8 (LXX 37:8)	555	4:15	616	1:18	33
31:9	613	5	223	2:19–23	571
31:10–20	769	5:9	1002	2:28	379–80, 465, 986, 992
31:17–20	790	5:16	616	2:31–45	985
31:20	785	7:2	563	2:34	955
46:1	785	7:2–3	992	2:37–38	573
47:4	556	7:6–7	563, 992	2:44–45	955
50:34	868	8:1–3	640	2:44	379–80, 953
51:36	868	9:4	476	3:28	592
52:34	616	9:10–14	950	4:12	728
30:7	1002	11:5	30	4:14	149
30:23	153	11:23	1227	4:19	67, 75
31:9	179	12	223	4:21	728
31:14	72	12:19	616	5:20	72
31:20	46	13:10–16	310	6:25	148
31:25	72	13:13	153	7	473
31:27	375	14:17	121–22	7:1–14	513
31:31–34	1042, 1045, 1054, 1057	16:4	105, 111	7:7–27	985
31:31	1137	16:59	87	7:9	473
31:34	89, 236	16:63	236	7:13–14	237
32:17	56	17:22–23	728–29	7:13	160, 328, 469, 471–73, 485,
32:22	87	17:24	1138		895–96, 1006–7, 1109
34:21	1001	18:10	1055, 1057	7:14	180, 573, 694, 696
36:3	142	18:23	773	7:15	29
37:11	1001	20:23	76	7:25	512–15
38:8	141	20:33–38	143	7:27	694, 696
38:14–15	1110	20:33	71	7:28	110–12, 133
38:31	1137	20:34	71	8–12	19, 32
39:21	71	20:47	1138	8:9–26	985
41:1	1000	21:7	534–35	8:13	1002
41:17	105	21:31	72	8:15	1212
43:3	142	22:10	817	8:17	29, 35, 469, 1212
46–51	71	24:9–10	1138	8:26	33, 36
48:1	280	24:15–24	542, 544	9–10	29, 35
50:6	1001	26:16	72	9:3	556
50:15	1001	28:2–19	555, 560	9:4	581
50:27	280	28:20–23	555	9:20	29, 35
50:51	1003	30:3	1003	9:20–21	28–29, 35
50:52	1004	31:5–6	728	9:21–24	116
51:5	1005	31:8	1152	9:23	33, 50, 58
51:6	1000, 1001	31:12	149, 932	9:24–27	985
51:22	1000	32:7	1005, 1007	9:24	29, 35, 197, 282

The New Testament

Mark

13:5	194	16:15	699	20:1	410
13:8	566	17:8	410	20:9	708
13:13–14	637, 643	18:4	668	20:10	411, 563
14:10–11	154	18:7	703	20:14	411
14:13	162	19:11	160	20:15	411
14:15–16	149	19:20	411, 678	21:8	411
14:18–19	149	20:1–3	563	22:16	899

The Apocrypha

1 Kingdoms

1:18	105
1:23	199
6:6	1012
19:23–24	140
21:13	996
23:8	932

2 Kingdoms

8:33–34	142
8:48–50	142
11:15	79
12:28	931
16:10	206

3 Kingdoms

2:12	129
13:21–22	191
14:6	266
17:18	207
19:6	1072

4 Kingdoms

3:13	207
4:9	207
6:14	931
10:1	79
10:6	79
15:5	1067
23:8	48
23:34	171

1 Esdras

8:49	122

2 Esdras

2:61	79
8:6	385
8:41	375–76
9:31	375
17:63	79

Tobit

1:1	143
3:6	119
3:13	119
4:8	149
4:11	149
5:4	48, 1212
5:10	104
12	1218
12:13	299

12:15	32
12:16	29, 1212
12:17	29
12:19	1215
13:14	279–80

Judith

6:19	69
8:6	123
13:8	75
13:18	66–67
15:2	29
16:14	45
16:17	154
16:21	33
16:22–23	122

Wisdom

1:5	30
1:15	967
3:1–9	1152
3:4	967
3:8	1067
3:9	1147
4:15	1147
7:2–3	34
7:4	105, 111
8:13	967
11:1	86
15:3	967
15:11	45, 68
19:10–12	442

Sirach

2:12–14	279
4:10	46
9:10	244
10:14	72
11:6	72
14:17	26
14:18	1053
14:25	105
17:31	1053
25:7–10	279
25:16	164
28:18	1002
31:8	280
36	282
36:11	46
38:33	380
39:2, 3	380
40:15	385
44:16	1228
48:9	1228
48:10	24, 31, 432
48:12	1228

48:22	51
49:12	32, 120
49:14	1228
50:20–22	1225, 1227, 1229
50:21	1228
51:11	29
51:12	964

Baruch

1:22	71
3:37	162
4:24	120
5:9	120

Susanna

3	26
28–62	1130
35	443

Bel and the Dragon

2	25
15	27

1 Maccabees

1:15	87
1:21–22	28
1:63	87
2:1–2	79
2:57	52
2:58	1228
4:11	1203
8:31	79
9:73	1067
10:47	164
11:33	299
11:57	79
11:67	221
14:41	164

2 Maccabees

2, 3, 4	25
3:2	988
5:2–3	992
7:27	34
9:16	988
10:19	904
15:11–16	430

3 Maccabees

5:24	65, 1159
5:27	66

Pseudepigrapha and Early Patristic Works

Dead Sea Scrolls and Related Texts

Rabbinic and Mishnaic Materials